THE AMERICAN CONVENTION ON HUMAN RIGHTS

The American Convention on Human Rights

ESSENTIAL RIGHTS

Thomas M. Antkowiak

Alejandra Gonza

OXFORD
UNIVERSITY PRESS

OXFORD
UNIVERSITY PRESS

Oxford University Press is a department of the University of Oxford. It furthers the University's objective of excellence in research, scholarship, and education by publishing worldwide. Oxford is a registered trademark of Oxford University Press in the UK and certain other countries.

Published in the United States of America by Oxford University Press
198 Madison Avenue, New York, NY 10016, United States of America.

Library of Congress Cataloging-in-Publication Data

Names: Antkowiak, Thomas M., author. | Gonza, Alejandra, author.
Title: The American Convention on Human Rights : essential rights / Thomas M. Antkowiak, Alejandra Gonza.
Description: First edition. | New York : Oxford University Press, 2017. | Includes bibliographical references and index.
Identifiers: LCCN 2016043883 | ISBN 9780199989683 (hardback)
Subjects: LCSH: American Convention on Human Rights (1969 November 22) | Human rights—America.
Classification: LCC KDZ574.A41969 A58 2017 | DDC 341.4/8097—dc23 LC record available at https://lccn.loc.gov/2016043883

Printed by Edwards Brothers Malloy, United States of America

Note to Readers

This publication is designed to provide accurate and authoritative information in regard to the subject matter covered. It is based upon sources believed to be accurate and reliable and is intended to be current as of the time it was written. It is sold with the understanding that the publisher is not engaged in rendering legal, accounting, or other professional services. If legal advice or other expert assistance is required, the services of a competent professional person should be sought. Also, to confirm that the information has not been affected or changed by recent developments, traditional legal research techniques should be used, including checking primary sources where appropriate.

(Based on the Declaration of Principles jointly adopted by a Committee of the American Bar Association and a Committee of Publishers and Associations.)

Para nuestros padres—Irene, Thomas, Lucía y Juan Guillermo—y nuestros hijos, Matías y Thomasito

Contents

1. Introduction 1
I. Overview of Book 1
II. The Inter-American Human Rights System's Impact, Major Institutions, and Legal Instruments 2
A. Impact and Importance of the Inter-American System 2
B. The Organization of American States, the American Convention, and Other Critical Human Rights Instruments 5
C. The Inter-American Commission on Human Rights 8
D. The Inter-American Court of Human Rights 11
1. Introduction 11
2. The Court in Relation to the Commission 13
3. The Court's *Ratione Materiae, Ratione Temporis, Ratione Personae,* and *Ratione Loci* Jurisdiction 14
4. Note on the Court's Assessment of Evidence and Burden of Proof 17
III. Key Developments and Critiques of the Inter-American Jurisprudence 18
A. Introduction 18
B. Extensive State Obligations to Respect and Ensure Rights 18
C. Article 63: Reparations 19
D. Article 24: Right to Equality 20
E. Article 4: Right to Life 21
F. Article 5: Right to Humane Treatment 22
G. Article 7: Right to Personal Liberty 23
H. Rights to Due Process and Judicial Protection 24
1. Article 8: Right to a Fair Trial 24
2. Article 25: Right to Judicial Protection 25

I. Article 13: Freedom of Expression 25
J. Article 21: Right to Property 26
IV. The Book's Structure and Methodology 27

2. *Equality* 31
Article 24: Right to Equal Protection 31
I. Introduction 32
II. Background 35
III. Scope of Protection 36
A. The Relationship of Article 24 and Article 1 36
B. The Assessment of Discrimination 40
1. Definitions and State Obligations 40
2. The Progression of the Court's Case Law: Discrimination in Law and in Fact 43
a. Introduction 43
b. Perceived Political Opponents 44
c. Disadvantaged Groups 45
d. Synthesis 48
3. *Atala Riffo* and the Court's Current Approach to Discrimination 49

3. *Life* 55
Article 4: Right to Life 55
I. Introduction 57
II. Background 59
III. Extensive State Obligations to Respect and Ensure the Right to Life 61
A. Introduction 61
B. Duty to Respect 62
C. Duty to Ensure (or "Protect") 65
1. Overview 65
2. Duty to Prevent through Legal Regulation 66
3. Duty to Adopt "Prevention and Protection Measures" in Threatening Circumstances 67
4. Duty to Investigate and Punish 68
IV. Scope of Protection 72
A. Meaning of "Every Person" and "In General, From the Moment of Conception" 72
B. Meaning of "No One Shall Be Arbitrarily Deprived" of Life 75
1. The Death Penalty 76
a. Introduction 76
b. "Only For The Most Serious Crimes" 77
c. The "Mandatory" Death Penalty 77

d. Due Process Requirements 78
e. Right to Apply for Pardon, Amnesty, or Commutation 81
2. Use of Lethal Force in Law Enforcement Scenarios 82
a. Introduction 82
b. The Principles of Legality, Necessity, and Proportionality 83
c. The Burden of Proof 85
d. State Duties after the Use of Force 85
3. Use of Lethal Force in Armed Conflicts 86
4. Arbitrary Deprivation of Life of Imprisoned Individuals 89
a. Introduction 89
b. Detention Conditions and Healthcare 90
c. Security Operations in Prisons 91
5. Forced Disappearances of Persons 92
a. Introduction and Definition 92
b. The Right to Life and *Ratione Temporis* Jurisdiction 94
C. The Concept of *Vida Digna* 97

4. Humane Treatment 101
Article 5: Right to Humane Treatment 101
I. Introduction 103
II. Background 105
III. Scope of Protection 106
A. A Broad Right with Uncertain Parameters 106
B. Definitions of Torture and the Inter-American Convention to Prevent and Punish Torture 108
C. The Inter-American Court's Three-Part Test for Torture 110
D. Involvement of State Actors: A Fourth Requirement? 114
E. Considerations of Evidence and Proof 116
F. Cruel, Inhuman, or Degrading Punishment or Treatment 117
1. Introduction 117
2. Sexual Violence and Violence against Women 118
3. State-Sanctioned Punishment 120
a. Corporal Punishment 120
b. The Death Penalty 120
c. Life Imprisonment: Children 121
4. Detention Conditions and Practices 122
5. Forced Disappearance 125
6. Threats of "Severe Physical Injuries" 126
7. Treatment of Children 127
G. Violations to Personal Integrity below the Threshold of Article 5(2) 127

H. Investigation and Prevention: State Obligations to Ensure the Rights of Article 5 130
I. Article 5(3): No Extension of Punishment beyond the Convicted Individual 132
J. Article 5(4): Separate Location and Treatment for Unconvicted Persons in Detention 132
K. Article 5(5): Separate Proceedings and Facilities for Children in the Criminal Justice System 134
L. Article 5(6): "Reform and Social Readaptation" of Prisoners 135

5. Personal Liberty 139
Article 7: Right to Personal Liberty 139
I. Introduction 141
II. Background 142
III. Scope of Protection 143
A. Overview 143
1. Right to Physical Liberty 143
2. Right to Personal Security 146
B. General Requirements to Deprive Liberty: The Principles of Legality and Arbitrariness 148
1. The Legality Principle 148
a. Restriction of Liberty Always the Exception 148
b. Ordered by a Competent Judicial Authority 150
i. Synthesis 150
ii. Detentions without Judicial Warrants: Exceptional Cases 151
c. State Obligation to Register Detentions 153
d. Detention Time Limits and Orders for Release 154
e. Pretrial Detention as Illegal Detention 154
f. Court's Increasing Reluctance to Find Violations of Article 7(2) 154
2. The Arbitrariness Principle 156
a. Synthesis 156
b. Forced Disappearances 156
c. Pretrial Detention as Arbitrary Detention 157
i. Sufficient Evidence of Criminal Responsibility 158
ii. Risks to the Criminal Proceeding 158
iii. Detention in Immigration Proceedings 159
iv. Pretrial Detention of Special Sectors of the Population 159
v. Time Limits for Pretrial Detention 160
3. Methodological Problems: Legality and Arbitrariness 160
C. The Specific Requirements of Paragraphs 4, 5, and 6 of Article 7 162
1. Article 7(4): Reasons for Detention and Notification of Charges 162
a. Reasons for Detention 162

b. Notification of Charges 163
2. Article 7(5): Judicial Supervision 164
a. Brought "Before a Judge or Other Officer Authorized by Law" 164
b. Right to Trial "Within a Reasonable Time" 166
3. Article 7(6): The Right to Habeas Corpus 167
4. Article 7(7): "No One Shall Be Detained for Debt" 169

6. Due Process and Judicial Protection 171
Article 8: Right to a Fair Trial 171
I. Introduction 174
A. Many Similarities among the Major Human Rights Treaties 174
B. Variances among the Human Rights Systems 176
C. Background 177
II. Article 8(1) 178
A. Introduction and Meaning of "Right to a Hearing" 178
B. Meaning of "With Due Guarantees" 181
C. Meaning of "Within a Reasonable Time" 183
D. Meaning of "Competent, Independent, and Impartial Tribunal, Previously Established by Law" 188
1. "Tribunal" 188
2. "Competent" 188
3. "Independent" 190
4. "Impartial" 191
5. "Previously Established by Law" 193
III. Article 8(2) and the Right to Be Presumed Innocent 194
A. Article 8(2)(a): The Right to be Assisted by a Translator or Interpreter 196
B. Article 8(2)(b): Prior Notification in Detail of Charges 197
C. Article 8(2)(c): Adequate Time and Means for Preparation of Defense 199
D. Article 8(2)(d): The Right to Defend Oneself Personally or to Be Assisted by Legal Counsel, and to Communicate Freely and Privately with Counsel 200
E. Article 8(2)(e): The Right to be Assisted by Counsel Provided by the State 202
F. Article 8(2)(f): The Right of the Defense to Present and Examine Witnesses 204
G. Article 8(2)(g) and Article 8(3): The Right Not to Be Compelled to Be a Witness against Oneself; Coercion and Confessions 206
H. Article 8(2)(h): The Right to Appeal a Judgment to a Higher Court 208
I. The Right to Effective Access to Consular Assistance 210
IV. Article 8(4): An Acquitted Person Shall Not Be Subjected to a New Trial for the Same Cause 211
V. Article 8(5): Public Criminal Proceedings 213

Article 25: Right to Judicial Protection 215
I. Introduction and Background 216
II. Article 25(1): "Simple, Prompt and Effective" Remedies 218
A. "Simple" and "Prompt" Remedies 218
B. "Effective" Remedies 220
III. Article 25(2): Enforcement of National Judgments 223
IV. The Boundaries of "Judicial Protection" 224
A. The Right of Access to Justice 224
B. Combining Articles 8 and 25: A Critique 225
C. The Court's Current, Broader View of Article 25 227

7. Freedom of Expression 229
Article 13: Freedom of Thought and Expression 229
I. Introduction 231
II. Background 234
III. Scope of Protection 235
A. Meaning of "Everyone" 235
B. Protected Expression 237
C. Safeguards for Journalists 239
D. Right of Access to State-Held Information 241
IV. Limitations to Article 13 243
A. Introduction 243
B. Prior Censorship 244
1. Overview 244
2. Prohibitions against Offensive Content 245
C. Subsequent Imposition of Liability 247
1. Overview and General Requirements 247
2. Subsequent Criminal Liability 249
a. Introduction 249
b. The Honor and Reputation of the Armed Forces 252
c. The Honor and Reputation of Public Officials 253
3. Subsequent Civil Liability 256
D. "Indirect" Restrictions 257
E. Cases of Persecution Leading to Generic Violations of Article 13(1) 259
F. Incitements to Violence: Article 13(5) 260

8. Property 263
Article 21: Right to Property 263
I. Introduction 265
II. Background 267

III. Scope of Protection 268
A. Many Forms of Property Recognized 268
B. Rights to Communal Property 271
IV. Limitations to the Right to Property 273
A. Right to Property Not Absolute 273
B. Meaning of "Just Compensation" 275
C. Meaning of "Reasons of Public Utility or Social Interest" 276
D. Meaning of "In the Cases and According to the Forms Established by Law" 278
E. Specific Approaches to Limitations 278
1. Restrictions during Criminal Investigations and Police Action 278
2. Protective Framework for Traditional Territories 279

9. Reparations 285
Article 63 285
I. Introduction 287
II. Background 289
III. The "Injured Party" of Article 63(1) and Related Topics 290
IV. Monetary Remedies 292
A. Pecuniary Damages 292
B. Moral Damages 296
1. In General 296
2. Community Development Programs 299
V. Non-Monetary Remedies 300
A. Background 300
B. Restitution 301
C. Rehabilitation 303
D. Recognition of Responsibility and Apologies 304
E. Memorials and Commemorations 304
F. Reform of Legislation and Policy, Training Programs 305
VI. Legal Fees and Expenses 307
VII. Supervision and Compliance with the Court's Judgments 308
A. Binding and Final Nature of Judgments 308
B. Introduction to Supervision 310
C. Cases of Noncompliance 311
D. Compliance Rates 313
VIII. Provisional Measures of Article 63(2) 314

APPENDIX: LIST OF INTER-AMERICAN COURT JUDGMENTS BY AMERICAN CONVENTION ARTICLE: ARTICLES 2–26 317
INDEX 405

1

Introduction

I. Overview of Book

Our book seeks to offer a thorough and critical analysis of selected rights of the American Convention on Human Rights. The Inter-American Court of Human Rights and Inter-American Commission on Human Rights are charged with interpreting the American Convention. Consequently, over the course of this volume, we will closely examine their assessment of these rights, with emphasis on the Court's binding decisions. We have chosen those American Convention rights that have been most developed by the Court and Commission, including the rights to equality, life, humane treatment, personal liberty, property, due process, and judicial protection, as well as freedom of expression and reparations. In this way, we do not suggest that other human rights are somehow "less essential"; to the contrary, we strongly support the current view in international human rights law that civil, political, social, economic, and cultural rights are all fundamental and indivisible.[1]

[1] *See, e.g.*, Vienna Declaration and Programme of Action, Adopted by the World Conference on Human Rights in Vienna on 25 June 1993, para. 5 ("All human rights are universal, indivisible and interdependent and interrelated); Suárez Peralta v. Ecuador, Preliminary Objections, Merits, Reparations, and Costs, Judgment, Inter-Am. Ct. H.R. (ser. C) No. 261, para. 131 (May 21, 2013) (recalling "the interdependence and indivisibility of civil and political rights, and economic, social and cultural rights, because they must be understood integrally as human rights without any specific ranking between them"); Airey v. Ireland, Eur. Ct. H.R., App. No. 6289/73, para. 26 (Oct. 9, 1979).

The American Convention on Human Rights. Thomas M. Antkowiak and Alejandra Gonza.

We examine the jurisprudence of the Court and Commission with a victim-centered lens. The Court has often championed a "*pro homine*" interpretation of the Convention; that is, the "most favorable" interpretation for the protection of human rights must always prevail.[2] Through bold rulings, both the Court and the Commission have strengthened individual and collective rights. Their interpretations have favored vulnerable petitioners over powerful States in numerous cases. The jurisprudence has also served countless other victims, and potential victims, across the Americas. However, other decisions have weakened Convention protections and distorted legal concepts. In fact, we have found a troubling divergence from the *pro homine* principle in recent case law. Principally, the Court's assessment of potential rights violations and reparations has become less transparent and rigorous, and, at the same time, more deferential to States. Throughout the book, we discuss these critical areas that neglect a victim-centered perspective or meticulous conceptual development, and we propose alternative approaches.

This Introduction briefly presents the Inter-American Human Rights System's impact, primary legal instruments, and its two key institutions, the Court and Commission. Next, we synthesize crucial developments in the System's jurisprudence and briefly refer to several of our critiques and alternative conceptual proposals—all of which are elaborated in the following chapters. Finally, we outline the structure and methodology of the book's remaining chapters.

II. The Inter-American Human Rights System's Impact, Major Institutions, and Legal Instruments

A. IMPACT AND IMPORTANCE OF THE INTER-AMERICAN SYSTEM

For decades the Inter-American Commission and Court have saved lives, secured redress for victims of rights violations, bolstered the rule of law, and provided critical opposition to despotic regimes in the Americas.[3] Through the 1980s, the Commission in

---

[2] *E.g.*, Juridical Condition & Rights of the Undocumented Migrants, Advisory Opinion OC-18/03, Inter-Am. Ct. H.R. (ser. A) No. 18, para. 21 (Sept. 17, 2003); Compulsory Membership in an Association Prescribed by Law for the Practice of Journalism (Arts. 13 and 29 American Convention on Human Rights), Advisory Opinion OC-5/85, Inter-Am. Ct. H.R. (ser. A) No. 5, para. 52 (Nov. 13, 1985).

[3] *See, e.g.*, Claudio Grossman, *The Inter-American System of Human Rights: Challenges for the Future,* 83 IND. L.J. 1267, 1268 (2008) (highlighting the System's accomplishments and explaining the region's three phases: dictatorships, transition to democracy, and the current phase that is particularly challenged by inequality and poverty); Larry Rohter, *After Decades, Nations Focus on Rights Abuses*, N.Y. TIMES, Sept. 1, 2005, http://www.nytimes.com/2005/09/01/world/americas/after-decades-nations-focus-on-rights-abuses.html?_r=0 (explaining the critical role of the Inter-American System in fostering accountability for human rights abuses). José Miguel Vivanco, the long-standing Americas Director of Human Rights Watch, has stated: "Everything we have achieved on human-rights issues in the region in the last 30 years is in some way a result of the work of the [Inter-American System]." *Chipping at the Foundations: The Regional Justice System Comes under Attack from the Countries Whose Citizens Need It Most*, THE ECONOMIST, June 9, 2012, http://www.economist.com/node/21556599/print.

particular shined a spotlight on the widespread abuses of Latin American dictatorships. Subsequently, during the region's transition to democracy, the Commission and the Court confronted the dark legacy of these regimes. By striking down amnesty laws and curtailing the jurisdiction of military courts, both institutions fostered accountability for serious rights violations. Currently, the Inter-American Human Rights System has sharpened its focus on the marginalized of the Americas: indigenous communities, victims of gender violence, and many others who suffer discrimination. Without a doubt, the System's accomplishments have been significant on individual, communal, and societal levels.

Over the years, the Court and Commission have unsurprisingly encountered fierce State resistance to their decisions and legal positions. In 1998, Trinidad and Tobago denounced the American Convention owing to disputes over the death penalty.[4] Under President Hugo Chávez, Venezuela followed suit in 2012, arguing that the Court and Commission had treated it unfairly in varied decisions.[5]

The year before, a group of States started a movement to "reform" the Inter-American Commission, an initiative that many perceived to be an attack on the institution's independence and powers.[6] Following the Commission's calls for Brazil to halt construction on a large power plant endangering indigenous groups,[7] that State withdrew its ambassador

---

[4] *See* Organization of American States, *Denunciation: Trinidad and Tobago*, *available at* http://www.oas.org/dil/treaties_B-32_American_Convention_on_Human_Rights_sign.htm#Trinidad and Tobago (last visited Nov. 21, 2016). *See also* Laurence R. Helfer, *Overlegalizing Human Rights: International Relations Theory and the Commonwealth Caribbean Backlash against Human Rights Regimes*, 102 COLUM. L. REV. 1832 (2002). In addition, Peru under Alberto Fujimori tried to withdraw from the Court's jurisdiction without denouncing the American Convention. *See* JO M. PASQUALUCCI, THE PRACTICE AND PROCEDURE OF THE INTER-AMERICAN COURT OF HUMAN RIGHTS 145 (2d ed. 2013). The Tribunal rejected this attempt, and continued to consider Peruvian cases before it. In 2001, after a change in government, Peru announced that it considered itself fully subject to the Court's jurisdiction. *See* PASQUALUCCI, *supra*, at 145–46. In a similar vein, in 2014, the Dominican Republic's Constitutional Court issued a ruling to withdraw from the Inter-American Court. *See, e.g.*, Amnesty International, *Dominican Republic: Withdrawal from Top Regional Human Rights Court Would Put Rights at Risk*, Nov. 6, 2014, https://www.amnesty.org/en/latest/news/2014/11/dominican-republic-withdrawal-top-regional-human-rights-court-would-put-rights-risk.

[5] *See* Organization of American States, *Letter to Secretary General José Miguel Insulza from Venezuelan Minister Nicolás Maduro Moros*, Sept. 6, 2012, *available at* http://www.oas.org/DIL/Nota_Rep%C3%BAblica_Bolivariana_Venezuela_to_SG.English.pdf; Inter-American Commission on Human Rights, *IACHR Deeply Concerned over Result of Venezuela's Denunciation of the American Convention*, Press Release No. 64/13 (2013), http://www.oas.org/en/iachr/media_center/PReleases/2013/064.asp.

[6] *See, e.g.*, Claudia Martin & Diego Rodríguez Pinzón, *Strengthening or Straining the Inter-American System on Human Rights*, *in* THE INTER-AMERICAN COURT OF HUMAN RIGHTS: THEORY AND PRACTICE, PRESENT AND FUTURE (Yves Haeck, Oswaldo Ruiz-Chiriboga & Clara Burbano Herrera eds., 2015); Katya Salazar & Daniel Cerqueira, *Las atribuciones de la Comisión Interamericana de Derechos Humanos*, *in* DESAFÍOS DEL SISTEMA INTERAMERICANO DE DERECHOS HUMANOS (Dejusticia ed., 2015); *Chipping at the Foundations*, *supra* note 3.

[7] Inter-Am. Comm'n H.R., *Precautionary Measures: Indigenous Communities of the Xingu River Basin, Pará, Brazil*, PM 382/10 (Apr. 1, 2011), *available at* http://www.oas.org/en/iachr/indigenous/protection/precautionary.asp.

to the Organization of American States (OAS), the Commission's parent institution, and stopped paying dues to the OAS.[8] Not long afterward, the OAS Permanent Council issued numerous recommendations, several of which aimed to restrict the Commission's mandate and activities.[9] Although the Commission and Court have weathered this tumultuous period, resulting changes to the Commission's procedures have, in some respects, weakened its authority.[10] Moreover, both institutions continue to suffer from a dearth of financial support; as of this writing, the Commission's budget problems have approached crisis levels.[11]

The Inter-American System's impact has varied throughout the hemisphere, owing to diverse national circumstances. States generally undertake to follow the Court's judgments against them, although particularly onerous or politically-sensitive orders trigger resistance and delay.[12] The Court's interpretations of the Convention and human rights norms have proven influential well beyond the confines of a specific case.[13] Other international human rights authorities increasingly follow its case law,[14] and some Latin

---

[8] *See, e.g., Chipping at the Foundations, supra* note 3. For more on the OAS, see the next section of this Introduction.

[9] Report of the Special Working Group to Reflect on the Workings of the Inter-American Commission on Human Rights with a View to Strengthening the Inter-American Human Rights System for Consideration by the Permanent Council (Dec. 13, 2011) GT/SIDH 13/11 rev. 2. For critiques of these recommendations, *see, e.g.*, Rodrigo Uprimny Yepes & Nelson Camilo Sanchez, *Human Rights: New Threats in the Hemisphere*, AMERICAS Q., Fall 2012, http://www.americasquarterly.org/human-rights-new-threats-in-the-hemisphere.

[10] A major concern involves modifications to the Commission's procedure on precautionary measures. *See* Inter-American Commission on Human Rights, *Reform of the Rules of Procedure, Policies and Practices*, Resolution 1/2013 (2013), *available at* https://www.oas.org/en/iachr/decisions/pdf/Resolution1-2013eng.pdf. The process to obtain these supposedly expedited measures is now more cumbersome, and has begun to resemble litigation on the merits.

[11] *See* Inter-American Commission on Human Rights, *Severe Financial Crisis of the IACHR Leads to Suspension of Hearings and Imminent Layoff of Nearly Half Its Staff*, Press Release No. 69/16 (2016), http://www.oas.org/en/iachr/media_center/PReleases/2016/069.asp.

[12] *See, e.g.*, this volume's Chapter 9, on reparations; Thomas M. Antkowiak, *An Emerging Mandate for International Courts: Victim-Centered Remedies and Restorative Justice*, 47 STAN. J. INT'L L. 279, 292–316 (2011) (assessing State compliance with various Court remedial orders); Douglas Cassel, *The Expanding Scope and Impact of Reparations Awarded by the Inter-American Court of Human Rights*, *in* OUT OF THE ASHES: REPARATION FOR VICTIMS OF GROSS AND SYSTEMATIC HUMAN RIGHTS VIOLATIONS 214 (Koen De Feyter ed., 2006).

[13] A lively debate exists about the extent to which national authorities should directly apply the American Convention and the Court's case law, a concept known as "conventionality control." *See, e.g.*, Sergio García Ramírez, *The Relationship between Inter-American Jurisdiction and States (National Systems): Some Pertinent Questions*, 5 NOTRE DAME J. INT'L COMP. L. 115, 137–48 (2015); Ariel E. Dulitzky, *An Inter-American Constitutional Court? The Invention of the Conventionality Control by the Inter-American Court of Human Rights*, 50 TEX. INT'L L.J. 46 (2015); Eduardo Ferrer Mac-Gregor, *Reflexiones sobre el control difuso de convencionalidad a la luz del caso Cabrera García y Montiel Flores vs. México*, XLIV BMDC 917 (2011).

[14] *See, e.g.*, Opuz v. Turkey, Eur. Ct. H.R., App. No. 33401/02, para. 83 (June 9, 2009); Centre for Minority Rights Development (Kenya) and Minority Rights Group International (on behalf of Endorois Welfare Council) v. Kenya, Comm. No. 276/2003, Afr. Comm'n on Human & Peoples' Rights (Feb. 4, 2010), paras. 233–38, 263–68, 294–98; Report of the Special Rapporteur on the situation of human rights and fundamental freedoms of indigenous people, James Anaya, A/HRC/15/37 (2010), para. 75. *See also* James L. Cavallaro & Stephanie Erin Brewer, *Reevaluating Regional Human Rights Litigation in the Twenty-First Century: The Case*

American States enable the Court's jurisprudence to deeply permeate national law, institutions, and politics.[15]

Readers from nations that have not yet accepted the Court's jurisdiction, such as the United States, may question the relevance of its case law.[16] Yet the Tribunal, through its interpretation of the Convention, has shaped crucial principles in international human rights law—commitments accepted by States Parties to widely-ratified treaties, such as the International Covenant on Civil and Political Rights. In fact, many such universal principles are applicable to all States through international customary law. Further, the Court's jurisprudence forcefully impacts the Inter-American Commission. The Commission, for its part, exercises jurisdiction over the OAS Member States—all 35 independent States of the Americas—by virtue of the OAS Charter.

B. THE ORGANIZATION OF AMERICAN STATES, THE AMERICAN CONVENTION, AND OTHER CRITICAL HUMAN RIGHTS INSTRUMENTS

In 1948, the Ninth International Conference of American States adopted the OAS Charter in Bogotá, Colombia. As noted, all 35 independent States of the region have ratified the Charter and joined the OAS, the world's oldest regional governmental organization, which serves as a forum for political, legal, and social issues. Although the OAS Charter calls for the "consolidation . . . of a system of individual liberty and social justice based on respect for the essential rights of man," it does not specify these "fundamental rights of the individual."[17]

During the 1948 Conference, the American Declaration on the Rights and Duties of Man was also approved, eight months before the United Nations' celebrated Universal Declaration of Human Rights.[18] The pioneering American Declaration proclaimed numerous civil, political, economic, social, and cultural rights. The Declaration stands

---

of the Inter-American Court, 102 AM. J. INT'L L. 768, 827 (2008) (the Court's "model of supranational litigation . . . will be increasingly relevant in other parts of the world").

[15] *See, e.g.*, Alexandra Huneeus, *Constitutional Lawyers and the Inter-American Court's Varied Authority*, 79 LAW & CONTEMP. PROBS. 179, 192 (2016) (with respect to Colombia, "the [Court's] judgments are frequently cited in domestic litigation over constitutional rights, and they continue to guide and constrain state actors while shaping public debates over certain policy matters"); Sergio García Ramírez, *Prólogo*, *in* LA CORTE INTERAMERICANA DE DERECHOS HUMANOS: UN CUARTO DE SIGLO vii (2005), *available at* http://www.corteidh.or.cr/docs/libros/cuarto%20de%20siglo.pdf (highlighting the increasing incorporation of the Court's jurisprudence into Latin American national law).

[16] The United States signed the American Convention in 1977, but it still has not ratified the treaty. American Convention on Human Rights, "Signatories and Ratifications," https://www.oas.org/dil/treaties_B-32_American_Convention_on_Human_Rights_sign.htm (last visited Nov. 21, 2016). On the other hand, the United States has participated in the Inter-American System in other ways, such as by providing financial support and presenting candidates to the Inter-American Commission.

[17] Charter of the Organization of American States, 119 UNTS 3, Preamble (1948).

[18] American Declaration of the Rights and Duties of Man, O.A.S. Official Rec., OEA/Ser.L./V./II.23, doc. 21 rev. 6 (1948).

as an important human rights instrument and source of legal obligations.[19] The Inter-American Court has affirmed that the American Declaration "contains and defines the fundamental human rights referred to in the [OAS] Charter."[20]

A binding treaty focusing on human rights, which also would establish the Inter-American Court to enforce its provisions, took longer to develop. In 1967, the Inter-American Commission on Human Rights revised an earlier draft prepared by the Inter-American Council of Jurists.[21] The Inter-American Commission's draft American Convention on Human Rights served as the basis for the Inter-American Specialized Conference on Human Rights, held in San José, Costa Rica, in November 1969. Delegates from two-dozen nations attended the San José Conference, where they negotiated and adopted the American Convention's final text. Of the 35 OAS Member States, 22 currently adhere to the Convention, which entered into force in 1978.[22]

In its first Part, the American Convention establishes State obligations to both respect and ensure the treaty's rights without discrimination. The Convention then enumerates those rights, including the rights to life, juridical personality, humane treatment, personal liberty, fair trial, compensation, privacy, reply, assembly, a name, nationality, property, government participation, equal protection, and judicial protection, as well as the freedoms of conscience, religion, thought, expression, association, movement, and residence. The Convention also establishes rights for children and the family, and sets out prohibitions against discrimination, slavery, and ex post facto laws.[23] Although the Convention focuses on civil and political rights, its Article 26 calls for States Parties "to achiev[e] progressively . . . the full realization of the rights implicit in the economic, social, educational, scientific, and cultural standards set forth in the Charter of the Organization of American States as amended by the Protocol of Buenos Aires."[24]

---

[19] *See* Douglass Cassel, *Inter-American Human Rights Law, Soft and Hard*, *in* COMMITMENT AND COMPLIANCE, THE ROLE OF NON-BINDING NORMS IN THE INTERNATIONAL LEGAL SYSTEM 394 (Dinah Shelton ed., 2000); Interpretation of the American Declaration of the Rights and Duties of Man within the Framework of Article 64 of the American Convention on Human Rights, Advisory Opinion OC-10/89, Inter-Am. Ct. H.R. (ser. A) No. 10, paras. 42–43 (July 14, 1989).

[20] *Id.* para. 43.

[21] *See* Inter-American Commission on Human Rights, "Introduction," *available at* http://www.oas.org/en/iachr/mandate/Basics/intro.asp (describing the history of the American Convention) (last visited Nov. 21, 2016).

[22] The States Parties to the American Convention are as follows: Argentina, Barbados, Bolivia, Brazil, Chile, Colombia, Costa Rica, Dominica, Dominican Republic, Ecuador, El Salvador, Guatemala, Haiti, Honduras, Jamaica, Mexico, Nicaragua, Panama, Paraguay, Peru, Suriname, and Uruguay. American Convention on Human Rights, "Signatories and Ratifications," https://www.oas.org/dil/treaties_B-32_American_Convention_on_Human_Rights_sign.htm (last visited Nov. 21, 2016).

[23] The American Convention's Article 9 actually encompasses much more than its title, Freedom from Ex Post Facto Laws, indicates: "No one shall be convicted of any act or omission that did not constitute a criminal offense, under the applicable law, at the time it was committed. A heavier penalty shall not be imposed than the one that was applicable at the time the criminal offense was committed. If subsequent to the commission of the offense the law provides for the imposition of a lighter punishment, the guilty person shall benefit therefrom."

[24] American Convention, art. 26.

In the Convention's Part II, "Means of Protection," the treaty creates the Inter-American Court of Human Rights and details the functions of the Inter-American Commission on Human Rights. These crucial supervisory institutions are further explained below. The Convention's final section, Part III, contains provisions on signature, ratification, reservations, amendments, protocols, and denunciation.

The American Convention's text drew from the American Declaration and the International Covenant on Civil and Political Rights, which had been adopted in 1966.[25] The European Convention for the Protection of Human Rights and Fundamental Freedoms was also influential, particularly with respect to the supervisory mechanisms established.[26] Nevertheless, the delegates at the San José Conference also adapted their Convention to the reality and priorities of the Americas.[27] These efforts are reflected in every Convention article examined in this book, and in numerous other Convention provisions. In every chapter, we indicate the distinctive terms found in each article; some of these formulations were subsequently emulated by other global rights instruments.

Two decades later, a pair of protocols to the American Convention were adopted: the first recognizes economic, social, and cultural rights; the second seeks to eliminate the death penalty. The Additional Protocol to the American Convention on Human Rights in the Area of Economic, Social and Cultural Rights, also known as the "Protocol of San Salvador," sets out rights to work, trade unions, social security, health, a "healthy environment," food, education, and "the benefits of culture," among others; the Protocol also features terms to protect families, children, the elderly, and the disabled.[28] As of this writing, 16 States of the Americas have ratified or acceded to the Protocol of San Salvador; it entered into force in November 1999.[29] Thirteen States have ratified or acceded to the Protocol to the American Convention on Human Rights to Abolish the Death Penalty,

---

[25] *See, e.g.*, Cecilia Medina, *Los 40 años de la Convención Americana sobre Derechos Humanos a la luz de cierta jurisprudencia de la Corte Interamericana*, ANUARIO DE DERECHOS HUMANOS 2009, at 16 (2009) [*Los 40 años*]; DINAH SHELTON, REGIONAL PROTECTION OF HUMAN RIGHTS 102 (2008).

[26] *See* SHELTON, *supra* note 25, at 102; HÉCTOR GROS ESPIELL, LA CONVENCIÓN AMERICANA Y LA CONVENCIÓN EUROPEA DE DERECHOS HUMANOS: ANÁLISIS COMPARATIVO (1991); Thomas Buergenthal, *The American and European Conventions on Human Rights: Similarities and Differences,* 30 AM. U. L. REV. 155, 156 (1981).

[27] *See, e.g.*, Minutes of the 2nd Session of Committee I, Doc. 36, Nov. 11, 1969, p. 160 (Brazilian delegate emphasizing that the San José Conference must not simply follow the ICCPR text); Minutes of the 11th Session of Committee I, Doc 52, Rev. 1, Nov. 17, 1969, pp. 238–39 (several State representatives considering the agrarian reform movements in Latin America when formulating the right to property); Report of Committee I "Protection." Rapporteur Juan Isaac Lovato, Doc. 60 (Revised) Nov. 19, 1969, p. 296 (noting that Conference debates on the death penalty responded to trends found in the region).

[28] Additional Protocol to the American Convention on Human Rights in the Area of Economic, Social and Cultural Rights ("Protocol of San Salvador"), OAS Treaty Series No. 69; 28 ILM 156 (1989), arts. 6–18, respectively.

[29] *General Information on the Treaty*, Additional Protocol to the American Convention on Human Rights in the Area of Economic, Social and Cultural Rights, *available at* http://www.oas.org/juridico/english/sigs/a-52.html (last visited Nov. 21, 2016).

which enters into force for a State as soon as it deposits its instrument of ratification or accession.[30]

Further, the OAS Member States have been engaged in a continuous process to create specialized treaties, building an extensive Inter-American framework on human rights: the Inter-American Convention to Prevent and Punish Torture (IACPPT);[31] the Inter-American Convention on the Prevention, Punishment and Eradication of Violence against Women, also known as the "Convention of Belém do Pará";[32] the Inter-American Convention on Forced Disappearance of Persons (IACFDP);[33] the Inter-American Convention on the Elimination of All Forms of Discrimination against Persons with Disabilities;[34] the Inter-American Convention Against Racism, Racial Discrimination, and Related Forms of Intolerance;[35] and the Inter-American Convention Against All Forms of Discrimination and Intolerance,[36] among others.[37] Of these treaties, the Convention of Belém do Pará currently boasts the highest number of ratifications, at 32 States.

C. THE INTER-AMERICAN COMMISSION ON HUMAN RIGHTS

In 1959, 10 years before the American Convention's adoption, the Fifth Meeting of Consultation of Ministers of Foreign Affairs established the Inter-American Commission on Human Rights.[38] The Commission, composed of seven members and based in Washington, DC, eventually became recognized by both the OAS Charter (through subsequent amendments) and the American Convention. In its early phase, the Commission

---

[30] *Signatories and Ratifications*, Protocol to the American Convention on Human Rights to Abolish the Death Penalty, *available at* http://www.oas.org/juridico/english/sigs/a-53.html (last visited Nov. 21, 2016).

[31] Inter-American Convention to Prevent and Punish Torture, O.A.S. Treaty Series No. 67 (1985).

[32] Inter-American Convention on the Prevention, Punishment and Eradication of Violence against Women, 33 ILM 1534 (1994).

[33] Inter-American Convention on Forced Disappearance of Persons, OAS Treaty Series No. 68, 33 ILM 1429 (1994).

[34] Inter-American Convention on the Elimination of All Forms of Discrimination against Person with Disabilities, AG/RES. 1608 (XXIX-1999).

[35] Inter-American Convention Against Racism, Racial Discrimination, and Related Forms of Intolerance, adopted in 2013.

[36] Inter-American Convention Against All Forms of Discrimination and Intolerance, adopted in 2013.

[37] Also of importance in the Inter-American System are the following instruments: Inter-American Democratic Charter, adopted in 2001; Declaration of Principles on Freedom of Expression, adopted in 2000; Principles and Best Practices on the Protection of Persons Deprived of Liberty in the Americas, adopted in 2008; and the newly-adopted American Declaration on the Rights of Indigenous Peoples, approved in 2016. *See* Inter-American Commission on Human Rights, *Basic Documents in the Inter-American System*, *available at* http://www.oas.org/en/iachr/mandate/basic_documents.asp (last visited Nov. 21, 2016).

[38] For more detailed information on the Inter-American Commission, *see* SHELTON, *supra* note 25, at 497–526; Inter-American Commission on Human Rights, *What Is the IACHR?*, *available at* http://www.oas.org/en/iachr/mandate/what.asp (last visited Nov. 21, 2016).

mainly promoted human rights in the region, investigated problematic situations within OAS Member States, and issued country or thematic reports.

After the entry into force of the American Convention and the establishment of the Inter-American Court, the Commission became much more involved in responding to individual petitions.[39] In the petition procedure, the Commission receives complaints that individuals, groups or nongovernmental organizations[40] have lodged against States (or inter-State petitions).[41] If the matters do not reach settlement, the Commission evaluates admissibility, establishes facts, and determines human rights violations and remedies, if applicable.[42] The Commission can also issue "precautionary measures" to address "serious and urgent situations presenting a risk of irreparable harm."[43] Its decisions have the force of recommendations; although not legally binding, the conclusions can be influential for both defendant States and the region as a whole.

In its reports and individual petition decisions, the Commission initially ascertains whether the State has ratified the American Convention. If not, for purposes of the Commission's analysis, the State's general human rights obligations derive from the American Declaration, which applies to all OAS Member States. To illustrate, the Commission has found the United States, which has not yet ratified the Convention, responsible for numerous human rights violations under the American Declaration.[44] On the other hand, the Commission employs the American Convention to assess the human rights obligations of States Parties to that treaty.

---

[39] The Commission currently has thousands of petitions before it. In 2015 alone, it received 2,164 petitions; there has been a pronounced upward trend in recent years. *See* Inter-American Commission on Human Rights, *Statistics*, *available at* http://www.oas.org/en/iachr/multimedia/statistics/statistics.html (last visited Nov. 21, 2016).

[40] Although the rights of legal persons or entities are not protected by the American Convention, the Court has stated, "this does not mean that . . . an individual may not resort to the Inter-American system . . . to enforce his fundamental rights, even when they are encompassed in a legal figure or fiction." Perozo et al. v. Venezuela, Preliminary Objections, Merits, Reparations, and Costs, Judgment, Inter-Am. Ct. H.R. (ser. C) No. 195, para. 399 (Jan. 28, 2009).

[41] Inter-State disputes in the Inter-American System are very rare. One example is the petition lodged by Nicaragua against Costa Rica in 2006. Report N° 11/07, Inter-State Case 01/06 Nicaragua v. Costa Rica, Mar. 8, 2007.

[42] The settlement procedure is an important tool in the Inter-American System to resolve a case more expeditiously; such settlements have included generous reparations packages for victims of human rights violations. *See* Inter-American Commission on Human Rights, *Impact of the Friendly Settlement Procedure, OEA/Ser.L/V/II. Doc. 45/13* (2013), *available at* www.oas.org/en/iachr/friendly_settlements/docs/Report-Friendly-Settlement.pdf; Laparra Martínez and family: Mexico, Report on Friendly Settlement, OEA/SER. L/ V/II. 157 (2016).

[43] Inter-American Commission on Human Rights, Rules of Procedure, Article 25 (2013), *available at* http://www.oas.org/en/iachr/mandate/Basics/rulesiachr.asp.

[44] *E.g.*, Abdur' Rahman v. United States, Case 12.422, Inter-Am. Comm'n H.R., Report No. 13/14, OEA/Ser.L/V/II.150, doc. 17, para. 94 (2014) ("United States is responsible for the violation of the right to a fair trial (Article XVIII) and right to due process of law (Article XXVI) guaranteed in the American Declaration"); Lackey et al. v. United States, Cases 11.575, 12.333, 12.341, Inter-Am. Comm'n H.R., Report No. 52/13, OEA/Ser.L./V/II, doc. 50 corr. 1, para. 250 (2013) (finding multiple violations to the American Declaration).

At this point, it is important to recall that the Commission and the Inter-American Court—like all international human rights mechanisms—play a subsidiary role in the protection of human rights. This means that these institutions cannot find a State responsible for breaching its international legal obligations until it first has had a fair opportunity to address and remedy the situation. As a result, both the Commission and Court, with certain exceptions, require the exhaustion of domestic remedies before their jurisdiction can be activated. Further, as human rights mechanisms, the Commission and Court only establish State responsibility for rights abuses; they never determine the criminal responsibility of individuals. Finally, the Commission and Court are not intended to function as appellate tribunals to review the judgments of national courts. When due process violations are alleged, nevertheless, the Commission and Court will frequently examine domestic proceedings "to establish their compatibility" with the American Convention or Declaration.[45]

Both the Commission and States can submit cases to the Inter-American Court under certain conditions.[46] First, the defendant State must have accepted the Court's jurisdiction; this is an additional step necessary upon ratification of the American Convention.[47] Second, the Commission must conclude that the defendant State has not sufficiently complied with the recommendations contained in its decision. If these two conditions apply, the Commission will refer the case to the Court—unless an absolute majority of the seven Commissioners decides against the referral. In making their decision to submit the case, the Commissioners consider the following factors: "a) the position of the petitioner; b) the nature and seriousness of the violation; c) the need to develop or clarify the case-law of the system; and d) the future effect of the decision within the legal systems of the Member States."[48]

The Commission sends to the Court, on average, about 14 cases per year,[49] and is obligated to appear in all cases before the Tribunal.[50] Yet the Commission is not the respondent or petitioner to any dispute. It transforms from a quasi-judicial body that assesses matters of fact and law to a "procedural" party before the Court.[51] The Commission's

[45] *E.g.*, Mohamed v. Argentina, Preliminary Objections, Merits, Reparations, and Costs, Judgment, Inter-Am. Ct. H.R. (ser. C) No. 255, para. 79 (Nov. 23, 2012); Herrera Ulloa v. Costa Rica, Preliminary Objections, Merits, Reparations, and Costs, Judgment, Inter-Am. Ct. H.R. (ser. C) No. 107, para. 146 (July 2, 2004).

[46] State referrals, however, are almost non-existent. *But see* In the Matter of Viviana Gallardo et al., Inter-Am. Ct. H.R. (ser. A) No. 101 (July 15, 1981). In this case, Costa Rica actually requested the Court to establish whether it was responsible for human rights violations, as a result of lethal violence in the State's prison.

[47] States may accept the Court's jurisdiction "unconditionally," or on an ad hoc basis: for a specified period, for specific cases, or by special agreement. American Convention, art. 62(2).

[48] Inter-American Commission on Human Rights, Rules of Procedure, Article 45 (2013), *available at* http://www.oas.org/en/iachr/mandate/Basics/rulesiachr.asp.

[49] *See* Inter-American Commission on Human Rights, *Statistics*, *available at* http://www.oas.org/en/iachr/multimedia/statistics/statistics.html (describing last 10 years) (last visited Nov. 21, 2016).

[50] American Convention art. 57.

[51] Inter-American Court of Human Rights, Rules of Procedure, Article 2(23) (former Rules, amended in 2000), *available at* http://www.corteidh.or.cr/sitios/reglamento/2000_eng.pdf.

role, "an auxiliary of the judiciary," has been described as akin to a *ministerio público* in Latin American criminal justice systems.[52] Yet, over the years, some were unsettled by the Commission's dual role: first adjudicator, and then victims' advocate—or unwanted representative—before the Court. Now, after the 2009 amendments to the Court's Rules of Procedure, the Commission may no longer present fact witnesses or victims' statements; these roles are reserved for the victims and their attorneys.[53] The Commission can only offer expert witnesses when "the Inter-American public order of human rights is affected in a significant manner."[54] Beyond involvement in cases, the Commission may request that the Court issue advisory opinions or binding "provisional measures" to avoid irreparable harm in urgent situations.[55]

D. THE INTER-AMERICAN COURT OF HUMAN RIGHTS

1. Introduction

In 1979, the OAS General Assembly elected the first seven judges of the Inter-American Court. However, the Tribunal, located in San José, Costa Rica, had only limited work until a substantial number of States accepted its jurisdiction and the Commission regularly referred cases.[56] Currently, 20 States of the Americas have accepted what is known as the Tribunal's "contentious jurisdiction": Argentina, Barbados, Bolivia, Brazil, Chile, Colombia, Costa Rica, Dominican Republic, Ecuador, El Salvador, Guatemala, Haiti, Honduras, Mexico, Nicaragua, Panama, Paraguay, Peru, Suriname, and Uruguay.[57] In

---

[52] Separate Opinion of Judge Rodolfo E. Piza E., para. 4, In the Matter of Viviana Gallardo et al., Inter-Am. Ct. H.R. (ser. A) No. 101 (July 15, 1981). This analogy emphasizes that the Commission strives to uphold the public interest, much like a public prosecutor's office purports to do.

[53] *See* Statement of Motives for the Reform of the Rules of Procedure (2009), *available at* http://www.corteidh.or.cr/sitios/reglamento/nov_2009_motivos_ing.pdf.

[54] Inter-American Court of Human Rights, Rules of Procedure, Article 35(1)(f) (current Rules, amended in 2009), *available at* http://www.corteidh.or.cr/sitios/reglamento/nov_2009_ing.pdf. In addition, the Commission previously assumed the representation of petitioners before the Court without attorneys. Now, the Court will appoint an "Inter-American defender," an attorney for petitioners without legal representation, so that "economic considerations will no longer impede access" to the Court. Statement of Motives for the Reform of the Rules of Procedure (2009), *available at* http://www.corteidh.or.cr/sitios/reglamento/nov_2009_motivos_ing.pdf.

[55] American Convention, art. 63(2); Inter-American Court of Human Rights, Rules of Procedure, Article 27(2) (current Rules, amended in 2009) ("With respect to matters not yet submitted to it, the Court may act at the request of the Commission.").

[56] In the Tribunal's first decade, advisory opinions constituted a significant portion of its work; in fact, it had issued nine of them before it handed down its first merits decision in a contentious case. Owing to "institutional rivalry," among other factors, the Inter-American Commission was initially reluctant to refer cases to the Court. Thomas Buergenthal, *New Upload: Remembering the Early Years of the Inter-American Court of Human Rights*, 37 N.Y.U. J. INT'L L. & POL. 259, 269 (2005).

[57] American Convention on Human Rights, "Signatories and Ratifications," https://www.oas.org/dil/treaties_B-32_American_Convention_on_Human_Rights_sign.htm (last visited Nov. 21, 2016).

addition to ruling on contentious cases and supervising State compliance with these judgments, the Tribunal issues advisory opinions and provisional measures in emergency situations.[58]

According to the Court, the American Convention "distinguishes very clearly" between the Tribunal's contentious proceedings, regulated by Convention Articles 61 to 63, and its advisory jurisdiction of Article 64.[59] The contentious case is "a dispute arising as a result of a claim initiated by an individual or State Party," alleging violations to the Convention.[60] In contentious proceedings, the Court interprets "the applicable norms," assesses the evidence submitted, and determines whether a State has violated the Convention.[61] If so, it will require the State to remedy the violations pursuant to the Convention's Article 63.[62]

Interpreting the Convention, the Tribunal has affirmed that all of its "decisions"—from judgments on the merits to orders on State compliance and provisional measures—are legally binding.[63] It has insisted that resulting State obligations may not be altered or mitigated "by invoking provisions or difficulties of domestic law."[64] As for the precedential value of its decisions, although the Tribunal lacks a formal rule on stare decisis, it generally follows its established case law.[65]

With respect to advisory opinions, Article 64 establishes that OAS Member States or authorized institutions, including the Inter-American Commission, "may consult the Court" on the American Convention or on "other treaties concerning the protection of human rights in the American states."[66] In addition, the Tribunal may issue "opinions regarding the compatibility" of national laws with human rights treaties.[67] In advisory proceedings, then, the Court primarily engages in the analysis and interpretation of legal

---

[58] American Convention, art. 63(2); Inter-American Court of Human Rights, Rules of Procedure, Article 27 (current Rules, amended in 2009).

[59] Restrictions to the Death Penalty (Arts. 4(2) and 4(4) American Convention on Human Rights), Advisory Opinion OC-3/83, Inter-Am. Ct. H.R. (ser. A) No. 3, para. 31 (Sept. 8, 1983).

[60] *Id.* para. 33.

[61] *Id.* para. 32.

[62] Article 63(1) of the American Convention establishes: "If the Court finds that there has been a violation of a right or freedom protected by this Convention, the Court shall rule that the injured party be ensured the enjoyment of his right or freedom that was violated. It shall also rule, if appropriate, that the consequences of the measure or situation that constituted the breach of such right or freedom be remedied and that fair compensation be paid to the injured party."

[63] Baena Ricardo et al. v. Panama, Competence, Judgment, Inter-Am. Ct. H.R. (ser. C) No. 104, para. 61 (Nov. 28, 2003) (stating "the obligation to comply with the provisions of the Court's decisions corresponds to a basic principle of the law on the international responsibility of the State"). Note also that the Spanish version of the Convention's Article 68(1) refers to a broader term, the Court's "decision," rather than its "judgment." Article 68(1) in Spanish provides: "*Los Estados Partes en la Convención se comprometen a cumplir la decisión de la Corte en todo caso en que sean partes.*"

[64] *Id.* para. 61.

[65] *See* Pasqualucci, *supra* note 4, at 48.

[66] American Convention, art. 64.

[67] *Id.*

norms.[68] As a result, the Tribunal has concluded that advisory and contentious proceedings are "parallel systems" and "alternate judicial methods."[69] A further distinction often made is that advisory opinions lack binding force. However, some scholars have argued that they are in fact obligatory for all States Parties to the Convention.[70] At the very least, the Court's advisory opinions constitute authoritative and far-reaching legal pronouncements.[71] When citing to its jurisprudence, the Court rarely distinguishes or prioritizes between contentious case judgments and advisory opinions.[72]

2. The Court in Relation to the Commission

As the "ultimate interpreter of the American Convention," the Inter-American Court is not bound by the Inter-American Commission's decisions with respect to that treaty.[73] The Commission is not technically a court of first instance, and so the Inter-American Court should not be considered its court of appeals; rather, the Court's authority "to examine and review all actions and decisions of the Commission derives from [the Court's] character as *sole judicial organ*" of the American Convention.[74] In this way, the Court has rejected the Commission's findings and analysis, and reviewed alleged procedural irregularities before the Commission.[75] It has even re-evaluated compliance with admissibility requirements, such as whether petitioners exhausted domestic remedies—issues often decided by the Commission several years before. This approach has been

---

[68] Restrictions to the Death Penalty (Arts. 4(2) and 4(4) American Convention on Human Rights), Advisory Opinion OC-3/83, Inter-Am. Ct. H.R. (ser. A) No. 3, para. 32 (Sept. 8, 1983).

[69] *Id.* para. 43.

[70] *See* HÉCTOR FAÚNDEZ LEDESMA, THE INTER-AMERICAN SYSTEM FOR THE PROTECTION OF HUMAN RIGHTS: INSTITUTIONAL AND PROCEDURAL ASPECTS 925 (3d ed. 2007).

[71] *See, e.g.*, Thomas Buergenthal, *The Advisory Practice of the Inter-American Human Rights Court*, 79 AM. J. INT'L L. 1, 25–27 (1985); LAURENCE BURGORGUE & AMAYA ÚBEDA DE TORRES, THE INTER-AMERICAN COURT OF HUMAN RIGHTS 96 (2011).

[72] *See also* Request for an Advisory Opinion Presented by the Inter-American Commission on Human Rights, Order of the Court, Inter-Am. Ct. H.R, para. 13 (June 24, 2005) (explaining the importance of advisory opinions for the Convention's interpretation), *available at* http://www.corteidh.or.cr./docs/opiniones/res_cor_24_06_05.pdf.

[73] *E.g.*, Article 55 of the American Convention on Human Rights, Advisory Opinion OC-20/09, Inter-Am. Ct. H.R. (ser. A) No. 20, para. 18 (Sept. 29, 2009); Almonacid Arellano et al. v. Chile, Preliminary Objections, Merits, Reparations, and Costs, Judgment, Inter-Am. Ct. H.R. (ser. C) No. 154, para. 124 (Sept. 26, 2006).

[74] 19 Merchants v. Colombia, Preliminary Objection, Judgment, Inter-Am. Ct. H.R. (ser. C) No. 93, para. 27 (June 12, 2002); Velásquez Rodríguez v. Honduras, Preliminary Objections, Judgment, Inter-Am. Ct. H.R. (ser. C) No. 1, para. 29 (June 26, 1987).

[75] The Court has considered alleged procedural irregularities before the Inter-American Commission, an issue that formed the basis of a State's preliminary objection before the Inter-American Court. Velásquez Rodríguez v. Honduras. Preliminary Objections, paras. 31–34. More recently, the Court expressly affirmed its authority to supervise due process of law in those Commission proceedings related to matters submitted to the Court. Control of Legality in the Practice of Authorities of the Inter-American Commission of Human Rights Advisory Opinion OC-19/05, Inter-Am. Ct. H.R. (ser. A) No. 19, para. 31 (Nov. 28, 2005).

criticized as an intrusion upon the Commission's domain.[76] Yet the Court will often concur with the Commission's decisions on admissibility, or rule that States tacitly waived their objections by failing to respond in a timely fashion.[77]

3. The Court's *Ratione Materiae, Ratione Temporis, Ratione Personae,* and *Ratione Loci* Jurisdiction

Like the International Court of Justice, the European Court of Human Rights, and other tribunals, the Inter-American Court has asserted "the inherent authority to determine the scope of its own competence."[78] The Tribunal has invoked this *compétence de la compétence* principle to affirm its jurisdiction in the face of vigorous State challenges.[79] The only way a State may withdraw from the Court's jurisdiction is "to denounce the Convention as a whole," pursuant to the treaty's applicable clause in Article 78.[80]

The Court's subject-matter (*ratione materiae*) competence centers on the American Convention, but is not limited to that treaty. Its jurisdiction is also established in legal instruments listed earlier, such as the Protocol of San Salvador, the Convention of Belém do Pará, the IACPPT, and the IACFDP. The Protocol of San Salvador grants jurisdiction to the Inter-American Commission and the Court over petitions alleging violations of the rights to unionize and education.[81] The IACFDP also authorizes the Commission and Court explicitly;[82] as a result, the Court has declared State violations of

---

[76] Concurring Opinion of Judge Cançado Trindade, Gangaram Panday v. Suriname, Preliminary Objections, Judgment, Inter-Am. Ct. H.R. (ser. C) No. 12, para. 6 (Dec. 4, 1991) (stating that the Commission and the Court "have defined powers, the former being entrusted with competence to decide on the admissibility of applications . . . the latter with jurisdiction (in contentious cases) to determine whether there had been a violation of the Convention").

[77] *E.g.*, Moiwana Cmty. v. Suriname, Preliminary Objections, Merits, Reparations, and Costs, Judgment, Inter-Am. Ct. H.R. (ser. C) No. 124, paras. 37–69 (June 15, 2005); Mayagna (Sumo) Awas Tingni Cmty. v. Nicaragua, Preliminary Objections, Judgment, Inter-Am. Ct. H.R. (ser. C) No. 66, para. 56 (Feb. 1, 2000).

[78] *E.g.*, Benjamin et al. v. Trinidad & Tobago, Preliminary Objections, Judgment, Inter-Am. Ct. H.R. (ser. C) No. 81, para. 69 (Sept. 1, 2001); Ivcher Bronstein v. Peru, Competence, Judgment, Inter-Am. Ct. H.R. (ser. C) No. 54, paras. 32–34 (Sept. 24, 1999). For the authority of the International Court of Justice and the European Court of Human Rights in this matter, see Statute of the International Court of Justice, Article 36(6); European Convention, Article 32(2). Interestingly, the Inter-American Commission's draft for the American Convention expressly stated this principle, but it was abruptly removed during the San José conference without explanation. Draft Inter-American Convention on Protection of Human Rights, art. 51, Doc. 5 (English). September 22, 1969.

[79] In 2003, Panama challenged the Court's competence to supervise judgment compliance. It argued that such monitoring is a "post-judgment stage" that "is not included in the norms that regulate the jurisdiction and procedure of the Court." Baena Ricardo et al. v. Panama, Competence, Judgment, Inter-Am. Ct. H.R. (ser. C) No. 104, para. 53 (Nov. 28, 2003).

[80] Constitutional Court v. Peru, Competence, Judgment, Inter-Am. Ct. H.R. (ser. C) No. 55, para. 39 (Sept. 24, 1999) (rejecting Peru's attempt to withdraw immediately from the Court's contentious jurisdiction); Ivcher Bronstein v. Peru, Competence, Judgment, Inter-Am. Ct. H.R. (ser. C) No. 54, para. 40 (Sept. 24, 1999) (same).

[81] Protocol of San Salvador, art. 19(6).

[82] Inter-American Convention on Forced Disappearance of Persons, art. XIII.

that instrument.[83] In several judgments, the Tribunal has found breaches to the IACPPT as well,[84] as that treaty grants competence to "the international fora" recognized by the respondent State Party.[85] Further, the Court aggressively assumed jurisdiction over the Convention of Belém do Pará in *González* et al. *v. Mexico*, over the State's detailed objections.[86]

Finally, the Court frequently refers to other international legal instruments in order to interpret the scope and content of the American Convention's rights. It does this in recognition of the Convention's progressive interpretation provision, Article 29,[87] and "the evolution of the fundamental rights of the human person in contemporary international law."[88] For example, on numerous occasions the Court has sought guidance from the Convention on the Rights of the Child to define the contours of the American Convention's Article 19 (Rights of the Child),[89] and has referred to the ILO Convention No. 169 to assess indigenous rights to property.[90] It has even employed non-binding international instruments—such as the U.N. Basic Principles on the Use of Force and Firearms by Law Enforcement Officials and the U.N. Guiding Principles on Internal Displacement—to interpret the Convention.[91] The Court's distinctive tendency to

[83] *E.g.*, Ticona Estrada et al. v. Bolivia, Merits, Reparations, and Costs, Judgment, Inter-Am. Ct. H.R. (ser. C) No. 191, para. 70 (Nov. 27, 2008); Molina Theissen v. Guatemala, Merits, Judgment, Inter-Am. Ct. H.R. (ser. C) No. 106, para. 43 (May 4, 2004).

[84] *E.g.*, Bayarri v. Argentina, Preliminary Objection, Merits, Reparations, and Costs, Judgment, Inter-Am. Ct. H.R. (ser. C) No. 187, para. 94 (Oct. 30, 2008); "Street Children" (Villagrán Morales et al.) v. Guatemala, Merits, Judgment, Inter-Am. Ct. H.R. (ser. C) No. 63, para. 252 (Nov. 19, 1999).

[85] Inter-American Convention to Prevent and Punish Torture, art. XIII.

[86] González et al. ("Cotton Field") v. Mexico, Preliminary Objections, Merits, Reparations, and Costs, Judgment, Inter-Am. Ct. H.R. (ser. C) No. 205, paras. 35–77 (Nov. 16, 2009).

[87] The Convention's Article 29 provides:

> No provision of this Convention shall be interpreted as: a. permitting any State Party, group, or person to suppress the enjoyment or exercise of the rights and freedoms recognized in this Convention or to restrict them to a greater extent than is provided for herein; b. restricting the enjoyment or exercise of any right or freedom recognized by virtue of the laws of any State Party or by virtue of another convention to which one of the said states is a party; c. precluding other rights or guarantees that are inherent in the human personality or derived from representative democracy . . . ; or d. excluding or limiting the effect that the American Declaration of the Rights and Duties of Man and other international acts of the same nature may have.

[88] *E.g.*, Yakye Axa Indigenous Cmty. v. Paraguay, Merits, Reparations, and Costs, Judgment, Inter-Am. Ct. H.R. (ser. C) No. 125, para. 127 (June 17, 2005); Juridical Condition & Rights of the Undocumented Migrants, Advisory Opinion OC-18/03, Inter-Am. Ct. H.R. (ser. A) No. 18, para. 120 (Sept. 17, 2003).

[89] *E.g.*, Chitay Nech et al. v. Guatemala, Preliminary Objections, Merits, Reparations, and Costs, Judgment, Inter-Am. Ct. H.R. (ser. C) No. 212, para. 165 (May 25, 2010); "Street Children" (Villagrán Morales et al.) v. Guatemala, Merits, Judgment, Inter-Am. Ct. H.R. (ser. C) No. 63, para. 194 (Nov. 19, 1999).

[90] *E.g.*, Saramaka People v. Suriname, Preliminary Objections, Merits, Reparations, and Costs, Judgment, Inter-Am. Ct. H.R. (ser. C) No. 172, para. 92 (Nov. 28, 2007); Yakye Axa Indigenous Cmty. v. Paraguay, Merits, Reparations, and Costs, Judgment, Inter-Am. Ct. H.R. (ser. C) No. 125, para. 127.

[91] *E.g.*, Landaeta Meijias Brothers et al. v. Venezuela, Preliminary Objections, Merits, Reparations, and Costs, Judgment, Inter-Am. Ct. H.R. (ser. C) No. 281, para. 124 (citing the U.N. Basic Principles on the Use of

incorporate international legal instruments has been considered controversial, particularly when the instruments have not been ratified by the defendant State or lack regional consent.[92] In addition, the Court's long-standing application of European Court standards has actually narrowed the American Convention's protections in areas such as freedom of speech and property rights.[93]

The Tribunal has explained its *ratione temporis* (temporal) jurisdiction, citing to the non-retroactivity principle of the Vienna Convention on the Law of Treaties.[94] The Court may only find violations "with regard to actions or omissions that have taken place following the date of recognition of the Tribunal's jurisdiction and with respect to any situations which have not ceased to exist by that date."[95] This allows for jurisdiction over violations, such as forced disappearances or displacement, which were committed prior to and continue after the State's acceptance. However, the Court has held that torture is not a continuing violation, as "each act of torture is consummated or terminated within itself, the perpetration thereof not extending over time."[96]

Ratione personae jurisdiction, for the Inter-American Court, includes two issues: whether a State can be properly brought before the Court as a respondent, and whether a party has standing to petition the Tribunal.[97] On the first count, as noted, a State must not only ratify the American Convention, but it must also expressly recognize the Tribunal's binding jurisdiction. With respect to standing, as mentioned, "only the States Parties and the Commission shall have the right to submit a case to the Court."[98]

Individuals, groups, and nongovernmental organizations cannot initiate a case before the Inter-American Tribunal. In contrast, victims may petition the European and African human rights tribunals directly.[99] Not surprisingly, commentators have criticized petitioners' lack of agency in this key respect.[100] Still, the petitioner's role before

---

Force and Firearms); Moiwana Cmty. v. Suriname, Preliminary Objections, Merits, Reparations, and Costs, Judgment, Inter-Am. Ct. H.R. (ser. C) No. 124, para. 111 (June 15, 2005) (citing the U.N. Guiding Principles on Internal Displacement).

[92] *See* Gerald L. Neuman, *Import, Export, and Regional Consent in the Inter-American Court of Human Rights*, 19 EUR. J. INT'L. L. 101 (2008) ("the Court has come to undervalue the consent of the relevant community of states as a factor in the interpretation of a human rights treaty").

[93] *See* this volume's Chapter 7, on the freedom of expression, and Chapter 8, on the right to property.

[94] Vienna Convention on the Law of Treaties art. 28, 1155 UNTS 331, 8 ILM 679 (1969).

[95] *E.g.*, Moiwana Cmty. v. Suriname, Preliminary Objections, Merits, Reparations, and Costs, Judgment, Inter-Am. Ct. H.R. (ser. C) No. 124, para. 70 (June 15, 2005); Serrano Cruz Sisters v. El Salvador, Preliminary Objections, Judgment, Inter-Am. Ct. H.R. (ser. C) No. 118, para. 65 (Nov. 23, 2004).

[96] Campo Dodd v. Mexico, Preliminary Objections, Judgment, Inter-Am. Ct. H.R. (ser. C) No. 113, para. 78 (Sept. 3, 2004). This contested holding barred the Court's *ratione temporis* jurisdiction over the violations alleged in the case. *Id.* para. 85.

[97] PASQUALUCCI, *supra* note 4, at 130.

[98] American Convention, art. 61(1).

[99] *See* Convention for the Protection of Human Rights and Fundamental Freedoms, Nov. 4, 1950, 213 U.N.T.S. 222, art. 34; Statute of the African Court of Justice and Human Rights, art. 30; Protocol to the African Charter on Human and Peoples' Rights on the Establishment of an African Court on Human and Peoples' Rights, art. 5.

[100] Antonio Cançado Trindade has called this a significant flaw of the System, "as it is not reasonable to conceive rights without the procedural capacity to vindicate them directly." Separate Opinion of Judge Cançado

the Inter-American Court has expanded significantly over the last two decades. First, the petitioner was allowed to independently submit evidence and claims at the reparations stage.[101] Currently, with the procedural reforms of 2000, they can also present their own legal arguments and evidence once the Commission sends the case to the Court.[102]

Finally, *ratione loci* competence requires that the alleged violation take place within the jurisdiction of the respondent State. In international law, this jurisdiction does not merely contemplate formal territorial boundaries; instead, the relevant question is whether the State exercises "authority and control" over the area.[103] In this way, the Inter-American Commission decided that the Guantánamo Bay detainees, although not held within the borders of the United States, nevertheless were under that State's *ratione loci* jurisdiction.[104]

4. Note on the Court's Assessment of Evidence and Burden of Proof

Generally, in the Inter-American System the party alleging rights violations must carry the burden of proof. However, there are situations when this burden is shifted, such as when the defendant State has superior access to evidence and information.[105] The Inter-American Court has often applied this doctrine when evaluating alleged mistreatment in State custody or forced disappearances.[106] Moreover, when States fail to refute or respond to the petitioner's allegations, the Court may presume their validity, provided that the submitted evidence is consistent with those allegations.[107] The Court has employed a variety of other presumptions in its judgments.[108]

Trindade, para. 14, Castillo Páez v. Peru, Preliminary Objections, Judgment, Inter-Am. Ct. H.R. (ser. C) No. 24 (Jan. 30, 1996).

[101] *See* Inter-American Court of Human Rights, Rules of Procedure, Article 23 (former Rules, amended in 1996), *available at* http://www.corteidh.or.cr/sitios/reglamento/1996_eng.pdf.

[102] This change was instituted by Article 23 of the Court's Rules of Procedure amended in 2000. Inter-American Court of Human Rights, Rules of Procedure, Article 23 (former Rules, amended in 2000), *available at* http://www.corteidh.or.cr/sitios/reglamento/2000_eng.pdf.

[103] *See, e.g.*, William A. Schabas, The European Convention on Human Rights: A Commentary 95 (2015); Pasqualucci, *supra* note 4, at 147.

[104] On this basis, the Inter-American Commission ordered precautionary measures for potential violations to the American Declaration and the Third Geneva Convention. Inter-American Commission on Human Rights, Precautionary Measures with respect to the United States and the Guantanamo Bay Detainees (Mar. 12, 2002), para. 80, *available at* http://www.cidh.oas.org/medidas/2002.eng.htm.

[105] *E.g.*, J. v. Peru, Preliminary Objections, Merits, Reparations, and Costs, Judgment, Inter-Am. Ct. H.R. (ser. C) No. 275, para. 306 (Nov. 27, 2013); Velásquez Rodríguez v. Honduras, Merits, Judgment, Inter-Am. Ct. H.R. (ser. C) No. 4, para. 135 (July 29, 1988).

[106] *Id.*

[107] *E.g.*, Vera Vera et al. v. Ecuador, Preliminary Objections, Merits, Reparations, and Costs, Judgment, Inter-Am. Ct. H.R. (ser. C) No. 226, para. 24 (May 19, 2011); "Street Children" (Villagrán Morales et al.) v. Guatemala, Reparations and Costs, Judgment, Inter-Am. Ct. H.R. (ser. C) No. 77, para. 68 (May 26, 2001).

[108] *See* Pasqualucci, *supra* note 4, at 169–71; Álvaro Paúl, *In Search of the Standards of Proof Applied by the Inter-American Court of Human Rights*, Revista IIDH (2012). We consider over the course of this volume various presumptions used by the Court.

There is no precise standard of proof for the Court to find States responsible for human rights violations. According to its settled case law, the Tribunal need not establish State liability "beyond all reasonable doubt," nor should it determine individual criminal responsibility.[109] It has indicated that, for international tribunals, "the criteria for the assessment of evidence are less rigid" than in the domestic legal sphere; in this way, the Court "freely" accepts and evaluates many forms of evidence and testimony.[110] In sum, the Court's flexible, if somewhat obscure, approach calls for evidence to be "sufficient, reliable, and pertinent to prove the facts that are the subject of the analysis."[111]

III. Key Developments and Critiques of the Inter-American Jurisprudence

A. INTRODUCTION

The Inter-American jurisprudence has proven distinctive in many respects. We already noted the Court's enthusiasm to incorporate other sources of international law into its interpretation of the American Convention, because it considers human rights treaties to be "living instruments whose interpretation must consider the changes over time and present-day conditions."[112] This section summarizes what we consider to be key developments concerning the rights to equality, life, humane treatment, personal liberty, due process, free expression, property, and reparations. Emphasizing a victim-centered perspective, we also point out critical areas where the Court's case law lacks consistency and clarity, and briefly mention some of our alternative conceptual proposals.

B. EXTENSIVE STATE OBLIGATIONS TO RESPECT AND ENSURE RIGHTS

To begin, the Court gives a robust reading to Article 1(1), the Convention's fundamental clause to "respect and ensure" the rights contained in the treaty. Similar to the United Nations, European, and African human rights regimes, States Parties to the Convention

---

[109] *E.g.*, J. v. Peru, Preliminary Objections, Merits, Reparations, and Costs, Judgment, Inter-Am. Ct. H.R. (ser. C) No. 275, para. 305 (Nov. 27, 2013); Velásquez Rodríguez v. Honduras, Merits, Judgment, Inter-Am. Ct. H.R. (ser. C) No. 4, paras. 127–28 (July 29, 1988).

[110] J. v. Peru, Preliminary Objections, Merits, Reparations, and Costs, Judgment, Inter-Am. Ct. H.R. (ser. C) No. 275, para. 305 (Nov. 27, 2013).

[111] *E.g.*, Vélez Restrepo and Family v. Colombia, Preliminary Objections, Merits, Reparations, and Costs, Judgment, Inter-Am. Ct. H.R. (ser. C) No. 248, para. 174 (Sept. 3, 2012); Velásquez Rodríguez v. Honduras, Merits, Judgment, Inter-Am. Ct. H.R. (ser. C) No. 4, para. 127 (July 29, 1988).

[112] *E.g.*, Yakye Axa Indigenous Cmty. v. Paraguay, Merits, Reparations, and Costs, Judgment, Inter-Am. Ct. H.R. (ser. C) No. 125, para. 125 (June 17, 2005); Right to Information on Consular Assistance in the Framework of the Guarantees of the Due Process of Law, Advisory Opinion OC-16/99, Inter-Am. Ct. H.R. (ser. A) No. 16, para. 114 (Oct. 1, 1999).

have both negative ("respect") and positive ("ensure") obligations. Negative obligations are generally understood to require States not to interfere in the exercise of rights, whereas positive obligations compel States to take action—affirmative steps to protect rights.[113] Positive obligations have expanded in international human rights jurisprudence, and the Inter-American System has driven many of these advances.[114]

Since its first contentious case, *Velásquez Rodríguez v. Honduras*, the Inter-American Court has held that "ensuring" human rights demands the positive State duty "to organize the governmental apparatus and, in general, all the structures through which public power is exercised" in order to safeguard the "free and full enjoyment" of the Convention's rights.[115] To comply with this sweeping "ensure" obligation, furthermore, "States must prevent, investigate and punish any violation of the rights recognized by the Convention and . . . attempt to restore the right violated and provide compensation as warranted for damages resulting from the violation."[116] Under this framework, States can readily be found responsible for the conduct of non-State actors, if States do not protect individuals under their jurisdiction according to a "reasonableness" standard—the rule of due diligence.[117]

C. ARTICLE 63: REPARATIONS

The Court's extensive reparations and interpretation of Convention Article 63[118] are widely hailed as trailblazing.[119] Its contemporary remedial approach comprises measures of restitution, rehabilitation, satisfaction, and guarantees of non-repetition, in conjunction with pecuniary and non-pecuniary damages. The Court is the only international body with binding jurisdiction that has consistently ordered this full range of reparations. Especially noteworthy is the Tribunal's focus upon exacting non-monetary remedies, in direct response to victims' repeated petitions.

---

[113] *See, e.g.*, Dinah Shelton & Ariel Gould, *Positive and Negative Obligations*, *in* THE OXFORD HANDBOOK OF INTERNATIONAL HUMAN RIGHTS LAW 562–63 (Dinah Shelton ed. 2013); MANFRED NOWAK, U.N. COVENANT ON CIVIL AND POLITICAL RIGHTS: CCPR COMMENTARY 123-124 (2d ed. 2005).

[114] *See id.* at 563, 579; Medina, *Los 40 años*, *supra* note 25, at 22.

[115] Velásquez Rodríguez v. Honduras, Merits, Judgment, Inter-Am. Ct. H.R. (ser. C) No. 4, para. 166 (July 29, 1988).

[116] *Id.*

[117] *E.g.*, Suárez Peralta v. Ecuador, Preliminary Objections, Merits, Reparations, and Costs, Judgment, Inter-Am. Ct. H.R. (ser. C) No. 261, para. 129 (May 21, 2013); Velásquez Rodríguez v. Honduras, Merits, Judgment, Inter-Am. Ct. H.R. (ser. C) No. 4, para. 172 (July 29, 1988). *See also* Shelton & Gould, *supra* note 113, at 577 (due diligence "is generally held to mean: the reasonable measures of prevention that a well-administered government could be expected to exercise under similar circumstances").

[118] *See* this volume's Chapter 9, on reparations, for a full discussion.

[119] *See, e.g.*, Sergio García Ramírez, *supra* note 13, at 148–49; BURGORGUE & ÚBEDA DE TORRES, *supra* note 71, at 224; Thomas M. Antkowiak, *Remedial Approaches to Human Rights Violations: The Inter-American Court of Human Rights and Beyond*, 46 COLUM. J. TRANSNAT'L L. 351, 386 (2008).

Of course, the Tribunal's reparations are not without their flaws. As for non-monetary remedies, the Court at times could require more intensive victim engagement in the design and implementation of reparations. Still, the Court's non-monetary reparations generally respond to victims' preferences for restoration, and even contemplate the complex realities of certain marginalized populations. In contrast, the Tribunal's inconsistent monetary reparations invite scrutiny. Particularly in the judgments involving groups, such as indigenous communities, the Court does not always respond to substantiated claims for monetary damages by both individuals and collectivities. If it neglects well-founded requests for material or moral compensation, the Court will compromise both individual and collective rights.

D. ARTICLE 24: RIGHT TO EQUALITY

Article 24[120]—despite its limited title, "Right to Equal Protection"—in fact establishes two critical, autonomous rights: the right to equality before the law and the right to equal protection of the law. The Inter-American equality jurisprudence has been dynamic over the last decade, considering varied forms of discrimination with both clarifying and confusing results. The Inter-American Court has declared equality to constitute a jus cogens principle, which would render it binding for all States, and expanded State obligations in this area—far surpassing the U.S. delegation's limited intentions during the Convention's negotiations. The Court broadly condemns indirect and private discrimination, and promotes affirmative action programs. However, its standards of review and even standards of proof for differential treatment remain uncertain.

The Court's interpretation of Article 24 and Article 1, both as separate concepts and in relation to each other, has been inconsistent and, more recently, problematic. The Tribunal now regards the scope of Article 24 as limited to "the application or interpretation of a specific domestic law."[121] We have objections to the Court's current approach, which overemphasizes the non-discrimination provision of Article 1(1). The approach conflicts with the Tribunal's prior jurisprudence, which in turn reflects international understandings of equality principles.

Further, an Article 24 violation clearly condemns discrimination, putting States on notice and likely providing more satisfaction to victims. In contrast, an Article 1(1) violation occurs in the Court's case law whenever a substantive right is breached (the violation necessarily results from the State's failure to respect or ensure the right in question). Merely finding yet another breach of Article 1(1) for discrimination obscures the Court's conclusion and diminishes its impact. To be clear, the Tribunal fully prohibits

---

[120] *See* this volume's Chapter 2, on the right to equality, for a full discussion.

[121] Artavia Murillo et al. (In-vitro Fertilization) v. Costa Rica, Preliminary Objections, Merits, Reparations, and Costs, Judgment, Inter-Am. Ct. H.R. (ser. C) No. 257, para. 285 (Nov. 28, 2012).

discrimination in law and in fact; however, for these and other reasons explained in Chapter 2, it should return to its former manner of interpreting Article 24.

E. ARTICLE 4: RIGHT TO LIFE

The American Convention is the only human rights treaty that expressly determines the point from which the right to life[122] must be protected: "in general, from the moment of conception."[123] In a surprising departure from its recent tendency to defer to States, the Court has established a firm rule for when "conception" occurs. *Artavia Murillo et al. v. Costa Rica*, a judgment from 2012, left little discretion to national authorities on this disputed matter, in contrast to the deferential approaches of the European Court of Human Rights and other tribunals.[124]

The Court has found arbitrary deprivations of life in numerous cases, such as when the death penalty has been applied under prohibited circumstances. In this area, the Inter-American System has played a key role in staying executions and in overturning "mandatory" death penalty statutes.[125] Of course, a State's use of disproportionate police or military force also imperils the right to life. In this context, the Court's case law has evolved, finding violations of Article 4 even when victims *survived* life-threatening situations. Further, internal armed conflicts in Latin America have obligated the Tribunal to analyze multiple killings under international humanitarian law. Yet it has not appeared well positioned to assess military objectives, technical weapon characteristics, and the notion of "excessive" civilian casualties.[126]

As is well known, the Court has been a pioneer in the conceptual development of the crime of forced disappearance. In 1988, the year of its first merits judgment *Velásquez Rodríguez v. Honduras*, there was scarce international law on disappearances.[127] Inter-American jurisprudence has established the crime as a violation of the rights to personal integrity, personal liberty, and the right to life; more recently, the Court has also affirmed that forced disappearance breaches the right to juridical personality, Article 3 of the Convention.

---

[122] *See* this volume's Chapter 3, on the right to life, for a full discussion.

[123] American Convention, art. 4(1).

[124] Artavia Murillo et al. (In-vitro Fertilization) v. Costa Rica, Preliminary Objections, Merits, Reparations, and Costs, Judgment, Inter-Am. Ct. H.R. (ser. C) No. 257, para. 189 (Nov. 28, 2012).

[125] *E.g.*, DaCosta Cadogan v. Barbados, Preliminary Objections, Merits, Reparations, and Costs, Judgment, Inter-Am. Ct. H.R. (ser. C) No. 204, para. 53 (Sept. 24, 2009); Hilaire, Constantine, and Benjamin et al. v. Trinidad & Tobago, Merits, Reparations, and Costs, Judgment, Inter-Am. Ct. H.R. (ser. C) No. 94, para. 104 (June 21, 2002).

[126] International Committee of the Red Cross, Customary International Humanitarian Law Database, Rule 14: Proportionality in Attack, *available at* https://www.icrc.org/customary-ihl/eng/docs/v1_cha_chapter4_rule14 (last visited Nov. 21, 2016).

[127] Velásquez Rodríguez v. Honduras, Merits, Judgment, Inter-Am. Ct. H.R. (ser. C) No. 4 (July 29, 1988).

Inter-American and international law demands significant positive obligations of States to safeguard life. At times, the Court's judgments blur positive and negative State duties in this area. Still, its case law clearly holds that States must adopt numerous positive measures, including legislative action, prevention of violence, and the investigation and punishment of crime—all according to the due diligence standard. Finally, international human rights bodies, foremost the Inter-American Court, have recognized the rights to health, education, culture, food, and clean water as components of the right to life. Much remains to be developed with regard to this key relationship between life and social, cultural and economic rights, as well as with respect to other complex Article 4 matters, such as abortion, genetic engineering, and euthanasia.

F. ARTICLE 5: RIGHT TO HUMANE TREATMENT

The American Convention's Article 5[128] provided an important contribution to international human rights law. Whereas other treaties only listed prohibited forms of conduct, Article 5 was innovative for general human rights treaties because, in addition to its other components, it established an autonomous *right*: "Every person has the right to have his physical, mental, and moral integrity respected."[129] Later, the African Charter on Human and Peoples' Rights and the European Union Charter followed this example and declared rights to personal integrity and human dignity.[130]

The Inter-American System's approach toward torture and other cruel, inhuman, and degrading treatment has often followed that of the European Court of Human Rights. Perhaps most importantly, the two Tribunals share the view that progressing standards for the protection of personal integrity require more rigorous safeguards of States and "greater firmness" of courts in finding violations.[131] What may be regarded as inhuman treatment today may constitute torture in the near future.

Human rights jurisprudence, at both the regional and United Nations levels, has converged significantly in this area. First, the prohibition of torture *and* cruel, inhuman or degrading treatment is absolute, even in the face of terrorism and threats to national security. Second, substantial positive State duties have emerged to protect personal integrity.

---

[128] *See* this volume's Chapter 4, on the right to humane treatment, for a full discussion.

[129] American Convention, art. 5. *See* CECILIA MEDINA, THE AMERICAN CONVENTION ON HUMAN RIGHTS: CRUCIAL RIGHTS AND THEIR THEORY AND PRACTICE 89 (2014).

[130] The African Charter's Article 4 establishes, in part: "Every human being shall be entitled to respect for his life and the integrity of his person. No one may be arbitrarily deprived of this right;" further, its Article 5 provides, in part: "Every individual shall have the right to the respect of the dignity inherent in a human being and to the recognition of his legal status." African Charter on Human and Peoples' Rights, art. 4-5, June 27, 1981, 1520 U.N.T.S. 217. In its Article 3(1), the Charter of Fundamental Rights of the European Union establishes, "Everyone has the right to respect for his or her physical and mental integrity." Charter of Fundamental Rights of the European Union, art. 3(1), 2010 O.J. C 83/02.

[131] Cantoral Benavides v. Peru, Merits, Judgment, Inter-Am. Ct. H.R. (ser. C) No. 69, para. 99 (Aug. 18, 2000) (citing to European Court judgments).

Third, poor detention conditions violate personal integrity, and prolonged solitary confinement is particularly dangerous. Although certain official sanctions are permissible, no punishments shall be "inconsistent with the spirit of the absolute prohibition of torture, inhuman and degrading treatment."[132]

Over the last two decades, the Inter-American Court—also drawing from the IACPPT, the Convention of Belém do Pará, and the Inter-American Commission's jurisprudence—has delivered a number of authoritative judgments, which have served to expand conceptions of torture and ill-treatment, broaden State obligations, condemn gender violence, and provide wide-ranging redress to victims. Nevertheless, the Court has not always been consistent in its approaches to Article 5, and more recently has shown a troubling reluctance to find torture and other violations in certain cases, as explained in Chapter 4.

G. ARTICLE 7: RIGHT TO PERSONAL LIBERTY

For most human rights treaties, a deprivation of liberty must meet two requirements in order to be permissible: its procedures and reasons must be established by law, and the detention or arrest cannot be arbitrary. Similarly, the American Convention's Article 7[133] establishes the general right of all persons to not be deprived illegally or arbitrarily of their liberty; in addition, it contains specific protections for individuals who have been deprived of their freedom. These detailed guarantees primarily contemplated criminal proceedings, but the Inter-American Court has now extended them to administrative deprivations of liberty, such as immigration detention.

To activate the protections of Article 7, the Court does not require a specific duration or location for the detention. In this way, the Tribunal has found violations to Article 7 in a wide range of detention scenarios, and denounces the widespread abuse of pre-trial detention in the Americas. Notably, the Court has even surpassed the Commission's broad interpretations by recognizing Article 7 protections in cases where deprivations of liberty were carried out by non-State actors, without the order or control of State authorities.

We consider the Tribunal's current method of interpreting legality and arbitrariness to be flawed in certain respects. First, when the Court finds an illegal detention, it frequently deems it unnecessary to examine arbitrariness. Although such an approach may appeal to notions of judicial economy, it fails to fully condemn detentions that are both illegal and arbitrary. The Tribunal cannot neglect its duty to rigorously analyze a case's facts in light of all the applicable Convention provisions. Second, unlike other international human rights tribunals, the Court often considers only the relevant domestic law,

---

[132] Association for the Prevention of Torture and the Center for Justice and International Law, Torture in International Law: a Guide to Jurisprudence 75 (2008).

[133] *See* this volume's Chapter 5, on the right to personal liberty, for a full discussion.

and not international law, in its assessment of a detention's legality. When the Court narrows its legality inquiry to the letter of national law, international human rights may be limited or distorted, and the State's discretion to restrict liberty may be increased. Finally, the Court appears increasingly reticent to criticize vague national laws regulating detention, even when the statutes plainly contravene the well-established legal certainty principle.

H. RIGHTS TO DUE PROCESS AND JUDICIAL PROTECTION

1. Article 8: Right to a Fair Trial

Article 8,[134] the Convention's primary due process provision, is called "Right to a Fair Trial." However, the Article goes far beyond trials and even judicial matters, regulating proceedings of "any public authority, whether administrative, legislative or judicial, which, through its decisions determines individual rights and obligations."[135] These broad protections have become more expansive still through numerous judgments of the Inter-American Court, consistent with its notion of the "evolutive nature of judicial process."[136]

Outside criminal cases, the Court appears to require the full range of criminal due process guarantees in administrative proceedings that "involve a manifestation of the punitive powers of the State," such as the process to deport or expel a migrant.[137] In addition, the Tribunal has commendably established that any proceeding that could result in an individual's deprivation of liberty or deportation calls for free legal representation, whenever necessary, as "an imperative for the interests of justice."[138]

Emerging from the region's history of forced disappearances and extrajudicial executions is a robust set of guarantees for victims and family members. The Court has established the overarching right to "justice": to have crimes effectively investigated and prosecuted, to learn the truth about what happened, and to receive reparation for harm suffered.[139] Such wide-ranging rights contrast with prosecutorial discretion and other constraints found in the criminal justice systems of the United States and other nations.

---

[134] *See* this volume's Chapter 6, on the rights to due process and judicial protection, for a full discussion.

[135] Constitutional Court v. Peru, Merits, Reparations, and Costs, Judgment, Inter-Am. Ct. H.R. (ser. C) No. 71, para. 71 (Jan. 31, 2001).

[136] Right to Information on Consular Assistance in the Framework of the Guarantees of the Due Process of Law, Advisory Opinion OC-16/99, Inter-Am. Ct. H.R. (ser. A) No. 16, para. 117 (Oct. 1, 1999).

[137] Separate Opinion of Judge Sergio García Ramírez, Claude Reyes et al. v. Chile, Merits, Reparations, and Costs, Judgment, Inter-Am. Ct. H.R. (ser. C) No. 151, para. 8 (Sept. 19, 2006).

[138] Pacheco Tineo Family v. Bolivia, Preliminary Objections, Merits, Reparations, and Costs, Judgment, Inter-Am. Ct. H.R. (ser. C) No. 272, para. 132 (Nov. 25, 2013).

[139] *E.g.*, Luna Lopez v. Honduras, Merits, Reparations, and Costs, Judgment, Inter-Am. Ct. H.R. (ser. C) No. 269, para. 188 (Oct. 10, 2013); Blake v. Guatemala, Merits, Judgment, Inter-Am. Ct. H.R. (ser. C) No. 36, para. 97 (Jan. 24, 1998).

In recent years, the Court has called for the exclusion of all evidence produced under "any form of duress"—a crucial advance for the Americas, where forced confessions and other statements are still accepted as valid evidence.[140] Although the American Convention does not specifically allude to consular assistance, the Court has developed the "right to effective access to consular assistance," in recognition of the vulnerability of detained foreign nationals and international legal developments.[141] Contemporary Court decisions have also condemned several amnesty laws and elaborated exceptions to the double jeopardy rule, in response to the impunity enjoyed by many rights abusers in the region. Now, spurious acquittals can be disregarded, and renewed prosecution may be permissible. Much remains for the Court to explain about its requirements for "effective" counsel, and the rights to translators and interpreters, among other essential topics.[142]

2. Article 25: Right to Judicial Protection

The Convention's Article 25,[143] Right to Judicial Protection, primarily referred to *amparo*, a "simple and prompt" judicial recourse of Latin American origin.[144] *Amparo* is designed to protect "fundamental rights" recognized in either State law or in the American Convention, and includes the writ of habeas corpus.[145] Yet the Court has expanded the remedies of Article 25 beyond *amparo*, and the Article's full content has become unsettled. This owes, at least in part, to the Court's frequent method of combining Articles 8 and 25 in its judgments; the practice has hindered the latter provision's meticulous development.

I. ARTICLE 13: FREEDOM OF EXPRESSION

The American Convention was designed to provide vibrant guarantees for the freedom of thought and expression.[146] Among international treaties, it contains the only prohibition

---

140 *E.g.*, Garcia Cruz and Sanchez Silvestre v. Mexico, Merits, Reparations, and Costs, Judgment, Inter-Am. Ct. H.R. (ser. C) No. 273, para. 58 (Nov. 26, 2013); Cabrera García and Montiel Flores v. Mexico, Preliminary Objections, Merits, Reparations, and Costs, Judgment, Inter-Am. Ct. H.R. (ser. C) No. 220, paras. 165–166 (Nov. 26, 2010).

141 *E.g.*, Vélez Loor v. Panama, Preliminary Objections, Merits, Reparations, and Costs, Judgment, Inter-Am. Ct. H.R. (ser. C) No. 218, paras. 151, 160 (Nov. 23, 2010); Right to Information on Consular Assistance in the Framework of the Guarantees of the Due Process of Law, Advisory Opinion OC-16/99, Inter-Am. Ct. H.R. (ser. A) No. 16, paras. 84 and 124 (Oct. 1, 1999).

142 *See* DaCosta Cadogan v. Barbados, Preliminary Objections, Merits, Reparations, and Costs, Judgment, Inter-Am. Ct. H.R. (ser. C) No. 204, para. 93 (Sept. 24, 2009) (beginning to set out parameters for "effective" counsel).

143 *See* this volume's Chapter 6, on the rights to due process and judicial protection, for a full discussion.

144 Habeas Corpus in Emergency Situations (Arts. 27(2), 25(1), and 7(6) American Convention on Human Rights), Advisory Opinion OC-8/87, Inter-Am. Ct. H.R. (ser. A) No. 8, para. 32 (Jan. 30, 1987).

145 American Convention, art. 25(1).

146 *See* this volume's Chapter 7, on the freedom of expression, for a full discussion.

against prior censorship and features an innovative provision on "indirect" restrictions to expression.[147] Interpreting Article 13, the Inter-American Court became the first international human rights tribunal to establish the right of all individuals to access State-held information—a right that was later recognized by other human rights authorities. The Court has issued several decisions that condemned censorship and disproportionate sanctions on expression, protecting the Article 13 rights of individuals and society at large. These judgments led to legislative reforms, the reversal of criminal convictions, and the lifting of bans on films and books, among other successes.

Until 2008, the Court conceived of the freedom of speech as a primary means to limit State power and foster democracy. Subsequently, however, the Tribunal began to allow more constraints on expression and to require more responsibilities of speakers. In doing so, it has often cited to European Court judgments, which interpret a treaty more restrictive of the freedom of speech. For example, contrary to the Inter-American Commission's position, the Court has held that criminal sanctions on expression are a legitimate means to protect honor and reputation, and that States have the obligation to establish such laws. The Court even accepted that protecting the honor of a State's armed forces was a legitimate objective to criminally punish speech.

In response, we argue that criminal sanctions on expression, in order to protect honor and reputation, should always violate Article 13. Among other reasons, this is because criminal punishment fails the proportionality requirement of Article 13(2). As a result, the Court must change its approach and prohibit the use of criminal law in these cases. Second, pursuant to the Convention, the Tribunal must develop clear definitions and rules concerning any sanctions on speech, with the goal to promote vigorous public debate. Otherwise, governments, domestic judges, and the Court itself will inevitably fail to honor Article 13's generous protections. Of course, speakers and journalists also require predictable standards to avoid chilling effects on the freedom of expression. Yet the Court's case law still permits, under uncertain circumstances, civil and even criminal sanctions for criticizing State institutions and public figures.

Also of concern, since 2006 the Court started finding violations of Article 13(1)'s general provision, without analyzing the Article's other paragraphs. As asserted above, the Tribunal cannot neglect its obligation to rigorously analyze a case's facts in light of the Convention's express terms and limitations. Otherwise, its assessment becomes opaque; again, this can result in greater discretion for the Court and States in this critical area.

J. ARTICLE 21: RIGHT TO PROPERTY

Among regional treaties, the American Convention provides a strong formulation of the right to property,[148] requiring, among other protections, "just compensation" upon

---

[147] American Convention, art. 13(3).

[148] *See* this volume's Chapter 8, on the right to property, for a full discussion.

property deprivation.[149] The Inter-American Court has elaborated a broad notion of property, including tangible and intangible property, as well as communal and private property. The Court's property case law has especially influenced international jurisprudence on indigenous rights.

In 2001, the Court decided *Mayagna (Sumo) Awas Tingni v. Nicaragua*; this ruling on an indigenous right to communal property was a first for an international human rights court.[150] Beginning with *Awas Tingni,* the Court has recognized "the unique and enduring ties that bind indigenous communities to their ancestral territory."[151] In the Inter-American System, even if non-native communities have occupied their lands "in accordance with customary practices," they may be entitled to official recognition of their ownership rights.[152] By requiring communities to follow a 'cultural script,' however, commentators have rightly criticized that the Court's approach limits the autonomy of indigenous peoples and their capacity for change.[153]

Throughout the Americas, States and private companies have extracted natural resources and developed commercial projects on lands belonging to indigenous peoples and Afro-Latin communities. In response, the Court has required that States comply with specific "safeguards"; with respect to "major" projects, they must even secure the community's free, prior, and informed consent.[154] Although this approach was pioneering for international tribunals, the Court's protections are easily evaded. To better safeguard vital ancestral lands and resources, we argue that the Court should adopt a robust right-to-life approach, rather than relying upon the modest right to property in these cases.

IV. The Book's Structure and Methodology

The following chapters examine each Convention right named above: the rights to equality, life, humane treatment, personal liberty, property, due process, and judicial protection, as well as freedom of expression and reparations. Although we have focused on those aspects of the Convention that have been most analyzed to date, there are still many gaps in the Inter-American jurisprudence, nearly five decades after the Convention's adoption.

---

[149] American Convention, art. 21(2).

[150] Mayagna (Sumo) Awas Tingni Cmty. v. Nicaragua, Merits, Reparations, and Costs, Judgment, Inter-Am. Ct. H.R. (ser. C) No. 79 (Aug. 31, 2001).

[151] *Id.* para. 149.

[152] *E.g.,* Xákmok Kásek Indigenous Cmty. v. Paraguay, Merits, Reparations, and Costs, Judgment, Inter-Am. Ct. H.R. (ser. C) No. 214, para. 93 (Aug. 24, 2010); Moiwana Cmty. v. Suriname, Preliminary Objections, Merits, Reparations, and Costs, Judgment, Inter-Am. Ct. H.R. (ser. C) No. 124, para. 131 (June 15, 2005).

[153] *See, e.g.,* Karen Engle, The Elusive Promise of Indigenous Development: Rights, Culture, Strategy 162–82 (2010); Ariel E. Dulitzky, *When Afro-Descendants Became "Tribal Peoples": The Inter-American Human Rights System and Rural Black Communities,* 15 UCLA J. Int'l L. & Foreign Aff. 29, 42 (2010).

[154] Saramaka People v. Suriname, Preliminary Objections, Merits, Reparations, and Costs, Judgment, Inter-Am. Ct. H.R. (ser. C) No. 172, para. 134 (Nov. 28, 2007).

By 1996, for example, the Court had fewer than 10 rulings on the merits. Further, its judgments, although lengthy, frequently lack in-depth conceptual development, a deficiency that often has constrained this book's analysis. Currently, however, with over 300 judgments on contentious cases and over 20 advisory opinions, the Tribunal's work has reached a critical mass.

Each chapter generally consists of the following: (1) an Introduction to compare the right's formulation with equivalent rights in other major international and regional treaties; (2) a Background section to consider the right's negotiation history; (3) a Scope of Protection section to analyze the right's provisions, paragraph by paragraph or topic by topic; and (4) a Limitations section, if applicable, to study any limitations to the right. The assessment centers on the judgments, advisory opinions, and other decisions of the Inter-American Court—the ultimate authority on the American Convention. The Inter-American Commission's relevant reports, published decisions, and other documents are also considered, especially with respect to issues that have not been addressed by the Court. At times, focused references are made to the decisions of other influential human rights authorities, such as the European Court of Human Rights and the United Nations Human Rights Committee, to draw significant comparisons and contrasts.

A Note on Judgment Citations

In its rulings, the Inter-American Court often repeats certain principles and observations. Due to space constraints, we cannot cite every judgment that states the repeated point. As a result, we have decided to use "e.g.," and then list two pertinent Court judgments: a recent decision and an earlier one. "E.g." indicates to readers that even more Court judgments contain the same point.

2

Equality

Article 24: Right to Equal Protection

All persons are equal before the law. Consequently, they are entitled, without discrimination, to equal protection of the law.

Chapter 2 Contents

I. Introduction 32
II. Background 35
III. Scope of Protection 36
   A. The Relationship of Article 24 and Article 1 36
   B. The Assessment of Discrimination 40
      1. Definitions and State Obligations 40
      2. The Progression of the Court's Case Law: Discrimination in Law and in Fact 43
         a. Introduction 43
         b. Perceived Political Opponents 44
         c. Disadvantaged Groups 45
         d. Synthesis 48
      3. *Atala Riffo* and the Court's Current Approach to Discrimination 49

The American Convention on Human Rights. Thomas M. Antkowiak and Alejandra Gonza.

I. Introduction

Equality constitutes an organizing principle for societies; it is the foundation upon which legal frameworks are—or should be—built.[1] As a consequence, it is prioritized in international law. The first two articles of the Universal Declaration of Human Rights are reserved for equality and non-discrimination.[2] Advancing these principles is among the primary objectives of the United Nations, according to its Charter.[3] The Inter-American Court has even held that "equality before the law, equal protection before the law and non-discrimination belong to *jus cogens*," international law's most authoritative classification.[4]

Despite its limited title, "Right to Equal Protection," Article 24 of the American Convention in fact establishes two key rights: (1) the enduring right to "equality before the law,"[5] and (2) the right to "equal protection of the law," a phrase introduced by the U.S. Constitution's Fourteenth Amendment.[6] But these two somewhat abstract concepts, along with non-discrimination and equality itself, have led to uncertainty—particularly at the international level. Differing opinions are held about their precise definitions; the concepts are even used interchangeably.[7] In this chapter, we employ the definitions shared

---

[1] *See* Juridical Condition & Rights of the Undocumented Migrants, Advisory Opinion OC-18/03, Inter Am. Ct. H.R. (ser. A) No. 18, para. 101 (Sept. 17, 2003).

[2] Article 1 provides: "All human beings are born free and equal in dignity and rights. They are endowed with reason and conscience and should act towards one another in a spirit of brotherhood." Article 2 establishes "Everyone is entitled to all the rights and freedoms set forth in this Declaration, without distinction of any kind, such as race, colour, sex, language, religion, political or other opinion, national or social origin, property, birth or other status. Furthermore, no distinction shall be made on the basis of the political, jurisdictional or international status of the country or territory to which a person belongs, whether it be independent, trust, non-self-governing or under any other limitation of sovereignty." Universal Declaration of Human Rights, G.A. Res. 217A (III), U.N. Doc. A/810 at 71 (1948) [Universal Declaration].

[3] Pursuant to the UN Charter, two purposes of the organization are "To develop friendly relations among nations based on respect for the principle of equal rights and self-determination of peoples, and to take other appropriate measures to strengthen universal peace;" and "To achieve international co-operation in solving international problems of an economic, social, cultural, or humanitarian character, and in promoting and encouraging respect for human rights and for fundamental freedoms for all without distinction as to race, sex, language, or religion." U.N. Charter art. 1.

[4] *E.g.*, Norín Catrimán et al. (Leaders, members, and activist of the Mapuche Indigenous People) v. Chile, Merits, Reparations, and Costs, Judgment, Inter-Am. Ct. H.R. (ser. C) No. 279, para. 197 (May 29, 2014); Juridical Condition & Rights of the Undocumented Migrants, Advisory Opinion OC-18/03, Inter-Am. Ct. H.R. (ser. A) No. 18, para. 101 (Sept. 17, 2003).

[5] *See, e.g.*, Manfred Nowak, U.N. Covenant on Civil and Political Rights: CCPR Commentary 598 ((2d ed. 2005) (stating that the principle can be found in many national bills of rights since the French Revolution).

[6] Section I of the Fourteenth Amendment to the U.S. Constitution provides, in part: "No state shall make or enforce any law which shall abridge the privileges or immunities of citizens of the United States; nor shall any state deprive any person of life, liberty, or property, without due process of law; nor deny to any person within its jurisdiction the equal protection of the laws." U.S. Const. amend. XIV, § 1.

[7] *See, e.g.*, Dinah Shelton, *Prohibited Discrimination in International Human Rights Law*, *in* The Diversity of International Law 266–67 (Aristotle Constantinides & Nikos Zaikos eds., 2010); Polyvios G.

by a number of global legal authorities.[8] According to these established views, the right to equality before the law requires equal application of the law. This means that judges and State officials must not act arbitrarily in enforcing laws. On the other hand, the right to equal protection of the law focuses upon the content of the law, and directs legislators to avoid all discrimination when drafting and enacting statutes.

When a law is formally equal, or neutral on its face, it seemingly treats everyone identically. Yet such formal equality may not result in real, or substantive, equality, because it may disregard social realities and actually disadvantage specific individuals or groups.[9] Legislators, courts, and human rights bodies have considered these disparate impacts and developed approaches on differential treatment—in pursuit of a truly "equal" protection of the law. Domestic and international frameworks, as a result, have enacted special measures, or affirmative action, for certain vulnerable groups.[10]

Pursuant to the text of Article 24, equal protection of the law—as indicated by the term "consequently"—*results from* equality before the law. Such a formulation is not found in Article 26 of the International Covenant on Civil and Political Rights (ICCPR), which provides in part: "All persons are equal before the law and are entitled without any discrimination to the equal protection of the law."[11] During the ICCPR negotiations, the relationship between the two principles was debated, and the delegates rightly—and overwhelmingly—chose to present them as conceptually independent from one another.[12]

Article 26 of the ICCPR also differs in that it illustrates forms of discrimination: "the law shall prohibit any discrimination and guarantee to all persons equal and effective protection against discrimination on any ground such as race, colour, sex, language, religion, political or other opinion, national or social origin, property, birth or other status."

POLYVIOU, THE EQUAL PROTECTION OF THE LAWS 1–2 (1980); Anja Seibert-Fohr, *The Rise of Equality in International Law and Its Pitfalls: Learning from Comparative Constitutional Law*, 35 BROOK. J. INT'L L. 1, 22 (2010).

[8] *See, e.g.*, NOWAK, *supra* note 5, at 604–608; UN Human Rights Committee, General Comment No. 18: Non-discrimination (1989), para. 12; UN Committee on Economic, Social and Cultural Rights, General Comment No. 16: The Equal Right of Men and Women to the Enjoyment of All Economic, Social and Cultural rights (2005), para. 9: YATAMA v. Nicaragua, Preliminary Objections, Merits, Reparations, and Costs, Judgment, Inter-Am. Ct. H.R. (ser. C) No. 127, para. 186 (June 23, 2005); African Commission on Human and Peoples' Rights 294/04: Zimbabwe Lawyers for Human Rights and Institute for Human Rights and Development in Africa (on behalf of Andrew Barclay Meldrum) v. Zimbabwe (2009), para. 96.

[9] *See, e.g.*, Charles Lawrence, *The Id, the Ego, and Equal Protection: Reckoning with Unconscious Racism*, 39 STAN. L. REV. 317, 330 (1987); Bruce Ackerman, *Beyond* Carolene Products, 98 HARV. L. REV. 713, 739 (1985); JOHN HART ELY, DEMOCRACY AND DISTRUST (1980).

[10] Such affirmative action approaches have sought to provide "equal opportunities" for group members, as well as, in some cases, "equality of results." The latter approach, and its use of quotas to achieve specific outcomes, has proven more controversial. *See, e.g.*, Richard Delgado, *Affirmative Action as a Majoritarian Device: Or, Do You Really Want to Be a Role Model?*, 89 MICH. L. REV. 1222, 1223–24 (1991); Kathleen Sullivan, *Sins of Discrimination: Last Term's Affirmative Action Cases*, 100 HARV. L. REV. 78, 80–96 (1986).

[11] International Covenant on Civil and Political Rights, Dec. 16, 1966, S. Treaty Doc. No. 95-20, 6 I.L.M. 368 (1967), 999 U.N.T.S. 171., art. 26 [ICCPR].

[12] *See* NOWAK, *supra* note 5, at 607.

In addition, this sentence creates a positive obligation for States Parties to prevent discrimination by enacting special laws and other protections.[13] Although Article 24 of the American Convention may not clearly establish such a positive obligation upon legislators, the Inter-American Court, as noted below, has nevertheless interpreted it as such.

Significantly, Article 24 of the American Convention and Article 26 of the ICCPR establish autonomous rights to equality, as do provisions in the Charter of Fundamental Rights of the European Union (EU Charter), the African Charter on Human and Peoples' Rights (African Charter), the Arab Charter on Human Rights (Arab Charter), and the Universal Declaration.[14] In contrast, the European Convention for the Protection of Human Rights and Fundamental Freedoms (European Convention) only provides an "accessory" right; its Article 14 stipulates:

> The enjoyment of the rights and freedoms set forth in this Convention shall be secured without discrimination on any ground such as sex, race, colour, language, religion, political or other opinion, national or social origin, association with a national minority, property, birth or other status.[15]

Such a clause prohibits discrimination, but only with regard to the rights enumerated in the treaty. Article 1(1) of the American Convention contains a similar provision.

Yet the guarantees of Article 24 of the American Convention, Article 26 of the ICCPR, Title III of the EU Charter, Article 11 of the Arab Charter, and Article 3 of the African Charter all stand alone; that is, according to these equality provisions, *all* rights and benefits found in a State Party's national legislation must be safeguarded without discrimination. This is so even if the State has no international treaty obligation to establish the right. To illustrate, the right to social security is not found in the ICCPR. Nevertheless, the UN Human Rights Committee found that the Netherlands, in breach of Article 26, had drawn impermissible gender distinctions to receive certain benefits provided by domestic law.[16]

---

[13] *Id.* at 607–608; UN Human Rights Committee, General Comment No. 18: Non-discrimination (Nov. 10, 1989), paras. 1, 12.

[14] Charter of Fundamental Rights of the European Union, 2000 O.J. (C 364), Title III [EU Charter]; Universal Declaration, art. 7; African Charter on Human and Peoples' Rights, CAB/LEG/67/3 rev. 5, 21 I.L.M. 58, art. 3 (1982) [African Charter]; Arab Charter on Human Rights, Council of the League of Arab States, art. 11 (2004), *available at* http://hrlibrary.umn.edu/instree/arabcharter2.html [Arab Charter].

[15] Convention for the Protection of Human Rights and Fundamental Freedoms, Nov. 4, 1950, 213 U.N.T.S. 222, art. 14 [European Convention]. Interestingly, the European Court has acknowledged that there could be a violation of Article 14 even if there is no breach of another Article of the Convention, despite Article 14's status as an accessory provision. DAVID HARRIS, MICHAEL O'BOYLE & COLIN WARBRICK, LAW OF THE EUROPEAN CONVENTION ON HUMAN RIGHTS 784 (3d ed. 2014).

[16] S.W.M. Broeks v. The Netherlands, Communication No. 172/1984, U.N. Doc. CCPR/C/OP/2 (1990), paras. 12.4, 15; F. H. Zwaan-de Vries v. The Netherlands, Communication No. 182/1984, U.N. Doc. CCPR/C/OP/2 (1990), paras. 12.4, 15.

In 2005, Protocol No. 12 entered into force, adding a general prohibition of discrimination to the European Convention. It provides: "the enjoyment of *any right set forth by law* shall be secured without discrimination."[17] However, the European treaty still lacks express recognitions of equality before the law and equal protection of the law.[18]

For its part, the Inter-American equality jurisprudence has been dynamic over the last decade, considering varied forms of discrimination with both clarifying and confusing results. Owing to the Inter-American Court's interpretations of Articles 24 and 1, State obligations have expanded—far surpassing the United States delegation's limited intentions during the Convention's negotiations. Many complex issues have yet to be fully analyzed, including indirect and private discrimination, as well as affirmative action. As discussed below, standards of review and even standards of proof for differential treatment remain uncertain. These challenging matters, as well as other crucial topics such as LGBT rights and same-sex marriage, will be further developed by the Inter-American System in its next decade of work.

II. Background

The Inter-American Commission on Human Rights prepared a draft of the American Convention to be negotiated by State representatives in San José, Costa Rica, during November 1969.[19] Surprisingly, the Inter-American Commission's draft omitted equal protection of the law. That glaring difference aside, the proposal resembled Article 26 of the ICCPR:

> All persons are equal before the law. The law shall prohibit discrimination and guarantee to all persons equal and effective protection against any discrimination for reasons of race, color, sex, language, religion, political or other opinion, national or social origin, economic status, birth, or any other social conditions.[20]

The U.S. delegation proposed to delete the entire second sentence, because "it creates the danger of wide divergence of opinion as to what constitutes compliance with the Article."[21] The President of Committee I designated a working group, which drafted the

---

[17] Protocol No. 12 to the Convention for the Protection of Human Rights and Fundamental Freedoms, Nov. 4, 2000, art. 1(1) (emphasis added).

[18] Explanatory Report, Protocol No. 12 to the Convention for the Protection of Human Rights and Fundamental Freedoms, para. 15. It should be noted that the Preamble to the Protocol nevertheless states: "Having regard to the fundamental principle according to which all persons are equal before the law and are entitled to the equal protection of the law."

[19] Draft Inter-American Convention on Protection of Human Rights, Doc. 5 (English), Sept. 22, 1969.

[20] Draft Inter-American Convention on Protection of Human Rights, Doc. 5 (English), art. 22, Sept. 22, 1969.

[21] Draft Inter-American Convention on Protection of Human Rights and Observations and Comments of the American Governments, Document 13, art. 22, Sept. 22, 1969 (English).

text that was unanimously accepted and became the final version.[22] Neither the fortunate insertion of "equal protection of the law," nor its formulation as a corollary to equality before the law (using the term "consequently"), was explained in the official conference records.

Later, the U.S. delegation's conference report noted that it had objected to the Inter-American Commission's draft because it had appeared to prohibit both private and public discrimination.[23] The delegation considered the final version to be more limited, and, as a result, more consistent with the Fourteenth Amendment to the U.S. Constitution.[24] Although U.S. objections removed Article 24's guidance on forms of discrimination, the Inter-American Court would subsequently address this omission by linking Article 24 to the non-discrimination clause of Article 1(1), as explained below.

III. Scope of Protection

A. THE RELATIONSHIP OF ARTICLE 24 AND ARTICLE 1

As noted above, the Convention's Article 24 constitutes an autonomous right to equality. In contrast, Article 1(1) is an accessory provision that, among other things, prohibits discrimination with respect to the rights of the American Convention.[25] Unfortunately, the Inter-American Court's interpretation of these two Articles—both as separate concepts and in relation to each other—has been inconsistent and, at times, problematic.

In an early advisory opinion, the Tribunal acknowledged that the two Articles "are conceptually not identical."[26] It continued:

> In recognizing equality before the law, [Article 24] prohibits all discriminatory treatment originating in a legal prescription. The prohibition against discrimination so broadly proclaimed in Article 1(1) with regard to the rights and guarantees enumerated in the Convention thus extends to the domestic law of the States Parties. . . .[27]

---

[22] *See* p. 259, Minutes of the 13th Session of Committee I, Doc 54 (Rev. 1), Nov. 18, 1969.

[23] Report of the United States Delegation to the Inter-American Conference on the Protection of Human Rights, p. 34, 1969.

[24] *Id.*

[25] Article 1(1) of the American Convention provides: "The States Parties to this Convention undertake to respect the rights and freedoms recognized herein and to ensure to all persons subject to their jurisdiction the free and full exercise of those rights and freedoms, without any discrimination for reasons of race, color, sex, language, religion, political or other opinion, national or social origin, economic status, birth, or any other social condition."

[26] Proposed Amendments of the Naturalization Provisions of the Constitution of Costa Rica, Advisory Opinion OC-4/84, Inter-Am. Ct. H.R. (ser. A) No. 4, para. 54 (Jan. 19, 1984).

[27] *Id.*

Here, despite using the term "equality before the law," the Court actually appears to refer to the equal protection properties of Article 24. It holds that Article 1's discrimination prohibition should extend to the law of States Parties, linking Article 1 and 24.

In *YATAMA v. Nicaragua*, the Tribunal set out a more meticulous explanation of the two Articles:

> Article 24 of the American Convention prohibits any type of discrimination, not only with regard to the rights embodied therein, but also with regard to all the laws that the State adopts and to their application. In other words, this Article does not merely reiterate the provisions of Article 1(1) of the Convention concerning the obligation of States to respect and ensure, without discrimination, the rights recognized therein, but, in addition, establishes a right that also entails obligations for the State to respect and ensure the principle of equality and non-discrimination in the safeguard of other rights and in all domestic laws that it adopts.[28]

Thus, the Court recognizes Article 24 as fully comprised of the independent rights to equality before the law and equal protection of the law. Article 24 forbids discrimination concerning all rights of the Convention. Additionally, Article 24 prohibits States from discrimination in the enactment and enforcement of their laws. In sum, Article 24's scope includes the anti-discrimination obligation of Article 1(1) and extends it beyond the Convention into State law and practice.

Yet the Court's case law takes an unexpected turn in *Apitz Barbera* et al. *v. Venezuela*.[29] In that judgment from 2008, the Tribunal considered that if the State discriminates with respect to rights in the Convention, "a violation of Article 1(1) and the substanti[ve] right involved would arise."[30] But if the "discrimination refers to unequal protection by domestic law, a violation of Article 24 would occur."[31] In the subsequent decision *Atala Riffo and Daughters v. Chile,* the Tribunal extended this approach: Article 24 does not only pertain to equal protection of national law, but also concerns its equal application.[32] In other words, the Court now regards the scope of Article 24 as limited to "the application or interpretation of a specific domestic law."[33]

---

[28] YATAMA v. Nicaragua, Preliminary Objections, Merits, Reparations, and Costs, Judgment, Inter-Am. Ct. H.R. (ser. C) No. 127, para. 186 (June 23, 2005).

[29] Apitz Barbera et al. ("First Court of Administrative Disputes") v. Venezuela, Preliminary Objection, Merits, Reparations, and Costs, Judgment, Inter-Am. Ct. H.R. (ser. C) No. 182 (Aug. 5, 2008).

[30] *Id.* para. 209.

[31] *Id.*

[32] Atala Riffo and Daughters v. Chile, Merits, Reparations, and Costs, Judgment, Inter-Am. Ct. H.R. (ser. C) No. 239, para. 82 (Feb. 24, 2012).

[33] Artavia Murillo et al. (In-vitro Fertilization) v. Costa Rica, Preliminary Objections, Merits, Reparations, and Costs, Judgment, Inter-Am. Ct. H.R. (ser. C) No. 257, para. 285 (Nov. 28, 2012). *See also* Duque v. Colombia, Preliminary Objections, Merits, Reparations and Costs, Judgment, Inter-Am. Ct. H.R. (ser. C) No. 310, para. 94 (Feb. 26, 2016) (making a similar statement).

Thus, discriminatory State laws and judicial actions have led to Article 24 violations.[34] Yet detentions and expulsions by State officials,[35] or "discriminatory acts based on expressions or statements" by paramilitary soldiers, have been excluded from the ambit of Article 24.[36] In *Expelled Dominicans and Haitians v. Dominican Republic*, the Court explained that the case's discriminatory detentions and expulsions impaired the victims' "substantive rights," such as Article 7 (Right to Personal Liberty) and Article 22 (Freedom of Movement and Residence), along with "the obligation established in Article 1(1) ... to respect the rights without discrimination."[37] It is not surprising that this tenuous distinction between Article 24 and Article 1(1) has not always been maintained, given that the Convention's numerous rights are invariably intertwined with State laws and their application.[38] The Tribunal's posture here draws a haphazard line in the sand.

There are certainly a number of objections to the Court's current approach, which places great emphasis on the accessory non-discrimination provision of Article 1(1) at the expense of Article 24. Above all, the approach is contrary to the Tribunal's jurisprudence in *YATAMA* and other cases, which in turn reflects international understandings of equality principles. The rights to equality before the law and equal protection of the law apply to *all* rights, not simply to the matters that fall out of the Convention's scope.[39] In this way, *YATAMA* found violations to both Article 24 and Article 23 (Political Rights) when an election law had a discriminatory impact upon voting rights.[40] The connection established between the two rights, which did not imply that Article 24 was

---

[34] Norín Catrimán et al. (Leaders, members, and activist of the Mapuche Indigenous People) v. Chile, Merits, Reparations, and Costs, Judgment, Inter-Am. Ct. H.R. (ser. C) No. 279, para. 228 (May 29, 2014); Atala Riffo and Daughters v. Chile, Merits, Reparations, and Costs, Judgment, Inter-Am. Ct. H.R. (ser. C) No. 239, para. 146 (Feb. 24, 2012).

[35] Expelled Dominicans and Haitians v. Dominican Republic, Preliminary Objections, Merits, Reparations, and Costs, Judgment, Inter-Am. Ct. H.R. (ser. C) No. 282, para. 404 (Aug. 28, 2014).

[36] Afro-Descendant Communities Displaced From the Cacarica River Basin (Operation Genesis) v. Colombia, Preliminary Objections, Merits, Reparations, and Costs, Judgment, Inter-Am. Ct. H.R. (ser. C) No. 270, para. 335 (Nov. 20, 2013).

[37] Expelled Dominicans and Haitians v. Dominican Republic, Preliminary Objections, Merits, Reparations, and Costs, Judgment, Inter-Am. Ct. H.R. (ser. C) No. 282, para. 404 (Aug. 28, 2014).

[38] *See* Veliz Franco et al. v. Guatemala, Preliminary Objections, Merits, and Reparations, Judgment, Inter-Am. Ct. H.R. (ser. C) No. 277 (May 19, 2014) (considering a defective criminal investigation, the Court avoided making the distinction and found a violation of Article 24 "in relation to the obligation of non-discrimination contained in Article 1(1)"); Artavia Murillo et al. (In-vitro Fertilization) v. Costa Rica, Preliminary Objections, Merits, Reparations, and Costs, Judgment, Inter-Am. Ct. H.R. (ser. C) No. 257 (Nov. 28, 2012) (finding that the Costa Rican Supreme Court's decision at issue was not related "to the application or interpretation of a specific domestic law that regulates [in-vitro fertilization]").

[39] *E.g.*, YATAMA v. Nicaragua, Preliminary Objections, Merits, Reparations, and Costs, Judgment, Inter-Am. Ct. H.R. (ser. C) No. 127, para. 186 (June 23, 2005) ("Article 24 of the American Convention prohibits any type of discrimination, not only with regard to the rights embodied therein, but also with regard to all the laws that the State adopts and to their application"); NOWAK, *supra* note 5, at 628.

[40] *Id.* para. 229.

merely accessory to Article 23, was commended in separate opinions by Judges Cançado Trindade and García Sayán.[41]

Similarly, when a prison regulation in *López Álvarez v. Honduras* unduly restricted the freedom of speech of Garifuna community members, the Tribunal found breaches of both Article 24 and Article 13 (Freedom of Speech) of the Convention.[42] In *Yean and Bosico v. Dominican Republic*, discriminatory practices that deprived two children of their nationality resulted in violations to Articles 24 and 20 (Right to Nationality).[43] Thus, in the Court's former approach, if discrimination resulted in the violation of a "substantive" Convention right, both Article 24 and the corresponding additional Article were found violated. If an additional Convention right was not violated, but the State still committed discrimination, then Article 24 was breached by itself.

The UN Human Rights Committee takes a similar stance. This is instructive because, as noted in the Introduction, the ICCPR's Article 26 features comparable autonomous rights to equality before the law and to equal protection of the law. Article 26, according to the Human Rights Committee, "prohibits discrimination in law or in fact in any field regulated and protected by public authorities."[44] Further, the ICCPR's Article 2 has an accessory provision similar to the American Convention's Article 1. When discrimination results in the breach of Covenant rights, the Human Rights Committee has found violations of the treaty's relevant substantive provisions along with Article 26.[45] This replicates the Inter-American Court's former approach: Article 26 of the ICCPR is understood to include all of the rights enumerated in its treaty.

Furthermore, the Inter-American Court's change in direction veers from the Tribunal's pro-victim path and *pro homine* interpretation of the Convention. The fact that Article 1(1) contains an anti-discrimination provision with respect to Convention

---

[41] *See id.*, Separate Opinion of Judge Antônio Cançado Trindade, para. 6, and Concurring Opinion of Diego García-Sayán, para. 31.

[42] López Álvarez v. Honduras, Merits, Reparations, and Costs, Judgment, Inter-Am. Ct. H.R. (ser. C) No. 141, para. 174 (Feb. 1, 2006).

[43] Yean and Bosico v. Dominican Republic, Preliminary Objections, Merits, Reparations, and Costs, Judgment, Inter-Am. Ct. H.R. (ser. C) No. 130, para. 174 (Sept. 8, 2005).

[44] UN Human Rights Committee, General Comment No. 18: Non-discrimination (Nov. 10, 1989), para. 12. *See also* Martínez de Irujo v. Spain, Views, U.N. Human Rights Committee, Commc'n No. 1008/2001, para. 6.5, U.N. Doc. CCPR/C/80/D/1008/2001 (June 15, 2004) (reiterating that Article 26 "is a free-standing provision which prohibits all discrimination in any sphere regulated by a State party to the Covenant").

[45] *E.g.*, Umarova v. Uzbekistan, Views, U.N. Human Rights Committee, Commc'n No. 1449/2006, para. 8.8, U.N. Doc. CCPR/C/100/D/1449/2006 (Oct. 19, 2010) ("The Committee considers that the arrest, trial and conviction of Mr. Umarov resulted in effectively preventing him from expressing his political views. Accordingly the Committee finds that the State party violated Mr. Umarov's rights under article 19, paragraph 2, and article 26 of the Covenant."); Sudalenko v. Belarus, Views, U.N. Human Rights Committee, Commc'n No. 1354/2005, para. 6.7, U.N. Doc. CCPR/C/100/D/1354/2005 (Nov. 1, 2010) ("the refusal to register the author as a candidate for the 2004 elections . . . was not based on objective and reasonable criteria and is, therefore, incompatible with the State party's obligations under article 25, paragraphs (a) and (b), read in conjunction with article 2, paragraph 1, and article 26 of the Covenant.").

rights should not subtract this quality from Article 24.[46] Article 24 encompasses broad, autonomous rights; its stature is greater and its scope is wider than Article 1(1)'s accessory discrimination prohibition.[47]

An Article 24 violation also clearly condemns discrimination, putting States on notice and likely providing more satisfaction to victims. In contrast, an Article 1(1) violation already occurs in the Court's case law whenever a substantive right is breached, whether or not discrimination is found. This is because a human rights violation necessarily results from the State's failure to respect or ensure the right in question, which are key obligations of Article 1(1).[48] Merely finding yet another breach of Article 1(1) obligations—even if the discrimination aspect is emphasized—obscures the Court's conclusion and diminishes its impact. In sum, it is true that under the current *Apitz Barbera* framework the Court still fully prohibits discrimination in law and in fact. However, for the conceptual and practical reasons described, the Tribunal should return to its former manner of interpreting Article 24.[49]

B. THE ASSESSMENT OF DISCRIMINATION

1. Definitions and State Obligations

To enforce equality principles, groups and individuals petition domestic or international courts and denounce instances of discrimination. Yet, as already pointed out, Article 24 lacks a definition of this principle. For many, discrimination means odious distinctions based on race, gender, ethnicity, sexual identity, or other status. However, discrimination also refers to many other unreasonable forms of differential treatment with regard to persons in similar situations.[50] For example, a State treated some individuals differently than others in the resolution of their compensation claims, although all were in comparable situations; this led to the Inter-American Court's finding of discrimination.[51]

---

[46] An approach bolstering human rights would seek to accumulate the protections of the American Convention. For an opposing view, *see* Marianne González Le Saux y Óscar Parra Vera, *Concepciones y cláusulas de igualdad en la jurisprudencia de la Corte Interamericana a propósito del Caso Apitz*, 47 REVISTA IIDH 127 (2008).

[47] *See* Separate Opinion of Judge Rodolfo E. Piza, Proposed Amendments of the Naturalization Provisions of the Constitution of Costa Rica, Advisory Opinion OC-4/84, Inter-Am. Ct. H.R. (ser. A) No. 4, para. 9 (Jan. 19, 1984); NOWAK, *supra* note 5, at 604–605; Anne Bayefsky, *The Principle of Equality or Non-discrimination in International Law*, 11 HRLJ 1, 3–4 (1990).

[48] *E.g.*, Supreme Court of Justice (Quintana Coello et al.) v. Ecuador, Preliminary Objections, Merits, Reparations, and Costs, Judgment, Inter-Am. Ct. H.R. (ser. C) No. 266, para. 183 (Aug. 23, 2013); Velásquez Rodríguez v. Honduras, 1988 Inter-Am. Ct. H.R. (ser. C) No. 4, para. 162 (July 29, 1988).

[49] If the Court returns to its former approach, it could also emphasize the non-discrimination provision of Article 1(1) whenever Convention rights are violated.

[50] *See, e.g.*, Shelton, *supra* note 7, at 261–62; Bayefsky, *supra* note 47, at 11–18.

[51] This is a simplified explanation of the judgment *Barbani Duarte* et al. *v. Uruguay*. *See* Barbani Duarte et al. v. Uruguay, Merits, Reparations, and Costs, Judgment, Inter. Am. Ct. H.R. (ser. C) No. 234, para. 185 (Oct. 13, 2011) ("the victims [suffered] arbitrary and discriminatory treatment, because the State did not guarantee an

The Inter-American Court and Commission prohibit all such forms of discrimination. They have generally followed European Court case law, also endorsed by the UN Human Rights Committee and other authorities, which broadly defines discrimination as differential treatment lacking a "reasonable and objective justification."[52] In this way, the Inter-American jurisprudence has held that such treatment is only permissible if it is "reasonable, objective, and proportionate and does not infringe upon human rights."[53]

Further, the Inter-American System forcefully condemns discrimination that harms disadvantaged social groups. As noted previously, the Court has linked Article 1(1) to Article 24. Accordingly, Article 24 applies the parameters of Article 1(1), prohibiting discrimination "for reasons of race, color, sex, language, religion, political or other opinion, national or social origin, economic status, birth, or any other social condition."[54] As signaled by "any other social condition," this is an open-ended list of criteria, which allows for the progression of human rights law. When interpreting this phrase, the Court has asserted, "it is always necessary to choose the alternative that is most favorable to the protection of the rights enshrined in said treaty, based on the principle of the rule most favorable to the human being."[55] Following this principle, the Tribunal has added sexual orientation, ethnic origin, disability, and HIV status to the list of prohibited categories.[56]

Currently, the Court also cites to the International Convention on the Elimination of All Forms of Racial Discrimination and the Convention on the Elimination of All

---

adequate reasoning of the decisions of the Central Bank that decided their claims . . . that would allow verification of the objective application of the criteria used to determine the requirement of absence of consent").

[52] *E.g.*, Belgian Linguistic case, Eur. Ct. H.R. (1968), para. 10; UN Human Rights Committee, General Comment No. 18: Non-discrimination (Nov. 10, 1989), para. 13 ("not every differentiation of treatment will constitute discrimination, if the criteria for such differentiation are reasonable and objective and if the aim is to achieve a purpose which is legitimate under the Covenant").

[53] *E.g.*, Vélez Loor v. Panama, Preliminary Objections, Merits, Reparations, and Costs, Judgment, Inter-Am. Ct. H.R. (ser. C) No. 218, para. 248 (Nov. 23, 2010); Proposed Amendments of the Naturalization Provisions of the Constitution of Costa Rica, Advisory Opinion OC-4/84, Inter-Am. Ct. H.R. (ser. A) No. 4, para. 56 (Jan. 19, 1984). The Inter-American Commission has stated that "a distinction based on reasonable and objective criteria (1) pursues a legitimate aim and (2) employs means which are proportional to the end sought." Morales de Sierra v. Guatemala, Case 11.625, Inter-Am. Comm'n H.R., Report No. 4/01, OEA/Ser. L./V/II.114, doc. 5 rev. (2002), para. 31. As explained later in this chapter, the Court has increasingly incorporated such an explicit analytical test into its case law.

[54] American Convention, art. 1(1).

[55] *E.g.*, Atala Riffo and Daughters v. Chile, Merits, Reparations, and Costs, Judgment, Inter-Am. Ct. H.R. (ser. C) No. 239, para. 84 (Feb. 24, 2012); Compulsory Membership in an Association Prescribed by Law for the Practice of Journalism (arts. 13 and 29 American Convention on Human Rights), Advisory Opinion OC-5/85, Inter-Am. Ct. H.R. (ser. A) No. 5, para. 52 (Nov. 13, 1985).

[56] Atala Riffo and Daughters v. Chile, Merits, Reparations, and Costs, Judgment, Inter-Am. Ct. H.R. (ser. C) No. 239, para. 93 (Feb. 24, 2012) (adding sexual orientation); Norín Catrimán et al. (Leaders, members, and activist of the Mapuche Indigenous People) v. Chile, Merits, Reparations, and Costs, Judgment, Inter-Am. Ct. H.R. (ser. C) No. 279, paras. 204–206 (May 29, 2014) (ethnic origin); Ximenes Lopes v. Brazil, Merits, Reparations, and Costs, Judgment, Inter-Am. Ct. H.R. (ser. C) No. 149, para. 105 (July 4, 2006) (disability); Gonzales Lluy et al. v. Ecuador, Preliminary Objections, Merits, Reparations and Costs, Judgment, Inter-Am. Ct. H.R. (ser. C) No. 298, para. 255 (Sept. 1, 2015) (HIV status).

Forms of Discrimination Against Women when assessing discrimination.[57] These treaties, according to the Tribunal,

> lead to the conclusion that discrimination is any distinction, exclusion, restriction or preference based on the prohibited reasons which has the purpose or effect of nullifying or impairing the recognition, enjoyment or exercise, on an equal footing, of human rights and fundamental freedoms in the political, economic, social, cultural or any other field.[58]

In addition, the Court and the Commission have drawn from specialized regional instruments to emphasize the strong connection between violence against women and discrimination.[59]

In the last several years, the Tribunal has outlined extensive State obligations in the field of equality law. States "must abstain from carrying out actions that are in any way directly or indirectly designed to create situations of *de jure* or *de facto* discrimination."[60] The Court, then, prohibits "indirect discrimination," which occurs when "laws, actions, policies or other measures," despite apparently neutral or general formulations, exert disproportionate impact upon "certain vulnerable groups."[61]

Moreover, States "are obliged to take affirmative action in order to reverse or change any discriminatory situations in their societies that prejudice a specific group of persons."[62] The Court has specified that such measures should contemplate "the situation of

---

[57] International Convention on the Elimination of All Forms of Racial Discrimination, 660 U.N.T.S. 195, G.A. Res. 2106 (XX), Annex, 20 U.N. GAOR Supp. (No. 14) at 47, U.N. Doc. A/6014 (1966); Convention on the Elimination of All Forms of Discrimination Against Women, 1249 U.N.T.S 13, G.A. Res. 34/180, 34 U.N. GAOR Supp. (No. 46) at 193, U.N. Doc. A/34/46 (1980).

[58] Norín Catrimán et al. (Leaders, members, and activist of the Mapuche Indigenous People) v. Chile, Merits, Reparations, and Costs, Judgment, Inter-Am. Ct. H.R. (ser. C) No. 279, para. 198 (May 29, 2014).

[59] *E.g.*, Veliz Franco et al. v. Guatemala, Preliminary Objections, Merits, and Reparations, Judgment, Inter-Am. Ct. H.R. (ser. C) No. 277, para. 207 (May 19, 2014) (citing, among others, the Inter-American Convention on the Prevention, Punishment and Eradication of Violence Against Women and the Council of Europe's Convention on Preventing and Combating Violence against Women and Domestic Violence); González et al. ("Cotton Field") v. Mexico, Preliminary Objections, Merits, Reparations, and Costs, Judgment, Inter-Am. Ct. H.R. (ser. C) No. 205, para. 394 (Nov. 16, 2009); Lenahan et al. v. United States, Case 12.626, Inter-Am. Comm'n H.R., Report No. 80/11, OEA/Ser.L/V/II, doc. 69, para. 110 (2011).

[60] *E.g.*, Norín Catrimán et al. (Leaders, members, and activists of the Mapuche Indigenous People) v. Chile, Merits, Reparations, and Costs, Judgment, Inter-Am. Ct. H.R. (ser. C) No. 279, para. 201 (May 29, 2014); Juridical Condition & Rights of the Undocumented Migrants, Advisory Opinion OC-18/03, Inter-Am. Ct. H.R. (ser. A) No. 18, para. 103 (Sept. 17, 2003).

[61] *E.g.*, Expelled Dominicans and Haitians v. Dominican Republic, Preliminary Objections, Merits, Reparations, and Costs, Judgment, Inter-Am. Ct. H.R. (ser. C) No. 282, para. 263 (Aug. 28, 2014); Nadege Dorzema et al. v. Dominican Republic, Merits, Reparations, and Costs, Judgment, Inter-Am. Ct. H.R. (ser. C) No. 251, para. 235 (Oct. 24, 2012).

[62] *E.g.*, Norín Catrimán et al. (Leaders, members, and activists of the Mapuche Indigenous People) v. Chile, Merits, Reparations, and Costs, Judgment, Inter-Am. Ct. H.R. (ser. C) No. 279, para. 201 (May 29, 2014);

weakness and destitution" of the members of these groups.[63] Significantly, the Tribunal also has interpreted Article 24 to prohibit private discrimination: the State has a "special duty of protection" against private actions that "create, maintain or encourage discriminatory situations" with the State's "tolerance or acquiescence."[64]

2. The Progression of the Court's Case Law: Discrimination in Law and in Fact

a. Introduction

Since Advisory Opinion No. 4 of 1984, the Inter-American Tribunal has recognized, like other courts, that determining "reasonable and objective" distinctions would require an analytical test.[65] It considered that there would be no discrimination "when the classifications selected are based on substantial factual differences and there exists a reasonable relationship of proportionality between these differences and the aims of the legal rule under review."[66] The aim cannot be "arbitrary, capricious, despotic or in conflict with the essential oneness and dignity of humankind."[67] That is, it should be fully aligned with the many human rights and freedoms established in international law.[68]

The Court offered examples of permissible distinctions. "It cannot be deemed discrimination on the grounds of age or social status" when the law limits "the legal capacity of minors or mentally incompetent persons who lack the capacity to protect their interests."[69] State mechanisms to control the entry and exit of migrants are acceptable, as long as "due process and human dignity" are ensured.[70]

Juridical Condition & Rights of the Undocumented Migrants, Advisory Opinion OC-18/03, Inter-Am. Ct. H.R. (ser. A) No. 18, para. 103 (Sept. 17, 2003).

63 Chitay Nech et al. v. Guatemala, Preliminary Objections, Merits, Reparations, and Costs, Judgment, Inter-Am. Ct. H.R. (ser. C) No. 212, para. 106 (May 25, 2010).

64 *E.g.*, Norín Catrimán et al. (Leaders, members, and activists of the Mapuche Indigenous People) v. Chile, Merits, Reparations, and Costs, Judgment, Inter-Am. Ct. H.R. (ser. C) No. 279, para. 201 (May 29, 2014); Juridical Condition & Rights of the Undocumented Migrants, Advisory Opinion OC-18/03, Inter-Am. Ct. H.R. (ser. A) No. 18, para. 104 (Sept. 17, 2003).

65 Proposed Amendments of the Naturalization Provisions of the Constitution of Costa Rica, Advisory Opinion OC-4/84, Inter-Am. Ct. H.R. (ser. A) No. 4, para. 57 (Jan. 19, 1984). Gerald Torres has observed that, during the litigation of the Court's early indigenous and Afro-Latin community cases, Article 24 violations were not claimed very often—although discrimination was a central issue. Gerald Torres, *Indigenous Peoples, Afro-Indigenous Peoples and Reparations*, *in* REPARATIONS FOR INDIGENOUS PEOPLES: INTERNATIONAL AND COMPARATIVE PERSPECTIVES 138 (Federico Lenzerini ed., 2008).

66 *Id.*

67 *Id.*

68 *See* Rodrigo Uprimny Yepes & Luz María Sánchez Duque, *Artículo 24: Igualdad ante la ley*, *in* LA CONVENCIÓN AMERICANA SOBRE DERECHOS HUMANOS COMENTADA 594 (Christian Steiner & Patricia Uribe eds., 2014).

69 Proposed Amendments of the Naturalization Provisions of the Constitution of Costa Rica, Advisory Opinion OC-4/84, Inter-Am. Ct. H.R. (ser. A) No. 4, para. 56 (Jan. 19, 1984).

70 Juridical Condition & Rights of the Undocumented Migrants, Advisory Opinion OC-18/03, Inter-Am. Ct. H.R. (ser. A) No. 18, para. 119 (Sept. 17, 2003).

In this way, the Court would evaluate whether the distinction in question pursues a legitimate governmental purpose in a proportionate manner. Of course, before this analysis begins, it needs to be shown that differential treatment has actually occurred. It is often more difficult to conclusively prove differential treatment in practice than when it is established by law. Identifying de facto discrimination can be a complex, factually-intensive exercise—an especially challenging enterprise for a remote, international tribunal with limited resources.[71] Owing to these practical obstacles, the Inter-American Court has found fewer instances of discrimination in fact.[72]

b. Perceived Political Opponents

Apitz Barbera et al. *v. Venezuela* involved judges who had been dismissed, allegedly "to pave the way for government-friendly judges and the political ideology of the [Chávez] Government."[73] The petitioners argued that their appeal was decided far more slowly than an appeal filed by another individual. The Inter-American Tribunal eventually concluded that the domestic court did not engage in differential treatment: the two appeals were "different in nature," as they involved different remedial issues and procedures.[74] Nevertheless, the Court still found violations to the judges' due process rights and ordered their reinstatement.[75]

Two more judgments against Venezuela, *Perozo* et al. and *Ríos* et al., concerned alleged discrimination against journalists in the access to information.[76] The petitioners had worked for television stations often critical of the Chávez government.[77] They claimed that the Chávez administration had blocked their coverage of official events, while State media outlets were granted access.[78] In neither case were the allegations proven to the Court's satisfaction. In *Perozo*, the Court observed that the only evidence furnished by petitioners, a video, appeared to show that *all* of the journalists attempting access to

---

[71] *See* De La Cruz Flores v. Peru, Merits, Reparations, and Costs, Judgment, Inter-Am. Ct. H.R. (ser. C) No. 115, para. 115 (Nov. 18, 2004) (showing restraint in this area).

[72] *Miranda Cortez* et al. *v. El Salvador* offers an interesting decision on de facto discrimination from the Inter-American Commission on Human Rights. Miranda Cortez et al. v. El Salvador, Case 12.249, Inter-Am. Comm'n H.R., Report No. 27/09, OEA/Serv.L/V/II, doc. 51 corr. 1, paras. 68–75 (2009). The case concerned an HIV patient who was obligated by State hospital employees to drink from a glass labeled "XXX." A general hospital regulation requiring such labels for HIV patients was not established. The Commission considered the discriminatory treatment to be "utterly unreasonable and demeaning," stigmatizing the victim; as a result, El Salvador was held in breach of Article 24. *Id.* para. 74.

[73] Apitz Barbera et al. ("First Court of Administrative Disputes") v. Venezuela, Preliminary Objection, Merits, Reparations, and Costs, Judgment, Inter-Am. Ct. H.R. (ser. C) No. 182, para. 4 (Aug. 5, 2008).

[74] *Id.* para. 215.

[75] *Id.* para. 267.

[76] Perozo et al. v. Venezuela, Preliminary Objections, Merits, Reparations, and Costs, Judgment, Inter-Am. Ct. H.R. (ser. C) No. 195 (Jan. 28, 2009); Ríos et al. v. Venezuela, Preliminary Objections, Merits, Reparations, and Costs, Judgment, Inter-Am. Ct. H.R. (ser. C) No. 194 (Jan. 28, 2009).

[77] Perozo et al. v. Venezuela, para. 380; Ríos et al. v. Venezuela, para. 349.

[78] Perozo et al. v. Venezuela, para. 382; Ríos et al. v. Venezuela, para. 342.

the Presidential Palace were forbidden entry, not merely the petitioners.[79] The Tribunal emphasized that no other evidence that might demonstrate differential treatment, such as official statements, had been submitted.[80]

In *Rios*, one of the journalist petitioners, Anahís Cruz, claimed that a military authority had prevented her from participating in a press conference. Cruz had submitted video evidence that depicted an interview with a high-ranking soldier, in which he states that another official asked Cruz to leave the conference.[81] The State disputed all allegations of discrimination. In its judgment, the Court did not closely study the video or explain why it offered insufficient proof of differential treatment. Also troublesome is the Court's conclusion on this point: "the existence of systematic hindrances on access to official sources of information was not proven in this case, nor was a discriminatory treatment by state authorities towards the alleged victims."[82] If the Tribunal implied that "systematic hindrances" need be shown, this would clearly comprise an unacceptably high burden of proof. Only one act of differential treatment should be sufficient for an Article 24 assessment.

c. *Disadvantaged Groups*

In contrast to the Venezuelan cases, de facto discrimination was proven in *Yean and Bosico v. Dominican Republic*.[83] The petitioners attempted to register their births and become nationals of the Dominican Republic. Both were under 13 years of age at the time, and, in the Court's view, fulfilled the State's legal requirements for that age category.[84] However, Dominican authorities required more extensive documentation of the petitioners, in line with the registration requirements of a different age category. The Tribunal found that "the circumstances of the Yean and Bosico children did not differ from other Dominican children under 13 years of age in a way that could justify increasing the requirements" for birth registration.[85]

As a result, the Court held that "the State acted arbitrarily, without using reasonable and objective criteria," leading to a violation of Article 24, among other rights.[86] The Court did not expressly consider whether a legitimate purpose had been articulated by the State or otherwise pursue an analytical test. Of note, however, the Tribunal observed

---

[79] Perozo et al. v. Venezuela, para. 393.

[80] *Id.*

[81] Ríos et al. v. Venezuela, Preliminary Objections, Merits, Reparations, and Costs, Judgment, Inter-Am. Ct. H.R. (ser. C) No. 194, para. 231 (Jan. 28, 2009) (in the original Spanish: "En el video presentado por los representantes, se observa una entrevista a un militar de alto rango, en la que éste se refiere a un incidente ocurrido entre la periodista Cruz y un oficial del Ejército y le solicita a la periodista retirarse.").

[82] *Id.* para. 351.

[83] Yean and Bosico v. Dominican Republic, Preliminary Objections, Merits, Reparations, and Costs, Judgment, Inter-Am. Ct. H.R. (ser. C) No. 130 (Sept. 8, 2005).

[84] *Id.* paras. 164–166.

[85] *Id.* para. 165.

[86] *Id.* para. 166.

that "the discriminatory treatment imposed . . . on the children" was "situated within the context of the vulnerable situation of the Haitian population and Dominicans of Haitian origin in the Dominican Republic, to which the alleged victims belong."[87]

In *López Álvarez v. Honduras*, a prison prohibited members of the Garifuna culture from speaking their native language within its confines.[88] The State offered no defense or justification for the differential treatment. The Court held

> the observance of rules in the collective treatment of the detainees within a criminal center does not give the State . . . the legal authority to limit, in an unjustified manner, the freedom of the people to express themselves through any means and in the language chosen by them.[89]

In finding that "the prohibition acquires a special seriousness, since the mother tongue represents an element of [the petitioner's] identity . . . as a Garifuna," it ruled violations of both Article 24 and Article 13, Freedom of Expression.[90] Again, there was no explicit test articulated to find discrimination. Still, it seemed implicit, as the Court considered whether the State had a purpose for the regulation, and then deemed the prison's measure disproportionate to public or security interests.

In another judgment involving ethnic populations, *YATAMA v. Nicaragua*, an election law required that candidates for municipal elections obtain the sponsorship of political parties. The Tribunal found that the restriction "imposed on the YATAMA candidates a form of organization alien to their practices, customs and traditions as a requirement to exercise the right to political participation."[91] Although the law's language was not as blatantly discriminatory as the classification in *López Álvarez*, it resulted in disparate impacts—that is, significant negative consequences for indigenous communities.

In *YATAMA*, the Court used a more detailed balancing test—although the analysis was simplified because the State, as in *López Álvarez*, did not defend the law under review. The Tribunal observed:

> The State has not justified that this restriction obeyed a useful and opportune purpose, which made it necessary so as to satisfy an urgent public interest. To the contrary, this restriction implied an impediment to the full exercise of the right to be elected of the members of the indigenous and ethnic communities. . . .[92]

---

[87] *Id.* para. 168.

[88] López Álvarez v. Honduras, Merits, Reparations, and Costs, Judgment, Inter-Am. Ct. H.R. (ser. C) No. 141 (Feb.1, 2006).

[89] *Id.* para. 168.

[90] *Id.* para. 169.

[91] YATAMA v. Nicaragua, Preliminary Objections, Merits, Reparations, and Costs, Judgment, Inter-Am. Ct. H.R. (ser. C) No. 127, para. 218 (June 23, 2005).

[92] *Id.*

Several criteria for a legitimate government objective are suggested here, including "useful," "opportune," and "urgent." Further, the legal classification apparently should be "necessary" to satisfy such an interest. The Court concluded that because political rights were limited "more than strictly necessary" by a "disproportionate restriction," the State violated both Article 23 (Political Rights) and Article 24, among other provisions of the Convention.[93]

Although a subsequent case, *González* et al. *("Cotton Field") v. Mexico*, did not further develop the emerging analysis and terminology of *YATAMA*, it provided a landmark ruling on the femicide of Ciudad Juarez.[94] This shocking cycle of violence began in the 1990s and left hundreds of women dead over a decade.[95] The Court condemned Mexico's "culture of discrimination against women that influenced the murders."[96] According to the Tribunal, widespread discrimination led to the State's "inaction" and "gender stereotyping," which ensured impunity for the crimes and triggered further attacks on women.[97] Issued after *Apitz Barbera* (*see* Section III(A) *supra*), the judgment did not conceptualize the discrimination as a violation of Article 24, but rather as a breach of Mexico's "obligation not to discriminate contained in Article 1(1) of the Convention, in relation to the obligation to guarantee [the rights to life, personal integrity, liberty and access to justice]."[98]

The *Fernández Ortega* et al. and *Rosendo Cantú* et al. judgments also involved chilling violence against women in Mexico.[99] Both cases addressed rapes perpetrated by Mexican soldiers against indigenous women, as well as the ongoing impunity for these crimes. The Court held, "in order to guarantee access to justice to members of indigenous communities," States must "offer effective protection that takes into account their particularities, social and economic characteristics, as well as their situation of special vulnerability,

---

[93] *Id.* para. 220. Of note, the Court observed that the candidates were affected by both "legal and real discrimination." *Id.* para. 224.

[94] González et al. ("Cotton Field") v. Mexico, Preliminary Objections, Merits, Reparations, and Costs, Judgment, Inter-Am. Ct. H.R. (ser. C) No. 205 (Nov. 16, 2009).

[95] Rampant gender violence has continued in Mexico. *See, e.g.*, Nina Lakhani, *Mexican State Known for Gender-Based Violence Issues Emergency Alert*, THE GUARDIAN (July 29, 2015), http://www.theguardian.com/world/2015/jul/29/mexico-gender-women-violence-emergency-alert-edomex; Damien Cave, *Wave of Violence Swallows More Women in Juárez*, N.Y. TIMES (June 23, 2012), http://www.nytimes.com/2012/06/24/world/americas/wave-of-violence-swallows-more-women-in-juarez-mexico.html?_r=0.

[96] González et al. ("Cotton Field") v. Mexico, Preliminary Objections, Merits, Reparations, and Costs, Judgment, Inter-Am. Ct. H.R. (ser. C) No. 205, para. 399 (Nov. 16, 2009).

[97] *Id.* paras. 400–401. *See also* Inter-American Commission on Human Rights, Access to Justice for Women Victims of Violence in the Americas, OEA/Ser.L/V/II. Doc. 68 (Jan. 20, 2007), *available at* http://www.cidh.org/women/Access07/tocaccess.htm (explaining, among other points, various governmental flaws in responding to cases of violence against women).

[98] *Id.* para. 402.

[99] Rosendo Cantú et al. v. Mexico, 2010 Inter-Am. Ct. H.R. (ser. C) No. 216 (Aug. 31, 2010); Fernández Ortega et al. v. Mexico, 2010 Inter-Am. Ct. H.R. (ser. C) No. 215 (Aug. 30, 2010).

customary law, values, customs and traditions."[100] The judgments noted that the victims, who did not speak Spanish, had been unable to file complaints or obtain relevant information in their native language.[101] For the Tribunal, these facts "implied treatment that did not consider [the victims'] situation of vulnerability based on [their] language and ethnicity," and were sufficient to constitute discrimination.[102] Similar to *González*, the judgments did not cite Article 24, but rather found violations of Mexico's "obligation to guarantee, without discrimination, the right to have access to justice, according to Articles 8(1) and 25 of the American Convention, in relation to Article 1(1)."[103]

In *Vélez Loor v. Panama*, petitioners alleged a "generalized" practice of discrimination against migrants in Panama, in addition to specific discrimination against Jesús Tranquilino Vélez Loor, an undocumented migrant from Ecuador.[104] The Court concluded that the petitioners did not submit sufficient evidence to prove a society-wide practice.[105] The UN reports and other documents presented on the subject did not address the claim with precision, according to the judgment. For example, some documents were prepared after the time of the case's facts, and others focused only upon refugees and migrants from Colombia. As for Vélez Loor in particular, the Court found that he had been denied consular assistance and legal counsel, among other due process protections.[106] Without much more, and despite the State's objections on the point, the Court held that the State failed to comply with "its obligation to guarantee, without discrimination, [his] right to access to justice under the terms of Articles 8(1) and 25 of the American Convention, in conjunction with Article 1(1)."[107]

d. Synthesis

Vélez Loor, like judgments before it, took notice of the petitioner's "serious vulnerable situation" as an "irregular migrant."[108] *López Álvarez, Yean and Bosico, YATAMA, González* et al., *Fernández Ortega* et al., and *Rosendo Cantú* also involved members of vulnerable groups, and resulted in Court findings of discrimination. The Tribunal did not rigorously articulate or apply an analytical test in these decisions, and its discussions were brief. Nevertheless, the results appear to indicate a more demanding standard of judicial review, recalling the U.S. Supreme Court's approach to "suspect classifications" such as race. The

---

[100] Rosendo Cantú et al. v. Mexico, para. 184; Fernández Ortega et al. v. Mexico, para. 200. *See also* Tiu Tojín v. Guatemala, Merits, Reparations, and Costs, Judgment, Inter-Am. Ct. H.R. (ser. C) No. 190, para. 96 (Nov. 26, 2008).

[101] Rosendo Cantú et al. v. Mexico, para. 185; Fernández Ortega et al. v. Mexico, para. 201.

[102] *Id.*

[103] *Id.*

[104] Vélez Loor v. Panama, Preliminary Objections, Merits, Reparations, and Costs, Judgment, Inter-Am. Ct. H.R. (ser. C) No. 218, para. 246 (Nov. 23, 2010).

[105] *Id.* para. 251.

[106] *Id.* paras. 148, 160, 181.

[107] *Id.* para. 254.

[108] *Id.*

Supreme Court's "strict scrutiny" test requires such classifications to be "narrowly tailored" to serve a "compelling" State interest.[109]

In the Venezuelan cases discussed above, the Inter-American Tribunal acknowledged the possibility of State discrimination based on political opinion, another forbidden category listed in Article 1(1).[110] Although a heightened form of scrutiny would have been appropriate, the Court never reached that point in its analysis, because differential treatment had not been proven to its satisfaction. In general, the Court should have offered more guidance in these cases on how to substantiate disparate treatment.

3. *Atala Riffo* and the Court's Current Approach to Discrimination

In the 2012 judgment *Atala Riffo and Daughters v. Chile*,[111] the Court advanced its equality jurisprudence in two respects: (1) it applied a more transparent and deliberate analytical test for assessing discrimination in general, and (2) it moved further toward the approaches of the U.S. Supreme Court and the European Court in the case of suspect categories.[112] *Atala Riffo* concerned, in part, the discriminatory treatment and interference in private and family life suffered by Karen Atala Riffo due to her sexual orientation. Among other aspects, the Inter-American Tribunal found that, owing to discriminatory treatment by Chilean courts, Atala Riffo lost custody of her daughters and was subject to a disciplinary proceeding that investigated her fitness as a criminal judge.[113]

After certain preliminary matters, the Court began its analysis by assessing whether differential treatment had occurred.[114] The Tribunal stated that it would be "sufficient to confirm that, to a certain extent, [her] sexual orientation was taken into account, either explicitly or implicitly, in adopting a specific [judicial] decision."[115] It proceeded to examine the Chilean courts' decisions, considering their "arguments," as well as "their actions,

---

[109] *E.g.*, Johnson v. California, 543 U.S. 499, 505 (2005); Adarand Constructors, Inc. v. Peña, 515 U.S. 200, 227 (1995).

[110] *E.g.*, Perozo et al. v. Venezuela, Preliminary Objections, Merits, Reparations, and Costs, Judgment, Inter-Am. Ct. H.R. (ser. C) No. 195, para. 380 (Jan. 28, 2009); Ríos et al. v. Venezuela, Preliminary Objections, Merits, Reparations, and Costs, Judgment, Inter-Am. Ct. H.R. (ser. C) No. 194, para. 349 (Jan. 28, 2009). *See also* Granier et al. (Radio Caracas Television) vs. Venezuela. Preliminary Objections, Merits, Reparations, Costs, Judgment, Inter-Am. Ct. H.R. (ser. C) No. 293, para. 235 (2015) (finding discriminatory treatment in the exercise of freedom of expression, on the basis of the petitioners' political opinion).

[111] Atala Riffo and Daughters v. Chile, Merits, Reparations, and Costs, Judgment, Inter-Am. Ct. H.R. (ser. C) No. 239 (Feb. 24, 2012).

[112] *See* Uprimny Yepes & Sánchez Duque, *supra* note 68, at 598 (stating that the Court uses a clearer test for discrimination in *Atala Riffo*).

[113] Atala Riffo and Daughters v. Chile, Merits, Reparations, and Costs, Judgment, Inter-Am. Ct. H.R. (ser. C) No. 239, paras. 30–222 (Feb. 24, 2012).

[114] In one key preliminary matter, as noted above, the Court determined that sexual orientation must be added to the list of prohibited categories of Article 1(1). *Id.* para. 93.

[115] *Id.* para. 94.

the language used, and the context in which the judicial decisions were made."[116] The Court found that "Ms. Atala's sexual orientation and the alleged effects that her living with her partner could have on the three girls . . . was central to the discussion between the parties and in the main judicial decisions made."[117] As a result, it concluded that "there was a difference in treatment based on [sexual orientation]."[118]

The Tribunal then considered the State's purpose for applying differential treatment. Chile argued that it was in the children's best interest; the Tribunal responded that a child's best interest was a "legitimate goal."[119] Having established a legitimate government aim that was "concrete" and not "abstract,"[120] the Court then examined whether the measure taken by Chilean courts—namely, revoking Atala Riffo's custody of her daughters—was "suitable" or "appropriate" to "fulfill the purpose stated."[121] The Court took the unusual step of reviewing the domestic courts' reasoning for their custody decisions. According to the Tribunal, their motives included:

> i) the alleged social discrimination suffered by the three girls due to Ms. Atala's expression of her sexual orientation; ii) the girls' alleged confusion regarding sexual roles as a consequence of their mother cohabiting with a partner of the same sex; iii) the alleged priority Ms. Atala gave to her personal life over the interests of her three daughters, and iv) the right of the girls to live in the bosom of a family with a father and a mother.[122]

The Inter-American Court remarked that the alleged harms "must be supported by technical evidence and reports from experts and researchers in order to reach conclusions that do not result in discriminatory decisions" and stereotyping.[123] Significantly, it stated that "the burden of proof here falls on the State, which must demonstrate that the judicial decision under consideration has been based on the existence of clear, specific and real harm to the children's development."[124] Because the Court found such evidentiary support lacking in the domestic judgments, it considered the loss of custody disproportionate and found Chile responsible for violating Articles 24 and 1(1) of the Convention.[125] The judgment followed a similar approach in examining other aspects of discrimination, such as the disciplinary investigation against Atala Riffo.

---

[116] *Id.* para. 95.
[117] *Id.* para. 96.
[118] *Id.* para. 98.
[119] *Id.* para. 110.
[120] *Id.* para. 221 (explaining these characteristics of a legitimate objective in another part of the judgment).
[121] *Id.* para. 114.
[122] *Id.* para. 113.
[123] *Id.* para. 124.
[124] *Id.* para. 125.
[125] *Id.* para. 146.

In this way, the Court proceeded through an identifiable analytical test for discrimination. It considered the government's purpose for the distinction, and whether the measure applied was appropriate to further that purpose. Following European case law, the Tribunal underscored that, once differential treatment has been established by the petitioner, the burden of proof shifts to the State to demonstrate a legitimate purpose and proportionality.[126]

However, the Tribunal's standard of review for suspect classifications still requires clarification. At one point, it asserted Chile "did not comply with the requirement to apply a strict scrutiny test," without explaining the origin of that test or what it specifically requires.[127] Elsewhere, the Court seemed to adopt European precedents to require "weighty reasons" for differential treatment involving suspect categories.[128] In fact, the Tribunal cited *Karner v. Austria*, where the European Court stated:

> where there is a difference in treatment based on sex or sexual orientation, the principle of proportionality does not merely require that the measure chosen is in principle suited for realising the aim sought. It must also be shown that it was *necessary* in order to achieve that aim to exclude certain categories of people.[129]

But it is unclear whether the Inter-American Court incorporates this standard that the measure must be "necessary" to achieve the State's aim. When such brief allusions are made to legal terms and standards, States are left with little direction. It is uncertain whether they should follow the U.S. Supreme Court's elaborate case law on levels of scrutiny, or whether they should assimilate the Strasbourg Court's approach. The European methodology, although comparable in certain respects to U.S. law, certainly is not identical.

Judgments following *Atala Riffo*, unfortunately, have not clarified the Inter-American Court's standard of review for suspect classifications. In fact, the Court has even avoided its analytical test on occasion. In *Norín Catrimán* et al. *v. Chile*, representatives of the Mapuche indigenous community complained of several violations, including that their rights to equality had been breached in terrorism convictions.[130] The Tribunal noted,

> Criminal law may be applied in a discriminatory manner if the judge or court convicts an individual on the basis of reasoning founded on negative stereotypes

---

[126] *Id.* para. 125 (citing to Case of D.H. and Others v. the Czech Republic of November 13, 2007).

[127] *Id.* para. 131.

[128] *Id.* para. 124. The Inter-American Commission has also referred to the "weighty reasons" standard. Morales de Sierra v. Guatemala, Case 11.625, Inter-Am. Comm'n H.R., Report No. 4/01, OEA/Ser.L./V/II.114, doc. 5 rev. para. 36 (2002) ("'very weighty reasons would have to be put forward' to justify a distinction based solely on the ground of sex").

[129] Karner v. Austria, 2003-IX Eur. Ct. H.R. 199, para. 41 (emphasis added).

[130] Norín Catrimán et al. (Leaders, members, and activists of the Mapuche Indigenous People) v. Chile, Merits, Reparations, and Costs, Judgment, Inter-Am. Ct. H.R. (ser. C) No. 279, para. 222 (May 29, 2014).

that associate an ethnic group with terrorism in order to determine any element of criminal responsibility.[131]

As in *Atala Riffo,* the Court proceeded to examine the language of the domestic judgments, and, without extensive analysis, found that the "mere use of [their] reasoning, which reveals stereotypes and biases as grounds for the judgments" violated Article 24.[132] The term "suspect category" was used in reference to the Mapuche, but neither its definition nor importance was explained.[133]

The Tribunal returned to a more disciplined use of its analytical test for one aspect of *Expelled Dominicans and Haitians v. Dominican Republic.*[134] It turned its attention to a judgment of the Dominican Constitutional Court, which plainly recognized differential treatment between individuals born in the Dominican Republic: (1) with undocumented parents; and (2) with documented parents. Having established this disparate treatment, which impacted rights to nationality as well as other rights, the Inter-American Court looked for a "reasonable and objective justification" or a "legitimate purpose."[135] It found that the Dominican judgment failed to "explain the objective sought by the distinction ... therefore [preventing] an assessment of whether it is reasonable and proportionate."[136] This led to a violation of Article 24, both with respect to the judgment and a related law.

Still, as seen in *Norín Catrimán*—and even in other sections of *Expelled Dominicans and Haitians*—the Court does not always apply *Atala Riffo*'s defined analytical test for discrimination. At times, the Tribunal perhaps omits the test when the established facts could hardly lead to another result.[137] For example, the Dominican Republic's violent expulsions of Haitian migrants and Dominicans of Haitian origin have been demonstrated several times before the Tribunal.[138] In similar fashion, deeply-flawed criminal investigations in cases of

[131] *Id.* para. 223.

[132] *Id.* para. 228.

[133] *Id.* para. 226.

[134] Expelled Dominicans and Haitians v. Dominican Republic, Preliminary Objections, Merits, Reparations, and Costs, Judgment, Inter-Am. Ct. H.R. (ser. C) No. 282 (Aug. 28, 2014).

[135] *Id.* para. 316.

[136] *Id.* para. 317.

[137] Of course, the test will also be omitted when differential treatment is not proven at the outset.

[138] *E.g.*, Expelled Dominicans and Haitians v. Dominican Republic, Preliminary Objections, Merits, Reparations, and Costs, Judgment, Inter-Am. Ct. H.R. (ser. C) No. 282, paras. 403–407 (Aug. 28, 2014); Nadege Dorzema et al. v. Dominican Republic, Merits, Reparations, and Costs, Judgment, Inter-Am. Ct. H.R. (ser. C) No. 251, paras. 237–238 (Oct. 24, 2012). However, the Court has shown reluctance to find racial discrimination in the Dominican cases, despite arguments and evidence submitted by the Inter-American Commission and petitioners. *Id.* paras. 330, 333, 399 (referring to these racial discrimination arguments). The Court has instead preferred to characterize the discrimination as based on national origin. *Id.* para. 404 ("This constituted a discriminatory action to the detriment of the victims due to their condition as Haitians and Dominicans of Haitian descent").

gender violence lack claims to any "legitimate purpose" or "proportionate" response for assessment by the Court.[139]

A finding of discrimination, however, is rarely a forgone conclusion for the Court. The Tribunal has rejected petitioners' claims to this effect several times since *Atala Riffo*.[140] In many of these judgments, it has tersely concluded that insufficient evidence was presented. Petitioners, according to the Court, simply did not substantiate "specific facts . . . from which supposed acts of discrimination could be derived,"[141] or explain "the specific actions that the State should have taken to comply" with its "obligation to ensure rights without discrimination."[142] As these important cases arrive in San José year after year, the Tribunal's discrimination analysis continues to be tested and refined.

---

[139] For examples of such flawed investigations, *see, e.g.*, Espinoza Gonzales v. Peru, Preliminary Objections, Merits, Reparations, Costs, Judgment, Inter-Am. Ct. H.R. (ser. C) No. 289, paras. 287–288 (Nov. 20, 2014); Veliz Franco et al. v. Guatemala, Preliminary Objections, Merits, and Reparations, Judgment, Inter-Am. Ct. H.R. (ser. C) No. 277, paras. 213–216 (May 19, 2014).

[140] *See, e.g.*, Kuna Indigenous People of Madungandi and Embera Indigenous People of Bayano and their Members v. Panama, Preliminary Objections, Merits, Reparations, and Costs, Judgment, Inter-Am. Ct. H.R. (ser. C) No. 284, para. 203 (Oct. 14, 2014) (finding insufficient evidence of discrimination); Afro-Descendant Communities Displaced From the Cacarica River Basin (Operation Genesis) v. Colombia, Preliminary Objections, Merits, Reparations, and Costs, Judgment, Inter-Am. Ct. H.R. (ser. C) No. 270, para. 337 (Nov. 20, 2013) (same); Constitutional Tribunal (Camba Campos et al.) v. Ecuador, Preliminary Objections, Merits, Reparations, and Costs, Judgment, Inter-Am. Ct. H.R. (ser. C) No. 268, para. 241 (Aug. 28, 2013) (same); Mémoli v. Argentina, Preliminary Objections, Merits, Reparations, and Costs, Judgment, Inter-Am. Ct. H.R. (ser. C) No. 265, para. 196 (Aug. 22, 2013) (same).

[141] Río Negro Massacres v. Guatemala, Preliminary Objections, Merits, Reparations, and Costs, Judgment, Inter-Am. Ct. H.R. (ser. C) No. 250, para. 232 (Sept. 4, 2012). In *Norín Catrimán*, petitioners also argued that the terrorism law had been selectively applied against the Mapuche community. Of 19 prosecutions based on the law, 12 had been directed against members of the community. Nevertheless, the Court responded that these results, by themselves, did not prove discriminatory enforcement; the Court would have needed additional information on crimes "of a similar nature at the time of the events of this case" that were allegedly perpetrated by individuals not belonging to the Mapuche community. Norín Catrimán et al. (Leaders, members, and activists of the Mapuche Indigenous People) v. Chile, Merits, Reparations, and Costs, Judgment, Inter-Am. Ct. H.R. (ser. C) No. 279, para. 219 (May 29, 2014).

[142] Afro-Descendant Communities Displaced From the Cacarica River Basin (Operation Genesis) v. Colombia, Preliminary Objections, Merits, Reparations, and Costs, Judgment, Inter-Am. Ct. H.R. (ser. C) No. 270, para. 337 (Nov. 20, 2013).

3

Life

Article 4: Right to Life

1. *Every person has the right to have his life respected. This right shall be protected by law and, in general, from the moment of conception. No one shall be arbitrarily deprived of his life.*
2. *In countries that have not abolished the death penalty, it may be imposed only for the most serious crimes and pursuant to a final judgment rendered by a competent court and in accordance with a law establishing such punishment, enacted prior to the commission of the crime. The application of such punishment shall not be extended to crimes to which it does not presently apply.*
3. *The death penalty shall not be reestablished in states that have abolished it.*
4. *In no case shall capital punishment be inflicted for political offenses or related common crimes.*
5. *Capital punishment shall not be imposed upon persons who, at the time the crime was committed, were under 18 years of age or over 70 years of age; nor shall it be applied to pregnant women.*
6. *Every person condemned to death shall have the right to apply for amnesty, pardon, or commutation of sentence, which may be granted in all cases. Capital punishment shall not be imposed while such a petition is pending decision by the competent authority.*

Chapter 3 Contents

I. Introduction 57
II. Background 59

The American Convention on Human Rights. Thomas M. Antkowiak and Alejandra Gonza.

III. Extensive State Obligations to Respect and Ensure the Right to Life 61
A. Introduction 61
B. Duty to Respect 62
C. Duty to Ensure (or "Protect") 65
1. Overview 65
2. Duty to Prevent through Legal Regulation 66
3. Duty to Adopt "Prevention and Protection Measures" in Threatening Circumstances 67
4. Duty to Investigate and Punish 68
IV. Scope of Protection 72
A. Meaning of "Every Person" and "In General, From the Moment of Conception" 72
B. Meaning of "No One Shall Be Arbitrarily Deprived" of Life 75
1. The Death Penalty 76
a. Introduction 76
b. "Only For The Most Serious Crimes" 77
c. The "Mandatory" Death Penalty 77
d. Due Process Requirements 78
e. Right to Apply for Pardon, Amnesty, or Commutation 81
2. Use of Lethal Force in Law Enforcement Scenarios 82
a. Introduction 82
b. The Principles of Legality, Necessity, and Proportionality 83
c. The Burden of Proof 85
d. State Duties after the Use of Force 85
3. Use of Lethal Force in Armed Conflicts 86
4. Arbitrary Deprivation of Life of Imprisoned Individuals 89
a. Introduction 89
b. Detention Conditions and Healthcare 90
c. Security Operations in Prisons 91
5. Forced Disappearances of Persons 92
a. Introduction and Definition 92
b. The Right to Life and *Ratione Temporis* Jurisdiction 94
C. The Concept of *Vida Digna* 97

I. Introduction

Life, of course, stands as one of the most fundamental human rights; without it, other rights are dispossessed of meaning.[1] Life is universally established in international law as a non-derogable right: Article 4 of the American Convention, Article 6 of the ICCPR, Article 2 of the European Convention, Article 2 of the EU Charter, Article 4 of the African Charter, and Article 5 (and others) of the Arab Charter, among other treaties.[2] Further, the right to life forms a part of customary international law, reaching the rank of jus cogens.[3]

Questions on the beginning of human life and abortion have long been divisive and controversial. The American Convention is the only human rights treaty that expressly determines the point from which the right to life must be safeguarded: "This right shall be protected . . . in general, from the moment of conception."[4] For its part, the ICCPR provides that a "sentence of death . . . shall not be carried out on pregnant women."[5] Thus, both treaties accord a level of protection to the fetus, although the ICCPR drafters rejected the proposed phrase "from the moment of conception," due to conflicting laws of States Parties.[6]

A recent Inter-American Court judgment, *Artavia Murillo* et al. *v. Costa Rica*, directly examined this significant phrase.[7] Surprisingly, the Court decided to establish a bright-line test for when "conception" occurs. *Artavia Murillo* held that "conception" should be understood as "from the moment at which implantation [of the embryo in the mother's uterus] occurs, and therefore . . . before this event, Article 4 of the American Convention cannot be applied."[8] The Court, then, appears to leave little discretion to States on this

---

[1] *See* Report of Committee I "Protection." Rapporteur Juan Isaac Lovato, Doc. 60 (Revised) November 19, 1969, p. 296 (reporting that most of the Article 4 discussion stressed the importance of this right for humanity); "Street Children" (Villagrán Morales et al.) v. Guatemala, Merits, Judgment, Inter-Am. Ct. H.R. (ser. C) No. 63, para. 144 (Nov. 19, 1999) ("The right to life is a fundamental human right, and the exercise of this right is essential for the exercise of all other human rights. If it is not respected, all rights lack meaning.").

[2] American Convention, art. 4; ICCPR, art. 6; European Convention, art. 2; EU Charter, art. 2; African Charter, art. 4; Arab Charter, arts. 5, 38, 40.

[3] *See, e.g.*, MANFRED NOWAK, U.N. COVENANT ON CIVIL AND POLITICAL RIGHTS: CCPR COMMENTARY 122 (2d ed. 2005); Human Rights Committee, General Comment 24 (52), General comment on issues relating to reservations made upon ratification or accession to the Covenant or the Optional Protocols thereto, or in relation to declarations under Article 41 of the Covenant, U.N. Doc. CCPR/C/21/Rev.1/Add.6, para. 10 (1994) ("And some non-derogable rights, which in any event cannot be reserved because of their status as peremptory norms, are also of this character—the prohibition of torture and arbitrary deprivation of life are examples"); Gómez Paquiyauri Brothers v. Peru, Merits, Reparations, and Costs, Judgment, Inter-Am. Ct. H.R. (ser. C) No. 110, para. 76 (July 8, 2004) ("extra-legal executions . . . violate international *jus cogens*" norms).

[4] American Convention, art. 4(1).

[5] ICCPR, art. 6(5).

[6] Niels Petersen, "Life, Right to, International Protection," MAX PLANCK ENCYCLOPEDIA OF PUBLIC INTERNATIONAL LAW, para. 8 (2012).

[7] Artavia Murillo et al. (In-vitro Fertilization) v. Costa Rica, Preliminary Objections, Merits, Reparations, and Costs, Judgment, Inter-Am. Ct. H.R. (ser. C) No. 257 (Nov. 28, 2012).

[8] *Id.* para. 189.

highly-disputed matter, in contrast to the deferential approaches of the European Court of Human Rights and other tribunals.

Despite its lofty status, the right to life is not absolute. The European Convention establishes a list of possible limitations:

> Deprivation of life shall not be regarded as inflicted in contravention of this article when it results from the use of force which is no more than absolutely necessary: a) in defence of any person from unlawful violence; b) in order to effect a lawful arrest or to prevent the escape of a person lawfully detained; c) in action lawfully taken for the purpose of quelling a riot or insurrection.[9]

To the contrary, the American Convention, the ICCPR, the African Charter, and the Arab Charter take a more flexible approach, prohibiting "arbitrary" deprivations of life. In the context of the ICCPR, "arbitrary" has been considered to mean "unlawfulness," "injustice," "capriciousness," and "unreasonableness."[10] The Inter-American Court has interpreted the term similarly, without arriving at a precise definition.[11] By not exhaustively specifying limitations, these treaties require a case-by-case analysis on the proportionality of the State measures adopted.[12]

Human rights conventions initially allowed for capital punishment. As made clear in the American Convention, the ICCPR, and the Arab Charter, however, it is reserved "only for the most serious crimes" and "pursuant to a final judgment rendered by a competent court."[13] These treaties also establish other restrictions—for example, capital punishment must not be applied to persons under 18 years of age and pregnant women.[14] Currently, the international trend points toward abolition.[15] The EU Charter and Protocol No. 13 to the European Convention fully prohibit the death penalty,[16] whereas the Second Optional Protocol to the ICCPR permits it only "in time of war pursuant to a conviction for a most serious crime of a military nature committed during wartime."[17] Over a dozen States of the Americas have ratified or acceded to the Protocol to the American Convention on Human Rights to Abolish the Death Penalty.[18]

---

[9] European Convention, art. 2(2).

[10] NOWAK, *supra* note 3, at 128.

[11] The Court has found arbitrary deprivations of life in five general situations. *See* Section IV(B), *infra*.

[12] *See* NOWAK, *supra* note 3, at 129; Petersen, *supra* note 6, para. 16.

[13] American Convention, art. 4(2); ICCPR, art. 6(2); Arab Charter, art. 6.

[14] American Convention, art. 4(5); ICCPR, art. 6(5); Arab Charter, art. 7.

[15] *See, e.g.*, Protocol to the American Convention on Human Rights to Abolish the Death Penalty (noting that "the tendency among the American States is to be in favor of abolition of the death penalty"); EU Charter, art. 2(2); Protocol No. 13 to the European Convention, art. 1; Second Optional Protocol to the ICCPR, art. 2(1); Eduardo Ferrer Mac-Gregor & Pablo González Domínguez, *Death Penalty, Amnesty Laws, and Forced Disappearances: Three Main Topics of the Inter-American* Corpus Juris *in Criminal Law*, 5 NOTRE DAME J. INT'L COMP. L. 1, 65, 83 (2015) (commenting on the "abolitionist trend" both within and beyond the Americas).

[16] EU Charter, art. 2(2); Protocol No. 13 to the European Convention, art. 1.

[17] Second Optional Protocol to the ICCPR, art. 2(1).

[18] *See* Signatories and Ratifications, Protocol to the American Convention on Human Rights to Abolish the Death Penalty, *available at* http://www.oas.org/juridico/english/sigs/a-53.html (last visited Nov. 21, 2016).

The American Convention itself limits capital punishment and forbids its re-establishment in States that have abolished it; as noted, the Convention also prohibits arbitrary deprivations of life, and generally provides that "every person has the right to have his life respected."[19] In addition, Inter-American and international law demands significant positive obligations of States for the protection of life. The American Convention, European Convention, the ICCPR, and the Arab Charter all expressly require States Parties to protect the right to life "by law."[20] Yet these treaties have been interpreted to require not only legislative action, but also the implementation of public health measures, the thorough investigation of deaths and disappearances, and the prevention of certain forms of violence—including acts of non-State actors.[21]

In fact, the right to life has expanded substantially in recent years. International human rights bodies, foremost the Inter-American Court, have recognized, among others, the rights to health, education, culture, food, and clean water as components of the right to life.[22] Much remains to be developed with regard to this key relationship between life and social, cultural, and economic rights, as well as with respect to other complex issues such as abortion, genetic engineering, and euthanasia. To the extent that international human rights bodies have considered these controversial issues, they have generally proceeded with caution; owing to divergent national approaches, international tribunals have often left a margin of discretion to States.[23]

II. Background

The Inter-American Commission's draft proposal on the right to life largely drew from the language and structure of the ICCPR's Article 6.[24] As noted above, the American Convention

---

[19] American Convention, art. 4(1).

[20] American Convention, art. 4(1); European Convention, art. 2(1); ICCPR, art. 6(1); Arab Charter, art. 5(2).

[21] *See, e.g.*, NOWAK, *supra* note 3, at 124; DAVID HARRIS, MICHAEL O'BOYLE & COLIN WARBRICK, LAW OF THE EUROPEAN CONVENTION ON HUMAN RIGHTS 203-234 (3d ed. 2014). For Inter-American Court cases, *see* the following discussion.

[22] *E.g.*, Yakye Axa Indigenous Cmty. v. Paraguay, Merits, Reparations and Costs, Judgment, Inter-Am. Ct. H.R. (ser. C) No. 125, paras. 167, 176 (June 17, 2005) (holding that the right to life was violated because the State had not taken sufficient "measures regarding the conditions that affected their possibility of having a decent life," such as access to healthcare, food, and clean water). The Human Rights Committee has comparably remarked that homelessness and health problems engage States' duties to ensure the right to life. U.N. Human Rights Comm., *Concluding Observations of the Human Rights Committee, Canada,* U.N. Doc CCPR/C/79/Add. 105 (Apr. 7 1999); U.N. Human Rights Comm., *General Comment No. 6: Article 6* (Right to Life), para. 5 (Apr. 30, 1982) in Compilation of General Comments and General Recommendations Adopted by Human Rights Treaty Bodies, U.N. Doc. HRI/GEN/1/Rev.9 (Vol. I), 176–78 (May 27, 2008).

[23] *See* Petersen, *supra* note 6, para. 36; WALTER KÄLIN & JÖRG KÜNZLI, THE LAW OF INTERNATIONAL HUMAN RIGHTS PROTECTION 274 (2009) (international human rights bodies usually leave States "basically free to settle the question themselves").

[24] *See* Draft Inter-American Convention on Protection of Human Rights, Doc. 5 (English). September 22, 1969, art. 3. However, the delegates rejected the Colombian proposal to conserve the ICCPR's "inherent" right to

did not follow the European Convention and establish specific limitations to the right. Instead, like the ICCPR, it simply provides, "No one shall be arbitrarily deprived of his life."[25]

Ultimately, the State delegates who gathered in Costa Rica to negotiate the Convention's final text only slightly modified the Commission's draft on the right to life. On the whole, the changes increased restrictions upon the use of capital punishment. At the initiative of the Uruguayan delegate,[26] the State representatives prohibited the extension of the death penalty to additional crimes and prevented its re-establishment "in States that have abolished it."[27] Although there were substantial efforts to ban capital punishment completely,[28] they were defeated due to laws permitting the practice in various States.[29]

As noted previously, the American Convention uniquely provides that the right to life "shall be protected . . . in general, from the moment of conception."[30] The Inter-American Commission's draft contained this formulation, and it was debated at the San José Conference. Although two delegates proposed its complete removal, the phrase received strong support from other representatives and remained unchanged. In opposition, Brazil opined that the phrase was vague and would not be "effective in preventing [States] from including the most varied reasons for abortion in their domestic laws."[31] For its part, the United States expressed preference for the language of the ICCPR's Article 6(1).[32] Both Brazil and the United States concluded that the matter of abortion would be best left to national legislators "in light of [the States'] own social development, experience and similar factors."[33] In contrast, the Venezuelan delegate declared that a treaty

life. P. 160, Minutes of the 2nd Session of Committee I, Doc. 36, Nov. 11, 1969 (delegates from Uruguay and Panama considering the term "inherent" to be "unnecessary").

[25] American Convention, art. 4(1).

[26] P. 161, Minutes of the 2nd Session of Committee I, Doc. 36, Nov. 11, 1969.

[27] American Convention, art. 4(2)–(3).

[28] P. 162, Minutes of the 2nd Session of Committee I, Doc. 36, Nov. 11, 1969 (Costa Rican delegate urging the elimination of the death penalty); p. 166, Minutes of the 3rd Session of Committee I, Doc. 38 (Rev. 1), Nov. 16, 1969 (Uruguayan delegate urging the same); p. 467, Minutes of the Concluding Plenary Session, Doc 84, November 22, 1969 (noting that the delegations of Costa Rica, Uruguay, Colombia, Ecuador, El Salvador, Panama, Honduras, Dominican Republic, Guatemala, Mexico, Venezuela, Nicaragua, Argentina, and Paraguay all expressed their desire to abolish the death penalty and resolved to establish a protocol to the American Convention to accomplish that objective); Report of the United States Delegation to the Inter-American Conference on the Protection of Human Rights, p. 19 ("In the Plenary Session, a number of delegations, led by Uruguay, attempted to make the article more sweeping by prohibiting application of the death penalty altogether").

[29] *See* p. 166, Minutes of the 3rd Session of Committee I, Doc. 38 (Rev. 1), Nov. 16, 1969 (Colombian delegate requesting that the proposal to abolish the death penalty be withdrawn, due to the conflict that would result with national laws).

[30] American Convention, art. 4(1).

[31] Amendments to the Draft Inter-American Convention on Protection of Human Rights (Brazil), Doc. 31 (English). Nov. 10, 1969. The delegation noted that Brazil "protected the rights of the fetus from the moment of conception," allowing for abortion only in cases of rape or to protect the mother's life. *Id.*

[32] P. 160, Minutes of the 2nd Session of Committee I, Doc. 36, Nov. 11, 1969.

[33] Report of the United States Delegation to the Inter-American Conference on the Protection of Human Rights, p. 19.

that did not establish the "from the moment of conception" principle would be "unacceptable."[34] The representative from Ecuador, joined by other delegates, even called for deleting "in general," in order to reduce any margin of discretion for States.[35]

The most discussed provision of Article 4 appeared to be its fourth paragraph: "In no case shall capital punishment be inflicted for political offenses or related common crimes."[36] The U.S. delegate proposed the elimination of this sentence; in the alternative, he requested that the drafters provide a precise definition for the offenses, so as to exclude crimes such as treason and political assassination.[37] The Brazilian representative again suggested that the meaning should be resolved by national legislators.[38] El Salvador proposed a political crimes definition for consideration; however, the various delegates could not agree.[39] The drafters eventually requested, by resolution, that the Inter-American Commission further study the subject.[40]

III. Extensive State Obligations to Respect and Ensure the Right to Life

A. INTRODUCTION

Article 4(1) establishes that "Every person has the right to have his life respected. This right shall be protected by law and, in general, from the moment of conception. No one shall be arbitrarily deprived of his life."[41] Thus, the text itself sets out both negative ("the right to have his life respected") and positive ("This right shall be protected by law . . . ") State duties. Interpreting Article 4, in relation to the respect and ensure provision of Article 1(1), the Inter-American Court has held that "compliance with" the right to life

> not only supposes that no one shall be deprived of his life arbitrarily (negative obligation), but also requires the State to adopt *all appropriate measures* to protect and preserve the right to life (positive obligation), in accordance with the obligation to ensure the free and full exercise of the rights of all those subject to its jurisdiction.[42]

---

[34] P. 160, Minutes of the 2nd Session of Committee I, Doc. 36, Nov. 11, 1969.

[35] *Id. See also* Report of the United States Delegation to the Inter-American Conference on the Protection of Human Rights, p. 19.

[36] American Convention, art. 4(4).

[37] P. 164, Minutes of the 3rd Session of Committee I, Doc. 38 (Rev. 1), Nov. 16, 1969; Report of the United States Delegation to the Inter-American Conference on the Protection of Human Rights, p. 18. Note that the U.S. delegate also unsuccessfully tried to delete the proscription of capital punishment for certain age groups. *Id.*

[38] *Id.* at p. 165.

[39] *Id.* at pp. 165–67.

[40] P. 513, Final Act, Doc. 70 (Rev. 1), Nov. 22, 1969.

[41] American Convention, art. 4(1).

[42] *E.g.*, Barrios Family v. Venezuela, Merits, Reparations, and Costs, Judgment, Inter-Am. Ct. H.R. (ser. C) No. 237, para. 48 (Nov. 24, 2011) (emphasis added); "Street Children" (Villagrán Morales et al.) v. Guatemala, Merits, Judgment, Inter-Am. Ct. H.R. (ser. C) No. 63, para. 139 (Nov. 19, 1999).

Thus, ensuring the right to life, according to the Court, requires more than mere protection "by law"; rather, "all appropriate measures" must be taken "to protect and to preserve the right." As a result, in cases where States have failed to prevent or investigate right-to-life violations, even by non-State actors, the Court has found breaches of Article 4 for failure to ensure the right. And clearly, when official agents are actually involved in an illegal death, this should amount to a violation of the State's negative obligation to respect the right to life. The Court's rich, albeit somewhat disordered, case law in this area has led to sweeping obligations for States.

B. DUTY TO RESPECT

The Convention's Article 4 prohibits the arbitrary deprivation of life by "acts of [State] agents carried out in their official capacity and . . . their omissions, even if they act outside the limits of their sphere of competence or in violation of domestic law."[43] In this way, the duty to respect the right to life "obliges States and all of their organs to refrain from killing" unless the circumstances are permissible under law.[44] The obligation is breached when State agents deprive individuals of life through, for example: unlawful use of force and extrajudicial executions,[45] forced disappearances,[46] and imposition of the death penalty without due process and other crucial restrictions.[47]

Further, the Court's case law has evolved: the duty to respect now forbids State actions that place lives in serious risk. The Tribunal has found a violation of Article 4 in cases where victims *survived* life-threatening situations, such as a massacre,[48] forced displacement,[49] birth in captivity,[50] or infection with a deadly disease.[51] To illustrate, in *Rochela Massacre v. Colombia* a commission that was investigating crimes of State security forces

---

[43] *E.g.*, Mapiripán Massacre v. Colombia, Merits, Reparations, and Costs, Judgment, Inter-Am. Ct. H.R. (ser. C) No. 134, para. 108 (Sept. 15, 2005); Rochela Massacre v. Colombia, Merits, Reparations, and Costs, Judgment, Inter-Am. Ct. H.R. (ser. C) No. 163, para. 67 (May 11, 2007).

[44] Kälin & Künzli, *supra* note 23, at 275.

[45] *E.g.*, Cruz Sánchez et al. v. Peru, Preliminary Objections, Merits, Reparations, Costs, Judgment, Inter-Am. Ct. H.R. (ser. C) No. 292 (Apr. 17, 2015); Landaeta Meijias Brothers et al. v. Venezuela, Preliminary Objections, Merits, Reparations, and Costs, Judgment, Inter-Am. Ct. H.R. (ser. C) No. 281 (Aug. 27, 2014).

[46] *E.g.*, Gelman v. Uruguay, Merits and Reparations, Judgment, Inter-Am. Ct. H.R. (ser. C) No. 221 (Feb. 24, 2011); Bámaca Velásquez v. Guatemala, Merits, Judgment, Inter-Am. Ct. H.R. (ser. C) No. 70 (Nov. 25, 2000).

[47] *E.g.*, DaCosta Cadogan v. Barbados, Preliminary Objections, Merits, Reparations, and Costs, Judgment, Inter-Am. Ct. H.R. (ser. C) No. 204, paras. 55 and 85 (Sept. 24, 2009); Boyce et al. v. Barbados, Preliminary Objections, Merits, Reparations, and Costs, Judgment, Inter-Am. Ct. H.R. (ser. C) No. 169, paras. 50 and 78 (Nov. 20, 2007).

[48] Rochela Massacre v. Colombia, Merits, Reparations, and Costs, Judgment, Inter-Am. Ct. H.R. (ser. C) No. 163, paras. 124 and 126 (May 11, 2007).

[49] Mapiripán Massacre v. Colombia, Merits, Reparations, and Costs, Judgment, Inter-Am. Ct. H.R. (ser. C) No. 134, para. 162 (Sept. 15, 2005).

[50] Gelman v. Uruguay, Merits and Reparations, Judgment, Inter-Am. Ct. H.R. (ser. C) No. 221 (Feb. 24, 2011).

[51] Gonzales Lluy et al. v. Ecuador, Preliminary Objections, Merits, Reparations and Costs, Judgment, Inter-Am. Ct. H.R. (ser. C) No. 298 (Sept. 1, 2015).

was brutally attacked; only three commission members survived.[52] The Court found violations of the right to life with respect to even the survivors, "taking into account the force employed, the intent and objective of the use of this force, and the situation in which the victims found themselves."[53] Nevertheless, in *Massacres of El Mozote and Nearby Places v. El Salvador*, the Tribunal did not find violations of the survivors' right to life, despite similar circumstances.[54]

According to the Court, a violation of the duty to respect life could also arise when the actions of non-State actors could be assimilated as official acts, attributable directly to the State, because: (1) the private actors were "empowered to act in State capacity," such as in the case of certain healthcare providers;[55] or (2) their illegal actions were carried out with the "collaboration, acquiescence, and tolerance" of State agents.[56] Thus, in cases involving even private health facilities, the Court found a breach of the obligation to *respect* the right to life, among other violations. In *Ximenes Lopes v. Brazil*, the Tribunal considered health to constitute a public interest that should be actively regulated by the State, especially in a case involving patients with disabilities.[57] The judgment concluded that, due to the inhuman treatment and death suffered by a patient in a private psychiatric facility, Brazil failed to comply with its "duties of respect, prevention, and protection."[58] Similarly, in *Gonzales Lluy* et al. *v. Ecuador*, the State failed to sufficiently regulate and supervise a private health service; a Red Cross blood bank had provided a three-year-old girl with blood infected with the HIV virus.[59] This resulted in a violation of Article 4, among other rights, for the serious risks imposed upon her life.

The Court has heard a series of cases concerning the armed conflict in Colombia. Paramilitary groups—with State "collaboration" or "tolerance"—perpetrated massacres,[60]

---

[52] Rochela Massacre v. Colombia, Merits, Reparations, and Costs, Judgment, Inter-Am. Ct. H.R. (ser. C) No. 163 (May 11, 2007).

[53] *Id.* para. 124.

[54] Massacres of El Mozote and Nearby Places v. El Salvador, Merits, Reparations, and Costs, Judgment, Inter-Am. Ct. H.R. (ser. C) No. 252, para. 201 (Oct. 25, 2012).

[55] Ximenes Lopes v. Brazil, Merits, Reparations, and Costs, Judgment, Inter-Am. Ct. H.R. (ser. C) No. 149, para. 87 (July 4, 2006); Gonzales Lluy et al. v. Ecuador, Preliminary Objections, Merits, Reparations and Costs, Judgment, Inter-Am. Ct. H.R. (ser. C) No. 298 (Sept. 1, 2015). *See also* Rochela Massacre v. Colombia, Merits, Reparations, and Costs, Judgment, Inter-Am. Ct. H.R. (ser. C) No. 163, para. 102 (May 11, 2007) (involving law enforcement personnel).

[56] Mapiripán Massacre v. Colombia, Merits, Reparations, and Costs, Judgment, Inter-Am. Ct. H.R. (ser. C) No. 134, para. 120 (Sept. 15, 2005).

[57] Ximenes Lopes v. Brazil, Merits, Reparations, and Costs, Judgment, Inter-Am. Ct. H.R. (ser. C) No. 149, paras. 88–90 (July 4, 2006).

[58] *Id.* para. 150.

[59] Gonzales Lluy et al. v. Ecuador, Preliminary Objections, Merits, Reparations and Costs, Judgment, Inter-Am. Ct. H.R. (ser. C) No. 298, paras. 189–91 (Sept. 1, 2015).

[60] *E.g.*, Rochela Massacre v. Colombia, Merits, Reparations, and Costs, Judgment, Inter-Am. Ct. H.R. (ser. C) No. 163 (May 11, 2007); Mapiripán Massacre v. Colombia, Merits, Reparations, and Costs, Judgment, Inter-Am. Ct. H.R. (ser. C) No. 134 (Sept. 15, 2005).

forced disappearances,[61] and assassinations of political leaders.[62] The Tribunal considered the degree of the Colombian army's support, "acquiescence," "collaboration" or "tolerance" to establish State responsibility in these deaths. However, it neglected to define these concepts clearly. In any event, the Court has required substantial evidence of the State's role to find a violation of the obligation to *respect* Article 4.[63] Otherwise, it may find a breach of the duty to *ensure* Article 4,[64] or will simply refuse any right-to-life violation.[65]

The Court appears overly cautious here, at times only determining a breach of the duty to *ensure* the right to life when active State "collaboration" with private actors was demonstrated.[66] For example, *Ituango Massacres v. Colombia* examined the murder of many "defenseless civilians" in 1996 and 1997.[67] The Court found that army soldiers "not only acquiesced to [these] acts perpetrated by the paramilitary groups, but at times collaborated with and took part in them directly."[68] Nevertheless, the judgment concluded that Colombia "failed to comply" only with its obligation to ensure Article 4.[69]

When assessing these complicated situations involving paramilitary groups, corporations, and others, the line between negative and positive obligations—the respect/ensure distinction—can become blurred.[70] For example, in one part of the *Ximenes Lopes* judgment, the Court considered a private psychiatric clinic as a proxy for the State in the

[61] 19 Merchants v. Colombia, Merits, Reparations, and Costs, Judgment, Inter-Am. Ct. H.R. (ser. C) No. 109 (July 5, 2004).

[62] Cepeda Vargas v. Colombia, Preliminary Objections, Merits, Reparations, and Costs, Judgment, Inter-Am. Ct. H.R. (ser. C.) No. 213 (May 26, 2010).

[63] *See* Mapiripán Massacre v. Colombia, Merits, Reparations, and Costs, Judgment, Inter-Am. Ct. H.R. (ser. C) No. 134, para 116 (Sept. 15, 2005) (reviewing, in detail, evidence of "logistic support and collaboration, acquiescence and omissions" by State agents).

[64] Pueblo Bello Massacre v. Colombia, Merits, Reparations, and Costs, Judgment, Inter-Am. Ct. H.R. (ser. C) No. 140 (Jan. 31, 2006).

[65] Castillo González et al. v. Venezuela, Merits, Judgment, Inter-Am. Ct. H.R. (ser. C) No. 256, paras. 113–116 (Nov. 27, 2012) (finding insufficient evidence of State responsibility with respect to alleged violations of Articles 4, 5, and 19 of the American Convention).

[66] Ituango Massacres v. Colombia, Preliminary Objections, Merits, Reparations, and Costs, Judgment, Inter-Am. Ct. H.R. (ser. C) No. 148, para. 133 (July 1, 2006). In *Kichwa Indigenous People of Sarayaku v. Ecuador*, a corporation had placed explosives in the community's ancestral territory for purposes of oil exploration. Kichwa Indigenous People of Sarayaku v. Ecuador, Merits and Reparations, Judgment Inter.-Am. Ct. H.R. (ser. C) No. 245 (June 27, 2012). The Tribunal determined that the explosives were placed there "with the State's acquiescence and protection"; consequently, Ecuador "created a permanent situation of risk and threat to the life and physical integrity" of the community members. *Id.* para. 248. Despite the State's apparently active role in interfering with their rights, the Court failed to find a clear violation to Ecuador's obligation to *respect* Article 4. *Id.* paras. 248–249.

[67] Ituango Massacres v. Colombia, Preliminary Objections, Merits, Reparations, and Costs, Judgment, Inter-Am. Ct. H.R. (ser. C) No. 148, para. 132 (July 1, 2006).

[68] *Id.* para. 133.

[69] *Id.* para. 138.

[70] *See* Dinah Shelton & Ariel Gould, *Positive and Negative Obligations, in* The Oxford Handbook of International Human Rights Law 565 (2013) ("With the passage of time, it has increasingly been recognized that the supposedly clear-cut distinctions between 'positive' and 'negative' obligations do not exist.")

provision of essential health services.[71] Alternatively, such a clinic can be conceived as a purely non-State actor that requires meticulous government regulation pursuant to the State's positive obligations to ensure life and other rights.

The Court's approach in this complex area has been somewhat confusing and imprecise. In fact, with some Article 4 judgments, it has merged negative and positive obligations under the duty to respect.[72] Several of these cases present challenges for a distant, international tribunal with limited fact-finding abilities. Still, the Court should strive for more conceptual clarity. Simply put, if a State has supported or collaborated with private actors in illegal killings, it has violated the negative duty to *respect* the right to life. On the other hand, if a State has failed to take appropriate, positive measures to protect life, then it has breached the duty to *ensure* Article 4. In various scenarios, in fact, both duties can be violated. As explained in the following section, the Court has linked many positive State obligations to the right to life.

C. DUTY TO ENSURE (OR "PROTECT")

1. Overview

As stated above, ensuring Article 4 demands that "all appropriate measures" must be taken "to protect and to preserve" the right to life. The Court has required several such "measures" with respect to Article 4, including the positive obligations to prevent, investigate, and criminally sanction. The State's duty to prevent still requires significant development by the Court, and occasionally is intertwined with the obligation to investigate.[73] The Inter-American jurisprudence has also elaborated an expansive duty to remedy violations to life and many other rights; that important aspect of the case law is examined in this volume's chapter on reparations.

These positive State obligations are regulated by the due diligence principle, which the Inter-American System has developed extensively.[74] As the Court stated in its first contentious case,

> the State has a legal duty to take *reasonable* steps to prevent human rights violations and to use the means at its disposal to carry out a serious investigation of violations

---

[71] Ximenes Lopes v. Brazil, Merits, Reparations, and Costs, Judgment, Inter-Am. Ct. H.R. (ser. C) No. 149, paras. 95–100 (July 4, 2006). *See also* Suárez Peralta v. Ecuador, Preliminary Objections, Merits, Reparations, and Costs, Judgment, Inter-Am. Ct. H.R. (ser. C) No. 261, para. 144 (May 21, 2013).

[72] The Tribunal has held that, in certain circumstances, the State's negative duty to respect life actually leads to a positive obligation to take measures to prevent threats and protect life. *See, e.g.*, Gómez Paquiyauri Brothers v. Peru, Merits, Reparations, and Costs, Judgment, Inter-Am. Ct. H.R. (ser. C) No. 110, paras. 124 and 171 (July 8, 2004).

[73] *See* Cecilia Medina, *Los 40 Años de la Convención Americana sobre Derechos Humanos a la Luz de Cierta Jurisprudencia de la Corte Interamericana*, ANUARIO DE DERECHOS HUMANOS 15, 25 (2009).

[74] *See, e.g.*, Shelton & Gould, *supra* note 70, at 579 ("Since the founding of modern human rights law, the Inter-American Commission and Court have been called upon more than other human rights bodies to apply the

committed within its jurisdiction, to identify those responsible, to impose the appropriate punishment and to ensure the victim adequate compensation.[75]

The Court and the Inter-American Commission have applied this key "reasonableness" standard to distinct contexts; the concept's parameters have depended upon the precise circumstances. Below we outline what due diligence has required of States in order to prevent, investigate, and punish possible violations to Article 4.

2. Duty to Prevent through Legal Regulation

The duty to prevent requires "an adequate regulatory framework that deters any threat to the right to life and safeguards the right to have access to conditions that ensure a decent life."[76] This obligation is grounded in Article 4 and Article 1(1), as well as in Article 2 (Domestic Legal Effects), by which States shall adopt "such legislative or other measures as may be necessary to give effect" to Convention rights.[77] Specifically, the Court has stressed repeatedly that abuses such as forced disappearances and torture must be strictly prohibited in domestic criminal law and prosecuted by State authorities.[78] Further, the Tribunal requires national law to establish limitations on the State's use of force,[79] independent systems of oversight for lethal force,[80] and relevant training programs for law enforcement officers.[81]

Yet the Court has, at times, sent incomplete or inconsistent messages about the far-reaching State obligation to protect life "by law." For example, it has heard several cases

---

due diligence standard to judge whether a state has lived up to its positive obligations in human rights cases."); Lenahan et al. v. United States, Case 12.626, Inter-Am. Comm'n H.R., Report No. 80/11, OEA/Ser.L/V/II, doc. 69, para. 111 (2011) ("the international and regional systems have pronounced on the strong link between discrimination, violence and due diligence, emphasizing that a State's failure to act with due diligence to protect women from violence constitutes a form of discrimination, and denies women their right to equality before the law").

[75] Velasquez Rodriguez v. Honduras, Merits, Judgment, Inter-Am. Ct. H.R. (ser. C) No. 4, para. 174 (July 29, 1988) (emphasis added).

[76] Artavia Murillo et al. (In-vitro Fertilization) v. Costa Rica, Preliminary Objections, Merits, Reparations, and Costs, Judgment, Inter-Am. Ct. H.R. (ser. C) No. 257, para. 172 (Nov. 28, 2012).

[77] American Convention, art. 2.

[78] *E.g.*, Contreras et. al. v. El Salvador, Merits, Reparations, and Costs, Judgment, Inter-Am. Ct. H.R. (ser. C) No. 232, para. 128 (Aug. 31, 2011); Goiburú et al. v. Paraguay, Merits, Reparations, and Costs, Judgment, Inter-Am. Ct. H.R. (ser. C) No. 153, para. 92 (Sept. 22, 2006).

[79] *E.g.*, Landaeta Meijias Brothers et al. v. Venezuela, Preliminary Objections, Merits, Reparations, and Costs, Judgment, Inter-Am. Ct. H.R. (ser. C) No. 281, para. 126 (Aug. 27, 2014) (and referring to the U.N. Basic Principles on the Use of Force and Firearms by Law Enforcement Officials and the U.N. Code of Conduct for Law Enforcement Officials); Montero Aranguren et al. (Det. Ctr. of Catia) v. Venezuela, Preliminary Objection, Merits, Reparations, and Costs, Judgment, Inter-Am. Ct. H.R. (ser. C) No. 150, para. 66 (July 5, 2006).

[80] Zambrano Vélez et al. v. Ecuador, Merits, Reparations, and Costs, Judgment, Inter-Am. Ct. H.R. (ser. C) No. 166, para. 86 (July 4, 2007).

[81] *E.g.*, Landaeta Meijias Brothers et al. v. Venezuela, Preliminary Objections, Merits, Reparations, and Costs, Judgment, Inter-Am. Ct. H.R. (ser. C) No. 281, para. 129 (Aug. 27, 2014); Nadege Dorzema et al. v. Dominican Republic, Merits, Reparations, and Costs, Judgment, Inter-Am. Ct. H.R. (ser. C) No. 251, para. 82 (Oct. 24, 2012).

considering amnesty laws and other legislation that preclude the criminal prosecution of serious human rights violations, such as extrajudicial executions and forced disappearances. The Court has held that these laws breach Convention Articles 1, 2, 8, and 25—but not Article 4.[82] In *Radilla Pacheco v. Mexico*, the Tribunal found that a Mexican law did not sufficiently define the crime of forced disappearance, and declared a breach of Article 2.[83] However, the judgment did not analyze the defective law's specific impact upon Article 4—that is, the State's failure to protect the right to life through legislation.

Among other crucial topics, the Court has not substantially developed the State's duty to protect, by law, the rights to life of pregnant women and the fetus. These subjects, and their associated cases, are discussed further in Section IV(A), *infra*.

3. Duty to Adopt "Prevention and Protection Measures" in Threatening Circumstances

To determine whether the State has fulfilled positive obligations to adopt "prevention and protection measures" in threatening scenarios, the Court analyzes

> whether, at the time of the events, a situation of real or imminent danger existed for the life of a specific individual or a group of individuals, whether the authorities were aware or should have been aware of this, and whether necessary measures were adopted within the scope of their authority which could be reasonably expected to prevent or avoid such danger.[84]

In *Luna López v. Honduras*, a judgment concerning a murdered environmental advocate, the Tribunal proceeded through this step-by-step analysis.[85] First, the Court established "the existence of a real and imminent danger" by observing that Carlos Luna López had been "threatened with a weapon pointed to his head and a shot fired into the air" after his complaints about illegal logging.[86] Second, as for the State's awareness of this danger, the Court noted how Luna López had reported the death threat, as well as other potential acts of theft and corruption, to prosecutors, courts, and the media.[87]

---

[82] *E.g.*, Gomes Lund et al. ("Guerrilha do Araguaia") v. Brazil, Preliminary Objections, Merits, Reparations, and Costs, Judgment, Inter-Am. Ct. H.R. (ser. C) No. 219, para. 172 (Nov. 24, 2010); Barrios Altos v. Peru, Merits, Judgment, Inter-Am. Ct. H.R. (ser. C) No. 75, paras. 41–44 (Mar. 14, 2001). *See also* Mac-Gregor & González Domínguez, *supra* note 15, at 85–87.

[83] Radilla Pacheco v. Mexico, Preliminary Objections, Merits, Reparations, and Costs, Judgment, Inter-Am. Ct. H.R. (ser. C) No. 209, para. 324 (Nov. 23, 2009).

[84] *E.g.*, Luna López v. Honduras, Merits, Reparations, and Costs, Judgment, Inter-Am. Ct. H.R. (ser. C) No. 269, para. 124 (Oct. 10, 2013); Pueblo Bello Massacre v. Colombia, Merits, Reparations, and Costs, Judgment, Inter-Am. Ct. H.R. (ser. C) No. 140, paras. 123–124 (Jan. 31, 2006).

[85] Luna López v. Honduras, Merits, Reparations, and Costs, Judgment, Inter-Am. Ct. H.R. (ser. C) No. 269, para. 124 (Oct. 10, 2013).

[86] *Id.* para. 125.

[87] *Id.*

In response, the Honduran prosecutor had convened an "informal" meeting to mediate between Luna López and the man who had threatened him.[88] The Court held that the meeting was far from an appropriate solution; instead, the State should have "maximized its efforts and used all its available and relevant resources to save his life."[89] More specifically, Honduras should have promptly adopted "security measures and personal protection to enable him to continue with his work, as well as [taken] the necessary steps to investigate immediately and effectively all other threats received."[90] Because the State "did not act with the due diligence required to counter the threat," the Court concluded that Honduras violated its duty to ensure his right to life.[91]

Human Rights Defender et al. *v. Guatemala*, concerning a human rights advocate's murder in 2004, led to a different result.[92] The petitioners argued that, at that time in Guatemala, "human rights defenders [faced] a context of threats and attacks on their lives and personal integrity."[93] The Court, as in other judgments, considered it relevant "to examine the contextual framework to facilitate a better understanding of the evidence and the arguments in order to assess the State's possible responsibility" in the case.[94] The Tribunal found this "context of vulnerability for human rights defenders" to have been established; nevertheless, it decided that evidence was lacking "to prove that the State knew, or should have known, of a situation of real and immediate danger to Mr. A.A.'s life prior to his death."[95] Thus, without enough evidence as to "the specific situation of danger facing Mr. A.A.," Article 4 was not found violated.[96]

4. Duty to Investigate and Punish

The State's duty to ensure the right to life includes the sweeping obligation to investigate every deprivation of life perpetrated by State agents or private parties.[97] When murders committed by non-State actors are not investigated, they "are aided in a sense by the

---

[88] *Id.* para. 135.

[89] *Id.* para. 137.

[90] *Id. See also* Cepeda Vargas v. Colombia, Preliminary Objections, Merits, Reparations, and Costs, Judgment, Inter-Am. Ct. H.R. (ser. C.) No. 213, para. 101 (May 26, 2010) (demanding "prompt and immediate action by the police, prosecutorial and judicial authorities ordering the opportune and necessary measures to determine the authors of the threats made and the crimes committed in this context").

[91] *Id.* para. 139.

[92] Human Rights Defender et al. v. Guatemala, Preliminary Objections, Merits, Reparations, and Costs, Judgment, Inter-Am. Ct. H.R. (ser. C) No. 283 (Aug. 28, 2014).

[93] *Id.* para. 78.

[94] *Id.* para. 73. *See also* Gudiel Alvarez et al. ("Diario Militar") v. Guatemala, Merits, Reparations, and Costs, Judgment, Inter-Am. Ct. H.R. (ser. C) No. 253, para. 52 (Nov. 20, 2012); Goiburú et al. v. Paraguay, Merits, Reparations, and Costs, Judgment, Inter-Am. Ct. H.R. (ser. C) No. 153, paras. 53, 63 (Sept. 22, 2006).

[95] *Id.* para. 149.

[96] *Id.* However, the Court found several other rights violations in the judgment. *Id.* para. 288.

[97] *E.g.*, Castillo González et al. v. Venezuela, Merits, Judgment, Inter-Am. Ct. H.R. (ser. C) No. 256, para. 122 (Nov. 27, 2012); Velasquez Rodriguez v. Honduras, Merits, Judgment, Inter-Am. Ct. H.R. (ser. C) No. 4, paras. 166, 176 (July 29, 1988).

government," engaging the State's liability.[98] Of course, criminal investigation is linked to the "prevention and protection measures" discussed above for threatened individuals: identifying and neutralizing the threat can save a life. Furthermore, investigations and criminal accountability will help prevent recurrence of crime, and likely will provide a degree of satisfaction to victims or their loved ones.[99]

The obligation to investigate "acquires special importance in relation to the severity of the crimes committed and the nature of the rights harmed."[100] In cases regarding violations of the right to life and "other grave human rights violations," the State has the obligation "to initiate, *ex officio* and immediately, a genuine, impartial and effective investigation."[101] Key objectives include the prosecution of all those with criminal responsibility and the elucidation of the truth.[102] While progressing within a reasonable time frame, authorities must also strictly observe the requirements of due process established in Article 8 of the American Convention.[103] It is important to note that the duty to investigate and pursue criminal accountability is not violated merely because the process "does not produce a satisfactory result"; official efforts only must comport with due diligence to discharge the State's obligation.[104]

---

[98] *E.g.*, Cruz Sánchez et al. v. Peru, Preliminary Objections, Merits, Reparations, Costs, Judgment, Inter-Am. Ct. H.R. (ser. C) No. 292, para. 348 (Apr. 17, 2015); Velasquez Rodriguez v. Honduras, Merits, Judgment, Inter-Am. Ct. H.R. (ser. C) No. 4, para. 177 (July 29, 1988).

[99] *E.g.*, Gomes Lund et al. ("Guerrilha do Araguaia") v. Brazil, Preliminary Objections, Merits, Reparations, and Costs, Judgment, Inter-Am. Ct. H.R. (ser. C) No. 219, para. 201 (Nov. 24, 2010) ("the obligation to investigate is a measure of reparation, given the need to remedy the violation of the right to know the truth in the specific case"); Mack Chang v. Guatemala, Merits, Reparations, and Costs, Judgment, Inter-Am. Ct. H.R. (ser. C) No. 101, para. 156 (Nov. 25, 2003) ("In cases of extra-legal executions, it is essential for the States to effectively investigate deprivation of the right to life and to punish all those responsible, especially when State agents are involved, as not doing so would create, within the environment of impunity, conditions for this type of facts to occur again").

[100] *E.g.*, Osorio Rivera and Family v. Peru, Preliminary Objections, Merits, Reparations, and Costs, Judgment, Inter-Am. Ct. H.R. (ser. C) No. 274, para. 177 (Nov. 26, 2013); Goiburú et al. v. Paraguay, Merits, Reparations, and Costs, Judgment, Inter-Am. Ct. H.R. (ser. C) No. 153, para. 128 (Sept. 22, 2006). As discussed in this volume's Chapter 4: Humane Treatment, the obligation to investigate has a specialized content in cases of gender violence.

[101] *E.g.*, Cruz Sánchez et al. v. Peru, Preliminary Objections, Merits, Reparations, Costs, Judgment, Inter-Am. Ct. H.R. (ser. C) No. 292, para. 348 (Apr. 17, 2015); Pueblo Bello Massacre v. Colombia, Merits, Reparations, and Costs, Judgment, Inter-Am. Ct. H.R. (ser. C) No. 140, para. 121 (Jan. 31, 2006).

[102] Cruz Sánchez et al. v. Peru, Preliminary Objections, Merits, Reparations, Costs, Judgment, Inter-Am. Ct. H.R. (ser. C) No. 292, para. 349 (Apr. 17, 2015).

[103] *E.g.*, Guidel Alvarez et al. ("Diario Militar") v. Guatemala, Merits, Reparations, and Costs, Judgment, Inter-Am. Ct. H.R. (ser. C) No. 253, paras. 259–262 (Nov. 20, 2012); Hilaire, Constantine, and Benjamin et al. v. Trinidad & Tobago, Merits, Reparations, and Costs, Judgment, Inter-Am. Ct. H.R. (ser. C) No. 94, para. 14 (June 21, 2002).

[104] *E.g.*, Cruz Sánchez et al. v. Peru, Preliminary Objections, Merits, Reparations, Costs, Judgment, Inter-Am. Ct. H.R. (ser. C) No. 292, para. 422 (Apr. 17, 2015); Velasquez Rodriguez v. Honduras, Merits, Judgment, Inter-Am. Ct. H.R. (ser. C) No. 4, para. 177 (July 29, 1988).

Citing to a United Nations text on the subject, the Court has set out basic due diligence standards for States to observe when investigating a death.[105] At minimum the authorities must seek:

> (a) to identify the victim; (b) to recover and preserve the probative material related to the death, in order to contribute to a potential criminal investigation of those responsible; (c) to identify possible witnesses and obtain their statements in relation to the death investigated; (d) to determine the cause, manner, place, and time of death, as well as any pattern or practice that may have resulted in the death, and (e) to distinguish between death from natural causes, accidental death, suicide and murder. In addition, the scene of the crime must be investigated exhaustively, and meticulous autopsies and analyses of human remains must be performed by competent professionals, using the most appropriate procedures.[106]

Even during armed conflict and other "difficult" circumstances, the Court has insisted that States have "obligations of due diligence" concerning the investigation of suspicious deaths.[107]

In potential cases of forced disappearances, the Court calls for search operations to begin immediately after the disappearance, under the presumption that the victim is still alive.[108] Several judgments have stated "it is essential that the judicial and prosecution authorities act promptly and immediately ordering the opportune and necessary measures to determine the whereabouts of the victim."[109] These measures must include all "the necessary logistic and scientific resources to collect and process the evidence and, in particular, the power to access the pertinent documentation and information."[110] When applicable, the recovery of the corpse clearly is "extremely important" for loved ones, as

---

[105] United Nations Manual on the Effective Prevention and Investigation of Extra-Legal, Arbitrary and Summary Executions, U.N. Doc. E/ST/CSDHA/.12 (1991).

[106] *E.g.*, Barrios Family v. Venezuela, Merits, Reparations, and Costs, Judgment, Inter-Am. Ct. H.R. (ser. C) No. 237, para. 235 (Nov. 24, 2011); Zambrano Vélez et al. v. Ecuador, Merits, Reparations, and Costs, Judgment, Inter-Am. Ct. H.R. (ser. C) No. 166, para. 121 (July 4, 2007).

[107] *E.g.*, Rodriguez Vera et al. (Persons Disappeared from the Palace of Justice) v. Colombia, Preliminary Objections, Merits, Reparations, and Costs, Judgment, Inter-Am. Ct. H.R. (ser. C) No. 287, para. 496 (Nov. 14, 2014) (considering international humanitarian law); Velásquez Rodríguez v. Honduras, Merits, Judgment, Inter-Am. Ct. H.R. (ser. C) No. 4, para. 177 (July 29, 1988).

[108] *E.g.*, Rodriguez Vera et al. (Persons Disappeared from the Palace of Justice) v. Colombia, Preliminary Objections, Merits, Reparations, and Costs, Judgment, Inter-Am. Ct. H.R. (ser. C) No. 287, para. 479 (Nov. 14, 2014); González et al. ("Cotton Field") v. Mexico, Preliminary Objections, Merits, Reparations, and Costs, Judgment, Inter-Am. Ct. H.R. (ser. C) No. 205, para. 283 (Nov. 16, 2009).

[109] *E.g.*, Rodriguez Vera et al. (Persons Disappeared from the Palace of Justice) v. Colombia, Preliminary Objections, Merits, Reparations, and Costs, Judgment, Inter-Am. Ct. H.R. (ser. C) No. 287, para. 479 (Nov. 14, 2014); Anzualdo Castro v. Peru, Preliminary Objections, Merits, Reparations, and Costs, Judgment, Inter-Am. Ct. H.R. (ser. C) No. 202, para. 134 (Sept. 22, 2009).

[110] *Id.* para. 487.

is learning the full truth about the circumstances of the disappearance.[111] The remains are also evidence, of course, and "can provide valuable information" to State authorities about the crime.[112]

Since *Velásquez Rodríguez v. Honduras*, the broad scope of the duty to investigate has been crucial to find violations of Article 4, particularly in cases where direct State involvement was difficult to prove.[113] The Court has attributed responsibility to the State for failure to protect women and girls facing gender violence[114] and civilians in conflict zones,[115] as well as endangered human rights defenders[116] and union leaders.[117] In these situations, States were aware of the prevailing danger; however, they neglected to conduct serious investigations and otherwise act appropriately to save the victims' lives. As a result, the Court found violations of the duty to ensure their rights to life, among other breaches to the Convention.[118]

In many other judgments concerning extrajudicial executions and forced disappearances, the Court has found defective investigations; however, it has assessed the State's lack of due diligence under Articles 8 (Right to a Fair Trial) and 25 (Right to Judicial Protection)—rather than under Article 4 and the duty to ensure the right to life.[119] Unaccountably, the Court resists a consistent approach in this area, as is found in the European human rights system.[120] The European Tribunal will, if applicable, find

[111] *Id.* paras. 480–481.

[112] *Id.*

[113] *See, e.g.*, González et al. ("Cotton Field") v. Mexico, Preliminary Objections, Merits, Reparations, and Costs, Judgment, Inter-Am. Ct. H.R. (ser. C) No. 205, paras. 242–248 (Nov. 16, 2009); Albán Cornejo et al. v. Ecuador, Merits, Reparations, and Costs, Judgment, Inter-Am. Ct. H.R. (ser. C) No. 171, paras. 42, 109 (Nov. 22, 2007).

[114] *E.g.*, Veliz Franco et al. v. Guatemala, Preliminary Objections, Merits, and Reparations, Judgment, Inter-Am. Ct. H.R. (ser. C) No. 277, paras. 151–158 (May 19, 2014); González et al. ("Cotton Field") v. Mexico, Preliminary Objections, Merits, Reparations, and Costs, Judgment, Inter-Am. Ct. H.R. (ser. C) No. 205, paras. 283–286 (Nov. 16, 2009).

[115] Pueblo Bello Massacre v. Colombia, Merits, Reparations, and Costs, Judgment, Inter-Am. Ct. H.R. (ser. C) No. 140, paras. 126, 151 (Jan. 31, 2006).

[116] Luna Lopez v. Honduras, Merits, Reparations, and Costs, Judgment, Inter-Am. Ct. H.R. (ser. C) No. 269, paras. 138–139 (Oct. 10, 2013).

[117] Cantoral Huamaní and García-Santa Cruz v. Peru, Preliminary Objections, Merits, Reparations, and Costs, Judgment, Inter-Am. Ct. H.R. (ser. C) No. 167, paras. 100–106 (July 10, 2007).

[118] Interestingly, in *Albán Cornejo* et al. *v. Ecuador*, the Court found a violation of Article 4 with respect to the *parents* of the deceased victim, due to the State's failure to investigate the case of medical malpractice adequately. Albán Cornejo et al. v. Ecuador, Merits, Reparations, and Costs, Judgment, Inter-Am. Ct. H.R. (ser. C) No. 171, para. 109 (Nov. 22, 2007).

[119] *E.g.*, Community of Santa Barbara v. Peru. Preliminary Objections, Merits, Reparations, and Costs, Judgment, Inter-Am. Ct. H.R. (ser. C) No. 299, para. 195 (Sept. 1, 2015); Osorio Rivera and Family v. Peru, Preliminary Objections, Merits, Reparations, and Costs, Judgment, Inter-Am. Ct. H.R. (ser. C) No. 274, para. 171 (Nov. 26, 2013).

[120] There are other Inter-American judgments that take a third approach: the defective investigation is established in the chapter on Articles 8 and 25, but then the Court refers back to the right to life (and other substantive rights as applicable, such as the right to personal liberty) to find a violation of the State's duty to

two violations of the right to life: one for failure to respect the right (for interference by the State) and another for failure to ensure the right (such as for a flawed criminal investigation).[121]

IV. Scope of Protection

A. Meaning of "Every Person" and "In General, from the Moment of Conception"

Article 4(1) provides: "Every person has the right to have his life respected. This right shall be protected by law and, in general, from the moment of conception."[122] It was not until 2012 that the Court, in *Artavia Murillo* et al. *v. Costa Rica*, began to interpret several key terms of this provision.[123] The case involved Costa Rica's ban on in vitro fertilization treatment; the State's Constitutional Court justified the prohibition due to the alleged "high loss of embryos" in the procedure.[124] The American Convention does not expressly allude to reproductive rights, but according to the Court they are safeguarded under Article 11 (right to privacy),[125] Article 17 (right to a family), Article 7 (right to personal liberty), and the right to health of the San Salvador Protocol.[126]

---

ensure those rights. *E.g.*, Gudiel Álvarez et al. ("Diario Militar") v. Guatemala, Merits, Reparations, and Costs, Judgment, Inter-Am. Ct. H.R. (ser. C) No. 253, para. 267 (Nov. 20, 2012) ("the State has violated its obligation to ensure the rights established in Articles 7, 5(1), 5(2), 4(1) and 3 of the Convention by an effective investigation of the forced disappearance"); Gonzalez Medina and Family v. Dominican Republic, Preliminary Objections, Merits, Reparations, and Costs, Judgment, Inter-Am. Ct. H.R. (ser. C) No. 240, para. 265 (Feb. 27, 2012) (similar).

121 *E.g.*, Mocanu and Others v. Romania, Eur. Ct. H.R., paras. 317–353 (Sept. 17, 2014) (explaining that the general duty under Article 1 of the European Convention and Articles 2 (Right to Life) and 3 (Prohibition of Torture) require "effective official investigations," and finding procedural violations of Articles 2 and 3 owing to the lack of such investigations); Akdeniz v. Turkey, Eur. Ct. H.R., paras. 103–112 (May 31, 2005) (similar). *See also* "Combining Articles 8 and 25: A Critique" in this book's Chapter 6: Due Process and Judicial Protection.

122 American Convention, art. 4(1).

123 Artavia Murillo et al. (In-vitro Fertilization) v. Costa Rica, Preliminary Objections, Merits, Reparations, and Costs, Judgment, Inter-Am. Ct. H.R. (ser. C) No. 257 (Nov. 28, 2012). Of course, for years the Court has affirmed that "[a]ny restrictive approach to the [right to life] is . . . inadmissible." *E.g.*, Zambrano Vélez et al. v. Ecuador, Merits, Reparations, and Costs, Judgment, Inter-Am. Ct. H.R. (ser. C) No. 166, para. 78 (July 4, 2007); "Street Children" (Villagrán Morales et al.) v. Guatemala, Reparations and Costs, Judgment, Inter-Am. Ct. H.R. (ser. C) No. 77, para. 144 (May 26, 2001).

124 Artavia Murillo et al. (In-vitro Fertilization) v. Costa Rica, Preliminary Objections, Merits, Reparations, and Costs, Judgment, Inter-Am. Ct. H.R. (ser. C) No. 257, para. 305 (Nov. 28, 2012).

125 The Court has stated that "the right to private life is related to: (i) reproductive autonomy, and (ii) access to reproductive health services, which includes the right to have access to the medical technology necessary to exercise this right." *Id.* para. 146.

126 *Id.* para. 150. The Tribunal has not yet explicitly linked reproductive rights to the right to life, although it has recognized the "connection between personal autonomy, reproductive freedom, and physical and mental integrity." *Id.* para. 147.

Artavia Murillo began by explaining that "every person," for the purposes of Article 4, refers to "every human being," based on the text of Article 1(2) of the Convention.[127] Next, the Court acknowledged that "there is no one agreed definition of the beginning of life," and that this matter has been "assessed in different ways from biological, medical, ethical, moral, philosophical and religious perspectives."[128] Nevertheless, it then set out to establish a bright-line test for when human "conception" occurs, in the terms of Article 4.

Artavia Murillo held that "conception" should be understood as "from the moment at which implantation [of the embryo in the mother's uterus] occurs, and therefore . . . before this event, Article 4 of the American Convention cannot be applied."[129] Costa Rica had maintained that "conception" occurs earlier, at fertilization;[130] however, according to the Court, Article 4 does not protect a fertilized egg that has not yet been implanted in the uterus.[131] Thus, the Court appears to leave little discretion to States on this highly-disputed matter, in contrast to the European Court of Human Rights and other tribunals.[132] The decision comprises a striking departure from the Inter-American Court's recent tendency, as noted elsewhere in this volume, to defer to State law.

As for the phrase "in general," the Court held that its "object and purpose" is to convey that the right to life "should not be understood as an absolute right, the alleged protection of which can justify the total negation of other rights."[133] Article 4 allows "as appropriate, an adequate balance between competing rights and interests."[134] In this way, the

---

[127] *Id.* paras. 176, 219.

[128] *Id.* para. 185.

[129] *Id.* para. 189.

[130] *Id.* para. 167.

[131] Curiously, the Court's judgment includes an extensive section where it balances various rights—the "rights to personal integrity, personal liberty, private life, intimacy, reproductive autonomy, access to reproductive health services, and to found a family"—against the "rights" of the un-implanted embryo, although it never conceded this embryo any rights at the outset. *Id.* paras. 314–315.

[132] *See* Harris, O'Boyle & Warbrick, *supra* note 21, at 220 (discussing *Vo v. France*: "given the absence of European legal, medical, ethical, or religious consensus as to when life begins, a margin of appreciation applies, even to the point where the Court doubted whether it was 'desirable, or even possible as matters stand, to answer in the abstract the question whether the unborn child is a person for the purposes of article 2.'"). In *Evans v. UK*, the European Court applied a similar margin of appreciation approach as in *Vo v. France*—deferring to State law—with respect to embryos created by IVF. *Id.* For further critiques and analysis of *Artavia Murillo*, from various perspectives, *see* Paolo Carozza, *The Anglo-Latin Divide and the Future of the Inter-American System of Human Rights*, 5 Notre Dame J. Int'l Comp. L. 153 (2015); Ligia De Jesus, *A Pro-choice Reading of a Pro-life Treaty: The Inter-American Court on Human Rights' Distorted Interpretation of the American Convention on Human Rights in* Artavia v. Costa Rica, 32 Wis. Int'l L.J. 223 (2014); Ciara O'Connell, *Engendering Reproductive Rights in the Inter-American System*, *in* Gender, Sexuality and Social Justice: What's Law Got to Do With It? (Kay Lalor, Elizabeth Mills, Arturo Sánchez García & Polly Haste eds. 2016); Álvaro Paúl, *Decision-Making Process of the Inter-American Court: An Analysis Prompted by the "In Vitro Fertilization" Case*, 21 ILSA J. Int'l & Comp. L. 87 (2014).

[133] Artavia Murillo et al. (In-vitro Fertilization) v. Costa Rica, Preliminary Objections, Merits, Reparations, and Costs, Judgment, Inter-Am. Ct. H.R. (ser. C) No. 257, para. 258 (Nov. 28, 2012).

[134] *Id.* para. 263.

judgment certainly leaves open the possibility to balance the rights of the unborn child with those of the mother. The Tribunal further held that protection of the right to life under Article 4 is "gradual and incremental according to its development."[135] Although the statement indicates that a later-stage fetus is entitled to "greater protection," the Court offers no specific guidance.

Both in *Artavia Murillo* and other judgments, the Court leaves the rights of unborn children in a state of significant uncertainty.[136] In *Gelman v. Uruguay*, María Claudia García Iruretagoyena de Gelman ("María Claudia"), who was seven-months pregnant, had been illegally detained in secret military facilities; as a result, her baby, María Macarena, was born in captivity.[137] The Tribunal recognized that the treatment "severely affected [the mother's] personal integrity . . . and caused . . . physical and psychological suffering."[138] Although in a footnote the Court acknowledged that such conditions could also seriously affect the child she was carrying, it did not find violations to María Macarena's right to personal integrity.[139] After María Macarena's birth, María Claudia was executed, and the child was illegally adopted by another family.[140] The Court considered the case's facts to constitute *two* forced disappearances—of both mother and child—leading to violations of Article 4, among other rights.[141] However, in the case of María Macarena, the Court found the human rights violations to have occurred *from her birth*—not from the earlier point when her mother was abducted.[142]

Although the Court has not directly dealt with abortion on the merits, the Inter-American Commission has indicated that the right to life, under the American

[135] *Id.* para. 264.

[136] *See also* Gelman v. Uruguay, Merits and Reparations, Judgment, Inter-Am. Ct. H.R. (ser. C) No. 221 (Feb. 24, 2011) (see discussion in following paragraph); Xákmok Kásek Indigenous Cmty. v. Paraguay, Merits, Reparations, and Costs, Judgment, Inter-Am. Ct. H.R. (ser. C) No. 214, para. 228 (Aug. 24, 2010) ("the representatives and the Commission have not presented arguments regarding the alleged violation of the right to life of the 'unborn,' so that, given the absence of grounds, the Court lacks facts on which to form an opinion as to the State's responsibility in these cases").

[137] Gelman v. Uruguay, Merits and Reparations, Judgment, Inter-Am. Ct. H.R. (ser. C) No. 221, para. 97 (Feb. 24, 2011).

[138] *Id.* para. 98.

[139] *See id.* note 128 ("Scientific evidence shows that diet, stress, physical and psychological stress experienced by the mother during pregnancy has systemic effects that affect children [. . .] that can even alter the child's subsequent physical development").

[140] María Macarena, who is still alive, only discovered her parents' fate years later (her biological father had also disappeared). *Id.* paras. 112–113.

[141] *Id.* paras. 101, 132.

[142] *Id.* para. 137 ("The Court declares that the State is responsible for having violated, from the birth of María Macarena Gelman García until the moment that she recovered her true and legitimate identity, the right to juridical personality, to life, to personal integrity, to personal liberty, to family, to a name, to the rights of the child, and to nationality, recognized in Articles 3, 4, 5, 7, 17, 18, 19, and 20(3) of the Convention, in relation to Articles 1(1) therein, and I and XI of the Inter-American Convention on the Forced Disappearance of Persons").

Declaration, allows for abortion in some circumstances.[143] As for the American Convention, the Commission's jurisprudence on abortion and the rights of unborn children is limited.[144] Still, during the *Artavia Murillo* litigation, the Commission asserted that Article 4 "does not establish an absolute or categorical right in relation to the prenatal stages of life" and that "an international and comparative recognition [exists] of the concept of gradual and incremental protection of life at the prenatal stage."[145] In addition, both the Court and the Commission have granted provisional and precautionary measures, respectively, to protect individuals seeking abortions when their health was in danger.[146] However, the provisional and precautionary measures—issued only after significant delays and containing ambiguous instructions—cast doubt upon the Inter-American System's current ability to provide prompt and effective remedies in this area.

B. MEANING OF "NO ONE SHALL BE ARBITRARILY DEPRIVED" OF LIFE

The Court has found arbitrary deprivations of life in five general situations. These include: (1) the application of the death penalty under certain circumstances, (2) the disproportionate use of force in law enforcement scenarios, (3) the disproportionate use of force during armed conflicts, (4) the deaths of imprisoned individuals, and (5) the forced disappearance of persons. The present section considers these situations, which can overlap to some extent.

---

[143] *See* Baby Boy v. United States, Case 2141, Inter-Am. Comm'n H.R., OEA/Ser.L/V/II.54, Doc. 9 rev. 1 (1981), para. 18. However, the Commission did not explain the precise circumstances; rather, in response to the petitioners' arguments, it reviewed the negotiation history of the American Declaration and American Convention.

[144] In *Baby Boy*, the Commission considers the Convention's negotiation history and concludes, "the implications of the clause '*in general*, from the moment of conception' are substantially different" from the more restrictive phrase "from the moment of conception" (emphasis added). *Id.* para. 30. In 2007, the Commission approved the settlement of an abortion case against Mexico. Paulina del Carmen Ramírez Jacinto v. Mexico, Case 161-02, Inter-Am. Comm. H.R., Report No. 21/07, OEA/Ser.L/V/II.130, doc. 22, rev.1 (2007), *available at* https://www.cidh.oas.org/annualrep/2007eng/Mexico161.02eng.htm. Although the Commission made no ruling on the merits of the dispute, it generally called for "de jure and de facto access to suitable and effective judicial remedies . . . for the protection of all the rights of women," as well as stressed the State's "obligation of acting with due diligence when violations of their human rights occur." *Id.* para. 26. *See also* Álvaro Paúl, *Controversial Conceptions: The Unborn and the American Convention on Human Rights*, 9 LOY. U. CHI. INT'L L. REV. 209 (2011) ("The Commission seems to grant the unborn legal personality for jurisdictional purposes, [and] it also endorses the unborn's capability of being injured by third parties. Nevertheless, the Commission seems to grant States a wide margin of appreciation for determining the protection given to the unborn.").

[145] Artavia Murillo et al. (In-vitro Fertilization) v. Costa Rica, Preliminary Objections, Merits, Reparations, and Costs, Judgment, Inter-Am. Ct. H.R. (ser. C) No. 257, para. 163 (Nov. 28, 2012).

[146] B. v El Salvador, Provisional Measures, Order of the Court, 2013 Inter-Am. Ct. H.R. (May 29, 2013); Inter-American Commission on Human Rights, Precautionary Measures, MC 178/15, Mainumby v. Paraguay (June 8, 2015), *available at* http://www.oas.org/es/cidh/decisiones/pdf/2015/MC178-15-ES.pdf (full order in Spanish). In both cases, the States in question prohibited abortion.

1. The Death Penalty

a. Introduction

Nearly two-thirds of all nations have now abolished the death penalty in law or practice.[147] Still, the Inter-American Court and Commission have confronted issues of capital punishment on several occasions. The Inter-American System has played a key role in staying executions in Caribbean States, and in overturning "mandatory" death penalty statutes in the region.[148] The Commission has also attempted, with little success, to stay executions in the United States.[149]

Article 4 of the Convention dedicates five paragraphs to limit the death penalty. For those States that did not permit capital punishment upon ratification, the Convention "imposes a definite prohibition [. . .] for all categories of offenses as far as the future is concerned."[150] The Court has not yet dealt with a case where a State sought to reinstitute the death penalty, and so has not found a violation of Article 4(3). However, in *Raxcacó Reyes v. Guatemala*, the Court determined that the State had extended capital punishment to the crime of kidnapping, and consequently declared a breach of Article 4(2).[151]

For retentionist States, the Convention "imposes restrictions designed to delimit strictly its application and scope, in order to reduce the application of the penalty to bring about its gradual disappearance."[152] The Tribunal's jurisprudence on capital punishment has concerned Barbados, Trinidad and Tobago, and Guatemala.[153] The case law can be arranged around four main themes: (1) the "most serious crimes" requirement, (2) a rejection of "mandatory" death penalty laws, (3) due process standards, and (4) full access to opportunities for commutation, amnesty, or pardon.

---

[147] Amnesty International, "Death Penalty," *available at* https://www.amnesty.org/en/what-we-do/death-penalty/ (last visited Nov. 21, 2016); Inter-American Commission on Human Rights, The Death Penalty in the Inter-American Human Rights System: From Restrictions to Abolition, paras. 23–38 (2011) (summarizing "significant developments in the region").

[148] *See* Brian D. Tittemore, *The Mandatory Death Penalty in the Commonwealth Caribbean and the Inter-American Human Rights System: An Evolution in the Development and Implementation of International Human Rights Protections*, 13 Wm. & Mary Bill Rts. J. 445, 484 (2004).

[149] Inter-American Commission on Human Rights, The Death Penalty in the Inter-American Human Rights System: From Restrictions to Abolition, para. 49 (2011) ("In dozens of instances the IACHR has issued precautionary measures requesting that the execution of death row inmates in the United States be stayed until the Commission had issued a determination on their petitions, and in dozens of instances the State has executed the prisoners in violation of those measures.").

[150] Restrictions to the Death Penalty (Arts. 4(2) and 4(4) American Convention on Human Rights), Advisory Opinion OC-3/83, Inter-Am. Ct. H.R. (ser. A) No. 3, paras. 56 and 68 (Sept. 8, 1983).

[151] Raxcacó Reyes v. Guatemala, Merits, Reparations, and Costs, Judgment, Inter-Am. Ct. H.R. (ser. C) No. 133, para. 66 (Sept. 15, 2005).

[152] *E.g.*, Hilaire, Constantine, and Benjamin et al. v. Trinidad & Tobago, Merits, Reparations, and Costs, Judgment, Inter-Am. Ct. H.R. (ser. C) No. 94, para. 99 (June 21, 2002); Restrictions to the Death Penalty (Arts. 4(2) and 4(4) American Convention on Human Rights), Advisory Opinion OC-3/83, Inter-Am. Ct. H.R. (ser. A) No. 3, para. 57 (Sept. 8, 1983).

[153] In 1998, Trinidad and Tobago denounced the American Convention, primarily because of the interventions of the Inter-American Commission and Court in this area.

b. "Only For The Most Serious Crimes"

The Court has reiterated the Convention's substantive limitations that the death penalty can only be applied to "the most serious crimes," and never to "political offenses or related common crimes."[154] Yet the Tribunal has not defined political offenses, nor has it listed "the most serious crimes." *Raxcacó Reyes* only indicated that the latter "affect most severely the most important individual and social rights and therefore merit the most vigorous censure and the most severe punishment."[155]

In *Raxcacó*, the Court decided that "simple kidnapping" would not belong to the "most serious" category.[156] Even when kidnapping is followed by death, the Tribunal considered that it would be necessary to examine all of the case's circumstances—and thus domestic law must grant courts "a margin of subjective appraisal."[157] Further, the Court cited a UN Human Rights Committee statement that crimes "that do not result in loss of life" may not be punished by the death penalty.[158] However, it is unclear if the Court has fully adopted this view, and if it considers that capital punishment should be possible only for certain types of intentional killings.

The Tribunal has not decided a case where an allegedly "political crime" led to the death penalty. For its part, the Inter-American Commission has also avoided defining political offenses. Still, it condemned Cuban legislation allowing for the application of capital punishment to a wide range of crimes.[159] Among them, the Commission criticized "crimes against the security of the State" as a particularly "broad and vague" category of offenses.[160] It has also denounced that political dissidents and "those who have attempted to flee the island" have been sentenced to death in Cuba.[161]

c. The "Mandatory" Death Penalty

The majority of relevant cases before the Inter-American Court have concerned the imposition of a "mandatory" death penalty. At issue in these judgments, beginning with *Hilarie, Constantine* et al *v. Trinidad and Tobago,* was "the automatic imposition" of the death penalty upon conviction for murder, without any consideration of mitigating

---

[154] Restrictions to the Death Penalty (Arts. 4(2) and 4(4) American Convention on Human Rights), Advisory Opinion OC-3/83, Inter-Am. Ct. H.R. (ser. A) No. 3, para. 54 (Sept. 8, 1983). In a recent judgment concerning a possible extradition from Peru to China, the Court was satisfied that China would not apply the death penalty for the crime of "smuggling common goods;" for these and other reasons, the judgment did not find a violation of Article 4. Wong Ho Wing v. Peru, Preliminary Objection, Merits, Reparations and Costs, Judgment, Inter-Am. Ct. H.R. (ser. C) No. 297, paras. 187–188 (June 30, 2015) (translation by authors).

[155] Raxcacó Reyes v. Guatemala, Merits, Reparations, and Costs, Judgment, Inter-Am. Ct. H.R. (ser. C) No. 133, para. 70 (Sept. 15, 2005).

[156] *Id.* para. 71.

[157] *Id.*

[158] *Id.* para. 69.

[159] Inter-American Commission on Human Rights, Annual Report 2014, paras. 158–166.

[160] *Id.* para. 162.

[161] Inter-American Commission on Human Rights, The Death Penalty in the Inter-American Human Rights System: From Restrictions to Abolition, para. 110, page 113 (2011) (referring to *Copello Castillo* et al. *v. Cuba*).

circumstances in the sentencing process.[162] The Tribunal found that "the law fails to distinguish the possibility of different degrees of culpability of the offender and fails to individually consider the particular circumstances of the crime."[163]

For the Court, "intentional or premeditated murder" must be addressed in criminal law "under various categories (criminal classes) that correspond with the wide range of seriousness of the surrounding facts, taking into account the different facets that can come into play."[164] As a result, the Tribunal has also found a violation of Article 2 in relation to Article 4, and required several changes to domestic law—including constitutional provisions.[165] The Court has also called for legislation to ensure "judicial protection against violations of [the] right to life."[166] In compliance with the Court's judgments, Barbados commuted capital punishment to life sentences for the petitioners; the State also expressed its commitment to abolish the mandatory death penalty and amend the problematic Constitutional norms.[167] Following the Inter-American System's decisions, the mandatory death penalty has been abandoned in various Caribbean States such as Saint Lucia, Dominica, Belize, the Bahamas, and Grenada.[168]

d. Due Process Requirements

Article 4(2) contains simple due process requirements for the death penalty: it may be imposed only "pursuant to a final judgment rendered by a competent court and in accordance with a law establishing such punishment, enacted prior to the commission of the crime."[169] The Court has clarified, however, that the Convention's full range of procedural guarantees must apply to capital punishment cases:

> If the due process of law, with all its rights and guarantees, must be respected regardless of the circumstances, then its observance becomes all the more important when

---

[162] *See, e.g.*, Tittemore, *supra* note 148, at 446.

[163] *E.g.*, DaCosta Cadogan v. Barbados, Preliminary Objections, Merits, Reparations, and Costs, Judgment, Inter-Am. Ct. H.R. (ser. C) No. 204, para. 53 (Sept. 24, 2009); Hilaire, Constantine, and Benjamin et al. v. Trinidad & Tobago, Merits, Reparations, and Costs, Judgment, Inter-Am. Ct. H.R. (ser. C) No. 94, para. 104 (June 21, 2002).

[164] DaCosta Cadogan v. Barbados, Preliminary Objections, Merits, Reparations, and Costs, Judgment, Inter-Am. Ct. H.R. (ser. C) No. 204, para. 50 (Sept. 24, 2009).

[165] *E.g.*, Boyce et al. v. Barbados, Preliminary Objections, Merits, Reparations, and Costs, Judgment, Inter-Am. Ct. H.R. (ser. C) No. 169, para. 79 (Nov. 20, 2007); Hilaire, Constantine, and Benjamin et al. v. Trinidad & Tobago, Merits, Reparations, and Costs, Judgment, Inter-Am. Ct. H.R. (ser. C) No. 94, para. 152(c) (June 21, 2002).

[166] Boyce et al. v. Barbados, Preliminary Objections, Merits, Reparations, and Costs, Judgment, Inter-Am. Ct. H.R. (ser. C) No. 169, para. 79 (Nov. 20, 2007).

[167] Boyce et al. v. Barbados, Monitoring Compliance with Judgment, Order of the Court, 2011 Inter-Am. Ct. H.R. (Nov. 21, 2011).

[168] Inter-American Commission on Human Rights, The Death Penalty in the Inter-American Human Rights System: From Restrictions to Abolition, para. 27 (2011).

[169] American Convention, art. 4(2).

that supreme entitlement that every human rights treaty and declaration recognizes and protects is at stake: human life.[170]

In this way, the Court and the Commission have looked to the Convention's due process provisions—Articles 8 and 25—as they seek to attain the "strictest and most rigorous enforcement of judicial guarantees" in this context.[171]

The Court's first decision on due process guarantees for the death penalty was *Advisory Opinion No. 16*, which dealt specifically with the right to consular notification and assistance. The Court clearly stated that non-observance of a detained foreign national's "right to consular information," defined in Article 36(1)(b) of the Vienna Convention on Consular Relations, violates due process of law; in such circumstances, imposition of the death penalty breaches the right not to be "arbitrarily" deprived of one's life.[172] Similarly, the Inter-American Commission, in several cases against the United States, has found the lack of consular notification to violate due process guarantees.[173]

The Court does not often discuss due process violations for death penalty cases under Article 4, preferring to reserve them for the judgment's chapter on Articles 8 and 25. In two judgments, *Hilaire* et al. *v Trinidad and Tobago* and *Fermin Ramirez v. Guatemala*, not only did the Tribunal find violations to Articles 8 or 25, but it also ordered a new trial for the petitioners.[174] In *Hilaire*, the Court found distinct procedural violations. For example, petitioners were denied "access to adequate legal assistance for the effective presentation of constitutional motions," which were cumbersome to file without counsel;[175] the Tribunal also concluded that domestic law did not recognize the right to trial "within a reasonable period of time."[176] Yet, because the Court ultimately ordered the State to retry all of the petitioners due to the application of the mandatory death penalty law, the specific due process violations "had little practical effect on the outcome of the case."[177]

---

[170] Right to Information on Consular Assistance in the Framework of the Guarantees of the Due Process of Law, Advisory Opinion OC-16/99, Inter-Am. Ct. H.R. (ser. A) No. 16, para. 135 (Oct. 1, 1999).

[171] *Id.* para. 136; Inter-American Commission on Human Rights, The Death Penalty in the Inter-American Human Rights System: From Restrictions to Abolition, paras. 40–43 (2011).

[172] Right to Information on Consular Assistance in the Framework of the Guarantees of the Due Process of Law, Advisory Opinion OC-16/99, Inter-Am. Ct. H.R. (ser. A) No. 16, para. 137 (Oct. 1, 1999).

[173] Inter-American Commission on Human Rights, The Death Penalty in the Inter-American Human Rights System: From Restrictions to Abolition, para. 121 (2011).

[174] Fermín Ramírez v. Guatemala, Merits, Reparations, and Costs, Judgment, Inter-Am. Ct. H.R. (ser. C) No. 126, para. 138 (June 20, 2005); Hilaire, Constantine, and Benjamin et al. v. Trinidad & Tobago, Merits, Reparations, and Costs, Judgment, Inter-Am. Ct. H.R. (ser. C) No. 94, para. 223 (June 21, 2002).

[175] Hilaire, Constantine, and Benjamin et al. v. Trinidad & Tobago, Merits, Reparations, and Costs, Judgment, Inter-Am. Ct. H.R. (ser. C) No. 94, para. 152(b) (June 21, 2002).

[176] *Id.* para. 152(a).

[177] Tittemore, *supra* note 148, at 496.

Fermin Ramirez involved a petitioner who had been convicted of murder and aggravated rape.[178] The Court held that Guatemala "violated the procedural rules of strict and necessary observance in cases of imposition of the death penalty." [179] Specifically, it found that the petitioner had not been notified adequately of the criminal charges, and that he had not been provided with sufficient opportunity to prepare a defense—in breach of paragraphs (b) and (c) of the Convention's Article 8(2). As mentioned below, his Article 4(6) right to apply for amnesty, pardon, or commutation of sentence was also violated. Curiously, the Court did not find a breach of Article 4(1), reasoning that Fermin Ramirez had not been executed.[180] Yet a violation of Article 4(6) should lead to the conclusion that the right to life was not respected, infringing the terms of Article 4(1).

DaCosta Cadogan v. Barbados, a subsequent judgment concerning a mandatory death penalty, did not lead the Court to order a retrial—although a domestic court hearing was ordered to determine a new sentence.[181] The Court found that due process was compromised because the defendant's mental health at the time of the facts was "never fully evaluated . . . in a case where the death penalty was the only possible sentence."[182] It considered that because DaCosta Cadogan's lawyer was appointed by the State, "the presiding judge had the duty to adopt a more active role in ensuring that all necessary measures were carried out in order to guarantee a fair trial."[183] As the trial judge could have ordered the free psychological examination, but chose not to do so, Barbados was held responsible for violations of both Article 8(1)[184] and paragraphs (f) and (c)[185] of Article 8(2).[186]

In summary, then, the Court demands rigorous due process guarantees in capital punishment cases, consistent with Articles 8 and 25. At this stage in the case law's development, however, it is unclear to what extent the procedural standards are stricter than

[178] Fermín Ramírez v. Guatemala, Merits, Reparations, and Costs, Judgment, Inter-Am. Ct. H.R. (ser. C) No. 126 (June 20, 2005).

[179] *Id.* para 79.

[180] In *Boyce* et al. *v. Barbados*, the Court found an Article 4 violation and cruel treatment for "any reading of death warrants or execution of a person whose petition is before the Inter-American System." Boyce et al. v. Barbados, Preliminary Objections, Merits, Reparations, and Costs, Judgment, Inter-Am. Ct. H.R. (ser. C) No. 169, para. 114 (Nov. 20, 2007). Thus, no actual death was necessary to find the State in violation of Article 4.

[181] DaCosta Cadogan v. Barbados, Preliminary Objections, Merits, Reparations, and Costs, Judgment, Inter-Am. Ct. H.R. (ser. C) No. 204 (Sept. 24, 2009).

[182] *Id.* para. 88.

[183] *Id.* para. 89.

[184] The Convention's Article 8(1) provides: "Every person has the right to a hearing, with due guarantees and within a reasonable time, by a competent, independent, and impartial tribunal, previously established by law, in the substantiation of any accusation of a criminal nature made against him or for the determination of his rights and obligations of a civil, labor, fiscal, or any other nature."

[185] The Convention's Article 8(2)(c) establishes "adequate time and means for the preparation of his defense"; Article 8(2)(f) provides for "the right of the defense to examine witnesses present in the court and to obtain the appearance, as witnesses, of experts or other persons who may throw light on the facts."

[186] DaCosta Cadogan v. Barbados, para. 90.

those of non-death-penalty criminal proceedings. When States fail to comply with procedural protections, the Court has ordered retrials or the commutation of sentences.[187]

The Inter-American Commission has similarly called for a "standard of strict, heightened scrutiny" in capital punishment cases.[188] It has condemned the practices of numerous States—prominent among them the United States—for insufficient due process, the execution of juvenile offenders, and racial discrimination in capital trials and sentencing.[189] The United States has resisted the Commission's direction in this area, to its "profound concern."[190] In fact, "in dozens of instances" the State has disregarded the Commission's precautionary measures that requested stays of execution.[191]

e. Right to Apply for Pardon, Amnesty, or Commutation

Article 4(6) of the Convention establishes the right of every person sentenced to the death penalty "to apply for pardon, amnesty or commutation of sentence"; the execution may not be carried out "while such a petition is pending decision by the competent authority." The Court found this provision to be violated in three cases.[192] In the first judgment, *Hilaire*, it held that Article 4(6), "when read together with Articles 8 and 1(1), places the State under the obligation to guarantee that an offender sentenced to death may effectively exercise this right."[193] Consequently, States must "implement a fair and transparent procedure by which an offender sentenced to death may make use of all favorable evidence deemed relevant to the granting of mercy."[194] The Court found

---

[187] Boyce et al. v. Barbados, Preliminary Objections, Merits, Reparations, and Costs, Judgment, Inter-Am. Ct. H.R. (ser. C) No. 169, para. 127 (Nov. 20, 2007) (the State must "formally commute the death sentence of Mr. Huggins"); Hilaire, Constantine, and Benjamin et al. v. Trinidad & Tobago, Merits, Reparations, and Costs, Judgment, Inter-Am. Ct. H.R. (ser. C) No. 94, para. 214 (June 21, 2002) (ordering a retrial). In *Wong Ho Wing v. Peru,* the Court considered an extradition procedure to China, which permits the death penalty. Wong Ho Wing v. Peru, Preliminary Objection, Merits, Reparations and Costs, Judgment, Inter-Am. Ct. H.R. (ser. C) No. 297 (June 30, 2015). The Court found that Article 4 was not violated because China had provided Peru sufficient assurances that it would not apply capital punishment. *Id.* paras. 151–152.

[188] Inter-American Commission on Human Rights, The Death Penalty in the Inter-American Human Rights System: From Restrictions to Abolition, para. 13 (2011).

[189] The Inter-American Commission also granted precautionary measures requesting the United States to stay the deportation of asylum seekers on the grounds that their lives would be in serious danger if returned to El Salvador. Inter-American Commission on Human Rights, Matter of E.G.S. and A.E.S.G. regarding the United States of America, Precautionary Measure 297-16 (May 11, 2016), *available at* http://www.oas.org/es/cidh/decisiones/pdf/2016/MC297-16-Es.pdf.

[190] Inter-American Commission on Human Rights, The Death Penalty in the Inter-American Human Rights System: From Restrictions to Abolition, para. 49 (2011).

[191] *Id.*

[192] Raxcacó Reyes v. Guatemala, Merits, Reparations, and Costs, Judgment, Inter-Am. Ct. H.R. (ser. C) No. 133, para. 90 (Sept. 15, 2005); Fermín Ramírez v. Guatemala, Merits, Reparations, and Costs, Judgment, Inter-Am. Ct. H.R. (ser. C) No. 126 (June 20, 2005), para. 110; Hilaire, Constantine, and Benjamin et al. v. Trinidad and Tobago, Merits, Reparations, and Costs, Judgment, Inter-Am. Ct. H.R. (ser. C) No. 94 (June 21, 2002).

[193] *Id.* para. 188.

[194] *Id.*

that the procedure in *Hilaire* "was characterized by a lack of transparency, lack of available information and lack of participation by the victims," violating Article 4(6).[195] In both *Fermín Ramírez* and *Raxcacó Reyes*, the Court ruled Guatemala in breach of the provision for eliminating, through a 2001 law, the State institution that decided pardon requests.[196]

2. Use of Lethal Force in Law Enforcement Scenarios

a. Introduction

Article 4 of the American Convention does not explicitly regulate the use of force by State agents. However, the Court has heard several cases on the use of lethal force by both police officers[197] and soldiers;[198] it recognizes that force is occasionally justified to maintain public safety and security. Yet lethal force must be exceptional and strictly obey the principles of legality, necessity, and proportionality.[199] If not, any resulting deprivation of life is arbitrary.[200] Accordingly, the Court has condemned a State's use of lethal force even in very dangerous contexts, such as terrorism, internal conflict, gang violence, and drug trafficking.[201]

Further, the Court requires a "clear demarcation between military and police duties."[202] That is, States "must restrict to the maximum extent the use of armed forces" outside of armed conflict, because "they are trained to fight against enemies and not to protect and control civilians."[203] Still, the Court has left the door open for the involvement of

---

[195] *Id.* para. 189.

[196] Raxcacó Reyes v. Guatemala, Merits, Reparations, and Costs, Judgment, Inter-Am. Ct. H.R. (ser. C) No. 133, paras. 83–86; Fermín Ramírez v. Guatemala, Merits, Reparations, and Costs, Judgment, Inter-Am. Ct. H.R. (ser. C) No. 126, paras. 107–110.

[197] *E.g.*, Landaeta Meijias Brothers et al. v. Venezuela, Preliminary Objections, Merits, Reparations, and Costs, Judgment, Inter-Am. Ct. H.R. (ser. C) No. 281 (Aug. 27, 2014); Uzcátegui et al. v. Venezuela, Merits and Reparations, Judgment, Inter-Am. Ct. H.R. (ser. C) No. 249 (Sept. 3, 2012).

[198] *E.g.*, Zambrano Vélez et al. v. Ecuador, Merits, Reparations, and Costs, Judgment, Inter-Am. Ct. H.R. (ser. C) No. 166 (July 4, 2007); Caracazo v. Venezuela, Merits, Judgment, Inter-Am. Ct. H.R. (ser. C) No. 58 (Nov. 11, 1999).

[199] *E.g.*, Landaeta Meijias Brothers et al. v. Venezuela, Preliminary Objections, Merits, Reparations, and Costs, Judgment, Inter-Am. Ct. H.R. (ser. C) No. 281, para. 134 (Aug. 27, 2014); Zambrano Vélez et al. v. Ecuador, Merits, Reparations, and Costs, Judgment, Inter-Am. Ct. H.R. (ser. C) No. 166, paras. 83–85 (July 4, 2007).

[200] *E.g.*, Zambrano Vélez et al. v. Ecuador, Merits, Reparations, and Costs, Judgment, Inter-Am. Ct. H.R. (ser. C) No. 166, para. 84 (July 4, 2007); Montero Aranguren et al. (Det. Ctr. of Catia) v. Venezuela, Preliminary Objection, Merits, Reparations, and Costs, Judgment, Inter-Am. Ct. H.R. (ser. C) No. 150, para. 68 (July 5, 2006).

[201] *E.g.*, Zambrano Vélez et al. v. Ecuador, Merits, Reparations, and Costs, Judgment, Inter-Am. Ct. H.R. (ser. C) No. 166, paras. 73–74, 110 (July 4, 2007) (1,200 State agents participated in an unlawful operation "to arrest criminals, drug traffickers and terrorists"); Servellón García et al. v. Honduras, Merits, Reparations, and Costs, Judgment, Inter-Am. Ct. H.R. (ser. C) No. 152, paras. 79(1)–(4) (Sept. 21, 2006) (considering aspects of widespread gang violence).

[202] Zambrano Vélez et al. v. Ecuador, Merits, Reparations, and Costs, Judgment, Inter-Am. Ct. H.R. (ser. C) No. 166, para. 51 (July 4, 2007).

[203] *Id.* In *Caracazo v. Venezuela*, the Court began to develop its case law in this area; there, the State recognized that 44 persons were killed by the Venezuelan Army and that "there was a common pattern of behavior

armed forces in law enforcement. When soldiers are employed as a means "for controlling social protests, domestic disturbances, internal violence, public emergencies and common crime," they must uphold a duty of "extreme care."[204] The content of this duty remains unclear. In addition, if States have justified military force by declaring a state of emergency, they must comply fully with the requirements of the Convention's Article 27 ("Suspension of Guarantees").[205]

b. The Principles of Legality, Necessity, and Proportionality

International human rights law requires at least three interrelated elements for the use of lethal force: legality, necessity, and proportionality.[206] In assessing use-of-force cases, the Court has applied the United Nations' Basic Principles on the Use of Force and Firearms by Law Enforcement Officials and the Code of Conduct for Law Enforcement Officials.[207] In its analysis, the Court increasingly examines three stages of the specific situation: before, during, and after the use of force.[208]

According to the Court, the principle of legality requires States to limit by law the situations where individuals may be justifiably deprived of life. States must have "an appropriate legal framework" that restricts "the use of lethal weapons that can cause injury or death to the greatest extent possible."[209] This legal framework must limit the legitimate purposes for the deadly use of force to

> self-defence or defence of others against the imminent threat of death or serious injury, to prevent the perpetration of a particularly serious crime involving grave threat to life, to arrest a person presenting such a danger and resisting their authority, or to prevent his or her escape, and only when less extreme means are insufficient to achieve these objectives. In any event, intentional lethal use of firearms may only be made when strictly unavoidable in order to protect life.[210]

---

characterized by the disproportionate use of the armed forces in the poorer residential districts." Caracazo v. Venezuela, Merits, Judgment, Inter-Am. Ct. H.R. (ser. C) No. 58, paras. 2(m), 37 (Nov. 11, 1999).

[204] *Id.*

[205] *Id.* paras. 42–71.

[206] *Id.* paras. 82–90; HARRIS, O'BOYLE & WARBRICK, *supra* note 21, at 226–33; Report of the Special Rapporteur on extrajudicial, summary or arbitrary executions, Christof Heyns, UN A/HRC/26/36, paras. 55–74 (2014).

[207] *E.g.*, Landaeta Meijias Brothers et al. v. Venezuela, Preliminary Objections, Merits, Reparations, and Costs, Judgment, Inter-Am. Ct. H.R. (ser. C) No. 281, para. 124 (Aug. 27, 2014); Nadege Dorzema et al. v. Dominican Republic, Merits, Reparations, and Costs, Judgment, Inter-Am. Ct. H.R. (ser. C) No. 251, para. 78 (Oct. 24, 2012).

[208] Landaeta Meijias Brothers et al. v. Venezuela, Preliminary Objections, Merits, Reparations, and Costs, Judgment, Inter-Am. Ct. H.R. (ser. C) No. 281, para. 124 (Aug. 27, 2014).

[209] *Id.* para. 126.

[210] *Id.* para. 131 (citing United Nations' Basic Principles on the Use of Force and Firearms by Law Enforcement Officials).

Moreover, State laws must require proper training for State agents,[211] and mandate independent reviews of lethal use of force,[212] among other elements.

Landaeta Meijias Brothers et al. *v. Venezuela* concerned a violation of the principle of legality. The Court found breaches of Articles 4 and 2 because Venezuela lacked legislation "establishing parameters for the use of force by State agents" and "failed to prove" that it had provided adequate training to its law enforcement agents.[213] The Tribunal arrived at a similar conclusion in *Nadege Dorzema* et al. *v. Dominican Republic* with respect to the Dominican army.[214]

The Court requires "absolute necessity" for the use of lethal force.[215] It "must be forbidden as a general rule" and only employed in "extraordinary" cases as a measure of "last resort."[216] In *Nadege Dorzema* et al., Dominican soldiers fired indiscriminately at a truck that failed to stop at an immigration checkpoint, killing several people.[217] The Court found that there was no evidence "that the migrants were armed or had attempted some kind of violent act against the agents."[218] It held that "even when abstaining from the use of force would have allowed the individuals . . . to escape, the agents should not have used lethal force," because the migrants "did not represent a threat or a real or imminent danger to the agents or third parties."[219] As a result, the Court found that this did not constitute a situation of absolute necessity.

The last step to assess use of force is the proportionality test. Referring to the UN Basic Principles on the Use of Force, the Court has indicated that "the level of force used must be in keeping with the level of resistance offered."[220] In this way, State agents must

---

211 Nadege Dorzema et al. v. Dominican Republic, Merits, Reparations, and Costs, Judgment, Inter-Am. Ct. H.R. (ser. C) No. 251, para. 81 (Oct. 24, 2012).

212 Zambrano Vélez et al. v. Ecuador, Merits, Reparations, and Costs, Judgment, Inter-Am. Ct. H.R. (ser. C) No. 166, para. 86 (July 4, 2007).

213 Landaeta Meijias Brothers et al. v. Venezuela, Preliminary Objections, Merits, Reparations, and Costs, Judgment, Inter-Am. Ct. H.R. (ser. C) No. 281, paras. 125, 129 (Aug. 27, 2014).

214 Nadege Dorzema et al. v. Dominican Republic, Merits, Reparations, and Costs, Judgment, Inter-Am. Ct. H.R. (ser. C) No. 251, para. 82 (Oct. 24, 2012). In *Zambrano Velez*, the Court found that Ecuador's law establishing a state of emergency failed to comply with the strict requirements of the Convention's Article 27. Zambrano Vélez et al. v. Ecuador, Merits, Reparations, and Costs, Judgment, Inter-Am. Ct. H.R. (ser. C) No. 166, paras. 42-71 (July 4, 2007). According to the Tribunal, the law lacked "geographical, time and material limits" for the suspension of rights, and permitted military action under vague objectives "to arrest criminals, drug dealers and terrorists." *Id.* para. 96.

215 *E.g.*, Landaeta Meijias Brothers et al. v. Venezuela, Preliminary Objections, Merits, Reparations, and Costs, Judgment, Inter-Am. Ct. H.R. (ser. C) No. 281, para. 134 (Aug. 27, 2014); Nadege Dorzema et al. v. Dominican Republic, Merits, Reparations, and Costs, Judgment, Inter-Am. Ct. H.R. (ser. C) No. 251, para. 85 (Oct. 24, 2012).

216 Zambrano Vélez et al. v. Ecuador, Merits, Reparations, and Costs, Judgment, Inter-Am. Ct. H.R. (ser. C) No. 166, para. 84 (July 4, 2007).

217 Nadege Dorzema et al. v. Dominican Republic, Merits, Reparations, and Costs, Judgment, Inter-Am. Ct. H.R. (ser. C) No. 251, para. 83 (Oct. 24, 2012).

218 *Id.*

219 *Id.* para. 85.

220 *Id.*

use a "criteria of differentiated and progressive use of force" and "employ negotiating tactics" when possible.[221] For example, in *Landaeta Meijias Brothers*, plainclothes detectives pursued Igmar Landaeta.[222] When he had already fallen down, the police fired on him, resulting in his death. The Court found that, under the circumstances, the shooting was clearly disproportionate to arrest Landaeta.[223] In *Nadege Dorzema,* which involved the immigration checkpoint killings, the State should have instead adopted proportionate measures such as "traffic controls with barricades, speed bumps, tire puncturing devices, and/or cameras."[224]

c. The Burden of Proof

In cases of alleged use of excessive force, the Court shifts the burden of proof to the State, which must furnish "a satisfactory and convincing explanation of the events and . . . rebut allegations of its liability."[225] States have failed to meet this standard on several occasions, resulting in Article 4 violations.[226] The UN Human Rights Committee has comparably shifted the burden of proof in these circumstances and found Article 6 violations when States fail to submit sufficient evidence.[227] However, the European Court generally requires more of petitioners to demonstrate the State's responsibility for a killing.[228]

d. State Duties after the Use of Force

As for State obligations after the use of force, the Court requires law enforcement to facilitate any necessary medical aid and to notify, "at the earliest possible moment," family members or other close contacts of the victim.[229] State agents must report the situation for administrative and judicial review; an investigation must "determine the level and

---

[221] *Id.*

[222] Landaeta Meijias Brothers et al. v. Venezuela, Preliminary Objections, Merits, Reparations, and Costs, Judgment, Inter-Am. Ct. H.R. (ser. C) No. 281, paras. 141–142 (Aug. 27, 2014).

[223] *Id.*

[224] Nadege Dorzema et al. v. Dominican Republic, Merits, Reparations, and Costs, Judgment, Inter-Am. Ct. H.R. (ser. C) No. 251, para. 88 (Oct. 24, 2012).

[225] *E.g.*, Uzcátegui et al. v. Venezuela, Merits and Reparations, Judgment, Inter-Am. Ct. H.R. (ser. C) No. 249, para. 135 (Sept. 3, 2012); Cabrera García and Montiel Flores v. Mexico, Preliminary Objections, Merits, Reparations, and Costs, Judgment, Inter-Am. Ct. H.R. (ser. C) No. 220, para. 134 (Nov. 26, 2010).

[226] *E.g.*, Gutiérrez and Family v. Argentina, Merits, Reparations, and Costs, Judgment, Inter-Am. Ct. H.R. (ser. C) No. 271, para. 141 (Nov. 25, 2013); Uzcátegui et al. v. Venezuela, Merits and Reparations, Judgment, Inter-Am. Ct. H.R. (ser. C) No. 249, paras. 135 and 141 (Sept. 3, 2012).

[227] *See* NOWAK, *supra* note 3, at 129–31.

[228] *See* HARRIS, O'BOYLE & WARBRICK, *supra* note 21, at 222 (for State liability under Article 2 "for the killing of any individual, it must first be shown beyond a reasonable doubt that the individual was killed by one of its agents," except when the victim dies "in an area within the exclusive control" of official authorities).

[229] *E.g.*, Landaeta Meijias Brothers et al. v. Venezuela, Preliminary Objections, Merits, Reparations, and Costs, Judgment, Inter-Am. Ct. H.R. (ser. C) No. 281, para. 143 (Aug. 27, 2014); Nadege Dorzema et al. v. Dominican Republic, Merits, Reparations, and Costs, Judgment, Inter-Am. Ct. H.R. (ser. C) No. 251, para. 100 (Oct. 24, 2012). In *Landaeta Meijias*, the Court chastised State agents for leaving the already-dead victim in an emergency room and failing to identify themselves. *Id.* para. 146.

manner of participation of each of those who intervened, whether directly or indirectly, so that the corresponding responsibilities may be established."[230] For more on the State's duty to investigate, see Section III(C)(4), *supra*.

3. Use of Lethal Force in Armed Conflicts

The Court has heard several cases concerning the right to life in the internal armed conflicts of Colombia, Peru, Guatemala, and El Salvador. Some have involved appalling military operations bringing about "the massive and indiscriminate destruction of civilians."[231] Similar to other international tribunals, the Inter-American Court has affirmed that the right to life is non-derogable and must also be respected in armed conflicts.[232] As held by the International Court of Justice, "the test of what is an arbitrary deprivation of life . . . falls to be determined by the applicable *lex specialis*, namely, the law applicable in armed conflict, which is designed to regulate the conduct of hostilities."[233] In this way, deaths during armed conflicts that breach international humanitarian law constitute violations of the right to life. The Court has analyzed killings perpetrated during hostilities by State agents and paramilitary soldiers; the latter have often been linked to the State.[234]

From an early stage, the Inter-American Commission argued for the Court to assess deaths during internal armed conflicts in light of international humanitarian law.[235] Yet the Tribunal showed reluctance to do so in *Las Palmeras v. Colombia*, a decision from 2000.[236] Only a few months later, however, the *Bámaca Velázquez v. Guatemala*

---

[230] *E.g.*, Landaeta Meijias Brothers et al. v. Venezuela, Preliminary Objections, Merits, Reparations, and Costs, Judgment, Inter-Am. Ct. H.R. (ser. C) No. 281, para. 143 (Aug. 27, 2014); Montero Aranguren et al. (Det. Ctr. of Catia) v. Venezuela, Preliminary Objection, Merits, Reparations, and Costs, Judgment, Inter-Am. Ct. H.R. (ser. C) No. 150, paras. 79–83 (July 5, 2006).

[231] Massacres of El Mozote and Nearby Places v. El Salvador, Merits, Reparations, and Costs, Judgment, Inter-Am. Ct. H.R. (ser. C) No. 252, para. 208 (Oct. 25, 2012).

[232] Cruz Sánchez et al. v. Peru, Preliminary Objections, Merits, Reparations, Costs, Judgment, Inter-Am. Ct. H.R. (ser. C) No. 292, para. 272 (Apr. 17, 2015) (affirming the right to life in armed conflicts and citing to similar holdings from the International Court of Justice and the European Court of Human Rights).

[233] Legality of the Threat or Use of Nuclear Weapons, Advisory Opinion, I.C.J, para. 25 (1996).

[234] The Court has often found States responsible for killings committed by paramilitary groups. *See, e.g.*, Rochela Massacre v. Colombia, Merits, Reparations, and Costs, Judgment, Inter-Am. Ct. H.R. (ser. C) No. 163 (May 11, 2007); Pueblo Bello Massacre v. Colombia, Merits, Reparations, and Costs, Judgment, Inter-Am. Ct. H.R. (ser. C) No. 140 (Jan. 31, 2006); Mapiripán Massacre v. Colombia, Merits, Reparations, and Costs, Judgment, Inter-Am. Ct. H.R. (ser. C) No. 134 (Sept. 15, 2005).

[235] For an early example of how the Inter-American Commission decided "to apply directly rules of international humanitarian law or to inform its interpretations of relevant provisions of the American Convention by reference to these rules," *see, e.g.*, Abella v. Argentina, Case 11.137, Inter-Am. Comm'n H.R., OEA/Ser.L/V/II.98 doc. 6 rev. 13, para. 157 (1998).

[236] The Court admitted the State's preliminary objection, reasoning that the American Convention "has only given the Court competence to determine whether the acts or the norms of the States are compatible with

judgment held "the relevant provisions of the Geneva Conventions may be taken into consideration as elements for the interpretation of the American Convention."[237]

Currently, the Court turns to three major principles from international humanitarian law to assess killings during armed conflict.[238] The principle of distinction establishes that parties to a conflict must always distinguish between civilians and combatants.[239] The principle of proportionality prohibits "an attack which may be expected to cause incidental loss of civilian life, injury to civilians, damage to civilian objects, or a combination thereof, which would be excessive in relation to the concrete and direct military advantage anticipated."[240] Finally, the principle of precaution requires that parties to a conflict "take all feasible precautions to protect the civilian population and civilian objects under their control against the effects of attacks."[241]

In *Santo Domingo Massacre v. Colombia*, within "the context of confrontations with the FARC guerrilla," the Colombian air force dropped a cluster bomb over the village of Santo Domingo, causing 17 deaths and many injuries.[242] The Court observed, among other points, that the particular bomb used was known to be inaccurate, and that the poorly-planned operation took little account of the nearby civilian population. As a result, it found that the State violated the principle of precaution in attack.[243]

As for the principle of distinction, the Court noted that domestic judicial and administrative authorities had already ruled that the State "failed to comply" with the principle.[244] It thus did not find it necessary to analyze the issue further. Finally, the judgment

---

the Convention itself, and not with the 1949 Geneva Conventions." Las Palmeras v. Colombia, Preliminary Objections, Judgment, Inter-Am. Ct. H.R. (ser. C) No. 67, para. 33 (Feb. 4, 2000).

[237] Bámaca Velásquez v. Guatemala, Merits, Judgment, Inter-Am. Ct. H.R. (ser. C) No. 70, para. 208 (Nov. 25, 2000).

[238] *E.g.*, Cruz Sánchez et al. v. Peru, Preliminary Objections, Merits, Reparations, Costs, Judgment, Inter-Am. Ct. H.R. (ser. C) No. 292, para. 273 (Apr. 17, 2015); Afro-Descendant Communities Displaced from the Cacarica River Basin (Operation Genesis) v. Colombia, Preliminary Objections, Merits, Reparations, and Costs, Judgment, Inter-Am. Ct. H.R. (ser. C) No. 270, para. 222 (Nov. 20, 2013).

[239] Cruz Sánchez et al. v. Peru, Preliminary Objections, Merits, Reparations, Costs, Judgment, Inter-Am. Ct. H.R. (ser. C) No. 292, para. 276 (Apr. 17, 2015); International Committee of the Red Cross, Customary International Humanitarian Law Database, Rule 1: The Principle of Distinction between Civilians and Combatants, *available at* https://www.icrc.org/customary-ihl/eng/docs/v1_cha_chapter1_rule1 (last visited Nov. 21, 2016).

[240] Cruz Sánchez et al. v. Peru, Preliminary Objections, Merits, Reparations, Costs, Judgment, Inter-Am. Ct. H.R. (ser. C) No. 292, note 343 (Apr. 17, 2015); International Committee of the Red Cross, Customary International Humanitarian Law Database, Rule 14: Proportionality in Attack, *available at* https://www.icrc.org/customary-ihl/eng/docs/v1_cha_chapter4_rule14 (last visited Nov. 21, 2016).

[241] Cruz Sánchez et al. v. Peru, Preliminary Objections, Merits, Reparations, Costs, Judgment, Inter-Am. Ct. H.R. (ser. C) No. 292, note 344 (Apr. 17, 2015); International Committee of the Red Cross, Customary International Humanitarian Law Database, Rule 22. Principle of Precautions against the Effects of Attacks, *available at* https://www.icrc.org/customary-ihl/eng/docs/v1_cha_chapter6_rule22 (last visited Nov. 21, 2016).

[242] Santo Domingo Massacre v. Colombia, Preliminary Objections, Merits, and Reparations, Judgment, Inter-Am. Ct. H.R. (ser. C) No. 259, paras. 70, 213 (Nov. 30, 2012).

[243] *Id.* para. 229.

[244] *Id.* para. 213.

avoided an examination of the bombing's proportionality, because the Court considered it unfeasible to assess "the specific and direct military advantage expected if it had hit a military objective, which did not occur in the circumstances of the case."[245] In sum, the flagrant bombing violated Article 4, but the Court did not appear well positioned for a new role assessing military plans and objectives, technical weapon characteristics, and the notion of "excessive" civilian casualties.

In contrast, Colombia was not found responsible for violating Article 4 during other bombings known as Operation Genesis.[246] In *Afro-Descendant Communities Displaced from the Cacarica River Basin*, the Court accepted the State's assertions that the bombings did not "directly affect" these communities, as they took place "several kilometers" away.[247] It was not even "alleged or reported that the said bombings directly caused the death or injury" of community members.[248] For these reasons, the Court concluded that the principle of distinction was respected during this particular military operation.

In the more recent judgment *Cruz Sánchez* et al. *v. Peru*, the Court examined the notorious Peruvian hostage crisis, when a guerilla group detained hundreds at the Japanese embassy in 1996.[249] After four months, the Peruvian army conducted an operation that freed the remaining hostages—at the same time killing all 14 participating members of the *Movimiento para la Revolución Tupac Amaru* (MRTA).[250] In the judgment, the Court quickly agreed that it was necessary to use force to save the hostages' lives, given the dire circumstances.[251]

It then considered whether Peru's rescue plan had sought to minimize the loss of life and adopt all possible precautions.[252] The Tribunal was satisfied, noting that negotiations were first pursued, the Peruvian military ensured the hostages' safety, and, according to various statements, the plan "contemplated" the capture of the MRTA members.[253]

---

245 *Id.* para. 215.

246 Afro-Descendant Communities Displaced from the Cacarica River Basin (Operation Genesis) v. Colombia, Preliminary Objections, Merits, Reparations, and Costs, Judgment, Inter-Am. Ct. H.R. (ser. C) No. 270 (Nov. 20, 2013).

247 *Id.* paras. 237–238.

248 *Id.* paras. 238–239.

249 Cruz Sánchez et al. v. Peru, Preliminary Objections, Merits, Reparations, Costs, Judgment, Inter-Am. Ct. H.R. (ser. C) No. 292 (Apr. 17, 2015).

250 *Id.* para. 164.

251 *Id.* paras. 274–275. In situations of armed conflict, the Tribunal has cited international humanitarian law to demand the principles of military necessity and humanity. In *Zambrano Vélez*, the Court explained that military necessity "justifies only those measures of military violence which are not forbidden by international law and which are relevant and proportionate to ensure the prompt subjugation of the enemy with the least possible cost of human and economic resources." Zambrano Vélez et al. v. Ecuador, Merits, Reparations, and Costs, Judgment, Inter-Am. Ct. H.R. (ser. C) No. 166, para. 85 (July 4, 2007). Further, the principle of humanity "complements and inherently limits the principle of necessity by forbidding those measures of violence which are not necessary . . . to the achievement of a definitive military advantage." *Id.*

252 Cruz Sánchez et al. v. Peru, Preliminary Objections, Merits, Reparations, Costs, Judgment, Inter-Am. Ct. H.R. (ser. C) No. 292, para. 283 (Apr. 17, 2015).

253 *Id.* paras. 147–150, 286.

Notwithstanding the petitioners' objections, the Court decided that the elements of "necessity, proportionality, and precaution in the use of force" were no longer in question.[254]

The Tribunal determined that nearly all of the MRTA victims were combatants actively participating in hostilities. However, one MRTA member, Eduardo Nicolás Cruz Sánchez, had been taken into custody while alive; soon after, he died of a gunshot wound. The Court found that Cruz Sánchez was in a situation of hors de combat, and thus was entitled to humane treatment under Article 4, "interpreted in light of Common Article 3 of the four Geneva Conventions."[255] Common Article 3 holds, in part:

> Persons taking no active part in the hostilities, including members of armed forces who have laid down their arms and those placed *hors de combat* by sickness, wounds, detention, or any other cause, shall in all circumstances be treated humanely. . . .[256]

Because petitioners alleged that Cruz Sánchez illegally died in the State's custody, Peru had the burden to provide a "satisfactory and convincing explanation" of how he was killed.[257] The State did not meet this standard, and the Court concluded that—based on the available evidence—Cruz Sánchez was likely executed by soldiers, in violation of Article 4.[258]

4. Arbitrary Deprivation of Life of Imprisoned Individuals

a. Introduction

The Court has heard several cases where the right to life of detained persons was jeopardized. One group of cases relates to distressing detention conditions and other structural

---

[254] *Id.* para. 287.

[255] *Id.* para. 316. "Common Article 3" refers to the Article that is common to all four Geneva Conventions. *See* Geneva Convention for the Amelioration of the Condition of the Wounded and Sick in Armed Forces in the Field art. 3, Aug. 12, 1949, 6 U.S.T. 3114, 75 U.N.T.S. 31; Geneva Convention for the Amelioration of the Condition of Wounded, Sick and Shipwrecked Members of Armed Forces at Sea art. 3, Aug. 12, 1949, 6 U.S.T. 3217, 75 U.N.T.S. 85; Geneva Convention Relative to the Protection of Civilian Persons in Time of War art. 3, Aug. 12, 1949, 6 U.S.T. 3516, 75 U.N.T.S. 287; Geneva Convention Relative to the Treatment of Prisoners of War art. 3, Aug. 12, 1949, 6 U.S.T. 3316, 75 U.N.T.S. 135.

[256] *Id.*

[257] Cruz Sánchez et al. v. Peru, Preliminary Objections, Merits, Reparations, Costs, Judgment, Inter-Am. Ct. H.R. (ser. C) No. 292, para. 317 (Apr. 17, 2015).

[258] *Id.* paras. 318–319. In another violent case, where M-19 guerillas occupied the Palace of Justice in Bogotá, Colombia, the Court condemned aspects of the State's response. Rodriguez Vera et al. (Persons Disappeared from the Palace of Justice) v. Colombia, Preliminary Objections, Merits, Reparations, and Costs, Judgment, Inter-Am. Ct. H.R. (ser. C) No. 287 (Nov. 14, 2014). The Court found that "a *modus operandi* existed aimed at the enforced disappearance of persons suspected of having participated in the taking of the Palace of Justice or of collaborating with the M-19"; it also concluded that State authorities "significantly altered the crime scene and committed numerous irregularities in the removal of the corpses." *Id.* para. 303.

problems within prison systems.[259] Another set of cases concerns the extrajudicial executions of prisoners during State security operations.[260]

b. Detention Conditions and Healthcare

The Court has held that the right to life "cannot be restricted under any circumstances during internment, and any such restriction is prohibited by international law."[261] It has stressed that the State "has a special role to play as guarantor of the rights of those deprived of their freedom, as the prison authorities exercise heavy control or command over the persons in their custody."[262] The right to life also requires "the right to live in prison conditions that are in keeping with [the prisoners'] dignity as human beings."[263]

In *Juvenile Reeducation Institute v. Paraguay*, the Court first affirmed the right to a "dignified" life for all detainees.[264] It found that the State exposed "all the inmates at the Center to cruel, inhuman and degrading treatment and to unfit living conditions that were prejudicial to their right to life, their growth and development and their life plans."[265] Consequently, it held that Paraguay violated Article 4 with respect to over 3,000 detainees—all inmates at the facility over a five-year period.

The Court also found a violation of Article 4 with respect to detainees who died in fires and violent episodes occurring at the prison. The fires were attributed to "gross negligence on the State's part," as it "did not take sufficient preventive measures to respond to the possibility of a fire at the Center."[266] The Court stressed that the State has an obligation "to design and apply" policies that prevent crises in prison.[267] Paraguay also had the "duty to create the conditions necessary to avoid, to the maximum extent possible, fighting among inmates."[268]

---

[259] *E.g.*, Pacheco Teruel et al. v. Honduras, Merits, Reparations, and Costs, Judgment, Inter-Am. Ct. H.R. (ser. C) No. 241 (Apr. 27, 2012); "Juvenile Reeducation Institute" v. Paraguay, Preliminary Objections, Merits, Reparations, and Costs, Judgment, Inter-Am. Ct. H.R. (ser. C) No. 112 (Sept. 2, 2004).

[260] *E.g.*, Miguel Castro Castro Prison v. Peru, Merits, Reparations, and Costs, Judgment, Inter-Am. Ct. H.R. (ser. C) No. 160 (Nov. 25, 2006); Montero Aranguren et al. (Det. Ctr. of Catia) v. Venezuela, Preliminary Objection, Merits, Reparations, and Costs, Judgment, Inter-Am. Ct. H.R. (ser. C) No. 150 (July 5, 2006).

[261] "Juvenile Reeducation Institute" v. Paraguay, Preliminary Objections, Merits, Reparations, and Costs, Judgment, Inter-Am. Ct. H.R. (ser. C) No. 112, para. 155 (Sept. 2, 2004).

[262] *Id.* para. 152. The Court has not yet found the deprivation of the right to life in immigration detention centers. In *Gangaram Panday v. Suriname*, which involved a victim detained in a place for deportees, the Court decided that there was insufficient evidence to link the State to his "suicide." Gangaram Panday v. Suriname, Merits, Reparations, and Costs, Judgment, Inter-Am. Ct. H.R. (ser. C) No. 16, para. 61 (Jan. 21, 1994).

[263] "Juvenile Reeducation Institute" v. Paraguay, Preliminary Objections, Merits, Reparations, and Costs, Judgment, Inter-Am. Ct. H.R. (ser. C) No. 112, para. 170 (Sept. 2, 2004).

[264] *Id.* paras. 151 and 155.

[265] *Id.* para. 176.

[266] *Id.* paras. 178–179.

[267] *Id.*

[268] *Id.* para. 184.

In *Pacheco Teruel* et al *v. Honduras*, the Court observed that the Honduran prison system "suffered from structural weaknesses," leading to "overcrowding, unsanitary conditions [and] conflicts."[269] In the case at hand, prison officials failed to respond to a major fire at San Pedro Sula Prison that left 107 inmates dead. Honduras acknowledged responsibility for the deaths and reached a settlement, by which the State committed, among other measures, to "improve the physical conditions" of nine national prisons, "taking into account the relevant international standards."[270]

Further, the Court has developed the State duty to provide detainees with "regular" medical monitoring, as well as "appropriate medical care and treatment when required."[271] In this way, there is a close relationship between the rights to life and personal integrity, following the European Court's case law.[272] In *Vera Vera* et al. *v. Ecuador,* police officers failed to obtain "appropriate and timely medical treatment" for a wounded victim, who was under their custody.[273] The Court held that Ecuador's "medical negligence" constituted inhuman and degrading treatment under Article 5(2), and also violated Vera Vera's right to life.[274]

c. Security Operations in Prisons

The second group of cases involves the extrajudicial executions of prisoners during security operations. In *Castro Castro Prison v. Peru*, police and soldiers conducted a violent operation within the prison, because they suspected that various prisoners were organizing a riot.[275] State agents killed 41 inmates who had been accused or convicted of terrorism-related crimes.[276] The Court found that "there was no riot of the inmates, or any other cause that could determine the legitimate use of force by state agents."[277] As a result, and after a partial acceptance of liability by Peru, the State was found to have violated Article 4, among other rights.[278]

---

[269] Pacheco Teruel et al. v. Honduras, Merits, Reparations, and Costs, Judgment, Inter-Am. Ct. H.R. (ser. C) No. 241, paras. 25, 29–35 (Apr. 27, 2012).

[270] *Id.* para. 95.

[271] *E.g.*, Vera Vera et al. v. Ecuador, Preliminary Objections, Merits, Reparations, and Costs, Judgment, Inter-Am. Ct. H.R. (ser. C) No. 226, para. 43 (May 19, 2011); Montero Aranguren et al. (Det. Ctr. of Catia) v. Venezuela, Preliminary Objection, Merits, Reparations, and Costs, Judgment, Inter-Am. Ct. H.R. (ser. C) No. 150, para. 102 (July 5, 2006).

[272] For more on how detention conditions and lack of access to medical care could constitute inhuman and degrading treatment, *see* this volume's Chapter 4: Humane Treatment.

[273] Vera Vera et al. v. Ecuador, Preliminary Objections, Merits, Reparations, and Costs, Judgment, Inter-Am. Ct. H.R. (ser. C) No. 226, para. 78 (May 19, 2011).

[274] *Id.* paras. 78–79.

[275] Miguel Castro Castro Prison v. Peru, Merits, Reparations, and Costs, Judgment, Inter-Am. Ct. H.R. (ser. C) No. 160, para. 213 (Nov. 25, 2006).

[276] *Id.* para. 197(10).

[277] *Id.* para. 234.

[278] *Id.* paras. 135–137, 258.

In *Neira Alegría* et al. *v. Peru*, the Peruvian military demolished a section of the San Juan Bautista Prison in response to a riot of "highly dangerous" and armed prisoners.[279] The operation killed numerous inmates, resulting in a disproportionate use of force against individuals who "would have eventually surrendered," according to the Court.[280] In addition, the State was "seriously negligent" for not adequately rescuing survivors or identifying the corpses.[281]

Montero Aranguren et al *v. Venezuela* examined the Catia prison, which was plagued by a very violent "subculture" of gangs and drug trafficking.[282] The Court stressed that, in such situations, the State has a "duty to take preventive measures" to protect detainees and prison officials.[283] To the contrary, the judgment found that Venezuela's passive role had allowed for the "creation" of the prison's brutal conditions.[284] Furthermore, State security forces eventually acted with "extreme force with lethal consequences" for numerous prisoners, as accepted by Venezuela during litigation, "which clearly violated Article 4" of the Convention.[285] The Court ordered the State to regulate the use of lethal force and firearms by security officers, pursuant to international standards such as the UN Basic Principles on the Use of Force and Firearms by Law Enforcement Officials.[286]

5. Forced Disappearances of Persons

a. Introduction and Definition

Forced disappearances plagued the Americas during the dark era of military dictatorships; even now, under several democratic governments, the crime continues to afflict the region.[287] In response, the Inter-American Court has been a pioneer in the conceptual development of this crime. Its first contentious judgment on the merits, *Velásquez Rodríguez v. Honduras* of 1988, found a violation of a student's right to life for his disappearance—occurring only days after Honduras had accepted the Court's jurisdiction.[288] At the time, there was scarce international law on forced

[279] Neira Alegría et al. v. Peru, Merits, Judgment, Inter-Am. Ct. H.R. (ser. C) No. 20, para. 74 (Jan. 19, 1995).

[280] *Id.*

[281] *Id.* paras. 71, 74.

[282] Montero Aranguren et al. (Det. Ctr. of Catia) v. Venezuela, Preliminary Objection, Merits, Reparations, and Costs, Judgment, Inter-Am. Ct. H.R. (ser. C) No. 150, para. 70 (July 5, 2006).

[283] *Id.*

[284] *Id.*

[285] *Id.* paras. 73–74.

[286] *Id.* para. 75.

[287] The Court has decided disappearance cases occurring during democratic governments. *E.g.*, Torres Millacura et al. v. Argentina, Merits, Reparations, and Costs, Judgment, Inter-Am. Ct. H.R. (ser. C) No. 229 (Aug. 26, 2011). Mexico, in particular, has been overwhelmed by forced disappearances. To investigate the notorious case of the 43 disappeared students of Ayotzinapa, the Interdisciplinary Group of Independent Experts was created in 2014 by the Inter-American Commission, the Mexican State, and representatives of the disappeared students. *See* "Interdisciplinary Group of Independent Experts," *available at* http://www.oas.org/en/iachr/activities/giei.asp (last visited Nov. 21, 2016).

[288] Velásquez Rodríguez v. Honduras, Merits, Judgment, Inter-Am. Ct. H.R. (ser. C) No. 4, para. 194 (July 29, 1988).

disappearances;[289] subsequently, in 1992, the United Nations approved its Declaration on the Protection of All Persons from Enforced Disappearance, and the Inter-American Convention on Forced Disappearance of Persons was adopted two years later.[290]

Through its numerous judgments concerning forced disappearances, the Court has incorporated aspects of these international legal definitions. Currently, the following elements constitute forced disappearance for the Court:

> a) the deprivation of liberty; b) the direct intervention of State agents or their acquiescence; and c) the refusal to acknowledge the detention and to reveal the fate or the whereabouts of the person concerned.[291]

The crime of forced disappearance breaches jus cogens norms,[292] and continues "until the whereabouts of the disappeared person are known and the facts are elucidated."[293] Inter-American jurisprudence recognizes the crime as a violation of the rights to personal integrity, personal liberty, and life. More recently, the Court has affirmed that forced disappearance also breaches the right to juridical personality, Article 3 of the Convention, after several judgments rejected arguments for this violation.[294] Article 3 is implicated

---

[289] Although in 1980, the U.N. Commission on Human Rights established the Working Group on Enforced or Involuntary Disappearances. *See* Resolution 20 (XXXVI) of 29 February 1980, *available at* http://www.ohchr.org/Documents/Issues/Disappearances/E-CN.4-RES-1980-20_XXXVI.pdf.

[290] Declaration on the Protection of All Persons from Enforced Disappearance, GA res. 47/133, 47 UN GAOR Supp. (No. 49) at 207, UN Doc. A/47/49 (1992); Inter-American Convention on Forced Disappearance of Persons, OAS Treaty Series No. 68, 33 ILM 1429 (1994).

[291] *E.g.*, Rodriguez Vera et al. (Persons Disappeared from the Palace of Justice) v. Colombia, Preliminary Objections, Merits, Reparations, and Costs, Judgment, Inter-Am. Ct. H.R. (ser. C) No. 287, para. 226 (Nov. 14, 2014); Gómez Palomino v. Peru, Merits, Reparations, and Costs, Judgment, Inter-Am. Ct. H.R. (ser. C) No. 136, para. 97 (Nov. 22, 2005). For its part, the International Convention for the Protection of All Persons from Enforced Disappearance defines this crime as "the arrest, detention, abduction or any other form of deprivation of liberty" by State agents or collaborators, "followed by a refusal to acknowledge the deprivation of liberty or by concealment of the fate or whereabouts of the disappeared person, which place such a person outside the protection of the law." International Convention for the Protection of All Persons from Enforced Disappearance, art. 2, A/RES/61/177, 14 IHRR 582 (2006).

[292] *E.g.*, Tiu Tojín v. Guatemala, Merits, Reparations, and Costs, Judgment, Inter-Am. Ct. H.R. (ser. C) No. 190, para. 91 (Nov. 26, 2008); Goiburú et al. v. Paraguay, Merits, Reparations, and Costs, Judgment, Inter-Am. Ct. H.R. (ser. C) No. 153, para. 84 (Sept. 22, 2006).

[293] *E.g.*, Radilla Pacheco v. Mexico, Preliminary Objections, Merits, Reparations, and Costs, Judgment, Inter-Am. Ct. H.R. (ser. C) No. 209, para. 140 (Nov. 23, 2009); Velásquez Rodríguez v. Honduras, Judgment, 1987 Inter-Am. Ct. H.R. (ser. C) No. 1, para. 153 (June 26, 1987). The forced disappearance continues until the victim's remains have been identified "with certainty." *E.g.*, Gomes Lund et al. ("Guerrilha do Araguaia") v. Brazil, Preliminary Objections, Merits, Reparations, and Costs, Judgment, Inter-Am. Ct. H.R. (ser. C) No. 219, para. 121 (Nov. 24, 2010); Ibsen Cardenas and Ibsen Peña v. Bolivia, Merits, Reparations, and Costs, Judgment, Inter-Am. Ct. H.R. (ser. C) No. 217, para. 82 (Sept. 1, 2010).

[294] *E.g.*, Gelman v. Uruguay, Merits and Reparations, Judgment, Inter-Am. Ct. H.R. (ser. C) No. 221, para. 77 (Feb. 24, 2011); Anzualdo Castro v. Peru, Preliminary Objections, Merits, Reparations, and Costs, Judgment,

because the crime "not only seeks to extract the person from the legal system, but also to deny his or her existence . . . leaving the person in a state of legal limbo."[295]

Since *Velásquez Rodríguez*, the Court has developed key presumptions when detainees are subjected to "repressive official bodies, State agents, or private persons who act under [State] acquiescence or tolerance, that with impunity carry out acts of torture and murder."[296] When time has passed without determining the detainee's fate, the Court has allowed for a "reasonable presumption of death."[297] Also, rampant disappearances and impunity violate, among other rights, the State's "obligation to prevent violations to the right to personal integrity and right to life," even when the abuses cannot be demonstrated in the particular case.[298]

b. The Right to Life and Ratione Temporis *Jurisdiction*

Defendant States began to object vigorously to the Court's temporal jurisdiction over forced disappearances. In 1996, with *Blake v. Guatemala*, the Court entered into an extended period of "fragmentation," in which it would rarely find a breach of Article 4 when temporal jurisdiction was at issue.[299] Judge Antonio Cançado Trindade, among others, criticized the Court for excluding right-to-life violations in various judgments, rather than treating forced disappearances as an inextricable bundle of violations—to Article 4 and other rights—that continued over time.[300] In *Blake*, Nicholas Blake, a U.S. journalist, had disappeared during Guatemala's internal conflict. The Court found that, according to his death certificate, Blake's execution was "completed" in 1985.[301] Because Guatemala did not accept the Court's jurisdiction until 1987, the Tribunal

---

Inter-Am. Ct. H.R. (ser. C) No. 202, para. 63 (Sept. 22, 2009). In *Gelman*, the Court also recognized that "the abduction and suppression of the identity [of children] can be qualified as a particular form of enforced disappearance of persons." *Id.* para. 132.

[295] *E.g.*, Gomes Lund et al. ("Guerrilha do Araguaia") v. Brazil, Preliminary Objections, Merits, Reparations, and Costs, Judgment, Inter-Am. Ct. H.R. (ser. C) No. 219, para. 122 (Nov. 24, 2010); Anzualdo Castro v. Peru, Preliminary Objections, Merits, Reparations, and Costs, Judgment, Inter-Am. Ct. H.R. (ser. C) No. 202, para. 90 (Sept. 22, 2009).

[296] *E.g.*, Gomes Lund et al. ("Guerrilha do Araguaia") v. Brazil, Preliminary Objections, Merits, Reparations, and Costs, Judgment, Inter-Am. Ct. H.R. (ser. C) No. 219, para. 122 (Nov. 24, 2010) (citing to Velásquez Rodríguez v. Honduras, Merits, Judgment, Inter-Am. Ct. H.R. (ser. C) No. 4 (July 29, 1988)).

[297] Velásquez Rodríguez v. Honduras, Merits, Judgment, Inter-Am. Ct. H.R. (ser. C) No. 4, para. 188 (July 29, 1988). In more recent disappearance cases against Russia, the European Court of Human Rights has also been willing to presume death in a similar manner. *See* HARRIS, O'BOYLE & WARBRICK, *supra* note 21, at 224.

[298] *E.g.*, Gomes Lund et al. ("Guerrilha do Araguaia") v. Brazil, Preliminary Objections, Merits, Reparations, and Costs, Judgment, Inter-Am. Ct. H.R. (ser. C) No. 219, para. 122; Velásquez Rodríguez v. Honduras, Merits, Judgment, Inter-Am. Ct. H.R. (ser. C) No. 4, para. 175 (July 29, 1988).

[299] Blake v. Guatemala, Reparations and Costs, Judgment, Inter-Am. Ct. H.R. (ser. C) No. 48, para. 36 (Jan. 22, 1999) (separate opinion of Judge Antonio Cançado Trindade).

[300] *Id. See also* U.N. Working Group on Enforced or Involuntary Disappearances, General Comment on Enforced Disappearance as a Continuous Crime, A/HRC/16/48 (2010) (criticizing this approach in general).

[301] Blake v. Guatemala, Preliminary Objections, Judgment, Inter-Am. Ct. H.R. (ser. C) No. 27, para. 33 (July 2, 1996).

decided that it lacked jurisdiction over the death, despite the fact that Blake's body was not found until 1992.[302]

Serrano Cruz Sisters v. El Salvador examined a different kind of temporal limitation on forced disappearances. Through an official declaration made when accepting the Court's competence, El Salvador attempted to exclude continuing violations by limiting the Tribunal's jurisdiction to "subsequent juridical facts and acts or juridical facts and acts which commence subsequent to the date" of acceptance.[303] Over Judge Cançado Trindade's dissent, the Court approved of the State's declaration as a valid limitation "for a specified period" under Article 62(2) of the Convention.[304] The violation in question was the forced disappearance of two girls during El Salvador's civil conflict.

One may rightly question whether the Convention's object and purpose would permit States, by declaration, to exclude the very serious and continuing crime of forced disappearance from the Tribunal's *ratione temporis* jurisdiction. The Court itself has qualified forced disappearances as crimes against humanity,[305] and has famously held:

> all amnesty provisions, provisions on prescription and the establishment of measures designed to eliminate responsibility are inadmissible, because they are intended to prevent the investigation and punishment of those responsible for serious human rights violations such as torture, extra-legal, summary or arbitrary execution and forced disappearance, all of them prohibited because they violate non-derogable rights recognized by international human rights law.[306]

This case law, similar contemporary legal advances, and the Convention's spirit all appear at odds with the *Serrano Cruz* judgment.[307]

---

[302] *Id.*

[303] Serrano Cruz Sisters v. El Salvador, Preliminary Objections, Judgment, Inter-Am. Ct. H.R. (ser. C) No. 118, para. 58 (Nov. 23, 2004).

[304] *Id.* para. 73.

[305] *E.g.*, Goiburú et al. v. Paraguay, Merits, Reparations, and Costs, Judgment, Inter-Am. Ct. H.R. (ser. C) No. 153, para. 82 (Sept. 22, 2006); 19 Merchants v. Colombia, Merits, Reparations, and Costs, Judgment, Inter-Am. Ct. H.R. (ser. C) No. 109, para. 142 (July 5, 2004).

[306] *E.g.*, Almonacid Arellano et al. v. Chile, Preliminary Objections, Merits, Reparations, and Costs, Judgment, Inter-Am. Ct. H.R. (ser. C) No. 154, para. 112 (Sept. 26, 2006); Barrios Altos v. Peru, Merits, Judgment, Inter-Am. Ct. H.R. (ser. C) No. 75, para. 41 (Mar. 14, 2001).

[307] The Court should have followed *Hilaire v. Trinidad and Tobago*, a judgment that rejected the State's attempted restriction of the Tribunal's jurisdiction, because it was "incompatible with the object and purpose of the Convention." Hilaire v. Trinidad & Tobago, Preliminary Objections, Judgment, Inter-Am. Ct. H.R. (ser. C) No. 80, para. 98 (Sept. 1, 2001) (assessing a different kind of State restriction). Since 2009, El Salvador fortunately adopted "a new state vision regarding international human rights obligations" and expressly recognized that "in the context of the armed conflict . . . between 1980 and 1991, there was a systematic pattern of forced disappearances of boys, girls, and youth, especially in the zones most affected by armed confrontations and military operations." Rochac Hernandez et al. v. El Salvador, Merits, Reparations, and Costs, Judgment, Inter-Am. Ct. H.R. (ser. C) No. 285, para. 18 (Oct. 14, 2014) (translation by authors).

In *Heliodoro Portugal v. Panama*, Heliodoro Portugal, a student leader and member of the *Movimiento de Unidad Revolucionaria*, disappeared in 1970, two decades before Panama accepted the Court's jurisdiction in 1990.[308] When Portugal's remains were discovered in 2000, a forensic examination concluded that he had died at least 20 years before—that is, nearly a decade before the Court exercised jurisdiction over Panama. As a result, the Court admitted the State's *ratione temporis* objection regarding the alleged violations to his rights to life and personal integrity. In contrast, the Tribunal decided, with little explanation, that Portugal's deprivation of liberty was a continuous element of his disappearance that fell within its temporal jurisdiction.[309]

In the period of fragmentation initiated by *Blake*, the Court—when faced with temporal limitations—found Article 4 violations only when the State admitted responsibility.[310] In *Radilla Pacheco v. México*, decided a year after *Heliodoro Portugal*, the Tribunal finally appeared to break with the *Blake* line of cases.[311] Mexico challenged the Court's temporal jurisdiction over the 1974 disappearance of Rosendo Radilla Pacheco. Because more than 24 years had passed before Mexico accepted the Court's competence in 1998, the State invoked the Tribunal's "reasonable presumption of death" doctrine to argue that Radilla Pacheco's death should fall outside its jurisdiction.[312]

The Court justifiably rejected this argument, recognizing that the presumption was created to level the playing field in cases where States have "alleged control over the detained person" and access to relevant information.[313] Permitting the State to shift the burden of proof back to the victim's family in these circumstances "invalidates the sense of [the presumption's] existence."[314] The Court has upheld this approach in *Gonzalez Medina and Family v. Dominican Republic.*[315] *Radilla Pacheco* eventually found that the forced disappearance of Radilla Pacheco violated his rights to life, personal liberty, humane treatment, and juridical personality.[316]

---

308 Heliodoro Portugal v. Panama, Preliminary Objections, Merits, Reparations, and Costs, Judgment, Inter-Am. Ct. H.R. (ser. C) No. 186, para. 87 (Aug. 12, 2008).

309 *Id.* para. 117.

310 *E.g.*, Ticona Estrada et al. v. Bolivia, Merits, Reparations, and Costs, Judgment, Inter-Am. Ct. H.R. (ser. C) No. 191, paras. 14, 188 (Nov. 27, 2008); Trujillo Oroza v. Bolivia, Merits, Judgment, Inter-Am. Ct. H.R. (ser. C) No. 64, para. 109 (Jan. 26, 2000).

311 Radilla Pacheco v. Mexico, Preliminary Objections, Merits, Reparations, and Costs, Judgment, Inter-Am. Ct. H.R. (ser. C) No. 209 (Nov. 23, 2009).

312 *Id.* para. 44.

313 *Id.* para. 47.

314 *Id.* para. 48.

315 Gonzalez Medina and Family v. Dominican Republic, Preliminary Objections, Merits, Reparations, and Costs, Judgment, Inter-Am. Ct. H.R. (ser. C) No. 240, para. 51 (Feb. 27, 2012).

316 Radilla Pacheco v. Mexico, Preliminary Objections, Merits, Reparations, and Costs, Judgment, Inter-Am. Ct. H.R. (ser. C) No. 209, para. 159 (Nov. 23, 2009).

In this way, it is hoped that the Court now considers the unique crime of forced disappearance as a whole, a fully "consolidated act."[317] As held by the UN Working Group on Enforced or Involuntary Disappearances in 2010:

> when a State is recognized as responsible for having committed an enforced disappearance that began before the entry into force of the relevant legal instrument and which continued after its entry into force, the State should be held responsible for all violations that result from the enforced disappearance, and not only for violations that occurred after the entry into force of the instrument.[318]

This means that the Court should no longer "fragment" the crime into its component violations; it cannot allow objections regarding temporal jurisdiction to prevent a breach of the right to life.

Finally, as mentioned above, both the Court and other international authorities have recognized forced disappearances, as well as extrajudicial executions, to constitute crimes against humanity when perpetrated in a widespread or systematic manner. According to well-established international criminal law and the Court's own jurisprudence, such serious crimes "shall not be subject to any statute of limitations" or benefit from other "measures designed to eliminate responsibility."[319] Thus, both the Court—through its interpretations of the Convention—and States Parties should make every effort to end impunity for these grave abuses.

C. THE CONCEPT OF *VIDA DIGNA*

Since 1999, the Court has developed the concept of *vida digna*, often translated as "the right to a dignified life" or "the right to a dignified existence."[320] This right, primarily

---

[317] U.N. Working Group on Enforced or Involuntary Disappearances, General Comment on Enforced Disappearance as a Continuous Crime, A/HRC/16/48, para. 2 (2010).

[318] *Id.* para. 4.

[319] Barrios Altos v. Peru, Merits, Judgment, Inter-Am. Ct. H.R. (ser. C) No. 75, para. 41 (Mar. 14, 2001); Rome Statute of the International Criminal Court, art. 29, July 17, 1998, 2187 U.N.T.S. 3. *See also* Updated Set of Principles for the Protection and Promotion of Human Rights through Action to Combat Impunity, UN Commission on Human Rights, E/CN.4/2005/102/Add.1 (2005) ("States should adopt and enforce safeguards against any abuse of rules such as those pertaining to prescription, amnesty, right to asylum, refusal to extradite, non bis in idem, due obedience, official immunities, repentance, the jurisdiction of military courts and the irremovability of judges that fosters or contributes to impunity.").

[320] *See generally* Steven R. Keener & Javier Vasquez, *A Life Worth Living: Enforcement of the Right to Health through the Right to Life in the Inter-American Court of Human Rights*, 40 COLUM. HUM. RTS. L. REV. 595 (2009); Jo M. Pasqualucci, *The Right to a Dignified Life* (Vida Digna): *The Integration of Economic and Social Rights with Civil and Political Rights in the Inter-American Human Rights System*, 31 HASTINGS INT'L & COMP. L. REV. 1 (2008). The principle of human dignity is found in many national constitutions in the Western Hemisphere. *See* Christopher McCrudden, *Human Dignity and Judicial Interpretation of Human Rights*, 19 EUR. J. INT'L L. 655, 664 (2008).

grounded in the Convention's Article 4, first appeared in the seminal judgment *Villagrán Morales* et al. *v. Guatemala*.[321] *Villagrán Morales* involved the murder of five "street children" at the hands of the Guatemalan national police. The Court asserted that States should seek to provide "at-risk children" with the "minimum conditions for a dignified life," promoting the "full and harmonious development of their personality."[322] This includes securing full access to education and "special assistance for children . . . who are abandoned or exploited."[323]

Five years later, *Juvenile Reeducation Institute v. Paraguay* held that States have the duty to ensure that incarcerated persons—both adults and children—can still enjoy a *vida digna*.[324] Detention conditions must allow for "opportunities for exercise or recreation," education, and "prompt and proper medical, dental and psychological care."[325] In this way, the Court primarily finds violations to *vida digna* when the petitioners belong to marginalized sectors, such as vulnerable children and detainees.

Judgments concerning indigenous groups have also emphasized *vida digna*. In *Yakye Axa v. Paraguay*, an indigenous community was denied entrance to its traditional territories for farming, hunting, and fishing.[326] Conditions in the community's temporary settlement were miserable. The Court condemned the situation, and further explained the content of *vida digna*:

> Special detriment to the right to health, and closely tied to this, detriment to the right to food and access to clean water, have a major impact on the right to a decent existence and basic conditions to exercise other human rights, such as the right to education or the right to cultural identity.[327]

---

[321] Villagrán Morales v. Guatemala, Merits, Judgment, Inter-Am. Ct. H.R. (ser. C) No. 63 (Nov. 19, 1999).

[322] *Id.* para. 191.

[323] *Id.* para. 196.

[324] "Juvenile Reeducation Institute" v. Paraguay, Preliminary Objections, Merits, Reparations and Costs, Judgment, Inter-Am. Ct. H.R. (ser. C) No. 112, para. 176 (Sept. 2, 2004).

[325] *Id.* paras. 164–166. Because the conditions were seriously deficient in *Juvenile Reeducation Institute*, the Court found Paraguay in breach of both Articles 4 and 5 (Right to Humane Treatment) with respect to all inmates—over 3,000 children and young adults. Although many of the detained were adolescents, the "decent living conditions" described are required for all incarcerated individuals. *Id.* para. 164. Similarly, the Human Rights Committee has employed the ICCPR's right to life provision to demand proper medical treatment and sanitary conditions for detainees. Lantsova v. Russian Fed'n, U.N. Human Rights Committee, Commc'n No. 763/1997, U.N. Doc. CCPR/C/74/D/763/1997 (Mar. 26, 2002). *See also* Martin Scheinin, *Human Rights Committee: Not Only a Committee on Civil and Political Rights, in* Social Rights Jurisprudence: Emerging Trends in International and Comparative Law 540, 548 (2008).

[326] Yakye Axa Indigenous Cmty. v. Paraguay, Merits, Reparations and Costs, Judgment, Inter-Am. Ct. H.R. (ser. C) No. 125 (June 17, 2005).

[327] *Id.* para. 167.

Because Paraguay had not taken sufficient "measures regarding the conditions that affected their possibility of having a decent life," the Tribunal held that Article 4 was violated.[328] It made a similar pronouncement with respect to the community in *Xákmok Kásek v. Paraguay*.[329]

Accordingly, the Court has recognized the rights to health, food, clean water, culture, and others under the framework of *vida digna*, and asserted that they are protected by Article 4, and, occasionally, Article 5 (Right to Humane Treatment). Thus, it regards *vida digna* as a means to protect a range of rights—including those of a social, economic, and cultural nature—under the right to life. The Court counts as one of many international and national tribunals that have stressed the concept of human dignity; moreover, it is certainly not the first to link dignity to the right to life.[330]

The right's exact parameters are not yet defined. Although some may consider *vida digna* as standing only for minimal life conditions, in *Sawhoyamaxa Indigenous Community. v. Paraguay* Judge García Ramírez remarked that the right to life

> is more than just a right to subsist, but is rather a right to self-development, which requires appropriate conditions. In such a framework, a single right with a double dimension is set, like the two-faced god Janus: one side, with a first-generation legal concept of the right to life; the other side, with the concept of a requirement to provide conditions for a feasible and full existence.[331]

---

[328] *Id.* para. 176. The Human Rights Committee has comparably remarked that homelessness and health problems engage States' duties to ensure the right to life. U.N. Human Rights Comm., *Concluding Observations of the Human Rights Committee, Canada,* U.N. Doc CCPR/C/79/Add. 105 (Apr. 7 1999). For its part, the European Court of Human Rights found degrading treatment and a violation to Article 3 of the European Convention when it observed that dire living conditions had a "detrimental effect on the applicants' health and well-being." Moldovan v. Romania (No. 2), Eur. Ct. H.R., App. No. 41138/98 and No. 64320/01, para. 110 (July 12, 2005).

[329] Xákmok Kásek Indigenous Community v. Paraguay, Merits, Reparations, and Costs, Judgment, Inter-Am. Ct. H.R. (ser. C) No. 214, para. 217 (Aug. 24, 2010).

[330] *See generally* ERIN DALY, DIGNITY RIGHTS: COURTS, CONSTITUTIONS, AND THE WORTH OF THE HUMAN PERSON (2013) (discussing how courts around the world interpret dignity). According to the European Court of Human Rights, "the very essence of [the European Convention system], as the Court has often stated, is respect for human dignity." Case of Vinter v. United Kingdom, Eur. Ct. H.R., App. No. 66069/09 and No. 3896/10, para. 113 (July 9, 2013). The Indian Supreme Court interpreted the constitutional guarantee of life and personal liberty to contain "the right to live with human dignity and all that goes along with it." McCrudden, *supra* note 320, at 693 (citing Mullin v. The Administrator, Union Territory of Delhi).

[331] Sawhoyamaxa Indigenous Cmty. v. Paraguay, Merits, Reparations, and Costs, Judgment, Inter-Am. Ct. H.R. (ser. C) No. 146, para. 18 (Mar. 29, 2006) (concurring opinion of Judge García Ramírez).

It would appear, especially after examining several of the Court's judgments on indigenous communities,[332] that Article 4's content has expanded beyond basic protections toward requirements for a "full existence."[333]

A common objection to *vida digna* concerns norm dilution. If Article 4 in fact protects a range of associated rights, the Court will find more violations of the provision—possibly diluting the meaning of the right to life.[334] Yet some commentators have embraced the use of *vida digna* to hold States accountable for breaches of social, economic, and cultural rights.[335] For now at least, Article 4 violations confer additional gravitas upon Court judgments. This demands the attention of offending States and the media, likely supporting victims' efforts to obtain redress.[336]

---

[332] When considering "the special protection required" for indigenous peoples, the *Yakye Axa* judgment discussed "the duty of progressive development" of Article 26; the rights to health, "a healthy environment," food, education, and "the benefits of culture" from the Additional Protocol to the American Convention; and "pertinent provisions" from ILO Convention No. 169. Yakye Axa Indigenous Cmty. v. Paraguay, Merits, Reparations, and Costs, Judgment, Inter-Am. Ct. H.R. (ser. C) No. 125, para. 163 (June 17, 2005).

[333] For more on *vida digna* and the rights of indigenous communities, *see* this volume's Chapter 8: Property, Section IV(E)(2), "Protective Framework for Traditional Territories."

[334] *See* Tara J. Melish, *The Inter-American Court of Human Rights: Beyond Progressivity*, *in* SOCIAL RIGHTS JURISPRUDENCE: EMERGING TRENDS IN COMPARATIVE AND INTERNATIONAL LAW 372, 407 (Malcolm Langford ed. 2008) (discussing a "threat of serious norm dilution" in reference to Article 4 of the Convention).

[335] *See* James L. Cavallaro & Emily Schaffer, *Rejoinder: Justice before Justiciability: Inter-American Litigation and Social Change*, 39 N.Y.U. J. INT'L L. & POL. 345, 382 (2006) ("The key . . . is to find ways to use this right-to-life focus to advance other aspects of social justice campaigns—including ESC rights"); James L. Cavallaro & Emily J. Schaffer, *Less as More: Rethinking Supranational Litigation of Economic and Social Rights in the Americas*, 56 HASTINGS L.J. 217, 272 (2004).

[336] *See* Rejoinder: Justice before Justiciability, *supra* note 335 at 381–82.

4

Humane Treatment

Article 5: Right to Humane Treatment

1. *Every person has the right to have his physical, mental, and moral integrity respected.*
2. *No one shall be subjected to torture or to cruel, inhuman, or degrading punishment or treatment. All persons deprived of their liberty shall be treated with respect for the inherent dignity of the human person.*
3. *Punishment shall not be extended to any person other than the criminal.*
4. *Accused persons shall, save in exceptional circumstances, be segregated from convicted persons, and shall be subject to separate treatment appropriate to their status as unconvicted persons.*
5. *Minors while subject to criminal proceedings shall be separated from adults and brought before specialized tribunals, as speedily as possible, so that they may be treated in accordance with their status as minors.*
6. *Punishments consisting of deprivation of liberty shall have as an essential aim the reform and social readaptation of the prisoners.*

Chapter 4 Contents

I. Introduction 103
II. Background 105

The American Convention on Human Rights. Thomas M. Antkowiak and Alejandra Gonza.

III. Scope of Protection 106
- A. A Broad Right with Uncertain Parameters 106
- B. Definitions of Torture and the Inter-American Convention to Prevent and Punish Torture 108
- C. The Inter-American Court's Three-Part Test for Torture 110
- D. Involvement of State Actors: A Fourth Requirement? 114
- E. Considerations of Evidence and Proof 116
- F. Cruel, Inhuman, or Degrading Punishment or Treatment 117
  1. Introduction 117
  2. Sexual Violence and Violence against Women 118
  3. State-Sanctioned Punishment 120
     - a. Corporal Punishment 120
     - b. The Death Penalty 120
     - c. Life Imprisonment: Children 121
  4. Detention Conditions and Practices 122
  5. Forced Disappearance 125
  6. Threats of "Severe Physical Injuries" 126
  7. Treatment of Children 127
- G. Violations to Personal Integrity below the Threshold of Article 5(2) 127
- H. Investigation and Prevention: State Obligations to Ensure the Rights of Article 5 130
- I. Article 5(3): No Extension of Punishment beyond the Convicted Individual 132
- J. Article 5(4): Separate Location and Treatment for Unconvicted Persons in Detention 132
- K. Article 5(5): Separate Proceedings and Facilities for Children in the Criminal Justice System 134
- L. Article 5(6): "Reform and Social Readaptation" of Prisoners 135

I. Introduction

The American Convention's Article 5 provided an important contribution to the international framework of human rights protection. The ICCPR's Article 7, the European Convention's Article 3, and the Arab Charter's Article 8 merely listed prohibited forms of conduct: torture or cruel,[1] inhuman or degrading treatment or punishment.[2] Yet Article 5 was innovative for general human rights treaties because, in addition to its other components, it established an autonomous *right*: "Every person has the right to have his physical, mental, and moral integrity respected."[3] The African Charter on Human and Peoples' Rights and the EU Charter followed suit and enumerated rights to personal integrity and human dignity.[4]

None of the cited human rights treaties defines the prohibited treatments and punishments.[5] For definitions of torture, one may turn to the United Nations' Convention Against Torture (CAT), adopted in 1984 and widely ratified, and the Inter-American Convention to Prevent and Punish Torture (IACPPT), among other instruments. The UN Committee against Torture (CAT Committee) interprets the CAT though the examination of State reports and individual communications. The IACPPT, adopted only one year after the CAT and influential within the Inter-American System, advances a broader notion of torture.[6]

The Inter-American System's approach toward torture and other cruel, inhuman, and degrading treatment has often followed that of the European Court of Human Rights. From the Inter-American Tribunal's early cases, it has cited and incorporated numerous aspects of the European jurisprudence. Perhaps most important, the Tribunals share the general view that progressing standards for the protection of personal integrity require

---

[1] To be precise, the European Convention's Article 3 prohibits only torture and "inhuman or degrading treatment or punishment," omitting the adjective "cruel." European Convention, art. 3.

[2] Article 8(1) of the Arab Charter also prohibits "humiliating" treatment: "No one shall be subjected to physical or psychological torture or to cruel, degrading, humiliating or inhuman treatment." Arab Charter on Human Rights, art. 8(1).

[3] Cecilia Medina, The American Convention on Human Rights: Crucial Rights and their Theory and Practice 89 (2014).

[4] The African Charter's Article 4 establishes: "Human beings are inviolable. Every human being shall be entitled to respect for his life and the integrity of his person. No one may be arbitrarily deprived of this right;" further, its Article 5 provides: "Every individual shall have the right to the respect of the dignity inherent in a human being and to the recognition of his legal status. All forms of exploitation and degradation of man particularly slavery, slave trade, torture, cruel, inhuman or degrading punishment and treatment shall be prohibited." African Charter on Human and Peoples' Rights, art. 4–5. In its Article 3(1), the Charter of Fundamental Rights of the European Union establishes: "Everyone has the right to respect for his or her physical and mental integrity." EU Charter, art. 3(1).

[5] Article 7 of the ICCPR, however, does contain an element not found in the American and European Conventions: "In particular, no one shall be subjected without his free consent to medical or scientific experimentation." ICCPR, art. 7.

[6] For a consideration of some significant differences between the two instruments, *see* Section III(B), *infra*.

more rigorous safeguards of States and "greater firmness" of courts in finding violations.[7] What may be regarded as inhuman treatment today may constitute torture in the near future.

Although the Inter-American Court, the European Tribunal, the UN Human Rights Committee, and the CAT Committee interpret separate instruments and have distinct jurisdictions, their principles and jurisprudence on the subject have converged substantially.[8] To begin, all four bodies have asserted clearly that the prohibition of torture *and* cruel, inhuman, or degrading treatment is absolute, even in the face of terrorism and threats to national security.[9] Second, they have established similar State duties to protect personal integrity.[10] As for positive obligations, States must reasonably protect persons under their jurisdiction from the actions of non-State actors, and States will be held responsible for violations to personal integrity if they fail to respond adequately to such actions, or fail to take sufficient measures to prevent them.[11]

Third, all four human rights institutions have examined various poor detention conditions and found them to constitute violations of their respective treaties.[12] They have expressed particular disapproval of certain practices such as prolonged solitary confinement.[13] Although certain official sanctions are permissible, no punishments shall be

---

[7] Cantoral Benavides v. Peru, Merits, Judgment, Inter-Am. Ct. H.R. (ser. C) No. 69, para. 99 (Aug. 18, 2000) (citing to European Court judgments).

[8] Of course, their respective treaties have a number of similarities as well, facilitating comparable jurisprudence.

[9] *See, e.g.*, ASSOCIATION FOR THE PREVENTION OF TORTURE AND THE CENTER FOR JUSTICE AND INTERNATIONAL LAW, TORTURE IN INTERNATIONAL LAW: A GUIDE TO JURISPRUDENCE 30, 72, 111 (2008); NIHAL JAYAWICKRAMA, THE JUDICIAL APPLICATION OF HUMAN RIGHTS LAW: NATIONAL, REGIONAL, AND INTERNATIONAL JURISPRUDENCE 298 (2002).

[10] Regarding State obligations to investigate, *see, e.g.*, UN Human Rights Committee, General Comment No. 20: Prohibition of torture or other cruel, inhuman or degrading treatment or punishment (article 7) (Mar. 10, 1992), para. 14; Bayarri v. Argentina, Preliminary Objection, Merits, Reparations, and Costs, Judgment, Inter-Am. Ct. H.R. (ser. C) No. 187, para. 88 (Oct. 30, 2008); Nechiporuk and Yonkalo v. Ukraine, Eur. Ct. H.R., App. No. 42310/04, para. 162 (Apr. 21, 2011); Convention against Torture and Other Cruel, Inhuman or Degrading Treatment or Punishment, Dec. 10, 1984, 1465 U.N.T.S. 85, art. 12 [CAT]. On State duties to legislate, *see, e.g.*, UN Human Rights Committee, General Comment No. 20: Prohibition of torture or other cruel, inhuman or degrading treatment or punishment (article 7) (Mar. 10, 1992), para. 13; Goiburú et al. v. Paraguay, Merits, Reparations, and Costs, Judgment, Inter-Am. Ct. H.R. (ser. C) No. 153, para. 92 (Sept. 22, 2006); M.C. v. Bulgaria, Eur. Ct. H.R., App. No. 39272/98, para. 153 (Dec. 4, 2003); CAT, art. 4. On State obligations to protect vulnerable populations, *see, e.g.*, UN Human Rights Committee, General Comment No. 20: Prohibition of torture or other cruel, inhuman or degrading treatment or punishment (article 7) (Mar. 10, 1992), para. 11; Vélez Loor v. Panama, Preliminary Objections, Merits, Reparations, and Costs, Judgment, Inter-Am. Ct. H.R. (ser. C) No. 218, para. 207 (Nov. 23, 2010); A v. United Kingdom, Eur. Ct. H.R., App. No. 35373/97, para. 22 (Dec. 17, 2002); UN Committee against Torture, General Comment No. 2: Implementation of Article 2 by States Parties (Jan. 24, 2008), para. 21.

[11] *See* Section III(H), *infra*.

[12] ASSOCIATION FOR THE PREVENTION OF TORTURE AND THE CENTER FOR JUSTICE AND INTERNATIONAL LAW, *supra* note 9, at 30, 72, 111; JAYAWICKRAMA, *supra* note 9, at 298; *see also* Section III(F)(4) on detention conditions, *infra*.

[13] *E.g.*, UN Human Rights Committee, General Comment No. 20: Prohibition of torture or other cruel, inhuman or degrading treatment or punishment (article 7) (Mar. 10, 1992), para. 6; UN Committee

"inconsistent with the spirit of the absolute prohibition of torture, inhuman and degrading treatment."[14]

Cross-fertilization has occurred among the globe's human rights tribunals, leading to increasingly stringent protections for personal integrity in each system.[15] Over the last two decades, the Inter-American Court—also drawing from the IACPPT, the Convention of Belém do Pará, and the Inter-American Commission's jurisprudence—has delivered a number of authoritative judgments, which have served to expand conceptions of torture and ill treatment, broaden State obligations, condemn gender violence, and provide wide-ranging redress to victims. Still, the Court has not always been consistent in its approaches to Article 5, and more recently has shown a troubling reluctance to find torture and other violations in certain cases.[16]

II. Background

The delegates in San José expanded the dimensions of this autonomous right from the Inter-American Commission's preliminary proposal. The draft provided only a right to "physical integrity."[17] Yet the majority of conference participants moved to protect the "duality of the human person"—that is, the psychological and physical facets of human beings.[18]

In contrast, there was a movement to eliminate paragraphs 4 through 6, which were largely borrowed from Article 10 of the ICCPR.[19] Chile's representative, for example, stated that the requirements were too detailed for a treaty on fundamental rights, and should be left to the discretion of national legislatures.[20] Other delegates showed concern with the provisions' compatibility with their domestic laws,[21] and the U.S. representative cautioned that obligations for the social rehabilitation of prisoners could be very costly for governments.[22]

---

against Torture, Concluding Observations on Japan, UN Doc. CAT/C/JPN/CO/1, para. 18 (Aug. 3, 2007); Mathew v. the Netherlands, Eur. Ct. H.R., App. No. 24919/03 (Sept. 29, 2005); De La Cruz Flores v. Peru, Merits, Reparations, and Costs, Judgment, Inter-Am. Ct. H.R. (ser. C) No. 115, para. 128 (Nov. 18, 2004).

[14] Association for the Prevention of Torture and the Center for Justice and International Law, *supra* note 9, at 75.

[15] *See id.*; Jayawickrama, *supra* note 9, at 298–352.

[16] *See* Sections III(C) and III(G), *infra*.

[17] Draft Inter-American Convention on Protection of Human Rights, Doc. 5 (English), art. 4(1), Sept. 22, 1969.

[18] Report of Committee I "Protection." Rapporteur Juan Isaac Lovato, Doc. 60 (Revised) Nov. 19, 1969, p. 296.

[19] Similar provisions are not found in the European Convention for the Protection of Human Rights and Fundamental Freedoms.

[20] P. 442, Minutes of the Second Plenary Session, Doc 86, Nov. 22, 1969.

[21] *Id.* (indicating comments from the Mexican and U.S. delegations).

[22] P. 175, Minutes of the 4th Session of Committee I, Doc 40 (Rev. 1), Nov. 16, 1969.

Other commentators also have expressed doubt that paragraphs 4–6 have a "fundamental connection" to the right to personal integrity.[23] However, emphasizing a relationship between personal integrity and personal liberty may in fact constitute an important step forward for the rights of detainees, both adults and children.[24] The Inter-American Court would later observe that "a person who is unlawfully detained is in an exacerbated situation of vulnerability creating a real risk that his other rights, such as the right to humane treatment . . . will be violated."[25] Ultimately, paragraphs 4–6 were approved at the San José Conference with only minimal changes.[26]

The title of Article 5 in Spanish reads "Right to Personal Integrity" (*Derecho a la Integridad Personal*), but the English version differs: "Right to Humane Treatment." Although this sense of the word "integrity" may have been less common in English—and the U.S. recommended "well-being" for the Article's text[27]—the term "integrity" was kept in the first paragraph of the English version. However, the Convention's Style Committee decided to change the U.S. proposal for the English title, "Freedom from Torture," to the current form.[28] Although "Right to Humane Treatment" is not as narrow as "Freedom from Torture," a more inclusive "Right to Personal Well-Being" or "Right to Personal Integrity" would have been preferable.

III. Scope of Protection

A. A BROAD RIGHT WITH UNCERTAIN PARAMETERS

As stated, Article 5 is notable because it provides for an autonomous right to personal integrity. This also suggests that Article 5(1) could be violated in circumstances that disrupt "physical, mental, and moral integrity" without reaching the threshold of the acts prohibited in Article 5(2). In fact, this is how the Inter-American Court has interpreted the provisions. However, the Tribunal has resisted explaining why an act can breach only Article 5(1) and not 5(2). As discussed below, the most egregious abuses are often

---

[23] MEDINA, *supra* note 3, at 133.

[24] *See* MANFRED NOWAK, U.N. COVENANT ON CIVIL AND POLITICAL RIGHTS: CCPR COMMENTARY 241–42 (2d ed. 2005) (discussing Article 10 of the ICCPR).

[25] *E.g.*, Tibi v. Ecuador, Preliminary Objections, Merits, Reparations, and Costs, Judgment, Inter-Am. Ct. H.R. (ser. C) No. 114, para. 147 (Sept. 7, 2004).; Sánchez v. Honduras, Preliminary Objection, Merits, Reparations, and Costs, Judgment, Inter-Am. Ct. H.R. (ser. C) No. 99, para. 96 (June 7, 2003).

[26] One of the more meaningful changes concerned Article 5(5): "Minors while subject to criminal proceedings shall be separated from adults and brought before specialized tribunals, as speedily as possible, so that they may be treated in accordance with their status as minors." This replaced a seemingly more punitive phrase "brought before special tribunals as speedily as possible for adjudication." Draft Inter-American Convention on Protection of Human Rights, Doc. 5 (English). Sept. 22, 1969, art. 4(4)(b).

[27] Draft Inter-American Convention on Protection of Human Rights and Observations and Comments of the American Governments, Document 13, Sept. 22, 1969 (English).

[28] American Convention on Human Rights (Final English Version, Revised by the Style Committee), Doc. 65 (Rev. 1), Jan. 7, 1970.

classified as torture, a term that certainly carries a stigma and special meaning.[29] Yet distinctions among the other forms of ill treatment are often ambiguous. And the boundary between "cruel, inhuman, or degrading punishments or treatments" and a "mere" Article 5(1) violation alone is even more uncertain. The Court has often followed a cautious approach, preferring a violation only to paragraph 1. In fact, its recent judgments have shown a troubling practice of rejecting Article 5 violations altogether.[30]

Significantly, Article 27 of the American Convention establishes that the entirety of Article 5 is non-derogable. The Inter-American Court has reiterated that "the right to humane treatment may not be suspended under any circumstance."[31] Similarly, according to the Tribunal, the prohibition against torture and cruel, inhuman, or degrading treatment or punishment

> is absolute and non-derogable, even under the most difficult circumstances, such as war, threat of war, the fight against terrorism and any other crimes, states of emergency, or internal unrest or conflict, suspension of constitutional guarantees, internal political instability or other public emergencies or catastrophes. Nowadays, this prohibition is part of international *jus cogens*.[32]

A strict interpretation of these statements leads to sweeping consequences: any intrusions upon "physical, mental, and moral integrity" cannot be tolerated. Nevertheless, similar to other human rights tribunals, the Court permits the "unavoidable level of suffering inherent in detention" and other State sanctions.[33] Of course, the State sanctions themselves must be consistent with international law; as discussed below, the Tribunal has held that certain punishments violate Article 5, regardless of their status in domestic law.

The principle of non-return or *non-refoulement* also forms an important part of the protections of Article 5. According to the Court, States Parties to the Convention cannot "deport, return, expel, extradite, or remove in any other way" individuals under their jurisdiction, "when there are grounds for believing that they would be in danger of being

---

[29] *See, e.g.*, Ireland v. the United Kingdom, Eur. Ct. H.R., App. No. 5310/71, para. 167 (Jan. 18, 1978) ("it was the intention that the Convention, with its distinction between 'torture' and 'inhuman or degrading treatment,' should by the first of these terms attach a special stigma to deliberate inhuman treatment causing very serious and cruel suffering").

[30] *See* Section III(G), *infra*.

[31] *E.g.*, Ximenes Lopes v. Brazil, Merits, Reparations, and Costs, Judgment, Inter-Am. Ct. H.R. (ser. C) No. 149, para. 126 (July 4, 2006); "Juvenile Reeducation Institute" v. Paraguay, Preliminary Objections, Merits, Reparations, and Costs, Judgment, Inter-Am. Ct. H.R. (ser. C) No. 112, para. 157 (Sept. 2, 2004).

[32] *E.g.*, Ruano Torres et al. v. El Salvador, Merits, Reparations and Costs, Judgment, Inter-Am. Ct. H.R. (ser. C) No. 292, para. 120 (Oct. 5, 2015); Caesar v. Trinidad and Tobago, Merits, Reparations, and Costs, Judgment, Inter-Am. Ct. H.R. (ser. C) No. 123, para. 100 (Mar. 11, 2005).

[33] *E.g.*, Vélez Loor v. Panama, Preliminary Objections, Merits, Reparations, and Costs, Judgment, Inter-Am. Ct. H.R. (ser. C) No. 218, para. 198 (Nov. 23, 2010); Neptune v. Haiti, Merits, Reparations, and Costs, Judgment, Inter-Am. Ct. H.R. (ser. C) No. 180, para. 130 (May 6, 2008).

subjected to torture, or cruel, inhuman or degrading treatment."[34] This principle has become as globally accepted as the prohibition against torture itself.[35]

B. DEFINITIONS OF TORTURE AND THE INTER-AMERICAN CONVENTION TO PREVENT AND PUNISH TORTURE

The Inter-American Court of Human Rights does not frequently qualify abusive acts as torture, although it finds Article 5 violations regularly in its judgments. To define torture, a term that is not explained in Article 5 itself, the Tribunal has often referred to Article 2 of the Inter-American Convention to Prevent and Punish Torture. Article 2 provides, in part:

> torture shall be understood to be any act intentionally performed whereby physical or mental pain or suffering is inflicted on a person for purposes of criminal investigation, as a means of intimidation, as personal punishment, as a preventive measure, as a penalty, or for any other purpose. Torture shall also be understood to be the use of methods upon a person intended to obliterate the personality of the victim or to diminish his physical or mental capacities, even if they do not cause physical pain or mental anguish.[36]

The IACPPT definition is generally broader than that of the widely-ratified UN Convention Against Torture.

In fact, there are a few significant differences between the two instruments. To illustrate, the IACPPT demands no specific purpose for torture.[37] Although the CAT provides for numerous possible objectives for torture, there are limits: only purposes that have "something in common with the purposes expressly listed" qualify.[38] These objectives are generally linked to the work of law enforcement authorities and comparable State agents.[39] Second, for the IACPPT "physical or mental pain or suffering" need not

---

[34] Wong Ho Wing v. Peru, Preliminary Objection, Merits, Reparations and Costs, Judgment, Inter-Am. Ct. H.R. (ser. C) No. 297, para. 127 (June 30, 2015); Rights and guarantees of children in the context of migration and/or in need of international protection, Advisory Opinion OC-21/14, Inter-Am. Ct. H.R. (ser. A) No. 21, para. 226 (Aug. 19, 2014).

[35] David Kretzmer, *Prohibition of Torture*, *in* MAX PLANCK ENCYCLOPEDIA OF PUBLIC INTERNATIONAL LAW para. 35 (2010).

[36] Inter-American Convention to Prevent and Punish Torture, art. 2, O.A.S. Treaty Series No. 67, *reprinted in* Basic Documents Pertaining to Human Rights in the Inter-American System, OEA/Ser.L.V/II.82 doc.6 rev.1 at 83 (1992) [IACPPT].

[37] *See id.*

[38] HERMAN BURGERS & HANS DANELIUS, UNITED NATIONS CONVENTION AGAINST TORTURE: A HANDBOOK ON THE CONVENTION AGAINST TORTURE AND OTHER, CRUEL, INHUMAN, OR DEGRADING TREATMENT OR PUNISHMENT 118 (1988).

[39] *Id.* at 119; Report of the UN Special Rapporteur on torture and other cruel, inhuman, or degrading treatment or punishment, Manfred Nowak, "Study on the Phenomena of Torture, Cruel, Inhuman or Degrading

be "severe," as required by the CAT.[40] Third, even if there is no "physical pain or mental anguish," pursuant to the IACPPT torture still can occur through another modality: "the use of methods upon a person intended to obliterate the personality of the victim or to diminish his physical or mental capacities."[41]

The Inter-American Court justifies its use of the IACPPT through its reading of the Vienna Convention on the Law of Treaties: "the interpretation of a treaty must take into account not only the agreements and instruments related to the treaty . . ., but also the system of which it is part."[42] This interpretive principle, according to the Court, is "particularly relevant" for international human rights law, "which has shown substantial progress through the evolution in the interpretation of international [treaties]."[43] As considered below, the Tribunal has now largely incorporated the IACPPT's definition of torture into its own case law.

Notably, since *Paniagua Morales v. Guatemala* the Court has actually declared violations of the IACPPT, although that instrument does not expressly grant it competence to do so.[44] The Tribunal explained its practice in *Villagrán Morales v. Guatemala*: the IACPPT provides that, once domestic remedies are exhausted, cases may be submitted to "an international organ, whether this was a commission, a committee, an existing tribunal or one that would be created in the future."[45] Because Guatemala had accepted the Court's jurisdiction and ratified the IACPPT, the Tribunal sensibly held that it was justified in finding violations of the treaty.

Since *Paniagua Morales*, whenever applicable in judgments against States Parties to the IACPPT, the Court will declare violations of Articles 1, 6, and 8.[46] These provisions

---

Treatment or Punishment in the World, Including an Assessment of Conditions of Detention," A/HRC/13/39/Add.5, para. 35 (Feb 5, 2010).

40 CAT, art. 1(1).

41 IACPPT, art. 2.

42 *E.g.*, Bueno Alves v. Argentina, Merits, Reparations, and Costs, Judgment, Inter-Am. Ct. H.R. (Ser. C) No. 164, para. 76 (May 11, 2007); Ituango Massacres v. Colombia, Preliminary Objections, Merits, Reparations, and Costs, Judgment, Inter-Am. Ct. H.R. (ser. C) No. 148, para. 156 (July 1, 2006). The Tribunal even turned to the IACPPT's torture definition in *Tibi v. Ecuador*, where the IACPPT had entered into force for the State over three years after the facts of the case (but nearly four years before the Court received the petition). Tibi v. Ecuador, Preliminary Objections, Merits, Reparations, and Costs, Judgment, Inter-Am. Ct. H.R. (ser. C) No. 114, para. 145 (Sept. 7, 2004). In contrast, in the 2005 judgment *Caesar v. Trinidad and Tobago*, the State still had not acceded to the IACPPT, and the Court avoided any mention of the instrument. Caesar v. Trinidad & Tobago, Merits, Reparations, and Costs, Judgment, Inter-Am. Ct. H.R. (ser. C) No. 123 (Mar. 11, 2005).

43 *E.g.*, Bueno Alves v. Argentina, Merits, Reparations, and Costs, Judgment, Inter-Am. Ct. H.R. (Ser. C) No. 164, para. 76 (May 11, 2007); Ituango Massacres v. Colombia, Preliminary Objections, Merits, Reparations, and Costs, Judgment, Inter-Am. Ct. H.R. (ser. C) No. 148, para. 156 (July 1, 2006).

44 *See* "White Van" (Paniagua Morales et al.) v. Guatemala, Merits, Judgment, Inter-Am. Ct. H.R. (ser. C) No. 37, para. 136 (Mar. 8, 1998).

45 Villagrán Morales et al. v. Guatemala, Preliminary Objections, Judgment, Inter-Am. Ct. H.R. (ser. C) No. 32, para. 248 (Sept. 11, 1997).

46 *E.g.*, Vélez Loor v. Panama, Preliminary Objections, Merits, Reparations, and Costs, Judgment, Inter-Am. Ct. H.R. (ser. C) No. 218, para. 245 (Nov. 23, 2010); Bayarri v. Argentina, Preliminary Objection, Merits,

involve a State's obligations to prevent and punish torture. Although other violations of the instrument are certainly possible, the Tribunal has centered on these aspects of the IACPPT.

C. THE INTER-AMERICAN COURT'S THREE-PART TEST FOR TORTURE

The Court has now largely assimilated the IACPPT's definition of torture into its own jurisprudence. Although the Court has considered some abuses as acts that attempted to "obliterate the personality" of a victim,[47] it has now mainly focused upon the IACPPT's three-part inquiry to find torture. As stated by the Tribunal, torture is "(i) intentional; (ii) causes severe physical or mental suffering, and (iii) is committed with an objective or purpose."[48] Intentionality requires that "the acts committed were deliberately inflicted upon the victim and not the result of negligent conduct, an accident or *force majeure*."[49]

Frequently the objective of torture before the Court is to extract an incriminating confession or statement against another.[50] The Tribunal has also accepted intimidation and punishment as aims for torture.[51] In fact, the Court has given every indication that it has espoused the open-ended purpose requirement of the IACPPT.[52] In the judgment *Bayarri v. Argentina*, it affirmed that torture is committed with "any aim or purpose."[53] If "any aim" is permissible, then there is really no purpose requirement at all. In contrast,

Reparations, and Costs, Judgment, Inter-Am. Ct. H.R. (ser. C) No. 187, para. 94 (Oct. 30, 2008). In *Tibi v. Ecuador*, the case's facts occurred before the IACPPT entered into force in Ecuador, but the Court held that the State's obligation to prevent and punish torture was ongoing from the time of the treaty's entry into force; thus, Articles 1, 6, and 8 were found violated. Tibi v. Ecuador, Preliminary Objections, Merits, Reparations, and Costs, Judgment, Inter-Am. Ct. H.R. (ser. C) No. 114, para. 159 (Sept. 7, 2004).

[47] Maritza Urrutia v. Guatemala, Merits, Reparations, and Costs, Judgment, Inter-Am. Ct. H.R. (ser. C) No. 103, para. 94 (Nov. 27, 2003).

[48] *E.g.*, Espinoza Gonzáles v. Peru, Preliminary Objections, Merits, Reparations, and Costs, Judgment, Inter-Am. Ct. H.R. (ser. C) No. 289, para. 143 (Nov. 20, 2014); Bueno Alves v. Argentina, Merits, Reparations, and Costs, Judgment, Inter-Am. Ct. H.R. (Ser. C) No. 164, para. 79 (May 11, 2007).

[49] *Id.* para. 81. *See also* Espinoza Gonzáles v. Peru, Preliminary Objections, Merits, Reparations, and Costs, Judgment, Inter-Am. Ct. H.R. (ser. C) No. 289, para. 189 (Nov. 20, 2014) (considering the "nature, repetition and duration over time" of the abuse to establish intentionality).

[50] *E.g.*, Bayarri v. Argentina, Preliminary Objection, Merits, Reparations, and Costs, Judgment, Inter-Am. Ct. H.R. (ser. C) No. 187, para. 81 (Oct. 30, 2008); Bámaca Velásquez v. Guatemala, Merits, Judgment, Inter-Am. Ct. H.R. (ser. C) No. 70, para. 158 (Nov. 25, 2000).

[51] *E.g.*, Gómez Paquiyauri Brothers v. Peru, Merits, Reparations, and Costs, Judgment, Inter-Am. Ct. H.R. (ser. C) No. 110, para. 116 (July 8, 2004) (intimidation); Caesar v. Trinidad & Tobago, Merits, Reparations, and Costs, Judgment, Inter-Am. Ct. H.R. (ser. C) No. 123, para. 88 (Mar. 11, 2005) (punishment).

[52] *E.g.*, Bayarri v. Argentina, Preliminary Objection, Merits, Reparations, and Costs, Judgment, Inter-Am. Ct. H.R. (ser. C) No. 187, para. 81 (Oct. 30, 2008); Gómez Paquiyauri Brothers v. Peru, Merits, Reparations, and Costs, Judgment, Inter-Am. Ct. H.R. (ser. C) No. 110, para. 116 (July 8, 2004).

[53] *Id.* para. 81. Note that the original Spanish is "*se cometa con cualquier fin o propósito*," whereas the Court's English translation—"with a purpose or objective"—omitted "any" or "whichever." *Id.*

the European Court adheres to the CAT's "purposive element to torture."[54] As would be expected, the CAT Committee similarly requires proof of that treaty's "impermissible purposes" to find torture.[55]

The Inter-American Court's third requisite for torture is "severe physical or mental suffering." As noted above, this terminology favors the CAT over the IACPPT, as the latter instrument does not use the adjective "severe." The Tribunal does not offer a bright-line test for severity. In evaluating the degree of suffering, it "must take into account the specific circumstances of each case, in view of objective and subjective factors."[56] It has explained that objective aspects include "the characteristics of mistreatment, such as the duration, the method or manner used to inflict harm, and the physical and psychological effects such harm may cause."[57] On the other hand, "subjective" factors involve "the characteristics of the individual undergoing mistreatment, including age, gender, health condition, and any other personal circumstance."[58] These personal factors could impact how victims experience the ordeal, and may "increase the suffering and the feeling of humiliation when they are subjected to certain treatments."[59] These various elements follow European case law.[60]

The Court found circumstances in the following selection of cases to pass the threshold of "severe" suffering to constitute torture.[61] They involve beatings, rape, psychological torment or deplorable detention conditions, among others.[62] In *Espinoza Gonzáles v. Peru*, police agents kicked and punched five inmates, Gladys Carol Espinoza Gonzáles among them; the police also struck them with blunt objects

---

[54] *E.g.*, Nechiporuk and Yonkalo v. Ukraine, Eur. Ct. H.R., App. No. 42310/04, para. 149 (Apr. 21, 2011); Talattin Akkoç v. Turkey, Eur. Ct. H.R., App. No. 50037/99, para. 115 (Nov. 10, 2005).

[55] UN Committee against Torture, General Comment No. 2: Implementation of Article 2 by States Parties (Jan. 24, 2008), para. 10.

[56] Bueno Alves v. Argentina, Merits, Reparations, and Costs, Judgment, Inter-Am. Ct. H.R. (Ser. C) No. 164, para. 83 (May 11, 2007). *See also* Loayza Tamayo v. Peru, Merits, Judgment, Inter-Am. Ct. H.R. (ser. C) No. 33, para. 57 (Sept. 17, 1997).

[57] Bueno Alves v. Argentina, Merits, Reparations, and Costs, Judgment, Inter-Am. Ct. H.R. (Ser. C) No. 164, para. 83 (May 11, 2007).

[58] *Id.*

[59] *E.g.*, Espinoza Gonzáles v. Peru, Preliminary Objections, Merits, Reparations, and Costs, Judgment, Inter-Am. Ct. H.R. (ser. C) No. 289, para. 142 (Nov. 20, 2014); Ximenes Lopes v. Brazil, Merits, Reparations, and Costs, Judgment, Inter-Am. Ct. H.R. (ser. C) No. 149, para. 127 (July 4, 2006).

[60] *See, e.g.*, Ireland v. the United Kingdom, Eur. Ct. H.R., App. No. 5310/71, para. 162 (Jan. 18, 1978).

[61] It should be noted that in some of the earlier cases the Inter-American Court still had not consolidated a uniform, three-part inquiry to find torture.

[62] For its part, the Inter-American Commission has repeatedly criticized the United States for its treatment of the Guantanamo Bay detainees, denouncing various acts of torture such as waterboarding and other "brutal interrogation techniques." Inter-American Commission on Human Rights, Towards the Closure of Guantanamo, OAS/Ser.L/V/II., Doc. 20/15, 3 June 2015, para. 108, *available at* http://www.oas.org/en/iachr/reports/pdfs/Towards-Closure-Guantanamo.pdf.

and exposed them to a powder used for tear gas.[63] In addition, Espinoza Gonzáles was "suspended in the air" with metal rods, causing her to faint.[64]

In *Bayarri v. Argentina*, the victim endured repeated beatings by police over three days—including the use of a cattle prod and plastic bag over his head. Also, Juan Carlos Bayarri's captors threatened to harm his father, "with whom he had a close relationship and whose whereabouts were unknown to him."[65] *Mendoza* et al. *v. Argentina* involved the practice of *falanga*, in which the soles of the feet are beaten.[66] The Court found that Claudio Núñez and Lucas Mendoza endured "strong blows" to their feet and elsewhere on their bodies while they were held in a federal prison.[67]

In *Bueno Alves v. Argentina*, the victim "was beaten on the ears and the stomach, insulted because of his nationality" and deprived of his ulcer medication while under police custody.[68] *Tibi v. Ecuador* involved a victim who, on several occasions, "suffered fist blows on the body and face, cigarette burns on his legs, and electrical discharges on his testicles."[69] Prison guards also struck Daniel Tibi with a heavy object and submerged his head in a water tank.

Surprisingly, however, the Court did not find torture in a later case where prisoners were forced to walk through two rows of guards who beat them with sticks and metal or rubber batons. The petitioners' expert witness concluded that the practice, which treated fallen victims even more brutally, amounted to torture.[70] Without much explanation, the Court decided that it was only inhuman treatment.[71] Similarly, in *Rodriguez Vera* et al. *v. Colombia*, the Tribunal did not find torture, although a victim was "obliged to remain standing with his hands on his head for several hours, subjected to numerous interrogations during which he was pressured to 'confess' supposed links" to a guerrilla group, and then transferred to a military base where he was interrogated again and held for several hours.[72] The Court considered it significant—perhaps overly so—that the victim himself stated

---

[63] Espinoza Gonzáles v. Peru, Preliminary Objections, Merits, Reparations, and Costs, Judgment, Inter-Am. Ct. H.R. (ser. C) No. 289, para. 210 (Nov. 20, 2014).

[64] *Id.*

[65] Bayarri v. Argentina, Preliminary Objection, Merits, Reparations, and Costs, Judgment, Inter-Am. Ct. H.R. (ser. C) No. 187, para. 87 (Oct. 30, 2008).

[66] Mendoza et al. v. Argentina, Preliminary Objections, Merits, and Reparations, Judgment, Inter-Am. Ct. H.R. (ser. C) No. 260, para. 209 (May 14, 2013).

[67] *Id.*

[68] Bueno Alves v. Argentina, Merits, Reparations, and Costs, Judgment, Inter-Am. Ct. H.R. (Ser. C) No. 164, para. 74 (May 11, 2007).

[69] Tibi v. Ecuador, Preliminary Objections, Merits, Reparations, and Costs, Judgment, Inter-Am. Ct. H.R. (ser. C) No. 114, para. 148 (Sept. 7, 2004).

[70] Miguel Castro Castro Prison v. Peru, Merits, Reparations, and Costs, Judgment, Inter-Am. Ct. H.R. (ser. C) No. 160, para. 297 (Nov. 25, 2006).

[71] *Id.* para. 300. However, the judgment classified as torture other instances of abuse, which are discussed below.

[72] Rodriguez Vera et al. v. Colombia, Preliminary Objections, Merits, Reparations, and Costs, Judgment, Inter-Am. Ct. H.R. (ser. C) No. 287, para. 423 (Nov. 14, 2014).

that "there was no torture," and characterized his treatment as "degrading."[73] It accepted this description, finding "cruel and degrading treatment" in violation of Article 5(2).[74]

Maritza Urrutia v. Guatemala referred specifically to psychological torture. In this case, Maritza Urrutia was "unlawfully and arbitrarily detained . . . [her] head was covered by a hood, she was kept handcuffed to a bed, in a room with the light on and the radio at full volume, which prevented her from sleeping."[75] In addition, military officials interrogated her for prolonged periods of time; during these sessions, the officials would show her photographs of tortured and killed persons, and inform her that she would suffer the same fate. They also threatened to kill or torture her family members. Eventually, Urrutia was forced to record a statement against her will; the video was subsequently broadcasted on national television. The Court considered that these acts were "prepared and inflicted deliberately to obliterate the victim's personality and demoralize her" and constituted "mental torture."[76]

Psychological torture was also found by the Court in a subsequent case, *Miguel Castro Castro Prison*. Among other abuses, this matter concerned a ruthless, four-day military operation against inmates at a Peruvian prison. The Court found that the operation was an unjustified "attack" by State agents that resulted in over 40 deaths and scores of injuries.[77] The assault involved bombs, grenades, automatic rifles, and other weapons. The Tribunal found that "the totality of the acts of aggression and the conditions [to] which the State deliberately [subjected] the inmates"—both the dead and the survivors—"caused all of them a serious psychological and emotional suffering" amounting to psychological torture.[78]

The shocking facts of *Miguel Castro Castro Prison* resulted in two additional findings of torture. One concerned the rape of a female inmate: State agents forcibly subjected her to a "vaginal inspection" with their fingers.[79] In *Castro Castro Prison* and subsequent judgments, the Court has asserted that "rape should also be understood to include acts of vaginal or anal penetration using other parts of the perpetrator's body or objects, as well as oral penetration by the male organ."[80] Citing international criminal law jurisprudence, *Espinoza Gonzáles v. Peru* later clarified, "for an act to be considered rape, it is sufficient

---

[73] *Id.* para. 428.

[74] *Id.*

[75] Maritza Urrutia v. Guatemala, Merits, Reparations, and Costs, Judgment, Inter-Am. Ct. H.R. (ser. C) No. 103, para. 85 (Nov. 27, 2003).

[76] *Id.* para. 94.

[77] Miguel Castro Castro Prison v. Peru, Merits, Reparations, and Costs, Judgment, Inter-Am. Ct. H.R. (ser. C) No. 160, paras. 242-243 (Nov. 25, 2006).

[78] *Id.* para. 293.

[79] *Id.* para. 309.

[80] *E.g.*, Espinoza Gonzáles v. Peru, Preliminary Objections, Merits, Reparations, and Costs, Judgment, Inter-Am. Ct. H.R. (ser. C) No. 289, para. 192 (Nov. 20, 2014); J. v. Peru, Preliminary Objections, Merits, Reparations, and Costs, Judgment, Inter-Am. Ct. H.R. (ser. C) No. 275, para. 359 (Nov. 27, 2013).

that penetration occurs, however slight this may be, in the terms described above."[81] It is entirely possible that the crime will not leave any "evidence of physical injury."[82]

The *Castro Castro Prison* Tribunal observed that the rape "of a detainee by a State agent is an especially gross and reprehensible act, taking into account the victim's vulnerability and the abuse of power displayed by the agent."[83] Since that judgment, the Court has consistently recognized that rape constitutes torture, as it is "an extremely traumatic experience" that leaves victims with "great physical and psychological damage," as well as emotional suffering and social stigma.[84] The Court's ruling in *Castro Castro Prison* followed the Inter-American Commission's groundbreaking decision from 1996.[85] In *Martí de Mejía v. Peru*, the Commission "became the first of the regional bodies explicitly to recognize that rape could constitute torture."[86]

The last finding of torture in *Miguel Castro Castro Prison* was triggered by the detention conditions suffered by the prison population after the assault. The inmates were transferred to overcrowded detention centers "without access to natural or artificial lighting."[87] The State provided inadequate meals and medical attention, despite the fact that several inmates were injured or sick. Guards beat a number of detainees, and subjected them to electrical shocks. Warm clothing was not supplied, despite freezing weather. Solitary confinement was ordered frequently. "Women's physiological needs" were ignored, such as "pre- and post-natal health needs" and necessary supplies for personal hygiene.[88] The sum of these deplorable conditions led the Court to conclude that the inmates had endured "physical and psychological torture."[89]

D. INVOLVEMENT OF STATE ACTORS: A FOURTH REQUIREMENT?

In most torture cases before the Court, State agents have directly perpetrated the violations. Yet, in *González* et al. *v. Mexico* of 2009, the Tribunal found that Mexico's role in

---

[81] Espinoza Gonzáles v. Peru, Preliminary Objections, Merits, Reparations, and Costs, Judgment, Inter-Am. Ct. H.R. (ser. C) No. 289, para. 192 (Nov. 20, 2014).

[82] *Id.* para. 193.

[83] Miguel Castro Castro Prison v. Peru, Merits, Reparations, and Costs, Judgment, Inter-Am. Ct. H.R. (ser. C) No. 160, para. 311 (Nov. 25, 2006).

[84] *E.g.*, Espinoza Gonzáles v. Peru, Preliminary Objections, Merits, Reparations, and Costs, Judgment, Inter-Am. Ct. H.R. (ser. C) No. 289, para. 193 (Nov. 20, 2014); Rosendo Cantu et al. v. Mexico, Preliminary Objections, Merits, Reparations, and Costs, Judgment, Inter-Am. Ct. H.R. (ser. C) No. 216, para. 114 (Aug. 31, 2010).

[85] Martí de Mejía v. Peru, Case 10.970, Inter-Am. Comm'n H.R., Report No. 5/96 (1996).

[86] Association for the Prevention of Torture and the Center for Justice and International Law, *supra* note 9, at 3. The next year, the European Court followed suit. Aydin v. Turkey, Eur. Ct. H.R., App. No. 23178/94 (Sept. 25, 1997).

[87] Miguel Castro Castro Prison v. Peru, Merits, Reparations, and Costs, Judgment, Inter-Am. Ct. H.R. (ser. C) No. 160, para. 319 (Nov. 25, 2006).

[88] *Id.*

[89] *Id.* para. 333.

three sexual assault-murders had not been confirmed, leaving open the possibility that non-State actors were solely responsible.[90] As a result, the Court refrained from defining the case's brutal acts as "torture," despite the fact that all three aspects of its test—intentionality, severity, and purpose—had apparently been met.

In the more recent judgment *Afro-Descendant Communities Displaced From the Cacarica River Basin (Operation Genesis) v. Colombia*, the Court found that members of a paramilitary group executed Marino López in "particularly cruel circumstances": they attacked his community, physically abused him, and, finally, decapitated him by machete.[91] The petitioners and Inter-American Commission, understandably, argued for torture. In response, the Court held Colombia responsible "for having failed to comply with its obligation to prevent violations and to protect the rights to life and to personal integrity of Marino López"—due to "the acquiescence or collaboration that . . . the Armed Forces provided to [the paramilitaries], which . . . encouraged and permitted the perpetration of this type of act."[92] However, the Court found that Colombian "military personnel were not involved in the events that . . . resulted in [his] death."[93] Ultimately, then, the Tribunal defined the acts as only "cruel, inhuman and degrading," and avoided discussion of the IACPPT.[94]

In this way, the Court may look for a certain degree of State involvement to qualify an Article 5 violation as torture. The IACPPT establishes that torture may be committed by a public employee or "a person who at the instigation of a public servant or employee . . . orders, instigates or induces the use of torture, directly commits it or is an accomplice thereto."[95] For its part, CAT defines torture as an act "inflicted by or at the instigation of or with the consent or acquiescence of a public official or other person acting in an official capacity."[96] In the case of López, it is difficult to conclude that the Court demanded more severe suffering to reach the torture threshold; moreover, as noted above, its case law is flexible with respect to a purpose requirement. Finally, his fate was obviously intentional: the paramilitary soldiers attacked him and hit him at least twice with the machete.[97] Thus, in order to establish torture, the Tribunal seems to have required a more direct role for the State in the victim's ordeal.

---

[90] González et al. ("Cotton Field") v. Mexico, Preliminary Objections, Merits, Reparations, and Costs, Judgment, Inter-Am. Ct. H.R. (ser. C) No. 205, para. 242 (Nov. 16, 2009).

[91] Afro-Descendant Communities Displaced From the Cacarica River Basin (Operation Genesis) v. Colombia, Preliminary Objections, Merits, Reparations, and Costs, Judgment, Inter-Am. Ct. H.R. (ser. C) No. 270, paras. 107–110, 476 (Nov. 20, 2013).

[92] *Id.* para. 281.

[93] *Id.* para. 110.

[94] *Id.* paras. 281–282.

[95] IACPPT, art. 3.

[96] CAT, art. 1.

[97] Afro-Descendant Communities Displaced From the Cacarica River Basin (Operation Genesis) v. Colombia, Preliminary Objections, Merits, Reparations, and Costs, Judgment, Inter-Am. Ct. H.R. (ser. C) No. 270, para. 108 (Nov. 20, 2013).

Judge Cecilia Medina Quiroga, in her separate opinion in *González*, disapproved of the Court's apparent requirement for State action, and rightly noted that the Tribunal need not follow the terms of the IACPPT or the CAT. [98] A number of international legal authorities, such as the European Court, the UN Human Rights Committee, and international criminal tribunals, have now recognized that private actors can commit torture—even when acting independently from State officials.[99] Given these significant global developments, an Inter-American requirement for State involvement would represent a jurisprudential reverse, as well as a grim disappointment for torture victims in the Americas.

E. CONSIDERATIONS OF EVIDENCE AND PROOF

When assessing evidence of potential violations to Article 5, the Court has noted that victims often do not submit complaints of ill treatment "out of fear," particularly when in detention.[100] It is "not reasonable" to require victims, each time they make a statement to authorities, to describe all abuse they have suffered.[101] The Tribunal has consistently recognized that a lack of visible marks is not conclusive, "because such acts of violence against the individual frequently do not leave permanent marks or scars."[102]

Detained persons face major obstacles proving ill treatment, especially if they lack access to independent medical examinations and the support of lawyers and family members.[103] In this situation, judges and other authorities must ensure that detainees have the ability to document any abuses they suffer, including access to adequate medical examinations.[104] Clearly, such examinations must be carried out promptly; if they are conducted

---

[98] Concurring opinion of Judge Medina Quiroga, González et al. ("Cotton Field") v. Mexico, paras. 5–20.

[99] *E.g.*, Opuz v. Turkey, Eur. Ct. H.R., App. No. 33401/02, para. 159 (June 9, 2009); UN Human Rights Committee, General Comment No. 20: Prohibition of torture or other cruel, inhuman or degrading treatment or punishment (article 7) (Mar. 10, 1992), para. 2; International Criminal Tribunal for the Former Yugoslavia (Prosecutor v. Kunarac, para. 148; Prosecutor v. Krnojelac, para. 187; Prosecutor v. Kvočka, para. 139); Rome Statute of the International Criminal Court (Rome, 17 July 1998) UN Doc. A/CONF.183/9 of 17 July 1998, *entered into force* 1 July 2002, art. 7(2)(e).

[100] *E.g.*, J. v. Peru, Preliminary Objections, Merits, Reparations, and Costs, Judgment, Inter-Am. Ct. H.R. (ser. C) No. 275, para. 337 (Nov. 27, 2013); Bayarri v. Argentina, Preliminary Objection, Merits, Reparations, and Costs, Judgment, Inter-Am. Ct. H.R. (ser. C) No. 187, para. 92 (Oct. 30, 2008).

[101] J. v. Peru, Preliminary Objections, Merits, Reparations, and Costs, Judgment, Inter-Am. Ct. H.R. (ser. C) No. 275, para. 351 (Nov. 27, 2013).

[102] *Id.* para. 329; U.N. Office of the High Commissioner for Human Rights, The Manual on Effective Investigation and Documentation of Torture and Other Cruel, Inhuman or Degrading Treatment or Punishment, para. 161, U.N. Doc. HR/P/PT/8/Rev.1 (Aug. 9, 1999), *available at* www.ohchr.org/Documents/Publications/training8Rev1en.pdf [Istanbul Protocol].

[103] *Id.* para. 333; Eldar Imanov and Azhdar Imanov v. Russia, Eur. Ct. H.R., App. No. 6887/02, para. 113 (Dec. 16, 2010).

[104] J. v. Peru, Preliminary Objections, Merits, Reparations, and Costs, Judgment, Inter-Am. Ct. H.R. (ser. C) No. 275, para. 333 (Nov. 27, 2013); Bayarri v. Argentina, Preliminary Objection, Merits, Reparations, and Costs, Judgment, Inter-Am. Ct. H.R. (ser. C) No. 187, para. 92 (Oct. 30, 2008). *See also* Istanbul Protocol, para. 77.

too long after the incident, or otherwise inappropriately, their results "cannot be used to question the veracity of the presumed victim's allegations of ill-treatment."[105] In any event, when individuals allege violations to their personal integrity while in custody, the burden shifts to the State to "provide a satisfactory and convincing explanation of the events and disprove the allegations against it through adequate proffer of evidence."[106] Thus, in these circumstances, the State is the special "guarantor" of these rights and there is a "presumption of liability" against it.[107]

As for sexual violence in particular, due to the typical characteristics of such assaults, it is generally very difficult to obtain evidence other than a victim's statement.[108] When evaluating these statements, the Court takes into account that victims usually do not report the crime in a complete manner, owing to post-traumatic stress and "the stigma that frequently results from this type of complaint."[109] It has also observed that medical examinations "will not necessarily reveal the occurrence of [sexual] violence or rape."[110]

F. CRUEL, INHUMAN, OR DEGRADING PUNISHMENT OR TREATMENT

1. Introduction

As in the case of torture, the American Convention does not explain which acts constitute cruel, inhuman, or degrading punishment or treatment. The Court acknowledges that these violations involve "several gradations . . . with varying degrees of physical and psychological effects . . . which must be proven in each specific situation."[111] Yet it rarely interprets or distinguishes among the terms "cruel, inhuman, or degrading." This is an understandable reticence, shared by authorities such as the CAT Committee and the UN Human Rights Committee.[112] Drawing fine distinctions in many cases would prove

---

[105] J. v. Peru, Preliminary Objections, Merits, Reparations, and Costs, Judgment, Inter-Am. Ct. H.R. (ser. C) No. 275, para. 333 (Nov. 27, 2013).

[106] *E.g.*, Baldeón García v. Peru, Merits, Reparations, and Costs, Judgment, Inter-Am. Ct. H.R. (ser. C) No. 147, para. 120 (Apr. 6, 2006); Sánchez v. Honduras, Preliminary Objection, Merits, Reparations, and Costs, Judgment, Inter-Am. Ct. H.R. (ser. C) No. 99, para. 111 (June 7, 2003).

[107] *Id.*

[108] *E.g.*, J. v. Peru, Preliminary Objections, Merits, Reparations, and Costs, Judgment, Inter-Am. Ct. H.R. (ser. C) No. 275, para. 323 (Nov. 27, 2013); Fernandez Ortega et al. v. Mexico, Preliminary Objections, Merits, Reparations, and Costs, Judgment, Inter-Am. Ct. H.R. (ser. C) No. 215, para. 100 (Aug. 30, 2010).

[109] *E.g.*, Espinoza Gonzáles v. Peru, Preliminary Objections, Merits, Reparations, and Costs, Judgment, Inter-Am. Ct. H.R. (ser. C) No. 289, para. 150 (Nov. 20, 2014); Rosendo Cantu et al. v. Mexico, Preliminary Objections, Merits, Reparations, and Costs, Judgment, Inter-Am. Ct. H.R. (ser. C) No. 216, paras. 91-95 (Aug. 31, 2010).

[110] Espinoza Gonzáles v. Peru, Preliminary Objections, Merits, Reparations, and Costs, Judgment, Inter-Am. Ct. H.R. (ser. C) No. 289, para. 153 (Nov. 20, 2014); J. v. Peru, Preliminary Objections, Merits, Reparations, and Costs, Judgment, Inter-Am. Ct. H.R. (ser. C) No. 275, para. 329 (Nov. 27, 2013).

[111] Loayza Tamayo v. Peru, Merits, Judgment, Inter-Am. Ct. H.R. (ser. C) No. 33, para. 57 (Sept. 17, 1997).

[112] The CAT Committee has recognized that "in practice, the definitional threshold between [such punishments and treatments] is often not clear." UN Committee against Torture, General Comment No. 2: Implementation of Article 2 by States Parties (Jan. 24, 2008) para. 3. The UN Human Rights Committee does not "consider

difficult or even arbitrary, and also would impede the Tribunal's case law from evolving in response to widening definitions in this field.[113]

Still, the Court has offered some basic guidelines, frequently borrowing from the European Tribunal's case law. Degrading treatment may be "characterized by the fear, anxiety and inferiority induced for the purpose of humiliating . . . the victim and breaking his physical and moral resistance."[114] In this way, the term "degrading" emphasizes humiliation and debasement, whereas inhuman treatment refers more to acute physical or mental suffering—although these concepts certainly overlap.[115] Additional Inter-American guidance, arranged by category, follows below.

2. Sexual Violence and Violence against Women

As discussed above, in *Miguel Castro Castro Prison* the Court held that State agents had committed torture by raping a female inmate. The Tribunal also found other instances of sexual violence in the case. "Following the line of international jurisprudence," such as the *Akayesu* judgment of the International Criminal Tribunal for Rwanda, and "taking into account" the Inter-American Convention on the Prevention, Punishment and Eradication of Violence Against Women (or the "Convention of Belém do Pará"),[116] the Court defined sexual violence as actions of "a sexual nature committed with a person without their consent, which besides including the physical invasion of the human body, may include acts that do not imply penetration or even any physical contact whatsoever."[117]

---

it necessary to draw up a list of prohibited acts or to establish sharp distinctions between the different kinds of punishment or treatment." UN Human Rights Committee, General Comment No. 20: Prohibition of torture or other cruel, inhuman or degrading treatment or punishment (article 7) (Mar. 10, 1992), para. 4. As a result, the HRC's decisions often limit themselves to a determination of whether the ICCPR's Article 7 has been violated. Association for the Prevention of Torture and the Center for Justice and International Law, *supra* note 9, at 8.

[113] *See, e.g.*, Cantoral Benavides v. Peru, Merits, Judgment, Inter-Am. Ct. H.R. (ser. C) No. 69, para. 99 (Aug. 18, 2000) (approving the European Court's observation that "certain acts that were classified in the past as inhuman or degrading treatment, but not as torture, may be classified differently in the future, that is, as torture, since the growing demand for the protection of fundamental rights and freedoms must be accompanied by a more vigorous response in dealing with infractions of the basic values of democratic societies.")

[114] *E.g.*, Caesar v. Trinidad & Tobago, Merits, Reparations, and Costs, Judgment, Inter-Am. Ct. H.R. (ser. C) No. 123, para. 69 (Mar. 11, 2005); Loayza Tamayo v. Peru, Merits, Judgment, Inter-Am. Ct. H.R. (ser. C) No. 33, para. 57 (Sept. 17, 1997). *See also* Ireland v. the United Kingdom, Eur. Ct. H.R., App. No. 5310/71, para. 167 (Jan. 18, 1978).

[115] *See* David Harris, Michael O'Boyle & Colin Warbrick, Law of the European Convention on Human Rights 261 (3d ed. 2014) (referring to European Court standards that are influential upon Inter-American case law).

[116] Inter-American Convention on the Prevention, Punishment and Eradication of Violence Against Women, 33 I.L.M. 1534, 1536 (1994).

[117] Miguel Castro Castro Prison v. Peru, Merits, Reparations, and Costs, Judgment, Inter-Am. Ct. H.R. (ser. C) No. 160, para. 306 (Nov. 25, 2006) (paraphrasing the ICTR judgment). *See also* Espinoza Gonzáles v. Peru, Preliminary Objections, Merits, Reparations, and Costs, Judgment, Inter-Am. Ct. H.R. (ser. C) No. 289, para. 191 (Nov. 20, 2014).

In *Miguel Castro Castro Prison*, several women confined in a police hospital were forced to remain nude, except for the cover of a sheet, and prevented from attending to their basic personal hygiene. Even during trips to the bathroom, they were constantly menaced by armed guards and denied all privacy. In the Court's view, such treatment constituted sexual violence. The Court held that this combination of factors caused "serious psychological and moral suffering" and amounted to "cruel treatment" in breach of Article 5(2).[118]

In *J. v. Peru*, "Ms. J. was subjected to sexual touching at the time of her arrest by a male State agent."[119] The Court concluded that the "inappropriate touching" of her genital area, without her consent, comprised an act of sexual violence.[120] Based on her statements and other evidence, the Tribunal was unable to determine whether rape had occurred in this case.[121] Nevertheless, it held that the abuse was "both physically and emotionally degrading and humiliating" in violation of Article 5(2).[122]

In various judgments on sexual violence, the Court has also found violations of Article 11 ("Right to Privacy").[123] Such was the case in *J. v. Peru*, where it held that the abuse constituted "interference in the most personal and intimate aspects of her private life."[124] Furthermore, when applicable, the Tribunal commonly finds States in breach of obligations established in the Convention of Belém do Pará and the Inter-American Convention against Torture, which provide for the prevention, investigation, and punishment of violence against women and other acts of torture.[125]

Both the Court and the Inter-American Commission have underscored the "inextricable link" between violence against women and gender discrimination, and have condemned extensive patterns of abuse in various cases.[126] The Commission has established

---

[118] *Id.* para. 308.

[119] J. v. Peru, Preliminary Objections, Merits, Reparations, and Costs, Judgment, Inter-Am. Ct. H.R. (ser. C) No. 275, para. 360 (Nov. 27, 2013).

[120] *Id.*

[121] *Id.* In the subsequent judgment that interpreted *J. v. Peru*, the Court stated that Peruvian authorities may eventually conclude, over the course of their investigations, that rape in fact occurred. J. v. Peru, Interpretation of the Judgment on Preliminary Objection, Merits, Reparations, and Costs, Judgment, Inter-Am. Ct. H.R. (ser. C) No. 291, para. 21 (Nov. 20, 2014).

[122] *Id.* para. 361.

[123] *E.g.*, Espinoza Gonzáles v. Peru, Preliminary Objections, Merits, Reparations, and Costs, Judgment, Inter-Am. Ct. H.R. (ser. C) No. 289, para. 197 (Nov. 20, 2014); J. v. Peru, Preliminary Objections, Merits, Reparations, and Costs, Judgment, Inter-Am. Ct. H.R. (ser. C) No. 275, para. 368 (Nov. 27, 2013).

[124] J. v. Peru, Preliminary Objections, Merits, Reparations, and Costs, Judgment, Inter-Am. Ct. H.R. (ser. C) No. 275, para. 367 (Nov. 27, 2013).

[125] *E.g., id.* para. 368; Rosendo Cantu et al. v. Mexico, Preliminary Objections, Merits, Reparations, and Costs, Judgment, Inter-Am. Ct. H.R. (ser. C) No. 216, para. 121 (Aug. 31, 2010).

[126] Lenahan et al. v. United States, Case 12.626, Inter-Am. Comm'n H.R., Report No. 80/11, OEA/Ser.L/V/II, doc. 69 (2011), para. 131; Fernandes v. Brazil, Case 12.051, Inter-Am. Comm'n H.R., Report No. 54/01, OEA/Ser.L./V/II.114, doc. 5 rev. (2002), paras. 55–56; Inter-Am. Comm'n H.R., Access to Justice for Women Victims of Violence in the Americas, OEA/Ser.L/V/II. Doc. 68 (Jan. 20, 2007), *available at* http://www.cidh.org/women/Access07/tocaccess.htm (explaining, among other points, various governmental flaws in responding to cases of violence against women). In *González* et al., the Court condemned

that States have the obligation to investigate and punish perpetrators of domestic violence, as well as other forms of gender violence, in accordance with the due diligence principle.[127] It has interpreted this State duty broadly, "encompassing not only the prompt investigation, prosecution, and sanction of these acts, but also the obligation to prevent these degrading practices."[128] This view comports with the obligations of Articles 5 and 1(1) of the American Convention, Article 7 of the Convention of Belém do Pará, and other international instruments.

3. State-Sanctioned Punishment

The Court has expressed special concern about corporal punishment, the death penalty, and life imprisonment.[129] Moreover, it has agreed with the European Tribunal that any severely disproportionate or "atrocious" punishment falls within the prohibition against torture and cruel, inhuman, and degrading treatment.[130]

a. Corporal Punishment

Corporal punishment, "in any circumstance," has been singled out to contravene Article 5(2). In *Caesar v. Trinidad and Tobago*, the Court held that States are under the "obligation *erga omnes* to abstain from imposing corporal punishment, as well as to prevent its administration, for constituting, *in any circumstance, a cruel, inhuman or degrading treatment or punishment*."[131] In *Caesar*, State officials flogged the victim with a "cat-o-nine tails."[132] After noting the "severe aggravating circumstances" that produced intense "physical and mental pain," the Court found that the corporal punishment applied in the case actually rose to the level of torture.[133]

b. The Death Penalty

In *Hilaire, Constantine and Benjamin* et al. *v. Trinidad and Tobago*, the Court observed that the petitioners, who had been sentenced to death, "live under the constant threat

---

Mexico's "culture of discrimination against women" that led to numerous killings; widespread discrimination encouraged the State's "inaction" and "gender stereotyping," which ensured impunity for the crimes and triggered further attacks on women. González et al. ("Cotton Field") v. Mexico, Preliminary Objections, Merits, Reparations, and Costs, Judgment, Inter-Am. Ct. H.R. (ser. C) No. 205, paras. 399-401 (Nov. 16, 2009).

[127] Lenahan et al. v. United States, Case 12.626, Inter-Am. Comm'n H.R., Report No. 80/11, OEA/Ser.L/V/II, doc. 69 (2011), para. 131.

[128] *Id.*

[129] Prolonged solitary confinement and other detention conditions are discussed in a subsequent section below.

[130] Mendoza et al. v. Argentina, Preliminary Objections, Merits, and Reparations, Judgment, Inter-Am. Ct. H.R. (ser. C) No. 260 (May 14, 2013); Harkins and Edwards v. United Kingdom, Eur. Ct. H.R., App. No. 9146/07 and No. 32650/07, para. 132 (Jan. 17, 2012).

[131] Caesar v. Trinidad & Tobago, Merits, Reparations, and Costs, Judgment, Inter-Am. Ct. H.R. (ser. C) No. 123, para. 70 (Mar. 11, 2005) (emphasis added).

[132] *Id.* para. 72.

[133] *Id.* para. 87.

that they may be taken to be hanged at any moment."[134] As stated by expert testimony, "the procedures leading up to the death by hanging . . . terrorize and depress the prisoners; others cannot sleep due to nightmares, much less eat."[135] Subsequently, in *Raxcacó Reyes v. Guatemala*, the Tribunal explicitly recognized the "death row phenomenon" after considering European jurisprudence. According to the Court, it consists of "a prolonged period of detention awaiting and prior to execution, during which the condemned man suffers mental anguish and is subject to extreme tension and psychological trauma."[136] Both *Hilaire* and *Raxcacó Reyes* found aggregate detention circumstances amounting to "cruel, inhuman and degrading treatment," although it is unclear if the Court considers the "death row phenomenon" by itself to constitute such treatment.[137] For its part, the Inter-American Commission has affirmed that the "death row phenomenon" per se amounts to "cruel, inhuman and degrading treatment."[138]

Two years later, in *Boyce* et al. *v. Barbados*, the Tribunal found that reading execution warrants to prisoners, while their domestic appeals and petitions before the Inter-American System were pending, constituted "cruel treatment."[139] The Court stressed that it was "fundamental" that all appeals and international litigation were completed before such warrants are read and, of course, any execution carried out.[140] It did not explain why this treatment was specifically "cruel," as opposed to "inhuman" or "degrading."

c. Life Imprisonment: Children

Mendoza et al. *v. Argentina* examined the "extreme psychological impact" upon five children who had been sentenced to life imprisonment.[141] The suffering they experienced led the Court to conclude that the punishment constituted cruel and inhuman treatment. Furthermore, it held that life imprisonment is never a proportionate punishment for children. Additional implications of life imprisonment for Article 5 are discussed *infra* in the section on Article 5(6).

---

[134] Hilaire, Constantine, and Benjamin et al. v. Trinidad & Tobago, Merits, Reparations, and Costs, Judgment, Inter-Am. Ct. H.R. (ser. C) No. 94, para. 168 (June 21, 2002).

[135] *Id.*

[136] Raxcacó Reyes v. Guatemala, Merits, Reparations, and Costs, Judgment, Inter-Am. Ct. H.R. (ser. C) No. 133, para. 97 (Sept. 15, 2005).

[137] *Id.* para. 102; Hilaire, Constantine, and Benjamin et al. v. Trinidad & Tobago, Merits, Reparations, and Costs, Judgment, Inter-Am. Ct. H.R. (ser. C) No. 94, para. 169 (June 21, 2002).

[138] Inter-American Commission on Human Rights, The Death Penalty in the Inter-American Human Rights System: From Restrictions to Abolition, OEA/Ser.L/V/II. Doc. 68, 31 December 2011, p. 185, *available at* https://www.oas.org/en/iachr/docs/pdf/deathpenalty.pdf

[139] Boyce et al. v. Barbados, Preliminary Objections, Merits, Reparations, and Costs, Judgment, Inter-Am. Ct. H.R. (ser. C) No. 169, para. 116 (Nov. 20, 2007).

[140] *Id.*

[141] Mendoza et al. v. Argentina, Preliminary Objections, Merits, and Reparations, Judgment, Inter-Am. Ct. H.R. (ser. C) No. 260, para. 183 (May 14, 2013).

4. Detention Conditions and Practices

Article 5(2) of the American Convention establishes, in its second sentence, that "[a]ll persons deprived of their liberty shall be treated with respect for the inherent dignity of the human person." Toward this end, the Court has emphasized that States must "safeguard the health and well-being of those deprived of liberty, and . . . ensure that the manner and method of deprivation of liberty does not exceed the inevitable level of suffering inherent in detention."[142] States "cannot invoke economic hardships" to justify substandard prison conditions.[143] As a result, the Tribunal has asserted that if "there is a deterioration of [the] physical, [psychological], and moral integrity" of a person owing to his or her conditions of detention, it will find, at a minimum, "cruel punishment" in breach of Article 5(2).[144]

Failure to provide "appropriate" medical care for a detained person may per se violate Article 5(2) "depending on the particular circumstances of the specific person, such as their state of health or type of ailment . . . the time that passes without such care, the accumulative physical and mental effects and, in some cases, the sex and age of the detainee."[145] The Court has stressed the State's duty "to provide detainees with regular medical checkups and adequate care and treatment when this is required."[146] Medical care must be free and provided "as promptly as possible" after detention.[147] Attention from independent, qualified physicians "is an important safeguard against torture and physical or mental ill treatment of inmates."[148] In *Espinoza Gonzáles v. Peru*, the Court observed that the detained victim's two medical examinations demonstrated "a progressive deterioration in her health"; in addition, the State did not follow the physician's recommendation for a neurological evaluation.[149] For this reason and others, the Court

---

[142] *E.g.*, Landaeta Meijias Brothers et al. v. Venezuela, Preliminary Objections, Merits, Reparations, and Costs, Judgment, Inter-Am. Ct. H.R. (ser. C) No. 281, para. 198 (Aug. 27, 2014); "Juvenile Reeducation Institute" v. Paraguay, Preliminary Objections, Merits, Reparations, and Costs, Judgment, Inter-Am. Ct. H.R. (ser. C) No. 112, para. 159 (Sept. 2, 2004).

[143] *E.g.*, Vélez Loor v. Panama, Preliminary Objections, Merits, Reparations, and Costs, Judgment, Inter-Am. Ct. H.R. (ser. C) No. 218, para. 198 (Nov. 23, 2010); Montero Aranguren et al. (Det. Ctr. of Catia) v. Venezuela, Preliminary Objection, Merits, Reparations, and Costs, Judgment, Inter-Am. Ct. H.R. (ser. C) No. 150, para. 85 (July 5, 2006).

[144] Miguel Castro Castro Prison v. Peru, Merits, Reparations, and Costs, Judgment, Inter-Am. Ct. H.R. (ser. C) No. 160, para. 314 (Nov. 25, 2006).

[145] *E.g.*, Espinoza Gonzáles v. Peru, Preliminary Objections, Merits, Reparations, and Costs, Judgment, Inter-Am. Ct. H.R. (ser. C) No. 289, para. 206 (Nov. 20, 2014); Vélez Loor v. Panama, Preliminary Objections, Merits, Reparations, and Costs, Judgment, Inter-Am. Ct. H.R. (ser. C) No. 218, para. 220 (Nov. 23, 2010).

[146] Espinoza Gonzáles v. Peru, Preliminary Objections, Merits, Reparations, and Costs, Judgment, Inter-Am. Ct. H.R. (ser. C) No. 289, para. 206 (Nov. 20, 2014).

[147] *E.g.*, Díaz Peña v. Venezuela, Preliminary Objections, Merits, Reparations, and Costs, Judgment, Inter-Am. Ct. H.R. (ser. C) No. 244, para. 137 (June 26, 2012); Vélez Loor v. Panama, Preliminary Objections, Merits, Reparations, and Costs, Judgment, Inter-Am. Ct. H.R. (ser. C) No. 218, para. 220 (Nov. 23, 2010).

[148] Díaz Peña v. Venezuela, Preliminary Objections, Merits, Reparations, and Costs, Judgment, Inter-Am. Ct. H.R. (ser. C) No. 244, para. 137 (June 26, 2012).

[149] Espinoza Gonzáles v. Peru, Preliminary Objections, Merits, Reparations, and Costs, Judgment, Inter-Am. Ct. H.R. (ser. C) No. 289, para. 208 (Nov. 20, 2014).

found that Espinoza Gonzáles "was subjected to cruel, inhuman and degrading treatment" in violation of Article 5(2).[150]

Other deplorable circumstances, by themselves, may violate Article 5(2). Cells that resemble cages, with bars instead of walls to eliminate privacy, "cannot but infringe the right to be treated humanely."[151] In the oft-cited judgment *Loayza Tamayo v. Peru*, the Court found that presenting María Elena Loayza Tamayo to the press as guilty of serious crimes—acts of terrorism for which she had not been tried—also violated Article 5(2).[152] During the State's publicity stunt, authorities had obligated her to wear a prisoner's uniform.

Incommunicado detention has been frequently condemned by the Tribunal, owing to the "extreme psychological and moral suffering" it can cause.[153] In *J. v. Peru*, the detained victim did not have contact with her family for 17 days, and was granted only limited access to her lawyer.[154] The Court found that the State had not proven that this "exceptional measure to safeguard the results of an investigation" was "essential" in the case; nor did Peru show that it was implemented in accord with national law.[155] Regular visits must be "guaranteed" to prisoners.[156] Further, prolonged solitary confinement is "strictly prohibited,"[157] because the detainee is placed in a "particularly vulnerable position" and endures severe psychological consequences.[158]

Overcrowding comprises "in itself, a violation of personal integrity."[159] Overcrowded conditions at detention facilities strain healthcare services, restrict recreational activities, and exacerbate "problems related to food, security, visitation schedules, education" and

---

[150] *Id. See also* Vera Vera et al. v. Ecuador, Preliminary Objections, Merits, Reparations, and Costs, Judgment, Inter-Am. Ct. H.R. (ser. C) No. 226, para. 75 (May 19, 2011).

[151] Boyce et al. v. Barbados, Preliminary Objections, Merits, Reparations, and Costs, Judgment, Inter-Am. Ct. H.R. (ser. C) No. 169, para. 97 (Nov. 20, 2007).

[152] Loayza Tamayo v. Peru, Merits, Judgment, Inter-Am. Ct. H.R. (ser. C) No. 33, para. 58 (Sept. 17, 1997).

[153] *E.g.*, Espinoza Gonzáles v. Peru, Preliminary Objections, Merits, Reparations, and Costs, Judgment, Inter-Am. Ct. H.R. (ser. C) No. 289, para. 186 (Nov. 20, 2014) (leading to a violation of Article 5(2)); Suárez Rosero v. Ecuador, Merits, Judgment, Inter-Am. Ct. H.R. (ser. C) No. 35, para. 90 (Nov. 12, 1997).

[154] J. v. Peru, Preliminary Objections, Merits, Reparations, and Costs, Judgment, Inter-Am. Ct. H.R. (ser. C) No. 275, para. 378 (Nov. 27, 2013). However, in this particular judgment, surprisingly only Article 5(1) was found violated due to the incommunicado detention. *Id.*

[155] *Id.* (noting that Peruvian law allowed 10 days of restricted communication, after judicial approval, provided that the detainee was given access to his or her attorney).

[156] Pacheco Teruel et al. v. Honduras, Merits, Reparations, and Costs, Judgment, Inter-Am. Ct. H.R. (ser. C) No. 241, para. 67 (Apr. 27, 2012).

[157] *Id.*

[158] Bámaca Velásquez v. Guatemala, Merits, Judgment, Inter-Am. Ct. H.R. (ser. C) No. 70, para. 150 (Nov. 25, 2000). *See also* Espinoza Gonzáles v. Peru, Preliminary Objections, Merits, Reparations, and Costs, Judgment, Inter-Am. Ct. H.R. (ser. C) No. 289, para. 186 (Nov. 20, 2014) ("starting with its first judgments, the Inter-American Court has considered that prolonged isolation and incommunicado [*sic*] represent, in themselves, forms of cruel and inhuman treatment, that are harmful to the mental and moral integrity of the individual").

[159] Pacheco Teruel et al. v. Honduras, Merits, Reparations, and Costs, Judgment, Inter-Am. Ct. H.R. (ser. C) No. 241, para. 67 (Apr. 27, 2012).

hygiene.[160] Moreover, overcrowding increases the risk of violence and speeds the deterioration of the facilities themselves. In *Vélez Loor v. Panama*, the Court considered that a "population density" more than "120% over its officially established housing capacity . . . reached dangerous levels."[161]

In *Pacheco Teruel* et al. *v. Honduras,* the Court examined the devastating consequences of a fire in an overcrowded prison.[162] It demanded that the State design and implement all necessary protocols for emergency response in detention centers, as well as install "all the physical mechanisms that minimize the risk of emergency situations or fire."[163] These mechanisms include, among others, adequate smoke detectors, alarms, and fire extinguishers.[164]

Other detention conditions can breach Article 5, in part because "they result in feelings of humiliation and inferiority."[165] In this regard, the Court has called for natural, adequate light and ventilation, as well as "regular and constant time out in the open air."[166] Latrines must be clean and offer privacy; prisoners must have access to water for personal hygiene.[167] Clearly, limited access to potable water constitutes "a serious failure" by the State.[168] The food provided in prisons "must be of good quality and sufficient nutritional value."[169] When studying aspects of a detainee's living conditions, the Court has frequently referred to the United Nations Body of Principles for the Protection of All Persons under Any Form of Detention or Imprisonment, as well as other UN and Inter-American Commission guidelines.[170]

---

160 Vélez Loor v. Panama, Preliminary Objections, Merits, Reparations, and Costs, Judgment, Inter-Am. Ct. H.R. (ser. C) No. 218, para. 204 (Nov. 23, 2010). With respect to personal hygiene, in *Vélez Loor* the Tribunal underscored that prisoners must have "sufficient safe water for daily personal needs, among them, the consumption of drinking water whenever they require it, as well as for personal hygiene." *Id.* para. 215.

161 *Id.* para. 203.

162 Pacheco Teruel et al. v. Honduras, Merits, Reparations, and Costs, Judgment, Inter-Am. Ct. H.R. (ser. C) No. 241 (Apr. 27, 2012).

163 *Id.* para. 68.

164 *Id.*

165 *E.g.*, Díaz Peña v. Venezuela, Preliminary Objections, Merits, Reparations, and Costs, Judgment, Inter-Am. Ct. H.R. (ser. C) No. 244, para. 135 (June 26, 2012); Montero Aranguren et al. (Detention Center of Catia) v. Venezuela, Preliminary Objections, Merits, Reparations, and Costs, Judgment, Inter-Am. Ct. H.R. (ser. C) No. 150, para. 97 (July 5, 2006).

166 Díaz Peña v. Venezuela, Preliminary Objections, Merits, Reparations, and Costs, Judgment, Inter-Am. Ct. H.R. (ser. C) No. 244, para. 136 (June 26, 2012).

167 Pacheco Teruel et al. v. Honduras, Merits, Reparations, and Costs, Judgment, Inter-Am. Ct. H.R. (ser. C) No. 241, para. 67 (Apr. 27, 2012).

168 Vélez Loor v. Panama, Preliminary Objections, Merits, Reparations, and Costs, Judgment, Inter-Am. Ct. H.R. (ser. C) No. 218, para. 216 (Nov. 23, 2010).

169 Pacheco Teruel et al. v. Honduras, Merits, Reparations, and Costs, Judgment, Inter-Am. Ct. H.R. (ser. C) No. 241, para. 67 (Apr. 27, 2012).

170 *E.g.*, Díaz Peña v. Venezuela, Preliminary Objections, Merits, Reparations, and Costs, Judgment, Inter-Am. Ct. H.R. (ser. C) No. 244, para. 137 (June 26, 2012) (citing the Body of Principles for the Protection of All Persons under Any Form of Detention or Imprisonment); Pacheco Teruel et al. v. Honduras, Merits,

In its Article 5 assessments, the Court usually considers conditions in the aggregate, as they are found in the detention centers under litigation. To illustrate, in *Boyce* et al. *v. Barbados*, the Court examined a prison that used "slop buckets" instead of bathrooms; detainees suffered overcrowding and inadequate lighting and ventilation, as well as confinement to their cells for 23 hours a day for over four years.[171] These "combined conditions" amounted to "treatment contrary to the dignity of every human being," and violated Article 5(2).[172]

In the same judgment, the Tribunal also considered a temporary facility in Barbados with even more dreadful conditions. There, the cells "resemble[d] cages."[173] The detainees were allowed to exercise only once a week; they were obligated to remain confined the rest of the time, except for 15 minutes each day when they could use the bathrooms and showers.[174] Finally, they were only allowed to communicate with visitors through a videoconferencing system. The ordeal lasted over two-and-a-half years for the petitioners; taking these various factors into account, the Court concluded that the detainees were victims of "inhuman and degrading treatment."[175]

5. Forced Disappearance

Similar to the international legal instruments on the subject, the Court has defined forced disappearance as a deprivation of liberty with the participation—or acquiescence—of State agents, followed by "the refusal to acknowledge the detention and to reveal the fate or the whereabouts of the person concerned."[176] The Tribunal has held that forced disappearance constitutes at least "cruel and inhuman treatment," due to "the mere fact of prolonged isolation and coercive solitary confinement."[177] Since its inception, the Court has roundly condemned this practice as a particularly grave human rights abuse,

---

Reparations, and Costs, Judgment, Inter-Am. Ct. H.R. (ser. C) No. 241, note 60 (citing same, as well as the U.N. Standard Minimum Rules for the Treatment of Prisoners, the U.N. Rules for the Protection of Juveniles Deprived of their Liberty, and the Inter-American Commission's Principles and Best Practices on the Protection of Persons Deprived of Liberty in the Americas, among others).

[171] Boyce et al. v. Barbados, Preliminary Objections, Merits, Reparations, and Costs, Judgment, Inter-Am. Ct. H.R. (ser. C) No. 169, para. 94 (Nov. 20, 2007).

[172] *Id.*

[173] *Id.* para. 97.

[174] *Id.*

[175] *Id.* para. 102.

[176] *E.g.*, Rodriguez Vera et al. (Persons Disappeared from the Palace of Justice) v. Colombia, Preliminary Objections, Merits, Reparations, and Costs, Judgment, Inter-Am. Ct. H.R. (ser. C) No. 287, para. 226 (Nov. 14, 2014); Gómez Palomino v. Peru, Merits, Reparations, and Costs, Judgment, Inter-Am. Ct. H.R. (ser. C) No. 136, para. 97 (Nov. 22, 2005). For an extensive discussion of forced disappearance, *see* this volume's Chapter 3 on the right to life.

[177] *E.g.*, Rodriguez Vera et al. (Persons Disappeared from the Palace of Justice) v. Colombia, Preliminary Objections, Merits, Reparations, and Costs, Judgment, Inter-Am. Ct. H.R. (ser. C) No. 287, para. 322 (Nov. 14, 2014); Anzualdo Castro v. Peru, Preliminary Objections, Merits, Reparations, and Costs, Judgment, Inter-Am. Ct. H.R. (ser. C) No. 202, para. 85 (Sept. 22, 2009).

whereby the victim's personal integrity is "violated in all its dimensions."[178] As discussed in this volume's chapter on the right to life, the Inter-American System typically considers forced disappearance to consist of "multiple acts that . . . violate permanently and simultaneously several rights protected by the Convention": Articles 5, 7 (Right to Personal Liberty), 4 (Right to Life), and 3 (Right to Juridical Personality).[179]

6. Threats of "Severe Physical Injuries"

Similar to its European counterpart, the Inter-American Tribunal has recognized that credibly threatening a person with "severe physical injuries" constitutes inhuman treatment and may rise to the level of psychological torture.[180] In the judgment *Ituango Massacres v. Colombia*, it was proven that the victims faced a harrowing ordeal before their death.[181] They witnessed a brutal massacre committed against their communities, and expected to be viciously killed at any moment. According to the Court, this anticipation and fear "constituted cruel and inhuman treatment."[182] In *Massacre of El Mozote and Nearby Places v. El Salvador*, the Tribunal considered that the massacre survivors suffered an Article 5(2) violation for "cruel, inhuman or degrading treatment," due to all they experienced "before, during, and after" the attacks.[183]

However, in related circumstances, the Tribunal has unjustifiably limited itself to finding only an Article 5(1) violation.[184] In *Valle Jaramillo v. Colombia*, attackers killed a victim in the presence of two other individuals, who were then tied up and menaced with guns.[185] The Court found that the situation for the two survivors was "agonizing and threatening," but did not classify it among the prohibited treatments of Article 5(2).[186]

---

[178] *E.g.*, Chitay Nech et al. v. Guatemala, 2010 Inter-Am. Ct. H.R. (ser. C) No. 212, para. 94 (May 25, 2010); Ticona Estrada et al. v. Bolivia, Merits, Reparations, and Costs, Judgment, Inter-Am. Ct. H.R. (ser. C) No. 191, para. 58 (Nov. 27, 2008).

[179] *E.g.*, Rodriguez Vera et al. (Persons Disappeared from the Palace of Justice) v. Colombia, Preliminary Objections, Merits, Reparations, and Costs, Judgment, Inter-Am. Ct. H.R. (ser. C) No. 287, para. 324 (Nov. 14, 2014); Anzualdo Castro v. Peru, Preliminary Objections, Merits, Reparations, and Costs, Judgment, Inter-Am. Ct. H.R. (ser. C) No. 202, paras. 89-103 (Sept. 22, 2009).

[180] *E.g.*, Espinoza Gonzáles v. Peru, Preliminary Objections, Merits, Reparations, and Costs, Judgment, Inter-Am. Ct. H.R. (ser. C) No. 289, para. 185 (Nov. 20, 2014); Valle Jaramillo et al. v. Colombia, Merits, Reparations, and Costs, Judgment, Inter-Am. Ct. H.R. (ser. C) No. 192, para. 108 (Nov. 27, 2008). *See also* Campbell and Cosans v. UK, Eur. Ct. H.R., App. No. 7511/76 and No. 7743/76, para. 26 (Feb. 25, 1982).

[181] Ituango Massacres v. Colombia, Preliminary Objections, Merits, Reparations, and Costs, Judgment, Inter-Am. Ct. H.R. (ser. C) No. 148 (July 1, 2006).

[182] *Id.* para. 256.

[183] Massacre of El Mozote and Nearby Places v. El Salvador, Merits, Reparations, and Costs, Judgment, Inter-Am. Ct. H.R. (ser. C) No. 252, para. 174 (Oct. 25, 2012).

[184] Valle Jaramillo et al. v. Colombia, Merits, Reparations, and Costs, Judgment, Inter-Am. Ct. H.R. (ser. C) No. 192, para. 110 (Nov. 27, 2008).

[185] *Id.* para. 70.

[186] *Id.* para. 109.

7. Treatment of Children

The Court has heard tragic cases involving the physical and psychological abuse of children, including their torture and extrajudicial killing. The leading judgment in this area is the 1997 decision in *Villagrán Morales v. Guatemala*, also known as the "case of the street children."[187] Matters involving the persecution of marginalized children, and of youth suspected of terrorist allegiances, have continued to arrive in San José.[188] The Tribunal has held that "the standard applied to classify treatment or punishment as cruel, inhuman or degrading must be higher in the case of children."[189] Also, when youth are in detention, States must exercise "the utmost care and responsibility, and must take special measures based on the principle of the best interests of the child."[190] In most circumstances, then, the Court will be more inclined to find a violation of Article 5(2) than it would under similar facts concerning adults.

G. VIOLATIONS TO PERSONAL INTEGRITY BELOW THE THRESHOLD OF ARTICLE 5(2)

As previously stated, the Inter-American Court will often limit itself to finding an Article 5(1) violation rather than a breach of Article 5(2). At times, the Court's reticence here is disappointing.[191] In any event, there are several scenarios where the Tribunal has often found, at a minimum, a violation of Article 5(1).

To begin, the Court has indicated that if an unlawful detention has occurred, even for a "short time," it will result in "a violation of mental and moral integrity."[192] Second, a State must prove that its use of force was "strictly necessary" in law enforcement actions; if not, the act "constitutes an affront to human dignity" in breach of Article 5.[193] Third, petitioners before the Court often have faced a long-standing denial of justice in their

---

[187] Villagrán Morales et al. v. Guatemala, Merits, Judgment, Inter-Am. Ct. H.R. (ser. C) No. 63 (Nov. 19, 1999).

[188] *E.g.*, Servellón García et al. v. Honduras, Merits, Reparations, and Costs, Judgment, Inter-Am. Ct. H.R. (ser. C) No. 152 (Sept. 21, 2006); Gómez Paquiyauri Brothers v. Peru, Merits, Reparations, and Costs, Judgment, Inter-Am. Ct. H.R. (ser. C) No. 110 (July 8, 2004).

[189] "Juvenile Reeducation Institute" v. Paraguay, Preliminary Objections, Merits, Reparations, and Costs, Judgment, Inter-Am. Ct. H.R. (ser. C) No. 112, para. 162 (Sept. 2, 2004).

[190] *E.g.*, Mendoza et al. v. Argentina, Preliminary Objections, Merits, and Reparations, Judgment, Inter-Am. Ct. H.R. (ser. C) No. 260, para. 191 (May 14, 2013); Villagrán Morales et al. v. Guatemala, Merits, Judgment, Inter-Am. Ct. H.R. (ser. C) No. 63, paras. 146, 191 (Nov. 19, 1999).

[191] *See, e.g.*, Landaeta Meijias Brothers et al. v. Venezuela, Preliminary Objections, Merits, Reparations, and Costs, Judgment, Inter-Am. Ct. H.R. (ser. C) No. 281, para. 203 (Aug. 27, 2014) (noting significant suffering for the youth victim, as well as several aggravating circumstances, yet only finding a violation of Article 5(1)).

[192] *E.g.*, Espinoza Gonzáles v. Peru, Preliminary Objections, Merits, Reparations, Costs, Judgment, Inter-Am. Ct. H.R. (ser. C) No. 289, para. 187 (Nov. 20, 2014); Sánchez v. Honduras, Preliminary Objections, Merits, Reparations, and Costs, Judgment, Inter-Am. Ct. H.R. (ser. C) No. 99, para. 98 (Nov. 26, 2003).

[193] *E.g.*, Espinoza Gonzáles v. Peru, Preliminary Objections, Merits, Reparations, Costs, Judgment, Inter-Am. Ct. H.R. (ser. C) No. 289, para. 184 (Nov. 20, 2014); Loayza Tamayo v. Peru, Merits, Judgment, Inter-Am. Ct. H.R.

cases, despite persistent efforts to obtain criminal accountability and reparations. When States are found responsible for these obstructions or delays, the victims' experiences of deep frustration and "powerlessness" translate into Article 5 violations.[194] Fourth, the Court has witnessed a troubling increase in cases involving the persecution of ethnic communities. When States are held liable for the forced displacement of these populations, among other abuses, Article 5 violations predictably result.[195]

Another commonly-applicable situation concerns family members. In cases of extrajudicial executions, forced disappearances, and torture, the Court will often decide that a "main" victim's family has suffered violations of the right to mental and moral integrity.[196] Over the last years, the Court has held that there is a rebuttable presumption of an Article 5(1) violation with regard to parents, children, spouses, and permanent companions, provided that the "main" victim has suffered one of these severe violations.[197]

Other petitioners—including siblings with some exceptions[198]—must submit evidence demonstrating a close relationship.[199] Relevant information includes: the relationship's specific characteristics and the petitioner's suffering; whether the petitioner was

---

(ser. C) No. 33, para. 57 (Sept. 17, 1997). *See also* Tarazona Arrieta et al. v. Peru, Preliminary Objections, Merits, Reparations, and Costs, Judgment, Inter-Am. Ct. H.R. (ser. C) No. 286, para. 169 (Oct. 15, 2014) (referring to State obligations when using force, which include precaution, prevention, and aiding those who have been "injured or affected" by such force).

[194] *E.g.,* Fernandez Ortega et al. v. Mexico, Preliminary Objections, Merits, Reparations, and Costs, Judgment, Inter-Am. Ct. H.R. (ser. C) No. 215, para. 137 (Aug. 30, 2010); Rosendo Cantu et al. v. Mexico, Preliminary Objections, Merits, Reparations, and Costs, Judgment, Inter-Am. Ct. H.R. (ser. C) No. 216, para. 131 (Aug. 31, 2010).

[195] *E.g.,* Afro-Descendant Communities Displaced From the Cacarica River Basin (Operation Genesis) v. Colombia, Preliminary Objections, Merits, Reparations, and Costs, Judgment, Inter-Am. Ct. H.R. (ser. C) No. 270, paras. 290, 324 (Nov. 20, 2013) (also indicating the State's obligation to provide protection to victims, following a displacement); Moiwana Community v. Suriname, Preliminary Objections, Merits, Reparations, and Costs, Judgment, Inter-Am. Ct. H.R. (ser. C) No. 124, paras. 102–103 (June 15, 2005).

[196] *E.g.,* Gómez Paquiyauri Brothers v. Peru, Merits, Reparations, and Costs, Judgment, Inter-Am. Ct. H.R. (ser. C) No. 110, paras. 118-119 (July 8, 2004) (extrajudicial executions); Sánchez v. Honduras, Preliminary Objections, Merits, Reparations, and Costs, Judgment, Inter-Am. Ct. H.R. (ser. C) No. 99, paras. 101-103 (Nov. 26, 2003) (forced disappearance); Tibi v. Ecuador, Preliminary Objections, Merits, Reparations, and Costs, Judgment, Inter-Am. Ct. H.R. (ser. C) No. 114, paras. 160-162 (Sept. 7, 2004) (torture).

[197] *E.g.,* Cruz Sánchez et al. v. Peru, Preliminary Objections, Merits, Reparations, Costs, Judgment, Inter-Am. Ct. H.R. (ser. C) No. 292, para. 444 (Apr. 17, 2015); Valle Jaramillo et al. v. Colombia, Merits, Reparations, and Costs, Judgment, Inter-Am. Ct. H.R. (ser. C) No. 192, para. 119 (Nov. 27, 2008). In other cases that do not involve "a grave violation of human rights in the terms of [the Court's] case law," this type of Article 5(1) violation must be proved. Suárez Peralta v. Ecuador, Preliminary Objections, Merits, Reparations, and Costs, Judgment, Inter-Am. Ct. H.R. (ser. C) No. 261, para. 158 (May 21, 2013) (finding the State responsible for not preventing medical malpractice).

[198] More recently, the Court has held that a rebuttable presumption of an Article 5(1) violation also applies to the siblings of disappeared victims, "unless the contrary is revealed by the specific circumstances of the case." *E.g.,* Osorio Rivera and Family v. Peru, Preliminary Objections, Merits, Reparations, and Costs, Judgment, Inter-Am. Ct. H.R. (ser. C) No. 274, para. 227 (Nov. 26, 2013); Guidel Alvarez et al. ("*Diario Militar*") v. Guatemala, Merits, Reparations, and Costs, Judgment, Inter-Am. Ct. H.R. (ser. C) No. 253, para. 286 (Nov. 20, 2012).

[199] *E.g.,* Cruz Sánchez et al. v. Peru, Preliminary Objections, Merits, Reparations, Costs, Judgment, Inter-Am. Ct. H.R. (ser. C) No. 292, para. 445 (Apr. 17, 2015). In *Mack Chang v. Guatemala*, a cousin of the murdered victim

actively involved in seeking justice in the case; whether, through acts or omissions, the State impeded the petitioner's efforts; and whether the loved one's whereabouts were unknown, as well as—in the case of death—whether the corpse was returned to the family.[200] Only in extreme circumstances will the Tribunal find that family members are victims of Article 5(2) violations.[201] Even in the face of violent deaths for "main" victims and ongoing impunity, the Court tends to find only Article 5(1) violations for family members and loved ones.[202]

Recently, the Court has shown a troubling tendency to disregard Article 5 violations altogether.[203] To illustrate, in *Expelled Dominicans and Haitians v. Dominican Republic*, it established that several victims had been first detained unlawfully, without being informed of the reasons for their arrest, and then arbitrarily expelled from their home nation.[204] In some cases, State agents separated their families and destroyed their identity documents, among other abuses.[205] However, the Court stated that the case's facts were already "analyzed" under other Convention rights—such as the rights to due process and personal liberty—so it did not find Article 5 violations.[206]

In other words, the Tribunal did not conclude that evidence was lacking on how the victims suffered severe abuses. Rather, it simply chose to assess the distressing experiences under other provisions of the American Convention. It is unclear why the Tribunal has occasionally become hesitant to declare an "autonomous" breach of Article 5 in this

---

was himself considered a victim of an Article 5(1) violation. Mack Chang v. Guatemala, Merits, Reparations, and Costs, Judgment, Inter-Am. Ct. H.R. (ser. C) No. 101, paras. 233, 244 (Nov. 25, 2003).

[200] *E.g.*, Cruz Sánchez et al. v. Peru, Preliminary Objections, Merits, Reparations, Costs, Judgment, Inter-Am. Ct. H.R. (ser. C) No. 292, para. 445 (Apr. 17, 2015); Valle Jaramillo et al. v. Colombia, Merits, Reparations, and Costs, Judgment, Inter-Am. Ct. H.R. (ser. C) No. 192, para. 119 (Nov. 27, 2008).

[201] *See, e.g.*, Rodriguez Vera et al. (Persons Disappeared from the Palace of Justice) v. Colombia, Preliminary Objections, Merits, Reparations, and Costs, Judgment, Inter-Am. Ct. H.R. (ser. C) No. 287, para. 539 (Nov. 14, 2014); González et al. ("Cotton Field") v. Mexico, Preliminary Objections, Merits, Reparations, and Costs, Judgment, Inter-Am. Ct. H.R. (ser. C) No. 205, para. 424 (Nov. 16, 2009); Bámaca Velásquez v. Guatemala, Merits, Judgment, Inter-Am. Ct. H.R. (ser. C) No. 70, para. 165 (Nov. 25, 2000).

[202] *See, e.g.*, Gutiérrez and Family v. Argentina, Merits, Reparations, and Costs, Judgment, Inter-Am. Ct. H.R. (ser. C) No. 271, paras. 145–146 (Nov. 25, 2013) (finding only an Article 5(1) violation after observing that "the extrajudicial execution of Jorge Omar Gutiérrez, attributable to the State, undoubtedly caused suffering, pain and anguish to his next of kin, particularly owing to the absence of a serious and effective investigation ... despite their continuous efforts to discover the truth about what happened, and the actual impunity in this case"); Veliz Franco et al. v. Guatemala, Preliminary Objections, Merits, and Reparations, Judgment, Inter-Am. Ct. H.R. (ser. C) No. 277, paras. 239, 242 (May 19, 2014); Kawas Fernández v. Honduras, Merits, Reparations, and Costs, Judgment, Inter-Am. Ct. H.R. (ser. C) No. 196, paras. 130-139 (Apr. 3, 2009).

[203] *E.g.*, Expelled Dominicans and Haitians v. Dominican Republic, Preliminary Objections, Merits, Reparations, and Costs, Judgment, Inter-Am. Ct. H.R. (ser. C) No. 282, para. 438 (Aug. 28, 2014); Norín Catrimán et al. (Leaders, members, and activist of the Mapuche Indigenous People) v. Chile, Merits, Reparations, and Costs, Judgment, Inter-Am. Ct. H.R. (ser. C) No. 279, para. 400 (May 29, 2014).

[204] *Id.*

[205] *Id.* paras. 418–420, 438.

[206] *Id.* para. 438.

way.[207] If it is for reasons of judicial efficiency, an extended analysis would certainly not be necessary in cases such as *Expelled Dominicans and Haitians*, which feature clear proof that personal integrity was compromised. By refusing to recognize this core human rights violation, the Court deprives victims of their due reparation, and neglects a full evaluation and condemnation of the State's unacceptable practices. The approach also clashes with the well-established case law mentioned above, which holds that any arbitrary detention violates "mental and moral integrity."[208]

H. INVESTIGATION AND PREVENTION: STATE OBLIGATIONS TO ENSURE THE RIGHTS OF ARTICLE 5

The Court has repeatedly stated that to ensure the rights of Article 5, States have the "obligation to investigate possible acts of torture or other cruel, inhuman or degrading treatment."[209] Even when the acts have not been reported to local authorities,

> whenever there are indications that [such violations have] occurred, the State must initiate, *ex officio* and immediately, an impartial, independent and meticulous investigation that allows the nature and origin of the injuries observed to be determined, those responsible to be identified, and their prosecution to commence.[210]

In addition, the Court's line of torture cases establishes that judicial authorities must make all efforts to promptly obtain relevant evidence and ensure its authenticity.[211] Testimony that has been coerced in any way is invalid.[212] With respect to medical evaluations, States must ensure "the independence of the medical and health care personnel

---

[207] Norín Catrimán et al. (Leaders, members, and activist of the Mapuche Indigenous People) v. Chile, Merits, Reparations, and Costs, Judgment, Inter-Am. Ct. H.R. (ser. C) No. 279, para. 400 (May 29, 2014) ("The Court understands the harm that the deprivation of liberty may have caused to the presumed victims, but considers that there has not been an autonomous violation of Article 5(1) of the American Convention").

[208] *E.g.,* Espinoza Gonzáles v. Peru, Preliminary Objections, Merits, Reparations, Costs, Judgment, Inter-Am. Ct. H.R. (ser. C) No. 289, para. 187 (Nov. 20, 2014); Sánchez v. Honduras, Preliminary Objections, Merits, Reparations, and Costs, Judgment, Inter-Am. Ct. H.R. (ser. C) No. 99, para. 98 (Nov. 26, 2003). As for Article 4, the Court has stated, "the declared violation of the right to life includes . . . as an inherent part of it, the consequences arising therefrom, including disregard for the personal integrity of the victim." Uzcátegui et al. v. Venezuela, Merits and Reparations, Judgment, Inter-Am. Ct. H.R. (ser. C) No. 249, para. 181 (Sept. 3, 2012). According to *Uzcátegui*, then, in order to find an Article 5 violation in addition to an Article 4 breach, there should be extra evidence of "fear and anguish" suffered by the victim before death. *Id.*

[209] *E.g.*, Bayarri v. Argentina, Preliminary Objection, Merits, Reparations, and Costs, Judgment, Inter-Am. Ct. H.R. (ser. C) No. 187, para. 88 (Oct. 30, 2008); Ximenes Lopes v. Brazil, Merits, Reparations, and Costs, Judgment, Inter-Am. Ct. H.R. (ser. C) No. 149, para. 147 (July 4, 2006).

[210] Bayarri v. Argentina, Preliminary Objection, Merits, Reparations, and Costs, Judgment, Inter-Am. Ct. H.R. (ser. C) No. 187, para. 92 (Oct. 30, 2008).

[211] *Id.*

[212] American Convention, art. 8(2)–(3).

responsible for examining and providing assistance to [victims]."[213] In these assessments and procedures, "the norms established for the practice of their profession," such as the Istanbul Protocol, must be followed.[214]

Over the last decade, the Tribunal has found Article 5 violations solely on the basis of the State's failure to ensure the right to personal integrity. For example, a failure to investigate serious allegations of ill treatment can result in an independent Article 5 violation—what the European Court has called a "procedural" breach to the corresponding provision of the European Convention.[215] For example, this occurred in *Bayarri*, where the Inter-American Court declared two violations to Article 5: the first for the torture perpetrated upon the victim, and the second for Argentina's deficient criminal investigation.[216]

The Court has held that the State obligation to investigate is "reinforced" by Articles 1, 6, and 8 of the IACPPT.[217] These three provisions are consonant with the Court's case law, as they require States to "take effective measures to prevent and punish" both torture and "other cruel, inhuman or degrading treatment or punishment."[218] Moreover, Article 8 replicates the Tribunal's mandate that a State immediately initiate a criminal investigation in response to allegations of torture. As noted above, the Court has frequently found violations of Articles 1, 6, and 8 of the IACPPT, provided that the respondent State is a party to the treaty.

More recently, the Court has asserted its jurisdiction to find violations of Article 7 of the Convention of Belém do Pará with respect to States Parties to the instrument.[219] The Inter-American Commission had already affirmed its competence to interpret and determine violations of the Convention of Belém do Pará.[220] As mentioned previously, the treaty's Article 7 seeks to "prevent, punish and eradicate" all forms of violence against women. In this way, its obligations are clearly consistent with State duties to ensure the rights of Article 5 of the American Convention.

State obligations to ensure Article 5 go beyond criminal investigation and prosecution. As discussed in this volume's chapter on the right to life, States must also protect

---

[213] Bayarri v. Argentina, Preliminary Objection, Merits, Reparations, and Costs, Judgment, Inter-Am. Ct. H.R. (ser. C) No. 187, para. 92 (Oct. 30, 2008).

[214] *Id. See also* Istanbul Protocol, paras. 104–106.

[215] *E.g.*, Nechiporuk and Yonkalo v. Ukraine, Eur. Ct. H.R., App. No. 42310/04, para. 165 (Apr. 21, 2011).

[216] Bayarri v. Argentina, Preliminary Objection, Merits, Reparations, and Costs, Judgment, Inter-Am. Ct. H.R. (ser. C) No. 187, paras. 87, 94 (Oct. 30, 2008).

[217] *E.g.*, *id.* para. 88; Gudiel Alvarez et al. ("Diario Militar") v. Guatemala, Merits, Reparations, and Costs, Judgment, Inter-Am. Ct. H.R. (ser. C) No. 253, para. 274 (Nov. 20, 2012).

[218] IACPPT, art. 6.

[219] *E.g.*, González et al. ("Cotton Field") v. Mexico, Preliminary Objections, Merits, Reparations, and Costs, Judgment, Inter-Am. Ct. H.R. (ser. C) No. 205, para. 52 (Nov. 16, 2009) ("The Court finds that, contrary to the arguments submitted by Mexico, the Convention of Belém do Pará mentions the Court's jurisdiction even more explicitly than the [IACPPT], because it alludes expressly to the provisions that allow the Commission to forward the said cases to the Court"); Miguel Castro Castro Prison v. Peru, Merits, Reparations, and Costs, Judgment, Inter-Am. Ct. H.R. (ser. C) No. 160, paras. 276, 470 (Nov. 25, 2006).

[220] Fernandes v. Brazil, Case 12.051, Inter-Am. Comm'n H.R., Report No. 54/01, OEA/Ser.L./V/II.114, doc. 5 rev. (2002), paras. 28, 60.

the rights to life and personal integrity through national legislation and urgent measures for individuals in danger. To illustrate, torture must be strictly prohibited in domestic criminal law, and States must carefully regulate the use of force by law enforcement.[221] To assess whether the State has positive obligations to adopt "prevention and protection measures" in threatening circumstances, the Court considers whether "a situation of real or imminent danger existed" for a specific person or group, whether State authorities were "aware or should have been aware" of the situation, and whether "necessary measures were adopted within the scope of their authority which could be reasonably expected to prevent or avoid such danger."[222]

I. Article 5(3): No Extension of Punishment Beyond the Convicted Individual

The Inter-American Court has resisted interpretation of Article 5(3). For example, in the 2005 judgment *García Asto and Ramírez Rojas v. Peru*, a violation to Article 5(3) was alleged.[223] Family members faced harsh restrictions when they visited their relative in prison. Once there, they were subjected to "humiliating treatment": they were "stigmatized" for having a family member accused of terrorism, and a sister of the victim was forced to "undergo a personal search which violated her privacy."[224] While the Court decided that these established facts amounted to a violation of Article 5(1) with respect to the family members, it did not address Article 5(3).[225]

J. Article 5(4): Separate Location and Treatment for Unconvicted Persons in Detention

The Inter-American Court has found a violation of Article 5(4) in a handful of judgments.[226] It has held that the provision imposes upon States the obligation "to establish a system for classifying prison inmates, in order to ensure that those who are

---

[221] *E.g.,* Landaeta Meijias Brothers et al. v. Venezuela, Preliminary Objections, Merits, Reparations, and Costs, Judgment, Inter-Am. Ct. H.R. (ser. C) No. 281, para. 126 (Aug. 27, 2014) (stressing that adequate State regulations must be adopted regarding the use of force); Goiburú et al. v. Paraguay, Merits, Reparations, and Costs, Judgment, Inter-Am. Ct. H.R. (ser. C) No. 153, para. 92 (Sept. 22, 2006) (affirming that torture must be fully prohibited by domestic criminal law).

[222] *E.g.,* Luna López v. Honduras, Merits, Reparations, and Costs, Judgment, Inter-Am. Ct. H.R. (ser. C) No. 269, para. 124 (Oct. 10, 2013); Pueblo Bello Massacre v. Colombia, Merits, Reparations, and Costs, Judgment, Inter-Am. Ct. H.R. (ser. C) No. 140, paras. 123–124 (Jan. 31, 2006).

[223] García Asto and Ramírez Rojas v. Peru, Preliminary Objection, Merits, Reparations, and Costs, Judgment, Inter-Am. Ct. H.R. (ser. C) No. 137 (Nov. 25, 2005).

[224] *Id.* para. 97(133)–(135).

[225] *Id.* para. 235.

[226] *E.g.,* J. v. Peru, Preliminary Objections, Merits, Reparations, and Costs, Judgment, Inter-Am. Ct. H.R. (ser. C) No. 275, para. 381 (Nov. 27, 2013); Tibi v. Ecuador, Preliminary Objections, Merits, Reparations, and Costs, Judgment, Inter-Am. Ct. H.R. (ser. C) No. 114, para. 158 (Sept. 7, 2004).

being prosecuted are segregated from those who have been convicted, and that the former are treated in a way that is appropriate to their status as [unconvicted] persons."[227] The Tribunal explains that these requirements are consistent with the right of the accused to be presumed innocent until found guilty.[228] Thus, if the State cannot demonstrate exceptional circumstances, it must show "the existence and operation of a classification system that respects [these] guarantees."[229] The Court has not clarified what may constitute "exceptional circumstances" in this respect.

In *Yvon Neptune v. Haiti*, the State did not dispute that the petitioner's individual cell was located near convicted prisoners.[230] The Court explained that a separate cell was not enough for adequate separation; the cells of unconvicted persons must be "located in different sections within a detention center, or in different institutions if this is possible."[231] As a result, in the judgment Article 5(4) was found to be violated.

Regarding the detention of migrants, *Vélez Loor v. Panama* concerned the holding of an undocumented immigrant in a Panamanian prison.[232] The Tribunal emphasized that States must protect immigrants, who experience significant vulnerability. In particular, their detention "solely for their irregular status should only be used as necessary and proportionately in the concrete case, only admissible for the shortest possible period of time and according to [defined] legal purposes."[233] The Inter-American Commission has similarly stated that "only in the most extreme cases" could the immigration detention of unaccompanied minors and migrant families be justified.[234] If detention is shown to be necessary and proportionate, according to *Vélez Loor*, "migrants must be held in facilities specifically destined for that purpose," and definitely not in prisons "or other places where placed together with those accused or convicted [of] crimes."[235] Whether the facilities are publicly or privately administered,

---

[227] *E.g.*, J. v. Peru, Preliminary Objections, Merits, Reparations, and Costs, Judgment, Inter-Am. Ct. H.R. (ser. C) No. 275, para. 380 (Nov. 27, 2013); Neptune v. Haiti, Merits, Reparations, and Costs, Judgment, Inter-Am. Ct. H.R. (ser. C) No. 180, para. 146 (May 6, 2008).

[228] J. v. Peru, Preliminary Objections, Merits, Reparations, and Costs, Judgment, Inter-Am. Ct. H.R. (ser. C) No. 275, para. 380 (Nov. 27, 2013).

[229] *Id.*

[230] Yvon Neptune v. Haiti, Merits, Reparations, and Costs, Judgment, Inter-Am. Ct. H.R. (ser. C) No. 180 (May 6, 2008).

[231] *Id.* para. 147.

[232] Vélez Loor v. Panama, Preliminary Objections, Merits, Reparations, and Costs, Judgment, Inter-Am. Ct. H.R. (ser. C) No. 218 (Nov. 23, 2010). The Court ultimately found a violation of Article 5(2) with respect to Vélez Loor. Presumably, Article 5(4) was not discussed because the Court did not consider him an "accused" person, but rather an undocumented immigrant.

[233] *Id.* para. 208.

[234] Inter-American Commission on Human Rights, Report on Immigration in the United States: Detention and Due Process, OEA/Ser.L/V/II, Doc. 78/10, 30 December 2010, paras. 51 and 368, *available at* http://www.oas.org/en/iachr/migrants/docs/pdf/migrants2011.pdf.

[235] Vélez Loor v. Panama, Preliminary Objections, Merits, Reparations, and Costs, Judgment, Inter-Am. Ct. H.R. (ser. C) No. 218, para. 208 (Nov. 23, 2010). The Court also held "in case of deprivation of liberty of persons

the State has the "essential obligation . . . to monitor these centers in order to ensure a real protection of the [detainees'] human rights" and provide all necessary services without discrimination.[236]

K. Article 5(5): Separate Proceedings and Facilities for Children in the Criminal Justice System

As underscored in the American Convention, numerous Inter-American decisions, and the influential Convention on the Rights of the Child—which the Court cites often—States owe children special measures of protection. In *"Juvenile Reeducation Institute" v. Paraguay*, the Tribunal recalled that one of these key measures is found in Article 5(5).[237] In that case, it was demonstrated that detained children had frequently been "transferred to adult prisons either as a form of punishment or because of overcrowding at the [youth detention center], and that at those adult penal institutions the children shared physical space with adults."[238] The Court asserted that such practices subject children "to conditions highly prejudicial to their development and made them vulnerable to others who, as adults, could prey upon them."[239]

In all cases, the imprisonment of a child "shall be used only as a measure of last resort"; children deprived of liberty must be uniformly separated from adults "unless it is considered in the child's best interest not to do so."[240] As for unaccompanied child migrants, they require special care from the State and "must never be lodged together with adults."[241] If the migrant children are with their families, they must remain with their parents or guardians, "avoiding the separation of the family unit insofar as possible . . . unless the best interest of the child advises otherwise."[242]

---

for immigration purposes, they should be accommodated in centers specifically designed for that purpose, offering material conditions and a regime appropriate to their legal situation and staffed by suitably-qualified personnel, avoiding, as far as possible, the disintegration of the family group." *Id.* para. 209. *See also* Rights and guarantees of children in the context of migration and/or in need of international protection, Advisory Opinion OC-21/14, Inter-Am. Ct. H.R. (ser. A) No. 21, para. 173 (Aug. 19, 2014).

[236] Rights and guarantees of children in the context of migration and/or in need of international protection, Advisory Opinion OC-21/14, Inter-Am. Ct. H.R. (ser. A) No. 21, para. 174 (Aug. 19, 2014).

[237] "Juvenile Reeducation Institute" v. Paraguay, Preliminary Objections, Merits, Reparations, and Costs, Judgment, Inter-Am. Ct. H.R. (ser. C) No. 112 (Sept. 2, 2004).

[238] *Id.* para. 175.

[239] *Id.* Curiously, the Court omitted a violation of Article 5(5) in *Juvenile Reeducation Institute v. Paraguay.*

[240] Convention on the Rights of the Child art. 37, G.A. res. 44/25, annex, 44 U.N. GAOR Supp. (No. 49) at 167, U.N. Doc. A/44/49 (1989). *See also* Rights and guarantees of children in the context of migration and/or in need of international protection, Advisory Opinion OC-21/14, Inter-Am. Ct. H.R. (ser. A) No. 21, para. 176 (Aug. 19, 2014) (holding, "based on Article 5(5) of the American Convention and 37(c) of the Convention on the Rights of the Child, that children should be separated from adults").

[241] *Id.* para. 177.

[242] *Id.*

Children subject to criminal proceedings must not be processed through the adult criminal justice system. According to the Court, the system for children requires distinct institutions, judges, procedures, and objectives that seek rehabilitation.[243] Presiding judges must have training in children's rights and psychology, among other requirements.[244] In fact, before utilizing judicial procedures at all, alternative proceedings such as restorative justice should be employed for children, provided that the methods "allow equitable decisions to be reached without detriment to [children's] rights."[245]

L. ARTICLE 5(6): "REFORM AND SOCIAL READAPTATION" OF PRISONERS

The Court does not refer to Article 5(6) very often. Even on the unusual occasion when it cites Article 5(6), and expressly finds detention conditions in conflict with this provision, it may not even declare a violation. Further, when the Tribunal actually does find a breach to Article 5(6), the detention conditions are not necessarily worse than those of other prison cases. Thus, references to Article 5(6) are infrequent and unpredictable, although one could argue that its violation should be found in most cases with inferior conditions of confinement.[246]

The Court has recognized that criminal punishment involves "a deprivation or alteration of the rights of persons, as a consequence of an unlawful conduct."[247] However, as already noted, the punishment cannot subject the prisoner to "distress or hardship of an intensity exceeding the unavoidable level of suffering inherent in detention."[248] That is,

---

[243] *E.g.*, "Juvenile Reeducation Institute" v. Paraguay, Preliminary Objections, Merits, Reparations, and Costs, Judgment, Inter-Am. Ct. H.R. (ser. C) No. 112, paras. 208-211 (Sept. 2, 2004); Juridical Condition & Human Rights of the Child, Advisory Opinion OC-17/02, Inter-Am. Ct. H.R. (ser. A) No. 17, para. 137(11) (Aug. 28, 2002).

[244] "Juvenile Reeducation Institute" v. Paraguay, Preliminary Objections, Merits, Reparations, and Costs, Judgment, Inter-Am. Ct. H.R. (ser. C) No. 112, para. 211 (Sept. 2, 2004).

[245] Juridical Condition & Human Rights of the Child, Advisory Opinion OC-17/02, Inter-Am. Ct. H.R. (ser. A) No. 17, para. 135 (Aug. 28, 2002).

[246] *See* "Juvenile Reeducation Institute" v. Paraguay, Preliminary Objections, Merits, Reparations, and Costs, Judgment, Inter-Am. Ct. H.R. (ser. C) No. 112, para. 168 (Sept. 2, 2004) ("the subhuman and degrading detention conditions that all the inmates at the Center were forced to endure inevitably affected their mental health, with adverse consequences for the psychological growth and development of their lives").

[247] *E.g.*, García Asto and Ramírez Rojas v. Peru, Preliminary Objection, Merits, Reparations, and Costs, Judgment, Inter-Am. Ct. H.R. (ser. C) No. 137, para. 223 (Nov. 25, 2005); Berenson Mejia v. Peru, Merits, Reparations, and Costs, Judgment, Inter-Am. Ct. H.R. (ser. C) No. 119, para. 101 (Nov. 25, 2004).

[248] "Juvenile Reeducation Institute" v. Paraguay, Preliminary Objections, Merits, Reparations, and Costs, Judgment, Inter-Am. Ct. H.R. (ser. C) No. 112, para. 159 (Sept. 2, 2004) (citing the European Court judgment *Kudla v. Poland*). *See also* Espinoza Gonzáles v. Peru, Preliminary Objections, Merits, Reparations, and Costs, Judgment, Inter-Am. Ct. H.R. (ser. C) No. 289, para. 206 (Nov. 20, 2014) (State must "ensure that the manner and method of deprivation of liberty do not exceed the inevitable level of suffering inherent in detention").

despite "the practical demands of imprisonment," the prisoner's "health and well-being [must be] adequately secured" by States.[249]

Still, the Court has not given much instruction on how States may best pursue the "reform and social readaptation" of prisoners. In *Pacheco Teruel* et al. *v. Honduras*, the Tribunal stated that education and recreation are "essential functions of a prison, and must be provided to all those deprived of liberty in order to promote the rehabilitation and social adjustment of inmates."[250] Similarly, in *Raxcacó Reyes v. Guatemala*, the Court ordered that the State adopt "the educational, work-related and other measures necessary to ensure the social readaptation" of the incarcerated petitioner, in accordance with Article 5(6).[251]

Rare specifics were offered in *"Juvenile Reeducation Institute" v. Paraguay*, which concerned both children and adults who endured "inhuman and degrading conditions" in "an atmosphere of violence, danger, abuse, corruption, mistrust and promiscuity."[252] The Court found that "rather than being rehabilitated at the Center to successfully rejoin society, the inmates . . . went through a counterproductive, brutal learning process, which in part explains the high recidivism rate among the inmates."[253] The Tribunal underscored that the State's obligations include "providing them with health care and education,"[254] and cited Rule 13(5) of the United Nations Standard Minimum Rules for the Administration of Juvenile Justice:

> While in custody, juveniles shall receive care, protection and all necessary individual assistance—social, educational, vocational, psychological, medical and physical—that they may require in view of their age, sex and personality.[255]

As detention conditions within the "Reeducation Institute" were abysmal, and its educational program lacked adequate resources, paragraphs 1, 2, and 6 of Article 5 were found violated, among other Convention provisions.[256] Notably, as a sweeping measure of

---

249 "Juvenile Reeducation Institute" v. Paraguay, Preliminary Objections, Merits, Reparations, and Costs, Judgment, Inter-Am. Ct. H.R. (ser. C) No. 112, para. 159 (Sept. 2, 2004) (citing the European Court judgment *Kudla v. Poland*).

250 Pacheco Teruel et al. v. Honduras, Merits, Reparations, and Costs, Judgment, Inter-Am. Ct. H.R. (ser. C) No. 241, para. 67 (Apr. 27, 2012).

251 Raxcacó Reyes v. Guatemala, Merits, Reparations, and Costs, Judgment, Inter-Am. Ct. H.R. (ser. C) No. 133, para. 135 (Sept. 15, 2005).

252 "Juvenile Reeducation Institute" v. Paraguay, Preliminary Objections, Merits, Reparations, and Costs, Judgment, Inter-Am. Ct. H.R. (ser. C) No. 112, para. 170 (Sept. 2, 2004).

253 *Id.* para. 134(24).

254 *Id.* para. 161.

255 *Id.* para. 163.

256 *Id.* para. 176.

reparation, the Court ordered Paraguay to provide "vocational assistance and a special education program" for numerous former inmates.[257]

In *Mendoza* et al. *v. Argentina*, the Court examined the life imprisonment of children under the lens of Article 5(6).[258] Unsurprisingly, the sentence was held inconsistent with the Convention provision, because life imprisonment involves the "maximum exclusion of the child from society, so that it functions in a purely retributive sense, because the expectations of re-socialization are annulled to their highest degree."[259] Under this rationale, considering these and the many other damaging aspects of such punishment, Article 5(6) should also prohibit life imprisonment for adults.[260]

---

[257] *Id.* para. 321.

[258] Mendoza et al. v. Argentina, Preliminary Objections, Merits, and Reparations, Judgment, Inter-Am. Ct. H.R. (ser. C) No. 260, para. 166 (May 14, 2013).

[259] *Id. See also* Inter-American Commission on Human Rights, Juvenile Justice and Human Rights in the Americas, OEA/Ser.L/V/II. Doc. 78, 13 July 2011, para. 366, *available at* http://www.oas.org/en/iachr/children/docs/pdf/JuvenileJustice.pdf (similar view with respect to life imprisonment).

[260] *See, e.g.*, Crime Prevention and Criminal Justice Branch, United Nations Centre for Social Development and Humanitarian Affairs, Life Imprisonment (1994), *available at* http://www.penalreform.org/wp-content/uploads/2013/06/UNODC-1994-Lifers.pdf.

5

Personal Liberty

Article 7: Right to Personal Liberty

1. *Every person has the right to personal liberty and security.*
2. *No one shall be deprived of his physical liberty except for the reasons and under the conditions established beforehand by the constitution of the State Party concerned or by a law established pursuant thereto.*
3. *No one shall be subject to arbitrary arrest or imprisonment.*
4. *Anyone who is detained shall be informed of the reasons for his detention and shall be promptly notified of the charge or charges against him.*
5. *Any person detained shall be brought promptly before a judge or other officer authorized by law to exercise judicial power and shall be entitled to trial within a reasonable time or to be released without prejudice to the continuation of the proceedings. His release may be subject to guarantees to assure his appearance for trial.*
6. *Anyone who is deprived of his liberty shall be entitled to recourse to a competent court, in order that the court may decide without delay on the lawfulness of his arrest or detention and order his release if the arrest or detention is unlawful. In States Parties whose laws provide that anyone who believes himself to be threatened with deprivation of his liberty is entitled to recourse to a competent court in order that it may decide on the lawfulness of such threat, this remedy may not be restricted or abolished. The interested party or another person in his behalf is entitled to seek these remedies.*
7. *No one shall be detained for debt. This principle shall not limit the orders of a competent judicial authority issued for nonfulfillment of duties of support.*

The American Convention on Human Rights. Thomas M. Antkowiak and Alejandra Gonza.

Chapter 5 Contents

- I. Introduction 141
- II. Background 142
- III. Scope of Protection 143
  - A. Overview 143
    - 1. Right to Physical Liberty 143
    - 2. Right to Personal Security 146
  - B. General Requirements to Deprive Liberty: The Principles of Legality and Arbitrariness 148
    - 1. The Legality Principle 148
      - a. Restriction of Liberty Always the Exception 148
      - b. Ordered by a Competent Judicial Authority 150
        - i. Synthesis 150
        - ii. Detentions without Judicial Warrants: Exceptional Cases 151
      - c. State Obligation to Register Detentions 153
      - d. Detention Time Limits and Orders for Release 154
      - e. Pretrial Detention as Illegal Detention 154
      - f. Court's Increasing Reluctance to Find Violations of Article 7(2) 154
    - 2. The Arbitrariness Principle 156
      - a. Synthesis 156
      - b. Forced Disappearances 156
      - c. Pretrial Detention as Arbitrary Detention 157
        - i. Sufficient Evidence of Criminal Responsibility 158
        - ii. Risks to the Criminal Proceeding 158
        - iii. Detention in Immigration Proceedings 159
        - iv. Pretrial Detention of Special Sectors of the Population 159
        - v. Time Limits for Pretrial Detention 160
    - 3. Methodological Problems: Legality and Arbitrariness 160
  - C. The Specific Requirements of Paragraphs 4, 5, and 6 of Article 7 162
    - 1. Article 7(4): Reasons for Detention and Notification of Charges 162
      - a. Reasons for Detention 162
      - b. Notification of Charges 163
    - 2. Article 7(5): Judicial Supervision 164
      - a. Brought "Before a Judge or Other Officer Authorized by Law" 164
      - b. Right to Trial "Within a Reasonable Time" 166
    - 3. Article 7(6): The Right to Habeas Corpus 167
    - 4. Article 7(7): "No One Shall Be Detained for Debt" 169

I. Introduction

Liberty stands as the quintessential right in the liberal philosophical tradition.[1] In current international law, however, the right refers specifically to physical liberty, rather than the fuller concepts of individual autonomy and human freedom.[2] All of the major human rights treaties recognize the "right to liberty and security of person": Article 9 of the ICCPR, Article 5 of the European Convention, Article 6 of the African Charter, Article 14 of the Arab Charter, Article 6 of the EU Charter, and Article 7 of the American Convention.[3] Although the right to security always accompanies the right to liberty, the Inter-American and European Courts of Human Rights have not emphasized an independent meaning for the former concept.[4] Yet the Human Rights Committee, interpreting the ICCPR, has held that the right to security obligates States to protect persons against diverse interferences by government officials and private actors.[5]

Of course, the right to physical liberty is not absolute. States commonly detain and imprison individuals to counter varied threats, real or perceived, to security. For most of the general human rights treaties, a deprivation of liberty must meet two requirements in order to be permissible: (1) its procedures and reasons must be established by law, and (2) the detention or arrest cannot be arbitrary. In contrast, the European Convention's approach is narrower: it lists acceptable scenarios for the deprivation of liberty and omits the open-ended principle of arbitrariness.[6] Although many human rights instruments make specific reference to "arrests" or "detentions," these terms have been interpreted broadly, and it has become clear that the provisions apply to diverse ways that an individual may be deprived of physical liberty.[7]

---

[1] *See, e.g.*, Cranston, Maurice, "Liberalism," *in* The Encyclopedia of Philosophy 458–61 (Paul Edwards ed., 1967) ("By definition, a liberal is a man who believes in liberty"); John Locke, The Second Treatise of Government in Two Treatises of Government 283–446 (Peter Laslett ed., 1960).

[2] *See, e.g.*, Manfred Nowak, U.N. Covenant on Civil and Political Rights: CCPR Commentary 212 (2d ed. 2005); David Harris, Michael O'Boyle & Colin Warbrick, Law of the European Convention on Human Rights 288 (3d ed. 2014).

[3] ICCPR, art. 9; European Convention, art. 5; African Charter, art. 6; Arab Charter, art. 14; EU Charter, art. 6; American Convention, art. 7.

[4] *See* Harris, O'Boyle & Warbrick, *supra* note 2, at 300. For discussion of the Inter-American Court's jurisprudence, *see* below.

[5] *See, e.g.*, Delgado Páez v. Colombia, Communication No. 195/1985, U.N. Doc. CCPR/C/39/D/195/1985 (1990), para. 5.6 ("Accordingly, while fully understanding the situation in Colombia, the Committee finds that the State party has not taken, or has been unable to take, appropriate measures to ensure Mr. Delgado's right to security of his person under article 9, paragraph 1").

[6] European Convention, art. 5(1).

[7] *See, e.g.*, Nowak, *supra* note 2, at 220–21 ("the holding of minors, mentally-ill persons, alcohol or drug addicts or vagrants, as well as deprivation of liberty by private persons, are to be understood as arrest or detention"); Harris, O'Boyle & Warbrick, *supra* note 2, at 288 (noting that all kinds of detention are controlled by Article 5 including "such matters as the detention of minors, the mentally disordered, and persons being deported or extradited"); Niels Petersen, "Liberty, Right to, International Protection," *in* Max Planck Encyclopedia of Public International Law, para. 6 (2012).

The American Convention's Article 7 establishes the general right of all persons to not be deprived illegally or arbitrarily of their liberty; in addition, it contains specific protections for individuals who have been deprived of their freedom.[8] These detailed guarantees primarily contemplated criminal proceedings, but now also extend to administrative deprivations of liberty, such as the detention of migrants or the mentally ill.[9] Paragraphs two and three of Article 7, which concern the principles of legality and arbitrariness, respectively, regulate all deprivations of liberty.[10] The Inter-American Court, like its international counterparts, has heard numerous cases concerning personal liberty, and has stressed the importance of this right for a democratic society, the rule of law, and the protection of other rights. Although the Court has advanced a variety of safeguards for personal liberty, we consider its current method of interpreting legality and arbitrariness to be flawed, as explained below.[11]

II. Background

In some respects, the Inter-American Commission's preliminary draft on the right to personal liberty resembled the ICCPR and the European Convention.[12] Yet neither the ICCPR nor the European Convention refers to detentions for debt. Both treaties also establish an "enforceable right to compensation" for victims of unlawful arrest or detention.[13] In contrast, the American Convention designated a separate provision, Article 10, to establish a right to compensation; however, Article 10 ultimately addressed a distinct situation: when an individual "has been sentenced by a final judgment through a miscarriage of justice."[14]

During the San José Conference, the representative from Ecuador added one of the first significant revisions: "Every person has the right to personal liberty and security."[15] This general affirmation of the two rights, although prominently featured in Article 9 of the ICCPR and Article 5 of the European Convention, had been omitted in the Inter-American Commission's initial proposal.[16] The Conference did not discuss personal security as a concept separate from personal liberty.

---

[8] *E.g.*, Neptune v. Haiti, Merits, Reparations, and Costs, Judgment, Inter-Am. Ct. H.R. (ser. C) No. 180, para. 89 (May 6, 2008); Chaparro Álvarez and Lapo Íñiguez v. Ecuador, Preliminary Objections, Merits, Reparations, and Costs, Judgment, Inter-Am. Ct. H.R. (ser. C) No. 170, para. 51 (Nov. 21, 2007).

[9] *See* discussion below.

[10] *See* Cecilia Medina, The American Convention on Human Rights: Crucial Rights and Their Theory and Practice 141 (2014).

[11] *See* "Methodological Problems: Legality and Arbitrariness" below.

[12] Draft Inter-American Convention on Protection of Human Rights, art. 6, Doc. 5 (English). Sept. 22, 1969.

[13] ICCPR, art. 9(5); European Convention, art. 5(5).

[14] American Convention, art. 10.

[15] P. 180, Minutes of the 5th Session of Committee I, Doc 43 (Rev. 1), Nov. 17, 1969.

[16] *See* Report of Committee I "Protection." Rapporteur Juan Isaac Lovato, Doc. 60 (Revised) Nov. 19, 1969, p. 297 (stating that the addition was "inspired" by Article 3 of the Universal Declaration of Human Rights).

The Brazilian delegate preferred to specify permissible scenarios for detention, as established by the European Convention's Article 5.[17] Yet Brazil's efforts to add an exhaustive list were defeated. The final version follows the ICCPR's reference to national law, but also adds a unique allusion to national constitutions: "No one shall be deprived of his physical liberty except for the reasons and under the conditions established beforehand *by the constitution of the State Party concerned* or by a law established pursuant thereto."[18]

The Commission's draft provided for judicial review even for those who believed themselves *threatened* with deprivation of liberty.[19] The US delegate objected to this provision out of concern that it could prevent a criminal investigation or proceeding.[20] Eventually, the approved version established that this judicial remedy "may not be restricted or abolished" in those States Parties whose legislation allows for this possibility.[21]

Article 7(7), the provision on debt, was debated extensively due to varying State laws in the Americas. A working group was formed; the group offered a simple proposal to forbid all deprivations of liberty for debt.[22] Yet some delegates responded that this proposal could prevent prison sentences for failure to pay child and spouse support.[23] The final version took these observations into account—establishing that "no one shall be detained for debt," but that "this principle shall not limit the orders of a competent judicial authority issued for nonfulfillment of duties of support."[24]

III. Scope of Protection

A. OVERVIEW

1. Right to Physical Liberty

The Inter-American Court has distinguished the right of Article 7 from the expansive notion of liberty "to do or not do all that is lawfully allowed."[25] Although every human right "protects an aspect" of this broader concept of individual freedom, the Court holds that Article 7 "protects exclusively the right to physical liberty."[26] In this way, the provision safeguards "physical conducts that presuppose the actual presence of the holder of the right and that

---

[17] P. 180, Minutes of the 5th Session of Committee I, Doc 43 (Rev. 1), November 17, 1969. The delegate also noted the Inter-American Commission draft's unique mention of national constitutions, a term that would eventually be conserved in the final version of Article 7(2). *Id.* at 184.

[18] American Convention, art. 7(2) (emphasis added).

[19] *See* Draft Inter-American Convention on Protection of Human Rights, art. 6(5) Doc. 5 (English). Sept. 22, 1969 (emphasis added).

[20] P. 182, Minutes of the 5th Session of Committee I, Doc 43 (Rev. 1), Nov. 17, 1969.

[21] American Convention, art. 7(6).

[22] P. 188, Minutes of the 6th Session of Committee I, Doc 44 (Rev. 1), Nov. 16, 1969.

[23] *Id.*

[24] American Convention, art. 7(7).

[25] Chaparro Álvarez and Lapo Íñiguez v. Ecuador, Preliminary Objections, Merits, Reparations, and Costs, Judgment, Inter-Am. Ct. H.R. (ser. C) No. 170, para. 52 (Nov. 21, 2007).

[26] *Id.*

are normally expressed in physical movement."[27] This ambiguous definition is not fully separated from the freedom of movement, Article 22 of the Convention.[28] The Court's Article 7 case law includes the technical concepts of arrest and detention, and encompasses many other forms of deprivation of liberty. For the Court, liberty is deprived when the individual "is unable to leave or abandon at will the place or establishment where she or he has been placed."[29]

The Tribunal has elaborated that "any deprivation of liberty, for the alleged commission of a crime or for any other reason, must be carried out in strict compliance with a series of guarantees that assure the protection of this fundamental right."[30] The Court has analyzed Article 7 in many criminal proceedings, but also in special legal regimes, such as military jurisdiction,[31] immigration contexts,[32] ad hoc terrorism processes,[33] and proceedings involving children.[34] The Tribunal has also frequently examined Article 7 in its vast jurisprudence on forced disappearances[35] and extrajudicial executions.[36]

For its part, the Inter-American Commission has held that Article 7 contemplates,

> Any form of detention, imprisonment, institutionalization, or custody of a person in a public or private institution which that person is not permitted to leave at will, by order of or under de facto control of a judicial, administrative or any other

---

[27] *Id.* para. 53.

[28] *See* Jesús María Casal, *Artículo 7: Derecho a la Libertad Personal*, *in* La Convención Americana Sobre Derechos Humanos Comentada 183 (Christian Steiner & Patricia Uribe eds., 2014).

[29] Rights & Guar. of Children in the Context of Migration and/or in Need of Int'l Prot., Advisory Opinion OC-21/14, Inter-Am. Ct. H.R. (ser. A) No. 21, para. 145 (Aug. 19, 2014).

[30] *E.g., id.*; Expelled Dominicans and Haitians v. Dominican Republic, Preliminary Objections, Merits, Reparations, and Costs, Judgment, Inter-Am. Ct. H.R. (ser. C) No. 282, para 359 (Aug. 28, 2014).

[31] *E.g.*, Usón Ramírez v. Venezuela, Preliminary Objection, Merits, Reparations, and Costs, Judgment, Inter-Am. Ct. H.R. (ser. C) No. 207, para. 148 (Nov. 20, 2009); Palamara Iribarne v. Chile, Merits, Reparations, Costs, Judgment, Inter-Am. Ct. H.R. (ser. C) No. 135, paras. 227–228 (Nov. 22, 2005).

[32] *E.g.*, Expelled Dominicans and Haitians v. Dominican Republic, Preliminary Objections, Merits, Reparations, and Costs, Judgment, Inter-Am. Ct. H.R. (ser. C) No. 282, para. 359 (Aug. 28, 2014); Vélez Loor v. Panama, Preliminary Objections, Merits, Reparations, and Costs, Judgment, Inter-Am. Ct. H.R. (ser. C) No. 218, para. 191 (Nov. 23, 2010).

[33] Galindo Cardenas et al. v. Peru, Preliminary Objections, Merits, Reparations and Costs, Inter-Am. Ct. H.R. (ser. C) No. 301, paras. 129–137 (Oct. 2, 2015).

[34] *E.g.*, Mendoza et al. v. Argentina, 2013 Inter-Am. Ct. H.R. (ser. C) No. 260, paras. 161–164 (May 14, 2013); Uzcátegui et al. v. Venezuela, 2012 Inter-Am. Ct. H.R. (ser. C) No. 249, paras. 152–159 (Sept. 3, 2012). *See also* Rights & Guar. of Children in the Context of Migration and/or in Need of Int'l Prot., Advisory Opinion OC-21/14, Inter-Am. Ct. H.R. (ser. A) No. 21, para. 144 (Aug. 19, 2014).

[35] *E.g.*, Rodriguez Vera et al. (Persons Disappeared from the Palace of Justice) v. Colombia, Preliminary Objections, Merits, Reparations, and Costs, Judgment, Inter-Am. Ct. H.R. (ser. C) No. 287, para. 226 (Nov. 14, 2014); Gómez Palomino v. Peru, Merits, Reparations, and Costs, Judgment, Inter-Am. Ct. H.R. (ser. C) No. 136, para. 97 (Nov. 22, 2005).

[36] *E.g.*, Massacres of El Mozote and Nearby Places v. El Salvador, Merits, Reparations, and Costs, Judgment, Inter-Am. Ct. H.R. (ser. C) No. 252, para. 203 (Oct. 25, 2012); Valle Jaramillo et al. v. Colombia, Merits, Reparations, and Costs, Judgment, Inter-Am. Ct. H.R. (ser. C) No. 192, paras. 105–106 (Nov. 27, 2008).

authority, for reasons of humanitarian assistance, treatment, guardianship, protection, or because of crimes or legal offenses.[37]

Notably, the Court has even gone beyond the Commission's wide interpretation by recognizing Article 7 protections in cases where deprivations of liberty were carried out by non-State actors, without the order or control of State authorities.[38]

In order to activate the protections of Article 7, the Inter-American Court does not require a specific duration for the detention. In this way, the Court has found violations to Article 7 in a wide range of detention scenarios. These may comprise a "brief period" or a simple "delay" for identification,[39] to a matter of days,[40] and finally to long terms of pretrial detention[41] and post-conviction incarceration.[42]

Some commentators consider that Article 7 primarily refers to confinement in a reduced space, such as a prison cell.[43] However, the Court has found violations for deprivations of liberty in a wide variety of settings beyond the typical jail cell, including: a military

---

[37] Principles and Best Practices on the Protection of Persons Deprived of Liberty in the Americas (2008), General Provision, OEA/Ser.L/V/II.131 doc. 26, *available at* http://www.oas.org/en/iachr/mandate/Basics/principlesdeprived.asp. Article 7 establishes that "every person" possesses the right to personal liberty and security; in this regard, the Inter-American Commission has elaborated that "this category of persons includes not only those deprived of their liberty because of crimes or infringements or non compliance with the law, whether they are accused or convicted, but also those persons who are under the custody and supervision of certain institutions." *Id.*

[38] Pueblo Bello Massacre v. Colombia, Merits, Reparations, and Costs, Judgment, Inter-Am. Ct. H.R. (ser. C) No. 140, para. 151 (Jan. 31, 2006). *But see* Veliz Franco et al. v. Guatemala, Preliminary Objections, Merits, and Reparations, Judgment, Inter-Am. Ct. H.R. (ser. C) No. 277, para. 144 (May 19, 2014) ("there is no conclusive evidence that [the victim] remained deprived of liberty prior to the moment at which she suffered the acts that resulted in her death").

[39] *E.g.*, Lysias Fleury et al. v. Haiti, Merits and Reparations, Judgment, Inter-Am. Ct. H.R. (ser. C) No. 236 (Nov. 23, 2011) ("a detention, whether for a brief period, or a 'delay,' even if merely for identification purposes, is a form of deprivation of physical liberty of the individual and, consequently, as a limitation of this liberty, it must adhere strictly to the relevant provisions of the American Convention and domestic law, provided that the latter is compatible with the Convention"); Torres Millacura et al. v. Argentina, Merits, Reparations, and Costs, Judgment, Inter-Am. Ct. H.R. (ser. C) No. 229, para. 76 (Aug. 26, 2011) (similar).

[40] *E.g.*, Palamara Iribarne v. Chile, Merits, Reparations, Costs, Judgment, Inter-Am. Ct. H.R. (ser. C) No. 135, para. 63 (Nov. 22, 2005) (4 days in one proceeding and 10 days in the other); Maritza Urrutia v. Guatemala, Merits, Reparations, and Costs, Judgment, Inter-Am. Ct. H.R. (ser. C) No. 103, para. 58(5) (Nov. 27, 2003) (eight days).

[41] In *Bayarri*, the victim endured 13 years of pretrial detention. Bayarri v. Argentina, Preliminary Objection, Merits, Reparations, and Costs, Judgment, Inter-Am. Ct. H.R. (ser. C) No. 187, para. 71 (Oct. 30, 2008). For detention during extradition proceedings, *see* Wong Ho Wing v. Peru, Preliminary Objection, Merits, Reparations and Costs, Judgment, Inter-Am. Ct. H.R. (ser. C) No. 297, para 235 (June 30, 2015).

[42] *E.g.*, Acosta Calderón v. Ecuador, Merits, Reparations, and Costs, Judgment, Inter-Am. Ct. H.R. (ser. C) No. 129, para. 50 (June 24, 2005) (six years and eight months); De La Cruz Flores v. Peru, Merits, Reparations, and Costs, Judgment, Inter-Am. Ct. H.R. (ser. C) No. 115, para. 73(53) (Nov. 18, 2004) (approximately eight years).

[43] *See* Medina, *supra* note 10, at 138 ("one could conclude that the right protected in this provision is principally the right to not be confined to a relatively small space").

base,[44] a customs facility,[45] an airport detention center,[46] a secret military detention site,[47] police stations and vehicles,[48] administrative offices of an intelligence agency,[49] and a military hospital.[50] Article 7 breaches have also been declared with respect to inmates who disappeared in prison.[51] The Court has even found violations for detentions in a church,[52] in a mine,[53] and "along the public roads" where individuals were forced to herd cattle.[54] Similar to other human rights tribunals,[55] the Court considers cases where persecuted victims have fled to other countries to implicate Article 22 rather than Article 7.[56]

2. Right to Personal Security

During many years, there was little discussion or Inter-American jurisprudence on the potentially-autonomous right to personal security. The European Court, for its part, has attributed little independent meaning to this right.[57] Nevertheless, some have argued that Article 7 still stands for the two separate concepts of security and liberty. Cecilia

---

[44] *E.g.*, Galindo Cardenas et al. v. Peru, Preliminary Objections, Merits, Reparations and Costs, Inter-Am. Ct. H.R. (ser. C) No. 301, para. 121 (Oct. 2, 2015); Cesti Hurtado v. Peru, Merits, Judgment, Inter-Am. Ct. H.R. (ser. C) No. 56, para. 76 (Sept. 29, 1999).

[45] Acosta Calderón v. Ecuador, Merits, Reparations, and Costs, Judgment, Inter-Am. Ct. H.R. (ser. C) No. 129, para. 50(9) (June 24, 2005) ("In custody of the Customs Military Police").

[46] Gangaram Panday v. Suriname, Merits, Reparations, and Costs, Judgment, Inter-Am. Ct. H.R. (ser. C) No. 16, para. 43 (Jan. 21, 1994).

[47] Maritza Urrutia v. Guatemala, Merits, Reparations, and Costs, Judgment, Inter-Am. Ct. H.R. (ser. C) No. 103, para. 58(5) (Nov. 27, 2003).

[48] *E.g.*, Gómez Paquiyauri Brothers v. Peru, Merits, Reparations, and Costs, Judgment, Inter-Am. Ct. H.R. (ser. C) No. 110, para. 67 (July 8, 2004) (trunk of a patrol car); Suárez Rosero v. Ecuador, Merits, Judgment, Inter-Am. Ct. H.R. (ser. C) No. 35, para. 46 (Nov. 12, 1997) (police station).

[49] Loayza Tamayo v. Peru, Merits, Judgment, Inter-Am. Ct. H.R. (ser. C) No. 33, para. 46(c) (Sept. 17, 1997).

[50] Bámaca Velásquez v. Guatemala, Merits, Judgment, Inter-Am. Ct. H.R. (ser. C) No. 70, para. 121(l) (Nov. 25, 2000) ("the infirmary of a military base").

[51] Neira Alegría et al. v. Peru, Merits, Judgment, Inter-Am. Ct. H.R. (ser. C) No. 20, para. 91 (Jan. 19, 1995).

[52] Baldeón García v. Peru, Merits, Reparations, and Costs, Judgment, Inter-Am. Ct. H.R. (ser. C) No. 147, paras. 2, 45 (Apr. 6, 2006).

[53] Peasant Community of Santa Barbara v. Peru, Preliminary Objections, Merits, Reparations and Costs, Judgment, Inter-Am. Ct. H.R. (ser. C) No. 299, para 168 (Sept. 1, 2015).

[54] Ituango Massacres v. Colombia, Preliminary Objections, Merits, Reparations, and Costs, Judgment, Inter-Am. Ct. H.R. (ser. C) No. 148, para. 150 (July 1, 2006).

[55] *See* NOWAK, *supra* note 2, at 212 (stating that the U.N. Human Rights Committee considers exile and expulsion from State territory to fall under the scope of freedom of movement rather than under the right to personal liberty).

[56] *E.g.*, Vélez Restrepo and Family v. Colombia, Preliminary Objections, Merits, Reparations, and Costs, Judgment, Inter-Am. Ct. H.R. (ser. C) No. 248, para. 224 (Sept. 3, 2012); Moiwana Cmty. v. Suriname, Preliminary Objections, Merits, Reparations, and Costs, Judgment, Inter-Am. Ct. H.R. (ser. C) No. 124, paras. 120–121 (June 15, 2005) (concerning both internally-displaced victims and victims exiled to another country). In *Gutiérrez Soler v. Colombia*, the Court found a violation of Article 7, among other rights; however, this was an acceptance of Colombia's recognition of liability, and was not expressly linked to the victim's exile. Gutiérrez Soler v. Colombia, Merits, Reparations, and Costs, Judgment, Inter-Am. Ct. H.R. (ser. C) No. 132, para. 52 (Sept. 12, 2005).

[57] HARRIS, O'BOYLE & WARBRICK, *supra* note 2 ; NOWAK, *supra* note 2, at 214.

Medina asserts that the right to personal security refers specifically to a detainee's right to physical integrity.[58]

To date, the Inter-American Court has not found a separate violation of the right to personal security. In *Chaparro Álvarez and Lapo Íñiguez v. Ecuador*, however, the Tribunal turned its direct attention to the principle.[59] The Court stated that security consists in "the absence of interferences that restrict or limit liberty beyond what is reasonable," and the "protection against all unlawful or arbitrary interference with physical liberty."[60] In this way, the Court closely links the concepts of physical liberty and personal security.

The Human Rights Committee takes a distinct view with wide ramifications. For the Committee, the right to security of person also applies outside the context of "formal" deprivations of liberty:

> An interpretation of article 9 which would allow a State party to ignore threats to the personal security of non-detained persons subject to its jurisdiction would render ineffective the guarantees of the Covenant. Moreover, States parties are under an obligation to take reasonable and appropriate measures to protect these persons.[61]

As a result, the Committee has applied the right to personal security to cases where either State or non-State actors have attacked or threatened non-detained individuals.[62] The Inter-American Court has not expressly taken up this interpretation of personal security, even when presented with similar circumstances.[63] Still, as noted above, the Convention's Article 7(6) protects "recourse to a competent court" for "anyone who believes himself to

[58] MEDINA, *supra* note 10, at 139.

[59] Chaparro Álvarez and Lapo Íñiguez v. Ecuador, Preliminary Objections, Merits, Reparations, and Costs, Judgment, Inter-Am. Ct. H.R. (ser. C) No. 170 (Nov. 21, 2007).

[60] *Id.* paras. 52–53.

[61] UN Human Rights Committee, Communication No. 1560/2007, Marcellana and Gumanoy v. The Philippines, Views adopted on 30 October 2008, para. 7.6. *See also* Communication No. 195/1985, Delgado Páez v. Colombia, Views adopted on 12 July 1990, para. 5.5; Communication No. 711/1996, Dias v. Angola, Views adopted on 20 March 2000, para. 8.3; Communication No. 821/1998, Chongwe v. Zambia, Views adopted on 25 October 2000, para. 5.3.

[62] *See* NOWAK, *supra* note 2, at 215.

[63] *See, e.g.*, Vélez Restrepo and Family v. Colombia, Preliminary Objections, Merits, Reparations, and Costs, Judgment, Inter-Am. Ct. H.R. (ser. C) No. 248, para. 175 (Sept. 3, 2012) (concluding that "the State can be attributed with international responsibility owing to the participation of State agents in the threats, harassment and attempted arbitrary deprivation of liberty perpetrated against [the victims]," but omitting any mention of the right to personal security). Still, there have been a couple of Court judgments involving threats and attacks where Article 7 also appears to encompass the meaning of personal security. *See, e.g.*, Valle Jaramillo et al. v. Colombia, Merits, Reparations, and Costs, Judgment, Inter-Am. Ct. H.R. (ser. C) No. 192, para. 105 (Nov. 27, 2008) (finding a violation of Colombia's obligation "to adopt the reasonable measures required to guarantee effectively the rights to personal liberty, humane treatment, and life" of a persecuted human rights advocate who was eventually executed by paramilitary agents).

be threatened with deprivation of his liberty," when such a remedy has been established in domestic law.[64]

B. GENERAL REQUIREMENTS TO DEPRIVE LIBERTY: THE PRINCIPLES OF LEGALITY AND ARBITRARINESS

1. The Legality Principle

Article 7(2) provides: "no one shall be deprived of his physical liberty except for the reasons and under the conditions established beforehand by the constitution of the State Party concerned or by a law established pursuant thereto." This reference to domestic law serves as an alternative to listing permissible scenarios for the deprivation of liberty, as provided by Article 5 of the European Convention. The ICCPR also alludes to domestic law; however, it is not as exacting as the American Convention, which demands that the relevant law form part of the State's constitution or at least be established pursuant to constitutional procedures. In this way, a detention could be considered illegal even if it follows a domestic statute, if the statute itself was inconsistent with the State's constitution.

Some commentators have criticized the Convention's reference to domestic law, and insist that the Court should not interpret national legislation except in rare cases.[65] It is true that establishing specific parameters and limitations in Article 7's text would have likely resulted in less discretion for States. In any event, the Inter-American Court has indicated some necessary elements for legal detentions, especially in its earlier judgments. In the following section, we consider situations where the Court has found illegal detentions and violations of Article 7(2).

a. *Restriction of Liberty Always the Exception*

The general principle in this area is that "liberty is always the rule, and its limitation or restriction always the exception."[66] This requirement must pervade national legislation and serve as the guiding principle for an analysis of legality. According to the Convention and Court, personal liberty can only be deprived according to a legislative statute or constitutional provision.[67] Moreover, the "reasons"

---

[64] American Convention, art. 7(6).

[65] *See* MEDINA, *supra* note 10, at 142; HÉCTOR GROS ESPIELL, LA CONVENCIÓN AMERICANA Y LA CONVENCIÓN EUROPEA DE DERECHOS HUMANOS: ANÁLISIS COMPARATIVO 89 (1991).

[66] *E.g.*, Norín Catrimán et al. (Leaders, members, and activists of the Mapuche Indigenous People) v. Chile, Merits, Reparations, and Costs, Judgment, Inter-Am. Ct. H.R. (ser. C) No. 279, para. 309 (May 29, 2014); Tibi v. Ecuador, Preliminary Objections, Merits, Reparations, and Costs, Judgment, Inter-Am. Ct. H.R. (ser. C) No. 114, para. 106 (Sept. 7, 2004).

[67] Such laws have been explained by the Court in an advisory opinion: "the word 'laws' in Article 30 of the Convention means a general legal norm tied to the general welfare, passed by democratically elected legislative

and "conditions" that permit such limitations must have a legitimate purpose and be previously[68] established in an express and detailed manner.[69] The Court has held that the following purposes are, in principle, legitimate for the deprivation of liberty: securing public safety,[70] preventing crime,[71] ensuring that "the accused does not prevent" criminal proceedings,[72] facilitating extradition processes,[73] and regulating migration.[74]

Considering that the majority of persons deprived of liberty are within the criminal justice system, it must be stressed that the Court condemns "general or specific preventive objectives" for detention.[75] For a domestic law to be compatible with the Convention, it must require "sufficient evidence" of criminal responsibility and follow a single objective: ensure that the accused "will not prevent the implementation of the proceeding or evade the action of justice."[76] In this way, "the personal characteristics of the supposed perpetrator and the seriousness of the offense" are not "sufficient justification for the preventive detention."[77] National law must provide alternative measures to pretrial detention to ensure a court appearance.[78]

---

bodies established by the Constitution, and formulated according to the procedures set forth by the constitutions of the States Parties for that purpose." The Word "Laws" in Article 30 of the American Convention on Human Rights, Advisory Opinion OC-6/86, Inter-Am. Ct. H.R. (ser. A) No. 6, para. 38 (May 9, 1986).

[68] Chaparro Álvarez and Lapo Íñiguez v. Ecuador, Preliminary Objections, Merits, Reparations, and Costs, Judgment, Inter-Am. Ct. H.R. (ser. C) No. 170, para. 57 (Nov. 21, 2007).

[69] Canese v. Paraguay, Merits, Reparations, and Costs, Judgment, Inter-Am. Ct. H.R. (ser. C) No. 111, para. 117 (Aug. 31, 2004).

[70] Servellón García et al. v. Honduras, Merits, Reparations, and Costs, Judgment, Inter-Am. Ct. H.R. (ser. C) No. 152, para. 92 (Sept. 21, 2006).

[71] *E.g.*, Torres Millacura et al. v. Argentina, Merits, Reparations, and Costs, Judgment, Inter-Am. Ct. H.R. (ser. C) No. 229, para. 69 (Aug. 26, 2011); Cabrera García and Montiel Flores v. Mexico, Preliminary Objections, Merits, Reparations, and Costs, Judgment, Inter-Am. Ct. H.R. (ser. C) No. 220 (Nov. 26, 2010).

[72] Chaparro Álvarez and Lapo Íñiguez v. Ecuador, Preliminary Objections, Merits, Reparations, and Costs, Judgment, Inter-Am. Ct. H.R., (ser. C) No. 170, para. 93 (Nov. 21, 2007).

[73] Wong Ho Wing v. Peru, Preliminary Objection, Merits, Reparations, and Costs, Judgment, Inter-Am. Ct. H.R. (ser. C) No. 297, para. 250 (June 30, 2015).

[74] *E.g.*, Nadege Dorzema et al. v. Dominican Republic, 2012 Inter-Am. Ct. H.R. (ser. C) No. 251, para. 124 (Oct. 24, 2012); Vélez Loor v. Panama, Preliminary Objections, Merits, Reparations, and Costs, Judgment, Inter-Am. Ct. H.R. (ser. C) No. 218, para. 169 (Nov. 23, 2010).

[75] *E.g.*, J. v. Peru, Preliminary Objections, Merits, Reparations, and Costs, Judgment, Inter-Am. Ct. H.R. (ser. C) No. 275, para. 159 (Nov. 27, 2013); Chaparro Álvarez and Lapo Íñiguez v. Ecuador, Preliminary Objections, Merits, Reparations, and Costs, Judgment, Inter-Am. Ct. H.R. (ser. C) No. 170, para. 103 (Nov. 21, 2007).

[76] J. v. Peru, Preliminary Objections, Merits, Reparations, and Costs, Judgment, Inter-Am. Ct. H.R. (ser. C) No. 275, para. 159 (Nov. 27, 2013).

[77] *E.g., id.*; López Álvarez v. Honduras, Merits, Reparations, and Costs, Judgment, Inter-Am. Ct. H.R. (ser. C) No. 141, para. 69 (Feb. 1, 2006).

[78] *E.g.*, J. v. Peru, Preliminary Objections, Merits, Reparations, and Costs, Judgment, Inter-Am. Ct. H.R. (ser. C) No. 275, para. 157 (Nov. 27, 2013); Tibi v. Ecuador, Preliminary Objections, Merits, Reparations, and Costs, Judgment, Inter-Am. Ct. H.R. (ser. C) No. 114, para. 106 (Sept. 7, 2004). Curiously, although these are all elements of legality, since *Norín Catrimán* et al. *v. Chile* the Court has assessed them under the concept of arbitrariness. *See* Norín Catrimán et al. (Leaders, members, and activists of the Mapuche Indigenous People)

Finally, the law must lack ambiguity such that it prevents arbitrary interpretations by State authorities—particularly undesirable when fundamental rights such as personal liberty may be curtailed.[79] This aspect of legality, more precisely called legal certainty (*nullum crimen, nulla poena sine lege certa*), holds an important place in the Court's case law and the Convention's Article 9.[80] As explained below and in the chapter on freedom of expression, however, it is currently uncommon for the Court to find violations when domestic law fails to comply with the principle of legal certainty.[81]

b. Ordered by a Competent Judicial Authority

I. SYNTHESIS According to Inter-American and global human rights law, a written and justified order, issued previous to the arrest by a competent judge, is indispensable for a legal detention.[82] The exception to this rule is when the individual has been caught in a criminal act, in flagrante delicto.[83] The judicial order or warrant provides fundamental safeguards; disregarding a warrant results in violations of the rights to due process (Article 8) and judicial protection (Article 25), in addition to personal liberty.[84]

In numerous cases the Court has found a violation of Article 7(2) for lack of judicial orders.[85] However, on occasion the Court skips an examination of the judicial order and the legal basis for the detention, proceeding directly to an analysis of arbitrariness.[86] It should be noted that arrests are not legal merely because they were carried out in

v. Chile, Merits, Reparations, and Costs, Judgment, Inter-Am. Ct. H.R. (ser. C) No. 279, paras. 310–312 (May 29, 2014).

[79] *E.g.*, Canese v. Paraguay, Merits, Reparations, and Costs, Judgment, Inter-Am. Ct. H.R. (ser. C) No. 111, para. 125 (Aug. 31, 2004); Cantoral Benavides v. Peru, Merits, Judgment, Inter Am. Ct. H.R. (ser. C) No. 69, para. 157 (Aug. 18, 2000).

[80] *See* Thomas M. Antkowiak, *Artículo 9: Principio de Legalidad y de Retroactividad, in* LA CONVENCIÓN AMERICANA SOBRE DERECHOS HUMANOS COMENTADA 257–59 (Christian Steiner & Patricia Uribe eds., 2014).

[81] *See also* this volume's Chapter 7: Freedom of Expression.

[82] *E.g.*, Chaparro Álvarez and Lapo Íñiguez v. Ecuador, Preliminary Objections, Merits, Reparations, and Costs, Judgment, Inter-Am. Ct. H.R. (ser. C) No. 170, para. 68 (Nov. 21, 2007) ("any arrest carried out without a written judicial order, except *in flagrante delicto,* would be unlawful"); Inter-Am. Comm'n H.R., Report on Terrorism and Human Rights, OEA/Ser.L/V/II.116, Doc. 5 rev. 1 corr. (22 October 2002), para. 121 (similar), *available at* http://www.cidh.org/terrorism/eng/part.d.htm#_ftnref331.

[83] Chaparro Álvarez and Lapo Íñiguez v. Ecuador, Preliminary Objections, Merits, Reparations, and Costs, Judgment, Inter-Am. Ct. H.R. (ser. C) No. 170, para. 68 (Nov. 21, 2007).

[84] *E.g.*, Ticona Estrada et al. v. Bolivia, Merits, Reparations, and Costs, Judgment, Inter-Am. Ct. H.R. (ser. C) No. 191, para. 61 (Nov. 27, 2008); Maritza Urrutia v. Guatemala, Merits, Reparations, and Costs, Judgment, Inter-Am. Ct. H.R. (ser. C) No. 103, para. 67 (Nov. 27, 2003).

[85] *E.g.*, Barrios Family v. Venezuela, Merits, Reparations, and Costs, Judgment, Inter-Am. Ct. H.R. (ser. C) No. 237, para. 65 (Nov. 24, 2011); La Cantuta v. Peru, Merits, Reparations, and Costs, Judgment, Inter-Am. Ct. H.R. (ser. C) No. 162, para. 109 (Nov. 29, 2006).

[86] *See* Cabrera García and Montiel Flores v. Mexico, Preliminary Objections, Merits, Reparations, and Costs, Judgment, Inter-Am. Ct. H.R. (ser. C) No. 220, para. 102 (Nov. 26, 2010).

conjunction with a distinct judicial order, such as a search warrant; judges must issue specific arrest warrants for the deprivation of liberty to be permissible.[87]

II. DETENTIONS WITHOUT JUDICIAL WARRANTS: EXCEPTIONAL CASES

The deprivation of liberty in flagrante delicto constitutes international law's central exception to the requirement for a judicial warrant. In many judgments the Court has determined that judicial orders and flagrante delicto have not been demonstrated.[88] However, it still has not explained what the American Convention precisely requires in order to qualify as a legitimate arrest in flagrante delicto. Normally, flagrante delicto calls for strict temporal and spatial proximity to the crime; that is, when the accused is surprised in the act of committing an offense, or is pursued and caught immediately after having done so.[89]

In two of four Court judgments where the State claimed a legal arrest based on flagrante delicto, the Tribunal referred to domestic law and denied the arguments.[90] It offered sparse reasoning for its conclusions, although in *Paniagua Morales* et al. *v. Guatemala* the Tribunal remarked, "the mere fact of [the victims'] acquittal . . . shows that they were not caught in the act."[91] In the other two judgments, the Court found the detentions legal owing to flagrante delicto.[92] For example, in *Acosta Calderón v. Ecuador*, customs police arrested Acosta Calderón, upon finding him in possession of a substance that appeared to be an illegal drug. The Court has emphasized that there must be "immediate" judicial supervision of flagrante delicto arrests, in order to comply with the protections of Article 7 against arbitrariness and illegality.[93] "The procedures regarding the verification of the elements of the crime" must of course be followed to justify any ongoing detention and the initiation of a criminal case against the accused person.[94]

---

[87] Uzcátegui et al. v. Venezuela, Merits and Reparations, Judgment, Inter-Am. Ct. H.R. (ser. C) No. 249, paras. 149–154 (Sept. 3, 2012).

[88] *E.g.*, Barrios Family v. Venezuela, Merits, Reparations, and Costs, Judgment, Inter-Am. Ct. H.R. (ser. C) No. 237, para. 65 (Nov. 24, 2011); Lysias Fleury et al. v. Haiti, Merits and Reparations, Judgment, Inter-Am. Ct. H.R. (ser. C) No. 236, para. 56 (Nov. 23, 2011).

[89] *E.g.*, Committee Against Torture, Report on Mexico Produced by the Committee under Article 20 of the Convention, and Reply from the Government Of Mexico, CAT/C/75, para. 177 (2003); BLACK'S LAW DICTIONARY (8th ed. 2004).

[90] "White Van" (Paniagua Morales et al.) v. Guatemala, Merits, Judgment, Inter-Am. Ct. H.R. (ser. C) No. 37, para. 111 (Mar. 8, 1998); Suárez Rosero v. Ecuador, Merits, Judgment, Inter-Am. Ct. H.R. (ser. C) No. 35, paras. 34, 44 (Nov. 12, 1997).

[91] "White Van" (Paniagua Morales et al.) v. Guatemala, Merits, Judgment, Inter-Am. Ct. H.R. (ser. C) No. 37, para. 111 (Mar. 8, 1998).

[92] López Álvarez v. Honduras, Merits, Reparations, and Costs, Judgment, Inter-Am. Ct. H.R. (ser. C) No. 141, para. 65 (Feb.1, 2006); Acosta Calderón v. Ecuador, Merits, Reparations, and Costs, Judgment, Inter-Am. Ct. H.R. (ser. C) No. 129, para. 61 (June 24, 2005).

[93] López Álvarez v. Honduras, Merits, Reparations, and Costs, Judgment, Inter-Am. Ct. H.R. (ser. C) No. 141, para. 64 (Feb.1, 2006).

[94] Acosta Calderón v. Ecuador, Merits, Reparations, and Costs, Judgment, Inter-Am. Ct. H.R. (ser. C) No. 129, para. 62 (June 24, 2005).

For many years the Court has analyzed the limits on State authority to detain in states of emergency, in order to maintain national security or public safety.[95] According to the American Convention, the right to personal liberty may be suspended in a "time of war, public danger, or other emergency that threatens the independence or security of a State Party."[96] These exceptional circumstances, then, may relax the requirements of legal detention, whereby domestic law must normally be followed, a judicial order issued, and the arrest primarily carried out by law enforcement officials. Nevertheless, the State Party may never suspend essential judicial guarantees such as habeas corpus.[97]

To analyze legality in these cases, the Court examines the decree that declares the state of emergency. In this way, the legal basis for detention changes: the executive order or decree temporarily replaces the relevant legislative statute. In these circumstances, pursuant to Article 27 of the American Convention, the State must "immediately inform the other States Parties . . . of the provisions . . . it has suspended, the reasons that gave rise to the suspension, and the date set for the termination of such suspension." The Court has repeatedly held that the suspension "must not exceed the limits strictly required"; further, "any action on the part of the public authorities that goes beyond those limits, which must be specified with precision in the decree," will be illegal.[98]

In this context, the Tribunal has conceded that the State's armed forces may take measures to restrict the personal liberty of civilians, provided that the military follows "strict criteria of exceptionality and due diligence" to respect human rights, "taking into account that the regime of the military forces is not in accordance with the functions intrinsic to civil authorities."[99] In *Osorio Rivera and Family v. Peru*, the Court found that the initial detention "was carried out in keeping with the attributes of the military forces

---

[95] *E.g.*, Galindo Cardenas et al. v. Peru, Preliminary Objections, Merits, Reparations and Costs, Judgment, Inter-Am. Ct. H.R. (ser. C) No. 301, para. 190 (Oct. 2, 2015); Castillo Páez v. Peru, Merits, Judgment, Inter-Am. Ct. H.R. (ser. C) No. 34, para. 56 (Nov. 3, 1997).

[96] American Convention, art. 27(1).

[97] *E.g.*, Osorio Rivera and Family v. Peru, Preliminary Objections, Merits, Reparations, and Costs, Judgment, Inter-Am. Ct. H.R. (ser. C) No. 274, para. 120 (Nov. 26, 2013); Habeas Corpus in Emergency Situations (Arts. 27(2), 25(1), and 7(6) American Convention on Human Rights), Advisory Opinion OC-8/87, Inter-Am. Ct. H.R. (ser. A) No. 8, para. 24 (Jan. 30, 1987).

[98] *E.g.*, Castillo Petruzzi et al. v. Peru, Merits, Reparations, and Costs, Judgment, Inter-Am. Ct. H.R. (ser. C) No. 52, para. 109 (May 30, 1999); Habeas Corpus in Emergency Situations (Arts. 27(2), 25(1), and 7(6) American Convention on Human Rights), Advisory Opinion OC-8/87, Inter-Am. Ct. H.R. (ser. A) No. 8, para. 38 (Jan. 30, 1987).

[99] Osorio Rivera and Family v. Peru, Preliminary Objections, Merits, Reparations, and Costs, Judgment, Inter-Am. Ct. H.R. (ser. C) No. 274, para. 122 (Nov. 26, 2013); Cabrera García and Montiel Flores v. Mexico, Preliminary Objections, Merits, Reparations, and Costs, Judgment, Inter-Am. Ct. H.R. (ser. C) No. 220, para. 89 (Nov. 26, 2010).

during the state of emergency" in Cajatambo Province.[100] However, it observed that Osorio Rivera was then transferred to a military base without bringing him before the competent authority and registering his detention. For the Tribunal, these circumstances amounted to an "abuse of power" and an illegitimate exercise of military force in the name of national security.[101]

As mentioned, critical judicial guarantees such as habeas corpus must still be available in states of emergency. When they are omitted, whether in the State's executive order or in practice, a violation to personal liberty results. According to the Court, the executive order, "whatever its breadth" or context, "cannot entail the suppression or ineffectiveness of the judicial guarantees that the Convention requires."[102]

The Court has also ruled on massive, indiscriminate detentions carried out by State security forces. States have arrested many individuals—often economically-disadvantaged youth or immigrants—suspected to "represent a risk or danger to the safety of others, without substantiated evidence that an offense has been committed."[103] The Court has held that these actions flout basic rights, such as the right to be presumed innocent, and elude fundamental protections, such as the judicial arrest warrant (except with flagrante delicto arrests).[104] Thus, in the absence of judicial oversight and "elements to individualize and separate the behaviors of each of the detainees," these operations constitute illegal and arbitrary detentions.[105]

c. State Obligation to Register Detentions

To protect against interferences with the right to personal liberty, the Tribunal has held that all detentions must be "duly registered in the pertinent record, indicating clearly, at a minimum, the reasons for the detention, who carried out the detention, the time of the

---

[100] Osorio Rivera and Family v. Peru, Preliminary Objections, Merits, Reparations, and Costs, Judgment, Inter-Am. Ct. H.R. (ser. C) No. 274, para. 167 (Nov. 26, 2013).

[101] *Id.* The Court declared only a generic Article 7 violation, and thus did not specify that Article 7(2) was breached.

[102] *E.g.*, Castillo Petruzzi et al. v. Peru, Merits, Reparations, and Costs, Judgment, Inter-Am. Ct. H.R. (ser. C) No. 52, para. 186 (May 30, 1999); Judicial Guarantees in States of Emergency (Arts. 27(2), 25, and 8 American Convention on Human Rights), Advisory Opinion OC-9/87, Inter-Am. Ct. H.R. (ser. A) No. 9, para. 25 (Oct. 6, 1987).

[103] *E.g.*, Pacheco Teruel et al. v. Honduras, Merits, Reparations, and Costs, Judgment, Inter-Am. Ct. H.R. (ser. C) No. 241, para. 108 (Apr. 27, 2012); Servellón García et al. v. Honduras, Merits, Reparations, and Costs, Judgment, Inter-Am. Ct. H.R. (ser. C) No. 152, para. 93 (Sept. 21, 2006). For a judgment concerning immigrants, *see* Expelled Dominicans and Haitians v. Dominican Republic, Preliminary Objections, Merits, Reparations, and Costs, Judgment, Inter-Am. Ct. H.R. (ser. C) No. 282, para. 348 (Aug. 28, 2014).

[104] *E.g.*, Pacheco Teruel et al. v. Honduras, Merits, Reparations, and Costs, Judgment, Inter-Am. Ct. H.R. (ser. C) No. 241, para. 108 (Apr. 27, 2012); Bulacio v. Argentina, Merits, Reparations, and Costs, Judgment, Inter-Am. Ct. H.R. (ser. C) No. 100, para. 137 (Sept. 18, 2003).

[105] Servellón García et al. v. Honduras, Merits, Reparations, and Costs, Judgment, Inter-Am. Ct. H.R. (ser. C) No. 152, paras. 92–93 (Sept. 21, 2006).

detention, and the time of release."[106] There also must be evidence that the judge with jurisdiction over the matter has been informed.[107] Failure to follow these requirements frequently has breached paragraphs 1 and 2 of Article 7.[108]

d. Detention Time Limits and Orders for Release

Unsurprisingly, the Court has found a violation to Article 7(2) when the length of the detention exceeded the limit specified in domestic law. In *Chaparro Álvarez*, for example, Ecuador's Code of Criminal Procedure established a maximum detention period of 48 hours for "investigative purposes."[109] Yet the two victims were detained for four days before they made their first statements before a prosecutor, and were held 22 days more before they could testify before a judge.[110] In *Cesti Hurtado v. Peru*, military authorities refused to obey a judicial order for the victim's release.[111] The Court found that Cesti Hurtado's continued detention violated his right to personal liberty in the terms of Article 7(2), among others.[112]

e. Pretrial Detention as Illegal Detention

In general, the Court conceptualizes pretrial detention as arbitrary detention under the framework of Article 7(3), as examined below. Still, there are Tribunal judgments that have held pretrial detention to be illegal. In *Palamara Iribarne v. Chile*, the Court found a violation of Article 7(2) along with Convention Article 8(2), which establishes the presumption of innocence, among other guarantees. The Tribunal concluded that insufficient evidence existed to rebut the presumption of innocence and arrest Palamara Iribarne, and thus his pretrial detention was contrary to domestic law and the American Convention.[113]

f. Court's Increasing Reluctance to Find Violations of Article 7(2)

The Court appears increasingly reticent to find violations of Article 7(2) and the legality principle, preferring instead to focus its analysis on Article 7(3). In a pair of judgments against Peru, the Tribunal concluded that the legality principle was not violated by a

---

[106] Guidel Alvarez et al. ("Diario Militar") v. Guatemala, Merits, Reparations, and Costs, Judgment, Inter-Am. Ct. H.R. (ser. C) No. 253, para. 197 (Nov. 20, 2012). *See also* Galindo Cardenas et al. v. Peru, Preliminary Objections, Merits, Reparations and Costs, Inter-Am. Ct. H.R. (ser. C) No. 301, para. 194 (Oct. 2, 2015).

[107] Guidel Alvarez et al. ("Diario Militar") v. Guatemala, Merits, Reparations, and Costs, Judgment, Inter-Am. Ct. H.R. (ser. C) No. 253, para. 197 (Nov. 20, 2012).

[108] *Id.*

[109] Chaparro Álvarez and Lapo Íñiguez v. Ecuador, Preliminary Objections, Merits, Reparations, and Costs, Judgment, Inter-Am. Ct. H.R. (ser. C) No. 170, para. 82 (Nov. 21, 2007).

[110] *Id.* para. 83.

[111] Cesti Hurtado v. Peru, Merits, Judgment, Inter-Am. Ct. H.R. (ser. C) No. 56, para. 143 (Sept. 29, 1999).

[112] *Id.* (violating paragraphs 1, 2, and 3 of Article 7).

[113] Palamara Iribarne v. Chile, Merits, Reparations, Costs, Judgment, Inter-Am. Ct. H.R. (ser. C) No. 135, para. 213 (Nov. 22, 2005).

vague law, which, according to Judge Cecilia Medina's dissent, "failed to distinguish the conduct described therein from other crimes that carry a lesser criminal sanction."[114] In *Torres Millacura* et al. *v. Argentina*, the Tribunal only based the violation of Article 7(2) on the failure to register the detention; it left for its Article 7(3) analysis the fact that the domestic law did not establish "concrete reasons" for arrest—and thus allowed police to act arbitrarily.[115]

Further, *Pacheco Teruel* et al. *v. Honduras* involved a vague, "anti-gang" criminal statute that granted wide discretion to law enforcement officials.[116] After assessing the law's text and the State's own admission of its ambiguity, the Court decided that it violated the Convention's Article 9 and Article 2 (Domestic Legal Effects). However, rather than considering the arrests resulting from this law as illegal in breach of Article 7(2), the Tribunal found them arbitrary in violation of Article 7(3).[117] Finally, in *Norín Catrimán* et al. *v. Chile*, the Court chose not to criticize a domestic law that allowed pretrial detention of persons deemed "dangerous for the security of society."[118] The law was not found per se incompatible with the American Convention because its terms "could be interpreted in a way that was consistent with it."[119] The Court concluded that Article 7(3)—not Article 7(2) or Article 2—was violated, among other Convention provisions, due to "the judicial interpretation and application of these norms."[120] In sum, these judgments should have found violations to Article 7(2), among other Convention terms, because the domestic laws in question ran afoul of the legality principle.[121] However, the Court—likely to avoid the politically-sensitive business of scrutinizing national legislation—has preferred to focus on the application of laws under Article 7(3).

---

[114] García Asto and Ramírez Rojas v. Peru, Preliminary Objection, Merits, Reparations, and Costs, Judgment, Inter-Am. Ct. H.R. (ser. C) No. 137, para. 4 (Nov. 25, 2005) (dissenting opinion of Judge Medina Quiroga); Berenson Mejia v. Peru, Merits, Reparations, and Costs, Judgment, Inter-Am. Ct. H.R. (ser. C) No. 119, para. 3 (Nov. 25, 2004) (dissenting opinion of Judge Medina Quiroga). *See also* Espinoza Gonzales v. Peru, Preliminary Objections, Merits, Reparations, Costs, Judgment, Inter-Am. Ct. H.R. (ser. C) No. 289, paras. 118 and 121 (Nov. 20, 2014) (also avoiding a legality assessment of Peruvian law); Usón Ramírez v. Venezuela, Preliminary Objection, Merits, Reparations, and Costs, Judgment, Inter-Am. Ct. H.R. (ser. C) No. 207, para. 155 (Nov. 20, 2009) (failing to consider the impact upon Article 7 of the ambiguous crime of "insult against the armed forces").

[115] Torres Millacura et al. v. Argentina, Merits, Reparations, and Costs, Judgment, Inter-Am. Ct. H.R. (ser. C) No. 229, para. 80 (Aug. 26, 2011).

[116] Pacheco Teruel et al. v. Honduras, Merits, Reparations, and Costs, Judgment, Inter-Am. Ct. H.R. (ser. C) No. 241, para. 61 (Apr. 27, 2012).

[117] *Id.*

[118] Norín Catrimán et al. (Leaders, members, and activist of the Mapuche Indigenous People) v. Chile, Merits, Reparations, and Costs, Judgment, Inter-Am. Ct. H.R. (ser. C) No. 279, para. 305 (May 29, 2014).

[119] *Id.* para. 364.

[120] *Id.*

[121] *See also* Cabrera García and Montiel Flores v. Mexico, Preliminary Objections, Merits, Reparations, and Costs, Judgment, Inter-Am. Ct. H.R. (ser. C) No. 220 (Nov. 26, 2010) (avoiding the opportunity to find a violation of Article 7(2) and confirm the illegal nature of most military arrests in Mexico).

2. The Arbitrariness Principle

a. Synthesis

Article 7(3), rather than specifying permissible detention scenarios, simply establishes "No one shall be subject to arbitrary arrest or imprisonment."[122] Interpreting the provision, the Inter-American Court has repeatedly held that no one may be arrested or detained

> for reasons and by methods which, although classified as legal, could be deemed incompatible with respect for the fundamental rights of the individual because, among other matters, they are unreasonable, unforeseeable or disproportionate.[123]

Similarly, the ICCPR drafters considered that arbitrariness "went beyond" unlawful and "contained elements of injustice, unpredictability, unreasonableness, capriciousness and disproportionality, as well as the Anglo-American principle of due process of law."[124] The Court has found many violations to Article 7(3), primarily in cases involving pretrial detention and forced disappearance.

b. Forced Disappearances

The Court has decided dozens of cases concerning the personal liberty of victims who were detained and subsequently disappeared. Its approach to Article 7 has varied in these judgments. The more recent tendency consists in finding a generic Article 7 violation and omitting an analysis of the Article's various paragraphs.[125] The Court has affirmed that any type of detention that initiates a forced disappearance is contrary to Article 7.[126]

The Inter-American System typically considers forced disappearance to consist of "multiple acts" that violate "simultaneously" several Convention rights: Articles 5 (Right

---

[122] American Convention, art. 7(3).

[123] *E.g.*, Neptune v. Haiti, Merits, Reparations, and Costs, Judgment, Inter-Am. Ct. H.R. (ser. C) No. 180, para. 97 (May 6, 2008); Gangaram Panday v. Suriname, Merits, Reparations, and Costs, Judgment, Inter-Am. Ct. H.R. (ser. C) No. 16, para. 47 (Jan. 21, 1994). More recently, the Court has explicitly considered the purpose and the proportionality of the restriction to liberty. *See* Wong Ho Wing v. Peru, Preliminary Objection, Merits, Reparations, and Costs, Judgment, Inter-Am. Ct. H.R. (ser. C) No. 297, para. 248 (June 30, 2015); Argüelles et al. v. Argentina, Preliminary Objections, Merits, Reparations, and Costs, Judgment, Inter-Am. Ct. H.R. (ser. C) No. 288, para. 120 (Nov. 20, 2014).

[124] NOWAK, *supra* note 2, at 225.

[125] *E.g.*, Rodriguez Vera et al. (Persons Disappeared from the Palace of Justice) v. Colombia, Preliminary Objections, Merits, Reparations, and Costs, Judgment, Inter-Am. Ct. H.R. (ser. C) No. 287, para. 324 (Nov. 14, 2014); La Cantuta v. Peru, Merits, Reparations, and Costs, Judgment, Inter-Am. Ct. H.R. (ser. C) No. 162, para. 116 (Nov. 29, 2006). In the case of massacres, when victims were briefly detained before execution, the Court's tendency also is to find a generic violation of Article 7. *See* Massacres of El Mozote and Nearby Places v. El Salvador, Merits, Reparations, and Costs, Judgment, Inter-Am. Ct. H.R. (ser. C) No. 252, para. 158 (Oct. 25, 2012).

[126] *E.g.*, Bámaca Velásquez v. Guatemala, Merits, Judgment, Inter-Am. Ct. H.R. (ser. C) No. 70, para. 142 (Nov. 25, 2000); Velasquez Rodriguez v. Honduras, Merits, Judgment, Inter-Am. Ct. H.R. (ser. C) No. 4, para.186 (July 29, 1988).

to Humane Treatment), 7, 4 (Right to Life), and 3 (Right to Juridical Personality).[127] In addition, the Tribunal considers forced disappearance to be a violation that continues in time until the corpse is recovered.[128] As a result, if a forced disappearance is proven, a State will usually be held responsible for all of its component violations—including Article 7—even if the detention occurred before the State accepted the Court's jurisdiction.[129]

c. *Pretrial Detention as Arbitrary Detention*

The Inter-American Commission has called "the excessive use of pretrial detention among the most serious and widespread problems" in the Americas.[130] It defines "pretrial" or "preventive" detention as "the whole period of deprivation of liberty of a suspected offender ordered by a judicial authority and prior to a final judgment."[131] Although most Inter-American cases concern pretrial detention in ordinary criminal proceedings, there are also instances of this practice ordered by military and immigration authorities.[132]

As noted previously, pretrial detention has not always been analyzed under the framework of arbitrariness, but the Court's most recent judgments have applied Article 7(3), as well as Article 7(5), to examine this phenomenon. A decision for pretrial detention must be exceptional, showing both sufficient evidence of criminal responsibility and verified risks to the criminal proceeding.[133] It must also uphold the presumption of innocence, as

---

[127] *E.g.*, Rodriguez Vera et al. (Persons Disappeared from the Palace of Justice) v. Colombia, Preliminary Objections, Merits, Reparations, and Costs, Judgment, Inter-Am. Ct. H.R. (ser. C) No. 287, para. 321 (Nov. 14, 2014); Anzualdo Castro v. Peru, Preliminary Objections, Merits, Reparations, and Costs, Judgment, Inter-Am. Ct. H.R. (ser. C) No. 202, paras. 89–103 (Sept. 22, 2009). For more on forced disappearance, *see* this volume's Chapter 3, on the right to life.

[128] Rodriguez Vera et al. (Persons Disappeared from the Palace of Justice) v. Colombia, Preliminary Objections, Merits, Reparations, and Costs, Judgment, Inter-Am. Ct. H.R. (ser. C) No. 287, paras. 321, 327 (Nov. 14, 2014).

[129] *See, e.g.*, Radilla Pacheco v. Mexico, Preliminary Objections, Merits, Reparations, and Costs, Judgment, Inter-Am. Ct. H.R. (ser. C) No. 209, paras. 150, 159 (Nov. 23, 2009) (holding Mexico responsible for forced disappearance although the detention occurred before it ratified American Convention and accepted Court's jurisdiction). However, in the earlier judgment *Blake v. Guatemala*, the Court had not yet developed this approach. Blake v. Guatemala, Merits, Judgment, Inter-Am. Ct. H.R. (ser. C) No. 36, para. 82 (Jan. 24, 1998). For a full discussion of these matters, *see* this volume's Chapter 3, on the right to life.

[130] Inter-Am. Comm'n H.R., Report on the Use of Pretrial Detention in the Americas, OEA/Ser.L/V/II., Doc. 46/13 (Dec. 30, 2013), para. 1, *available at* www.oas.org/en/iachr/pdl/reports/pdfs/Report-PD-2013-en.pdf.

[131] *Id.* para. 37.

[132] *See, e.g.*, Vélez Loor v. Panama, Preliminary Objections, Merits, Reparations, and Costs, Judgment, Inter-Am. Ct. H.R. (ser. C) No. 218, para. 169 (Nov. 23, 2010) (regarding immigration detention); Palamara Iribarne v. Chile, Merits, Reparations, Costs, Judgment, Inter-Am. Ct. H.R. (ser. C) No. 135 (Nov. 22, 2005) (concerning pretrial detention in military proceedings).

[133] *E.g.*, Norín Catrimán et al. (Leaders, members, and activist of the Mapuche Indigenous People) v. Chile, Merits, Reparations, and Costs, Judgment, Inter-Am. Ct. H.R. (ser. C) No. 279, paras. 310–312 (May 29, 2014); J. v. Peru, Preliminary Objections, Merits, Reparations, and Costs, Judgment, Inter-Am. Ct. H.R. (ser. C) No. 275, para. 159 (Nov. 27, 2013).

well as the principles of legality, necessity, and proportionality.[134] A judge must periodically review a continuing case of pretrial detention.[135]

I. SUFFICIENT EVIDENCE OF CRIMINAL RESPONSIBILITY According to the Court, sufficient evidence must permit "the reasonable supposition that the individual . . . has taken part in the unlawful act under investigation."[136] Similarly, the European Convention allows for arrest "on reasonable suspicion of having committed an offence or when it is reasonably considered necessary to prevent his committing an offence or fleeing after having done so."[137] The European Court interprets "reasonable suspicion" in this context as "the existence of facts or information which would satisfy an objective observer that the person concerned may have committed an offence."[138]

The Inter-American Court has found pretrial detention to be arbitrary in cases where insufficient proof of the crime was shown.[139] To illustrate, in *Acosta Calderón v. Ecuador*, Acosta Calderón was held for over five years in pretrial detention for alleged cocaine possession.[140] However, the State had never complied with its own laws to demonstrate, through chemical analysis, that the "substance in question" was in fact cocaine.[141] The only evidentiary basis offered was a police statement; as a result, the Court found the detention to be arbitrary. In *Norín Catrimán* et al. *v. Chile*, the Court determined that pretrial detention had been ordered based on uncorroborated, "confidential testimony," which the defense had been unable to challenge.[142] Consequently, the pretrial detention was found arbitrary, in violation of Article 7(3), among other provisions.

II. RISKS TO THE CRIMINAL PROCEEDING Even when sufficient evidence exists, pretrial detention "can only be based on one legitimate goal: to ensure that the accused will not prevent the implementation of the proceeding or evade the action of justice."[143] The individual's personal characteristics or the seriousness of the

---

[134] Norín Catrimán et al. v. Chile, Merits, Reparations, and Costs, Judgment, Inter-Am. Ct. H.R. (ser. C) No. 279, para. 310 (May 29, 2014).

[135] Argüelles et al. v. Argentina, Preliminary Objections, Merits, Reparations, and Costs, Judgment, Inter-Am. Ct. H.R. (ser. C) No. 288, paras. 121–122 and 128 (Nov. 20, 2014).

[136] *Id.* para. 311.

[137] European Convention, art. 5(1)(c).

[138] HARRIS, O'BOYLE & WARBRICK, *supra* note 2, at 317.

[139] *E.g.*, Acosta Calderón v. Ecuador, Merits, Reparations, and Costs, Judgment, Inter-Am. Ct. H.R. (ser. C) No. 129, para. 70 (June 24, 2005); Tibi v. Ecuador, Preliminary Objections, Merits, Reparations, and Costs, Judgment, Inter-Am. Ct. H.R. (ser. C) No. 114, para. 107 (Sept. 7, 2004).

[140] Acosta Calderón v. Ecuador, Merits, Reparations, and Costs, Judgment, Inter-Am. Ct. H.R. (ser. C) No. 129, para. 70 (June 24, 2005).

[141] *Id.*

[142] Norín Catrimán et al. (Leaders, members, and activist of the Mapuche Indigenous People) v. Chile, Merits, Reparations, and Costs, Judgment, Inter-Am. Ct. H.R. (ser. C) No. 279, para. 334 (May 29, 2014).

[143] *E.g.*, J. v. Peru, Preliminary Objections, Merits, Reparations, and Costs, Judgment, Inter-Am. Ct. H.R. (ser. C) No. 275, para. 159 (Nov. 27, 2013); Barreto Leiva v. Venezuela, Merits, Reparations, and Costs, Judgment, Inter-Am. Ct. H.R. (ser. C) No. 206, para. 111 (Nov. 17, 2009).

criminal charges "are not, in themselves, sufficient justification" for pretrial detention.[144] "Procedural risks" should not be presumed, "but must be verified in each case, based on the real and objective circumstances of the specific case."[145] The Court has found violations of Article 7(3) when these requirements are neglected in the decision to detain or in the domestic law itself.[146]

III. DETENTION IN IMMIGRATION PROCEEDINGS Although the Inter-American Commission asserts that pretrial detention is only permissible in criminal proceedings, the Inter-American Court unfortunately appears not to agree. In *Vélez Loor v. Panama*, the Tribunal indicated that the practice "may be suitable to regulate and control irregular immigration in order to ensure that the individual appears before the immigration proceeding" or to ensure "the application of an order for deportation."[147] Nevertheless, it found that Panama did not pursue those "lawful purposes" in holding Vélez Loor, and instead followed a "punitive" objective.[148] The State had imprisoned him for re-entering the country without documents, after having been deported; consequently, the detention was found arbitrary in violation of Article 7(3). The Court stressed that migrants can only be held "for the shortest period of time," and that "the detention of people for non-compliance with immigration laws should never involve punitive purposes."[149] As for the detention of child migrants in particular, the Tribunal has urged "a general principle of non-deprivation of liberty."[150]

IV. PRETRIAL DETENTION OF SPECIAL SECTORS OF THE POPULATION *Juvenile Reeducation Institute* involved the pretrial detention of numerous children and adults in Paraguay. The Court declined to consider a collective Article 7 violation,

---

[144] *E.g.*, J. v. Peru, para. 159; López Álvarez v. Honduras, Merits, Reparations, and Costs, Judgment, Inter-Am. Ct. H.R. (ser. C) No. 141, para. 69 (Feb. 1, 2006).

[145] *E.g.*, J. v. Peru, para. 159; Barreto Leiva v. Venezuela, Merits, Reparations, and Costs, Judgment, Inter-Am. Ct. H.R. (ser. C) No. 206, para. 115 (Nov. 17, 2009).

[146] *E.g.*, Wong Ho Wing v. Peru, Preliminary Objection, Merits, Reparations, and Costs, Judgment, Inter-Am. Ct. H.R. (ser. C) No. 297, para. 253 (June 30, 2015) (finding the pretrial detention arbitrary in violation of Article 7(3), when it was shown that the domestic court failed to evaluate the procedural risk involved); Barreto Leiva v. Venezuela, Merits, Reparations, and Costs, Judgment, Inter-Am. Ct. H.R. (ser. C) No. 206, para. 116 (Nov. 17, 2009) (finding violations to Articles 7(3) and 2, among others, owing to flaws in the relevant national law). *But see* Norín Catrimán et al. (Leaders, members, and activist of the Mapuche Indigenous People) v. Chile, Merits, Reparations, and Costs, Judgment, Inter-Am. Ct. H.R. (ser. C) No. 279, para. 364 (May 29, 2014) (holding that the Chilean law that allowed pretrial detention in cases of alleged "danger to the security of society" was not "per se contrary to the American Convention, because [it] could be interpreted in a way that was consistent" with the Convention and "the evaluation of whether there was a procedural risk").

[147] Vélez Loor v. Panama, Preliminary Objections, Merits, Reparations, and Costs, Judgment, Inter-Am. Ct. H.R. (ser. C) No. 218, para. 169 (Nov. 23, 2010).

[148] *Id.* para. 172.

[149] *Id.* para. 171.

[150] Rights & Guar. of Children in the Context of Migration and/or in Need of Int'l Prot., Advisory Opinion OC-21/14, Inter-Am. Ct. H.R. (ser. A) No. 21, para. 163 (Aug. 19, 2014).

as it required specific evidence on each individual's case.[151] Still, citing the Convention on the Rights of the Child, the Court emphasized that the pretrial detention of children should be done "only as a measure of last resort and for the shortest appropriate period of time."[152] In its advisory opinion on children's rights, the Court made a similar pronouncement.[153]

In *Norín Catrimán v. Chile*, the Court recognized that "prolonged" pretrial detention "may have different effects" on indigenous persons "owing to their economic, social and cultural characteristics."[154] As for indigenous leaders, their detention "may also have negative consequences on the values, practices and customs of the community or communities in which they exercise their leadership."[155] In this way, "when interpreting and applying their domestic laws," States "must take into consideration" these distinct characteristics to ensure the rights of indigenous peoples to personal liberty.[156]

V. TIME LIMITS FOR PRETRIAL DETENTION In *Wong Ho Wing v. Peru*, the petitioner was detained pending extradition to China.[157] However, as accepted by Peru, the pertinent domestic law did not establish a time limit for detention under these circumstances. The Court held that time limits for pretrial detention serve as a key "safeguard" against arbitrary detentions.[158] The absence of such a limit led to the excessive pretrial detention of Wong Ho Wing, and "constituted an additional element" in the arbitrariness of his detention, in violation of Article 7(3).[159]

3. Methodological Problems: Legality and Arbitrariness

The Court's approach to the principles of legality and arbitrariness has been inconsistent over the years. More recently, the Tribunal has attempted to draw a sharp distinction between the two concepts. Yet the principles are closely linked: after all, many

---

[151] "Juvenile Reeducation Institute" v. Paraguay, Preliminary Objections, Merits, Reparations, and Costs, Judgment, Inter-Am. Ct. H.R. (ser. C) No. 112, para. 233 (Sept. 2, 2004).

[152] *Id.* para. 231 (citing Article 37 of the Convention on the Rights of the Child).

[153] Juridical Condition & Human Rights of the Child, Advisory Opinion OC-17/02, Inter-Am. Ct. H.R. (ser. A) No. 17, para. 126 (Aug. 28, 2002) (citing to the United Nations Rules for the Protection of Juveniles Deprived of their Liberty).

[154] Norín Catrimán et al. (Leaders, members, and activists of the Mapuche Indigenous People) v. Chile, Merits, Reparations, and Costs, Judgment, Inter-Am. Ct. H.R. (ser. C) No. 279, para. 357 (May 29, 2014).

[155] *Id.*

[156] *Id.*

[157] Wong Ho Wing v. Peru, Preliminary Objection, Merits, Reparations, and Costs, Judgment, Inter-Am. Ct. H.R. (ser. C) No. 297 (June 30, 2015).

[158] *Id.* para. 255.

[159] *Id. See also* García Asto and Ramírez Rojas v. Peru, Preliminary Objection, Merits, Reparations, and Costs, Judgment, Inter-Am. Ct. H.R. (ser. C) No. 137, para. 143 (Nov. 25, 2005) (finding a violation of Article 7(3), because the Peruvian court, "after more than fourteen years [since] the issuance of said precautionary measure, did not submit sufficient arguments to maintain Urcesino Ramírez-Rojas' detention").

forms of detention are prohibited in national law precisely because they are arbitrary in some sense.

Often, when the Court finds an illegal detention, it considers it unnecessary to examine arbitrariness.[160] In *Bayarri v. Argentina*, the Tribunal explained, "the arbitrariness mentioned in Article 7(3) of the Convention has its own legal content, which only needs to be analyzed in the case of detentions that are considered lawful."[161] Although such an approach may appeal to notions of judicial economy, it fails to fully condemn detentions that are both illegal and arbitrary. For example, the Court would send a confusing message if it found excessive pretrial detention to be merely illegal—due to the particular State's national law—and not arbitrary, despite the Court's tendency to rule that prolonged pretrial detention violates Article 7(3). The Tribunal must strive for clear, consistent jurisprudence, and cannot neglect its duty to rigorously analyze a case's facts in light of all the applicable Convention provisions.

Even more troubling is the Court's recent approach to assessing legality under Article 7(2). As described above, the Tribunal initially looked to international legal principles and jurisprudence to establish certain core elements for a legal detention. These include certainty in relevant national law, and requirements for judicial warrants and the official registration of all detentions, among others.

However, in contrast to other human rights tribunals, the Court currently focuses almost exclusively on the text of national law to assess a detention's legality.[162] It does so without critically analyzing the law in view of international law and its own jurisprudence on Article 7. Following this approach, a problematic detention that still complies with a State's deficient national law can nevertheless be found "legal" and consistent with Article 7(2).[163] When the Inter-American Court narrows its legality inquiry to the letter

---

[160] *But see* Expelled Dominicans and Haitians v. Dominican Republic, Preliminary Objections, Merits, Reparations, and Costs, Judgment, Inter-Am. Ct. H.R. (ser. C) No. 282, para. 368. (Aug. 28, 2014) (finding detentions to be illegal and arbitrary); Neptune v. Haiti, Merits, Reparations, and Costs, Judgment, Inter-Am. Ct. H.R. (ser. C) No. 180, para. 100 (May 6, 2008) (same).

[161] Bayarri v. Argentina, Preliminary Objection, Merits, Reparations, and Costs, Judgment, Inter-Am. Ct. H.R. (ser. C) No. 187, para. 62 (Oct. 30, 2008). *See also* Wong Ho Wing v. Peru, Preliminary Objection, Merits, Reparations and Costs, Judgment, Inter-Am. Ct. H.R. (ser. C) No. 297, para 238 (June 30, 2015).

[162] In this context, both the European Court and the Human Rights Committee demand that domestic legislation comply with international law, especially with the protections set out in their respective treaties. *See* HARRIS, O'BOYLE & WARBRICK, *supra* note 2, at 301 (stating that the concept of "lawfulness" requires, among other things, "compliance with general principles expressed or implied in the [European] Convention"); NOWAK, *supra* note 2, at 224 (describing cases where the Human Rights Committee held that "judicial review of the lawfulness of detention under Article 9(4) must also include the compatibility with international law, above all the Covenant itself").

[163] In *Torres Millacura*, the Court recognized that the domestic law did not establish "concrete reasons" for arrests—and thus allowed police to act arbitrarily—but did not find a violation of Article 7(2) in this respect. Torres Millacura et al. v. Argentina, Merits, Reparations, and Costs, Judgment, Inter-Am. Ct. H.R. (ser. C) No. 229, para. 80 (Aug. 26, 2011).

of national law, international human rights may be limited or distorted, and the State's discretion to restrict liberty may be increased.

C. THE SPECIFIC REQUIREMENTS OF PARAGRAPHS 4, 5, AND 6 OF ARTICLE 7

The Court has held that these three provisions establish positive obligations for State agents and private persons acting with the State's "tolerance or acquiescence and who are responsible for the detention."[164]

1. Article 7(4): Reasons for Detention and Notification of Charges

Article 7(4) establishes: "Anyone who is detained shall be informed of the reasons for his detention and shall be promptly notified of the charge or charges against him."[165] The Court has specified that this provision "entails two obligations: (a) the need for written or oral information on the reasons for the detention, and (b) notice, in writing, of the charges."[166] In this way, Article 7(4) establishes "a mechanism to avoid unlawful or arbitrary conduct" from the moment liberty is deprived.[167] Detainees and their representatives, including those persons with legal custody over the detainees, must be informed of this information to enable an adequate legal defense.[168]

a. Reasons for Detention

This basic requirement has been expanded over the years, following the European Convention,[169] and now demands that the detaining agent, at the time of the arrest, explain "in simple language, free of technical terms, . . . the essential legal grounds and facts on which the arrest is based."[170] The Court has indicated that this right applies to

---

[164] *E.g.*, Tibi v. Ecuador, Preliminary Objections, Merits, Reparations, and Costs, Judgment, Inter-Am. Ct. H.R. (ser. C) No. 114, para. 108 (Sept. 7, 2004); Sánchez v. Honduras, Preliminary Objection, Merits, Reparations, and Costs, Judgment, Inter-Am. Ct. H.R. (ser. C) No. 99, para. 81 (June 7, 2003).

[165] American Convention, art. 7(4). Note that the Spanish version states "detained or retained," although the records at the San José Conference do not explain why "retained" was added.

[166] *E.g.*, Expelled Dominicans and Haitians v. Dominican Republic, Preliminary Objections, Merits, Reparations, and Costs, Judgment, Inter-Am. Ct. H.R. (ser. C) No. 282, para. 369 (Aug. 28, 2014); Cabrera García and Montiel Flores v. Mexico, 2010 Inter-Am. Ct. H.R. (ser. C) No. 220, para. 106 (Nov. 26, 2010).

[167] *E.g.*, Tibi v. Ecuador, Preliminary Objections, Merits, Reparations, and Costs, Judgment, Inter-Am. Ct. H.R. (ser. C) No. 114, para. 109 (Sept. 7, 2004); Bulacio v. Argentina, Merits, Reparations, and Costs, Judgment, Inter-Am. Ct. H.R. (ser. C) No. 100, para. 128 (Sept. 18, 2003).

[168] Tibi v. Ecuador, Preliminary Objections, Merits, Reparations, and Costs, Judgment, Inter-Am. Ct. H.R. (ser. C) No. 114, para. 109 (Sept. 7, 2004).

[169] *See* European Convention, art. 5(2) (stating "Everyone who is arrested shall be informed promptly, in a language which he understands, of the reasons for his arrest and of any charge against him.")

[170] Chaparro Álvarez and Lapo Íñiguez v. Ecuador, Preliminary Objections, Merits, Reparations, and Costs, Judgment, Inter-Am. Ct. H.R. (ser. C) No. 170, para. 71 (Nov. 21, 2007). Presumably, an interpreter should be available to ensure an explanation "in a language which [the individual] understands." European Convention, art. 5(2).

all forms of arrest, whether by judicial warrant or in flagrante delicto.[171] However, it did not find a violation to Article 7(4) in *Acosta Calderón v. Ecuador*, where it was "assumed that Mr. Acosta Calderón knew the reason for his arrest to be drug trafficking."[172] Such assumptions have left both the Inter-American and European Courts open to criticism, as their respective treaties both unconditionally require an explanation of the reasons for an arrest.[173] Criminal defendants cannot be expected to glean that key information only on the basis of the interrogation or general situation.

Article 7(4), according to the Court, also demands that the detainee must be informed of the right to establish contact with "another person"—such as an attorney, a relative, or a consular official—before making his or her first statement before the authorities.[174] This notification will facilitate the accused's access to "the appropriate assistance and protection."[175] In *Vélez Loor v. Panama*, the State did not inform Vélez Loor of his right to consular assistance in a timely manner; as a result, the Court found that Articles 7(4) and 8 (Right to a Fair Trial) were breached.[176] The burden of proof on this point rests upon the State. If the State does not show that its authorities informed the detainee of this information, it violates Article 7(4).[177]

b. Notification of Charges

Another, distinct element of Article 7(4) is the right to be promptly notified of the charges. For some, it may be acceptable that this notification occurs at a stage subsequent to the initial arrest, owing to the charges' technical and legal nature. However, if a judge has ordered the arrest—as should be the situation in most cases—it is reasonable to provide information on the legal charges. This will enhance, from the very beginning, the ability of accused individuals to defend themselves.

---

[171] López Álvarez v. Honduras, Merits, Reparations, and Costs, Judgment, Inter-Am. Ct. H.R. (ser. C) No. 141, para. 83 (Feb. 1, 2006).

[172] Acosta Calderón v. Ecuador, Merits, Reparations, and Costs, Judgment, Inter-Am. Ct. H.R. (ser. C) No. 129, para. 73 (June 24, 2005).

[173] *See* HARRIS, O'BOYLE & WARBRICK, *supra* note 2, at 334.

[174] *E.g.*, Tibi v. Ecuador, Preliminary Objections, Merits, Reparations, and Costs, Judgment, Inter-Am. Ct. H.R. (ser. C) No. 114, para. 112 (Sept. 7, 2004); Bulacio v. Argentina, Merits, Reparations, and Costs, Judgment, Inter-Am. Ct. H.R. (ser. C) No. 100, para. 130 (Sept. 18, 2003).

[175] Tibi v. Ecuador, Preliminary Objections, Merits, Reparations, and Costs, Judgment, Inter-Am. Ct. H.R. (ser. C) No. 114, para. 112 (Sept. 7, 2004).

[176] Vélez Loor v. Panama, Preliminary Objections, Merits, Reparations, and Costs, Judgment, Inter-Am. Ct. H.R. (ser. C) No. 218, para. 160 (Nov. 23, 2010). *See also* Tibi v. Ecuador, Preliminary Objections, Merits, Reparations, and Costs, Judgment, Inter-Am. Ct. H.R. (ser. C) No. 114, paras. 112–113 (Sept. 7, 2004). The right to effective access to consular assistance and other due process rights are examined in this volume's Chapter 6.

[177] Galindo Cardenas et al. v. Peru, Preliminary Objections, Merits, Reparations and Costs, Inter-Am. Ct. H.R. (ser. C) No. 301, para. 212 (Oct. 2, 2015); Chaparro Álvarez and Lapo Íñiguez v. Ecuador, Preliminary Objections, Merits, Reparations, and Costs, Judgment, Inter-Am. Ct. H.R. (ser. C) No. 170, para. 73 (Nov. 21, 2007). In *Chaparro Álvarez*, the Court found a violation of Article 7(2) as well, because States must provide this information pursuant to domestic law. *Id.*

Similarly, the Convention's Article 8(2)(b) guarantees "prior notification in detail to the accused of the charges against him."[178] As explained in the subsequent chapter on Article 8 and due process, the Court has held that States must notify individuals in writing of the actions or omissions attributed to them, the reasons and evidence that led to the charge, and the crime's legal definition.[179] If the accused is not notified in a timely fashion, such as before giving his or her first statement to the authorities, both Article 7(4) and Article 8(2)(b) can be violated.[180]

2. Article 7(5): Judicial Supervision

On numerous occasions, the Inter-American Court has affirmed that "immediate" judicial oversight guards against arbitrary or illegal detentions and upholds the rights of the detainee, including the presumption of innocence.[181]

a. Brought "Before a Judge or Other Officer Authorized by Law"

In the first place, the Court has established that the judge "or other officer authorized by law" must fulfill the requirements set out in the Convention's Article 8(1)—that is, competence, independence, and impartiality.[182] Thus, in order to examine the detention's legality and reasonableness, the judicial officer must have full jurisdiction over the matter and authority to order a release. In this way, the Inter-American Tribunal has condemned the State practices of putting detainees before prosecutors and military authorities; these methods jeopardize their rights to personal liberty, personal integrity, and due process.[183]

---

[178] American Convention, art. 8(2)(b).

[179] *E.g.*, J. v. Peru, Preliminary Objections, Merits, Reparations, and Costs, Judgment, Inter-Am. Ct. H.R. (ser. C) No. 275, paras. 198–199 (Nov. 27, 2013); López Álvarez v. Honduras, Merits, Reparations, and Costs, Judgment, Inter-Am. Ct. H.R. (ser. C) No. 141, para. 149 (Feb. 1, 2006).

[180] *See* Palamara Iribarne v. Chile, Merits, Reparations, Costs, Judgment, Inter-Am. Ct. H.R. (ser. C) No. 135, para. 227 (Nov. 22, 2005) ("Mr. Palamara-Iribarne provided his first statement without being first given prior notice of the crimes he was being charged with, and the State thus violated Articles 7(4) and 8(2)(b) of the Convention").

[181] *E.g.*, Galindo Cardenas et al. v. Peru, Preliminary Objections, Merits, Reparations and Costs, Inter-Am. Ct. H.R. (ser. C) No. 301, para. 202 (Oct. 2, 2015); Neptune v. Haiti, Merits, Reparations, and Costs, Judgment, Inter-Am. Ct. H.R. (ser. C) No. 180, para. 107 (May 6, 2008).

[182] *E.g.*, Palamara Iribarne v. Chile, Merits, Reparations, Costs, Judgment, Inter-Am. Ct. H.R. (ser. C) No. 135, para. 222 (Nov. 22, 2005); Tibi v. Ecuador, Preliminary Objections, Merits, Reparations, and Costs, Judgment, Inter-Am. Ct. H.R. (ser. C) No. 114, para. 119 (Sept. 7, 2004).

[183] *See, e.g.*, Acosta Calderón v. Ecuador, Merits, Reparations, and Costs, Judgment, Inter-Am. Ct. H.R. (ser. C) No. 129, para. 80 (June 24, 2005) (victim brought before prosecutor); Palamara Iribarne v. Chile, Merits, Reparations, Costs, Judgment, Inter-Am. Ct. H.R. (ser. C) No. 135, para. 223 (Nov. 22, 2005) ("Considering that it was the Naval Prosecutor who ordered that Mr. Palamara-Iribarne be held in preventive detention in both cases, said officer cannot review the legality of his own orders"); Cantoral Benavides v. Peru, Merits, Judgment, Inter-Am. Ct. H.R. (ser. C) No. 69, para. 76 (Aug. 18, 2000) (finding a violation of Article 7(5) because, among other reasons, victim was brought before a military judge instead of a civilian judge).

Second, the Tribunal has held that judicial supervision must be "effective" in both examining the actions of the arresting authorities and in "reestablishing" the rights of the detainee.[184] In *Bayarri*, the Court found that the judge did not fully review the detention's legality, neglected to order a medical examination despite signs of physical abuse, and required detention without following all aspects of the Argentine Code of Criminal Procedure.[185] The State, then, failed to exercise effective judicial supervision of the detention, in violation of Article 7(5) and other Convention provisions.

Third, the Court has stressed that the judge must hear detainees personally and examine all information that they provide, in order to decide upon the appropriateness of the detention.[186] In *Chaparro Álvarez*, the judge had been present during the arrests; thus, the State maintained that there was "no need to bring the victims before her again."[187] The Inter-American Tribunal rejected this argument: although the judge's initial presence "could be described as an additional guarantee, it was not, by itself, sufficient to satisfy the requirement of Article 7(5) of being 'brought' before a judge" to "evaluate all the explanations" of the detainee.[188]

Fourth, Article 7(5) contains demanding temporal requirements. The English text provides that "any person detained shall be brought *promptly* before a judge."[189] However, the Court has called for "immediate" judicial oversight, a standard more consistent with the Spanish version of Article 7(5)—requiring a judicial hearing "without delay" (*sin demora*).[190] Yet the Tribunal has not specified the maximum permissible time frame in these circumstances, preferring instead to refer to national law.[191] It has condemned many flagrant delays;[192] the shortest period breaching Article 7(5) in the case law appears to be 38 hours, in the case of a detained child.[193]

---

[184] Bayarri v. Argentina, Preliminary Objection, Merits, Reparations, and Costs, Judgment, Inter-Am. Ct. H.R. (ser. C) No. 187, para. 67 (Oct. 30, 2008). *See also* Argüelles et al. v. Argentina, Preliminary Objections, Merits, Reparations, and Costs, Judgment, Inter-Am. Ct. H.R. (ser. C) No. 288, para. 133 (Nov. 20, 2014).

[185] Bayarri v. Argentina, Preliminary Objection, Merits, Reparations, and Costs, Judgment, Inter-Am. Ct. H.R. (ser. C) No. 187, para. 67 (Oct. 30, 2008).

[186] *Id.* para. 65; Chaparro Álvarez and Lapo Íñiguez v. Ecuador, Preliminary Objections, Merits, Reparations, and Costs, Judgment, Inter-Am. Ct. H.R. (ser. C) No. 170, para. 85 (Nov. 21, 2007).

[187] Chaparro Álvarez and Lapo Íñiguez v. Ecuador, Preliminary Objections, Merits, Reparations, and Costs, Judgment, Inter-Am. Ct. H.R. (ser. C) No. 170, para. 85 (Nov. 21, 2007).

[188] *Id.*

[189] American Convention, art. 7(5) (emphasis added).

[190] *Id.* (providing, in Spanish: "*Toda persona detenida o retenida debe ser llevada, sin demora, ante un juez u otro funcionario autorizado por la ley para ejercer funciones judiciales* . . .").

[191] *See* MEDINA, *supra* note 10, at 158–59.

[192] *E.g.*, Acosta Calderón v. Ecuador, Merits, Reparations, and Costs, Judgment, Inter-Am. Ct. H.R. (ser. C) No. 129, para. 79 (June 24, 2005) ("There is no evidence in the case file that Mr. Acosta Calderón gave any statement before a judge until almost two years after his arrest"); Tibi v. Ecuador, Preliminary Objections, Merits, Reparations, and Costs, Judgment, Inter-Am. Ct. H.R. (ser. C) No. 114, paras. 117–121 (Sept. 7, 2004).

[193] Landaeta Meijias Brothers et al. v. Venezuela, Preliminary Objections, Merits, Reparations, and Costs, Judgment, Inter-Am. Ct. H.R. (ser. C) No. 281, para. 178 (Aug. 27, 2014). *See also* Bayarri v. Argentina, Preliminary Objection, Merits, Reparations, and Costs, Judgment, Inter-Am. Ct. H.R. (ser. C) No. 187,

Only rarely, such as in some blatant Peruvian cases, has the Tribunal expressly found domestic law to contravene this requirement.[194] The Court's approach here is overly deferential to States; it should establish a maximum rule such as 48 hours. When the limit is exceeded, either in law or in practice, an Article 7(5) violation should result.

b. Right to Trial "Within a Reasonable Time"

These terms relate to Article 7(3); recently, the Court has also analyzed Article 7(5) in cases of pretrial detention.[195] The provision is key because it upholds the presumption of innocence and demands a detainee's release if the trial does not occur after a "reasonable time." Perhaps for this significant consequence, the Court has not found a violation of this provision often; even less common is an order for a detainee's freedom.

It must be emphasized that—even when there may exist reasons to keep an individual detained—if a "reasonable time" has expired, that person must be released. State authorities must not unduly prolong a detention, according to the Court.[196] Medina argues that the time period to be measured should begin with the arrest or detention, and continue until the conviction is firm—because the defendant has the presumption of innocence until that moment.[197] However, as before, the Court has provided little explicit guidance for this situation, and prefers to remit to national law. In fact, the Tribunal occasionally is hesitant to rule on this point at all. In *Acosta Calderón*, the Tribunal avoided examining whether the length of pretrial detention was "reasonable," considering it sufficient to find a violation of Article 7(3).[198]

The Court has established one relevant time limit: pretrial detention cannot reach or exceed the sentence of the charged crime upon conviction. In this way, Suárez Rosero's right to trial within a reasonable time was clearly violated in *Suárez Rosero v. Ecuador*, when he was detained for nearly two years more than the maximum sentence for the crime in question.[199] Still, the Court's standard does not prove very useful, especially in cases where a detainee is charged with a very serious crime or multiple offenses that would carry a significant sentence.

---

para. 66 (Oct. 30, 2008) (describing a delay of five to six days). As for the European Court, even in cases of potential terrorism, "the concept of promptness could not properly be stretched so as to permit a delay of four days and six hours or more." HARRIS, O'BOYLE & WARBRICK, *supra* note 2, at 340.

[194] *See, e.g.*, Castillo Petruzzi et al. v. Peru, Merits, Reparations, and Costs, Judgment, Inter-Am. Ct. H.R. (ser. C) No. 52, para. 110 (May 30, 1999) ("those Peruvian laws that allow the authorities to hold a person suspected of the crime of treason in preventive custody for 15 days, with the possibility of a 15-day extension, without bringing that person before a judicial authority, are contrary to the [Convention]").

[195] Norín Catrimán et al. (Leaders, members, and activist of the Mapuche Indigenous People) v. Chile, Merits, Reparations, and Costs, Judgment, Inter-Am. Ct. H.R. (ser. C) No. 279, para. 310 (May 29, 2014).

[196] Sánchez v. Honduras, Preliminary Objection, Merits, Reparations, and Costs, Judgment, Inter-Am. Ct. H.R. (ser. C) No. 99, para. 84 (June 7, 2003).

[197] MEDINA, *supra* note 10, at 159–60.

[198] Acosta Calderón v. Ecuador, Merits, Reparations, and Costs, Judgment, Inter-Am. Ct. H.R. (ser. C) No. 129, para. 82 (June 24, 2005).

[199] Suárez Rosero v. Ecuador, Merits, Judgment, Inter-Am. Ct. H.R. (ser. C) No. 35, paras. 74–75 (Nov. 12, 1997).

In *Bayarri*, the Tribunal unsurprisingly found that 13 years of pretrial detention was "clearly excessive" in breach of Article 7(5).[200] The domestic proceedings had ended with the Bayarri's acquittal. The Court asserted that a release certainly need not await an acquittal; rather judges must "periodically assess" the "reasons," "need," and "proportionality" of the detention, as well as the reasonableness of its duration.[201] When the pretrial detention "does not fulfill these conditions, the release of the person detained should be ordered, without detriment to the continuation of the respective proceedings."[202]

The Tribunal noted in *Bayarri* that Argentine legislation allowed for up to 3 years of pretrial detention. Curiously, despite examining the law's text, the Court did not criticize this excessive time frame or find it contrary to the Convention. The Tribunal has only very rarely condemned national law in this context.[203] In *Suárez Rosero*, the State's criminal code established limits for pretrial detention; however, the limits did not apply to those charged with drug-related offenses.[204] The Court found the law's exception to "deprive a part of the prison population of a fundamental right."[205] As a result, the provision violated both Article 7(5) and Article 2, "whether or not it was enforced in the instant case."[206]

3. Article 7(6): The Right to Habeas Corpus

Article 7(6) contains the right to habeas corpus, which establishes:

> Anyone who is deprived of his liberty shall be entitled to recourse to a competent court, in order that the court may decide without delay on the lawfulness of his arrest or detention and order his release if the arrest or detention is unlawful.[207]

For the Court, the well-known habeas corpus remedy is an example of *amparo*—a "simple and prompt" judicial recourse that is widespread in Latin America.[208] The Convention's

---

[200] Bayarri v. Argentina, Preliminary Objection, Merits, Reparations, and Costs, Judgment, Inter-Am. Ct. H.R. (ser. C) No. 187, para. 75 (Oct. 30, 2008).

[201] *Id.* para. 76.

[202] *Id.*

[203] *See* Suárez Rosero v. Ecuador, Merits, Judgment, Inter-Am. Ct. H.R. (ser. C) No. 35, para. 98 (Nov. 12, 1997) (case discussed in text); Hilaire, Constantine, and Benjamin et al. v. Trinidad & Tobago, Merits, Reparations, and Costs, Judgment, Inter-Am. Ct. H.R. (ser. C) No. 94, para. 124 (June 21, 2002) ("The delays caused by Trinidad and Tobago throughout the judicial proceedings of the twenty-four mentioned victims . . . constitute a violation of the right to trial within a reasonable time, guaranteed in Articles 7(5) and 8(1) of the American Convention. Such delays likewise violate Article 2 since the State did not adopt the necessary measures in its domestic law to make effective the guarantees protected in these provisions.").

[204] Suárez Rosero v. Ecuador, Merits, Judgment, Inter-Am. Ct. H.R. (ser. C) No. 35, para. 95 (Nov. 12, 1997).

[205] *Id.* para. 98.

[206] *Id.*

[207] American Convention, art. 7(6).

[208] Habeas Corpus in Emergency Situations (Arts. 27(2), 25(1), and 7(6) American Convention on Human Rights), Advisory Opinion OC-8/87, Inter-Am. Ct. H.R. (ser. A) No. 8, para. 32 (Jan. 30, 1987); ALLAN R. BREWER

Article 25 contains the "whole series of remedies" represented by *amparo,* whereas the specific recourse of habeas corpus is found in Article 7(6).[209] The Court has held that *amparo* and habeas corpus are among the "judicial guarantees" of Article 27(2) that cannot be suspended in times of emergency.[210] They are essential to protect the rights to personal liberty, life, and personal integrity, as well as to prevent forced disappearances.[211] When habeas corpus is denied, the Court may find violations of both Articles 7(6) and 25, or simply Article 7(6).[212]

A first requirement for the right to habeas corpus is that the court be competent. Only the judiciary has jurisdiction for these petitions, according to the Inter-American Court. It has rejected the competency of military and administrative authorities, as well as political figures such as a mayor, to decide habeas petitions—even when domestic law vests them with this power.[213] Second, the habeas petition must be resolved "without delay." As stated above, the Court has not set an explicit time limit, but clearly "almost one week" violates the "without delay" principle.[214] It has also found several longer delays to breach Article 7(6); as in other situations, the Court usually refers to domestic law as a basis for comparison.[215]

Third, the judicial examination of the habeas petition must be "effective." *López Álvarez v. Honduras* held that a judge must fully examine the detainee's circumstances and expressly respond, on record, to the petitioner's arguments.[216] In other judgments, the Court stressed that the judge's examination must be "serious," "independent," and "impartial."[217]

Carías, Constitutional Protection of Human Rights in Latin America: A Comparative Study of *Amparo* Proceedings 163 (2009); Gros Espiell, *supra* note 65, at 116.

[209] Habeas Corpus in Emergency Situations (Arts. 27(2), 25(1), and 7(6) American Convention on Human Rights), Advisory Opinion OC-8/87, Inter-Am. Ct. H.R. (ser. A) No. 8, para. 34 (Jan. 30, 1987).

[210] *Id.* para. 44.

[211] *Id.* para. 35. *See also* Galindo Cardenas et al. v. Peru, Preliminary Objections, Merits, Reparations and Costs, Inter-Am. Ct. H.R. (ser. C) No. 301, para. 44 (Oct. 2, 2015).

[212] *E.g.*, Cesti Hurtado v. Peru, Merits, Judgment, Inter-Am. Ct. H.R. (ser. C) No. 56, para. 133 (Sept. 29, 1999) (both articles found violated); Rochac Hernandez et al. v. El Salvador, Merits, Reparations, and Costs, Judgment, Inter-Am. Ct. H.R. (ser. C) No. 285 (Oct. 14, 2014) (only Article 7(6)).

[213] *See* Vélez Loor v. Panama, Preliminary Objections, Merits, Reparations, and Costs, Judgment, Inter-Am. Ct. H.R. (ser. C) No. 218, para. 126 (Nov. 23, 2010) (concerning an immigration official); Chaparro Álvarez and Lapo Íñiguez v. Ecuador, Preliminary Objections, Merits, Reparations, and Costs, Judgment, Inter-Am. Ct. H.R. (ser. C) No. 170, para. 116 (Nov. 21, 2007) (involving a mayor); Palamara Iribarne v. Chile, Merits, Reparations, Costs, Judgment, Inter-Am. Ct. H.R. (ser. C) No. 135, para. 223 (Nov. 22, 2005) (concerning military authorities).

[214] Bayarri v. Argentina, Preliminary Objection, Merits, Reparations, and Costs, Judgment, Inter-Am. Ct. H.R. (ser. C) No. 187, para. 66 (Oct. 30, 2008).

[215] *E.g.*, Tibi v. Ecuador, Preliminary Objections, Merits, Reparations, and Costs, Judgment, Inter-Am. Ct. H.R. (ser. C) No. 114, para. 134 (Sept. 7, 2004); "Juvenile Reeducation Institute" v. Paraguay, Preliminary Objections, Merits, Reparations, and Costs, Judgment, Inter-Am. Ct. H.R. (ser. C) No. 112, para. 250 (Sept. 2, 2004).

[216] López Álvarez v. Honduras, Merits, Reparations, and Costs, Judgment, Inter-Am. Ct. H.R. (ser. C) No. 141, paras. 96–98 (Feb. 1, 2006). *See also* Wong Ho Wing v. Peru, Preliminary Objection, Merits, Reparations, and Costs, Judgment, Inter-Am. Ct. H.R. (ser. C) No. 297, paras. 289–292 (June 30, 2015).

[217] *E.g.*, Peasant Community of Santa Barbara v. Peru, Preliminary Objections, Merits, Reparations and Costs, Inter-Am. Ct. H.R. (ser. C) No. 299, para. 234 (Sept. 1, 2015); Mack Chang v. Guatemala, Merits, Reparations, and Costs, Judgment, Inter-Am. Ct. H.R. (ser. C) No. 101, para. 181 (Nov. 25, 2003).

The Tribunal's enduring case law on effective remedies requires that they provide suitable "results or answers to the violations."[218] In the case of habeas petitions, this clearly requires that, upon finding an impermissible detention, the judge must immediately secure the detainee's freedom.[219] The Inter-American Court has found violations to Article 7(6) when the right was rendered ineffective either in law or in practice.[220]

4. Article 7(7): "No One Shall Be Detained for Debt"

It does not appear that the Inter-American Court and Commission have yet discussed Article 7(7) in their case law. For more information on this provision, see this chapter's Introduction.

---

[218] *E.g.*, Usón Ramírez v. Venezuela, Preliminary Objections, Merits, Reparations, and Costs, Judgment, Inter-Am. Ct. H.R. (ser. C) No. 207, para. 128 (Nov. 20, 2009); Acevedo Buendía et al. ("Discharged and Retired Employees of the Office of the Comptroller") v. Peru, Preliminary Objection, Merits, Reparations, and Costs, Judgment, Inter-Am. Ct. H.R. (ser. C) No. 198, para. 69 (July 1, 2009).

[219] *E.g.*, Neptune v. Haiti, Merits, Reparations, and Costs, Judgment, Inter-Am. Ct. H.R. (ser. C) No. 180, para. 114 (May 6, 2008); López Álvarez v. Honduras, Merits, Reparations, and Costs, Judgment, Inter-Am. Ct. H.R. (ser. C) No. 141, paras. 97–98 (Feb. 1, 2006).

[220] *E.g.*, Anzualdo Castro v. Peru, Preliminary Objections, Merits, Reparations, and Costs, Judgment, Inter-Am. Ct. H.R. (ser. C) No. 202, para. 76 (Sept. 22, 2009) (finding a restriction in a Peruvian law to impede the exercise of the right to habeas corpus); Acosta Calderón v. Ecuador, Merits, Reparations, and Costs, Judgment, Inter-Am. Ct. H.R. (ser. C) No. 129, para. 97 (June 24, 2005) ("even when the [habeas petition] does exist formally, it was not effective in the present case, since it was not fulfilled with the objective of obtaining, without delay, a decision regarding the legality of the arrest or detention of the alleged victim").

6

Due Process and Judicial Protection

Article 8: Right to a Fair Trial

1. *Every person has the right to a hearing, with due guarantees and within a reasonable time, by a competent, independent, and impartial tribunal, previously established by law, in the substantiation of any accusation of a criminal nature made against him or for the determination of his rights and obligations of a civil, labor, fiscal, or any other nature.*
2. *Every person accused of a criminal offense has the right to be presumed innocent so long as his guilt has not been proven according to law. During the proceedings, every person is entitled, with full equality, to the following minimum guarantees:*
   a. *the right of the accused to be assisted without charge by a translator or interpreter, if he does not understand or does not speak the language of the tribunal or court;*
   b. *prior notification in detail to the accused of the charges against him;*
   c. *adequate time and means for the preparation of his defense;*
   d. *the right of the accused to defend himself personally or to be assisted by legal counsel of his own choosing, and to communicate freely and privately with his counsel;*
   e. *the inalienable right to be assisted by counsel provided by the state, paid or not as the domestic law provides, if the accused does not defend himself personally or engage his own counsel within the time period established by law;*
   f. *the right of the defense to examine witnesses present in the court and to obtain the appearance, as witnesses, of experts or other persons who may throw light on the facts;*
   g. *the right not to be compelled to be a witness against himself or to plead guilty; and*
   h. *the right to appeal the judgment to a higher court.*

The American Convention on Human Rights. Thomas M. Antkowiak and Alejandra Gonza.

3. *A confession of guilt by the accused shall be valid only if it is made without coercion of any kind.*
4. *An accused person acquitted by a nonappealable judgment shall not be subjected to a new trial for the same cause.*
5. *Criminal proceedings shall be public, except insofar as may be necessary to protect the interests of justice.*

Chapter 6 Contents

I. Introduction 174
  A. Many Similarities among the Major Human Rights Treaties 174
  B. Variances among the Human Rights Systems 176
  C. Background 177
II. Article 8(1) 178
  A. Introduction and Meaning of "Right to a Hearing" 178
  B. Meaning of "With Due Guarantees" 181
  C. Meaning of "Within a Reasonable Time" 183
  D. Meaning of "Competent, Independent, and Impartial Tribunal, Previously Established by Law" 188
    1. "Tribunal" 188
    2. "Competent" 188
    3. "Independent" 190
    4. "Impartial" 191
    5. "Previously Established by Law" 193
III. Article 8(2) and the Right to Be Presumed Innocent 194
  A. Article 8(2)(a): The Right to be Assisted by a Translator or Interpreter 196
  B. Article 8(2)(b): Prior Notification in Detail of Charges 197
  C. Article 8(2)(c): Adequate Time and Means for Preparation of Defense 199
  D. Article 8(2)(d): The Right to Defend Oneself Personally or to Be Assisted by Legal Counsel, and to Communicate Freely and Privately with Counsel 200
  E. Article 8(2)(e): The Right to be Assisted by Counsel Provided by the State 202
  F. Article 8(2)(f): The Right of the Defense to Present and Examine Witnesses 204
  G. Article 8(2)(g) and Article 8(3): The Right Not to Be Compelled to Be a Witness against Oneself; Coercion and Confessions 206

H. Article 8(2)(h): The Right to Appeal a Judgment to a Higher Court 208
I. The Right to Effective Access to Consular Assistance 210
IV. Article 8(4): An Acquitted Person Shall Not Be Subjected to a New Trial for the Same Cause 211
V. Article 8(5): Public Criminal Proceedings 213

I. Introduction

Article 8's title, "Right to a Fair Trial," belies the breadth of its due process protections. The purpose of this provision, as explained by a former president of the Inter-American Court, is to ensure that State authorities who determine an individual's rights "will do so using a procedure that provides the necessary means to defend [his or her] legitimate interests and obtain duly reasoned rulings," in order that he or she "is protected by the law and safeguarded from arbitrariness."[1] Similar to other human rights tribunals, the Court offers extensive jurisprudence in this area. Still, much remains for the Court to develop, such as the key concepts of "effective" counsel and adequate language access.

A. MANY SIMILARITIES AMONG THE MAJOR HUMAN RIGHTS TREATIES

The primary regional human rights treaties and the ICCPR establish a number of judicial guarantees and due process protections. Although the language and degree of detail varies from treaty to treaty, most require: an independent and impartial tribunal,[2] a tribunal established by law,[3] and public criminal hearings.[4] Furthermore, all persons accused of a criminal offense have the following rights: to be presumed innocent,[5] to be informed of the charges in a language they understand,[6] to have enough time and resources to prepare their defense,[7] to be tried within a reasonable time,[8] to defend themselves personally or to use the services of a lawyer of their own choosing,[9] to use the services of an interpreter if they do not understand or speak the official language,[10] to question the witnesses called

---

[1] Separate Opinion of Judge García Ramírez, para. 4, Claude Reyes et al. v. Chile, Merits, Reparations, and Costs, Judgment, Inter-Am. Ct. H.R. (ser. C) No. 151 (Sept. 19, 2006).

[2] ICCPR, art. 14(1); European Convention, art. 6(1); American Convention, art. 8(1); African Charter, art. 7; Arab Charter, art. 13; EU Charter, art. 47.

[3] ICCPR, art. 14(1); European Convention, art. 6(1); American Convention, art. 8(1); Arab Charter, art. 13; EU Charter, art. 47.

[4] ICCPR, art. 14(1); European Convention, art. 6(1); American Convention, art. 8(5); Arab Charter, art. 13; EU Charter, art. 47; LOUISE DOSWALD-BECK & ROBERT KOLB, JUDICIAL PROCESS AND HUMAN RIGHTS: UNITED NATIONS, EUROPEAN, AMERICAN AND AFRICAN SYSTEMS 122 (2004).

[5] ICCPR, art. 14(2); European Convention, art. 6(2); American Convention, art. 8(2); African Charter, art. 7; Arab Charter, art. 16; EU Charter, art. 48.

[6] ICCPR, art. 14(3)(a); European Convention, art. 6(3)(a); American Convention, art. 8(2)(a–b); Arab Charter, art. 16.

[7] ICCPR, art. 14(3)(b); European Convention, art. 6(3)(b); American Convention, art. 8(2)(d); Arab Charter, art. 16.

[8] ICCPR, art. 14(3)(c); European Convention, art. 6(1); American Convention, art. 8(1); African Charter, art. 7; Arab Charter, art. 14; EU Charter, art. 47.

[9] ICCPR, art. 14(3)(d); European Convention, art. 6(3)(c); American Convention, art. 8(2)(d); African Charter, art. 7; Arab Charter, art. 16; EU Charter, art. 47.

[10] ICCPR, art. 14(3)(f); European Convention, art. 6(3)(e); American Convention, art. 8(2)(a); Arab Charter, art. 16.

by the opposing party and to present their own witnesses,[11] to appeal to a higher court,[12] to not be tried again for a crime after final acquittal,[13] and to not be tried for an offense that was not criminal at the time of commission.[14]

As in the case of other rights where the European case law is well developed, the Inter-American Court has cited often to its counterpart when considering due process matters. Consequently, the European Court has influenced the Inter-American Tribunal's interpretations of the American Convention with respect to judicial impartiality[15] and independence,[16] its "reasonable time" standard for various proceedings,[17] "effective" legal assistance,[18] and the examination of witnesses,[19] among others. Moreover, in the *Vélez Loor v. Panama* judgment, the Inter-American Court, citing to *Benham v. The United Kingdom*,[20] held that individuals—including undocumented immigrants—who cannot afford counsel must have free legal representation in proceedings where their physical liberty is at stake.[21]

United Nations Human Rights Committee (HRC) decisions and UN principles have also been persuasive for the Inter-American Court on the subject of due process. For example, the important case *Herrera Ulloa v. Costa Rica* relied heavily on HRC jurisprudence to develop the characteristics of an adequate review by an appeals court.[22] The Inter-American Tribunal has also referred to HRC General Comments,[23] the

---

[11] ICCPR, art. 14(3)(e); European Convention, art. 6(3)(d); American Convention, art. 8(2)(f); Arab Charter, art. 16.

[12] ICCPR, art. 14(5); Protocol 7 to European Convention, art. 2; American Convention, art. 8(2)(h); African Charter, art. 7; Arab Charter, art. 16.

[13] ICCPR, art. 14(7); Protocol 7 to European Convention, art. 4; American Convention, art. 8(4); Arab Charter, art. 19; EU Charter, art. 50.

[14] ICCPR, art. 15(1); European Convention, art. 7(1); American Convention, art. 9; Arab Charter, art. 15; African Charter, art. 7; EU Charter, art. 49; DOSWALD-BECK & KOLB, *supra* note 4, at 122–23.

[15] Apitz Barbera et al. ("First Court of Administrative Disputes") v. Venezuela, Preliminary Objection, Merits, Reparations, and Costs, Judgment, Inter-Am. Ct. H.R. (ser. C) No. 182, para. 56 (Aug. 5, 2008).

[16] Reverón Trujillo v. Venezuela, Preliminary Objections, Merits, Reparations, and Costs, Judgment, Inter-Am. Ct. H.R. (ser. C) No. 197, para. 70 (June 30, 2009).

[17] Genie Lacayo v. Nicaragua, Merits, Reparations, and Costs, Judgment, Inter-Am. Ct. H.R. (ser. C) No. 30, para. 77 (Jan. 29, 1997).

[18] Chaparro Álvarez and Lapo Íñiguez v. Ecuador, Preliminary Objections, Merits, Reparations, and Costs, Judgment, Inter-Am. Ct. H.R. (ser. C) No. 170, para. 159 (Nov. 21, 2007).

[19] Berenson Mejia v. Peru, Merits, Reparations, and Costs, Judgment, Inter-Am. Ct. H.R. (ser. C) No. 119, para. 184 (Nov. 25, 2004).

[20] Benham v. The United Kingdom, Eur. Ct. H.R., App. No. 19380/92, para. 64 (June 10, 1996).

[21] Vélez Loor v. Panama, Preliminary Objections, Merits, Reparations, and Costs, Judgment, Inter-Am. Ct. H.R. (ser. C) No. 218, para. 146 (Nov. 23, 2010). *See also* Juridical Condition & Rights of the Undocumented Migrants, Advisory Opinion OC-18/03, Inter-Am. Ct. H.R. (ser. A) No. 18, para. 126 (Sept. 17, 2003).

[22] Herrera Ulloa v. Costa Rica, Preliminary Objections, Merits, Reparations, and Costs, Judgment, Inter-Am. Ct. H.R. (ser. C) No. 107, para. 166 (July 2, 2004) (citing HRC Communication No 1007/2001: Spain. 19/09/2003, CCPR/C/78/D/1007/2001).

[23] Tibi v. Ecuador, Preliminary Objections, Merits, Reparations, and Costs, Judgment, Inter-Am. Ct. H.R. (ser. C) No. 114, para. 186 (Sept. 7, 2004).

Body of Principles for the Protection of All Persons under Any Form of Detention or Imprisonment,[24] and the Basic Principles on the Independence of the Judiciary, among others.[25]

B. VARIANCES AMONG THE HUMAN RIGHTS SYSTEMS

Despite numerous convergences, there still are differences among the systems. To begin, Article 8 provides for a right to a hearing "in the substantiation of any accusation of a criminal nature . . . or for the determination of . . . rights and obligations of a civil, labor, fiscal, or any other nature."[26] A glance at the other instruments shows a more limited right to a hearing. The European Convention refers only to "the determination of . . . civil rights and obligations or of any criminal charge."[27] The ICCPR, although broader than the European text, still restricts the right to "the determination of any criminal charge" or "rights and obligations in a suit at law"[28]—a phrase that, according to the HRC, introduces inconsistency and complexity.[29] Nevertheless, the HRC has accepted a range of issues as "rights and obligations in a suit at law."[30] Similarly, over the years the European Court has significantly extended the reach of Article 6's right to a hearing, closing the gap between the European approach and that of the other two systems.[31]

The European Convention, unlike the other two treaties, fails to establish the defendant's right not to be compelled to be a witness against himself or to plead guilty. Moreover, this exclusion was ratified by the Council of Europe States during the drafting of the Seventh Protocol to the Convention, which added other rights of the accused.[32] However, through judgments such as *Saunders v. UK*, the European Court has fortunately read the freedom from self-incrimination into Article 6.[33] Although this freedom is not absolute, many forms of "improper compulsion" are prohibited.[34]

In some respects the American Convention is not as broad as the European Convention and the ICCPR. Article 8 only requires that criminal proceedings be public, whereas the

---

[24] Acosta Calderón v. Ecuador, Merits, Reparations, and Costs, Judgment, Inter-Am. Ct. H.R. (ser. C) No. 129, para. 122 (June 24, 2005).

[25] Reverón Trujillo v. Venezuela, Preliminary Objections, Merits, Reparations, and Costs, Judgment, Inter-Am. Ct. H.R. (ser. C) No. 197, para. 70 (June 30, 2009).

[26] American Convention, art. 8.

[27] European Convention, art. 6(1).

[28] ICCPR, art. 14(1).

[29] General Comment No. 32, Article 14: Right to equality before courts and tribunals and to a fair trial, CCPR/C/GC/32, 23 August 2007, para. 16.

[30] *Id.*

[31] *See* David Harris, Michael O'Boyle & Colin Warbrick, Law of the European Convention on Human Rights 409 (3d ed. 2014).

[32] *See id.* at 422.

[33] *See id.*

[34] *Id.*

European and UN instruments extend that obligation to hearings on other matters.[35] Further, the American Convention's text does not guarantee free legal aid to indigents. As noted, however, the Court has issued a critical ruling in this regard. *Vélez Loor* held that whenever "decisions may be taken by which an accused may be deported, expelled, or deprived of freedom, the provision of free public legal aid service is necessary to avoid the violation of the right to due process."[36]

Another noteworthy difference among human rights treaties concerns the *ne bis in idem* principle. The American Convention grants more robust protection than its peer instruments by prohibiting another trial based on the same "cause" or facts, as opposed to merely the same "offense" or *delito* ("crime"). Yet Article 8 only refers to persons "acquitted by a nonappealable judgment." In contrast, Protocol 7 to the European Convention provides: "No one shall be liable to be tried or punished again in criminal proceedings . . . for an offence for which he has already been finally acquitted *or convicted* in accordance with the law and penal procedure of that State."[37] The ICCPR's text is similar.[38] In this way, the American Convention overlooks the rights of those who may be prosecuted or punished again for crimes for which they have already been convicted.

Furthermore, the American Convention's Article 8 does not include the stipulation of the ICCPR and the European Convention that the conviction or acquittal occur "under the jurisdiction of the same State" or "in accordance with the law and penal procedure of that State."[39] Thus, the American Convention could obligate a State Party to respect the final conviction or acquittal reached by courts of another sovereign State. On the contrary, the *ne bis in idem* provisions of the European Convention and the ICCPR prohibit double jeopardy only with respect to offenses adjudicated in the same State.

C. BACKGROUND

The Inter-American Commission's preliminary draft primarily borrowed from Article 6 of the European Convention and Article 14 of the ICCPR. The San José Conference expanded some aspects of the Commission's proposal. In paragraph 1, the right to a hearing was broadly extended to matters of "labor, fiscal, or any other nature."[40] Moreover, key requirements for hearings were elaborated in greater detail: they must be carried out

---

[35] *Compare* Art. 8(5) of the American Convention *with* Art. 14(1) of the ICCPR and Art. 6(1) of the European Convention.

[36] Vélez Loor v. Panama, Preliminary Objections, Merits, Reparations, and Costs, Judgment, Inter-Am. Ct. H.R. (ser. C) No. 218, para. 146 (Nov. 23, 2010). *See also* Juridical Condition & Rights of the Undocumented Migrants, Advisory Opinion OC-18/03, Inter-Am. Ct. H.R. (ser. A) No. 18, para. 126 (Sept. 17, 2003).

[37] Protocol 7 to European Convention, art. 4(1) (emphasis added).

[38] *See* ICCPR, art. 14(7).

[39] ICCPR, art. 14(7); Protocol 7 to ECHR, art. 4(1).

[40] Pp. 194–95, Minutes of the 6th Session of Committee I, Doc 44 (Rev. 1), Nov. 16, 1969.

"with due guarantees and within a reasonable time, by a competent, independent, and impartial tribunal, previously established by law."[41]

Paragraph 2 complements paragraph 1 and refers specifically to criminal proceedings.[42] Here, the delegates strengthened the Commission's text by establishing that the assistance of a translator or interpreter must be free of charge.[43] However, they could not agree to require free legal counsel for the economically disadvantaged, because some States objected to the consequent financial burden.[44] As a result, Article 8(2)(e) provides for "the inalienable right to be assisted by counsel provided by the state, paid or not as the domestic law provides, if the accused does not defend himself personally or engage his own counsel . . . ."[45]

Also of much concern, the Conference changed "legal counsel" to "counsel" in this provision. Although this may not seem significant in English, the Spanish terms better reveal the delegates' intentions: they eliminated "attorney" (*abogado*) and replaced it with "defender" (*defensor*), who is not necessarily a lawyer.[46] Fortunately, the Inter-American Court later emphasized that criminal cases and any proceeding that could result in deprivation of liberty or deportation all require the services of an attorney, paid by the State whenever necessary, if the defendant does not represent him- or herself.[47] Finally, the content of paragraphs 3, 4, and 5 of Article 8 was largely unmodified from the Inter-American Commission's initial proposal.

II. Article 8(1)

A. INTRODUCTION AND MEANING OF "RIGHT TO A HEARING"

Article 8(1) regulates all proceedings, whether they concern State actions toward the individual or matters between private parties.[48] Possible subject matter is vast: criminal, civil, or "any other nature." Although the Article as a whole is called "Right to a Fair Trial" in English and "Judicial Guarantees" in Spanish, the provision goes beyond judicial matters, encompassing proceedings of "any public authority, whether administrative,

---

41 *Id.* at pp. 191, 195.

42 CECILIA MEDINA, LA CONVENCIÓN AMERICANA: TEORÍA Y JURISPRUDENCIA 267 (2003).

43 Pp. 199–200, Minutes of the 6th Session of Committee I, Doc 44 (Rev. 1), Nov. 16, 1969.

44 *Id.* at 202, 224.

45 American Convention, art. 8(2)(e).

46 Pp. 200–01, Minutes of the 6th Session of Committee I, Doc 44 (Rev. 1), Nov. 16, 1969.

47 *E.g.*, Argüelles et al. v. Argentina, Preliminary Objections, Merits, Reparations, and Costs, Judgment, Inter-Am. Ct. H.R. (ser. C) No. 288, para. 175 (Nov. 20, 2014) (affirming that the accused must have access to an attorney from the moment that a criminal investigation is ordered); Vélez Loor v. Panama, Preliminary Objections, Merits, Reparations, and Costs, Judgment, Inter-Am. Ct. H.R. (ser. C) No. 218, para. 146 (Nov. 23, 2010).

48 *See* Juridical Condition & Rights of the Undocumented Migrants, Advisory Opinion OC-18/03, Inter-Am. Ct. H.R. (ser. A) No. 18, para. 173(7) (Sept. 17, 2003)("The broad scope of the preservation of due process encompasses all matters and all persons, without any discrimination," including undocumented migrants.).

legislative or judicial, which, through its decisions determines individual rights and obligations."[49]

These broad protections have become more expansive still through the interpretations of the Inter-American Court, consistent with its notion of the "evolutive nature of judicial process."[50] In *Claude Reyes* et al. *v. Chile*, petitioners requested information from the State, and an administrative authority denied the request. The Court decided that this request constituted a "proceeding," and thus activated the protections of Article 8(1): "the guarantees established in Article 8(1) . . . are also applicable when a public authority adopts decisions that determine such rights."[51] In contrast, the two-judge dissent in *Claude Reyes* argued that an official's simple refusal to provide information does not amount to a determination of the petitioner's rights, and so is not a matter regulated by the provision.[52]

The right to a hearing presupposes that States have established appropriate procedures for petitioners. The Court has explained that Article 8(1) does not always require oral proceedings, but such proceedings are necessary in various contexts, especially in criminal matters.[53] In *Barbani Duarte* et al. *v. Uruguay*, it indicated that the right to a hearing includes two elements: a "formal" or "procedural" element that "ensures access to the competent body to determine the right that is claimed," and a "material aspect," whereby the State must ensure that the eventual decision is implemented.[54]

If participation in proceedings were too costly, this would constitute a denial of the procedural aspect of the right to a hearing.[55] Also, vulnerable sectors such as migrants

---

[49] Constitutional Court v. Peru, Merits, Reparations, and Costs, Judgment, Inter-Am. Ct. H.R. (ser. C) No. 71, para. 71 (Jan. 31, 2001). *See also* Claude Reyes et al. v. Chile, Merits, Reparations, and Costs, Judgment, Inter-Am. Ct. H.R. (ser. C) No. 151, para. 118 (Sept. 19, 2006) ("The guarantees established in this provision must be observed during the different procedures in which State entities adopt decisions that determine the rights of the individual, because the State also empowers administrative, collegiate, and uni-personal authorities to adopt decisions that determine rights.").

[50] Right to Information on Consular Assistance in the Framework of the Guarantees of the Due Process of Law, Advisory Opinion OC-16/99, Inter-Am. Ct. H.R. (ser. A) No. 16, para. 117 (Oct. 1, 1999).

[51] Claude Reyes et al. v. Chile, Merits, Reparations, and Costs, Judgment, Inter-Am. Ct. H.R. (ser. C) No. 151, para. 119 (Sept. 19, 2006).

[52] *Id.*, Dissenting Opinion of Judges Alirio Abreu Burelli and Cecilia Medina Quiroga, para. 3 ("A request for access to information and the refusal to grant it is not a juridical situation in which a legally-empowered State body determines the application of the right in a specific situation in which the norm embodying the right has been contested or violated. To the contrary, the act of refusing access to information creates the dispute and this gives rise to the right of those affected to resort to a body that will decide it, that will settle the dispute, based on its jurisdiction and competence.").

[53] *See* Apitz Barbera et al. ("First Court of Administrative Disputes") v. Venezuela, Preliminary Objections, Merits, Reparations, and Costs, Judgment, Inter-Am. Ct. H.R. (ser. C) No. 182, para. 75 (Aug. 5, 2008). *See also* the below analysis of Article 8(5).

[54] Barbani Duarte et al. v. Uruguay, Merits, Reparations, and Costs, Judgment, Inter. Am. Ct. H.R. (ser. C) No. 234, para. 122 (Oct. 13, 2011).

[55] *See* Cantos v. Argentina, Merits, Reparations, and Costs, Judgment, Inter-Am. Ct. H.R. (ser. C) No. 97, para. 55 (Nov. 28, 2002).

and indigenous persons have other disadvantages that necessitate "countervailing measures that help to reduce or eliminate the obstacles and deficiencies that impair or diminish an effective defense of one's interests."[56] Without such measures "in various stages of the proceeding, one could hardly say that those who have the disadvantages enjoy a true opportunity for justice and the benefit of the due process of law."[57] Thus, States "must guarantee that access to justice is genuine and not merely formal."[58]

In the Inter-American experience, there have been many situations of active obstruction of justice. State agents and accomplices have not only manipulated evidence, but also have threatened, killed, or forced into exile petitioners, attorneys, investigators, and judges seeking to hold rights abusers accountable.[59] As would be expected, such cases lead to violations of Article 8, as well as Article 25 (Right to Judicial Protection) in some instances.

Emerging from the region's history of forced disappearances and extrajudicial executions is a robust set of guarantees for victims and family members. The Court has established the rights of relatives to have crimes effectively investigated and prosecuted, to learn the truth about what happened, and to receive reparation for harm suffered.[60] Such expansive rights contrast sharply with prosecutorial discretion and other constraints found in the criminal justice systems of the United States and other nations.[61]

In numerous judgments, the Court calls this constellation of guarantees for victims and family members "the right of access to justice," and finds its basis in Articles 8 and 25 of the American Convention.[62] An analysis of the Tribunal's recurrent combination of these two provisions is located in the below section on Article 25. For present purposes, it is suffice to say that some have objected to using Article 8 as a source for these

---

[56] Right to Information on Consular Assistance in the Framework of the Guarantees of the Due Process of Law, Advisory Opinion OC-16/99, Inter-Am. Ct. H.R. (ser. A) No. 16, para. 119 (Oct. 1, 1999).

[57] *Id.*

[58] Juridical Condition & Rights of the Undocumented Migrants, Advisory Opinion OC-18/03, Inter-Am. Ct. H.R. (ser. A) No. 18, para. 126 (Sept. 17, 2003).

[59] *E.g.*, Moiwana Cmty. v. Suriname, Preliminary Objections, Merits, Reparations, and Costs, Judgment, Inter-Am. Ct. H.R. (ser. C) No. 124, paras. 139–167 (June 15, 2005); Mack Chang v. Guatemala, Merits, Reparations, and Costs, Judgment, Inter-Am. Ct. H.R. (ser. C) No. 101, paras. 165–218 (Nov. 25, 2003).

[60] *E.g.*, Luna Lopez v. Honduras, Merits, Reparations, and Costs, Judgment, Inter-Am. Ct. H.R. (ser. C) No. 269, para. 188 (Oct. 10, 2013); Blake v. Guatemala, Merits, Judgment, Inter-Am. Ct. H.R. (ser. C) No. 36, para. 97 (Jan. 24, 1998).

[61] *See, e.g.*, Allison Marston Danner, *Enhancing the Legitimacy and Accountability of Prosecutorial Discretion at the International Criminal Court*, 97 AM. J. INT'L L. 510, 512–13 (2003) (noting a number of States where prosecutors have a wide degree of discretion on whether crimes should be pursued).

[62] *E.g.*, Cruz Sánchez et al. v. Peru, Preliminary Objections, Merits, Reparations, Costs, Judgment, Inter-Am. Ct. H.R. (ser. C) No. 292, para. 398 (Apr. 17, 2015); Landaeta Meijias Brothers et al. v. Venezuela, Preliminary Objections, Merits, Reparations, and Costs, Judgment, Inter-Am. Ct. H.R. (ser. C) No. 281, para. 265 (Aug. 27, 2014).

wide-ranging rights. Article 8, it has been argued, instead establishes the *manner* of determining rights and obligations, without actually creating such rights.[63]

B. MEANING OF "WITH DUE GUARANTEES"

The Court has also broadly interpreted the term "due guarantees" of Article 8(1). Construing this undefined phrase,[64] the Tribunal has held:

> although this article does not stipulate minimum guarantees in matters which concern the determination of the rights and obligations of a civil, labor, fiscal or any other nature, the minimum guarantees established in paragraph 2 of the article should also apply to those categories.[65]

Thus, in non-criminal proceedings, an individual still has the right to due process "in the terms recognized for criminal matters, to the extent that it is applicable to the respective procedure."[66]

Such an expansive conclusion is certainly surprising, if not "excessive" and "erroneous," as argued by Cecilia Medina.[67] However, in its case law the Court appears to require a full panoply of criminal due process guarantees only in administrative proceedings that "involve a manifestation of the punitive powers of the State."[68] A common example is the process to deport or expel a migrant.[69]

---

63 *See, e.g.*, MEDINA, *supra* note 42, at 281. For an opposing view, *see* Concurring Vote of Judge Antonio Cançado Trindade, López Álvarez v. Honduras, Merits, Reparations, and Costs, Judgment, Inter-Am. Ct. H.R. (ser. C) No. 141 (Feb. 1, 2006).

64 During the debates at San José, H. Robertson, Director of the Legal Department of the European Commission on Human Rights, cautioned that the phrase "with due guarantees" was too "general" and "vague," and recommended that the delegates instead opt for the phrasing of the ICCPR. P. 191, Minutes of the 6th Session of Committee I, Doc 44 (Rev. 1), Nov. 16, 1969.

65 *E.g.*, Constitutional Court v. Peru, Merits, Reparations, and Costs, Judgment, Inter-Am. Ct. H.R. (ser. C) No. 71, para. 70 (Jan. 31, 2001); Ivcher Bronstein v. Peru, Merits, Reparations, and Costs, Judgment, Inter-Am. Ct. H.R. (ser. C) No. 74, para. 103 (Feb. 6, 2001).

66 Ivcher Bronstein v. Peru, Merits, Reparations, and Costs, Judgment, Inter-Am. Ct. H.R. (ser. C) No. 74, para. 103 (Feb. 6, 2001).

67 MEDINA, *supra* note 42, at 291. Rather than requiring the "minimum guarantees" of Article 8(2) in all of the procedures of Article 8(1), Medina argues that the Court should further develop Article 8(1)'s concept of the "accusation of a criminal nature." *Id.* She states that Article 8(2)'s minimum guarantees may more sensibly apply to that limited subset of procedures.

68 Separate Opinion of Judge Sergio García Ramírez, para. 8, Claude Reyes et al. v. Chile, Merits, Reparations, and Costs, Judgment, Inter-Am. Ct. H.R. (ser. C) No. 151 (Sept. 19, 2006).

69 Pacheco Tineo Family v. Bolivia, Preliminary Objections, Merits, Reparations, and Costs, Judgment, Inter-Am. Ct. H.R. (ser. C) No. 272, para. 132 (Nov. 25, 2013) (calling for guarantees that are "substantially the same" as those established in Article 8(2)).

According to the Tribunal, these proceedings must assess the individual circumstances of each person and be free of all discrimination.[70] The migrant has the right to be informed of any charges, if applicable, and of the reasons for the expulsion or deportation.[71] The State must also provide information on how to challenge the deportation, and on how to receive legal representation, translation and interpretation services, and consular assistance.[72] The migrant has the right to appeal an unfavorable decision, and to "appear or to be represented before the competent authorities for this purpose."[73] Deportation "may only be carried out following a reasoned decision in keeping with the law, which has been duly notified."[74] Finally, when a migrant informs the State that he or she would be at risk of harm if returned, the competent authorities must make an assessment; if the danger is verified, the migrant cannot be returned to that nation.[75] The Court has outlined additional protections for child migrants[76] and asylum seekers.[77]

---

[70] *Id.* para. 133. *See also* Juridical Condition & Rights of the Undocumented Migrants, Advisory Opinion OC-18/03, Inter-Am. Ct. H.R. (ser. A) No. 18, para. 173 (Sept. 17, 2003).

[71] *Id.*

[72] *Id. See also* Nadege Dorzema et al. v. Dominican Republic, Merits, Reparations, and Costs, Judgment, Inter-Am. Ct. H.R. (ser. C) No. 251, paras. 160–178 (Oct. 24, 2012).

[73] Pacheco Tineo Family v. Bolivia, Preliminary Objections, Merits, Reparations, and Costs, Judgment, Inter-Am. Ct. H.R. (ser. C) No. 272, para. 133 (Nov. 25, 2013).

[74] *Id.*

[75] *Id.* para. 136.

[76] The Court has held that the following due process protections "must govern any immigration proceedings, whether administrative or judicial, that involve children: the right to be notified of the existence of a proceeding and of the decision adopted in the context of the immigration proceedings; the right that the immigration proceedings are conducted by a specialized official or judge; the right to be heard and to take part in the different procedural stages; the right to be assisted without charge by a translator and/or interpreter; effective access to communication with consular officials and consular assistance; the right to be assisted by a legal representative and to communicate freely with the representative; the obligation to appoint a guardian in the case of children who are unaccompanied or separated; the right that the decision adopted takes into consideration the best interest of the child and is duly reasoned; the right to appeal the decision before a higher court with suspensive effect, and a reasonable time for the duration of the proceedings." Rights & Guar. of Children in the Context of Migration and/or in Need of Int'l Prot., Advisory Opinion OC-21/14, Inter-Am. Ct. H.R. (ser. A) No. 21, para. 283(5) (Aug. 19, 2014). *See also* Pacheco Tineo Family v. Bolivia, Preliminary Objections, Merits, Reparations, and Costs, Judgment, Inter-Am. Ct. H.R. (ser. C) No. 272, paras. 216–229 (Nov. 25, 2013).

[77] The Court has held that States have the following obligations with respect to asylum seekers, in accordance with the American Convention and other international instruments: "a) They must guarantee the applicant the necessary facilities, including the services of a competent interpreter, as well as, if appropriate, access to legal assistance and representation, in order to submit their request to the authorities. . . b) The request must be examined, objectively, within the framework of the relevant procedure, by a competent and clearly identified authority, and requires a personal interview; c) The decisions adopted by the competent organs must be duly and expressly founded; d) In order to protect the rights of applicants who may be in danger, all stages of the asylum procedure must respect the protection of the applicant's personal information and the application, and the principle of confidentiality; e) If the applicant is denied refugee status, he should be provided with information on how to file an appeal under the prevailing system and granted a reasonable period for this, so that the decision adopted can be formally adopted, and f) The appeal for review must have suspensive effects and must allow the applicant to remain in the country until the competent authority has adopted the required

Beyond the immigration context, the Court appears to determine what due process protections are necessary on a case-by-case basis: "the circumstances of a particular case or proceeding—its significance, its legal character, and its context in a particular legal system—are among the factors" to be considered.[78] In *Claude Reyes*, the minimal guarantees required of the administrative authority, which had received the request for information, were to issue a "duly justified written decision."[79] Such a decision must provide "information regarding the reasons and norms on which [the official] based his decision not to disclose . . . the information in [the] specific case."[80] By not providing such a response, the Court determined that the decision was arbitrary and in breach of Article 8(1).

In this way, as an essential "due guarantee," the Tribunal has consistently required explicit reasoning for "the decisions adopted by the domestic organs of the States that may have an impact on human rights."[81] The reasoning of a decision "should reveal the facts, grounds and norms" that form its basis, "so that any sign of arbitrariness can be excluded."[82] It should be clear that the parties have been able to submit all of their arguments and evidence, and that these submissions have been duly evaluated.[83]

C. MEANING OF "WITHIN A REASONABLE TIME"

The "reasonable time" standard considers the total duration of the proceedings, until a "final and firm judgment is delivered and the jurisdiction thereby ceases."[84] The Court has stated that "particularly in criminal matters, that time must [include] any appeals that may be filed."[85] The time period also includes the execution of civil judgments for damages that are

decision." Pacheco Tineo Family v. Bolivia, Preliminary Objections, Merits, Reparations, and Costs, Judgment, Inter-Am. Ct. H.R. (ser. C) No. 272, para. 159 (Nov. 25, 2013).

78 Exceptions to the Exhaustion of Domestic Remedies (Arts. 46(1), 46(2)(a), and 46(2)(b) American Convention on Human Rights), Advisory Opinion OC-11/90, Inter-Am. Ct. H.R. (ser. A) No. 11, para. 28 (Aug. 10, 1990).

79 Claude Reyes et al. v. Chile, Merits, Reparations, and Costs, Judgment, Inter-Am. Ct. H.R. (ser. C) No. 151, para. 122 (Sept. 19, 2006).

80 *Id.*

81 *E.g.*, J. v. Peru, Preliminary Objections, Merits, Reparations, and Costs, Judgment, Inter-Am. Ct. H.R. (ser. C) No. 275, para. 224 (Nov. 27, 2013); YATAMA v. Nicaragua, Preliminary Objections, Merits, Reparations, and Costs, Judgment, Inter-Am. Ct. H.R. (ser. C) No. 127, para. 125 (June 23, 2005).

82 *E.g.*, J. v. Peru, Preliminary Objections, Merits, Reparations, and Costs, Judgment, Inter-Am. Ct. H.R. (ser. C) No. 275, para. 224 (Nov. 27, 2013); Claude Reyes et al. v. Chile, Merits, Reparations, and Costs, Judgment, Inter-Am. Ct. H.R. (ser. C) No. 151, para. 122 (Sept. 19, 2006).

83 *E.g.*, J. v. Peru, Preliminary Objections, Merits, Reparations, and Costs, Judgment, Inter-Am. Ct. H.R. (ser. C) No. 275, para. 224 (Nov. 27, 2013); López Mendoza. v. Venezuela, Merits, Reparations, and Costs, Judgment, Inter-Am. Ct. H.R. (ser. C) No. 233, para. 141 (Sept. 1, 2011).

84 *E.g.*, Tarazona Arrieta et al. v. Peru, Preliminary Objections, Merits, Reparations, and Costs, Judgment, Inter-Am. Ct. H.R. (ser. C) No. 286, para. 98 (Oct. 15, 2014); Suárez Rosero v. Ecuador, Merits, Judgment, Inter-Am. Ct. H.R. (ser. C) No. 35, para. 71 (Nov. 12, 1997).

85 Suárez Rosero v. Ecuador, Merits, Judgment, Inter-Am. Ct. H.R. (ser. C) No. 35, para. 71 (Nov. 12, 1997).

contingent upon criminal proceedings.[86] With respect to criminal processes, the clock starts "when the first procedural act" against a suspect occurs.[87]

Prior to *López Álvarez v. Honduras*, the period started either at the moment of arrest or detention, or, if inapplicable, when "the judicial authority takes cognizance of the case."[88] But *López Álvarez* recognized that many more State actions can infringe upon the rights of an individual suspected of a crime, leading to a "substantial expansion" of the time frame.[89] As a result, any initial actions by the prosecutor or other authorities that restrict the rights of the suspect may be considered as the "first procedural act."[90] In contrast, when the Court is assessing a State's due diligence in investigating crimes, it starts counting time from the moment the crimes occurred.[91] In administrative procedures, the calculation begins with the submission of a claim or, again, the "first procedural act."[92]

Since *Genie Lacayo v. Nicaragua*, the Court has considered three elements, borrowed from European case law, in order to determine whether the duration is reasonable: (1) the complexity of the matter, (2) the conduct of the judicial authorities, and (3) the procedural activity of the interested party.[93] *Valle Jaramillo* et al. *v. Colombia* introduced a fourth element: the "effect on the person involved in the procedure."[94] These four criteria have been applied to both criminal and administrative proceedings, and have led the Court to find many violations of Article 8 over the years.

The Tribunal has recognized a number of situations as containing "complexity": prosecuting armed groups (such as insurgents or paramilitaries), soldiers, or police;[95]

---

[86] Tarazona Arrieta et al. v. Peru, Preliminary Objections, Merits, Reparations, and Costs, Judgment, Inter-Am. Ct. H.R. (ser. C) No. 286, para. 98 (Oct. 15, 2014); Furlan and Family v. Argentina, Preliminary Objections, Merits, Reparations, and Costs, Judgment, Inter-Am. Ct. H.R. (ser. C) No. 246, para. 151 (Aug. 31, 2012).

[87] López Álvarez v. Honduras, Merits, Reparations, and Costs, Judgment, Inter-Am. Ct. H.R. (ser. C) No. 141, para. 129 (Feb. 1, 2006).

[88] *E.g.*, Tibi v. Ecuador, Preliminary Objections, Merits, Reparations, and Costs, Judgment, Inter-Am. Ct. H.R. (ser. C) No. 114, para. 168 (Sept. 7, 2004); Suárez Rosero v. Ecuador, Merits, Judgment, Inter-Am. Ct. H.R. (ser. C) No. 35, para. 70 (Nov. 12, 1997).

[89] Concurring Opinion of Judge Sergio García Ramírez, para. 43, López Álvarez v. Honduras, Merits, Reparations, and Costs, Judgment, Inter-Am. Ct. H.R. (ser. C) No. 141 (Feb. 1, 2006).

[90] *Id.*

[91] *E.g.*, González et al. ("Cotton Field") v. Mexico, Preliminary Objections, Merits, Reparations, and Costs, Judgment, Inter-Am. Ct. H.R. (ser. C) No. 205, paras. 290, 294 (Nov. 16, 2009); Anzualdo Castro v. Peru, Preliminary Objections, Merits, Reparations, and Costs, Judgment, Inter-Am. Ct. H.R. (ser. C) No. 202, para. 131 (Sept. 22, 2009).

[92] Tibi v. Ecuador, Preliminary Objections, Merits, Reparations, and Costs, Judgment, Inter-Am. Ct. H.R. (ser. C) No. 114, para. 168 (Sept. 7, 2004).

[93] Genie Lacayo v. Nicaragua, Merits, Reparations, and Costs, Judgment, Inter-Am. Ct. H.R. (ser. C) No. 30, para. 77 (Jan. 29, 1997).

[94] Valle Jaramillo et al. v. Colombia, Merits, Reparations, and Costs, Judgment, Inter-Am. Ct. H.R. (ser. C) No. 192, para. 155 (Nov. 27, 2008).

[95] *E.g.*, *id.* para. 156; Moiwana Cmty. v. Suriname, Preliminary Objections, Merits, Reparations, and Costs, Judgment, Inter-Am. Ct. H.R. (ser. C) No. 124, para. 162 (June 15, 2005).

investigating multiple crimes and/or perpetrators;[96] failing to locate suspects, witnesses, and other evidence;[97] restoring extensive indigenous territories;[98] navigating various jurisdictions and remedies;[99] and probing into crimes of the distant past,[100] among others. Still, when weighed against the other circumstances, these situations rarely persuade the Court to conclude that a State's delay was reasonable.[101]

The Tribunal often points to the conduct of judges and other authorities as the primary explanation for an unreasonable length of proceedings. In *Las Dos Erres Massacre v. Guatemala*, it lamented the "pattern of judicial delay in Guatemala in investigations of grave human rights violations."[102] The Court cited to a half-dozen cases before it that demonstrated "the lack of will and interest" of State officials to prosecute these serious crimes, leading to a paralysis of proceedings and the spread of impunity in Guatemala.[103]

The Court has also dealt with poorly managed administrative procedures. A trilogy of cases against Paraguay sought the restitution of ancestral lands.[104] Delays occurred at every turn; recovery proceedings had taken 11 years in the shortest case. Upon finding violations of Article 8 in the last judgment, *Xákmok Kásek Indigenous Community*, the Tribunal chastised Paraguay for its "passivity, inactivity, little diligence, and lack of responsiveness."[105]

---

[96] *E.g.*, Rochela Massacre v. Colombia, Merits, Reparations, and Costs, Judgment, Inter-Am. Ct. H.R. (ser. C) No. 163, para. 158 (May 11, 2007); Moiwana Cmty. v. Suriname, Preliminary Objections, Merits, Reparations, and Costs, Judgment, Inter-Am. Ct. H.R. (ser. C) No. 124, para. 162 (June 15, 2005).

[97] *E.g.*, Valle Jaramillo et al. v. Colombia, Merits, Reparations, and Costs, Judgment, Inter-Am. Ct. H.R. (ser. C) No. 192, para. 156 (Nov. 27, 2008); Moiwana Cmty. v. Suriname, Preliminary Objections, Merits, Reparations, and Costs, Judgment, Inter-Am. Ct. H.R. (ser. C) No. 124, para. 162 (June 15, 2005).

[98] *E.g.*, Xákmok Kásek Indigenous Cmty. v. Paraguay, Merits, Reparations, and Costs, Judgment, Inter-Am. Ct. H.R. (ser. C) No. 214, para. 134 (Aug. 24, 2010); Yakye Axa Indigenous Cmty. v. Paraguay, Merits, Reparations, and Costs, Judgment, Inter-Am. Ct. H.R. (ser. C) No. 125, para. 87 (June 17, 2005).

[99] *E.g.*, Luna Lopez v. Honduras, Merits, Reparations, and Costs, Judgment, Inter-Am. Ct. H.R. (ser. C) No. 269, para. 190 (Oct. 10, 2013); La Cantuta v. Peru, Merits, Reparations, and Costs, Judgment, Inter-Am. Ct. H.R. (ser. C) No. 162, paras. 159–160 (Nov. 29, 2006).

[100] *E.g.*, Radilla Pacheco v. Mexico, Preliminary Objections, Merits, Reparations, and Costs, Judgment, Inter-Am. Ct. H.R. (ser. C) No. 209, para. 245 (Nov. 23, 2009); Heliodoro Portugal v. Panama, Preliminary Objections, Merits, Reparations, and Costs, Judgment, Inter-Am. Ct. H.R. (ser. C) No. 186, para. 150 (Aug. 12, 2008).

[101] *See, e.g.*, Valle Jaramillo et al. v. Colombia, Merits, Reparations, and Costs, Judgment, Inter-Am. Ct. H.R. (ser. C) No. 192, para. 159 (Nov. 27, 2008); Yakye Axa Indigenous Cmty. v. Paraguay, Merits, Reparations, and Costs, Judgment, Inter-Am. Ct. H.R. (ser. C) No. 125, para. 98 (June 17, 2005).

[102] "Las Dos Erres" Massacre v. Guatemala, Preliminary Objections, Merits, Reparations, and Costs, Judgment, Inter-Am. Ct. H.R. (ser. C) No. 211, para. 134 (Nov. 24, 2009).

[103] *Id.* para. 135.

[104] Xákmok Kásek Indigenous Cmty. v. Paraguay, Merits, Reparations, and Costs, Judgment, Inter-Am. Ct. H.R. (ser. C) No. 214, para. 137 (Aug. 24, 2010); Sawhoyamaxa Indigenous Cmty. v. Paraguay, Merits, Reparations, and Costs, Judgment, Inter-Am. Ct. H.R. (ser. C) No. 146, para. 97 (Mar. 29, 2006); Yakye Axa Indigenous Cmty. v. Paraguay, Merits, Reparations, and Costs, Judgment, Inter-Am. Ct. H.R. (ser. C) No. 125, para. 98 (June 17, 2005).

[105] Xákmok Kásek Indigenous Cmty. v. Paraguay, Merits, Reparations, and Costs, Judgment, Inter-Am. Ct. H.R. (ser. C) No. 214, para. 134 (Aug. 24, 2010).

In contrast, Colombian officials satisfied the due diligence standard in *Valle Jaramillo* when responding to an extrajudicial execution. The State had convicted two persons for the murder, a third for a lesser offense, and acquitted seven others of all charges. As "only slightly more than three years" elapsed between the crime and the convictions, the Court considered that "the measures taken by the Colombian State's prosecutors and judiciary were in keeping with criteria of diligence and reasonableness."[106] In *Kuna Indigenous People of Madungandi v. Panama*, three years were also deemed reasonable for the criminal proceedings regarding trespass and logging of the community's lands.[107]

In very difficult circumstances, even longer delays have been considered permissible for official investigations. *Luna López v. Honduras* involved the murder of an environmental activist in 1998.[108] One person was convicted for the killing in 2002; another was acquitted in 2006.[109] A third suspect fled the country; he was returned in 2008 and prosecuted.[110] A judge ultimately convicted him in 2013 for involvement in the murder.[111] In view of the flight from Honduras, threats against judges and prosecutors during the proceedings, and other complications, the overall achievements of State authorities "occurred within a reasonable period of time," according to the Court.[112]

As for the third element to determine reasonable time, "the procedural activity of the interested party," the Court does not require that victims or family members take the lead in criminal investigations and prosecutions. On the contrary, it has repeatedly held that the criminal justice process "is the State's responsibility, and decidedly does not depend upon the initiative of victims and their family members or upon their submission of evidence."[113] In such cases, the Tribunal only verifies whether they have actively hindered the proceedings.[114] Many times, the victims' perseverance and courage have alone kept the investigations open.[115]

---

[106] Valle Jaramillo et al. v. Colombia, Merits, Reparations, and Costs, Judgment, Inter-Am. Ct. H.R. (ser. C) No. 192, para. 158 (Nov. 27, 2008).

[107] Kuna Indigenous People of Madungandi and Embera Indigenous People of Bayano and their Members v. Panama, Preliminary Objections, Merits, Reparations, and Costs, Judgment, Inter-Am. Ct. H.R. (ser. C) No. 284, para. 186 (Oct. 14, 2014).

[108] Luna Lopez v. Honduras, Merits, Reparations, and Costs, Judgment, Inter-Am. Ct. H.R. (ser. C) No. 269 (Oct. 10, 2013).

[109] *Id.* para. 193.

[110] *Id.*

[111] *Id.*

[112] *Id.*

[113] *E.g.*, Serrano Cruz Sisters v. El Salvador, Merits, Reparations, and Costs, Judgment, Inter-Am. Ct. H.R. (ser. C) No. 120, para. 61 (Mar. 1, 2005); 19 Merchants v. Colombia, Merits, Reparations, and Costs, Judgment, Inter-Am. Ct. H.R. (ser. C) No. 109, para. 184 (July 5, 2004).

[114] *E.g.*, Xákmok Kásek Indigenous Cmty. v. Paraguay, Merits, Reparations, and Costs, Judgment, Inter-Am. Ct. H.R. (ser. C) No. 214, para. 134 (Aug. 24, 2010); Moiwana Cmty. v. Suriname, Preliminary Objections, Merits, Reparations, and Costs, Judgment, Inter-Am. Ct. H.R. (ser. C) No. 124, para. 161 (June 15, 2005).

[115] *See, e.g.*, Moiwana Cmty. v. Suriname, Preliminary Objections, Merits, Reparations, and Costs, Judgment, Inter-Am. Ct. H.R. (ser. C) No. 124, para. 161 (June 15, 2005); Mack Chang v. Guatemala, Merits, Reparations, and Costs, Judgment, Inter-Am. Ct. H.R. (ser. C) No. 101, para. 226 (Nov. 25, 2003).

Otherwise, an inquiry into procedural activity considers whether the interested party in the proceedings has acted in good faith. A criminal defendant's use of all the recourses provided by law cannot be deemed bad faith.[116] It is the judge's responsibility to ensure that zealous defense does not lead to abuses of process and unacceptable delays.[117]

At the end of 2008, as noted, the Court wisely added a fourth element to its analysis of reasonableness: the "effect on the person involved in the procedure."[118] Thus, "if the passage of time has a relevant impact on the judicial situation of the individual, the proceedings should be carried out more promptly so that the case is decided as soon as possible."[119] Under this framework, in *Xákmok Kásek* the Tribunal found that Paraguay's delay in returning the community's ancestral territories "has directly affected its way of life."[120] *Furlan and Family v. Argentina* reprimanded national judges for disregarding the disabilities of the petitioner, who required expedited resolution to his civil suit for damages, in order to afford necessary medical treatment.[121]

For years, the Court has stated "in certain cases, a prolonged delay may, in itself, constitute a violation of judicial guarantees."[122] Yet even with flagrant delays it would still proceed to analyze the factors discussed above. More recently, however, the Tribunal has appeared to adopt something akin to a strict liability standard. In *Landaeta Meijias Brothers* et al. *v. Venezuela*, after 17 years, the State had not proceeded beyond an initial investigation for an extrajudicial execution.[123] This delay, by itself, violated Article 8, and the Court "[did] not find it necessary to include any further considerations on the other elements relating to the reasonable time."[124] Such an approach certainly seems appropriate

---

[116] *See* MEDINA, *supra* note 42, at 309.

[117] *E.g.*, Mack Chang v. Guatemala, Merits, Reparations, and Costs, Judgment, Inter-Am. Ct. H.R. (ser. C) No. 101, paras. 209–211 (Nov. 25, 2003); Genie Lacayo v. Nicaragua, Merits, Reparations, and Costs, Judgment, Inter-Am. Ct. H.R. (ser. C) No. 30, para. 79 (Jan. 29, 1997).

[118] Valle Jaramillo et al. v. Colombia, Merits, Reparations, and Costs, Judgment, Inter-Am. Ct. H.R. (ser. C) No. 192, para. 155 (Nov. 27, 2008).

[119] *Id.*

[120] Xákmok Kásek Indigenous Cmty. v. Paraguay, Merits, Reparations, and Costs, Judgment, Inter-Am. Ct. H.R. (ser. C) No. 214, para. 136 (Aug. 24, 2010).

[121] Furlan and Family v. Argentina, Preliminary Objections, Merits, Reparations, and Costs, Judgment, Inter-Am. Ct. H.R. (ser. C) No. 246, paras. 201–203 (Aug. 31, 2012).

[122] *E.g.*, Radilla Pacheco v. Mexico, Preliminary Objections, Merits, Reparations, and Costs, Judgment, Inter-Am. Ct. H.R. (ser. C) No. 209, para. 191 (Nov. 23, 2009); Anzualdo Castro v. Peru, Preliminary Objections, Merits, Reparations, and Costs, Judgment, Inter-Am. Ct. H.R. (ser. C) No. 202, para. 124 (Sept. 22, 2009).

[123] Landaeta Meijias Brothers et al. v. Venezuela, Preliminary Objections, Merits, Reparations, and Costs, Judgment, Inter-Am. Ct. H.R. (ser. C) No. 281, para. 265 (Aug. 27, 2014).

[124] *Id.* para. 267. *See also* Rodriguez Vera et al. (Persons Disappeared from the Palace of Justice) v. Colombia, Preliminary Objections, Merits, Reparations, and Costs, Judgment, Inter-Am. Ct. H.R. (ser. C) No. 287, para. 506 (Nov. 14, 2014) (observing that, after 29 years, little progress had been made with the criminal investigations, and holding that "it is not necessary to make a detailed analysis of the previously mentioned criteria concerning the reasonable time"); García and Family Members v. Guatemala, Merits, Reparations, and Costs, Judgment, Inter-Am. Ct. H.R. (ser. C) No. 258, para. 153 (Nov. 29, 2012) (similar).

in extreme scenarios, to facilitate the Tribunal's work and to take a firmer position against the extended delays that have dismayed many petitioners in the Americas.

D. MEANING OF "COMPETENT, INDEPENDENT, AND IMPARTIAL TRIBUNAL, PREVIOUSLY ESTABLISHED BY LAW"

1. "Tribunal"

As discussed above, Article 8 guarantees are triggered when any public authority adopts decisions that affect rights and obligations. The official designation of the public authority in domestic law, whether as a "tribunal" or something else, is not significant according to the Inter-American jurisprudence.[125] If the body is authorized to make determinations on rights, the Court holds that Article 8 will apply.

2. "Competent"

Competent tribunals appropriately exercise *ratione personae, ratione materiae, ratione temporis*, and *ratione loci* jurisdiction—that is, jurisdiction over the person, subject matter, time, and place, respectively. In assessing competence, then, the Court has considered, among other aspects, "the nature of the crime and the legal interest affected."[126] Because "the existence and jurisdiction of the competent tribunal derives from" a State's legislation, "only the legislative branch is able to regulate . . . the jurisdiction of the courts."[127] When the Inter-American Court finds a lack of competence, a violation to Article 8 is declared, and the Court generally considers it unnecessary to analyze the other elements of Article 8(1), such as a court's independence and impartiality.[128]

The Tribunal has most often explained competence in the context of military jurisdiction, frequently asserted against civilians accused of terrorism.[129] In the 2015 judgment *Cruz Sánchez* et al. *v. Peru*, the Court reviewed its long-standing case law on the

---

[125] *E.g.*, Baena Ricardo et al. v. Panama, Merits, Reparations, and Costs, Judgment, Inter-Am. Ct. H.R. (ser. C) No. 72, paras. 124–134 (Feb. 2, 2001); Constitutional Court v. Peru, Merits, Reparations, and Costs, Judgment, Inter-Am. Ct. H.R. (ser. C) No. 71, para. 71 (Jan. 31, 2001).

[126] Escué Zapata v. Colombia, Merits, Reparations, and Costs, Judgment, Inter-Am. Ct. H.R. (ser. C) No. 165, para. 105 (July 4, 2007).

[127] Barreto Leiva v. Venezuela, Merits, Reparations, and Costs, Judgment, Inter-Am. Ct. H.R. (ser. C) No. 206, para. 76 (Nov. 17, 2009).

[128] *E.g.*, Supreme Court of Justice (Quintana Coello et al.) v. Ecuador, Preliminary Objections, Merits, Reparations, and Costs, Judgment, Inter-Am. Ct. H.R. (ser. C) No. 266, para. 181 (Aug. 23, 2013) ("Having determined that the body that carried out the process was not competent, it is unnecessary to examine the other guarantees established in Article 8(1) of the Convention."); Cabrera García and Montiel Flores v. Mexico, Preliminary Objections, Merits, Reparations, and Costs, Judgment, Inter-Am. Ct. H.R. (ser. C) No. 220, para. 201 (Nov. 26, 2010).

[129] Beyond the military jurisdiction context, *see, e.g.*, Supreme Court of Justice (Quintana Coello et al.) v. Ecuador, Preliminary Objections, Merits, Reparations, and Costs, Judgment, Inter-Am. Ct. H.R. (ser. C) No. 266, para.

subject.[130] To begin, "military criminal jurisdiction shall have a restrictive and exceptional scope and be directed toward the protection of special juridical interests, related to the tasks characteristic of the military forces."[131] The Court has clarified that only active soldiers shall be prosecuted in this forum for offenses strictly concerning the "military order."[132]

As a result, military jurisdiction is *not* the appropriate jurisdiction for the investigation and prosecution of human rights violations, *even if* they are committed by active military personnel. The State's ordinary criminal justice system must process those matters.[133] If the military jurisdiction hears such cases, "it is violating the right to a competent tribunal and, *a fortiori*, to a due process."[134]

In *Radilla Pacheco v. Mexico*, the Court also specified that it is not sufficient for civilian courts to review the decisions of military tribunals in cases of human rights violations; the right to a competent tribunal is still breached, as "the judge shall be competent since the first instance."[135] Another practice in violation of this principle is the use of "faceless" or secret judges and prosecutors in terrorism trials. The Court has ruled that this prevents defendants from learning the identity of their judges, and thus—among other problems—they cannot evaluate the tribunal's competency, independence, or impartiality.[136]

---

162 (Aug. 23, 2013) (finding Ecuador's Congress not competent to dismiss Supreme Court justices, "given that the new Constitution had removed its power to do so").

[130] Cruz Sánchez et al. v. Peru, Preliminary Objections, Merits, Reparations, Costs, Judgment, Inter-Am. Ct. H.R. (ser. C) No. 292 (Apr. 17, 2015).

[131] *Id.* para. 397 (translation by authors based on previous case law); Radilla Pacheco v. Mexico, Preliminary Objections, Merits, Reparations, and Costs, Judgment, Inter-Am. Ct. H.R. (ser. C) No. 209, para. 272 (Nov. 23, 2009). In *Palamara Iribarne v. Chile*, the Court asserted that military jurisdiction "should be reduced to the minimum and be inspired in the principles and guarantees prevailing in modern criminal law." Palamara Iribarne v. Chile, Merits, Reparations, Costs, Judgment, Inter-Am. Ct. H.R. (ser. C) No. 135, para. 132 (Nov. 22, 2005).

[132] Cruz Sánchez et al. v. Peru, Preliminary Objections, Merits, Reparations, Costs, Judgment, Inter-Am. Ct. H.R. (ser. C) No. 292, para. 397 (Apr. 17, 2015). In *Usón Ramírez v. Venezuela*, the petitioner was retired, and the Court underlined that retired service members, who "do not exercise particular functions of defense or national security," should not be tried by military courts. Usón Ramírez v. Venezuela, Preliminary Objection, Merits, Reparations, and Costs, Judgment, Inter-Am. Ct. H.R. (ser. C) No. 207, para. 115 (Nov. 20, 2009).

[133] *E.g., id.* para. 398; Durand and Ugarte v. Peru, Merits, Judgment, Inter-Am. Ct. H.R. (ser. C) No. 68, para. 118 (Aug. 16, 2000).

[134] *E.g.*, Cruz Sánchez et al. v. Peru, Preliminary Objections, Merits, Reparations, Costs, Judgment, Inter-Am. Ct. H.R. (ser. C) No. 292, para. 398 (Apr. 17, 2015)(translation by authors based on previous case law); Tiu Tojín v. Guatemala, Merits, Reparations, and Costs, Judgment, Inter-Am. Ct. H.R. (ser. C) No. 190, para. 118 (Nov. 26, 2008). The Court has specified several detailed characteristics for laws that establish military tribunals. *See* Usón Ramírez v. Venezuela, Preliminary Objection, Merits, Reparations, and Costs, Judgment, Inter-Am. Ct. H.R. (ser. C) No. 207, para. 110 (Nov. 20, 2009); Palamara Iribarne v. Chile, Merits, Reparations, Costs, Judgment, Inter-Am. Ct. H.R. (ser. C) No. 135, para. 126 (Nov. 22, 2005).

[135] Radilla Pacheco v. Mexico, Preliminary Objections, Merits, Reparations, and Costs, Judgment, Inter-Am. Ct. H.R. (ser. C) No. 209, para. 281 (Nov. 23, 2009).

[136] *E.g.*, J. v. Peru, Preliminary Objections, Merits, Reparations, and Costs, Judgment, Inter-Am. Ct. H.R. (ser. C) No. 275, para. 184 (Nov. 27, 2013) (clarifying that "the intervention of the 'faceless' prosecutor in the criminal

3. "Independent"

A tribunal's *independence* primarily refers to its autonomy in relation to other branches of government and their members; whereas the tribunal's *impartiality* mainly concerns its relationship with the parties to the specific matter before it.[137] The Inter-American Court has emphasized that the State must ensure both an independent judiciary and independent individual judges.[138] The Court has frequently dealt with independence and impartiality; however, it does not always sufficiently distinguish between the two concepts, preferring instead to highlight their interrelated nature.[139]

Still, *Quintana Coello* et al. *v. Ecuador, Camba Campos* et al. *v. Ecuador*, and *Reverón Trujillo v. Venezuela* discussed judicial independence at some length.[140] The Court held that two obligations arise from the right to a hearing by an independent tribunal: the first obligation corresponds to the judge, and the second to the State. The judge's duty of independence is fulfilled only when he or she "rules pursuant to—and moved by—the Law."[141] For their part, States must respect and ensure the right to be heard by an independent judge:

> The duty of respect consists in the negative obligation of public authorities to abstain from illegally interfering in the Judicial Power or with its members, that is, with regard to the specific judge. The duty of [ensure] consists in preventing those interferences and investigating and punishing those that commit them.[142]

Prevention of interferences and external pressure also entails the adoption of laws and regulations "that ensure an adequate process for the appointment and tenure of the judges."[143]

---

proceeding against Ms. J. also constitutes a violation of Article 8(1)"); Cantoral Benavides v. Peru, Merits, Judgment, Inter-Am. Ct. H.R. (ser. C) No. 69, para. 127 (Aug. 18, 2000).

[137] Apitz Barbera et al. ("First Court of Administrative Disputes") v. Venezuela, Preliminary Objection, Merits, Reparations, and Costs, Judgment, Inter-Am. Ct. H.R. (ser. C) No. 182, paras. 55–56 (Aug. 5, 2008). *See also* Argüelles et al. v. Argentina, Preliminary Objections, Merits, Reparations, and Costs, Judgment, Inter-Am. Ct. H.R. (ser. C) No. 288, para. 147 (Nov. 20, 2014).

[138] *E.g.*, Argüelles et al. v. Argentina, Preliminary Objections, Merits, Reparations, and Costs, Judgment, Inter-Am. Ct. H.R. (ser. C) No. 288, para. 147 (Nov. 20, 2014); Reverón Trujillo v. Venezuela, Preliminary Objections, Merits, Reparations, and Costs, Judgment, Inter-Am. Ct. H.R. (ser. C) No. 197, para. 67 (June 30, 2009).

[139] *See, e.g.*, Apitz Barbera et al. ("First Court of Administrative Disputes") v. Venezuela, Preliminary Objection, Merits, Reparations, and Costs, Judgment, Inter-Am. Ct. H.R. (ser. C) No. 182, para. 55 (Aug. 5, 2008).

[140] Constitutional Tribunal (Camba Campos et al.) v. Ecuador, Preliminary Objections, Merits, Reparations, and Costs, Judgment, Inter-Am. Ct. H.R. (ser. C) No. 268 (Aug. 28, 2013); Supreme Court of Justice (Quintana Coello et al.) v. Ecuador, Preliminary Objections, Merits, Reparations, and Costs, Judgment, Inter-Am. Ct. H.R. (ser. C) No. 266 (Aug. 23, 2013); Reverón Trujillo v. Venezuela, Preliminary Objections, Merits, Reparations, and Costs, Judgment, Inter-Am. Ct. H.R. (ser. C) No. 197 (June 30, 2009).

[141] Reverón Trujillo v. Venezuela, Preliminary Objections, Merits, Reparations, and Costs, Judgment, Inter-Am. Ct. H.R. (ser. C) No. 197, para. 146 (June 30, 2009).

[142] *Id.*

[143] *Id.*

The Court has approved European and UN standards on the appointment process and tenure.[144] It has affirmed that judges must be selected "exclusively based on their personal merits and professional qualifications, through objective selection and continuance mechanisms" that consider the "specific nature of the duties to be fulfilled."[145] Competitions shall be open and announced publicly, and details regarding requirements shall be communicated in a clear and transparent fashion.[146] Finally, all applicants, including those who currently occupy the positions, shall compete for the posts in equal conditions.[147]

As regards the judicial term of office, it shall be secured by law until a mandatory retirement age or the end of the term, where applicable.[148] Promotion of judges, where applicable, shall be "based on objective factors, in particular on ability, integrity and experience."[149] Judges may be dismissed "only on grounds of serious misconduct or incompetence, in accordance with fair procedures ensuring objectivity and impartiality set out in the Constitution or the law."[150] In this situation, the judge must always be given the right to defense.[151] The Inter-American Court has indicated that when a judge's tenure "is affected in an arbitrary manner," the right to judicial independence is violated "in conjunction with" Article 23(1)(c) of the American Convention (Right to Participate in Government).[152] That provision establishes a citizen's right "to have access, under general conditions of equality, to the public service of [his or her] country."[153]

4. "Impartial"

The Court has held that impartiality, "a fundamental guarantee of due process,"[154] means that a tribunal's members should not have any vested interest, premeditated decision, or preference for any of the parties involved in a case.[155] Clearly, judges cannot be personally

---

[144] Constitutional Tribunal (Camba Campos et al.) v. Ecuador, Preliminary Objections, Merits, Reparations, and Costs, Judgment, Inter-Am. Ct. H.R. (ser. C) No. 268, para. 188 (Aug. 28, 2013) (citing to the case law of the European Court of Human Rights and to the United Nations' Basic Principles on the Independence of the Judiciary).

[145] Reverón Trujillo v. Venezuela, Preliminary Objections, Merits, Reparations, and Costs, Judgment, Inter-Am. Ct. H.R. (ser. C) No. 197, para. 72 (June 30, 2009).

[146] *Id.* para. 73; Supreme Court of Justice (Quintana Coello et al.) v. Ecuador, para. 150.

[147] Reverón Trujillo v. Venezuela, Preliminary Objections, Merits, Reparations, and Costs, Judgment, Inter-Am. Ct. H.R. (ser. C) No. 197, para. 73 (June 30, 2009); Supreme Court of Justice (Quintana Coello et al.) v. Ecuador, para. 145.

[148] *Id.* para. 75; Supreme Court of Justice (Quintana Coello et al.) v. Ecuador, para. 145.

[149] *Id.* para. 76.

[150] *Id.* para. 77; Supreme Court of Justice (Quintana Coello et al.) v. Ecuador, para. 145.

[151] *Id.*

[152] Supreme Court of Justice (Quintana Coello et al.) v. Ecuador, para. 155.

[153] American Convention, art. 23(1)(c).

[154] Usón Ramírez v. Venezuela, Preliminary Objection, Merits, Reparations, and Costs, Judgment, Inter-Am. Ct. H.R. (ser. C) No. 207, para. 117 (Nov. 20, 2009).

[155] *E.g.*, Argüelles et al. v. Argentina, Preliminary Objections, Merits, Reparations, and Costs, Judgment, Inter-Am. Ct. H.R. (ser. C) No. 288, para. 168 (Nov. 20, 2014); Palamara Iribarne v. Chile, Merits, Reparations, Costs, Judgment, Inter-Am. Ct. H.R. (ser. C) No. 135, para. 146 (Nov. 22, 2005).

involved in the dispute.[156] Thus, the judge must evaluate a case's facts "*subjectively* free of all prejudice, and also offer sufficient *objective* guarantees to exclude any doubt the parties or the community might entertain as to his or her lack of impartiality."[157]

Personal or subjective impartiality is to be presumed unless there is evidence to the contrary.[158] Such evidence could include "whether the judge has displayed hostility or ill will" toward the parties or whether he or she arranged to take the case "for personal reasons."[159] On the other hand, the so-called "objective test" consists in determining whether the judge in question "offered sufficient convincing elements to exclude any legitimate misgivings or well-grounded suspicion of partiality."[160] In this way, appearances matter: a judge "must appear to act without being subject to influences, incentives, pressures, threats, or interference, direct or indirect, but instead only and exclusively according to the Law."[161]

The Court has demanded that judges recuse themselves from cases where their impartiality could be "legitimately" doubted.[162] In *Usón Ramírez v. Venezuela*, one of the Venezuelan judges who heard the appeal filed by Usón Ramírez was the very same individual who, in his capacity as a military prosecutor, had ordered the criminal investigation.[163] The judge was not prevented from hearing the case, nor did he accept the motion to disqualify him. The Inter-American Tribunal concluded, "his participation in the trial against Mr. Usón-Ramírez, first as an accuser and then as a judge, raises serious doubts about his impartiality," leading to a breach of the right to be tried by an impartial tribunal and a violation of Article 8(1).[164]

---

[156] Argüelles et al. v. Argentina, Preliminary Objections, Merits, Reparations, and Costs, Judgment, Inter-Am. Ct. H.R. (ser. C) No. 288, para. 168 (Nov. 20, 2014).

[157] Apitz Barbera et al. ("First Court of Administrative Disputes") v. Venezuela, Preliminary Objection, Merits, Reparations, and Costs, Judgment, Inter-Am. Ct. H.R. (ser. C) No. 182, para. 56 (Aug. 5, 2008) (emphasis added). *See also* Argüelles et al. v. Argentina, Preliminary Objections, Merits, Reparations, and Costs, Judgment, Inter-Am. Ct. H.R. (ser. C) No. 288, para. 167 (Nov. 20, 2014).

[158] Apitz Barbera et al. ("First Court of Administrative Disputes") v. Venezuela, Preliminary Objection, Merits, Reparations, and Costs, Judgment, Inter-Am. Ct. H.R. (ser. C) No. 182, para. 56 (Aug. 5, 2008).

[159] Atala Riffo and Daughters v. Chile, Merits, Reparations, and Costs, Judgment, Inter-Am. Ct. H.R. (ser. C) No. 239, para. 234 (Feb. 24, 2012).

[160] Apitz Barbera et al. ("First Court of Administrative Disputes") v. Venezuela, Preliminary Objection, Merits, Reparations, and Costs, Judgment, Inter-Am. Ct. H.R. (ser. C) No. 182, para. 56 (Aug. 5, 2008). *See also* Usón Ramírez v. Venezuela, Preliminary Objection, Merits, Reparations, and Costs, Judgment, Inter-Am. Ct. H.R. (ser. C) No. 207, para. 117 (Nov. 20, 2009).

[161] Atala Riffo and Daughters v. Chile, Merits, Reparations, and Costs, Judgment, Inter-Am. Ct. H.R. (ser. C) No. 239, para. 189 (Feb. 24, 2012) (citing Principle 2 of the United Nations' Basic Principles on the Independence of the Judiciary).

[162] *Id.* para. 238. *See also* Usón Ramírez v. Venezuela, Preliminary Objection, Merits, Reparations, and Costs, Judgment, Inter-Am. Ct. H.R. (ser. C) No. 207, para. 118 (Nov. 20, 2009).

[163] Usón Ramírez v. Venezuela, Preliminary Objection, Merits, Reparations, and Costs, Judgment, Inter-Am. Ct. H.R. (ser. C) No. 207, para. 118 (Nov. 20, 2009).

[164] *Id.* para. 119.

The Tribunal has stressed that the ability to disqualify a judge is "a procedural means of protecting the right to a hearing by an impartial body."[165] This recourse should not be considered as a challenge to the judge's "moral rectitude," but rather "as a tool to build trust in those turning to the State" for justice.[166] In *Apitz Barbera* et al. *v. Venezuela*, the Court found that, because Venezuelan law did not permit motions to disqualify the judges at issue, the State failed to ensure the petitioners' right to a hearing before an impartial tribunal.[167]

The Court has also required impartiality beyond judicial proceedings.[168] In *Constitutional Court v. Peru*, constitutional court justices were dismissed by a congressional commission.[169] However, some commission members had already expressed views related to the justices in question, tainting the impeachment procedure and leading to Peru's violation of Article 8.[170] The judgment *Albán Cornejo* et al. *v. Ecuador* called for impartiality in the supervisory proceedings of professional associations, such as those that impose disciplinary sanctions on physicians.[171] The Tribunal remarked that the decisions of such associations "may become highly influential" in subsequent litigation, "even though said decisions are not formally conclusive, mandatory or binding" on the courts.[172]

5. "Previously Established by Law"

According to the Court, "a basic principle of the independence of the judiciary is that every person has the right to be heard by regular courts, following procedures previously established by law."[173] States are not to create "[t]ribunals that do not use the duly established procedures of the legal process [. . .] to displace the jurisdiction belonging to the ordinary courts or judicial tribunals."[174] As the ordinary jurisdiction was usurped by

---

[165] *E.g.*, Argüelles et al. v. Argentina, Preliminary Objections, Merits, Reparations, and Costs, Judgment, Inter-Am. Ct. H.R. (ser. C) No. 288, para. 167 (Nov. 20, 2014); Apitz Barbera et al. ("First Court of Administrative Disputes") v. Venezuela, Preliminary Objection, Merits, Reparations, and Costs, Judgment, Inter-Am. Ct. H.R. (ser. C) No. 182, para. 64 (Aug. 5, 2008).

[166] Apitz Barbera et al. ("First Court of Administrative Disputes") v. Venezuela, Preliminary Objection, Merits, Reparations, and Costs, Judgment, Inter-Am. Ct. H.R. (ser. C) No. 182, para. 63 (Aug. 5, 2008).

[167] *Id.* para. 67.

[168] *See* Juana María Ibáñez Rivas, *Artículo 8: Garantías Judiciales*, *in* La Convención Americana Sobre Derechos Humanos Comentada 225-26 (Christian Steiner & Patricia Uribe eds., 2014).

[169] The Constitutional Court v. Peru, Merits, Reparations, and Costs, Judgment, Inter-Am. Ct. H.R. (ser. C) No. 71 (Jan. 31, 2001).

[170] *Id.* para. 78.

[171] Albán Cornejo et al. v. Ecuador, Merits, Reparations, and Costs, Judgment, Inter-Am. Ct. H.R. (ser. C) No. 171, para. 78 (Nov. 22, 2007).

[172] *Id.*

[173] Castillo Petruzzi et al. v. Peru, Merits, Reparations, and Costs, Judgment, Inter-Am. Ct. H.R. (ser. C) No. 52, para. 129 (May 30, 1999).

[174] *Id.* (citing the United Nations' Basic Principles on the Independence of the Judiciary).

military tribunals in *Castillo Petruzzi* et al. *v. Peru*, the Court found a violation of Article 8(1) in that judgment.[175]

This issue also came to the fore against Peru two years later, in *Ivcher Bronstein*. There, a "First Temporary Commercial Public Law Court" had been established to hear matters associated with Ivcher Bronstein's rights as a shareholder of a large media company.[176] The Inter-American Court concluded that, "by creating temporary public law chambers and courts and appointing judges to them at the time that the facts of the case *sub judice* occurred," Peru breached Ivcher Bronstein's "right to be heard by judges or courts 'previously established by law.' "[177]

In its attempts to counter terrorism, the United States established special military commissions to try the detainees at Guantánamo Bay, Cuba.[178] Since 2002, the Inter-American Commission on Human Rights—along with many other international legal authorities[179]—has criticized many aspects of this "global war on terror," including the ad hoc commissions.[180] The Inter-American Commission has called on the United States to "ensure that any criminal cases against [these] detainees . . . are dealt with through the [ordinary] criminal justice system rather than military commissions."[181] Otherwise, the detainees suffer violations of their right to be tried by a competent, independent, and impartial tribunal, previously established by law.[182]

III. Article 8(2) and the Right to Be Presumed Innocent

Article 8(2) outlines several familiar protections for criminal defendants. In cases where the Court has found a judge or tribunal to lack competence, independence, or impartiality, it has often found it "unnecessary to rule on other aspects of the criminal proceeding,"

---

[175] *Id.* paras. 132–134.

[176] Ivcher Bronstein v. Peru, Merits, Reparations, and Costs, Judgment, Inter-Am. Ct. H.R. (ser. C) No. 74, para. 113 (Feb. 6, 2001).

[177] *Id.* para. 114.

[178] *See* Military Order on the Detention, Treatment and Trial of Certain Non-Citizens in the War Against Terrorism of 13 November 2001. This Order was revised by several subsequent orders.

[179] *See, e.g.*, Report of the Chairperson-Rapporteur of the Working Group on Arbitrary Detention, the Special Rapporteur on the independence of judges and lawyers, the Special Rapporteur on torture and other cruel, inhuman or degrading treatment or punishment, the Special Rapporteur on freedom of religion or belief, and the Special Rapporteur on the right of everyone to the enjoyment of the highest attainable standard of physical and mental health, Situation of Detainees at Guantánamo Bay, Comm'n on Human Rights, U.N. Doc. E/CN.4/2006/120 (Feb. 27, 2006).

[180] Inter-American Commission on Human Rights, Towards the Closure of Guantánamo, OEA/Ser.L/V/II. Doc.20/15, paras. 219–220 (June 3, 2015), *available at* http://www.oas.org/en/iachr/reports/thematic.asp. Note that the Inter-American Commission cannot strictly interpret the U.S. actions in light of the American Convention, because the United States has not ratified the Convention.

[181] *Id.* para. 220 (reiterating the U.N. Human Rights Committee's statement).

[182] *Id.*

and thus has avoided an assessment of Article 8(2).[183] Still, there remain numerous judgments that have studied its provisions.

To begin, the Tribunal has stressed, "the principle of presumption of innocence constitutes a basis for the right to a fair trial."[184] A defendant is innocent until proven guilty beyond any reasonable doubt.[185] This core principle also requires that State authorities be "discreet and prudent" when commenting on suspects and open criminal investigations.[186] To illustrate, during press conferences, Peruvian officials would introduce detained individuals as terrorists—well before they had been convicted.[187] This practice, as well as other "categorical and unqualified statements of diverse State officials at different times," influenced public opinion as to the defendant's guilt and "prejudged the evaluation of the facts" by the courts, violating Article 8(2).[188]

Also comporting with the presumption of innocence is the State's obligation to avoid restricting the liberty of an accused person "beyond the limits strictly necessary to ensure that he will not impede the efficient development of an investigation and that he will not evade justice."[189] Because it is "the most severe measure that may be applied" to a person suspected of a crime, pretrial detention must be used only exceptionally.[190] When pretrial detention is abused, it becomes "the equivalent of advance punishment," in contravention of the presumption of innocence.[191]

---

[183] *E.g.*, Usón Ramírez v. Venezuela, Preliminary Objection, Merits, Reparations, and Costs, Judgment, Inter-Am. Ct. H.R. (ser. C) No. 207, para. 120 (Nov. 20, 2009); Cantoral Benavides v. Peru, Merits, Judgment, Inter-Am. Ct. H.R. (ser. C) No. 69, para. 115 (Aug. 18, 2000).

[184] Tibi v. Ecuador, Preliminary Objections, Merits, Reparations, and Costs, Judgment, Inter-Am. Ct. H.R. (ser. C) No. 114, para. 180 (Sept. 7, 2004).

[185] *E.g.*, Argüelles et al. v. Argentina, Preliminary Objections, Merits, Reparations, and Costs, Judgment, Inter-Am. Ct. H.R. (ser. C) No. 288, para. 130 (Nov. 20, 2014); J. v. Peru, Preliminary Objections, Merits, Reparations, and Costs, Judgment, Inter-Am. Ct. H.R. (ser. C) No. 275, para. 228 (Nov. 27, 2013).

[186] J. v. Peru, Preliminary Objections, Merits, Reparations, and Costs, Judgment, Inter-Am. Ct. H.R. (ser. C) No. 275, para. 244 (Nov. 27, 2013).

[187] *See, e.g.*, J. v. Peru, Preliminary Objections, Merits, Reparations, and Costs, Judgment, Inter-Am. Ct. H.R. (ser. C) No. 275, para. 237 (Nov. 27, 2013); Berenson Mejia v. Peru, Merits, Reparations, and Costs, Judgment, Inter-Am. Ct. H.R. (ser. C) No. 119, para. 158 (Nov. 25, 2004); Cantoral Benavides v. Peru, Merits, Judgment, Inter-Am. Ct. H.R. (ser. C) No. 69, para. 119 (Aug. 18, 2000).

[188] J. v. Peru, Preliminary Objections, Merits, Reparations, and Costs, Judgment, Inter-Am. Ct. H.R. (ser. C) No. 275, para. 248 (Nov. 27, 2013).

[189] *E.g.*, Argüelles et al. v. Argentina, Preliminary Objections, Merits, Reparations, and Costs, Judgment, Inter-Am. Ct. H.R. (ser. C) No. 288, para. 130 (Nov. 20, 2014); Tibi v. Ecuador, Preliminary Objections, Merits, Reparations, and Costs, Judgment, Inter-Am. Ct. H.R. (ser. C) No. 114, para. 180 (Sept. 7, 2004).

[190] *E.g.*, Barreto Leiva v. Venezuela, Merits, Reparations, and Costs, Judgment, Inter-Am. Ct. H.R. (ser. C) No. 206, para. 121 (Nov. 17, 2009); Neptune v. Haiti, Merits, Reparations, and Costs, Judgment, Inter-Am. Ct. H.R. (ser. C) No. 180, para. 107 (May 6, 2008).

[191] *E.g.*, Argüelles et al. v. Argentina, Preliminary Objections, Merits, Reparations, and Costs, Judgment, Inter-Am. Ct. H.R. (ser. C) No. 288, para. 130 (Nov. 20, 2014); Suárez Rosero v. Ecuador, Merits, Judgment, Inter-Am. Ct. H.R. (ser. C) No. 35, para. 77 (Nov. 12, 1997). For more on pretrial detention, *see* this volume's Chapter 5 on personal liberty.

As established by Article 8(2), "every person [accused of a criminal offense] is entitled, with full equality, to the following minimum guarantees." The Court has emphasized that they are called "*minimum* guarantees" because States may of course develop additional due process protections in view of national preferences or special circumstances.[192] One such special circumstance entails the participation of children in judicial or administrative proceedings, which require heightened diligence on the part of State officials. When children—defined as under 18 years of age—are accused of crimes, the Court has held that States should try to avoid judicial proceedings altogether, and seek alternative processes such as counseling and restorative justice.[193] Should judicial proceedings be necessary, special courts and procedures are essential.[194] These proceedings must have the capacity to ensure privacy, psychological assistance, and other support and protections for children.[195] Judges and officials must be specifically trained in children's rights and child psychology "to avoid any abuse of [their] discretionary authority and to ensure that the measures ordered in any case are appropriate and proportionate."[196]

The various provisions of Article 8(2), which plainly relate to each other and are often assessed in combination, are considered in order below.

A. Article 8(2)(a): The Right to Be Assisted by a Translator or Interpreter

Though the Court has recognized this right, it has not directly assessed Article 8(2)(a).[197] It is surprising, given the increasing numbers of cases arriving to the Inter-American System dealing with migrants and indigenous populations, some of whom do not fluently speak the official language of the domestic court system.[198] As translators and interpreters

---

[192] *E.g.*, DaCosta Cadogan v. Barbados, Preliminary Objections, Merits, Reparations, and Costs, Judgment, Inter-Am. Ct. H.R. (ser. C) No. 204, para. 84 (Sept. 24, 2009) (emphasis added); Exceptions to the Exhaustion of Domestic Remedies (Arts. 46(1), 46(2)(a), and 46(2)(b) American Convention on Human Rights), Advisory Opinion OC-11/90, Inter-Am. Ct. H.R. (ser. A) No. 11, para. 24 (Aug. 10, 1990).

[193] "Juvenile Reeducation Institute" v. Paraguay, Preliminary Objections, Merits, Reparations, and Costs, Judgment, Inter-Am. Ct. H.R. (ser. C) No. 112, paras. 210–211 (Sept. 2, 2004); Juridical Condition & Human Rights of the Child, Advisory Opinion OC-17/02, Inter-Am. Ct. H.R. (ser. A) No. 17, para. 137 (Aug. 28, 2002).

[194] *Id. See also* Article 5(5) of the American Convention ("Minors while subject to criminal proceedings shall be separated from adults and brought before specialized tribunals, as speedily as possible, so that they may be treated in accordance with their status as minors.").

[195] "Juvenile Reeducation Institute" v. Paraguay, Preliminary Objections, Merits, Reparations, and Costs, Judgment, Inter-Am. Ct. H.R. (ser. C) No. 112, paras. 210–211 (Sept. 2, 2004).

[196] *Id.*

[197] *See* Vélez Loor v. Panama, Preliminary Objections, Merits, Reparations, and Costs, Judgment, Inter-Am. Ct. H.R. (ser. C) No. 218, FN 129 (Nov. 23, 2010); Concurring Opinion of Judge Sergio García-Ramírez, para. 49, López Álvarez v. Honduras, Merits, Reparations, and Costs, Judgment, Inter-Am. Ct. H.R. (ser. C) No. 141 (Feb. 1, 2006).

[198] *Yakye Axa Indigenous Community v. Paraguay* examines a criminal proceeding concerning members of an indigenous community, but Article 8(2)(a) is not alleged or assessed. *See* Yakye Axa Indigenous Cmty. v. Paraguay, Merits, Reparations, and Costs, Judgment, Inter-Am. Ct. H.R. (ser. C) No. 125, paras. 106–119 (June 17, 2005).

are not always provided to criminal defendants of the Americas,[199] both the Court and victims' attorneys should stress this key right more.

Although no violations have yet been declared, the Court has supported this principle through its jurisprudence. In a recent advisory opinion, it explicitly called for a child's "right to be assisted without charge by a translator and/or interpreter" in any immigration proceedings, "whether administrative or judicial."[200] In *Pacheco Tineo Family v. Bolivia*, the Tribunal required translation and interpretation services for deportation and expulsion proceedings.[201] More broadly, it has stated: "the judicial process must recognize and correct any real disadvantages that those brought before the bar might have, thus observing the principle of equality before the law and the courts."[202] In this vein, considering indigenous community members, the Court instructed Guatemala to "ensure that they understand and are understood in the legal proceedings . . . offering them interpreters or other effective means for said purpose."[203]

The Tribunal should clarify the ambiguity left in the provision's text, which states "translator *or* interpreter." If this meant that providing only one of the two services would be sufficient, the Article would be unsatisfactory—because defendants require full comprehension of both oral and written elements of their defense.[204] That is, both translation and interpretation likely would be necessary for those without a full command of the language, unless a particular defendant showed otherwise.

B. ARTICLE 8(2)(B): PRIOR NOTIFICATION IN DETAIL OF CHARGES

The Court has indicated that, in accordance with Article 8(2)(b), States must notify individuals in writing of the actions or omissions attributed to them, the reasons and evidence that led to the charge, and the crime's legal definition.[205] All of this

---

[199] *See, e.g.*, Expert Opinion of Lottie Marie Cunningham de Aguirre, Mayagna (Sumo) Awas Tingni Cmty. v. Nicaragua, Merits, Reparations, and Costs, Judgment, Inter-Am. Ct. H.R. (ser. C) No. 79, para. 83 (Aug. 31, 2001) (explaining that judges often do not appoint translators or interpreters for members of indigenous communities in Nicaragua); HOLLY MIKKELSON, INTRODUCTION TO COURT INTERPRETING (2014) (noting that Latin American nations with large indigenous populations are struggling to provide sufficient language services).

[200] Rights & Guar. of Children in the Context of Migration and/or in Need of Int'l Prot., Advisory Opinion OC-21/14, Inter-Am. Ct. H.R. (ser. A) No. 21, para. 283(5) (Aug. 19, 2014).

[201] Pacheco Tineo Family v. Bolivia, Preliminary Objections, Merits, Reparations, and Costs, Judgment, Inter-Am. Ct. H.R. (ser. C) No. 272, para. 133 (Nov. 25, 2013).

[202] *E.g.*, Vélez Loor v. Panama, Preliminary Objections, Merits, Reparations, and Costs, Judgment, Inter-Am. Ct. H.R. (ser. C) No. 218, para. 152 (Nov. 23, 2010); Juridical Condition & Rights of the Undocumented Migrants, Advisory Opinion OC-18/03, Inter-Am. Ct. H.R. (ser. A) No. 18, para. 121 (Sept. 17, 2003).

[203] Tiu-Tojín v. Guatemala, Merits, Reparations, and Costs, Judgment, Inter-Am. Ct. H.R. (ser. C) No. 190, para. 100 (Nov. 26, 2008).

[204] *See* MEDINA, *supra* note 42, at 323–24.

[205] *E.g.*, J. v. Peru, Preliminary Objections, Merits, Reparations, and Costs, Judgment, Inter-Am. Ct. H.R. (ser. C) No. 275, paras. 198–199 (Nov. 27, 2013); López Álvarez v. Honduras, Merits, Reparations, and Costs, Judgment, Inter-Am. Ct. H.R. (ser. C) No. 141, para. 149 (Feb. 1, 2006).

information must be timely, clear, complete, and sufficiently detailed to allow individuals to fully exercise their right to defense and to explain their version of the facts to the judge.[206] It must be conveyed directly, through official channels; learning the information through the media or inferring it through the questions of State agents is not sufficient.[207] Although criminal charges may be modified during the proceedings by the prosecutor or judge, their underlying factual basis must remain unaltered, and the defendant's right to defense must be fully guaranteed with any change.[208] Naturally, the right to notification acquires special urgency when States take measures to restrict personal liberty.[209]

The Court has clarified that Article 8(2)(b) applies even before charges are filed, considering that the suspect's rights could be "affected by acts of authority that he is unaware of or that he cannot control or oppose effectively, which is evidently contrary to the Convention."[210] It has recognized that an individual can transition from a "person of interest" to formally charged very quickly; as a consequence, the State cannot "wait until someone is formally accused to provide him with the information on which the timely exercise of the right of defense depends."[211] Further, the Tribunal has asserted, "to ensure that [Article 8(2)(b)] can meet its intrinsic objectives, the notification must take place before the accused gives his first statement before any public authority."[212] If formal charges have not yet been made by that point, "as a minimum" persons under investigation "must learn about, in as much detail as possible," the facts imputed to them.[213]

---

206 J. v. Peru, Preliminary Objections, Merits, Reparations, and Costs, Judgment, Inter-Am. Ct. H.R. (ser. C) No. 275, paras. 199, 288 (Nov. 27, 2013); Barreto Leiva v. Venezuela, Merits, Reparations, and Costs, Judgment, Inter-Am. Ct. H.R. (ser. C) No. 206, para. 28 (Nov. 17, 2009). It appears that this provision requires more detail than Article 7(4) of the American Convention. *See* MEDINA, *supra* note 42, at 325.

207 *E.g.*, J. v. Peru, Preliminary Objections, Merits, Reparations, and Costs, Judgment, Inter-Am. Ct. H.R. (ser. C) No. 275, para. 199 (Nov. 27, 2013); Barreto Leiva v. Venezuela, Merits, Reparations, and Costs, Judgment, Inter-Am. Ct. H.R. (ser. C) No. 206, para. 47 (Nov. 17, 2009).

208 Fermín Ramírez v. Guatemala, Merits, Reparations, and Costs, Judgment, Inter-Am. Ct. H.R. (ser. C) No. 126, paras. 65–80 (June 20, 2005). In *Fermín Ramírez*, the State had modified both the legal and factual basis for the prosecution during the trial, resulting in flagrant violations of Article 8(2)(b) and (c). *Id.*

209 *E.g.*, J. v. Peru, Preliminary Objections, Merits, Reparations, and Costs, Judgment, Inter-Am. Ct. H.R. (ser. C) No. 275, para. 199 (Nov. 27, 2013); Palamara Iribarne v. Chile, Merits, Reparations, Costs, Judgment, Inter-Am. Ct. H.R. (ser. C) No. 135, para. 225 (Nov. 22, 2005).

210 J. v. Peru, Preliminary Objections, Merits, Reparations, and Costs, Judgment, Inter-Am. Ct. H.R. (ser. C) No. 275, para. 194 (Nov. 27, 2013); Barreto Leiva v. Venezuela, Merits, Reparations, and Costs, Judgment, Inter-Am. Ct. H.R. (ser. C) No. 206, para. 30 (Nov. 17, 2009).

211 J. v. Peru, Preliminary Objections, Merits, Reparations, and Costs, Judgment, Inter-Am. Ct. H.R. (ser. C) No. 275, para. 197 (Nov. 27, 2013); Barreto Leiva v. Venezuela, Merits, Reparations, and Costs, Judgment, Inter-Am. Ct. H.R. (ser. C) No. 206, para. 46 (Nov. 17, 2009).

212 *E.g.*, J. v. Peru, Preliminary Objections, Merits, Reparations, and Costs, Judgment, Inter-Am. Ct. H.R. (ser. C) No. 275, para. 195 (Nov. 27, 2013); López Álvarez v. Honduras, Merits, Reparations, and Costs, Judgment, Inter-Am. Ct. H.R. (ser. C) No. 141, para. 149 (Feb. 1, 2006).

213 J. v. Peru, Preliminary Objections, Merits, Reparations, and Costs, Judgment, Inter-Am. Ct. H.R. (ser. C) No. 275, para. 199 (Nov. 27, 2013); Barreto Leiva v. Venezuela, Merits, Reparations, and Costs, Judgment, Inter-Am. Ct. H.R. (ser. C) No. 206, para. 31 (Nov. 17, 2009).

In both *J. v. Peru* and *Barreto Leiva v. Venezuela*, the Tribunal acknowledged that "certain cases" may justify keeping criminal investigations confidential to a degree, "in order to guarantee the effectiveness of the administration of justice."[214] In such scenarios, "necessary" measures can be taken to impede the destruction or tampering of evidence.[215] Nevertheless, the State's investigation authority "must be harmonized with the right of defense of the person investigated, which supposes the possibility of knowing the facts of which he or she is accused."[216] Because the Tribunal dismissed the States' secrecy arguments without further discussion, the judgments did not develop the precise circumstances under which information may be properly withheld from the suspect under investigation.

C. ARTICLE 8(2)(C): ADEQUATE TIME AND MEANS FOR PREPARATION OF DEFENSE

This "fundamental" right ensures the defendant's "access to the record of the case and to the evidence gathered against him."[217] The individual under investigation must be able to fully participate in the analysis of the evidence. In *Palamara Iribarne v. Chile*, the defense counsel had unsuccessfully attempted several times to obtain pertinent information.[218] Once the investigation was referred to a military court, the attorney finally gained access to the case file—but he was then given only six days to submit a response.[219] These circumstances triggered a violation of Article 8(2)(c), among other provisions.[220]

The Court has not provided detailed guidance on an "adequate time" standard, at least in the context of defense preparation. Another case that dealt with the issue was *Castillo Petruzzi v. Peru*. There, defendants charged with terrorism-related crimes only had access to the case file the day before the court issued their conviction. Peruvian law granted defense attorneys only 12 hours to consult the file. Clearly, a number of due process violations resulted, including a breach of Article 8(2)(c).[221] The Inter-American Court should clarify

---

[214] J. v. Peru, Preliminary Objections, Merits, Reparations, and Costs, Judgment, Inter-Am. Ct. H.R. (ser. C) No. 275, para. 196 (Nov. 27, 2013); Barreto Leiva v. Venezuela, Merits, Reparations, and Costs, Judgment, Inter-Am. Ct. H.R. (ser. C) No. 206, para. 45 (Nov. 17, 2009).

[215] J. v. Peru, Preliminary Objections, Merits, Reparations, and Costs, Judgment, Inter-Am. Ct. H.R. (ser. C) No. 275, para. 196 (Nov. 27, 2013).

[216] *Id.*; Barreto Leiva v. Venezuela, Merits, Reparations, and Costs, Judgment, Inter-Am. Ct. H.R. (ser. C) No. 206, para. 53 (Nov. 17, 2009).

[217] Barreto Leiva v. Venezuela, Merits, Reparations, and Costs, Judgment, Inter-Am. Ct. H.R. (ser. C) No. 206, para. 54 (Nov. 17, 2009); Palamara Iribarne v. Chile, Merits, Reparations, Costs, Judgment, Inter-Am. Ct. H.R. (ser. C) No. 135, para. 170 (Nov. 22, 2005).

[218] Palamara Iribarne v. Chile, Merits, Reparations, Costs, Judgment, Inter-Am. Ct. H.R. (ser. C) No. 135, para. 172 (Nov. 22, 2005).

[219] Palamara Iribarne's attorney was then forced to wait four months before he was allowed to offer evidence in defense of his client. *Id.* para. 177.

[220] *Id.* para. 181 (concluding that Chile "violated Article 8 of the Convention in relation to subparagraphs (1), (5), (2)(c), (2)(d), (2)(f) and (2)(g), to the detriment of Mr. Humberto Antonio Palamara Iribarne").

[221] Castillo Petruzzi et al. v. Peru, Merits, Reparations, and Costs, Judgment, Inter-Am. Ct. H.R. (ser. C) No. 52, para. 142 (May 30, 1999). However, in *López Mendoza v. Venezuela*, the Court remarked that the petitioners

here that domestic tribunals must grant continuances when shown to be important for adequate criminal defense.

In the more recent judgments *J. v. Peru* and *Barreto Leiva*, as mentioned above, the State kept the investigation secret from the defendants. Consequently, the Inter-American Court found that the defense was undermined, in breach of Article 8(2)(c). It held that if a State wishes to limit this right, "it must do so in keeping with the principle of legality," and "present the legitimate objective that it seeks to achieve, and prove that the means used to this end is suitable, necessary and strictly proportionate."[222] In *J.*, the Tribunal observed that the restrictions imposed upon the petitioner's defense were not even permitted by Peruvian law.[223] Further, her attorney visits were limited (see next section) to a "clearly disproportionate" extent; as a result, Peru failed the Court's balancing test in violation of both paragraphs (c) and (d) of Article 8(2).[224]

D. Article 8(2)(d): The Right to Defend Oneself Personally or to Be Assisted by Legal Counsel, and to Communicate Freely and Privately with Counsel

Consistent with the American Convention, the Court has acknowledged that individuals may choose to defend themselves. Nevertheless, it has underscored the importance of a "technical defense."[225] Such a defense, according to the Tribunal, is conducted by a legal professional, "who advises the accused on his rights and duties and who also exercises, *inter alia*, a critical control over lawfulness in the production of evidence."[226]

The Court has ruled that the accused must have access to an attorney from the moment that a criminal investigation is ordered, and especially during the first statement.[227] In

"did not show how [15 working days to submit evidence] limited the possibility of an adequate defense." López Mendoza v. Venezuela, Merits, Reparations, and Costs, Judgment, Inter-Am. Ct. H.R. (ser. C) No. 233, para. 121 (Sept. 1, 2011).

[222] J. v. Peru, Preliminary Objections, Merits, Reparations, and Costs, Judgment, Inter-Am. Ct. H.R. (ser. C) No. 275, para. 206 (Nov. 27, 2013). In *Barreto Leiva*, the Court was particularly critical of the Venezuelan law that prevented a suspect's access to the criminal investigation. Barreto Leiva v. Venezuela, Merits, Reparations, and Costs, Judgment, Inter-Am. Ct. H.R. (ser. C) No. 206, para. 56 (Nov. 17, 2009). According to the Tribunal, the law failed to take into account the individual characteristics of criminal cases, and thus violated Articles 8(2)(c) and 2 of the American Convention. *Id.* para. 57.

[223] J. v. Peru, Preliminary Objections, Merits, Reparations, and Costs, Judgment, Inter-Am. Ct. H.R. (ser. C) No. 275, para. 207 (Nov. 27, 2013).

[224] *Id.*

[225] *E.g.*, Argüelles et al. v. Argentina, Preliminary Objections, Merits, Reparations, and Costs, Judgment, Inter-Am. Ct. H.R. (ser. C) No. 288, paras. 176–177 (Nov. 20, 2014); Barreto Leiva v. Venezuela, Merits, Reparations, and Costs, Judgment, Inter-Am. Ct. H.R. (ser. C) No. 206, para. 61 (Nov. 17, 2009).

[226] Barreto Leiva v. Venezuela, Merits, Reparations, and Costs, Judgment, Inter-Am. Ct. H.R. (ser. C) No. 206, paras. 61-62 (Nov. 17, 2009).

[227] *E.g., id.*; Argüelles et al. v. Argentina, Preliminary Objections, Merits, Reparations, and Costs, Judgment, Inter-Am. Ct. H.R. (ser. C) No. 288, para. 175 (Nov. 20, 2014).

Barreto Leiva, Venezuela had claimed that the prosecutor's presence during the defendant's statements was sufficient. Clearly, the Court concluded otherwise, holding that "it is not reasonable to entrust naturally opposed" functions—that is, prosecution and defense—in the same person.[228] In *Chaparro Álvarez and Lapo Íñiguez v. Ecuador*, Chaparro Álvarez's defense lawyer was present for his statement, but the police forbade the attorney from advising him during the interrogation.[229] In this case, "the presence of a defense lawyer was a mere formality," and Ecuador "violated the right embodied in Article 8(2)(d)" as a consequence.[230]

The defendant has the right "to communicate freely and privately" with counsel.[231] In a handful of cases involving terrorism suspects in Peru, the Court found that the State had impeded this right to free and private legal consultation.[232] In *Castillo Petruzzi* et al. *v. Peru*, the petitioners were prohibited legal counsel from the time they were detained until they gave statements to the authorities; only then were they assigned lawyers.[233] Thus, the role of these attorneys was "peripheral at best," leading to a violation of Article 8(2)(d).[234] In *J. v. Peru*, the petitioner demonstrated that, over a 14-month period of pre-trial detention, she was only able to meet with her lawyer three times for between 15 and 25 minutes; these meetings with her attorney were never private.[235] The Court found violations of paragraphs (c) and (d) of Article 8(2).[236]

Vélez Loor v. Panama examined the question of when attorneys are required in non-criminal contexts.[237] The Court explained that the proceeding's "significance, its legal character, and its context in a particular legal system" figure "among the factors" that determine whether legal representation is necessary for due process.[238] Specifically,

---

228 Barreto Leiva v. Venezuela, Merits, Reparations, and Costs, Judgment, Inter-Am. Ct. H.R. (ser. C) No. 206, para. 63 (Nov. 17, 2009).

229 Chaparro Álvarez and Lapo Íñiguez v. Ecuador, Preliminary Objections, Merits, Reparations, and Costs, Judgment, Inter-Am. Ct. H.R. (ser. C) No. 170, para. 158 (Nov. 21, 2007).

230 *Id.*

231 American Convention, art. 8(2)(d).

232 *See* Cantoral Benavides v. Peru, Merits, Judgment, Inter-Am. Ct. H.R. (ser. C) No. 69, para. 128 (Aug. 18, 2000), and judgments discussed in text.

233 Castillo Petruzzi et al. v. Peru, Merits, Reparations, and Costs, Judgment, Inter-Am. Ct. H.R. (ser. C) No. 52, para. 146 (May 30, 1999).

234 *Id.* Note, however, that the Court decided that the Peruvian law prohibiting an attorney from assisting more than one defendant at the same time "does not represent, per se, a violation of Article 8(2)(d)." *Id.* para. 147. It arrived at this conclusion despite recognizing that the law "does have the effect of limiting the accused's choices of defense attorneys." *Id.*

235 J. v. Peru, Preliminary Objections, Merits, Reparations, and Costs, Judgment, Inter-Am. Ct. H.R. (ser. C) No. 275, para. 202 (Nov. 27, 2013).

236 *Id.* para. 207.

237 Vélez Loor v. Panama, Preliminary Objections, Merits, Reparations, and Costs, Judgment, Inter-Am. Ct. H.R. (ser. C) No. 218, para. 145 (Nov. 23, 2010).

238 *Id. See also* Exceptions to the Exhaustion of Domestic Remedies (Arts. 46(1), 46(2)(a), and 46(2)(b) American Convention on Human Rights), Advisory Opinion OC-11/90, Inter-Am. Ct. H.R. (ser. A) No. 11, para. 28 (Aug. 10, 1990).

whenever "decisions may be taken by which an accused may be deported, expelled, or deprived of freedom, the provision of free public legal aid service is necessary to avoid the violation of the right to due process."[239] To reiterate, this commendable judgment established that any proceeding that could result in an individual's deprivation of liberty or deportation calls for free legal representation, whenever necessary, as "an imperative for the interests of justice."[240]

E. Article 8(2)(e): The Right to Be Assisted by Counsel Provided by the State

During the Conference of San José it was indicated that the Latin American tradition was to obligate defendants to be represented by an attorney, at least when they did not defend themselves.[241] At the same time, certain delegates were worried by the economic burden of granting free legal service.[242] Owing to these circumstances and Article 8's final text, there existed an unfortunate possibility in the region that indigent defendants could be compelled to hire attorneys that are not funded by the State.

Subsequently, in *Advisory Opinion 11*, the Inter-American Court held that such a scenario is impermissible, as it would discriminate against the indigent "for reason of his economic status."[243] The Court then asserted that States that do not provide the poor with free counsel cannot subsequently claim, in a case before the Inter-American System, that appropriate domestic legal remedies existed but were not exhausted by these petitioners.[244] The Court also recognized that when defendants are permitted to represent themselves because they cannot afford counsel, "a violation of Article 8 of the Convention could be said to exist if it can be proved that the lack of legal counsel affected the right to a fair hearing."[245]

Currently, when the defendant is denied access to any attorney, the Court finds violations of both paragraphs (d) and (e) of Article 8(2).[246] In contrast, if the State impedes

---

[239] Vélez Loor v. Panama, Preliminary Objections, Merits, Reparations, and Costs, Judgment, Inter-Am. Ct. H.R. (ser. C) No. 218, para. 146 (Nov. 23, 2010). *See also* Juridical Condition & Rights of the Undocumented Migrants, Advisory Opinion OC-18/03, Inter-Am. Ct. H.R. (ser. A) No. 18, para. 126 (Sept. 17, 2003).

[240] Vélez Loor v. Panama, Preliminary Objections, Merits, Reparations, and Costs, Judgment, Inter-Am. Ct. H.R. (ser. C) No. 218, para. 146 (Nov. 23, 2010).

[241] P. 201, Minutes of the 7th Session of Committee I, Doc 45, Nov. 14, 1969.

[242] P. 202, Minutes of the 7th Session of Committee I, Doc 45, November 14, 1969.

[243] Exceptions to the Exhaustion of Domestic Remedies (Arts. 46(1), 46(2)(a), and 46(2)(b) American Convention on Human Rights), Advisory Opinion OC-11/90, Inter-Am. Ct. H.R. (ser. A) No. 11, para. 25 (Aug. 10, 1990). *See also* Acosta Calderón v. Ecuador, Merits, Reparations, and Costs, Judgment, Inter-Am. Ct. H.R. (ser. C) No. 129, para. 122 (June 24, 2005) (citing the United Nations' Body of Principles for the Protection of All Persons under Any Form of Detention or Imprisonment, which provides for free legal assistance to indigent detained persons, among other principles).

[244] Exceptions to the Exhaustion of Domestic Remedies, Advisory Opinion OC-11/90, Inter-Am. Ct. H.R. (ser. A) No. 11, para. 26 (Aug. 10, 1990).

[245] *Id.* para. 27.

[246] *E.g.*, Argüelles et al. v. Argentina, Preliminary Objections, Merits, Reparations, and Costs, Judgment, Inter-Am. Ct. H.R. (ser. C) No. 288, paras. 181–182 (Nov. 20, 2014) (finding that the "defenders" were not licensed

the services and counsel of a private attorney, only paragraph (d) is breached.[247] Still, the Tribunal has not differentiated much between the two paragraphs, and has interpreted the terms of Article 8(2)(e) only a few times.

In *Chaparro Álvarez and Lapo Íñiguez v. Ecuador*, the public defender assigned to one of the petitioners, Freddy Lapo Íñiguez, was absent during his interrogation and pretrial statement, only appearing "so that he could begin [the] statement and at the end of it, in order to sign it."[248] The Court found the public defender's "attitude" to be "clearly incompatible with the State's obligation to provide an acceptable defense lawyer to anyone who is unable to defend himself or appoint a private defense lawyer," in breach of Article 8(2)(e).[249] The Tribunal further held: "the legal assistance provided by the State must be effective and, to this end, the State must adopt all appropriate measures."[250] In this way, Article 8(2)(e) does not merely require a State-appointed attorney under the appropriate circumstances. For the Court, it also demands "effective" legal assistance by that lawyer.

In *DaCosta Cadogan v. Barbados*, the Tribunal began to set out parameters for effective counsel. There, petitioners alleged that State-appointed counsel was "grossly incompetent," and, as a consequence, this should amount to a violation of Article 8(2)(e).[251] They argued that "an independent forensic psychiatric or psychological assessment" was critical to demonstrate a defense of "diminished responsibility" in the death-penalty case.[252] The Court accepted the possibility that incompetent attorneys could violate Article 8(2)(e). However, it appeared to endorse a demanding standard for finding such a violation: "gross incompetence," taking the phrase of petitioners.[253] The Tribunal decided that the lawyer's "failure to pursue a defense of diminished responsibility and his decision to choose instead other available defenses" did not meet this standard.[254]

Instead, the Inter-American Court pinned the blame on the trial judge. It remarked that, as the case involved a possible death sentence, "such proceedings require the most ample and strict observation of due process rights."[255] In addition, "considering that Mr. DaCosta Cadogan was afforded state-appointed legal counsel, the presiding judge had

---

attorneys); Acosta Calderón v. Ecuador, Merits, Reparations, and Costs, Judgment, Inter-Am. Ct. H.R. (ser. C) No. 129, paras. 124, 126 (June 24, 2005).

[247] Chaparro Álvarez and Lapo Íñiguez v. Ecuador, Preliminary Objections, Merits, Reparations, and Costs, Judgment, Inter-Am. Ct. H.R. (ser. C) No. 170, paras. 155, 158 (Nov. 21, 2007). Although both paragraphs (d) and (e) of Article 8(2) could have been found violated in this judgment, as no lawyer assisted Chaparro Álvarez during his first police interview. *Id.* para. 156.

[248] *Id.* para. 156.

[249] *Id.* para. 159.

[250] *Id.*

[251] DaCosta Cadogan v. Barbados, Preliminary Objections, Merits, Reparations, and Costs, Judgment, Inter-Am. Ct. H.R. (ser. C) No. 204, para. 91 (Sept. 24, 2009).

[252] *Id.*

[253] *Id.* para. 93.

[254] *Id.*

[255] *Id.* para. 89.

the duty to adopt a more active role in ensuring that all necessary measures were carried out in order to guarantee a fair trial."[256] Because the trial judge could have ordered the psychological examination, but chose not to do so, Barbados was held responsible for other due process violations: paragraphs (c) and (f) of Article 8(2) and Article 8(1).[257]

Much remains for the Court to explain about its requirement for "effective" counsel. It is true that a defendant can take certain actions with respect to his or her underperforming lawyer. However, once a threshold has been crossed, the State should be held responsible—whether in the case of an appointed attorney or private counsel. To illustrate, as in *DaCosta Cadogan*, the State must intervene if defense counsel fails to act for the accused in key situations or neglects to comply with important procedural requirements.[258] The concept of effective counsel must also include sufficient opportunity to build the case and to communicate adequately with the client, along the entire course of the representation.[259] Although some flaws in legal strategy may not violate a standard for effective counsel, the Inter-American Court clearly must demand that State-appointed lawyers be fully qualified for the type of case at hand and its specific stage of proceedings.[260]

F. Article 8(2)(f): The Right of the Defense to Present and Examine Witnesses

The Inter-American Court has held on a number of occasions that "one of the prerogatives of the accused must be the opportunity to examine or have examined witnesses against him and to obtain the attendance and examination of witnesses on his behalf, under the same conditions as witnesses against him."[261] In order to find a violation of this provision, the Tribunal requires detailed information regarding the defense's witnesses

---

[256] *Id.*

[257] *Id.* para. 90.

[258] *See* Harris, O'Boyle & Warbrick, *supra* note 2, at 481 (explaining how the European Court has interpreted its own standard for "practical and effective" legal assistance). In *Tibi v. Ecuador*, court-appointed defense counsel did not visit Tibi, nor did the attorney "intervene in his defense," violating paragraphs (d) and (e) of Article 8(2). Tibi v. Ecuador, Preliminary Objections, Merits, Reparations, and Costs, Judgment, Inter-Am. Ct. H.R. (ser. C) No. 114, para. 194 (Sept. 7, 2004).

[259] *See, e.g.*, American Bar Association, The Ten Principles of a Public Defense Delivery System (2002), *available at* http://www.americanbar.org/content/dam/aba/administrative/legal_aid_indigent_defendants/ls_sclaid_def_tenprinciplesbooklet.authcheckdam.pdf.

[260] *See id.*; Harris, O'Boyle & Warbrick, *supra* note 2, at 482–83.

[261] *E.g.*, Berenson Mejia v. Peru, Merits, Reparations, and Costs, Judgment, Inter-Am. Ct. H.R. (ser. C) No. 119, para. 184 (Nov. 25, 2004); Castillo Petruzzi et al. v. Peru, Merits, Reparations, and Costs, Judgment, Inter-Am. Ct. H.R. (ser. C) No. 52, para. 154 (May 30, 1999). *See also* Norín Catrimán et al. (Leaders, members and activist of the Mapuche Indigenous People) v. Chile, Merits, Reparations, and Costs, Judgment, Inter-Am. Ct. H.R. (ser. C) No. 279, para. 242 (May 29, 2014). Article 8(2)(f) has been violated in several cases against Peru. *See, e.g.*, J. v. Peru, Preliminary Objections, Merits, Reparations, and Costs, Judgment, Inter-Am. Ct. H.R. (ser. C) No. 275, para. 210 (Nov. 27, 2013); García Asto and Ramírez Rojas v. Peru, Preliminary Objection, Merits, Reparations, and Costs, Judgment, Inter-Am. Ct. H.R. (ser. C) No. 137, para. 161 (Nov. 25, 2005); Berenson Mejía v. Peru, *supra*, para. 186; Castillo Petruzzi et al. v. Peru, *supra*, para. 156.

or evidence.[262] In some instances, petitioners were unable to provide testimony or evidence for their defense in domestic proceedings. In *Canese v. Paraguay*, Ricardo Canese had attempted to secure the participation of witnesses and experts in the criminal trial against him, but the judge prevented their testimony.[263] The Court found that Canese was not allowed to present "probative material in his defense that could 'throw light on the facts,'" in violation of Article 8(2)(f).[264]

In *DaCosta Cadogan*, as mentioned above, the Inter-American Tribunal found that the trial judge had failed to order a key psychiatric evaluation

> in order to determine, *inter alia*, the existence of a possible alcohol dependency or other "personality disorders" that could have affected Mr. DaCosta Cadogan at the time of the offense, and . . . also failed to ensure that Mr. DaCosta and his counsel were aware of the availability of a free, voluntary, and detailed mental health evaluation in order to prepare his defense in the trial.[265]

As a result, the defendant's mental health was "never fully evaluated . . . in a case where the death penalty was the only possible sentence."[266] Under these grave circumstances, the Court held this omission to constitute violations of both Article 8(1) and paragraphs (f) and (c) of Article 8(2).[267]

A more recent judgment against Chile, *Norín Catrimán* et al., closely examined the use of anonymous witnesses in prosecutions for terrorism-related charges.[268] The Court began by approving relevant European jurisprudence, which requires "judicial control, based on the principles of necessity and proportionality, taking into account that this is

---

[262] *E.g.*, Norín Catrimán et al. (Leaders, members and activist of the Mapuche Indigenous People) v. Chile, Merits, Reparations, and Costs, Judgment, Inter-Am. Ct. H.R. (ser. C) No. 279, paras. 244–260 (May 29, 2014); Barreto Leiva v. Venezuela, Merits, Reparations, and Costs, Judgment, Inter-Am. Ct. H.R. (ser. C) No. 206, paras. 65–66 (Nov. 17, 2009).

[263] Canese v. Paraguay, Merits, Reparations, and Costs, Judgment, Inter-Am. Ct. H.R. (ser. C) No. 111, para. 164 (Aug. 31, 2004).

[264] *Id.*

[265] DaCosta Cadogan v. Barbados, Preliminary Objections, Merits, Reparations, and Costs, Judgment, Inter-Am. Ct. H.R. (ser. C) No. 204, para. 88 (Sept. 24, 2009).

[266] *Id.*

[267] *Id.* para. 90.

[268] Norín Catrimán et al. (Leaders, members and activist of the Mapuche Indigenous People) v. Chile, Merits, Reparations, and Costs, Judgment, Inter-Am. Ct. H.R. (ser. C) No. 279 (May 29, 2014). Also, in three cases against Peru, a domestic law on terrorism prohibited defendants from cross-examining and challenging the State authorities who had prepared the reports and provided testimony that formed the basis for the charges. Violations to Article 8(2)(f) resulted. García Asto and Ramírez Rojas v. Peru, Preliminary Objection, Merits, Reparations, and Costs, Judgment, Inter-Am. Ct. H.R. (ser. C) No. 137, para. 153 (Nov. 25, 2005); Berenson Mejia v. Peru, Merits, Reparations, and Costs, Judgment, Inter-Am. Ct. H.R. (ser. C) No. 119, para. 183 (Nov. 25, 2004); Castillo Petruzzi et al. v. Peru, Merits, Reparations, and Costs, Judgment, Inter-Am. Ct. H.R. (ser. C) No. 52, para. 153 (May 30, 1999).

an exceptional measure and verifying the existence of a situation of risk for the witness."[269] It also considered whether Chile employed "counterbalancing measures," such as:

> (a) the judicial authority must be aware of the identity of the witness and be able to observe his demeanor under questioning . . . and (b) the defense must be granted every opportunity to examine the witness directly at some stage of the proceedings on matters that are not related to his identity or actual residence . . . .[270]

Even when such measures have been taken, however, the Court asserted that a conviction cannot be based "either solely or to a decisive extent on anonymous statements."[271]

Norín Catrimán assessed distinct proceedings that had used anonymous witnesses. In the first, against Segundo Norín Catrimán, the Court found the judicial control "insufficient," because the judge, in accepting the prosecutor's request, did not specify "the objective criteria, the reasoning, and the verifiable evidence that, in the specific case, would substantiate the alleged risk for the witnesses and their families."[272] Despite these flaws, Article 8(2)(f) was not declared violated, because the anonymous testimony was not decisive in the conviction, and "specific counterbalancing measures were guaranteed so that the defense could examine the anonymous witness and contest his testimony."[273] In contrast, as regards the proceedings against two other defendants, the Court found that "decisive significance was given to the statements of anonymous witnesses," leading to breaches of Article 8(2)(f).[274]

G. Article 8(2)(g) and Article 8(3): The Right Not to Be Compelled to Be a Witness against Oneself; Coercion and Confessions

These two provisions are clearly related and thus are considered together in this section.[275] Article 8(2)(g) establishes a well-accepted *right* of the accused, whereas Article 8(3) is a corollary of this right: a more specific principle that regulates coerced evidence. This principle is of crucial importance in the Americas, where forced confessions and other statements are still regularly accepted as valid evidence.[276]

---

[269] Norín Catrimán et al. v. Chile, Merits, Reparations, and Costs, Judgment, Inter-Am. Ct. H.R. (ser. C) No. 279, para. 245 (May 29, 2014).

[270] *Id.* para. 246.

[271] *Id.* para. 247.

[272] *Id.* para. 249.

[273] *Id.* para. 251(a).

[274] *Id.* paras. 251(b)–260.

[275] *See* Judge García Ramírez Concurring Opinion, para. 8, Maritza Urrutia v. Guatemala, Merits, Reparations, and Costs, Judgment, Inter-Am. Ct. H.R. (ser. C) No. 103 (Nov. 27, 2003) (linking the two provisions).

[276] *See, e.g.*, "US Foreign Policy, Human Rights and Public Security in Colombia and Mexico," Written Testimony Before the United States Senate Subcommittee on Human Rights and the Law of José Miguel Vivanco, Executive Director of the Americas Division, Human Rights Watch (May 18, 2010) (describing how police and other State authorities regularly coerce confessions and other testimony in Latin America).

The language of the two provisions suggests that whenever a suspect is coerced to be a witness against him- or herself, Article 8(2)(g) is breached—whether or not a confession is produced.[277] In contrast, Article 8(3) is activated only with a confession of guilt. The Court's judgments are consistent with this interpretation. Therefore, when coercion to make a statement is found, the Court has declared a violation of Article 8(2)(g).[278] Yet when tainted evidence had been rejected by an appeals court,[279] or when the defendant had refused to confess despite pressure, and even torture,[280] Article 8(3) was not breached. Finally, when the coerced confession is employed as valid evidence against the defendant, both provisions are held violated.[281]

In a judgment from 2003, *Maritza Urrutia v. Guatemala*, both Article 8(2)(g) and Article 8(3) were violated in notable circumstances.[282] Maritza Urrutia was detained, tortured, and forced to film a statement whereby she confessed to her role as a guerilla and "urged her companions to abandon the armed fight."[283] The statement was broadcast on Guatemalan television. The Court remarked that

> although it appears that [Article 8(2)(g) and Article 8(3)] are limited to the protection of persons subject to judicial proceedings . . . the Court considers that they must be respected in proceedings or procedures before or accompanying the judicial proceedings, which, should these guarantees not be respected, could have an unfavorable and unjustified impact on the juridical status of the person in question.[284]

As a result, although Urrutia's self-incriminating statement was not made within criminal proceedings, the Court found that both provisions were still breached.[285]

---

[277] In fact, it appears that for a violation of Article 8(2)(g), no statement at all is necessary by the accused; the act of coercion itself is the only required element. *See* López Álvarez v. Honduras, Merits, Reparations, and Costs, Judgment, Inter-Am. Ct. H.R. (ser. C) No. 141, para. 155 (Feb. 1, 2006); Tibi v. Ecuador, Preliminary Objections, Merits, Reparations, and Costs, Judgment, Inter-Am. Ct. H.R. (ser. C) No. 114, para. 181 (Sept. 7, 2004).

[278] *E.g.*, Bayarri v. Argentina, Preliminary Objection, Merits, Reparations, and Costs, Judgment, Inter-Am. Ct. H.R. (ser. C) No. 187, para. 109 (Oct. 30, 2008); López Álvarez v. Honduras, Merits, Reparations, and Costs, Judgment, Inter-Am. Ct. H.R. (ser. C) No. 141, para. 155 (Feb. 1, 2006).

[279] Bayarri v. Argentina, Preliminary Objection, Merits, Reparations, and Costs, Judgment, Inter-Am. Ct. H.R. (ser. C) No. 187, para. 108 (Oct. 30, 2008).

[280] López Álvarez v. Honduras, Merits, Reparations, and Costs, Judgment, Inter-Am. Ct. H.R. (ser. C) No. 141, para. 107 (Feb. 1, 2006); Tibi v. Ecuador, Preliminary Objections, Merits, Reparations, and Costs, Judgment, Inter-Am. Ct. H.R. (ser. C) No. 114, para. 162 (Sept. 7, 2004).

[281] Cantoral Benavides v. Peru, Merits, Judgment, Inter-Am. Ct. H.R. (ser. C) No. 69, para. 133 (Aug. 18, 2000).

[282] Maritza Urrutia v. Guatemala, Merits, Reparations, and Costs, Judgment, Inter-Am. Ct. H.R. (ser. C) No. 103 (Nov. 27, 2003).

[283] *Id.* para. 58(8).

[284] *Id.* para. 120.

[285] *Id.* para. 121.

In recent years, the Court has called for the exclusion of *all* evidence—not only confessions and statements against oneself—produced under "any form of duress."[286] The Tribunal prohibits both the evidence "obtained directly under duress" and any evidence that subsequently "derives from" the coercion.[287] If criminal courts do not block the tainted evidence, a violation of Article 8 will result.[288] Further, the Court has clarified that duress or abuse need not occur immediately before or during the particular statement to render it invalid, as prior mistreatment could obtain a similar effect.[289]

H. Article 8(2)(h): The Right to Appeal a Judgment to a Higher Court

As explained previously in this volume, the Inter-American Court does not usually review whether a national court has interpreted and applied domestic law correctly; it focuses on whether States have violated the American Convention.[290] The Tribunal has stated that the right to appeal "is an essential guarantee that must be respected within the framework of due process of law in order to permit a guilty verdict to be reviewed by a different and higher judge or court."[291] Specifically, the Court has explained that the appellate procedure "must be an ordinary, accessible and effective remedy that permits a comprehensive review or examination of the appealed ruling;" also, an appeal must be "available to anyone who has been convicted," and must respect "basic procedural guarantees."[292] The appeal must result in a judicial ruling that "provides clear, complete and logical grounds" for its decision on criminal responsibility.[293]

---

286 *E.g.*, Garcia Cruz and Sanchez Silvestre v. Mexico, Merits, Reparations, and Costs, Judgment, Inter-Am. Ct. H.R. (ser. C) No. 273, para. 58 (Nov. 26, 2013); Cabrera García and Montiel Flores v. Mexico, Preliminary Objections, Merits, Reparations, and Costs, Judgment, Inter-Am. Ct. H.R. (ser. C) No. 220, paras. 165–166 (Nov. 26, 2010).

287 Cabrera García and Montiel Flores v. Mexico, Preliminary Objections, Merits, Reparations, and Costs, Judgment, Inter-Am. Ct. H.R. (ser. C) No. 220, para. 167 (Nov. 26, 2010).

288 Despite finding that confessions were coerced in *Cabrera García and Montiel Flores v. Mexico*, the Court refused the victims' requests to order the State to remove their names "from any criminal records as well as to permanently eliminate any criminal record related to the facts reported in this case." Cabrera García and Montiel Flores v. Mexico, Preliminary Objections, Merits, Reparations, and Costs, Judgment, Inter-Am. Ct. H.R. (ser. C) No. 220, para. 222 (Nov. 26, 2010).

289 *E.g.*, Garcia Cruz and Sanchez Silvestre v. Mexico, Merits, Reparations, and Costs, Judgment, Inter-Am. Ct. H.R. (ser. C) No. 273, para. 58 (Nov. 26, 2013); Cabrera García and Montiel Flores v. Mexico, Preliminary Objections, Merits, Reparations, and Costs, Judgment, Inter-Am. Ct. H.R. (ser. C) No. 220, para. 175 (Nov. 26, 2010).

290 Norín Catrimán et al. v. Chile, Merits, Reparations, and Costs, Judgment, Inter-Am. Ct. H.R. (ser. C) No. 279, para. 287 (May 29, 2014).

291 *E.g., id.* para. 269; Herrera Ulloa v. Costa Rica, Preliminary Objections, Merits, Reparations, and Costs, Judgment, Inter-Am. Ct. H.R. (ser. C) No. 107, para. 158 (July 2, 2004).

292 *E.g.*, Norín Catrimán et al. v. Chile, Merits, Reparations, and Costs, Judgment, Inter-Am. Ct. H.R. (ser. C) No. 279, para. 270 (May 29, 2014); Liakat Ali Alibux v. Suriname, Preliminary Objections, Merits, Reparations, and Costs, Judgment, Inter-Am. Ct. H.R. (ser. C) No. 276, paras. 84–87 (Jan. 30, 2014).

293 Norín Catrimán et al. v. Chile, Merits, Reparations, and Costs, Judgment, Inter-Am. Ct. H.R. (ser. C) No. 279, para. 288 (May 29, 2014).

An "ordinary" remedy for the Court is one that can be filed before the judgment becomes final.[294] A procedure is "accessible" in this sense when it features "minimal formalities"[295] and is not "so complex that it makes this right illusory."[296] Regardless of the particular appellate system adopted by States, it must be "effective"; that is, it must "constitute an appropriate mechanism to rectify an erroneous conviction."[297] For example, "the higher court must have the jurisdictional authority to take up the particular case in question."[298] Thus, a military court was inappropriate to consider an appeal of the conviction of civilians in *Castillo Petruzzi* et al. *v. Peru*.[299]

Further, the appeal must allow for a "comprehensive review" of the previous judgment.[300] The key case *Herrera Ulloa v. Costa Rica* examined the Costa Rican courts of cassation, which, as in various countries, provided only limited review of criminal convictions.[301] As a result, the Inter-American Court held that such tribunals did not satisfy Article 8(2)(h).[302] Similarly, in *Norín Catrimán* et al. *v. Chile*, the appeals court failed to achieve a "comprehensive examination of the ruling appealed, because it did not analyze all the contested factual, evidentiary and legal issues on which the guilty verdict . . . was based."[303] The Inter-American Tribunal explained that the appeals court neglected the

---

294 *E.g., id.* para. 270; Herrera Ulloa v. Costa Rica, Preliminary Objections, Merits, Reparations, and Costs, Judgment, Inter-Am. Ct. H.R. (ser. C) No. 107, para. 158 (July 2, 2004).

295 *E.g.*, Norín Catrimán et al. v. Chile, Merits, Reparations, and Costs, Judgment, Inter-Am. Ct. H.R. (ser. C) No. 279, para. 270 (May 29, 2014); Liakat Ali Alibux v. Suriname, Preliminary Objections, Merits, Reparations, and Costs, Judgment, Inter-Am. Ct. H.R. (ser. C) No. 276, para. 86 (Jan. 30, 2014).

296 *E.g.*, Norín Catrimán et al. v. Chile, Merits, Reparations, and Costs, Judgment, Inter-Am. Ct. H.R. (ser. C) No. 279, para. 270 (May 29, 2014); Herrera Ulloa v. Costa Rica, Preliminary Objections, Merits, Reparations, and Costs, Judgment, Inter-Am. Ct. H.R. (ser. C) No. 107, para. 164 (July 2, 2004).

297 *E.g.*, Norín Catrimán et al. v. Chile, Merits, Reparations, and Costs, Judgment, Inter-Am. Ct. H.R. (ser. C) No. 279, para. 270 (May 29, 2014); Liakat Ali Alibux v. Suriname, Preliminary Objections, Merits, Reparations, and Costs, Judgment, Inter-Am. Ct. H.R. (ser. C) No. 276, para. 86 (Jan. 30, 2014).

298 *E.g.*, Vélez Loor v. Panama, Preliminary Objections, Merits, Reparations, and Costs, Judgment, Inter-Am. Ct. H.R. (ser. C) No. 218, para. 179 (Nov. 23, 2010); Castillo Petruzzi et al. v. Peru, Merits, Reparations, and Costs, Judgment, Inter-Am. Ct. H.R. (ser. C) No. 52, para. 161 (May 30, 1999).

299 Castillo Petruzzi et al. v. Peru, Merits, Reparations, and Costs, Judgment, Inter-Am. Ct. H.R. (ser. C) No. 52, para. 161 (May 30, 1999).

300 *E.g.*, Norín Catrimán et al. v. Chile, Merits, Reparations, and Costs, Judgment, Inter-Am. Ct. H.R. (ser. C) No. 279, para. 270 (May 29, 2014); Herrera Ulloa v. Costa Rica, Preliminary Objections, Merits, Reparations, and Costs, Judgment, Inter-Am. Ct. H.R. (ser. C) No. 107, para. 165 (July 2, 2004).

301 *See* Concurring Opinion of Judge García Ramírez, para. 34, Herrera Ulloa v. Costa Rica, Preliminary Objections, Merits, Reparations, and Costs, Judgment, Inter-Am. Ct. H.R. (ser. C) No. 107 (July 2, 2004) (describing the tradition of courts of cassation).

302 *Id.* para. 167. *See also* Mendoza et al. v. Argentina, Preliminary Objections, Merits, and Reparations, Judgment, Inter-Am. Ct. H.R. (ser. C) No. 260, para. 261 (May 14, 2013) ("because the appeal in cassation of the judgment was not sufficient to guarantee . . . the right to appeal the judgment, the Court considers that Argentina violated the right recognized in Article 8(2)(h) of the American Convention").

303 Norín Catrimán et al. v. Chile, Merits, Reparations, and Costs, Judgment, Inter-Am. Ct. H.R. (ser. C) No. 279, para. 280 (May 29, 2014).

"interdependence" between factual findings and legal conclusions, in that "an erroneous determination of the facts entails an erroneous or incorrect application of the law."[304]

The right to appeal must be available to anyone who has been convicted.[305] This right remains fully intact in those States that allow the government to appeal acquittals. In *Mohamed v. Argentina*, the Court clarified that the right to appeal still must be ensured to an individual who was initially acquitted at the trial level, but then convicted by a higher court.[306] "To interpret it otherwise," according to the Tribunal, would leave him or her "without the right to an appeal against the conviction."[307]

Finally, appellate proceedings "must respect the minimum procedural guarantees that . . . are pertinent and necessary to decide the errors asserted by the appellant, without this entailing the need to conduct a new oral trial."[308] Of course, this implies that an independent, impartial and competent court decides the matter after evaluating all arguments. On this point, the Tribunal has stressed that an appellate court's composition must be entirely different from that of the initial court. Thus, when a supreme court has exclusive jurisdiction over special criminal proceedings, the trial could be heard by the chief justice or a panel of judges, and the appeal should be decided by the full court—with the exception of those judges who already participated.[309]

I. THE RIGHT TO EFFECTIVE ACCESS TO CONSULAR ASSISTANCE

Although the American Convention does not specifically allude to this matter, the Court has established the "right to effective access to consular assistance" as "an individual right," "a minimum guarantee protected within the Inter-American system," and "a component of the right to defense and due process" that "should be granted without delay."[310] This right seeks to address the vulnerability of detained foreign nationals by providing

---

[304] *Id.*

[305] *E.g.*, *id.* para. 270; Mohamed v. Argentina, Preliminary Objections, Merits, Reparations, and Costs, Judgment, Inter-Am. Ct. H.R. (ser. C) No. 255, para. 92 (Nov. 23, 2012).

[306] Mohamed v. Argentina, Preliminary Objections, Merits, Reparations, and Costs, Judgment, Inter-Am. Ct. H.R. (ser. C) No. 255, para. 92 (Nov. 23, 2012).

[307] *Id.*

[308] *E.g.*, Norín Catrimán et al. v. Chile, Merits, Reparations, and Costs, Judgment, Inter-Am. Ct. H.R. (ser. C) No. 279, para. 270 (May 29, 2014); Mohamed v. Argentina, Preliminary Objections, Merits, Reparations, and Costs, Judgment, Inter-Am. Ct. H.R. (ser. C) No. 255, para. 101 (Nov. 23, 2012).

[309] Liakat Ali Alibux v. Suriname, Preliminary Objections, Merits, Reparations, and Costs, Judgment, Inter-Am. Ct. H.R. (ser. C) No. 276, para. 105 (Jan. 30, 2014). In *Liakat Ali Alibux*, the Court found that the use of Suriname's High Court of Justice as the criminal tribunal with sole jurisdiction over high-ranking ministers was "compatible, in principle, with the American Convention." *Id.* para 102. Nevertheless, Suriname did not provide a manner of appealing the High Court's decision, and thus violated Article 8(2)(h). *Id.* para. 106.

[310] Vélez Loor v. Panama, Preliminary Objections, Merits, Reparations, and Costs, Judgment, Inter-Am. Ct. H.R. (ser. C) No. 218, paras. 151, 160 (Nov. 23, 2010); Right to Information on Consular Assistance in the Framework of the Guarantees of the Due Process of Law, Advisory Opinion OC-16/99, Inter-Am. Ct. H.R. (ser. A) No. 16, paras. 84 and 124 (Oct. 1, 1999). *See also* Rights & Guar. of Children in the Context of Migration and/or in Need of Int'l Prot., Advisory Opinion OC-21/14, Inter-Am. Ct. H.R. (ser. A) No. 21, paras. 116, 126–128

"the fundamental guarantee of . . . access to justice."[311] Consular officials may assist the detainee in various ways, such as providing an attorney, obtaining evidence and information in the country of origin, and monitoring his or her health.[312]

According to the Tribunal, there are "three essential components" of this right due to a detained foreign national: "1) the right to be informed of his rights under the Vienna Convention [on Consular Relations]; 2) the right to have effective access to communication with the consular official; and 3) the right to the assistance itself."[313] Referring to the Vienna Convention on Consular Relations, the Court has further explained that "effective access" must include the ability to receive timely visits from consular officials and to freely communicate with them.[314] It has held that these three components safeguard an individual's rights to personal liberty and humane treatment, in addition to the right to due process.[315]

In *Vélez Loor v. Panama*, the Court required the State to show if it had complied with the obligation to inform the petitioner of his right to consular assistance.[316] Panama merely had sent notice to the Embassy of Ecuador, his State of origin, and Jesús Tranquilino Vélez Loor only received consular assistance—helping him obtain medical attention—after he had already received a detention order. Consequently, the Court decided that he had been unable to exercise "his right to defense," among other reasons, for having lacked an effective access to consular assistance.[317] It concluded that Article 8(1) and 8(2)(d), as well as Article 7(4) (Right to Personal Liberty) were violated.[318]

IV. Article 8(4): An Acquitted Person Shall Not Be Subjected to a New Trial for the Same Cause

The *ne bis in idem* principle, or the prohibition against double jeopardy, is well accepted in international law.[319] According to Inter-American jurisprudence, three elements must

---

(Aug. 19, 2014); Pacheco Tineo Family v. Bolivia, Preliminary Objections, Merits, Reparations, and Costs, Judgment, Inter-Am. Ct. H.R. (ser. C) No. 272, para. 133 (Nov. 25, 2013).

[311] Vélez Loor v. Panama, Preliminary Objections, Merits, Reparations, and Costs, Judgment, Inter-Am. Ct. H.R. (ser. C) No. 218, para. 154 (Nov. 23, 2010).

[312] *Id.*; The Right to Information on Consular Assistance in the Framework of the Guarantees of the Due Process of Law, Advisory Opinion OC-16/99, Inter-Am. Ct. H.R. (ser. A) No. 16, para. 86 (Oct. 1, 1999).

[313] Vélez Loor v. Panama, Preliminary Objections, Merits, Reparations, and Costs, Judgment, Inter-Am. Ct. H.R. (ser. C) No. 218, para. 153 (Nov. 23, 2010).

[314] *Id.* para. 158.

[315] *Id.*

[316] *Id.* para. 155.

[317] *Id.* para. 159.

[318] *Id.* para. 160. In a previous judgment, *Chaparro Álvarez and Lapo Íñiguez. v. Ecuador*, the State had not notified Juan Carlos Chaparro, a foreign detainee, of his right to communicate with a consular official of his country; as a result, the Court only declared a violation of Article 8(1). Chaparro Álvarez and Lapo Íñiguez v. Ecuador, Preliminary Objections, Merits, Reparations, and Costs, Judgment, Inter-Am. Ct. H.R. (ser. C) No. 170, para. 165 (Nov. 21, 2007).

[319] *See, e.g.*, Rome Statute of the International Criminal Court, art. 20; 7th Protocol to the European Convention, art. 4; ICCPR, art. 14(7).

be present to violate Article 8(4): (1) the accused must have been acquitted, (2) the acquittal must be the result of a final judgment, and (3) the new proceedings must be based on the same facts that constituted the grounds for the first trial.[320] The Tribunal has asserted that the formulation in the American Convention is more protective than that of the ICCPR, in that Article 8(4) prohibits another trial based on the same "cause" or facts, as opposed to the (more narrow) same "offense" or "crime."[321] In this way, the American Convention prevents prosecutors from reconfiguring the same facts into a new criminal charge for trial.

This is what happened in *Loayza Tamayo v. Peru*, where the petitioner was tried and acquitted by a military court for treason.[322] Then, María Elena Loayza Tamayo was brought before an ordinary criminal court for the "closely linked" crime of terrorism.[323] The Inter-American Court found that neither crime was "strictly defined, so that they may be interpreted similarly."[324] As a result, the Court held that the laws establishing the crimes were inconsistent with Article 8(4), and that Peru violated this provision for trying Loayza Tamayo again for the same facts of which she had been acquitted.[325]

In *Berenson Mejía v. Peru*, the Tribunal observed that the Supreme Council of Military Justice had waived jurisdiction in Lori Berenson Mejía's case, sending it to a civilian criminal court.[326] Without a decision on the merits, according to the Inter-American Court, there could be no violation of Article 8(4).[327] The Court also stated that military trials of civilians, which violate the "principle of access to a competent, independent and impartial tribunal," cannot "constitute a real proceeding under Article 8(4)."[328] In contrast, the earlier *Loayza Tamayo* judgment, for effects of Article 8(4), had considered the prior military court ruling—an acquittal—to be valid.

Subsequent Court decisions have further developed the exceptions to the *ne bis in idem* principle, in recognition of the impunity enjoyed by many rights abusers in the Americas. In contexts where there was never any real intention of holding the

---

[320] J. v. Peru, Preliminary Objections, Merits, Reparations, and Costs, Judgment, Inter-Am. Ct. H.R. (ser. C) No. 275, para. 262 (Nov. 27, 2013); Alan García v. Peru, Case No. 11.006, Inter-Am. Comm'n H.R., Report No. 1/95, OEA/Ser.L/V/II.88 Doc. 9 rev. (1995).

[321] *E.g.*, J. v. Peru, Preliminary Objections, Merits, Reparations, and Costs, Judgment, Inter-Am. Ct. H.R. (ser. C) No. 275, para. 259 (Nov. 27, 2013); Loayza Tamayo v. Peru, Merits, Judgment, Inter-Am. Ct. H.R. (ser. C) No. 33, para. 66 (Sept. 17, 1997).

[322] Loayza Tamayo v. Peru, Merits, Judgment, Inter-Am. Ct. H.R. (ser. C) No. 33, para. 67 (Sept. 17, 1997).

[323] *Id.*

[324] *Id.* para. 68.

[325] *Id.* paras. 68 and 77.

[326] Berenson Mejia v. Peru, Merits, Reparations, and Costs, Judgment, Inter-Am. Ct. H.R. (ser. C) No. 119, para. 208 (Nov. 25, 2004).

[327] *Id.*

[328] *Id.* para. 206. *See also* Cantoral Benavides v. Peru, Merits, Judgment, Inter-Am. Ct. H.R. (ser. C) No. 69, para. 138 (Aug. 18, 2000).

perpetrator accountable,[329] or when the "non-appealable judgment was delivered in contravention of the guarantees of competence, independence and impartiality," the double jeopardy rule is not applicable.[330] That is, spurious acquittals can be disregarded, and renewed prosecution may be permissible. Moreover, if new evidence surfaces that makes it possible to identify perpetrators of human rights violations or crimes against humanity, "investigations can be reopened, even if the case ended in an acquittal with the authority of a final judgment."[331] According to the Court, this action is demanded by "the dictates of justice, the rights of the victims, and the spirit and the wording of the American Convention."[332]

V. Article 8(5): Public Criminal Proceedings

This "essential element . . . of criminal procedure in a democratic State" is ensured, according to the Court, "by holding an oral stage in which the accused is able to have direct access to the judge and the evidence, and which provides access to the public."[333] The Inter-American case law endorses the "general move in the [Latin American] region towards oral, adversarial trials" and away from the emphasis on written proceedings.[334] In this way, according to the Tribunal, "the secret administration of justice is prohibited"; it must be transparent and subject to "the scrutiny of the parties and of the public."[335] Article 8(5) promotes impartiality, public trust, and access to information.[336]

Berenson Mejía v. Peru, as noted above, considered in detail the Peruvian military trials of civilians who were accused of terrorism and treason. Hooded judges presided over these proceedings, which were closed to the public. The hearings were held on military

---

329 *E.g.*, J. v. Peru, Preliminary Objections, Merits, Reparations, and Costs, Judgment, Inter-Am. Ct. H.R. (ser. C) No. 275, para. 267 (Nov. 27, 2013); Carpio Nicolle et al. v. Guatemala, Merits, Reparations, and Costs, Judgment, Inter-Am. Ct. H.R. (ser. C) No. 117, paras. 131–132 (Nov. 22, 2004).

330 *E.g.*, J. v. Peru, Preliminary Objections, Merits, Reparations, and Costs, Judgment, Inter-Am. Ct. H.R. (ser. C) No. 275, para. 267 (Nov. 27, 2013); La Cantuta v. Peru, Merits, Reparations, and Costs, Judgment, Inter-Am. Ct. H.R. (ser. C) No. 162, para. 153 (Nov. 29, 2006).

331 Almonacid Arellano et al. v. Chile, Preliminary Objections, Merits, Reparations, and Costs, Judgment, Inter-Am. Ct. H.R. (ser. C) No. 154, para. 154 (Sept. 26, 2006).

332 *Id.*

333 *E.g.*, J. v. Peru, Preliminary Objections, Merits, Reparations, and Costs, Judgment, Inter-Am. Ct. H.R. (ser. C) No. 275, para. 217 (Nov. 27, 2013); Castillo Petruzzi et al. v. Peru, Merits, Reparations, and Costs, Judgment, Inter-Am. Ct. H.R. (ser. C) No. 52, para. 172 (May 30, 1999).

334 *A Broken System*, THE ECONOMIST, July 12, 2014, http://www.economist.com/news/americas/21606864-citizens-security-regions-biggest-problem-time-improve-criminal-justice-broken.

335 *E.g.*, J. v. Peru, Preliminary Objections, Merits, Reparations, and Costs, Judgment, Inter-Am. Ct. H.R. (ser. C) No. 275, para. 217 (Nov. 27, 2013); Palamara Iribarne v. Chile, Merits, Reparations, Costs, Judgment, Inter-Am. Ct. H.R. (ser. C) No. 135, para. 168 (Nov. 22, 2005).

336 J. v. Peru, Preliminary Objections, Merits, Reparations, and Costs, Judgment, Inter-Am. Ct. H.R. (ser. C) No. 275, para. 217 (Nov. 27, 2013).

bases, in "circumstances of secrecy and isolation."[337] Consequently, the Inter-American Court ruled that "evidently the right to the public nature of the proceeding embodied in the Convention was not respected," in breach of Article 8(5).[338]

In contrast, when Berenson Mejía's case was transferred to the ordinary criminal courts, "identifiable" judges presided over publicly-accessible proceedings, which were transmitted through the media.[339] Under those circumstances, the Court decided that Article 8(5) was upheld. In another judgment against Peru, Luis Cantoral Benavides's terrorism case had also been moved to civilian jurisdiction; however, several hearings were conducted within jails—sufficient for the Tribunal to conclude that Article 8(5) was violated.[340]

The Court has offered little to explain when closed proceedings are "necessary to protect the interests of justice," in the terms of Article 8(5). In *J. v. Peru*, the State attempted to justify its use of private proceedings for terrorist offenses as "an exceptional circumstance" that was "required by national security" and for the protection of the prosecutors and judges involved.[341] With little analysis, the Court held that the State failed to prove "the need and proportionality" of closing the trial in J's case, and also disapproved of the Peruvian law (prior to 2003) that mandated such restricted proceedings.[342] As Cecilia Medina notes, Article 8(5)'s phrase "interests of justice" perhaps does not aptly describe those situations in which privacy would significantly benefit the participants, such as children in criminal proceedings.[343] Still, the Court has stated that publicity should in fact be limited within this context, in observance of the best interests of the child.[344]

---

[337] Berenson Mejia v. Peru, Merits, Reparations, and Costs, Judgment, Inter-Am. Ct. H.R. (ser. C) No. 119, para. 198 (Nov. 25, 2004).

[338] *Id. See also* Castillo Petruzzi et al. v. Peru, Merits, Reparations, and Costs, Judgment, Inter-Am. Ct. H.R. (ser. C) No. 52, paras. 172–173 (May 30, 1999); Cantoral Benavides v. Peru, Merits, Judgment, Inter-Am. Ct. H.R. (ser. C) No. 69, para. 115 (Aug. 18, 2000).

[339] *Id.* para. 200.

[340] Cantoral Benavides v. Peru, Merits, Judgment, Inter-Am. Ct. H.R. (ser. C) No. 69, paras. 146–147 (Aug. 18, 2000).

[341] J. v. Peru, Preliminary Objections, Merits, Reparations, and Costs, Judgment, Inter-Am. Ct. H.R. (ser. C) No. 275, para. 216 (Nov. 27, 2013). Previously, Peru did not appear to argue this point vigorously. *See, e.g.*, Cantoral Benavides v. Peru, Merits, Judgment, Inter-Am. Ct. H.R. (ser. C) No. 69, para. 148 (Aug. 18, 2000); Castillo Petruzzi et al. v. Peru, Merits, Reparations, and Costs, Judgment, Inter-Am. Ct. H.R. (ser. C) No. 52, para. 171 (May 30, 1999).

[342] *Id.* para. 220.

[343] Medina, *supra* note 42, at 337.

[344] Juridical Condition & Human Rights of the Child, Advisory Opinion OC-17/02, Inter-Am. Ct. H.R. (ser. A) No. 17, para. 134 (Aug. 28, 2002) ("These limits take into account the best interests of the child, insofar as they protect him or her from opinions, judgments or stigmatization that may have a substantial bearing on his or her future life.").

Article 25: Right to Judicial Protection

1. *Everyone has the right to simple and prompt recourse, or any other effective recourse, to a competent court or tribunal for protection against acts that violate his fundamental rights recognized by the constitution or laws of the state concerned or by this Convention, even though such violation may have been committed by persons acting in the course of their official duties.*
2. *The States Parties undertake:*
   a. *to ensure that any person claiming such remedy shall have his rights determined by the competent authority provided for by the legal system of the state;*
   b. *to develop the possibilities of judicial remedy; and*
   c. *to ensure that the competent authorities shall enforce such remedies when granted.*

Chapter 6 Contents (*Continued*)

I. Introduction and Background 216
II. Article 25(1): "Simple, Prompt and Effective" Remedies 218
A. "Simple" and "Prompt" Remedies 218
B. "Effective" Remedies 220
III. Article 25(2): Enforcement of National Judgments 223
IV. The Boundaries of "Judicial Protection" 224
A. The Right of Access to Justice 224
B. Combining Articles 8 and 25: A Critique 225
C. The Court's Current, Broader View of Article 25 227

I. Introduction and Background

Article 25 of the American Convention primarily refers to *amparo*, a "simple and prompt" judicial recourse of Latin American origin that is widespread in the hemisphere.[345] *Amparo* literally means "protection." Appropriately, this versatile action, guaranteed in many constitutions of the region, safeguards a broad range of human rights.[346] According to Allan Brewer Carías, it "is always conceived as a judicial proceeding initiated by means of an action or recourse filed by a party, which finishes with a judicial order or writ."[347] Article 25's remedy protects "fundamental rights" recognized in either State law or in the American Convention.[348]

The Inter-American Commission's preliminary proposal for the Article mirrored the "classic" *amparo* remedy:[349] "Everyone has the right to effective, simple and prompt recourse to the competent national judges and courts, to protect him against acts that violate his fundamental rights recognized by the constitution or by law."[350] The San José Conference, however, introduced modifications that weakened the Article's protections and muddled its original purpose.

First, the United States suggested the phrase "or any other effective recourse," after "simple and prompt recourse," arguing that "the one necessary criterion is whether the recourse is 'effective.'"[351] Yet this comment overlooks the central function of *amparo*: a rapid judicial response to imminent or already-occurring violations to fundamental rights. The inclusion of the new phrase casts doubt upon whether the recourse need be at all simple or prompt. Still, in urgent circumstances, an "effective" response would imply an expedited proceeding.

Second, Chile, with the support of the United States, convinced delegates to merge elements of Article 2(3) of the ICCPR to Article 25's text.[352] These became the State duties of Article 25(2). Adding them seems unnecessary, as general obligations are already established in Articles 1 and 2 of the American Convention.[353] Chile

---

[345] Habeas Corpus in Emergency Situations (Arts. 27(2), 25(1), and 7(6) American Convention on Human Rights), Advisory Opinion OC-8/87, Inter-Am. Ct. H.R. (ser. A) No. 8, para. 32 (Jan. 30, 1987); ALLAN R. BREWER CARÍAS, CONSTITUTIONAL PROTECTION OF HUMAN RIGHTS IN LATIN AMERICA: A COMPARATIVE STUDY OF *AMPARO* PROCEEDINGS 163 (2009); HÉCTOR GROS ESPIELL, LA CONVENCIÓN AMERICANA Y LA CONVENCIÓN EUROPEA DE DERECHOS HUMANOS: ANÁLISIS COMPARATIVO 116 (1991).

[346] BREWER CARÍAS, *supra* note 345, at 163–67.

[347] *Id.* at 77.

[348] American Convention, art. 25(1).

[349] P. 261, Minutes of the 14th Session of Committee I, Doc 53 (Rev. 1), Nov. 18, 1969 (the president of Committee I described it as "enshrining the classic right of amparo").

[350] Draft Inter-American Convention on Protection of Human Rights, Doc. 5 (English), art. 23 Sept. 22, 1969.

[351] Draft Inter-American Convention on Protection of Human Rights and Observations and Comments of the American Governments, Document 13 (English), art. 23, Sept. 22, 1969.

[352] P. 262–263, Minutes of the 14th Session of Committee I, Doc 53 (Rev. 1), Nov. 18, 1969.

[353] *See* p. 262, Minutes of the 14th Session of Committee I, Doc 53 (Rev. 1), Nov. 18, 1969 (the Colombian delegate made a similar observation in response to the Chilean proposal).

claimed that the addition would "clearly establish" State commitments in this area.[354] However, borrowing the ICCPR's phrase "States Parties undertake . . . to develop the possibilities of judicial remedy" actually confuses Article 25's original objective, which is to provide judicial protection through *amparo*. The ICCPR's Article 2(3) does not go so far as to require judicial remedies; it merely urges States to develop them in the future.

As a result—despite the very title of the Article, "Right to Judicial Protection," and a common acknowledgment that Article 25 granted the right to *amparo*—the final text leaves ambiguous whether judicial protection is actually required in all instances, or whether administrative proceedings may also suffice. The United States reported after the conference that the delegates' addition of the term "tribunal" to paragraph 1 indicated "that the recourse may be to [an] administrative or a judicial body."[355] However, the practical effect of this ambiguity has been limited, as *amparo* actions in the Americas generally have required the involvement of first instance or higher courts, rather than administrative bodies.[356] Further, in the Inter-American Court's first binding judgment it dispelled misunderstandings on this point, holding that Article 25 requires States Parties "to provide effective *judicial* remedies to victims of human rights violations."[357]

The Inter-American Court has stated that Article 25 "is one of the fundamental pillars not only of the American Convention, but of the very rule of law in a democratic society in the terms of the Convention."[358] Accordingly, it has held that Article 25's right to *amparo* is among the "judicial guarantees" of Article 27(2) that cannot be suspended in times of emergency.[359] Although the writ of habeas corpus is expressly established in a distinct provision of the Convention, Article 7(6), the Court recognizes habeas corpus as a specific example of the "whole series of remedies" represented by *amparo*.[360] Thus, habeas corpus, unsurprisingly, is also non-derograble according to the Tribunal.[361] When habeas corpus is denied, the Court may find violations of both Articles 7(6) and 25, or only Article 7(6).[362]

---

[354] P. 263, Minutes of the 14th Session of Committee I, Doc 53 (Rev. 1), Nov. 18, 1969.

[355] P. 35, Report of the United States Delegation to the Inter-American Conference on Protection of Human Rights.

[356] *See* Brewer Carías, *supra* note 345, at 107.

[357] Velásquez Rodríguez v. Honduras, Preliminary Objections, Judgment, Inter-Am. Ct. H.R. (ser. C) No. 1, para. 91 (June 26, 1987) (emphasis added).

[358] *E.g.*, Kuna Indigenous People of Madungandi and Embera Indigenous People of Bayano and their Members v. Panama, Preliminary Objections, Merits, Reparations, and Costs, Judgment, Inter-Am. Ct. H.R. (ser. C) No. 284, para. 167 (Oct. 14, 2014); Castillo Páez v. Peru, Merits, Judgment, Inter-Am. Ct. H.R. (ser. C) No. 34, para. 82 (Nov. 3, 1997).

[359] Habeas Corpus in Emergency Situations (Arts. 27(2), 25(1), and 7(6) American Convention on Human Rights), Advisory Opinion OC-8/87, Inter-Am. Ct. H.R. (ser. A) No. 8, para. 44 (Jan. 30, 1987).

[360] *Id.* para. 34.

[361] *Id.* para. 44.

[362] *E.g.*, Cesti Hurtado v. Peru, Merits, Judgment, Inter-Am. Ct. H.R. (ser. C) No. 56, para. 133 (Sept. 29, 1999 (finding both articles violated); Rochac Hernandez et al. v. El Salvador, Merits, Reparations, and Costs,

There is no direct equivalent to *amparo* found in the European Convention, EU Charter, the ICCPR, the African Charter, or the Arab Charter.[363] Article 13 of the European Convention, Article 2(3) of the ICCPR, and Article 23 of the Arab Charter are all general provisions that only require "effective" remedies—with no reference to simplicity and promptness—and they do not mandate judicial involvement.[364] Article 47 of the EU Charter grants the "right to an effective remedy before a tribunal"; however, it refers to a "reasonable time" standard, often associated with non-urgent proceedings such as a typical criminal investigation and trial.[365]

II. Article 25(1): "Simple, Prompt and Effective" Remedies

A. "SIMPLE" AND "PROMPT" REMEDIES

As mentioned above, the drafters of the Convention left some uncertainty as to the characteristics of Article 25's judicial protection. The Inter-American System has filled in some of the gaps over the years. First, there is significant support for the proposition that the Article's remedies must unite all three qualities: simplicity, promptness, *and* efficacy. In fact, despite the ambiguity of the text, the Rapporteur of Committee I arrived at this same conclusion after the provision's negotiations.[366]

The Inter-American Court and Commission agree on this point. The Court has referred to Article 25 as establishing "the obligation to provide a prompt, simple and effective recourse to the alleged victims in order to guarantee their rights."[367] Similarly,

---

Judgment, Inter-Am. Ct. H.R. (ser. C) No. 285, para. 162 (Oct. 14, 2014) (choosing to evaluate a potential violation of Article 7(6) rather than of Article 25).

363 *See* Acevedo Jaramillo et al. v. Peru, Preliminary Objections, Merits, Reparations, and Costs, Judgment, Inter-Am. Ct. H.R. (ser. C) No. 144, para. 71 (Feb. 7, 2006); MEDINA, *supra* note 42, at 367; GROS ESPIELL, *supra* note 345, at 116.

364 Article 23 of the Arab Charter states: "Each State party to the present Charter undertakes to ensure that any person whose rights or freedoms as herein recognized are violated shall have an effective remedy, notwithstanding that the violation has been committed by persons acting in an official capacity." Article 13 of the European Convention provides: "Everyone whose rights and freedoms as set forth in this Convention are violated shall have an effective remedy before a national authority notwithstanding that the violation has been committed by persons acting in an official capacity." Article 2(3) of the ICCPR establishes: "Each State Party to the present Covenant undertakes: (a) To ensure that any person whose rights or freedoms as herein recognized are violated shall have an effective remedy, notwithstanding that the violation has been committed by persons acting in an official capacity; (b) To ensure that any person claiming such a remedy shall have his right thereto determined by competent judicial, administrative or legislative authorities, or by any other competent authority provided for by the legal system of the State, and to develop the possibilities of judicial remedy; (c) To ensure that the competent authorities shall enforce such remedies when granted." *See also* HARRIS, O'BOYLE & WARBRICK, *supra* note 31, at 772 (affirming that "a variety of non-judicial authorities have been accepted as satisfying Article 13" of the European Convention).

365 EU Charter, art. 47.

366 Report of Committee I "Protection." Rapporteur Juan Isaac Lovato, Doc. 60 (revised) Nov. 19, 1969, p. 302.

367 Acevedo Buendía et al. ("Discharged & Retired Employees of the Office of the Comptroller") v. Peru, Preliminary Objection, Merits, Reparations, and Costs, Judgment, Inter-Am. Ct. H.R. (ser. C) No. 198, para.

the Commission has stated that the provision "creates the obligation to provide simple, prompt, and effective remedies against violations of human rights."[368]

Yet there is less guidance as to the precise meaning of the terms "simple" and "prompt." Still, in *Aguado Alfaro* et al. *v. Peru*, the Court found an Article 25 violation after observing "it is clear that the [victims] had no certainty about the proceeding they should or could use" to redress the violations they suffered.[369] Available remedies, then, should be understandable for potential litigants. Brewer Carías refers to another connotation of "simple": streamlined recourses that "must lack the dilatory procedural formalities of ordinary judicial means."[370]

With regard to "prompt," it is obvious that too much delay will defeat the purpose of any legal remedy.[371] The Court decided in *Acosta Calderón v. Ecuador* that 44 days to resolve an *amparo* was excessive.[372] Other judgments have found longer delays in violation of the promptness requirement.[373] Although the Tribunal offers no bright-line test, it often refers to domestic law as a basis for comparison. It noted in *Constitutional Court v. Peru*, for example, that the six-month amparo proceeding flagrantly disregarded the maximum period of 20 days permitted by Peruvian law.[374]

The Convention uses distinct language in Article 7(6) with respect to habeas corpus petitions, requiring that courts resolve such petitions "without delay." The Court has interpreted this phrase more frequently than "prompt." "Without delay" (*sin demora*) also appears in the Spanish version of Article 7(5)—but not the English version—so it has been considered often in that context by the largely Spanish-speaking Tribunal. In *Bayarri v.*

---

77 (July 1, 2009). Further, Advisory Opinion 9/87 reiterated that Article 25(1) "gives expression to the procedural institution known as *amparo*, which is a simple and prompt remedy"; in the next sentence, the Court affirmed that the provision "also establishes in broad terms the obligation of the States to provide to all persons within their jurisdiction an effective judicial remedy to violations of their fundamental rights." Judicial Guarantees in States of Emergency (Arts. 27(2), 25, and 8 American Convention on Human Rights), Advisory Opinion OC-9/87, Inter-Am. Ct. H.R. (ser. A) No. 9, para. 23 (Oct. 6, 1987).

[368] Inter-American Commission on Human Rights, Access to Justice as a Guarantee of Economic, Social, and Cultural Rights: A Review of the Standards Adopted by the Inter-American System of Human Rights, OEA/Ser.L/V/II.129, Doc. 4, 7 Sept. 2007, para. 244.

[369] Dismissed Cong. Emp. (Aguado Alfaro et al.) v. Peru, Preliminary Objections, Merits, Reparations, and Costs, Judgment, Inter-Am. Ct H.R. (ser. C) No. 158, para. 129 (Nov. 24, 2006).

[370] Brewer Carías, *supra* note 345, at 170.

[371] *See, e.g.*, "Juvenile Reeducation Institute" v. Paraguay, Preliminary Objections, Merits, Reparations, and Costs, Judgment, Inter-Am. Ct. H.R. (ser. C) No. 112, para. 245 (Sept. 2, 2004) ("Clearly, a remedy will not be 'truly effective' if it is not decided within a time frame that enables the violation being claimed to be corrected in time.").

[372] Acosta Calderón v. Ecuador, Merits, Reparations, and Costs, Judgment, Inter-Am. Ct. H.R. (ser. C) No. 129, para. 97 (June 24, 2005).

[373] *E.g.*, Acevedo Buendía et al. v. Peru, Preliminary Objection, Merits, Reparations, and Costs, Judgment, Inter-Am. Ct. H.R. (ser. C) No. 198, para. 74 (July 1, 2009); Constitutional Court v. Peru, Merits, Reparations, and Costs, Judgment, Inter-Am. Ct. H.R. (ser. C) No. 71, para. 91 (Jan. 31, 2001).

[374] Constitutional Court v. Peru, Merits, Reparations, and Costs, Judgment, Inter-Am. Ct. H.R. (ser. C) No. 71, para. 91 (Jan. 31, 2001).

Argentina, the Court held that "almost one week" violated the "without delay" principle.[375] On the other hand, the *López Álvarez v. Honduras* judgment indicated that seeing a judge the day after a detention satisfied the standard.[376] As in the case of Article 25, the Court will frequently look to national law when assessing observance of the "without delay" principle.

It appears, then, that the "without delay" standard of Article 7 is somewhat more demanding than the "prompt" rule of Article 25(1). Yet the boundaries are not clear, and the Court may at times apply the "without delay" rule beyond habeas corpus to the other remedies of Article 25.[377] Occasionally, the Tribunal makes a troubling error by conflating the more forgiving "reasonable time" standard of Article 8 ("Right to a Fair Trial") with the faster requirements of Articles 25 and 7(6).[378] As Cecilia Medina points out, "the simplicity and promptness of an *amparo* remedy [cannot] be measured" with the same time standard for the completion of a trial.[379]

B. "EFFECTIVE" REMEDIES

Article 25(1), according to the Court, "sets forth the obligation of the State Parties to guarantee, to all persons under their jurisdiction, an effective judicial recourse against acts that violate their fundamental rights."[380] The Tribunal has explained that "effectiveness" goes far beyond the mere "formal existence" of the recourses in national law.[381] The remedies must actually establish whether there has been a human rights violation and then "ensure what is necessary to provide redress."[382] The Court has clarified that

---

[375] Bayarri v. Argentina, Preliminary Objection, Merits, Reparations, and Costs, Judgment, Inter-Am. Ct. H.R. (ser. C) No. 187, para. 66 (Oct. 30, 2008).

[376] López Álvarez v. Honduras, Merits, Reparations, and Costs, Judgment, Inter-Am. Ct. H.R. (ser. C) No. 141, para. 91 (Feb. 1, 2006).

[377] *See* Juana María Ibáñez Rivas, *Artículo 25: Protección Judicial*, *in* La Convención Americana Sobre Derechos Humanos Comentada 610, 615 (Christian Steiner & Patricia Uribe eds., 2014) (remarking on shared standards between Articles 25 and 7); Concurring Opinion of Judge García Ramírez, paras. 23–25, Tibi v. Ecuador, Preliminary Objections, Merits, Reparations, and Costs, Judgment, Inter-Am. Ct. H.R. (ser. C) No. 114 (Sept. 7, 2004) (referring to the relationships between Article 25 and other rights and provisions of the American Convention). The matter is made more uncertain by the differing usage of "without delay" in the Spanish and English versions of the American Convention.

[378] Cantos v. Argentina, Merits, Reparations, and Costs, Judgment, Inter-Am. Ct. H.R. (ser. C) No. 97, para. 57 (Nov. 28, 2002).

[379] Medina, *supra* note 42, at 371. *See also* Ad Hoc Judge Diego Rodríguez Pinzón, Partially Dissenting Opinion, para. 10, Salvador Chiriboga v. Ecuador, Preliminary Objections and Merits, Judgment, Inter-Am. Ct. H.R. (ser. C) No. 179 (May 6, 2008).

[380] *E.g.*, Argüelles et al. v. Argentina, Preliminary Objections, Merits, Reparations, and Costs, Judgment, Inter-Am. Ct. H.R. (ser. C) No. 288, para. 145 (Nov. 20, 2014); Velásquez Rodríguez v. Honduras, Preliminary Objections, Judgment, Inter-Am. Ct. H.R. (ser. C) No. 1, para. 91 (June 26, 1987).

[381] *E.g.*, Kuna Indigenous People of Madungandi and Embera Indigenous People of Bayano and their Members v. Panama, Preliminary Objections, Merits, Reparations, and Costs, Judgment, Inter-Am. Ct. H.R. (ser. C) No. 284, para. 165 (Oct. 14, 2014); Judicial Guarantees in States of Emergency, Advisory Opinion OC-9/87, Inter-Am. Ct. H.R. (ser. A) No. 9, para. 24 (Oct. 6, 1987).

[382] *Id.*

an unfavorable ruling for petitioners "does not necessarily signify the ineffectiveness of the remedy filed, or that [they] did not have access to an effective remedy."[383]

Whether the remedy is "adequate" is also a central part of this discussion—although the Court does not always distinguish this concept from "effective" remedies. Since its first contentious case, the Court has held that a remedy is "adequate" or appropriate when it is "suitable to address the infringement of a legal right."[384] In this way, the remedy of habeas corpus is the adequate remedy for a disappearance, and *amparo* is appropriate for the expedited protection of fundamental rights in other situations.[385]

Article 25 "is closely linked" to the general obligations under Articles 1(1) and 2 and requires multiple duties of States: "not only [to] draft and enact an effective remedy, but to also ensure the due application of this remedy by its judicial authorities," including the full execution of the judgment.[386] If the law or regulation establishing the remedy is deficient, a violation of Article 25 will result.[387] In addition, a number of circumstances render codified remedies "illusory" and, as a consequence, equally ineffective, such as

> when the Judicial Power lacks the necessary independence to render impartial decisions or the means to carry out its judgments; or in any other situation that constitutes a denial of justice, as when there is an unjustified delay in the decision. . . .[388]

Following this long-standing jurisprudence, the Court has declared violations of Article 25 when victims sought remedies before courts that were not competent, independent, or impartial.[389]

---

[383] *E.g.*, Mémoli v. Argentina, Preliminary Objections, Merits, Reparations, and Costs, Judgment, Inter-Am. Ct. H.R. (ser. C) No. 265, para. 195 (Aug. 22, 2013); Fermín Ramírez v. Guatemala, Merits, Reparations, and Costs, Judgment, Inter-Am. Ct. H.R. (ser. C) No. 126, para. 83 (June 20, 2005).

[384] Velásquez Rodríguez v. Honduras, Merits, Judgment, Inter-Am. Ct. H.R. (ser. C) No. 4, para. 64 (July 29, 1988).

[385] *Id.* para. 65 ("habeas corpus would be the normal means of finding a person presumably detained by the authorities, of ascertaining whether he is legally detained and, given the case, of obtaining his liberty"). *See also* Supreme Court of Justice (Quintana Coello et al.) v. Ecuador, Preliminary Objections, Merits, Reparations, and Costs, Judgment, Inter-Am. Ct. H.R. (ser. C) No. 266, para. 194 (Aug. 23, 2013) ("the judges were prevented from making use of the amparo remedy and . . . the unconstitutionality suit was neither appropriate nor effective to protect the violated rights of the Supreme Court judges").

[386] *E.g.*, Liakat Ali Alibux v. Suriname, Preliminary Objections, Merits, Reparations, and Costs, Judgment, Inter-Am. Ct. H.R. (ser. C) No. 276, para. 33 (Jan. 30, 2014); "Street Children" (Villagrán Morales et al.) v. Guatemala, Merits, Judgment, Inter-Am. Ct. H.R. (ser. C) No. 63, para. 237 (Nov. 19, 1999).

[387] *E.g.*, Castillo Petruzzi et al. v. Peru, Merits, Reparations, and Costs, Judgment, Inter-Am. Ct. H.R. (ser. C) No. 52, paras. 180, 188 (May 30, 1999); Loayza Tamayo v. Peru, Merits, Judgment, Inter-Am. Ct. H.R. (ser. C) No. 33, paras. 52–55 (Sept. 17, 1997).

[388] Judicial Guarantees in States of Emergency, Advisory Opinion OC-9/87, Inter-Am. Ct. H.R. (ser. A) No. 9, para. 24 (Oct. 6, 1987).

[389] *E.g.*, Usón Ramírez v. Venezuela, Preliminary Objection, Merits, Reparations, and Costs, Judgment, Inter-Am. Ct. H.R. (ser. C) No. 207, para. 130 (Nov. 20, 2009); Durand and Ugarte v. Peru, Merits, Judgment, Inter-Am. Ct. H.R. (ser. C) No. 68, paras. 125, 131 (Aug. 16, 2000).

The Tribunal has also recognized cases where individuals, as a practical matter, have been unable to access judicial remedies at all, leading to an Article 25 violation. To illustrate, when persons have been expelled from a country or secretly detained, the Court has noted the impossibility of exercising the right to judicial protection.[390] In *Castillo Páez v. Peru*, the police not only hid the victim and officially denied his arrest, but also furnished the judge with falsified detention records.[391] Such disappearance cases before the Court, characterized by protracted delays and blatant obstruction of justice, have led to many breaches of Article 25.[392]

Pervasive denials of judicial protection have also occurred in the global efforts to counter terrorism after September 11, 2001. According to the Inter-American Commission:

> While the nature of the courts or tribunals may vary, depending in particular upon the applicability of international humanitarian law as the *lex specialis* in situations of armed conflict, the availability of recourse to judicial protection to persons affected by anti-terrorist initiatives cannot be suspended insofar as they are necessary for the protection of the rights not subject to derogation in times of emergency.[393]

In 2002, the Commission authorized precautionary measures in favor of detainees at Guantánamo Bay, Cuba. The Commission considered that, "absent clarification of the legal status of the detainees," their rights under various legal regimes "could not be said to be the subject of effective legal protection by the [United States]."[394] Consequently, it urged the United States to ensure that competent tribunals immediately determine the detainees' legal status.[395] In 2015, the Commission issued a special report in which it criticized, in detail, the detainees' lack of judicial protection and due process, and renewed its calls for the closure of the facility.[396]

---

390 *See, e.g.*, Expelled Dominicans and Haitians v. Dominican Republic, Preliminary Objections, Merits, Reparations, and Costs, Judgment, Inter-Am. Ct. H.R. (ser. C) No. 282, para. 396 (Aug. 28, 2014) ("in view of the particular circumstances of this case, specifically the way in which the expulsions were implemented, the presumed victims were unable to file the remedies mentioned by the Dominican Republic, and no effective proceedings were available to them").

391 Castillo Páez v. Peru, Merits, Judgment, Inter-Am. Ct. H.R. (ser. C) No. 34, para. 58 (Nov. 3, 1997).

392 *E.g.*, Anzualdo Castro v. Peru, Preliminary Objections, Merits, Reparations, and Costs, Judgment, Inter-Am. Ct. H.R. (ser. C) No. 202, para. 169 (Sept. 22, 2009); Bámaca Velásquez v. Guatemala, Merits, Judgment, Inter-Am. Ct. H.R. (ser. C) No. 70, para. 196 (Nov. 25, 2000).

393 Inter-American Commission on Human Rights, Report on Terrorism and Human Rights, OEA/Ser.L/V/II.116, Doc. 5 rev. 1 corr. 22, para. 352 (Oct. 2002), *available at* http://www.cidh.org/terrorism/eng/toc.htm.

394 Inter-American Commission on Human Rights, Precautionary Measures Granted by the IACHR during 2002, para. 80, *available at* http://www.cidh.org/medidas/2002.eng.htm.

395 The Inter-American Commission made this statement under the authority of the American Declaration of the Rights and Duties of Man, as the United States has not ratified the American Convention. In any event, it is fully consistent with the Commission's views on judicial protection under the Convention.

396 Inter-American Commission on Human Rights, Towards the Closure of Guantanamo, OAS/Ser.L/V/II., Doc. 20/15 (June 3, 2015), *available at* http://www.oas.org/en/iachr/reports/pdfs/Towards-Closure-Guantanamo.pdf.

III. Article 25(2): Enforcement of National Judgments

The State obligations outlined by Article 25(2), as noted above, reiterate duties already established in more general form by Articles 1(1) and 2 of the Convention. Appropriating the phrases from the ICCPR, the Chilean delegate believed that further emphasis would strengthen the protections of Article 25.[397] In practice, the Inter-American Court refers infrequently to these provisions. The Court has cited to Article 25(2)(b) to remind State Parties to the Convention that, if they do not have an effective judicial remedy to protect a particular right, they must create one. It rarely declares an express breach of Article 25(2)(a).[398] Even after finding that specific national courts are not competent, the Court generally limits itself to a reference to Article 25(1).

Nevertheless, the Tribunal has alluded to Article 25(2)(c) and even found violations of this provision.[399] This has occurred when the judgments of domestic courts were not enforced. A clear example is *Acevedo Buendía* et al. *v. Peru*, where nearly 300 individuals had demanded their unpaid pensions through the courts, arriving as high as Peru's Constitutional Court.[400] Citing budgetary constraints, the State still had not complied with the national judicial rulings, incurring in violation of Article 25, paragraphs (1) and 2(c).[401]

In this line of judgments on Article 25(2)(c), the Court has emphasized that "State responsibility does not end when the competent authorities issue the decision or judgment"; rather, "the State must also guarantee the means to execute [these] decisions."[402] This requires that "all public authorities, within the framework of their jurisdiction, must take heed of judicial decisions and promote their execution."[403] Following European Court case law, the Inter-American Tribunal calls for judgment implementation to be "without delay," as well as "complete, perfect, and comprehensive," including opportunities for participation of the parties.[404]

---

[397] P. 263, Minutes of the 14th Session of Committee I, Doc 53 (Rev. 1), Nov. 18, 1969.

[398] *But see* Afro-Descendant Communities Displaced From the Cacarica River Basin (Operation Genesis) v. Colombia, Preliminary Objections, Merits, Reparations, and Costs, Judgment, Inter-Am. Ct. H.R. (ser. C) No. 270, para. 410 (Nov. 20, 2013) (finding Article 25(2)(a) violation, but offering little explanation).

[399] *E.g., id.*; Mejía Idrovo v. Ecuador, Preliminary Objections, Merits, Reparations, and Costs, Judgment, Inter-Am. Ct. H.R. (ser. C) No. 228, para. 111 (July 5, 2011).

[400] Acevedo Buendía et al. ("Discharged and Retired Employees of the Office of the Comptroller") v. Peru, Preliminary Objections, Merits, Reparations, and Costs, Judgment, Inter-Am. Ct. H.R. (ser. C) No. 198 (July 1, 2009).

[401] *Id.* para. 79. *But see* "Five Pensioners" v. Peru, Merits, Reparations, and Costs, Judgment, Inter-Am. Ct. H.R. (ser. C) No. 98, para. 141 (Feb. 28, 2003) (although finding a scenario similar to *Acevedo Buendía*, the Court did not refer to Article 25(2)(c)).

[402] Acevedo Jaramillo et al. v. Peru, Preliminary Objections, Merits, Reparations, and Costs, Judgment, Inter-Am. Ct. H.R. (ser. C) No. 144, para. 216 (Feb. 7, 2006); Baena Ricardo et al. v. Panama, Competence, Judgment, Inter-Am. Ct. H.R. (ser. C) No. 104, para. 79 (Nov. 28, 2003).

[403] Furlan and Family v. Argentina, Preliminary Objections, Merits, Reparations, and Costs, Judgment, Inter-Am. Ct. H.R. (ser. C) No. 246, para. 211 (Aug. 31, 2012); Mejía Idrovo v. Ecuador, Preliminary Objections, Merits, Reparations, and Costs, Judgment, Inter-Am. Ct. H.R. (ser. C) No. 228, para. 106 (July 5, 2011).

[404] Furlan and Family v. Argentina, Preliminary Objections, Merits, Reparations, and Costs, Judgment, Inter-Am. Ct. H.R. (ser. C) No. 246, para. 210 (Aug. 31, 2012).

IV. The Boundaries of "Judicial Protection"

A. THE RIGHT OF ACCESS TO JUSTICE

Yet to be addressed is the important and disputed matter of how Article 25 relates to Article 8, the due process provision of the American Convention. Since *Velásquez-Rodríguez v. Honduras*, its first contentious case, the Court has explained, "States Parties have an obligation to provide effective judicial remedies to victims of human rights violations (Art. 25), remedies that must be substantiated in accordance with the rules of due process of law (Art. 8(1))."[405] This well-established case law has not been challenged.

What has been subject to dispute, however, is the manner that the contemporary Court has combined Articles 8 and 25 to undergird the State obligation to investigate and punish human rights abuses. A great number of judgments now hold that Articles 8 and 25 together provide for "the right of access to justice," which includes criminal investigation and accountability.[406] In cases of forced disappearances and extrajudicial executions, this meta-right also requires that loved ones are fully informed of the circumstances surrounding the victim's fate—what the Court, the Inter-American Commission, and many others have denominated "the right to the truth."[407]

Throughout its case law, the Court has stressed that State obligations in this area are "of means and not of results"; the investigation must be "serious, impartial and effective, and be aimed at . . . the pursuit, capture, prosecution and eventual punishment of the perpetrators," whether State agents or private individuals.[408] Due diligence requires that the authorities conducting the investigation "take all the actions and make all the inquiries

---

[405] *E.g.*, Cruz Sánchez et al. v. Peru, Preliminary Objections, Merits, Reparations, Costs, Judgment, Inter-Am. Ct. H.R. (ser. C) No. 292, para. 346 (Apr. 17, 2015); Velásquez Rodríguez v. Honduras, Preliminary Objections, Judgment, Inter-Am. Ct. H.R. (ser. C) No. 1, para. 91 (June 26, 1987).

[406] *E.g.*, Cruz Sánchez et al. v. Peru, Preliminary Objections, Merits, Reparations, Costs, Judgment, Inter-Am. Ct. H.R. (ser. C) No. 292, para. 398 (Apr. 17, 2015); Anzualdo Castro v. Peru, Preliminary Objections, Merits, Reparations, and Costs, Judgment, Inter-Am. Ct. H.R. (ser. C) No. 202, para. 124 (Sept. 22, 2009).

[407] *E.g.*, Cruz Sánchez et al. v. Peru, Preliminary Objections, Merits, Reparations, Costs, Judgment, Inter-Am. Ct. H.R. (ser. C) No. 292, para. 428 (Apr. 17, 2015) (explaining that the right to the truth is usually "subsumed" in the Court's analysis of Articles 8 and 25); Inter-American Commission on Human Rights, The Right to Truth in the Americas, OEA/Ser.L/V/II.152, Doc. 2, 13, para. 65 (Aug. 2014) ("That right is couched in terms of the right of access to justice and the obligation to investigate"), *available at* http://www.oas.org/en/iachr/reports/pdfs/Right-to-Truth-en.pdf; Basic Principles and Guidelines on the Right to a Remedy and Reparation for Victims of Gross Violations of International Human Rights Law and Serious Violations of International Humanitarian Law, G.A. Res. 60/147, at 24, U.N. Doc A/RES/60/147 (Mar. 21, 2006) ("victims and their representatives should be entitled to seek and obtain information on the causes leading to their victimization and on the causes and conditions pertaining to the [violations] and to learn the truth in regard to these violations.").

[408] *E.g.*, Cruz Sánchez et al. v. Peru, Preliminary Objections, Merits, Reparations, Costs, Judgment, Inter-Am. Ct. H.R. (ser. C) No. 292, paras. 351–352 (Apr. 17, 2015); Espinoza Gonzales v. Peru, Preliminary Objections, Merits, Reparations, Costs, Judgment, Inter-Am. Ct. H.R. (ser. C) No. 289, para. 238 (Nov. 20, 2014).

required to achieve the result sought."[409] To illustrate, in the case of a possible extrajudicial killing, the Court has outlined minimal requirements for due diligence: authorities must (1) identify the victim; (2) recover and preserve relevant evidence,[410] maintaining the chain of custody; (3) identify witnesses and obtain their statements; and (4) through autopsies and other scientific analysis, determine the cause, manner, location, and time of death, as well as any pattern or practice that may have caused the death.[411] Regarding other serious rights violations, such as forced disappearance, torture, and gender violence, the Tribunal has developed additional investigation standards,[412] drawing from specialized instruments of the Inter-American and global human rights systems.[413]

B. COMBINING ARTICLES 8 AND 25: A CRITIQUE

Cecilia Medina has found fault with the Court's constant integration of Articles 8 and 25. She asserts that this practice shows how the Tribunal ascribes too many judicial recourses and meanings to Article 25, despite its original conception as protection exclusively through *amparo*.[414] Although Medina concedes that the text of Article 25 leaves the possibility open for other "effective" judicial recourses, she believes the Article has a limited scope.[415] On the other hand, the duty to investigate and numerous other judicial remedies are rooted in the American Convention's Article 1(1), which requires States to

---

[409] *E.g.*, Espinoza Gonzales v. Peru, Preliminary Objections, Merits, Reparations, Costs, Judgment, Inter-Am. Ct. H.R. (ser. C) No. 289, para. 238 (Nov. 20, 2014); Serrano Cruz Sisters v. El Salvador, Merits, Reparations, and Costs, Judgment, Inter-Am. Ct. H.R. (ser. C) No. 120, para. 83 (Mar. 1, 2005).

[410] The Court explains that, at a minimum, the investigator must: restrict access to the scene of the crime; "photograph [the scene], and any other physical evidence and the body as it was found and after it has been moved; collect and preserve any samples of blood, hair, fibers and threads or other clues; examine the scene for shoe impressions or any other impressions of an evidentiary nature, and prepare a report detailing any observations at the scene, actions of investigators and disposition of all evidence recovered." *E.g.*, Landaeta Meijias Brothers et al. v. Venezuela, Preliminary Objections, Merits, Reparations, and Costs, Judgment, Inter-Am. Ct. H.R. (ser. C) No. 281, paras. 227–228 (Aug. 27, 2014); Veliz Franco et al. v. Guatemala, Preliminary Objections, Merits, and Reparations, Judgment, Inter-Am. Ct. H.R. (ser. C) No. 277, paras. 191–194 (May 19, 2014).

[411] Landaeta Meijias Brothers et al. v. Venezuela, Preliminary Objections, Merits, Reparations, and Costs, Judgment, Inter-Am. Ct. H.R. (ser. C) No. 281, paras. 227–228 (Aug. 27, 2014).

[412] *See, e.g.*, Espinoza Gonzales v. Peru, Preliminary Objections, Merits, Reparations, Costs, Judgment, Inter-Am. Ct. H.R. (ser. C) No. 289, para. 242 (Nov. 20, 2014) (concerning violence against women and torture); Rodriguez Vera et al. (Persons Disappeared from the Palace of Justice) v. Colombia, Preliminary Objections, Merits, Reparations, and Costs, Judgment, Inter-Am. Ct. H.R. (ser. C) No. 287, para. 480 (Nov. 14, 2014) (concerning forced disappearances).

[413] *Id.* paras. 239–264 (citing, among others, the Inter-American Convention to Prevent and Punish Torture, the Inter-American Convention on the Prevention, Punishment and Eradication of Violence against Women, and the Istanbul Protocol: Manual on the Effective Investigation and Documentation of Torture and Other Cruel, Inhuman or Degrading Treatment or Punishment).

[414] Judge Medina Concurring Opinion, paras. 3–4, Gómez Palomino v. Peru, Merits, Reparations, and Costs, Judgment, Inter-Am. Ct. H.R. (ser. C) No. 136 (Nov. 22, 2005); MEDINA, *supra* note 42, at 363–365.

[415] Judge Medina Partially Dissenting Opinion, paras. 3–5, Salvador Chiriboga v. Ecuador, Preliminary Objections and Merits, Judgment, Inter-Am. Ct. H.R. (ser. C) No. 179 (May 6, 2008).

respect and ensure the rights of the treaty.[416] This was also the Court's interpretation in *Velásquez Rodríguez*, which held that Article 1's duty to ensure rights:

> implies the duty of States Parties to organize the governmental apparatus and, in general, all the structures through which public power is exercised, so that they are capable of juridically ensuring the free and full enjoyment of human rights. As a consequence of this obligation, the States must prevent, investigate and punish any violation of the rights recognized by the Convention and, moreover, if possible, attempt to restore the right violated and provide compensation as warranted for damages resulting from the violation.[417]

Furthermore, in this landmark judgment and other early decisions, the Tribunal did not conceive of Article 25's judicial remedies as open-ended.[418]

These interpretations lost influence, but, under the leadership of then-judge Medina, the Court took them up once again for a time. It regarded deficient criminal investigations as violating Article 1(1) and the substantive right in question, such as Article 4 (Right to Life) or Article 5 (Right to Humane Treatment).[419] To illustrate, in *Bayarri v. Argentina*, Juan Carlos Bayarri was tortured by police and the State did not sufficiently investigate the crime; as a result, the Court held Argentina responsible for two violations of Articles 5 and 1: the first for failing to *respect* the right to humane treatment (the act of torture), and the second for failing to *ensure* the right (the flawed criminal investigation).[420] Finding "procedural violations" of substantive rights in this way is a well-established practice at the European Court of Human Rights.[421]

Yet the Court has apparently returned to its method of considering faulty investigations under Articles 8 and 25—the right of access to justice. As a measure of compromise,

---

[416] Judge Medina Concurring Opinion, para. 4, Gómez Palomino v. Peru, Merits, Reparations, and Costs, Judgment, Inter-Am. Ct. H.R. (ser. C) No. 136 (Nov. 22, 2005); MEDINA, *supra* note 42, at 364.

[417] Velásquez Rodríguez v. Honduras, Merits, Judgment, Inter-Am. Ct. H.R. (ser. C) No. 4, para. 166 (July 29, 1988).

[418] *See* Habeas Corpus in Emergency Situations, Advisory Opinion OC-8/87, Inter-Am. Ct. H.R. (ser. A) No. 8, para. 32 (Jan. 30, 1987) (stating that Article 25(1) "gives expression to the procedural institution known as '*amparo*'").

[419] *E.g.*, Bayarri v. Argentina, Preliminary Objections, Merits, Reparations, and Costs, Judgment, Inter-Am. Ct. H.R. (ser. C) No. 187, paras. 87, 94 (Oct. 30, 2008) (concluding that "the State did not investigate with due diligence the torture to which Juan Carlos Bayarri was subjected in violation of the right to humane treatment embodied in Article 5(1) and 5(2) of the American Convention, in relation to Article 1(1) thereof"); Valle Jaramillo et al. v. Colombia, Merits, Reparations, and Costs, Judgment, Inter-Am. Ct. H.R. (ser. C) No. 192, paras. 105–106 (Nov. 27, 2008) (finding procedural violations of Articles 4, 5, and 7 because the State had neglected to ensure these rights by, among other things, conducting an adequate investigation).

[420] Bayarri v. Argentina, Preliminary Objections, Merits, Reparations, and Costs, Judgment, Inter-Am. Ct. H.R. (ser. C) No. 187, paras. 87, 94 (Oct. 30, 2008).

[421] *E.g.*, Mocanu and Others v. Romania, Eur. Ct. H.R., App. Nos. 10865/09, 45886/07 and 32431/08, paras. 317–353 (Sept. 17, 2014) (explaining that the general duty under Article 1 of the European Convention and Articles 2 (Right to Life) and 3 (Prohibition of Torture) require "effective official investigations," and finding procedural violations of Articles 2 and 3 due to the lack of such investigations); Akdeniz v. Turkey, Eur. Ct. H.R., App. No. 25165/94, paras. 103–112 (May 31, 2005).

perhaps, it still recognizes that the underlying basis for such investigations is found in Article 1(1) and the relevant substantive right. For example, in *Espinoza Gonzales v. Peru*, the Court found that the State failed to ensure the Article 5 right to humane treatment by undertaking a serious criminal investigation, but then declared violations of Articles 8 and 25, rather than a procedural breach of Article 5.[422]

Also compelling is Medina's critique that assessing combinations of Articles, such as 8 and 25, hinders the understanding and development of each individual provision.[423] The Tribunal's judgments often analyze rights together, rather than using discrete sections. In one single chapter of *González* et al. *("Cotton Field") v. Mexico*, for instance, the Court discussed, among others, the rights to life, humane treatment, personal liberty, judicial protection, and due process.[424] This practice has tended to distort the structure of rights and evade a rigorous elaboration of concepts—including those associated with the right to judicial protection.

C. THE COURT'S CURRENT, BROADER VIEW OF ARTICLE 25

Thus, the contemporary Court does not limit the remedies of Article 25 to simply *amparo* and habeas corpus. With respect to a range of criminal procedures and motions, for example, it has stated, "the right to effective judicial protection requires the judges to direct the proceedings in a way that avoids undue delays," impunity, and other injustice.[425] The full content of Article 25, however, remains unclear.

In some situations, such as when criminal accountability and fundamental rights are at stake, the Court has admonished States for providing only administrative remedies. In *Mapiripán Massacre v. Colombia*, some survivors of the massacre had received monetary compensation, through state administrative proceedings, for pecuniary and non-pecuniary damages.[426] But the Tribunal found that cash compensation alone amounted to inadequate redress. It stated:

> When it assesses the effectiveness of domestic remedies sought under national administrative-law jurisdiction, the Court must establish whether the decisions taken by the latter have in fact contributed to ending impunity, to insuring

---

[422] Espinoza Gonzales v. Peru, Preliminary Objections, Merits, Reparations, Costs, Judgment, Inter-Am. Ct. H.R. (ser. C) No. 289, paras. 239, 287 (Nov. 20, 2014).

[423] Judge Medina Partially Dissenting Opinion, para. 5, Salvador Chiriboga v. Ecuador, Preliminary Objections and Merits, Judgment, Inter-Am. Ct. H.R. (ser. C) No. 179 (May 6, 2008). *See also* Ad Hoc Judge Diego Rodríguez Pinzón Partially Dissenting Opinion, para. 12, Salvador Chiriboga v. Ecuador (May 6, 2008).

[424] González et al. ("Cotton Field") v. Mexico, Preliminary Objections, Merits, Reparations, and Costs, Judgment, Inter-Am. Ct. H.R. (ser. C) No. 205, paras. 109–402 (Nov. 16, 2009).

[425] *E.g.*, Landaeta Meijias Brothers et al. v. Venezuela, Preliminary Objections, Merits, Reparations, and Costs, Judgment, Inter-Am. Ct. H.R. (ser. C) No. 281, para. 218 (Aug. 27, 2014); Mack Chang v. Guatemala, Merits, Reparations, and Costs, Judgment, Inter-Am. Ct. H.R. (ser. C) No. 101, para. 211 (Nov. 25, 2003).

[426] Mapiripán Massacre v. Colombia, Merits, Reparations, and Costs, Judgment, Inter-Am. Ct. H.R. (ser. C) No. 134, paras. 207–209 (Sept. 15, 2005).

non-recidivism of injurious acts, and to guaranteeing free and full exercise of the rights protected by the Convention.[427]

This holding, followed in several subsequent judgments, requires criminal justice through the courts, among other remedial measures, after serious rights abuses.[428]

Other cases before the Tribunal have examined how indigenous communities attempted to recover their crucial rights to ancestral lands, often through administrative mechanisms. In the recent judgment *Kuna Indigenous People of Madungandi and Embera Indigenous People of Bayano v. Panama*, the communities had petitioned various nonjudicial authorities for their territories, with little success.[429] The Tribunal found a violation of Article 25, along with Article 8, deciding that the recourses used by the petitioners "did not obtain a response that permitted an adequate determination of their rights and obligations."[430] Further, the Tribunal emphasized that, under Article 25, these proceedings must "take into account [indigenous communities'] specificities, their economic and social characteristics, as well as their situation of special vulnerability, their customary law, values, and customs."[431]

As discussed in the above section on Article 8, the Court has developed broad due process rights. By being frequently combined with Article 8, Article 25 also has expanded in scope beyond the initial *amparo* concept. Of course, because the Court has recognized that Article 25 remedies must be simple, prompt, and effective, there are limits to the kinds of recourses contained in this provision. For example, the Tribunal has more recently held that the right to appeal a criminal conviction "embodies a specific type of remedy" found in Article 8, but is "not provided for" in Article 25(1)."[432] Hopefully, in the next years the Court will continue to explain the key content and widening parameters of Article 25.

---

427 *Id.* para. 210.

428 For a full discussion of the remedies required by the Court after rights violations, *see* this volume's chapter on reparations.

429 Kuna Indigenous People of Madungandi and Embera Indigenous People of Bayano and their Members v. Panama, Preliminary Objections, Merits, Reparations, and Costs, Judgment, Inter-Am. Ct. H.R. (ser. C) No. 284 (Oct. 14, 2014).

430 *Id.* para. 173. In *Barbani Duarte* et al. *v. Uruguay*, the Court considered what Article 25 requires for the adequate judicial review of administrative decisions. Barbani Duarte et al. v. Uruguay, Merits, Reparations, and Costs, Judgment, Inter. Am. Ct. H.R. (ser. C) No. 234, para. 203 (Oct. 13, 2011).

431 *E.g.*, Kuna Indigenous People of Madungandi and Embera Indigenous People of Bayano & their Members v. Panama, Preliminary Objections, Merits, Reparations, and Costs, Judgment, Inter-Am. Ct. H.R. (ser. C) No. 284, para. 167 (Oct. 14, 2014); Yakye Axa Indigenous Cmty. v. Paraguay, Merits, Reparations, and Costs, Judgment, Inter-Am. Ct. H.R. (ser. C) No. 125, para. 63 (June 17, 2005).

432 Barreto Leiva v. Venezuela, Merits, Reparations, and Costs, Judgment, Inter-Am. Ct. H.R. (ser. C) No. 206, para. 102 (Nov. 17, 2009).

7

Freedom of Expression

Article 13: Freedom of Thought and Expression

1. *Everyone has the right to freedom of thought and expression. This right includes freedom to seek, receive, and impart information and ideas of all kinds, regardless of frontiers, either orally, in writing, in print, in the form of art, or through any other medium of one's choice.*
2. *The exercise of the right provided for in the foregoing paragraph shall not be subject to prior censorship but shall be subject to subsequent imposition of liability, which shall be expressly established by law to the extent necessary to ensure:*
   a. *respect for the rights or reputations of others; or*
   b. *the protection of national security, public order, or public health or morals.*
3. *The right of expression may not be restricted by indirect methods or means, such as the abuse of government or private controls over newsprint, radio broadcasting frequencies, or equipment used in the dissemination of information, or by any other means tending to impede the communication and circulation of ideas and opinions.*
4. *Notwithstanding the provisions of paragraph 2 above, public entertainments may be subject by law to prior censorship for the sole purpose of regulating access to them for the moral protection of childhood and adolescence.*
5. *Any propaganda for war and any advocacy of national, racial, or religious hatred that constitute incitements to lawless violence or to any other similar action against any person or group of persons on any grounds including those of race, color, religion, language, or national origin shall be considered as offenses punishable by law.*

The American Convention on Human Rights. Thomas M. Antkowiak and Alejandra Gonza.

Chapter 7 Contents

I. Introduction 231
II. Background 234
III. Scope of Protection 235
A. Meaning of "Everyone" 235
B. Protected Expression 237
C. Safeguards for Journalists 239
D. Right of Access to State-Held Information 241
IV. Limitations to Article 13 243
A. Introduction 243
B. Prior Censorship 244
1. Overview 244
2. Prohibitions against Offensive Content 245
C. Subsequent Imposition of Liability 247
1. Overview and General Requirements 247
2. Subsequent Criminal Liability 249
a. Introduction 249
b. The Honor and Reputation of the Armed Forces 252
c. The Honor and Reputation of Public Officials 253
3. Subsequent Civil Liability 256
D. "Indirect" Restrictions 257
E. Cases of Persecution Leading to Generic Violations of Article 13(1) 259
F. Incitements to Violence: Article 13(5) 260

I. Introduction

Reiterating the enduring views of many tribunals and scholars,[1] the Inter-American Court has held

> Freedom of expression is a cornerstone upon which the very existence of a democratic society rests. It is indispensable for the formation of public opinion. It is also a *conditio sine qua non* for the development of political parties, trade unions, scientific and cultural societies and, in general, those who wish to influence the public. It represents, in short, the means that enable the community, when exercising its options, to be sufficiently informed. Consequently, it can be said that a society that is not well informed is not a society that is truly free.[2]

The fundamental nature of this freedom has been recognized internationally by the American and Universal Declarations, the ICCPR, the European Convention, the Arab Charter, the African Charter, and the EU Charter.[3] In the Inter-American System, the Inter-American Democratic Charter and the Inter-American Commission's Declaration of Principles on Freedom of Expression ("Principles") also affirm and elaborate upon the freedom of expression.[4]

There are many aspects to this freedom. It safeguards the individual's right to hold an opinion and to share information and ideas. The American Convention and the ICCPR further specify that information and ideas "of all kinds" may be communicated.[5] Further, the freedom comprises the right to "receive" this information—and, in the American Convention and other select instruments—to "seek" it.[6] Consequently, the right is not only for those who wish to disseminate ideas and information; it also belongs to the potential audience, from the individual to society as a whole.[7] Relying on this key term

---

[1] *See, e.g.*, New York Times Co. v. Sullivan, 376 U.S. 254, 271 (1964) ("in spite of the probability of excesses and abuses, these liberties are, in the long view, essential to enlightened opinion and right conduct on the part of the citizens of a democracy"); Handyside v. the United Kingdom, Eur. Ct. H.R., App. No. 5493/72, para. 49 (Dec. 7, 1976) ("Freedom of expression constitutes one of the essential foundations of such a society, one of the basic conditions for its progress and for the development of every man"); John Stuart Mill, On Liberty and Considerations on Representative Government 14–15 (1859) (stating that freedom of expression is necessary to uncover the truth).

[2] Compulsory Membership in an Association Prescribed by Law for the Practice of Journalism (Arts. 13 and 29 American Convention on Human Rights), Advisory Opinion OC-5/85, Inter-Am. Ct. H.R. (ser. A) No. 5, para. 70 (Nov. 13, 1985).

[3] American Declaration, art. IV; Universal Declaration, art. 19; ICCPR, art. 19; European Convention, art. 10; Arab Charter, art. 32; African Charter, art. 9; EU Charter, art. 11.

[4] Inter-American Democratic Charter, adopted in 2001; Declaration of Principles on Freedom of Expression, adopted in 2000.

[5] American Convention, art. 13; ICCPR, art. 19.

[6] American Convention, art. 13; Universal Declaration, art. 19; ICCPR, art. 19; Arab Charter, art. 32.

[7] *E.g.*, Mémoli v. Argentina, Preliminary Objections, Merits, Reparations, and Costs, Judgment, Inter-Am. Ct. H.R. (ser. C) No. 265, para. 119 (Aug. 22, 2013); Compulsory Membership in an Association Prescribed by Law

"seek," the Inter-American Court became the first international human rights tribunal to establish the right of all individuals to access State-held information[8]—a right that was later recognized by other human rights authorities.[9]

The American Convention was designed to provide robust guarantees for the freedom of thought and expression. Among international treaties, it contains the only prohibition against prior censorship, and features an innovative provision on "indirect" restrictions.[10] In *Advisory Opinion No. 5*, the Inter-American Tribunal's first interpretation of Article 13, the Court recognized the Article's provisions as more "generous" than other treaties and thus rejected attempts "to invoke restrictions contained in those other international instruments . . . to limit the exercise of the rights and freedoms that the [American Convention] recognizes."[11] Following the advisory opinion, the Court issued several decisions that condemned prior censorship and disproportionate sanctions on expression, protecting the Article 13 rights of individuals and society at large.[12] These judgments led to legislative reforms, the reversal of criminal convictions, and the lifting of bans on films and books, among other successes.[13]

Although freedom of expression is often understood as a negative right, the Court has also required several positive State obligations in this area. Among other duties,[14] States must ensure pluralism and diversity of viewpoints in the media.[15] Second, State officials, given their influential roles, must "verify reasonably, though not necessarily in

for the Practice of Journalism (Arts. 13 and 29 American Convention on Human Rights), Advisory Opinion OC-5/85, Inter-Am. Ct. H.R. (ser. A) No. 5, para. 140 (Nov. 13, 1985).

[8] Claude Reyes et al. v. Chile, Merits, Reparations, and Costs, Judgment, Inter-Am. Ct. H.R. (ser. C) No. 151, para. 77 (Sept. 19, 2006).

[9] *See* Alejandra Gonza, *El derecho a la información en el artículo 13 de la Convención Americana*, 99–100, Biblioteca Jurídica Virtual de la UNAM, *available at* http://biblio.juridicas.unam.mx/libros/5/2465/8.pdf (last visited Nov. 25, 2016); Nicola Wenzel, *Freedom of Opinion and Expression*, *in* Max Planck Encyclopedia of Public International Law (2014), at para. 20.

[10] *See* Sergio García Ramírez, Alejandra Gonza & Erendira Ramos Vásquez, Freedom of Thought and Expression in the Case Law of the Inter-American Court of Human Rights 48 (4th ed. 2016).

[11] Compulsory Membership in an Association Prescribed by Law for the Practice of Journalism, Advisory Opinion OC-5/85, Inter-Am. Ct. H.R. (ser. A) No. 5, para. 50 (Nov. 13, 1985).

[12] *E.g.*, Palamara Iribarne v. Chile, Merits, Reparations, Costs, Judgment, Inter-Am. Ct. H.R. (ser. C) No. 135 (Nov. 22, 2005); "The Last Temptation of Christ" (Olmedo Bustos et al.) v. Chile, Merits, Reparations, and Costs, Judgment, Inter-Am. Ct. H.R. (ser. C) No. 73 (Feb. 5, 2001).

[13] *Olmedo Bustos et al. v. Chile*, although one of the best-known cases, counts as only one of several success stories. *Id. See also* this book's chapter on reparations.

[14] For additional State obligations, *see, e.g.*, Perozo et al. v. Venezuela, Preliminary Objections, Merits, Reparations, and Costs, Judgment, Inter-Am. Ct. H.R. (ser. C) No. 195, para. 375 (Jan. 28, 2009) ("with respect to the accreditations or authorizations necessary for the media to participate in official events, which imply a possible restriction to [Article 13], it is essential to prove that their application is legal and legitimate and necessary and proportionate to the goal in question in a democratic society.").

[15] *E.g.*, Granier et al. (Radio Caracas Television) v. Venezuela, Preliminary Objections, Merits, Reparations, Costs, Judgment, Inter-Am. Ct. H.R. (ser. C) No. 293, paras. 143–145 (June 22, 2015); Kimel v. Argentina, Merits, Reparations, and Costs, Judgment, Inter-Am. Ct. H.R. (ser. C) No. 177, para. 57 (May 2, 2008).

an exhaustive manner, the truthfulness of the facts supporting their opinions";[16] and their statements should not "amount to a form of interference with or pressure impairing the rights of those" who wish to participate in public debate and discourse.[17] Third, States must "adopt reasonable and appropriate measures to enable lawful demonstrations to proceed peacefully."[18] Fourth, States must implement "special measures of prevention and protection for journalists subject to special risk," including the prompt investigation and punishment of rights violations against journalists.[19]

Until 2008, the Court conceived of the freedom of speech as a primary means to limit State power and foster democracy. Subsequently, the Tribunal modified its posture; it began to allow more limitations on expression and to require more responsibilities of speakers.[20] In doing so, it has often cited to European Court judgments, which interpret a treaty more restrictive of the freedom of expression.[21] For example, contrary to the Inter-American Commission's position, the Court has held that criminal sanctions on expression are a legitimate means to protect honor and reputation, and that States have the obligation to establish such laws.[22] The Court even accepted that protecting the honor of a State's armed forces was a legitimate objective to criminally punish speech.[23]

---

[16] *E.g.*, Perozo et al. v. Venezuela, Preliminary Objections, Merits, Reparations, and Costs, Judgment, Inter-Am. Ct. H.R. (ser. C) No. 195, para. 151 (Jan. 28, 2009) (noting "this verification should be performed subject to a higher standard than that used by private parties . . . and with a view to keeping citizens from receiving a distorted version of the facts."); Ríos et al. v. Venezuela, Preliminary Objections, Merits, Reparations, and Costs, Judgment, Inter-Am. Ct. H.R. (ser. C) No. 194 (Jan. 28, 2009) (similar).

[17] Perozo et al. v. Venezuela, Preliminary Objections, Merits, Reparations, and Costs, Judgment, Inter-Am. Ct. H.R. (ser. C) No. 195, para. 151 (Jan. 28, 2009) (observing also that "this duty of special care is particularly emphasized in those situations of greater social conflict, disorderly conducts or social and political bias, precisely because of the risks entailed for certain people or groups at a given time."). The Inter-American Commission has stated that public officials have additional duties "to ensure that their statements do not interfere with the independence and autonomy of judicial authorities"; to keep confidential "certain sensitive information in the possession of the State, within the framework established by Article 13.2 of the Convention"; and to "denounce human rights violations of which they are aware." Gallo et al. v. Argentina, Case 12.632, Inter-Am. Comm'n H.R., Report No. 43/15, OEA/Ser.L/V/II.155, Doc. 23, para. 226 (2015).

[18] Perozo et al. v. Venezuela, Preliminary Objections, Merits, Reparations, and Costs, Judgment, Inter-Am. Ct. H.R. (ser. C) No. 195, para. 166 (Jan. 28, 2009).

[19] Vélez Restrepo and Family v. Colombia, Preliminary Objections, Merits, Reparations, and Costs, Judgment, Inter-Am. Ct. H.R. (ser. C) No. 248, para. 194 (Sept. 3, 2012).

[20] Kimel v. Argentina, Merits, Reparations, and Costs, Judgment, Inter-Am. Ct. H.R. (ser. C) No. 177, para. 71 (May 2, 2008).

[21] The European Convention's Article 10 establishes, in part: "The exercise of these freedoms, since it carries with it duties and responsibilities, may be subject to such formalities, conditions, restrictions or penalties as are prescribed by law and are necessary in a democratic society, in the interests of national security, territorial integrity or public safety, for the prevention of disorder or crime, for the protection of health or morals, for the protection of the reputation or rights of others, for preventing the disclosure of information received in confidence, or for maintaining the authority and impartiality of the judiciary."

[22] Mémoli v. Argentina, Preliminary Objections, Merits, Reparations, and Costs, Judgment, Inter-Am. Ct. H.R. (ser. C) No. 265, paras. 125–126 (Aug. 22, 2013).

[23] Usón Ramírez v. Venezuela, Preliminary Objection, Merits, Reparations, and Costs, Judgment, Inter-Am. Ct. H.R. (ser. C) No. 207, para. 66 (Nov. 20, 2009).

In these cases involving criminal and civil sanctions, the Court balances the freedom of expression against the rights to honor, reputation, or privacy. An Article 13 violation often hinges on whether the restriction on speech is considered disproportionate. This ad hoc examination, in turn, depends upon whether the Court characterizes the expressions as opinions or facts, as well as whether they involve the "public interest," criminal accusations, and "malice," among other elements. However, the Court has not fully defined these vital terms nor used them in a consistent manner.

In response, we argue that criminal sanctions on expression, in order to protect honor and reputation, should always violate Article 13. Among other reasons, this is because criminal punishment fails the proportionality requirement of Article 13(2). As a result, the Court must change its approach and prohibit the use of criminal law in these cases. Second, pursuant to the American Convention, the Tribunal must develop clear definitions and rules regarding any sanctions on speech, with the goal to promote vigorous public debate. Otherwise, governments, domestic judges, and the Court itself will inevitably fail to honor Article 13's generous protections. Of course, speakers and journalists also require predictable standards to avoid chilling effects on the freedom of expression. Yet the Court's case law still permits, under uncertain circumstances, civil and even criminal sanctions for criticizing State institutions and public figures.

Also of concern, since 2006 the Court started finding violations of Article 13(1)'s general provision, without analyzing the Article's other paragraphs.[24] As stated elsewhere in this volume, the Tribunal cannot neglect its duty to rigorously analyze a case's facts in light of the Convention's express terms and limitations. Otherwise, its assessment becomes opaque; again, this can result in greater discretion for the Court and States in this critical area.

II. Background

The delegates in San José largely maintained the Inter-American Commission's preliminary proposal on freedom of expression.[25] The discussion centered more on technical modifications, rather than substantive changes.[26] The most significant revision concerned Article 13(5). The Commission's original draft allowed for wider restrictions on speech, specifically on expressions that "constitute incitement to discrimination, hostility or violence," such as the ICCPR's Article 20(2).[27] The U.S. representative opposed this formulation as overly restrictive on freedom of expression, and inconsistent with the First

---

[24] López Álvarez v. Honduras, Merits, Reparations, and Costs, Judgment, Inter-Am. Ct. H.R. (ser. C) No. 141, para. 174 (Feb. 1, 2006).

[25] Draft Inter-American Convention on Protection of Human Rights, Doc. 5 (English), art. 12, Sept. 22, 1969.

[26] Report of Committee I "Protection." Rapporteur Juan Isaac Lovato, Doc. 60 (Revised) Nov. 19, 1969, p. 298.

[27] Draft Inter-American Convention on Protection of Human Rights, Doc. 5 (English), art. 12(5)(b), Sept. 22, 1969.

Amendment of the U.S. Constitution.[28] Consequently, the Convention's final version of Article 13(5) only limited expressions that amount to incitements to violence.[29]

As for the Article's first paragraph, Colombia proposed the addition of a phrase similar to the ICCPR's Article 19(1): "Everyone shall have the right to hold opinions without interference."[30] There is no record as to why the suggestion was not accepted. Before approving Article 13(2), the delegates considered the possibility of modifying or even eliminating the strong prohibition of prior censorship, as some States allowed it in their legislation.[31]

Select delegations showed concern that Article 13(3), the provision on "indirect" restrictions, offered inadequate or uncertain definitions.[32] Although the Commission's draft was approved in Committee I, a few modifications were made before the plenary vote.[33] "The use of government and private monopolies" was replaced by "the abuse of government or private controls."[34] According to the U.S. representative, the new text was preferable because "a licensed operation such as a television station by its very nature has a monopoly on the use of a public resource, such as a broadcasting frequency."[35]

III. Scope of Protection

A. MEANING OF "EVERYONE"

Article 13 establishes that "everyone" holds the right to freedom of thought and expression; in this way, "there are no individuals or groups that, a priori, are excluded."[36] Although the rights of legal persons or entities are not protected by the American Convention,[37] the Court has stated: "this does not mean that . . . an individual may not resort to the Inter-American system . . . to enforce his fundamental rights, even when they are encompassed in a legal figure or fiction."[38] On occasion, the Court has found

---

[28] P. 26, Report of the United States Delegation to the Inter-American Conference on Protection of Human Rights (1969).

[29] P. 444, Minutes of the Second Plenary Session, Doc. 86, Nov. 22, 1969.

[30] P. 213, Minutes of the 8th Session of Committee I, Doc. 48, Nov. 15, 1969.

[31] *See id.*

[32] *See, e.g.*, p. 40, Observations of the Government of Chile to the Draft Convention, Doc. 7, Sept. 26, 1969; p. 46, Observations of the Government of Argentina to the Draft Convention, Doc. 8, Sept. 26, 1969.

[33] P. 444, Minutes of the Second Plenary Session, Doc. 86, Nov. 22, 1969.

[34] *Id.*

[35] P. 25, Report of the United States Delegation to the Inter-American Conference on Protection of Human Rights (1969).

[36] *E.g.*, Granier et al. (Radio Caracas Television) v. Venezuela, Preliminary Objections, Merits, Reparations, Costs, Judgment, Inter-Am. Ct. H.R. (ser. C) No. 293, para. 142 (June 22, 2015); Compulsory Membership in an Association Prescribed by Law for the Practice of Journalism, Advisory Opinion OC-5/85, Inter-Am. Ct. H.R. (ser. A) No. 5, para. 34 (Nov. 13, 1985).

[37] Entitlement of Legal Entities to Hold Rights under the Inter-American Human Rights System, Advisory Opinion OC-22/16, Inter-Am. Ct. H.R. (ser. A) No. 22, para. 140(2) (Feb. 26, 2016).

[38] *E.g.*, Perozo et al. v. Venezuela, Preliminary Objections, Merits, Reparations, and Costs, Judgment, Inter-Am. Ct. H.R. (ser. C) No. 195, para. 399 (Jan. 28, 2009); Cantos v. Argentina, Merits, Reparations, and Costs, Judgment, Inter-Am. Ct. H.R. (ser. C) No. 97, para. 29 (Nov. 28, 2002).

journalists and others associated with media companies to have suffered Article 13 violations, owing to acts directed against those companies.[39]

When a legal entity, such as a TV station or newspaper, has been attacked, the Court requires that petitioners demonstrate a "negative, certain and substantial impact" upon a natural person, in order to assess a potential violation to that individual's freedom of expression.[40] The Tribunal has also considered the petitioner's role in the media enterprise, looking for "real involvement in the business's communicational mission."[41] Originally, for these complaints to be admissible, petitioners needed to file domestic remedies in their own names, and not only in the names of the affected businesses.[42] Currently, however, the petitioner need only show that the appropriate domestic remedies pursued on behalf of the legal entity have a connection to the human rights violations alleged before the Inter-American System.[43]

The Court's various requirements in this area can impede victims from holding States accountable for these troubling acts of intimidation and aggression. For example, in *Perozo* et al. *v. Venezuela* the Court concluded that the various damages caused to the office and property of the TV channel *Globovision* were directed only to the business itself, without a sufficient showing of how the damages affected the petitioners' rights.[44] In contrast, the Inter-American Commission's Principles declare that "the material destruction of communications media violate the fundamental rights of individuals and strongly restrict freedom of expression."[45]

---

[39] *E.g.*, Perozo et al. v. Venezuela, Preliminary Objections, Merits, Reparations, and Costs, Judgment, Inter-Am. Ct. H.R. (ser. C) No. 195, para. 362 (Jan. 28, 2009); Ríos et al. v. Venezuela, Preliminary Objections, Merits, Reparations, and Costs, Judgment, Inter-Am. Ct. H.R. (ser. C) No. 194, para. 334 (Jan. 28, 2009).

[40] Granier et al. (Radio Caracas Television) vs. Venezuela, Preliminary Objections, Merits, Reparations, Costs, Judgment, Inter-Am. Ct. H.R. (ser. C) No. 293, para. 151 (June 22, 2015) (translation by authors). *See also* Entitlement of Legal Entities to Hold Rights under the Inter-American Human Rights System, Advisory Opinion OC-22/16, Inter-Am. Ct. H.R. (ser. A) No. 22, para. 119 (Feb. 26, 2016) (requiring a "direct and essential relationship" between the natural person and the legal entity) (translation by authors).

[41] Granier et al. (Radio Caracas Television) vs. Venezuela, Preliminary Objections, Merits, Reparations, Costs, Judgment, Inter-Am. Ct. H.R. (ser. C) No. 293, para. 153 (June 22, 2015).

[42] *See* Cantos v. Argentina, Preliminary Objections, Judgment, Inter-Am. Ct. H.R. (ser. C) No. 85, para. 30 (Sept. 7, 2001).

[43] *See* Entitlement of Legal Entities to Hold Rights under the Inter-American Human Rights System, Advisory Opinion OC-22/16, Inter-Am. Ct. H.R. (ser. A) No. 22, para. 136 (Feb. 26, 2016); William Gómez Vargas v. Costa Rica, Petition 1164/05, Inter-Am. Comm'n H.R, Report No. 72/11, para. 43 (Mar. 31, 2011).

[44] Perozo et al. v. Venezuela, Preliminary Objections, Merits, Reparations, and Costs, Judgment, Inter-Am. Ct. H.R. (ser. C) No. 195, para. 402 (Jan. 28, 2009). *See also* Herrera Ulloa v. Costa Rica, Preliminary Objections, Merits, Reparations, and Costs, Judgment, Inter-Am. Ct. H.R. (ser. C) No. 107 (July 2, 2004) (failing to conclude that the newspaper's legal representative suffered a violation of Article 13); Granier et al. (Radio Caracas Television) v. Venezuela, Preliminary Objections, Merits, Reparations, Costs, Judgment, Inter-Am. Ct. H.R. (ser. C) No. 293, para. 342 (June 22, 2015) (after establishing abuse of power and discriminatory treatment regarding Article 13, Court did not find a property violation to be actionable).

[45] Declaration of Principles on Freedom of Expression, Principle 9.

B. PROTECTED EXPRESSION

Article 13 establishes that everyone has the "freedom to seek, receive, and impart information and ideas of *all kinds*."[46] According to the Inter-American Court and Commission, this provision safeguards

> not only the dissemination of ideas and information that are received favorably or considered inoffensive or indifferent but also those that are offensive, shocking, unsettling, unpleasant or disturbing to the State or to any sector of the population, as this is required by the principles of pluralism and tolerance inherent in a democracy.[47]

In this way, the Inter-American Commission's Special Rapporteur on Freedom of Expression ("Special Rapporteur") has stated that there should be a general presumption that all speech is protected by Article 13.[48]

Article 13 prohibits all prior censorship, except that "public entertainments may be subject by law to prior censorship for the sole purpose of regulating access to them for the moral protection of childhood and adolescence."[49] The Inter-American Court has emphasized that "in all other cases," any censorship "implies the impairment of freedom of thought and expression."[50] Thus, Article 13's coverage of expression is very broad, and problematic speech—even "propaganda for war and any advocacy of national, racial, or religious hatred that constitute incitements to lawless violence"[51]—can only be limited by subsequent sanctions.[52]

The Court's Article 13 case law has not yet reached diverse forms of expression; it has mainly assessed information and speech concerning typical public affairs. To illustrate, its judgments have considered: journalism exposing a public official's corruption,[53] TV stations

---

[46] American Convention, art. 13(1) (emphasis added).

[47] *E.g.*, Office of the Special Rapporteur on Freedom of Expression, Inter-American Commission on Human Rights, *A Hemispheric Agenda for the Defense of Freedom of Expression*, OEA/Ser.L/V/II CIDH/RELE/INF. 4/09 (2009), para. 21 ["Hemispheric Agenda"]; "The Last Temptation of Christ" (Olmedo Bustos et al.) v. Chile, Merits, Reparations, and Costs, Judgment, Inter-Am. Ct. H.R. (ser. C) No. 73, para. 69 (Feb. 5, 2001) (citing the European Court of Human Rights).

[48] Hemispheric Agenda, para. 21.

[49] American Convention, art. 13(4).

[50] "The Last Temptation of Christ" (Olmedo Bustos et al.) v. Chile, Merits, Reparations, and Costs, Judgment, Inter-Am. Ct. H.R. (ser. C) No. 73, para. 70 (Feb. 5, 2001).

[51] American Convention, art. 13(5).

[52] Yet here the Special Rapporteur appears to take a different view, and considers that Article 13 excludes certain speech: "speech advocating violence, war propaganda, the incitement of hatred for discriminatory reasons, the direct and public incitement of genocide, and child pornography." Hemispheric Agenda, para. 21. However, the Inter-American Court has not specified that these forms of expression fall outside the coverage of Article 13.

[53] Herrera Ulloa v. Costa Rica, Preliminary Objections, Merits, Reparations, and Costs, Judgment, Inter-Am. Ct. H.R. (ser. C) No. 107 (July 2, 2004).

and newspapers critical of government administrations,[54] a presidential candidate who published a column against his rival,[55] retired military officers who denounced the armed forces through their interviews or books,[56] a lawyer who referred to the illicit acts of a public official during a press conference, [57] judges who expressed opposition to the Honduran coup d'état,[58] and other political leaders and rights advocates who criticized the government.[59]

The Court, similar to the United States Supreme Court, holds that "it is logical and appropriate that statements concerning public officials" should be given "a certain latitude in the broad debate on matters of public interest that is essential for the functioning of a truly democratic system."[60] Although the honor and reputation of public officials should be respected, a higher "threshold of protection" must apply to such statements.[61] This is only fair, according to the Inter-American Court, as these officials—public figures whose "activities . . . belong to the realm of public debate"—have "voluntarily" opened themselves to "a more intense public scrutiny."[62] Special protection even extends to statements about private persons and entities, as long as the expressions are relevant to the public interest.[63] The Court, however, has been unable to arrive at a precise definition for "public interest" in this context, so the actual scope of protection is uncertain.[64]

---

[54] *E.g.*, Granier et al. (Radio Caracas Television) v. Venezuela, Preliminary Objections, Merits, Reparations, Costs, Judgment, Inter-Am. Ct. H.R. (ser. C) No. 293 (June 22, 2015); Ivcher Bronstein v. Peru, Merits, Reparations, and Costs, Judgment, Inter-Am. Ct. H.R. (ser. C) No. 74 (Feb. 6, 2001).

[55] Canese v. Paraguay, Merits, Reparations, and Costs, Judgment, Inter-Am. Ct. H.R. (ser. C) No. 111 (Aug. 31, 2004).

[56] Usón Ramírez v. Venezuela, Preliminary Objection, Merits, Reparations, and Costs, Judgment, Inter-Am. Ct. H.R. (ser. C) No. 207 (Nov. 20, 2009); Palamara Iribarne v. Chile, Merits, Reparations, Costs, Judgment, Inter-Am. Ct. H.R. (ser. C) No. 135 (Nov. 22, 2005).

[57] Tristán Donoso v. Panama, Preliminary Objections, Merits, Reparations, and Costs, Judgment, Inter-Am. Ct. H.R. (ser. C) No. 193 (Jan. 27, 2009).

[58] López Lone et al. v. Honduras, Preliminary Objection, Merits, Reparations and Costs. Judgment Inter-Am. Ct. H.R. (ser. C) No. 302 (Oct. 5, 2015).

[59] *E.g.*, Manuel Cepeda Vargas v. Colombia, Preliminary Objections, Merits, Reparations, and Costs, Judgment, Inter-Am. Ct. H.R. (ser. C.) No. 213 (May 26, 2010); Uzcátegui et al. v. Venezuela, Merits and Reparations, Judgment, Inter-Am. Ct. H.R. (ser. C) No. 249 (Sept. 3, 2012).

[60] Herrera Ulloa v. Costa Rica, Preliminary Objections, Merits, Reparations, and Costs, Judgment, Inter-Am. Ct. H.R. (ser. C) No. 107, para. 128 (July 2, 2004). *See also* Granier et al. (Radio Caracas Television) v. Venezuela, Preliminary Objections, Merits, Reparations, Costs, Judgment, Inter-Am. Ct. H.R. (ser. C) No. 293, para. 140 (June 22, 2015). For similar U.S. Supreme Court case law, *see, e.g.*, New York Times Co. v. Sullivan, 376 U.S. 254.

[61] *Id.* paras. 128–129.

[62] *Id.* para. 129.

[63] *See* Canese v. Paraguay, Merits, Reparations, and Costs, Judgment, Inter-Am. Ct. H.R. (ser. C) No. 111, para. 103 (Aug. 31, 2004) ("a different threshold of protection should be applied, which is not based on the nature of the subject, but on the characteristic of public interest inherent in the activities or acts of a specific individual"); Mémoli v. Argentina, Preliminary Objections, Merits, Reparations, and Costs, Judgment, Inter-Am. Ct. H.R. (ser. C) No. 265, para. 147 (Aug. 22, 2013) ("certain information concerning private individuals or organizations may be classified as information of public interest").

[64] In *Mémoli v. Argentina*, three judges attempted a definition. *See* Joint Partially Dissenting Opinion of Judges Manuel E. Ventura Robles, Eduardo Vio Grossi and Eduardo Ferrer Mac-Gregor Poisot, Mémoli v. Argentina (Aug. 22, 2013) (proposing a means for determining issues in the "public interest").

In fact, this higher "threshold of protection" has appeared to make little practical difference in the Court's recent decisions. Rather than according clear preferential status to statements concerning the public interest, since 2007 the Court has found that the right to honor and freedom of expression "deserve equal protection and must coexist harmoniously."[65] As discussed below, when the rights conflict the Tribunal engages in an ad hoc balancing test.[66]

Further, when expression conveys an essential aspect of "identity and dignity," the Court and the Special Rapporteur have also granted it "a special level of protection."[67] In the key judgment *López Álvarez v. Honduras*, the Court found an Article 13 violation when a detained individual was prohibited from speaking his native language in prison.[68] It affirmed that Article 13 includes "the right of people to use the language of their choice when expressing their thoughts."[69] More recently, the Special Rapporteur declared that freedom of expression "encompasses the right to express one's own sexual orientation and gender identity."[70] In *Atala Riffo v. Chile*, the Court agreed that "sexual orientation is an essential component of a person's identity"; however, it conceptualized the "conduct associated with the expression of homosexuality" under the right to equality, rather than under Article 13.[71]

C. SAFEGUARDS FOR JOURNALISTS

In the Americas, journalists are frequently the target of attacks, intimidation, and persecution. The Inter-American Commission has evaluated many such situations,[72]

---

[65] Kimel v. Argentina, Merits, Reparations, and Costs, Judgment, Inter-Am. Ct. H.R. (ser. C) No. 177, para. 51 (May 2, 2008); Mémoli v. Argentina, Preliminary Objections, Merits, Reparations, and Costs, Judgment, Inter-Am. Ct. H.R. (ser. C) No. 265, para. 142 (Aug. 22, 2013).

[66] Kimel v. Argentina, Merits, Reparations, and Costs, Judgment, Inter-Am. Ct. H.R. (ser. C) No. 177, para. 51 (May 2, 2008) ("the prevalence of either of [the rights] in a particular case will depend on the considerations made as to proportionality").

[67] Office of the Special Rapporteur on Freedom of Expression, Annual Report 2015, p. 362.

[68] López Álvarez v. Honduras, Merits, Reparations, and Costs, Judgment, Inter-Am. Ct. H.R. (ser. C) No. 141 (Feb. 1, 2006).

[69] *Id.* para. 164.

[70] Office of the Special Rapporteur on Freedom of Expression, Annual Report 2015, p. 362.

[71] Atala Riffo and Daughters v. Chile, Merits, Reparations, and Costs, Judgment, Inter-Am. Ct. H.R. (ser. C) No. 239, para. 139 (Feb. 24, 2012). In *Velásquez Paiz* et al. *v. Guatemala*, the Court declined another opportunity to expand concepts of expression under Article 13. Velásquez Paiz et al. v. Guatemala, Preliminary Objections, Merits, Reparations and Costs, Judgment, Inter-Am. Ct. H.R. (ser. C) No. 307 (Nov. 19, 2015). The victim's lawyers argued that the flawed investigation into Claudina Velásquez's death owed to authorities' "prejudices associated with her style of dress" and the poor neighborhood where her body was found. *Id.* para. 139 (translation by authors). The Court refused to consider whether an individual's clothing and personal style could constitute a form of expression under Article 13. In response, Judge Roberto Caldas asserted that "the implicit message in the ineffective investigation of these cases is that expressing control over one's own body by the free choice of clothing can place a woman in a situation of special vulnerability." Partially Dissenting Opinion, Judge Roberto Caldas, para. 21(translation by authors).

[72] *See, e.g.*, Office of the Special Rapporteur for Freedom of Expression, Inter-American Commission Human Rights, Violence against Journalists and Media Workers: Inter-American Standards and National Practices on

which are now increasingly arriving at the Inter-American Court.[73] Both institutions have expressed alarm about this crisis, and in some cases have issued urgent measures to protect journalists.[74]

Without attempting the difficult task of defining "journalists," the Court has called it "essential" that they "enjoy the necessary protection and independence to exercise their functions comprehensively."[75] In this regard, "States have the obligation to adopt special measures of prevention and protection for journalists subject to special risk owing to the exercise of their profession."[76] The Court also has emphasized "the importance of effectively and diligently investigating" rights violations against journalists, whether committed by State agents or private actors.[77] While these abuses remain unpunished, journalists will "reasonably fear that this type of human rights violation might be repeated, and this could lead to self-censorship of their work."[78] In addition, the Tribunal has urged public officials to condemn attacks on the press.[79]

As for other impediments to the free practice of journalism, the Court has ruled that mandatory licensing violates Article 13(2).[80] Licensing or requiring university degrees for journalists would breach "not only the right of each individual to seek and impart information and ideas through any means of his choice, but also the right of the public at large

---

Prevention, Protection and Prosecution of Perpetrators, OEA/Ser.L/V/II. CIDH/RELE/INF. 12/13 (2013); Office of the Special Rapporteur for Freedom of Expression, Inter-American Commission Human Rights, Special Study on the Status of Investigations into the Murder of Journalists OEA/Ser.L/V/II.131. Doc. 35 (2008).

[73] *E.g.*, Vélez Restrepo and Family v. Colombia, Preliminary Objections, Merits, Reparations, and Costs, Judgment, Inter-Am. Ct. H.R. (ser. C) No. 248 (Sept. 3, 2012); Perozo et al. v. Venezuela, Preliminary Objections, Merits, Reparations, and Costs, Judgment, Inter-Am. Ct. H.R. (ser. C) No. 195 (Jan. 28, 2009).

[74] *E.g.*, Sánchez Cerezo v. Mexico, Precautionary Measures 5/15, Inter-Am. Comm'n H.R. (2015); "Globovisión" Television Station v. Venezuela, Provisional Measures, Order, Inter-Am. Ct. H.R. (Sept. 4, 2004); Luisiana Ríos et al. v. Venezuela, Provisional Measures, Order, Inter-Am. Ct. H.R. (Sept. 8, 2004).

[75] Ivcher Bronstein v. Peru, Merits, Reparations, and Costs, Judgment, Inter-Am. Ct. H.R. (ser. C) No. 74, para. 150 (Feb. 6, 2001).

[76] Vélez Restrepo and Family v. Colombia, Preliminary Objections, Merits, Reparations, and Costs, Judgment, Inter-Am. Ct. H.R. (ser. C) No. 248, paras. 189–194 (Sept. 3, 2012).

[77] *Id.* para. 191.

[78] *Id.* para. 212. *See also* Office of the Special Rapporteur for Freedom of Expression, Inter-American Commission Human Rights, Impunity, Self-Censorship and Armed Internal Conflict: An Analysis of the State of Freedom of Expression in Colombia, OEA/Ser.L/V/II Doc. 51 (2005), para. 99.

[79] Perozo et al. v. Venezuela, Preliminary Objections, Merits, Reparations, and Costs, Judgment, Inter-Am. Ct. H.R. (ser. C) No. 195, para. 151 (Jan. 28, 2009); Ríos et al. v. Venezuela, Preliminary Objections, Merits, Reparations, and Costs, Judgment, Inter-Am. Ct. H.R. (ser. C) No. 194, para. 139 (Jan. 28, 2009).

[80] Compulsory Membership in an Association Prescribed by Law for the Practice of Journalism, Advisory Opinion OC-5/85, Inter-Am. Ct. H.R. (ser. A) No. 5, para. 81 (Nov. 13, 1985). The Court has also indicated that the processes for granting licenses and concessions should be fair, "clear and precise." Granier et al. (Radio Caracas Television) v. Venezuela, Preliminary Objections, Merits, Reparations, Costs, Judgment, Inter-Am. Ct. H.R. (ser. C) No. 293, para. 171 (June 22, 2015).

to receive information without any interference."[81] The Commission's Principles share this view, and also declare that ethical rules governing "journalistic activities . . . should in no case be imposed by the State."[82]

However, with *Kimel v. Argentina*, the Court began to limit the practice of journalism.[83] In consideration of "the great responsibility" belonging to "professionals in the field of social communications," *Kimel* held:

> journalists have the duty to verify reasonably, though not necessarily in an exhaustive manner, the truthfulness of the facts supporting their opinion. Therefore, it is valid to claim equity and diligence in the search for information and the verification of the sources. . . . Therefore, journalists have the duty to keep a critical distance from sources and match the information against other relevant data.[84]

In developing these duties, the Court has been influenced by international authorities such as the European Court, which preside over regimes that are more restrictive of freedom of expression. In contrast, the Principles reject requirements for "truthfulness, timeliness or impartiality,"[85] because "the right to information encompasses all information, including that which we might term 'erroneous,' 'untimely,' or 'incomplete.' "[86] In the Court's subsequent judgment *Mémoli v. Argentina*, it even upheld criminal sanctions against journalists, when the right to honor was at issue.[87]

D. RIGHT OF ACCESS TO STATE-HELD INFORMATION

In *Claude Reyes v. Chile*, a landmark decision from 2006, the Court interpreted Article 13 to include the right of all persons to access State-held information, subject to the usual limitations of Article 13(2).[88] In *Claude Reyes*, the petitioners had requested information

---

[81] Compulsory Membership in an Association Prescribed by Law for the Practice of Journalism, Advisory Opinion OC-5/85, Inter-Am. Ct. H.R. (ser. A) No. 5, para. 81 (Nov. 13, 1985). Similarly, the UN Human Rights Committee has stated that "general State systems of registration or licensing of journalists are incompatible with [Article 19]." UN Human Rights Committee, General Comment No. 34, Article 19, Freedoms of Opinion and Expression, CCPR/C/GC/34, para. 44 (2011).

[82] Declaration of Principles on Freedom of Expression, Principle 6.

[83] Kimel v. Argentina, Merits, Reparations, and Costs, Judgment, Inter-Am. Ct. H.R. (ser. C) No. 177 (May 2, 2008).

[84] *Id.* paras. 57, 79.

[85] Declaration of Principles on Freedom of Expression, Principle 7.

[86] Office of the Special Rapporteur for Freedom of Expression, Inter-American Commission Human Rights, Background and Interpretation of the Declaration of Principles, para. 31 (2000), *available at* http://www.oas.org/en/iachr/expression/showarticle.asp?artID=132&lID=1.

[87] Mémoli v. Argentina, Preliminary Objections, Merits, Reparations, and Costs, Judgment, Inter-Am. Ct. H.R. (ser. C) No. 265 (Aug. 22, 2013). *See* discussion below.

[88] Claude Reyes et al. v. Chile, Merits, Reparations, and Costs, Judgment, Inter-Am. Ct. H.R. (ser. C) No. 151 (Sept. 19, 2006).

from a State institution about a controversial development project, but the official response addressed only part of the request.[89]

Recognizing that Article 13 establishes the right to "to seek" and "receive . . . information and ideas of all kinds," the Court held that the American Convention

> protects the right of the individual to receive [State-held] information and the positive obligation of the State to provide it, so that the individual may have access to such information or receive an answer that includes a justification when, for any reason permitted by the Convention, the State is allowed to restrict access to the information in a specific case.[90]

Further, the individual who requests information need not "prove direct interest or personal involvement in order to obtain it."[91]

In this way, *Claude Reyes* stressed that "State authorities are governed by the principle of maximum disclosure, which establishes the presumption that all information is accessible, subject to a limited system of exceptions."[92] The Court recognized the dual nature of this right of access: once the individual gains access to information, he or she may circulate it widely, so that society may assess and respond to the information. In addition, when access to such information is hindered, the State must ensure that "there is a simple, prompt and effective recourse that permits determining whether there has been a violation of the right of the person requesting information," and, if applicable, that the State institution disclose the information at issue.[93] Subsequently, the Court has linked Article 13's right to access information to a victim's rights to "truth" and to "justice," finding additional violations to Articles 8 and 25 of the Convention.[94]

---

[89] *Id.* para. 66.

[90] *Id.* para. 77.

[91] *Id.*

[92] *Id.* para. 92. The Court also has held that, in cases of human rights violations, "State authorities cannot resort to mechanisms such as official secret or confidentiality of the information, or reasons of public interest or national security, to refuse to supply the information required by the judicial or administrative [investigation]." Gomes Lund et al. ("Guerrilha do Araguaia") v. Brazil, Preliminary Objections, Merits, Reparations, and Costs, Judgment, Inter-Am. Ct. H.R. (ser. C) No. 219, para. 202 (Nov. 24, 2010). Further, as concerns "the investigation of punishable facts, the decision to qualify the information as secretive or to refuse to hand it over cannot stem solely from a State organ whose members are charged with committing the wrongful acts." *Id.*

[93] Claude Reyes et al. v. Chile, Merits, Reparations, and Costs, Judgment, Inter-Am. Ct. H.R. (ser. C) No. 151, para. 137 (Sept. 19, 2006).

[94] Gomes Lund et al. ("Guerrilha do Araguaia") v. Brazil, Preliminary Objections, Merits, Reparations, and Costs, Judgment, Inter-Am. Ct. H.R. (ser. C) No. 219, paras. 201–212 (Nov. 24, 2010) (linking Article 13 to the right to truth and Articles 8 and 25); Kaliña and Lokono Peoples v. Suriname, Merits, Reparations and Costs, Judgment, Inter-Am. Ct. H.R. (ser. C) No. 309, paras. 267–268 (Nov. 25, 2015) (connecting Article 13 to the right to justice and Article 25). For more on "the right of access to justice" and "the right to the truth," *see* this volume's Chapter 6: Due Process and Judicial Protection.

IV. Limitations to Article 13

A. INTRODUCTION

Freedom of expression is not an absolute right. Article 13(2) permits its restriction in the form of "subsequent imposition of liability, which shall be expressly established by law to the extent necessary to ensure" the rights of others or the "protection of national security, public order, or public health or morals."[95] Initially, the Court established that the permissible limitations are only those strictly enumerated in Article 13, terms that themselves should be interpreted restrictively.[96] Because Article 13 contains its own limitations, the American Convention's general provision on limitations, found in Article 32, does not apply.[97] The Court has stressed that restrictions to the freedom of expression found in other international treaties should never be applied to the American Convention.[98]

Since its first analysis of Article 13(2), the Court has set out two categories for impermissible interferences with the freedom of expression.[99] The first consists in its "extreme violation": when the right is denied through various forms of prior censorship.[100] The second category involves the range of other restrictions forbidden by the Convention. These include cases when States unjustifiably impose civil or criminal liability, as well as the "indirect" restrictions of Article 13(3).[101]

Yet the Court's strict approach to limitations has relaxed in recent years, as discussed below. Since 2006, the Court began to find violations of Article 13(1)'s general provision, without analyzing the Article's other paragraphs.[102] In this way, it has found violations of Article 13(1) in cases of political assassination,[103] persecution of journalists,[104] and a prison's ban of the Garifuna language, among others.[105] The Court's change in methodology is significant, because it allows both the Tribunal and States greater discretion in

---

95 American Convention, art. 13(2).

96 Compulsory Membership in an Association Prescribed by Law for the Practice of Journalism, Advisory Opinion OC-5/85, Inter-Am. Ct. H.R. (ser. A) No. 5, para. 65 (Nov. 13, 1985); Lopez Lone et al. v. Honduras, Preliminary Objection, Merits, Reparations and Costs, Judgment, Inter-Am. Ct. H.R. (ser. C) No. 302, para. 172 (Oct. 5, 2015).

97 Compulsory Membership in an Association Prescribed by Law for the Practice of Journalism, Advisory Opinion OC-5/85, Inter-Am. Ct. H.R. (ser. A) No. 5, para. 65 (Nov. 13, 1985).

98 *Id.* para. 51.

99 *Id.* para 53.

100 *Id.* para 54.

101 *Id.* para. 47.

102 López Álvarez v. Honduras, Merits, Reparations, and Costs, Judgment, Inter-Am. Ct. H.R. (ser. C) No. 141, para. 174 (Feb. 1, 2006).

103 Cepeda Vargas v. Colombia, Preliminary Objections, Merits, Reparations, and Costs, Judgment, Inter-Am. Ct. H.R. (ser. C.) No. 213 (May 26, 2010).

104 Vélez Restrepo and Family v. Colombia, Preliminary Objections, Merits, Reparations, and Costs, Judgment, Inter-Am. Ct. H.R. (ser. C) No. 248 (Sept. 3, 2012).

105 López Álvarez v. Honduras, Merits, Reparations, and Costs, Judgment, Inter-Am. Ct. H.R. (ser. C) No. 141 (Feb. 1, 2006).

this critical area. This discretion and lack of rigor can destabilize the Court's case law and diminish Article 13 protections.

B. PRIOR CENSORSHIP

1. Overview

As noted, the American Convention stands as the only international human rights treaty that prohibits prior censorship, rendering the Convention more protective than other instruments.[106] As a result, the Commission's Principles demand that States forbid censorship by law.[107] Yet the Convention itself and subsequent interpretations have not defined censorship very precisely or detailed which exact controls are prohibited. The Court takes a case-by-case approach, explaining censorship broadly as "the seizing or barring of publications and, generally, any procedure that subjects the expression or dissemination of information to governmental control."[108] It has recognized that any branch of government—executive, judicial, or legislative—is capable of censorship.[109]

The consensus is that Article 13 bans practically all forms of prior censorship.[110] Still, Article 13(4) articulates one exception: "public entertainments may be subject by law to prior censorship for the sole purpose of regulating access to them for the moral protection of childhood and adolescence."[111] The Inter-American Court and Commission have shown reticence to develop this limited exception, and the Tribunal has emphasized that "in all other cases," any censorship "implies the impairment of freedom of thought and expression."[112] Thus, as mentioned previously, "propaganda for war and any advocacy of national, racial, or religious hatred that constitute incitements to lawless violence" can only be limited by subsequent imposition of liability.[113]

---

[106] *See, e.g.*, García Ramírez, Gonza & Ramos Vásquez, *supra* note 10, at 48; David John Harris, Donna Gomien & Leo Zwaak, Law and Practice of the European Convention on Human Rights and the European Social Charter 274 (1996). In contrast, the European human rights system allows prior restraints in limited circumstances. *See* David Harris, Michael O'Boyle & Colin Warbrick, Law of the European Convention on Human Rights 640 (3d ed. 2014).

[107] Declaration of Principles on Freedom of Expression, Principle 5.

[108] Compulsory Membership in an Association Prescribed by Law for the Practice of Journalism, Advisory Opinion OC-5/85, Inter-Am. Ct. H.R. (ser. A) No. 5, para. 54 (Nov. 13, 1985).

[109] "The Last Temptation of Christ" (Olmedo Bustos et al.) v. Chile, Merits, Reparations, and Costs, Judgment, Inter-Am. Ct. H.R. (ser. C) No. 73, para. 72 (Feb. 5, 2001).

[110] *See, e.g.*, Eduardo Bertoni & Carlos Zelada, *Artículo 13: Libertad de Pensamiento y de Expresión*, *in* La Convención Americana Sobre Derechos Humanos Comentada 325 (Christian Steiner & Patricia Uribe eds., 2014); Gregorio Badeni, Tratado de Libertad de Prensa 218 (2002); Hemispheric Agenda, para. 24.

[111] American Convention, art. 13(4).

[112] "The Last Temptation of Christ" (Olmedo Bustos et al.) v. Chile, Merits, Reparations, and Costs, Judgment, Inter-Am. Ct. H.R. (ser. C) No. 73, para. 70 (Feb. 5, 2001).

[113] American Convention, art.13(5).

The Inter-American jurisprudence has examined censorship by domestic law and by various State institutions, including the armed forces. To date the Court's judgments have evaluated relatively simple censorship cases, which have not fully assessed imminent danger to life or national security. Notably, it has chosen to consider some potential cases of censorship as "indirect" restrictions of Article 13(3)—such as when Venezuela refused to renew a television station's license, due to its critical government views, forcing its closure.[114] Further, in cases when journalists and opposition politicians were killed or persecuted, the Court found violations to Article 13(1), without considering these acts to constitute censorship.[115] The Court, then, avoids an expansive concept of censorship, likely because the consequences are severe: censorship almost always violates Article 13, and States cannot escape responsibility by arguing a "legitimate" objective or the presence of mitigating circumstances.[116]

2. Prohibitions against Offensive Content

The Court and Commission have heard cases where films and books were banned in consideration of individuals' privacy and the reputation of religious and State institutions. The Court's leading censorship judgment, *Olmedo Bustos* et al. *v. Chile*, involved the State's prohibition on the film *The Last Temptation of Christ*.[117] The Chilean Supreme Court approved the ban, reasoning that censorship was permitted in the State's Constitution, and that the film "deforms the figure of Jesus Christ, offends his honor and in consequence the honor of . . . members of the Catholic Church, Christians in general."[118]

With little analysis, the Inter-American Court found an Article 13(2) violation for prior censorship; the victims were identified members of the Chilean public who claimed

---

[114] Granier et al. (Radio Caracas Television) v. Venezuela, Preliminary Objections, Merits, Reparations, Costs, Judgment, Inter-Am. Ct. H.R. (ser. C) No. 293 (June 22, 2015). *See also* Ivcher Bronstein v. Peru, Merits, Reparations, and Costs, Judgment, Inter-Am. Ct. H.R. (ser. C) No. 74 (Feb. 6, 2001) (finding violation of Article 13(3) when Peru revoked the citizenship of a television director to obstruct his influence over the network's programs).

[115] Vélez Restrepo and Family v. Colombia, Preliminary Objections, Merits, Reparations, and Costs, Judgment, Inter-Am. Ct. H.R. (ser. C) No. 248 (Sept. 3, 2012); Cepeda Vargas v. Colombia, Preliminary Objections, Merits, Reparations, and Costs, Judgment, Inter-Am. Ct. H.R. (ser. C.) No. 213 (May 26, 2010). In its merits decisions, the Inter-American Commission also does not appear to consider murder and attacks specifically as censorship in violation of Article 13(2). *E.g.*, Oliveira v. Brazil, Case 12.308, Inter-Am. Comm'n H.R., Report No. 37/10, OEA/Ser.L/V/II, doc. 5 rev. 1, para. 103 (2011); Héctor Félix Miranda v. México, Case 11.739, Inter-Am. Comm'n H.R., Report No. 50/99, para. 56 (1999).

[116] Note that previously the Inter-American Commission gave States the opportunity to demonstrate that censored material was "found within the exceptions established in the Convention." Clark v. Grenada, Case 10.325, Inter-Am. Comm'n H.R., Report No. 2/96, OEA/Ser.L./V/II.95, doc. 7 rev. (1997).

[117] "The Last Temptation of Christ" (Olmedo Bustos et al.) v. Chile, Merits, Reparations, and Costs, Judgment, Inter-Am. Ct. H.R. (ser. C) No. 73 (Feb. 5, 2001).

[118] "The Last Temptation of Christ" (Olmedo Bustos et al.) v. Chile, Inter-Am. Comm. H.R., Application, p. 13 (1999), *available at* http://www.corteidh.or.cr/docs/casos/olmedobu/demanda.PDF.

their right to watch the film.[119] Notably, *Olmedo Bustos* ordered constitutional reform, but failed to evaluate the film's content or explore topics of artistic expression and potential blasphemy. It also passed on the opportunity to interpret the Convention's exception to censorship in Article 13(4). Chile eventually reformed its Constitution and domestic legislation on censorship.[120]

Another judgment against Chile, *Palamara Iribarne*, concerned a retired Navy officer's book titled *Ethics and Intelligence Services*.[121] The military had prohibited its publication, arguing that it would endanger national security. The Court found that various measures to suppress the book resulted in prior censorship, in violation of Humberto Palamara Iribarne's "right to disseminate information and ideas."[122] These measures included the ban on publishing and distributing the book, as well as other aggressive State actions, such as attempts to delete electronic files and orders to prohibit Palamara Iribarne from "making negative comments" about the Navy or the proceedings initiated against him.[123]

On the other hand, the Court noted that "employees or officers of an institution have the duty to maintain the confidentiality of certain information to which they have access in the course of their duties."[124] Further, "under certain circumstances, a breach of the duty of confidentiality may result in administrative, tort or disciplinary liability."[125] Yet the Court found that Palamara Iribarne used publicly-available information to write his book; as a result, it decided that the duty of confidentiality did not apply, and it was unnecessary to examine the duty's parameters. It remains unclear how the Court will resolve a national security case with more complex characteristics.

For its part, the Inter-American Commission also has heard emblematic censorship cases against Chile.[126] A year after *Palamara*, the Commission decided *Matus Acuña et al. v. Chile*.[127] The journalist Alejandra Matus Acuña authored a book titled *The Black Book of Chilean Justice*; subsequently, a judge named in the book filed a complaint

---

[119] "The Last Temptation of Christ" (Olmedo Bustos et al.) v. Chile, Merits, Reparations, and Costs, Judgment, Inter-Am. Ct. H.R. (ser. C) No. 73, para. 73 (Feb. 5, 2001). For a distinct result from the European Court, *see* Wingrove v. the United Kingdom, Eur. Ct. H.R., App. No. 17419/90 (Nov. 25, 1996) (deferring to UK authorities' decision to censor an allegedly blasphemous film).

[120] "The Last Temptation of Christ" (Olmedo Bustos et al.) v. Chile, Merits, Reparations, and Costs, Judgment, Inter-Am. Ct. H.R. (ser. C) No. 73, para. 82(c) (Feb. 5, 2001); "The Last Temptation of Christ" (Olmedo-Bustos et al.) v. Chile, Monitoring Compliance with Judgment, Order, Inter-Am. Ct. H.R. (Nov. 28, 2003).

[121] Palamara Iribarne v. Chile, Merits, Reparations, Costs, Judgment, Inter-Am. Ct. H.R. (ser. C) No. 135 (Nov. 22, 2005).

[122] *Id.* para. 74.

[123] *Id.*

[124] *Id.* para. 77.

[125] *Id.*

[126] *See* Matus Acuña et al. v. Chile, Case 12.142, Inter-Am. Comm'n H.R. Report No. 90/05, OEA/Ser.L/II.124, doc. 5 (2006); Martorell v. Chile, Case 11.230, Inter-Am. Comm'n H.R., Report No. 11/96, OEA/Ser.L./V/II.95, doc. 7 rev. (1997).

[127] Matus Acuña et al. v. Chile, Case 12.142, Inter-Am. Comm'n H.R. Report No. 90/05, OEA/Ser.L/II.124, doc. 5 (2006).

against Matus Acuña for having committed a crime "against the security of the State."[128] A Chilean court then prohibited the book's further publication and required "confiscation of all copies of the book."[129] The Commission found prior censorship and that the national security law allowing censorship violated Article 13.

C. SUBSEQUENT IMPOSITION OF LIABILITY

1. Overview and General Requirements

Although censorship is generally prohibited, Article 13(2) allows for "subsequent imposition of liability."[130] The Court has held that sanctions on expression are only permitted when States comply with the provision's requirements, explained as follows:

> (i) [the sanction] must be expressly established by law, in both the formal and substantial sense; (ii) it must respond to an objective permitted by [Article 13(2) of] the American Convention . . . and (iii) it must be necessary in a democratic society (and to this end must comply with the requirements of suitability, necessity and proportionality).[131]

In interpreting both the limitations of Article 13 and other Convention Articles, the Court employs terms that are often redundant or ambiguous. To better understand these provisions, a review of the relevant case law is necessary.

As for the first requirement, the sanctions must be previously and expressly established by law;[132] such laws must be "passed by the legislature and promulgated by the Executive Branch."[133] The Court does not always apply the legality requirement;[134] when it does, even somewhat ambiguous laws may pass its review.[135] In fact, the judgment *Fontevecchia*

---

[128] *Id.* para. 36.

[129] *Id.*

[130] American Convention, art. 13(2).

[131] *E.g.*, Mémoli v. Argentina, Preliminary Objections, Merits, Reparations, and Costs, Judgment, Inter-Am. Ct. H.R. (ser. C) No. 265, para. 130 (Aug. 22, 2013); Tristán Donoso v. Panama, Preliminary Objections, Merits, Reparations, and Costs, Judgment, Inter-Am. Ct. H.R. (ser. C) No. 193, para. 56 (Jan. 27, 2009).

[132] Palamara Iribarne v. Chile, Merits, Reparations, Costs, Judgment, Inter-Am. Ct. H.R. (ser. C) No. 135, para. 79 (Nov. 22, 2005).

[133] The Word "Laws" in Article 30 of the American Convention on Human Rights, Advisory Opinion OC-6/86, Inter-Am. Ct. H.R. (ser. A) No. 6, para 27 (May 9, 1986). *See also* Claude Reyes et al. v. Chile, Merits, Reparations, and Costs, Judgment, Inter-Am. Ct. H.R. (ser. C) No. 151, para. 89 (Sept. 19, 2006).

[134] *E.g.*, Herrera Ulloa v. Costa Rica, Preliminary Objections, Merits, Reparations, and Costs, Judgment, Inter-Am. Ct. H.R. (ser. C) No. 107, para. 136 (July 2, 2004); Canese v. Paraguay, Merits, Reparations, and Costs, Judgment, Inter-Am. Ct. H.R. (ser. C) No. 111, paras. 96, 104, 109 (Aug. 31, 2004).

[135] *See* Tristán Donoso v. Panama, Preliminary Objections, Merits, Reparations, and Costs, Judgment, Inter-Am. Ct. H.R. (ser. C) No. 193, paras. 117, 132 (Jan. 27, 2009). Since *Kimel v. Argentina,* the Court analyzes these laws under Articles 9 and 2 of the Convention. Kimel v. Argentina, Merits, Reparations, and Costs, Judgment, Inter-Am. Ct. H.R. (ser. C) No. 177, para. 67 (May 2, 2008).

and D'Amico v. Argentina, which concerned civil sanctions for speech, revealed quite flexible criteria.[136] The Court stated, "while the certainty of the law is highly desirable, it may bring with it excessive rigidity."[137] Citing the European Court, *Fontevecchia* noted "many laws are formulated in terms, that to a greater or lesser extent, are vague and whose interpretation and application are questions of practice."[138] Later, the Inter-American Court even applied a flexible standard for legality in a case involving criminal sanctions, *Mémoli v. Argentina*.[139] In contrast, the Special Rapporteur has definitively rejected vague legislation that punishes expression.[140]

The second requirement for sanctions on expression is that the restriction must pursue "an objective permitted by the American Convention," called "a compelling governmental interest" by the Court.[141] As stated above, Article 13 establishes as permissible purposes the "respect for the rights or reputations of others" or "the protection of national security, public order, or public health or morals."[142] To date, the Court has interpreted the "rights of others" exception in contentious cases, discussed below, concerning the rights to honor, reputation, and privacy. As for "public order," it has explained that the concept refers to "the conditions that assure the normal and harmonious functioning of institutions based on a coherent system of values and principles."[143] The Court declined opportunities to consider the national security exception in both *Palamara* and *Usón Ramírez*.[144]

In *Usón Ramírez*, the Court surprisingly accepted that protecting the honor of the State's armed forces was a legitimate objective to restrict expression.[145] In arriving at this conclusion—which had been opposed by the Inter-American Commission—the judgment reasoned that domestic law protected the military's honor and that, "in general, such right is set forth in the American Convention regarding natural persons."[146] Further,

---

136 Fontevecchia & D`Amico v. Argentina, Merits, Reparations, and Costs, Judgment, Inter-Am. Ct. H.R. (ser. C) No. 238 (Nov. 29, 2011).

137 *Id.* para. 90

138 *Id.*

139 Mémoli v. Argentina, Preliminary Objections, Merits, Reparations, and Costs, Judgment, Inter-Am. Ct. H.R. (ser. C) No. 265, para. 137 (Aug. 22, 2013).

140 Hemispheric Agenda, paras. 53–73.

141 Compulsory Membership in an Association Prescribed by Law for the Practice of Journalism, Advisory Opinion OC-5/85, Inter-Am. Ct. H.R. (ser. A) No. 5, para. 46 (Nov. 13, 1985). *See also* Hemispheric Agenda, para. 24.

142 American Convention, art. 13(2).

143 Compulsory Membership in an Association Prescribed by Law for the Practice of Journalism, Advisory Opinion OC-5/85, Inter-Am. Ct. H.R. (ser. A) No. 5, para. 64 (Nov. 13, 1985).

144 Palamara Iribarne v. Chile, Merits, Reparations, Costs, Judgment, Inter-Am. Ct. H.R. (ser. C) No. 135 (Nov. 22, 2005); Usón Ramírez v. Venezuela, Preliminary Objection, Merits, Reparations, and Costs, Judgment, Inter-Am. Ct. H.R. (ser. C) No. 207.

145 Usón Ramírez v. Venezuela, Preliminary Objection, Merits, Reparations, and Costs, Judgment, Inter-Am. Ct. H.R. (ser. C) No. 207, para. 66 (Nov. 20, 2009).

146 *Id.*

the Tribunal cited European Court precedents for the proposition that "protection of the right to the reputation of companies, not only of individuals, may be a legitimate purpose to restrict the right to the freedom of expression."[147]

Third, the sanction must be "necessary in a democratic society."[148] According to the Court, this requirement prompts a proportionality analysis: the "restriction must be proportionate to the underlying interest and in direct furtherance of such legitimate purpose, interfering as little as possible with the effective exercise of the right to freedom of thought and expression."[149] In the subsequent liability cases, most of the breaches to Article 13 are owed to a violation of this requirement: the Court considered the sanction in question to be disproportionate.

2. Subsequent Criminal Liability

a. Introduction

In the view of many experts, criminal sanctions on expression chill the freedom of speech, weaken democracy, and "protect power and privilege."[150] Yet some States of the Americas have not rejected the use of criminal law to limit expression, often with the objective to protect personal honor and reputation.[151] The Court and the Commission sharply disagree on this subject.

In 1994, the Commission approved an important settlement regarding the case of the Argentine journalist Horacio Verbitsky,[152] and issued a key thematic report.[153] In these documents, the Commission condemned "laws of contempt" (*leyes de desacato*) that "criminalize expression which offends, insults, or threatens a public functionary in the performance of his or her official duties," when there is no identifiable danger of imminent violence.[154] Currently, both the Commission and the Special Rapporteur broadly denounce the criminalization of

---

[147] *Id.* para. 65.

[148] *E.g.*, Mémoli v. Argentina, Preliminary Objections, Merits, Reparations, and Costs, Judgment, Inter-Am. Ct. H.R. (ser. C) No. 265, para. 130 (Aug. 22, 2013); Tristán Donoso v. Panama, Preliminary Objections, Merits, Reparations, and Costs, Judgment, Inter-Am. Ct. H.R. (ser. C) No. 193, para. 56 (Jan. 27, 2009).

[149] *E.g.*, Palamara Iribarne v. Chile, Merits, Reparations, Costs, Judgment, Inter-Am. Ct. H.R. (ser. C) No. 135, para. 85 (Nov. 22, 2005); Compulsory Membership in an Association Prescribed by Law for the Practice of Journalism, Advisory Opinion OC-5/85, Inter-Am. Ct. H.R. (ser. A) No. 5, para. 46 (Nov. 13, 1985).

[150] Gregory C. Lisby, *No Place in the Law: The Ignominy of Criminal Libel in American Jurisprudence*, 9 COMM. LAW & POL'Y 433, 438 (2004). *See also* THOMAS I. EMERSON, THE SYSTEM OF FREEDOM OF EXPRESSION 390 (1970); GARCÍA RAMÍREZ, GONZA & RAMOS VÁSQUEZ, *supra* note 10, at 58–59. Some authors have argued for the partial decriminalization of speech. *See, e.g.*, ERNESTO VILLANUEVA, DERECHO DE LA INFORMACION 351 (2006); EDUARDO BERTONI, LIBERTAD DE EXPRESIÓN EN EL ESTADO DE DERECHO 7–10 (2000).

[151] *See, e.g.*, Hemispheric Agenda, paras. 55–57.

[152] Verbitsky v. Argentina, Case 11.012, Inter-Am. Comm'n H.R., Report No. 22/94, Friendly Settlement (1994).

[153] Inter-American Commission on Human Rights, Report on the Compatibility of Laws of Contempt with the American Convention on Human Rights, OAS/ser L/VII.88, Doc. 9, rev (1995), pp. 210–223.

[154] *Id.*

expression, and urge that States eliminate crimes against honor and reputation. As stated by the Special Rapporteur,

> The use of the corrective means of the State to . . . discourage the open and vigorous deliberation of all matters of public relevance is incompatible with the guiding principles of democratic regimes and, in particular, with the right to freedom of expression enshrined in Article 13 of the American Convention.[155]

The Commission and the Special Rapporteur also object to disproportionate civil sanctions on expression.[156] In this regard, the Principles have specified that, for civil sanctions in public interest cases to be permissible, it must be proven that the journalist "had the specific intent to inflict harm, was fully aware that false news was disseminated, or acted with gross negligence in efforts to determine the truth or falsity of such news."[157]

In contrast, the Court holds that criminal sanctions on speech are a legitimate means to protect honor and reputation, and has even asserted that States have the obligation to establish such laws.[158] The Court has decided seven cases of criminal sanctions concerning six different States.[159] In six judgments, it found the specific criminal punishment to be disproportionate, violating Article 13(2); in three of those, the Tribunal ordered legislative reform.[160] To date, it has only heard one case involving civil sanctions.[161]

The Commission's perseverance in this area, coupled with earlier Court decisions, has led to legislative reform in the region. However, State officials and others continue to

---

155 Hemispheric Agenda, para. 55.

156 *See, e.g.*, Office of the Special Rapporteur on Freedom of Expression, Annual Report 2015, Chapter V, Conclusions and Recommendations, para. 9 ("Promote the inclusion of inter-American standards in civil legislation so that civil proceedings against individuals who have made statements about public officials or about matters of public interest apply the standard of actual malice, in accordance with principle 10 of the Declaration of Principles, and are proportionate and reasonable").

157 Declaration of Principles on Freedom of Expression, Principle 10.

158 Mémoli v. Argentina, Preliminary Objections, Merits, Reparations, and Costs, Judgment, Inter-Am. Ct. H.R. (ser. C) No. 265, paras. 125–126 (Aug. 22, 2013).

159 *Id.*; Usón Ramírez v. Venezuela, Preliminary Objection, Merits, Reparations, and Costs, Judgment, Inter-Am. Ct. H.R. (ser. C) No. 207 (Nov. 20, 2009); Tristán Donoso v. Panama, Preliminary Objections, Merits, Reparations, and Costs, Judgment, Inter-Am. Ct. H.R. (ser. C) No. 193 (Jan. 27, 2009); Kimel v. Argentina, Merits, Reparations, and Costs, Judgment, Inter-Am. Ct. H.R. (ser. C) No. 177 (May 2, 2008); Palamara Iribarne v. Chile, Merits, Reparations, Costs, Judgment, Inter-Am. Ct. H.R. (ser. C) No. 135 (Nov. 22, 2005); Canese v. Paraguay, Merits, Reparations, and Costs, Judgment, Inter-Am. Ct. H.R. (ser. C) No. 111 (Aug. 31, 2004); Herrera Ulloa v. Costa Rica, Preliminary Objections, Merits, Reparations, and Costs, Judgment, Inter-Am. Ct. H.R. (ser. C) No. 107 (July 2, 2004). In *Uzcátegui* et al. *v. Venezuela*, the petitioner was sued for criminal defamation by a military officer, but the Court did not analyze the subsequent liability aspect of the case. Uzcátegui et al. v. Venezuela, Merits and Reparations, Judgment, Inter-Am. Ct. H.R. (ser. C) No. 249 (Sept. 3, 2012).

160 Only in *Mémoli* was the criminal sanction upheld by the Court. Mémoli v. Argentina, Preliminary Objections, Merits, Reparations, and Costs, Judgment, Inter-Am. Ct. H.R. (ser. C) No. 265 (Aug. 22, 2013).

161 Fontevecchia and D`Amico v. Argentina, Merits, Reparations, and Costs, Judgment, Inter-Am. Ct. H.R. (ser. C) No. 238 (Nov. 29, 2011).

use criminal and civil actions to impede critical expression and robust public debate.[162] According to the requirements reviewed above, it is reasonable to conclude that these criminal sanctions are inconsistent with Article 13.

In particular, Article 13(2)(a) lists "respect for the rights or reputations of others" as a permissible purpose to restrict speech. As a result, we will presume that protecting honor, reputation, and privacy consist in "overriding public interests" or "compelling objectives" to limit expression—although the Court has not clearly defined these terms. Nevertheless, the specific restriction used by the State still must "interfere as little as possible with the effective exercise of the right to freedom of thought and expression."[163] The "least restrictive" means to protect honor and reputation is certainly not criminal law; the Court itself has reiterated that criminal punishment is the most severe legal response available to States.[164] Even civil sanctions can be disproportionate and seriously inhibit expression.[165] In this way, we argue that criminal sanctions in these cases should always fail the proportionality test of Article 13(2)—and possibly even disregard the legality and "compelling objective" requirements as well.[166] Consequently, to safeguard the critical rights of Article 13, as well as democracy in the Americas, the Court must change its approach and prohibit the use of criminal law to protect honor and reputation.

---

[162] *See, e.g.*, Office of the Special Rapporteur on Freedom of Expression, Annual Report 2015, Chapter V, Conclusions and Recommendations, paras. 8–9; Hemispheric Agenda, para. 57. Recently, Chilean president Michelle Bachelet brought a criminal libel suit against journalists of the magazine *Qué Pasa*. *See Declaración de Revista Qué Pasa ante querella de presidenta Bachelet*, May 31, 2016, *available at* http://www.quepasa.cl/articulo/politica/2016/05/declaracion-de-revista-que-pasa-ante-querella-de-presidenta-bachelet.shtml/.

[163] *E.g.*, Palamara Iribarne v. Chile, Merits, Reparations, Costs, Judgment, Inter-Am. Ct. H.R. (ser. C) No. 135, para. 85 (Nov. 22, 2005); Compulsory Membership in an Association Prescribed by Law for the Practice of Journalism, Advisory Opinion OC-5/85, Inter-Am. Ct. H.R. (ser. A) No. 5, para. 46 (Nov. 13, 1985).

[164] *E.g.*, Usón Ramírez v. Venezuela, Preliminary Objection, Merits, Reparations, and Costs, Judgment, Inter-Am. Ct. H.R. (ser. C) No. 207, para. 73 (Nov. 20, 2009) ("The Court has pointed out that Criminal Law is the most restrictive and severe means to establish liabilities for illicit behavior, particularly when sanctions involve deprivation of liberty. Therefore, the use of the criminal way shall respond to the principle of minimum intervention, due to the nature of criminal law as *ultima ratio*."); Canese v. Paraguay, Merits, Reparations, and Costs, Judgment, Inter-Am. Ct. H.R. (ser. C) No. 111, para. 104 (Aug. 31, 2004) (similar).

[165] Fontevecchia and D'Amico v. Argentina, Merits, Reparations, and Costs, Judgment, Inter-Am. Ct. H.R. (ser. C) No. 238, para. 74 (Nov. 29, 2011) ("the fear of a disproportionate civil sanction may clearly be as or more intimidating and inhibiting for the exercise of freedom of expression than a criminal sanction, as it has the potential to compromise the personal and family life of those who complain, or as in the present case, those who publish information about a public official, with the obvious and unmerited result of self-censorship for the affected and for other potential critics of the performance of a public official"); Tristán Donoso v. Panama, Preliminary Objections, Merits, Reparations, and Costs, Judgment, Inter-Am. Ct. H.R. (ser. C) No. 193, para. 129 (Jan. 27, 2009) (similar).

[166] For more on how these concepts are linked, *see* Compulsory Membership in an Association Prescribed by Law for the Practice of Journalism, Advisory Opinion OC-5/85, Inter-Am. Ct. H.R. (ser. A) No. 5, para. 46 (Nov. 13, 1985) ("the 'necessity' and, hence, the legality of restrictions imposed under Article 13(2) on freedom of expression, depend upon a showing that the restrictions are required by a compelling governmental interest"); Palamara Iribarne v. Chile, Merits, Reparations, Costs, Judgment, Inter-Am. Ct. H.R. (ser. C) No. 135, para. 85 (similar).

b. The Honor and Reputation of the Armed Forces

In the 2005 judgment *Palamara Iribarne*, the Court denounced "laws of contempt" and asserted that expressions in the public interest, such as criticism of State institutions like the Navy, should enjoy enhanced protection.[167] In this way, "all persons are allowed to exercise democratic control over all State institutions and officials," without fearing retaliation for their disapproving views.[168] Nevertheless, four years later, in *Usón Ramírez*, the Court essentially reversed aspects of *Palamara*.[169] Francisco Usón Ramírez, a retired military officer, criticized Venezuela's armed forces on television. In response, a military court convicted him for the crime of "slander against the National Armed Forces"; he was imprisoned for over three years.[170]

As noted above, the Court controversially accepted that protecting the honor of the State's armed forces was a legitimate objective to restrict expression. It made this decision taking into account that Venezuelan law recognized the military's right to honor—and despite holding that the military is not a natural person, and thus is not protected by the Convention.[171] Usón Ramírez had not been prosecuted for compromising national security, and thus the Court decided that the Article 13 national security objective was not at issue in this case.

The judgment accepted the criminal sanctions on expression as legitimate in principle. However, assessing the specific criminal law at issue, the Court found that the crime's definition was "too vague and ambiguous," breaching Article 13 and other Convention provisions.[172] It also considered that Usón Ramírez had expressed an opinion about a subject of public interest—namely, "military institutions and their members"— and "lacked any specific intention to insult, offend, or disparage."[173] As a result, it concluded that the criminal sanctions were disproportionate, violating Article 13 again.

In sum, despite finding violations to Article 13, the judgment ultimately condoned a military's use of criminal law to silence its critics. Under this precedent, the Court could find a speaker's "intention to offend" in a future case and uphold the sanction. *Usón Ramírez* disregards the vital role of public scrutiny over State institutions and political leaders. It also neglects the vulnerability of individuals before these powerful institutions and figures. The

---

167 Palamara Iribarne v. Chile, Merits, Reparations, Costs, Judgment, Inter-Am. Ct. H.R. (ser. C) No. 135 (Nov. 22, 2005).

168 *Id.* para. 254.

169 Usón Ramírez v. Venezuela, Preliminary Objection, Merits, Reparations, and Costs, Judgment, Inter-Am. Ct. H.R. (ser. C) No. 207 (Nov. 20, 2009).

170 *Id.* para. 88.

171 *Id.* para. 63.

172 *Id.* para. 57.

173 *Id.* para. 86. Although *Usón Ramírez* affirmed that opinions "cannot be the object of any sanction," the judgment ignored the contradiction that Francisco Usón Ramírez had been imprisoned for over three years, precisely for expressing his opinion. *Id.*

case represents one of the various ways that oppressive regimes have controlled speech in the region.[174]

c. *The Honor and Reputation of Public Officials*

Herrera Ulloa v. Costa Rica was the first case where the Commission asked the Court to strike down laws criminalizing defamatory statements against public officials.[175] Mauricio Herrera Ulloa, a newspaper journalist, published articles that "partially reproduced news reports" about the "alleged illicit activities" of a Costa Rican diplomatic representative.[176] Subsequently, in *Ricardo Canese v. Paraguay*, the Court assessed the criminal conviction of a presidential candidate for publicly stating that a rival candidate was involved in corrupt business activities.[177] Both judgments recognized the expressions as protected speech in the public interest, denounced the criminal prosecutions, and found violations to Article 13.[178]

In *Kimel v. Argentina*, however, the Court's case law takes a turn.[179] Eduardo Kimel, a journalist and historian, authored a book that found fault with criminal investigations into a notorious murder of five Catholic priests. A judge mentioned in the book brought a criminal action for "defamation," and Kimel was convicted.[180] For the first time, the Court held that "criminal proceedings are suitable" to protect a person's honor and reputation, even when that person is a public official.[181] The judgment, citing to the European Court,[182] explained that "by threatening to impose sanctions, [criminal proceedings] serve the purpose of preserving the legal right whose protection is sought."[183] The Inter-American Court even declared that it does not consider criminal sanctions "regarding the right to . . . give one's opinion" to violate the Convention, despite holding in the same

---

[174] For a relevant Commission case, *see* Robles Espinoza and Sons v. Peru, Case 11.317, Inter-Am. Comm'n H.R., Report No. 20/99, para. 175 (1999) (concluding that "through the imposition of enforced retirement as a disciplinary measure, the filing of two criminal suits, and other threats . . . the Peruvian State has submitted General Rodolfo Robles Espinoza to a process of harassment and intimidation in retaliation for his revelations regarding human rights violations committed by members of the Peruvian Armed Forces").

[175] Herrera Ulloa v. Costa Rica, Preliminary Objections, Merits, Reparations, and Costs, Judgment, Inter-Am. Ct. H.R. (ser. C) No. 107 (July 2, 2004).

[176] *Id.* para. 105.

[177] Canese v. Paraguay, Merits, Reparations, and Costs, Judgment, Inter-Am. Ct. H.R. (ser. C) No. 111 (Aug. 31, 2004).

[178] *Id.* paras. 106–108; Herrera Ulloa v. Costa Rica, Preliminary Objections, Merits, Reparations, and Costs, Judgment, Inter-Am. Ct. H.R. (ser. C) No. 107, para 135 (July 2, 2004).

[179] Kimel v. Argentina, Merits, Reparations, and Costs, Judgment, Inter-Am. Ct. H.R. (ser. C) No. 177 (May 2, 2008).

[180] *Id.* para. 43.

[181] *Id.* para. 71

[182] The Inter-American Court cited the European Tribunal's decision *Mamere v. France* for the proposition that "the eminent value of freedom of expression, especially in debates on subjects of general concern, cannot take precedence in all circumstances over the need to protect the honor and reputation of others, be they ordinary citizens or public officials." *Id.* para. 78, FN 57.

[183] *Id.*

judgment that "an opinion cannot be subjected to sanctions, even more so where it is a value judgment on the actions of a public official."[184]

The Court achieved consensus in *Kimel* by placing conditions on the use of criminal sanctions, stating that they should be:

> carefully analyzed, pondering the extreme seriousness of the conduct of the individual who expressed the opinion, his actual malice, the characteristics of the unfair damage caused, and other information which shows the absolute necessity to resort to criminal proceedings as an exception.[185]

In his separate opinion, Judge García Ramírez wrote that these conditions are not sufficient for protecting the freedom of expression, and recommended that the Court rule out criminal law as a means to protect honor and reputation.[186] Eventually, the *Kimel* Court found a violation to Article 13 due to the law's lack of precision, which had been already expressly accepted by Argentina.[187] Finally, reasoning that Kimel's opinion "had no bearing on the . . . judge's personal life, nor did it impute an illegal conduct," it held the criminal sanction to be disproportionate.[188]

In 2013, a sharply-divided Court decided *Mémoli v. Argentina*, its first judgment to uphold criminal sanctions against a journalist for "defamation."[189] The controversial decision appeared to ignore *Kimel*'s conditions requiring only exceptional use of criminal punishment.[190] Instead, the Court stated that it was "sufficiently foreseeable" that criminal accusations of "fraud" and "deceit," among others, "could result in a judicial action for the alleged harm to the honor or reputation of the complainants"—three members of a private association.[191]

Mémoli deferred to the decisions of the domestic courts, which "examined the statements made by [Carlos and Pablo Mémoli] and their impact on the honor and reputation"

---

184 *Id.* paras. 78, 93.

185 *Id.* para. 78.

186 Judge García Ramírez Concurring Opinion, para. 26, Kimel v. Argentina (stating that it is "necessary to advance" from criminal to civil proceedings in this area).

187 *Id.* para. 67.

188 *Id.* para. 91.

189 Mémoli v. Argentina, Preliminary Objections, Merits, Reparations, and Costs, Judgment, Inter-Am. Ct. H.R. (ser. C) No. 265, para. 131 (Aug. 22, 2013).

190 Although it is true that the *Mémoli* judgment cited the conditions. *Id.* para. 139. For additional critiques of the *Mémoli* judgment, *see, e.g.*, José Miguel Vivanco, *Un caso argentino, fiel reflejo de las limitaciones a la prensa en la región*, Diario La Nación, Argentina, Nov. 11, 2013, http://www.lanacion.com.ar/1637121-un-caso-argentino-fiel-reflejo-de-las-limitaciones-a-la-prensa-en-la-region; Eduardo Bertoni, *Retroceso y tensión en la Corte Interamericana*, La Nación, Costa Rica, Nov. 28, 2013, http://www.nacion.com/opinion/foros/Retroceso-Corte-Interamericana-Derechos-Humanos_0_1381061885.html.

191 Mémoli v. Argentina, Preliminary Objections, Merits, Reparations, and Costs, Judgment, Inter-Am. Ct. H.R. (ser. C) No. 265, para. 137 (Aug. 22, 2013).

of the three individuals.[192] The Inter-American Court decided, "this examination constituted a reasonable and sufficient weighing up of the two rights in conflict, which justified the subsequent imposition of liability."[193] Next, the Court considered the proportionality of the sanctions, suspended sentences of one and five months of prison, respectively. It concluded that the punishments "were not excessive or manifestly disproportionate in a way that affected their right to freedom of expression."[194] Surprisingly, the Tribunal disregarded the fact that the criminal law applied in *Mémoli* was the same law that the *Kimel* Court had found incompatible with the American Convention.[195]

A central dispute was whether the statements concerned the public interest, which would require a higher standard of protection. The Commission, petitioners, and the three-judge dissent all argued that the corrupt "administration of public property," such as that alleged in this case, impacted the public interest;[196] other factors also indicated that the statements were in the community's interest.[197] However, the Court's majority, although acknowledging that "certain information concerning private individuals or organizations may be classified as information of public interest," observed that "in this case two domestic courts analyzed and rejected this argument."[198] It decided not to "annul the decision of the domestic courts in this regard" and refused to find a violation of Article 13.[199]

Because the Court has not prohibited criminal sanctions in these cases, it must engage in a balancing test each time. For the Tribunal, the Article 13 violation often hinges on whether the restriction is considered disproportionate. This examination, in turn, depends upon whether the Court—and increasingly domestic courts—characterize the expressions as opinions or facts, as well as whether they involve the public interest, criminal accusations, and "malice," among other concepts. However, unlike other tribunals, the Court has not fully defined these essential terms in its case law nor used them in a consistent manner. By applying opaque standards in this way, its method is discretional and unpredictable. In judgments such as *Mémoli* and *Usón Ramírez*, this approach permitted the Court to defer to States on certain key determinations—such as legitimate objectives to restrict Article 13 and the meaning of "public interest"—leading to conflict with the American Convention and its own jurisprudence.

---

[192] *Id.* para. 143.

[193] *Id.*

[194] *Id.* para. 144.

[195] Kimel v. Argentina, Merits, Reparations, and Costs, Judgment, Inter-Am. Ct. H.R. (ser. C) No. 177, para. 67 (May 2, 2008).

[196] *Id.* para. 114.

[197] *See* Joint Partially Dissenting Opinion of Judges Manuel E. Ventura Robles, Eduardo Vio Grossi and Eduardo Ferrer Mac-Gregor Poisot, Mémoli v. Argentina (proposing a means for determining issues in the "public interest," and arguing that this matter fell within the public interest).

[198] *Id.* para. 147.

[199] *Id.*

3. Subsequent Civil Liability

To date, the Court has only heard one case concerning civil sanctions on expression. In *Fontevecchia and D'Amico v. Argentina*, journalists published articles and photography about President Carlos Menem's son from an extramarital affair.[200] Menem sued for the invasion of his privacy; the resulting civil judgment ordered various fines and penalties. *Fontevecchia* recognized that civil sanctions can readily inhibit freedom of expression and "compromise the personal and family life" of those who publish information.[201] The Court outlined criteria similar to *Kimel*: civil penalties "should be carefully analyzed, considering the conduct displayed by the person making the statements, the characteristics of the damage allegedly caused, and other information that demonstrates the need to resort to the civil forum."[202]

The Tribunal recalled that a different threshold of protection applies to public officials. It also expressly found that the published articles related to the public interest, as they concerned "the integrity of political leaders," the president's gifts of "large sums of money" to his son and his son's mother, and the "possible existence of . . . interference in a judicial investigation."[203] As a result, and because there was "no unreasonable or arbitrary interference in the private life of Mr. Menem," Article 13 was violated in detriment of the petitioner journalists.[204] Despite the vagueness of Argentina's legislation, the Court did not rule it incompatible with the Convention. Instead, it found fault with domestic tribunals, stating that they must better weigh the public interest and different threshold of protection in this context. Ultimately, the Inter-American Court revoked the civil sanctions, but unaccountably failed to order moral damages for the victims.

Much remains for the Court to address in the area of civil sanctions on expression. *Fontevecchia*, for example, eluded an assessment of the proportionality of the rather severe fine imposed; the Inter-American Commission has also avoided this key issue.[205] Moving forward, the Court should adopt standards to foster vigorous public debate similar to the Commission's Principles and U.S. Supreme Court case law. Specifically, as regards the alleged defamation of public figures, plaintiffs should shoulder a substantial burden: prove by convincing evidence that the defendant knew the defamatory statement

---

[200] Fontevecchia and D`Amico v. Argentina, Merits, Reparations, and Costs, Judgment, Inter-Am. Ct. H.R. (ser. C) No. 238 (Nov. 29, 2011).

[201] *Id.* para. 74.

[202] *Id.* para. 56.

[203] *Id.* para. 62.

[204] *Id.* para. 75.

[205] *See* Stokes v. Jamaica, Case 12.468, Inter-Am. Comm'n. H.R., Report No. 23/08, OEA/Ser.L/V/II.134, doc. 5 rev. 1 (2009) (finding no Article 13 violation for a severe civil libel judgment (approx. GBP £533,000) and holding "absent clear errors or due process violations, the Commission finds that the domestic courts were in the best position to determine the amount, and to assess the proportionality of the award with respect to the harm suffered").

was false or acted with reckless disregard of the truth.[206] In fact, the Court should encourage alternative mechanisms to protect honor and reputation. Procedures to obtain retractions, corrections, replies, or apologies could replace costly and protracted litigation, benefiting both parties to a dispute.[207]

D. "INDIRECT" RESTRICTIONS

The American Convention's Article 13(3) establishes that the "right of expression may not be restricted by indirect methods or means."[208] The Court has explained that this broad provision targets State and private restrictions,[209] including abusive controls over media and "any other means tending to impede the communication and circulation of ideas and opinions."[210] In this way, these cases can prove complex for the Court and Commission, as Article 13(3) encompasses public and private acts committed against both legal persons, such as media companies, and natural persons.

Currently, there are two groups of "indirect" restrictions cases in the Court's jurisprudence. In the first group, such restrictions are found in cases that also involve severe violations to Article 13(2). With little additional analysis or explanation, the Court found the following situations to constitute indirect restrictions: an international travel ban,[211] dismissal from State employment,[212] criminal and administrative proceedings,[213] and interferences with the right to intellectual property, among others.[214]

The second group of cases concerns the State's abusive control of television stations. In *Ivcher Bronstein v. Peru*, a director of a television channel had approved of numerous reports critical of the Fujimori regime, denouncing torture, killings, and corruption.[215]

---

[206] *See, e.g.*, DANIEL A. FARBER, THE FIRST AMENDMENT 91 (2010) (summarizing and analyzing the U.S. Supreme Court rule); Declaration of Principles on Freedom of Expression, Principle 10 (stating a somewhat similar principle).

[207] *See* DARIO MILO, DEFAMATION AND FREEDOM OF SPEECH 256–79 (2008). The American Convention's Article 14, Right of Reply, establishes in part: "Anyone injured by inaccurate or offensive statements or ideas disseminated to the public in general by a legally regulated medium of communication has the right to reply or to make a correction using the same communications outlet, under such conditions as the law may establish."

[208] American Convention, art. 13(3).

[209] Compulsory Membership in an Association Prescribed by Law for the Practice of Journalism, Advisory Opinion OC-5/85, Inter-Am. Ct. H.R. (ser. A) No. 5, paras. 47–48 (Nov. 13, 1985).

[210] American Convention, art. 13(3). Principles 12 and 13 also offer examples of "indirect" restrictions. Declaration of Principles on Freedom of Expression, Principles 12 and 13.

[211] Canese v. Paraguay, Merits, Reparations, and Costs, Judgment, Inter-Am. Ct. H.R. (ser. C) No. 111, para. 107 (Aug. 31, 2004).

[212] *Id.*

[213] *Id.*; Palamara Iribarne v. Chile, Merits, Reparations, Costs, Judgment, Inter-Am. Ct. H.R. (ser. C) No. 135, para. 94 (Nov. 22, 2005).

[214] Palamara Iribarne v. Chile, Merits, Reparations, Costs, Judgment, Inter-Am. Ct. H.R. (ser. C) No. 135, paras. 100, 106–107 (Nov. 22, 2005).

[215] Ivcher Bronstein v. Peru, Merits, Reparations, and Costs, Judgment, Inter-Am. Ct. H.R. (ser. C) No. 74, para. 155 (Feb. 6, 2001).

Fujimori's government issued an order that allowed for the revocation of naturalized Peruvians' citizenship. Baruch Ivcher Bronstein's citizenship was soon revoked, preventing him from continuing his work at the channel. The Court found this State action to constitute an "indirect means of restricting his freedom of expression, as well as that of the journalists" who worked with him.[216]

In *Granier v. Venezuela*, the Venezuelan station RCTV, broadcasting since 1953, had to close because the State refused to renew its license.[217] The Court noted a general "deterioration in the protection of the freedom of expression" in Venezuela, and observed that there were many clear, public warnings by President Hugo Chávez and other State officials that television licenses—including that of RCTV—would not be renewed if they continued to criticize the government. [218] The judgment then stated that such licensing procedures must be "clear and precise" and respect "general guarantees of due process," such as independence and impartiality.[219]

Venezuela responded that its objective in closing RCTV was to protect a "pluralism" of viewpoints.[220] Given the numerous public statements on record undermining this stated purpose, among other evidence, the Court found that the State abused its power and had applied indirect restrictions in breach of Article 13(3).[221] The judgment emphasized that the victims in the case were not only the individuals associated with RCTV, but also included Venezuelan society as a whole, as that society was deprived of access to the station's point of view. Consequently, as in *Ivcher Bronstein v. Peru*, the Court ordered the State to return the victims to broadcasting.[222]

Granier fails to assess the State restrictions on Article 13 in a complete, methodical fashion. It remains ambiguous how the Court defines "abuses of power" or "indirect" restrictions to the freedom of expression.[223] Clearly, Venezuela's flagrant actions violated Article 13; however, the Court does not indicate why they did not rise to the level of censorship. Further, the Tribunal unaccountably held that the many public declarations by President Chávez and other officials "could not autonomously configure facts constitutive of a violation of the American Convention."[224] Yet these statements, orders, and warnings determined RCTV's fate and restricted freedom of expression; Chávez often

[216] *Id.* para. 162.

[217] Granier et al. (Radio Caracas Television) v. Venezuela, Preliminary Objections, Merits, Reparations, Costs, Judgment, Inter-Am. Ct. H.R. (ser. C) No. 293 (June 22, 2015).

[218] *Id.* para. 197 (translation by authors).

[219] *Id.* para. 171 (translation by authors).

[220] *Id.* para. 188 (translation by authors).

[221] *Id.* para. 199. It is also important to note that the Court found discriminatory treatment in the exercise of freedom of expression, on the basis of the petitioners' political opinion. *Id.* para. 235.

[222] *Id.* paras. 380–382; Ivcher Bronstein v. Peru, Merits, Reparations, and Costs, Judgment, Inter-Am. Ct. H.R. (ser. C) No. 74, paras. 181–182 (Feb. 6, 2001).

[223] The Court did not consider, for example, that the State's seizure and subsequent use of RCTV's broadcasting facilities resulted in violations of the freedom of expression and the right to property. *Id.* para. 359.

[224] *Id.* para. 193.

made governmental decisions in public fashion, during television programs. The Court should have considered these statements as State acts; then, it should have applied a careful analysis to those acts—assessing their legality, objective, and proportionality.

E. CASES OF PERSECUTION LEADING TO GENERIC VIOLATIONS OF ARTICLE 13(1)

Recently, the Court has heard several cases involving persecution and violence against individuals, often journalists or political leaders. These judgments have held that freedom of expression may be violated by "*de facto* conditions that put, directly or indirectly, in a situation of risk or greater vulnerability those who exercise or attempt to exercise such freedom, by actions or omissions of state agents or private individuals."[225] In these cases, non-State actors obstructed the work of journalists at television stations;[226] a cameraman was attacked by soldiers while filming a protest; [227] a human rights advocate endured threats, harassment, and a criminal suit for defamation;[228] and a political leader was assassinated.[229] The Court has found these flagrant acts to breach Article 13(1), without considering the Article's other paragraphs.

López Lone et al. *v. Honduras* concerned a different kind of persecution.[230] Four judges had opposed the coup against President Zelaya in Honduras. They had participated in public protests, initiated lawsuits, or otherwise spoken out against the coup. As a result, all judges faced disciplinary proceedings, and three were dismissed. The Court found that the judges' acts, including the initiation of criminal and constitutional legal actions, constituted expression protected by Article 13.[231] It concluded that the disciplinary proceedings and dismissals violated Article 13(1), in addition to other Articles of the Convention.[232]

It is problematic that these various cases of persecution have led only to generic violations of Article 13(1). The Special Rapporteur has denounced extrajudicial killings and

---

[225] Perozo et al. v. Venezuela, Preliminary Objections, Merits, Reparations, and Costs, Judgment, Inter-Am. Ct. H.R. (ser. C) No. 195, para. 118 (Jan. 28, 2009); Ríos et al. v. Venezuela, Preliminary Objections, Merits, Reparations, and Costs, Judgment, Inter-Am. Ct. H.R. (ser. C) No. 194, para. 107 (Jan. 28, 2009).

[226] *Id.*

[227] Vélez Restrepo and Family v. Colombia, Preliminary Objections, Merits, Reparations, and Costs, Judgment, Inter-Am. Ct. H.R. (ser. C) No. 248 (Sept. 3, 2012).

[228] Uzcátegui et al. v. Venezuela, Merits and Reparations, Judgment, Inter-Am. Ct. H.R. (ser. C) No. 249 (Sept. 3, 2012).

[229] Cepeda Vargas v. Colombia, Preliminary Objections, Merits, Reparations, and Costs, Judgment, Inter-Am. Ct. H.R. (ser. C.) No. 213 (May 26, 2010).

[230] López Lone et al. v. Honduras, Preliminary Objection, Merits, Reparations and Costs, Inter-Am. Ct. H.R. (ser. C) No. 302 (Oct. 5, 2015).

[231] On the other hand, the Court noted that certain types of "conduct" of judges may be limited, in order to protect Article 8 of the American Convention and the independence and impartiality of judicial proceedings. *Id.* para. 171 (translation by authors).

[232] *Id.* para. 341 (not finding violations to other paragraphs of Article 13, but finding breaches to distinct Convention provisions, such as Article 15 (Right of Assembly) and 23 (Right to Participate in Government)).

attacks as the "most extreme form of censorship."[233] If not censorship in breach of Article 13(2), some of the circumstances could have been conceptualized as the "indirect" restrictions of Article 13(3). The cases involving criminal and disciplinary proceedings should have been analyzed pursuant to Article 13(2)'s subsequent liability provision. In sum, these situations doubtlessly violated the freedom of expression. Nevertheless, the Court cannot neglect its duty to closely analyze the facts in light of the Convention's terms. Otherwise, its assessment becomes concealed; as discussed above, this could result in greater discretion for the Court and for States.

F. INCITEMENTS TO VIOLENCE: ARTICLE 13(5)

The American Convention contains narrow limitations on propaganda and hate speech. The Convention only specifies "propaganda for war" and "incitements to lawless violence" or to "similar action," whereas the ICCPR and the European Convention permit wider restrictions on expression.[234] To date, neither the Inter-American Court nor the Commission has offered detailed jurisprudence on Article 13(5).[235] Still, the Special Rapporteur has recently studied the subject with respect to lesbian, gay, bisexual, trans and intersex (LGBTI) persons.[236] The Special Rapporteur explained that sanctions under Article 13(5) require a "high threshold":

> Such sanctions must be backed by truthful, objective, and strong proof that the person was not simply issuing an opinion (even if that opinion was unfair or

[233] Office of the Special Rapporteur for Freedom of Expression, Inter-American Commission Human Rights, Violence against Journalists and Media Workers: Inter-American Standards and National Practices on Prevention, Protection and Prosecution of Perpetrators, OEA/Ser.L/V/II. CIDH/RELE/INF. 12/13, para. 1 (2013).

[234] The ICCPR's Article 20 provides: "1. Any propaganda for war shall be prohibited by law. 2. Any advocacy of national, racial or religious hatred that constitutes incitement to discrimination, hostility or violence shall be prohibited by law." The European Convention's Article 10 establishes, in part: "The exercise of these freedoms, since it carries with it duties and responsibilities, may be subject to such formalities, conditions, restrictions or penalties as are prescribed by law and are necessary in a democratic society, in the interests of national security, territorial integrity or public safety, for the prevention of disorder or crime, for the protection of health or morals, for the protection of the reputation or rights of others, for preventing the disclosure of information received in confidence, or for maintaining the authority and impartiality of the judiciary."

[235] In a case involving Cuban dissidents, the Inter-American Commission assessed Cuba's criminal laws punishing "Acts against the Independence or Territorial Integrity of the State." Oscar Elías Biscet et al. v. Cuba, Case 12.476, Inter-Am. Comm'n H.R., Report No. 67/06, para. 191 (2006). Cuba is not a State Party to the American Convention, so the Commission applied the American Declaration of the Rights and Duties of Man. It held that the criminal laws at issue were "a means to silence ideas and opinions because they discourage any type of criticism for fear of the aforementioned penalties." *Id.* para. 209. As a result, the laws "impair the essence of the right of freedom of investigation, opinion, expression, and dissemination established in Article IV of the American Declaration." *Id.*

[236] Among other points, the Special Rapporteur has expressed concern that regional legislation to prohibit hate speech against LGBTI persons suffers from vagueness, "which could compromise the effective enjoyment of

> disturbing), but that the person had: (a) the clear intention of promoting lawless violence or any other similar action against LGBTI persons; and (b) the capacity to achieve this objective and create an actual risk of harm to LGBTI persons.[237]

The Special Rapporteur has also stressed that "in order to effectively combat hate speech, a comprehensive and sustained approach that goes beyond legal measures and includes preventive and educational mechanisms should be adopted."[238]

In the Venezuelan judgments *Perozo* et al. and *Ríos* et al., the Court declined the opportunity to interpret Article 13(5) when it considered incendiary public statements made by various political leaders.[239] These statements identified certain media companies and their staff as "enemies of the Venezuelan people" who had plotted subversive actions, among other accusations.[240] The petitioners argued that these statements provoked the subsequent attacks against RCTV and *Globovisión*. Ultimately, the Court, having found the attackers to be non-State actors, concluded that Venezuela was responsible "for non-compliance with the obligation contained in Article 1(1) of the Convention to ensure the right to freely seek, receive and impart information and the right to humane treatment."[241]

---

the right to freedom of expression on issues of public interest." Office of the Special Rapporteur on Freedom of Expression, Annual Report 2015, p. 361.

[237] *Id.* at p. 367.

[238] *Id.* at p. 371.

[239] Perozo et al. v. Venezuela, Preliminary Objections, Merits, Reparations, and Costs, Judgment, Inter-Am. Ct. H.R. (ser. C) No. 195 (Jan. 28, 2009); Ríos et al. v. Venezuela, Preliminary Objections, Merits, Reparations, and Costs, Judgment, Inter-Am. Ct. H.R. (ser. C) No. 194 (Jan. 28, 2009).

[240] Perozo et al. v. Venezuela, Preliminary Objections, Merits, Reparations, and Costs, Judgment, Inter-Am. Ct. H.R. (ser. C) No. 195, para. 139 (Jan. 28, 2009).

[241] *Id.* para. 426(5).

8

Property

Article 21: Right to Property

1. *Everyone has the right to the use and enjoyment of his property. The law may subordinate such use and enjoyment to the interest of society.*
2. *No one shall be deprived of his property except upon payment of just compensation, for reasons of public utility or social interest, and in the cases and according to the forms established by law.*
3. *Usury and any other form of exploitation of man by man shall be prohibited by law.*

Chapter 8 Contents

I. Introduction 265
II. Background 267
III. Scope of Protection 268
  A. Many Forms of Property Recognized 268
  B. Rights to Communal Property 271
IV. Limitations to the Right to Property 273
  A. Right to Property Not Absolute 273
  B. Meaning of "Just Compensation" 275
  C. Meaning of "Reasons of Public Utility or Social Interest" 276

The American Convention on Human Rights. Thomas M. Antkowiak and Alejandra Gonza.

D. Meaning of "In the Cases and According to the Forms Established by Law" 278
E. Specific Approaches to Limitations 278
1. Restrictions during Criminal Investigations and Police Action 278
2. Protective Framework for Traditional Territories 279

I. Introduction

Both the American and Universal Declarations of Human Rights established the right to property.[1] However, universal commitment to private property rights waned during the ideological disputes of the Cold War. Neither the International Covenant on Civil and Political Rights nor the International Covenant on Economic, Social and Cultural Rights provides for the right to property. The European Convention originally excluded the right, but it surfaced in Article 1 of the First Protocol to the Convention:

> Every natural or legal person is entitled to the peaceful enjoyment of his possessions. No one shall be deprived of his possessions except in the public interest and subject to the conditions provided for by law and by the general principles of international law.
>
> The preceding provisions shall not, however, in any way impair the right of a State to enforce such laws as it deems necessary to control the use of property in accordance with the general interest or to secure the payment of taxes or other contributions or penalties.[2]

This provision, the subject of much debate during the drafting process, formulates a more constrained right than its analog of the American Convention on Human Rights.[3] Article 1 of the First Protocol sets out a pronounced "right of a State to enforce such laws to control the use of property"; in the event of property interference, it considers "the public interest" and does not explicitly reference a right to compensation. The European Court, interpreting these terms, has permitted States wide latitude to infringe upon the right when deemed in the public interest.[4]

The Arab Charter, for its part, refers to "private property:" "Everyone has a guaranteed right to own private property, and shall not under any circumstances be arbitrarily or unlawfully divested of all or any part of his property."[5] The African Charter establishes: "The right to property shall be guaranteed. It may only be encroached upon in the interest of public need or in the general interest of the community and in accordance with the provisions of appropriate laws."[6] Like the European Convention's Protocol, both the African and Arab instruments omit an express right to compensation.

---

[1] American Declaration of the Rights and Duties of Man, art. XXIII; Universal Declaration, art. 17.

[2] Protocol to the Convention for the Protection of Human Rights and Fundamental Freedoms, Mar. 20, 1952, 213 U.N.T.S. 262, art. 1.

[3] *See* Secretary General's Memorandum, Protocol to the Convention for the Protection of Human Rights and Fundamental Freedoms 134–136.

[4] *See* David Harris, Michael O'Boyle & Colin Warbrick, Law of the European Convention on Human Rights 874 (3d ed. 2014). *See also* James and Others v. UK, Eur. Ct. H.R., App. No. 8793/79 (Feb. 21, 1986).

[5] Arab Charter on Human Rights, art. 31.

[6] African Charter on Human and Peoples' Rights, art. 14.

In this sense, then, the American Convention provides a stronger formulation of the right. Among other protections, it requires "just compensation" upon deprivation of property. The EU Charter of Fundamental Rights takes this guarantee a step further: if one is "deprived of his or her possessions," then "fair compensation" must be paid "in good time."[7]

As for collective property rights, prominent legal instruments—such as the UN Declaration on the Rights of Indigenous Peoples[8] and the ILO Convention No. 169[9]—set out broad protections for indigenous communities. These instruments, along with various UN human rights bodies, advance positions that are generally consistent with the leading Inter-American jurisprudence.[10] One of the Court's landmark judgments in this area, *Saramaka People v. Suriname*, established "safeguards" for States to implement before development projects commence on community lands, and called for the "free, prior, and informed consent" of communities in certain situations.[11] Yet, as these protections are limited, we argue below that the Court should adopt a demanding right-to-life approach in these cases, rather than rely on the modest right to property.

The African regional human rights system has followed the Inter-American Court's lead and called for similar protections for indigenous territories and resources.[12] In contrast, the European Court and the European Convention itself have generally not stressed group rights.[13] The European Tribunal lacks this robust case law guaranteeing communal rights to ancestral lands and resources.[14]

---

[7] EU Charter, art. 17.

[8] United Nations Declaration on the Rights of Indigenous Peoples, G.A. Res. 61/295, U.N. Doc. A/RES/61/295 (Sept. 13, 2007), 46 I.L.M. 1013 (2007).

[9] Convention concerning Indigenous and Tribal Peoples in Independent Countries (ILO No. 169), 72 ILO Official Bull. 59; 28 ILM 1382 (1989).

[10] *See, e.g.*, Committee on the Elimination of Racial Discrimination, General Recommendation No. 23 (1997) on Indigenous Peoples (CERD/C/51/Misc. 13/Rev.4), para. 5 ("The Committee especially calls upon States parties to recognize and protect the rights of indigenous peoples to own, develop, control and use their communal lands, territories and resources and, where they have been deprived of their lands and territories traditionally owned or otherwise inhabited or used without their free and informed consent, to take steps to return those lands and territories."); Report of the Special Rapporteur on the Situation of Human Rights and Fundamental Freedoms of Indigenous People, James Anaya, A/HRC/12/34 (July 2009), paras. 36–57 (explaining how several international legal instruments and human rights bodies support indigenous collective property rights and the State's duty to consult these communities).

[11] Saramaka People v. Suriname, Preliminary Objections, Merits, Reparations, and Costs, Judgment, Inter-Am. Ct. H.R. (ser. C) No. 172, paras. 128-129 (Nov. 28, 2007).

[12] *See* African Comm'n on Human and Peoples' Rights, Resolution on a Human Rights-Based Approach to Natural Resources Governance, 51st Sess., Apr. 18–May 2, 2012, *available at* http://www.achpr.org/sessions/51st/resolutions/224 ("[A]ll necessary measures must be taken by the State to ensure participation, including the free, prior and informed consent of communities, in decision-making related to natural resources governance."); Afr. Comm'n on Human & Peoples' Rights, Ctr. for Minority Rights Dev. (Kenya) v. Kenya, Comm. No. 276/2003, para. 291 (Feb. 4, 2010) (holding that, with respect to "any development or investment projects that would have a major impact within the Endorois territory, the State has a duty not only to consult with the community, but also to obtain their free, prior, and informed consent, according to their customs and traditions").

[13] *See generally* 48 Kalderas Gipsies v. FRG and Netherlands, Eur. Ct. H.R., App. No. 7827/77 (July 6, 1977).

[14] The European Court of Human Rights has infrequently considered cases involving indigenous communities. *See* European Court of Human Rights, Cultural Rights in the Case-Law of the European

II. Background

The right to property was one of the most contested provisions of the American Convention. The Specialized Conference in San José debated three distinct possibilities: (1) eliminate the right entirely, following the International Covenant on Civil and Political Rights; (2) adopt the Inter-American Commission's preliminary proposal; or (3) pursue a definition that "would strengthen the social function of property."[15] The Inter-American Commission's moderate proposal, with the addition of a prohibition against usury and other forms of exploitation, prevailed during the Committee debates.

Subsequently, a plenary session amended the text: instead of "everyone has the right to private property," the final version provided "everyone has the right to the use and enjoyment of his property."[16] The US delegate had objected to these changes. He opposed a more inclusive notion of property that would encompass "cooperative as well as private property."[17] Moreover, he argued that there is more to property than its mere use and enjoyment.[18] That is, by these terms, a State could allow use of property without ceding a full right to it. The Venezuelan representative, one of the amendment's sponsors, defended it on the grounds that it offered the most advanced expression of "man's progress."[19]

Additional modifications during the plenary removed the term "public interest" from Article 21.[20] The delegates preferred "the law may subordinate such use and enjoyment to the *interest of society*," rather than "to the public interest."[21] Also, "public utility or social interest" replaced "public interest" in the following provision: "no one shall be deprived of his property except upon payment of just compensation, for reasons of *public utility or social interest*, and in the cases and according to the forms established by law."[22] Several delegates appeared to share the opinion that references to "social interest" better accommodated the agrarian reform movements occurring in Latin American countries.[23]

The final title of Article 21 in all official languages other than English remained "Right to Private Property," despite the removal of the term "private" from the Article's text, and the efforts of various delegates to change the title to "Right to the Use and Enjoyment of

---

COURT OF HUMAN RIGHTS 19–21 (2011) (referring only to a limited number of cases), *available at* http://www.echr.coe.int; Timo Koivurova, *Jurisprudence of the European Court of Human Rights Regarding Indigenous Peoples: Retrospect and Prospects*, 18 INT'L J. MINORITY & GRP. RTS. 1 (2011) (stating that "there have been no landmark cases decided by the European Court of Human Rights . . . in favour of indigenous peoples").

[15] Report of the Rapporteur of Committee I, Juan Isaac Lovato, Doc. 60 (English), Nov. 19, 1969.

[16] P. 446, Minutes of the Second Plenary Session, Doc. 86, Nov. 22, 1969 (Spanish).

[17] P. 31, Report of the United States Delegation to the Inter-American Conference on Protection of Human Rights (1969).

[18] P. 446, Minutes of the Second Plenary Session, Doc. 86, Nov. 22, 1969 (Spanish).

[19] *Id.* at p. 447 (the Venezuelan delegate stated that the amendment represented "*la manifestación última del progreso del hombre*").

[20] *Id.* at p. 446.

[21] *Id.* (emphasis added).

[22] *Id.* (emphasis added).

[23] Pp. 238–39, Minutes of the 11th Session of Committee I, Doc 52, Rev. 1, Nov. 17, 1969.

Property (*Bienes*)."[24] The official English title, "Right to Property," conveys a broader concept, notwithstanding the United States' position favoring only private property.[25] These inconsistencies were not explained in official documents.[26]

The Inter-American Court's first judgment on the merits concerning an alleged Article 21 violation, *Cesti Hurtado v. Peru*, did not appear until 1999.[27] Property cases are now more frequently litigated before the Tribunal; in particular, community land matters are increasingly common. Yet Article 21(3), concerning usury and other forms of "exploitation of man by man," apparently has not yet been examined by the Court or the Inter-American Commission. This is not surprising, as the provision, rather than articulating a right, directs States to prohibit these practices among private persons.[28] In fact, some delegates in San José considered Article 21(3) to be "mere rhetoric" that was unsuitable for the Convention.[29] Still, a petitioner could operationalize this provision by challenging a State's inadequate legal protections from usury before the Inter-American System.

III. Scope of Protection

A. MANY FORMS OF PROPERTY RECOGNIZED

The Inter-American Court has developed a broad notion of property, including communal and private property. In this way, it has recognized that both individuals and communities hold property rights. Corporations possess property rights in the Inter-American System, but these rights are only relevant for the Court to the extent that they "encompass" human rights, such as a shareholder's right to property.[30] The Inter-American concept includes tangible and intangible property: "all movable and immovable property, corporeal and incorporeal elements, and any other immaterial object that may have a value."[31] In arriving at this wide-ranging definition, the Inter-American Court has

---

[24] P. 446, Minutes of the Second Plenary Session, Doc. 86, Nov. 22, 1969 (Spanish) (the delegations of Brazil, Chile, Ecuador, Guatemala, Uruguay, and Venezuela were involved in this proposal). *See also* Mayagna (Sumo) Awas Tingni Cmty. v. Nicaragua, Merits, Reparations, and Costs, Judgment, Inter-Am. Ct. H.R. (ser. C) No. 79, FN 55 (Aug. 31, 2001).

[25] *See* pp. 31–32, Report of the United States Delegation to the Inter-American Conference on the Protection of Human Rights (1969).

[26] *See* Jo Pasqualucci, *International Indigenous Land Rights: A Critique of the Jurisprudence of the Inter-American Court of Human Rights in Light of the United Nations Declaration on the Rights of Indigenous Peoples*, 27 WISC. INT'L L.J. 51, 65 (2009); Mayagna (Sumo) Awas Tingni Cmty. v. Nicaragua, Merits, Reparations, and Costs, Judgment, Inter-Am. Ct. H.R. (ser. C) No. 79, FN 55 (Aug. 31, 2001).

[27] Cesti Hurtado v. Peru, Merits, Judgment, Inter-Am. Ct. H.R. (ser. C) No. 56 (Sept. 29, 1999).

[28] *See* HÉCTOR GROS ESPIELL, LA CONVENCIÓN AMERICANA Y LA CONVENCIÓN EUROPEA DE DERECHOS HUMANOS: ANÁLISIS COMPARATIVO 112 (1991).

[29] Pp. 31–32, Report of the United States Delegation to the Inter-American Conference on the Protection of Human Rights (1969).

[30] Perozo et al. v. Venezuela, Preliminary Objections, Merits, Reparations, and Costs, Judgment, Inter-Am. Ct. H.R. (ser. C) No. 195, paras. 399-400 (Jan. 28, 2009).

[31] *E.g.*, Mémoli v. Argentina, Preliminary Objections, Merits, Reparations, and Costs, Judgment, Inter-Am. Ct. H.R. (ser. C) No. 265, para. 170 (Aug. 22, 2013); Ivcher Bronstein v. Peru, Merits, Reparations, and Costs, Judgment, Inter-Am. Ct. H.R. (ser. C) No. 74, para. 122 (Feb. 6, 2001).

employed a number of rationales, starting, of course, with the intentionally-expansive text of Article 21 itself.

The Tribunal also frequently cites to Article 29(b) of the American Convention, which establishes that no Convention provision may be interpreted as "restricting the enjoyment or exercise of any right or freedom recognized by virtue of the laws of any State Party or by virtue of another convention to which one of the said states is a party." In several cases, the Court has referred to Article 29(b) when it expands its jurisprudence on property. For example, it has adopted principles on pensions and communal property that belonged to respondent States' national legislation.[32]

In 2001, the Inter-American Court issued its first judgment on indigenous land rights, *Mayagna (Sumo) Awas Tingni v. Nicaragua*.[33] *Awas Tingni*'s ruling on an indigenous right to communal property was a first for an international human rights court.[34] The Tribunal cited Article 29 as a major justification for this advance. Because Nicaraguan law recognized communal property, the Court reasoned that it could not exclude this dimension from Article 21.[35] In *Yakye Axa Indigenous Community v. Paraguay*, the Tribunal examined ILO Convention No. 169, an international treaty that had been ratified by the State.[36] The Court considered that several of the treaty's provisions offered further support and development of indigenous communal property rights. Further, in *Saramaka People v. Suriname*, the Court cited to Articles 1 and 27 of the ICCPR, which had been ratified by Suriname, to reinforce the same principle.[37]

In *Ituango Massacres v. Colombia*, paramilitary forces destroyed houses and robbed livestock with the "acquiescence" of the Colombian Army.[38] As Colombia had acceded to Protocol II to the Geneva Conventions, the Court considered Articles 13(2) and 14 of Protocol II, which prohibit, respectively, acts that "spread terror among the civilian

---

[32] *E.g.*, "Five Pensioners" v. Peru, Merits, Reparations, and Costs, Judgment, Inter-Am. Ct. H.R. (ser. C) No. 98, para. 103 (Feb. 28, 2003) (pensions); Mayagna (Sumo) Awas Tingni Cmty. v. Nicaragua, Inter-Am. Ct. H.R. (ser. C) No. 79, para. 148 (Aug. 31, 2001) (communal property).

[33] Mayagna (Sumo) Awas Tingni Cmty. v. Nicaragua, Inter-Am. Ct. H.R. (ser. C) No. 79 (Aug. 31, 2001).

[34] The African human rights courts were not yet in operation, and the European Court of Human Rights still has not rendered a comparable interpretation. The non-binding Human Rights Committee, for its part, does not even have competence to find violations of the right to property, because that right was omitted from the ICCPR. For more commentary on *Awas Tingni v. Nicaragua, see* S. James Anaya & Maia S. Campbell, *Gaining Legal Recognition of Indigenous Land Rights: The Story of the* Awas Tingni *Case in Nicaragua, in* HUMAN RIGHTS ADVOCACY STORIES 117 (Deena R. Hurwitz & Margaret L. Satterthwaite eds., 2009); S. James Anaya & Claudio Grossman, *The Case of* Awas Tingni v. Nicaragua: *A New Step in the International Law of Indigenous Peoples*, 19 ARIZ. J. INT'L & COMP. L. 1 (2002).

[35] Mayagna (Sumo) Awas Tingni Cmty. v. Nicaragua, Inter-Am. Ct. H.R. (ser. C) No. 79, para. 148 (Aug. 31, 2001).

[36] Yakye Axa Indigenous Cmty. v. Paraguay, Merits, Reparations, and Costs, Judgment, Inter-Am. Ct. H.R. (ser. C) No. 125, paras. 127, 130, 136, 150–151 (June 17, 2005).

[37] Saramaka People v. Suriname, Preliminary Objections, Merits, Reparations, and Costs, Judgment, Inter-Am. Ct. H.R. (ser. C) No. 172, paras. 93-95 (Nov. 28, 2007).

[38] Ituango Massacres v. Colombia, Preliminary Objections, Merits, Reparations, and Costs, Judgment, Inter-Am. Ct. H.R. (ser. C) No. 148, paras. 176-180 (July 1, 2006).

population," and actions that "destroy . . . objects indispensable to the survival of the civilian population."[39] The Tribunal concluded that the offenses in question contravened both of these provisions, thus rendering the Article 21 violation "particularly grave."[40]

To complement its application of Article 29, the Court has repeatedly held that "human rights treaties are living instruments whose interpretation must consider the changes over time and present-day conditions."[41] As a result of its broad interpretive approach, the Court has recognized all the following as examples of property requiring protection under Article 21: all intellectual property rights associated with the authorship of a book;[42] shares of a company and all associated rights;[43] vested retirement pensions;[44] earned salaries, benefits and raises;[45] court judgments awarding compensation;[46] traditional territories of indigenous and "tribal" populations;[47]

---

[39] *Id.* paras. 179–180. *See also* Santo Domingo Massacre v. Colombia, Preliminary Objections, Merits, and Reparations, Judgment, Inter-Am. Ct. H.R. (ser. C) No. 259, paras. 270-272 (Nov. 30, 2012); Massacres of El Mozote and Nearby Places v. El Salvador, Merits, Reparations, and Costs, Judgment, Inter-Am. Ct. H.R. (ser. C) No. 252, para. 179 (Oct. 25, 2012) (both using the Geneva Conventions to interpret the scope of Article 21).

[40] Ituango Massacres v. Colombia, Preliminary Objections, Merits, Reparations, and Costs, Judgment, Inter-Am. Ct. H.R. (ser. C) No. 148, para. 182 (July 1, 2006).

[41] *E.g.*, Yakye Axa Indigenous Cmty. v. Paraguay, Merits, Reparations, and Costs, Judgment, Inter Am. Ct. H.R. (ser. C) No. 125, para. 125 (June 17, 2005); Right to Information on Consular Assistance in the Framework of the Guarantees of the Due Process of Law, Advisory Opinion OC-16/99, Inter-Am. Ct. H.R. (ser. A) No. 16, para. 114 (Oct. 1, 1999).

[42] According to the Court, there are both "tangible and intangible aspects" associated with authorship: "the tangible dimension of such property rights includes, among other aspects, the publication, exploitation, assignment, or transfer of the works, while the intangible dimension of such rights is related to the safeguard of the authorship of the works and the protection of the integrity thereof." Palamara Iribarne v. Chile, Merits, Reparations, Costs, Judgment, Inter-Am. Ct. H.R. (ser. C) No. 135, para. 103 (Nov. 22, 2005). Furthermore, the exercise of both dimensions "is susceptible of having value and becomes part of a person's assets"; thus, "the use and enjoyment of intellectual works is also protected by Article 21." *Id.*

[43] *E.g.*, Chaparro Álvarez and Lapo Íñiguez v. Ecuador, Preliminary Objections, Merits, Reparations, and Costs, Judgment, Inter-Am. Ct. H.R. (ser. C) No. 170, para. 209 (Nov. 21, 2007); Ivcher Bronstein v. Peru, Merits, Reparations, and Costs, Judgment, Inter-Am. Ct. H.R. (ser. C) No. 74, paras. 123, 127 (Feb. 6, 2001). However, Alejandra Gonza criticized the Court's reluctance to find a violation to a shareholder's right to property in *Perozo and Others v. Venezuela*. Alejandra Gonza, *Artículo 21: El Derecho a la Propiedad, in* La Convención Americana sobre Derechos Humanos Comentada 512 (Christian Steiner & Patricia Uribe eds., 2014). There, the Court found insufficient evidence that the shareholder's rights were affected by proven damage to the business, a television station. This view, Gonza points out, makes it easier for States to persecute shareholders by targeting their corporations. *Id.*

[44] "Five Pensioners" v. Peru, Merits, Reparations, and Costs, Judgment, Inter-Am. Ct. H.R. (ser. C) No. 98, para. 103 (Feb. 28, 2003).

[45] Abrill Alosilla et al. v. Peru, 2011 Inter-Am. Ct. H.R. (ser. C) No. 223, para. 83 (Mar. 4, 2011).

[46] Furlan and Family v. Argentina, Preliminary Objections, Merits, Reparations, and Costs, Judgment, Inter-Am. Ct. H.R. (ser. C) No. 246, para. 222 (Aug. 31, 2012).

[47] *E.g.*, Mayagna (Sumo) Awas Tingni Cmty. v. Nicaragua, Merits, Reparations, and Costs, Judgment, Inter-Am. Ct. H.R. (ser. C) No. 79, paras. 142-155 (Aug. 31, 2001); Moiwana Cmty. v. Suriname, Preliminary Objections, Merits, Reparations, and Costs, Judgment, Inter-Am. Ct. H.R. (ser. C) No. 124, paras. 129–135 (June 15, 2005) (regarding nonnative "tribal" populations in particular).

privately-owned parcels of land;[48] houses;[49] stores;[50] crops;[51] livestock;[52] as well as other personal possessions.[53] Rights to these properties and belongings were infringed by States through seizures[54] and expropriations,[55] arbitrary pension reductions,[56] flawed or disregarded judicial decisions,[57] a long-standing injunction preventing the sale of property,[58] as well as acts of theft and willful destruction,[59] among others.

B. RIGHTS TO COMMUNAL PROPERTY

Beginning with *Awas Tingni*, the Court has recognized "the unique and enduring ties that bind indigenous communities to their ancestral territory."[60] According to the Tribunal, such a people's relationship to traditional lands should be understood as "the fundamental basis

---

48 Salvador Chiriboga v. Ecuador, Preliminary Objections and Merits, Judgment, Inter-Am. Ct. H.R. (ser. C) No. 179, paras. 116-118 (May 6, 2008).

49 Ituango Massacres v. Colombia, Preliminary Objections, Merits, Reparations, and Costs, Judgment, Inter-Am. Ct. H.R. (ser. C) No. 148, paras. 174-183 (July 1, 2006).

50 Santo Domingo Massacre v. Colombia, Preliminary Objections, Merits, and Reparations, Judgment, Inter-Am. Ct. H.R. (ser. C) No. 259, para. 282 (Nov. 30, 2012).

51 Massacres of El Mozote and Nearby Places v. El Salvador, Merits, Reparations, and Costs, Judgment, Inter-Am. Ct. H.R. (ser. C) No. 252, para. 168 (Oct. 25, 2012).

52 *E.g.*, *id.*; Ituango Massacres v. Colombia, Preliminary Objections, Merits, Reparations, and Costs, Judgment, Inter-Am. Ct. H.R. (ser. C) No. 148, paras. 174-183 (July 1, 2006).

53 *E.g.*, Barrios Family v. Venezuela, Merits, Reparations, and Costs, Judgment, Inter-Am. Ct. H.R. (ser. C) No. 237, paras. 149-150 (Nov. 24, 2011); Tibi v. Ecuador, Preliminary Objections, Merits, Reparations, and Costs, Judgment, Inter-Am. Ct. H.R. (ser. C) No. 114, paras. 213-221 (Sept. 7, 2004). In *Tibi,* the Court also noted that "possession in itself establishes the presumption of ownership in favor of the possessor." *Id.* para 218.

54 Tibi v. Ecuador, Preliminary Objections, Merits, Reparations, and Costs, Judgment, Inter-Am. Ct. H.R. (ser. C) No. 114, para. 159, paras. 213-221 (Sept. 7, 2004).

55 Salvador Chiriboga v. Ecuador, Preliminary Objections and Merits, Judgment, Inter-Am. Ct. H.R. (ser. C) No. 179, paras. 116-118 (May 6, 2008).

56 "Five Pensioners" v. Peru, Merits, Reparations, and Costs, Judgment, Inter-Am. Ct. H.R. (ser. C) No. 98, para. 109 (Feb. 28, 2003).

57 *E.g.*, Ivcher Bronstein v. Peru, Merits, Reparations, and Costs, Judgment, Inter-Am. Ct. H.R. (ser. C) No. 74, para. 130 (Feb. 6, 2001) (flawed decision); Furlan and Family v. Argentina, Preliminary Objections, Merits, Reparations, and Costs, Judgment, Inter-Am. Ct. H.R. (ser. C) No. 246, paras 213–214 (Aug. 31, 2012) (judgment for compensation not fully complied with by State).

58 Mémoli v. Argentina, Preliminary Objections, Merits, Reparations, and Costs, Judgment, Inter-Am. Ct. H.R. (ser. C) No. 265, para. 183 (Aug. 22, 2013) (the injunction was in force for more than 17 years).

59 *E.g.*, Afro-Descendant Communities Displaced From the Cacarica River Basin (Operation Genesis) v. Colombia, Preliminary Objections, Merits, Reparations, and Costs, Judgment, Inter-Am. Ct. H.R. (ser. C) No. 270, para. 353 (Nov. 20, 2013); Ituango Massacres v. Colombia, Preliminary Objections, Merits, Reparations, and Costs, Judgment, Inter-Am. Ct. H.R. (ser. C) No. 148, paras. 174-183 (July 1, 2006).

60 Moiwana Cmty. v. Suriname, Preliminary Objections, Merits, Reparations, and Costs, Judgment, Inter-Am. Ct. H.R. (ser. C) No. 124, para. 131 (June 15, 2005); Mayagna (Sumo) Awas Tingni Cmty. v. Nicaragua, Merits, Reparations, and Costs, Judgment, Inter-Am. Ct. H.R. (ser. C) No. 79, para. 149 (Aug. 31, 2001).

of its culture, spiritual life, integrity, and economic survival."[61] In *Moiwana Community v. Suriname*, the Court decided that the N'djuka community, a nonnative population of African descent, had a similar relationship with its lands.[62] Although the community had lived in Moiwana Village for only a century, the Tribunal found a significant spiritual and cultural nexus to the territory—describing the connection as "all-encompassing."[63] In this way, the Court has concluded that collective ownership of community lands may be protected by Article 21.

In the Inter-American System, if the communities have occupied their lands "in accordance with customary practices," they are generally entitled to official recognition of their ownership rights.[64] The Court is receptive to such claims of "traditional" occupation. By requiring communities to follow a "cultural script," however, commentators have rightly criticized that the Court's approach limits the autonomy of indigenous peoples and their capacity for change.[65] Petitioners have satisfied the Tribunal's standard by submitting the testimony of community members themselves, as well as reports by anthropologists and other experts. Surprisingly, States have not generally offered much expert opinion to challenge "traditional" use and occupancy.[66]

---

[61] Mayagna (Sumo) Awas Tingni Cmty. v. Nicaragua, Merits, Reparations, and Costs, Judgment, Inter-Am. Ct. H.R. (ser. C) No. 79, para. 149 (Aug. 31, 2001).

[62] Moiwana Cmty. v. Suriname, Preliminary Objections, Merits, Reparations, and Costs, Judgment, Inter-Am. Ct. H.R. (ser. C) No. 124, para. 133 (June 15, 2005). For other Court judgments protecting the collective land rights of Afro-Latin populations, *see, e.g.,* Afro-Descendant Communities Displaced From the Cacarica River Basin (Operation Genesis) v. Colombia, Preliminary Objections, Merits, Reparations, and Costs, Judgment, Inter-Am. Ct. H.R. (ser. C) No. 270 (Nov. 20, 2013); Saramaka People v. Suriname, Preliminary Objections, Merits, Reparations, and Costs, Judgment, Inter-Am. Ct. H.R. (ser. C) No. 172 (Nov. 28, 2007).

[63] Moiwana Cmty. v. Suriname, Preliminary Objections, Merits, Reparations, and Costs, Judgment, Inter-Am. Ct. H.R. (ser. C) No. 124, para. 133 (June 15, 2005).

[64] *E.g., id.* para. 131; Xákmok Kásek Indigenous Community v. Paraguay, 2010 Inter-Am. Ct. H.R. (ser. C) No. 214, para. 93 (Aug. 24, 2010). In *Xákmok Kásek Indigenous Community*, the Court utilized four factors to assess the "traditional character" of the lands in question: "a) the Community's occupation and trajectory of the land and its surrounding areas; b) the toponymy of the area; c) technical studies prepared on the matter, and d) the alleged suitability of the land being claimed." *Id.*

[65] *See* RICHARD PRICE, RAINFOREST WARRIORS: HUMAN RIGHTS ON TRIAL 238–39 (2011) (finding "disturbingly essentialist" *Saramaka*'s requirement that natural resources must be "traditionally used" for Article 21 protections); Ariel E. Dulitzky, *When Afro-Descendants Became "Tribal Peoples": The Inter-American Human Rights System and Rural Black Communities*, 15 UCLA J. INT'L L. & FOREIGN AFF. 29, 42 (2010) (explaining that to obtain property protection, groups are pressured to show the Court an "essentialized and frozen culture"); KAREN ENGLE, THE ELUSIVE PROMISE OF INDIGENOUS DEVELOPMENT: RIGHTS, CULTURE, STRATEGY 162–82 (2010).

[66] In *Saramaka*, Suriname used expert testimony, but the evidence presented did not appear to relate directly to this subject. *See* Saramaka People v. Suriname, Preliminary Objections, Merits, Reparations, and Costs, Judgment, Inter-Am. Ct. H.R. (ser. C) No. 172, paras. 64-65 (Nov. 28, 2007). In *Xákmok Kásek*, the State's expert, Sergio Iván Braticevic, actually confirmed the "traditional character" of the lands for the petitioners. Xákmok Kásek Indigenous Community v. Paraguay, 2010 Inter-Am. Ct. H.R. (ser. C) No. 214, para. 102 (Aug. 24, 2010). *But see* Garifuna Community Triunfo de la Cruz & its Members v. Honduras, Merits, Reparations, and Costs, Judgment, 2015 Inter-Am. Ct. H.R. (ser. C) No. 305, paras. 96–98, 112 (Oct. 8, 2015) (State presented various challenges to petitioners' claims).

Once this standard is deemed fulfilled, the Court has ordered States, where applicable, to delimit, demarcate, and grant collective title over the territories in question, within a reasonable amount of time.[67] When necessary, States are required to amend relevant domestic legislation and practices in order to ensure such collective rights to land.[68] Until these measures are adopted, the Tribunal often forbids States, "or third parties acting with [their] acquiescence or tolerance," from engaging in acts that would affect the ancestral lands in any form.[69]

In a trilogy of cases against Paraguay, indigenous communities had lost possession of their ancestral territories against their will, and the lands were eventually transferred to third parties.[70] In such a situation, the Court orders the prompt return of the lands; if restitution is not possible, the Tribunal requires that the State deliver similarly-valued plots of land, chosen with the affected communities' approval.[71] Thus, current occupation of ancestral territories is not necessary to claim communal property rights over them.

IV. Limitations to the Right to Property

A. RIGHT TO PROPERTY NOT ABSOLUTE

Similar to other legal instruments, the American Convention's right to property is not absolute. Article 21(1) holds "the law may subordinate such use and enjoyment to the interest of society." Article 21(2) establishes that deprivation of property is only permissible "upon payment of just compensation, for reasons of public utility or social interest,

---

[67] *E.g.*, Kuna Indigenous People of Madungandi and Embera Indigenous People of Bayano and their Members v. Panama, Preliminary Objections, Merits, Reparations and Costs, Judgment, 2014 Inter-Am. Ct. H.R. (ser. C) No. 284, paras. 117, 134, 232 (Oct. 14, 2014); Mayagna (Sumo) Awas Tingni Cmty. v. Nicaragua, Merits, Reparations, and Costs, Judgment, Inter-Am. Ct. H.R. (ser. C) No. 79, para. 173 (Aug. 31, 2001).

[68] *E.g.*, Saramaka People v. Suriname, Preliminary Objections, Merits, Reparations, and Costs, Judgment, Inter-Am. Ct. H.R. (ser. C) No. 172, para. 214 (Nov. 28, 2007); Mayagna (Sumo) Awas Tingni Cmty. v. Nicaragua, Merits, Reparations, and Costs, Judgment, Inter-Am. Ct. H.R. (ser. C) No. 79, para. 173 (Aug. 31, 2001). When domestic legislation and procedures fail to ensure these rights, the Court also may declare a violation of Article 2 (Domestic Legal Effects) of the American Convention. *E.g.*, Kuna Indigenous People of Madungandi and Embera Indigenous People of Bayano and their Members v. Panama, 2014 Inter-Am. Ct. H.R. (ser. C) No. 284, para. 157 (Oct. 14, 2014); Mayagna (Sumo) Awas Tingni Cmty. v. Nicaragua, Merits, Reparations, and Costs, Judgment, Inter-Am. Ct. H.R. (ser. C) No. 79, para. 155 (Aug. 31, 2001).

[69] *E.g.*, Kuna Indigenous People of Madungandi and Embera Indigenous People of Bayano and their Members v. Panama, 2014 Inter-Am. Ct. H.R. (ser. C) No. 284, para. 232 (Oct. 14, 2014); Mayagna (Sumo) Awas Tingni Cmty. v. Nicaragua, Merits, Reparations, and Costs, Judgment, Inter-Am. Ct. H.R. (ser. C) No. 79, para. 173 (Aug. 31, 2001).

[70] Yakye Axa Indigenous Cmty. v. Paraguay, Merits, Reparations, and Costs, Judgment, Inter-Am. Ct. H.R. (ser. C) No. 125 (June 17, 2005); Sawhoyamaxa Indigenous Cmty. v. Paraguay, Merits, Reparations, and Costs, Judgment, Inter-Am. Ct. H.R. (ser. C) No. 146 (Mar. 29, 2006); Xákmok Kásek Indigenous Cmty. v. Paraguay, Merits, Reparations, and Costs, Judgment, Inter-Am. Ct. H.R. (ser. C) No. 214 (Aug. 24, 2010).

[71] Yakye Axa Indigenous Cmty. v. Paraguay, Merits, Reparations, and Costs, Judgment, Inter-Am. Ct. H.R. (ser. C) No. 125, para. 217 (June 17, 2005); Sawhoyamaxa Indigenous Cmty. v. Paraguay, Merits, Reparations, and Costs, Judgment, Inter-Am. Ct. H.R. (ser. C) No. 146, para. 212 (Mar. 29, 2006); Xákmok Kásek Indigenous

and in the cases and according to the forms established by law." These two provisions, read together, could have indicated that only an outright deprivation of property—as opposed to a mere interference with the right—requires additional State obligations, most notably the payment of just compensation. Yet the Court does not emphasize a distinction between deprivations and other kinds of interference to property.[72]

In several indigenous rights cases, the Court has applied the following test both to apparent deprivations and to other property infringements. The test requires restrictions on property rights to be: (1) previously established by law, (2) necessary, (3) proportional, and (4) with the aim of achieving a legitimate objective in a democratic society.[73] In addition, the measure cannot constitute "a denial of [the indigenous community's] traditions and customs in a way that endangers the very survival of the group and of its members."[74]

This analysis of legality, necessity, proportionality, and legitimacy has also been used in the Inter-American System to scrutinize possible violations of other human rights. It requires the infringement to be "closely adjusted to the attainment of a legitimate objective, interfering as little as possible with the effective exercise of the restricted right."[75] However, outside the indigenous land context, the test is infrequently employed for property matters.[76] This is unfortunate, considering that such a test obligates the Tribunal to complete a more structured, balanced, and transparent analysis.

Cmty. v. Paraguay, Merits, Reparations, and Costs, Judgment, Inter-Am. Ct. H.R. (ser. C) No. 214, para. 109 (Aug. 24, 2010).

[72] For example, in *Chaparro Álvarez*, the Court held that the failure to return seized company property "had an impact on [the company's] value and productivity, which, in turn, prejudiced its shareholders." Chaparro Álvarez and Lapo Íñiguez v. Ecuador, 2007 Inter-Am. Ct. H.R. (ser. C) No. 170, para. 209 (Nov. 21, 2007). The Tribunal characterized these facts "as an arbitrary interference in the 'enjoyment' of the property under the provisions of Article 21(1)." *Id.* No further explanation was offered. On the other hand, in the same judgment, the State's failure to return an unlawfully-seized private car constituted a "deprivation" pursuant to Article 21(2). *Id.* para. 218. An apparent difference here is corporate versus individual property, but it was not clarified by the Court.

[73] *E.g.*, Yakye Axa Indigenous Cmty. v. Paraguay, Merits, Reparations, and Costs, Judgment, Inter-Am. Ct. H.R. (ser. C) No. 125, para. 144 (June 17, 2005); Saramaka People v. Suriname, Preliminary Objections, Merits, Reparations, and Costs, Judgment, Inter-Am. Ct. H.R. (ser. C) No. 172, para. 127 (Nov. 28, 2007).

[74] Saramaka People v. Suriname, Preliminary Objections, Merits, Reparations, and Costs, Judgment, Inter-Am. Ct. H.R. (ser. C) No. 172, para. 128 (Nov. 28, 2007). *See* discussion on "Protective Framework for Traditional Territories," *infra*.

[75] Yakye Axa Indigenous Cmty. v. Paraguay, Merits, Reparations, and Costs, Judgment, Inter-Am. Ct. H.R. (ser. C) No. 125, para. 145 (June 17, 2005). *See also* Salvador Chiriboga v. Ecuador, Preliminary Objections and Merits, Judgment, Inter-Am. Ct. H.R. (ser. C) No. 179, para. 63 (May 6, 2008) (holding that if an infringement of the right is to be permissible, it must prove to be the "least costly" means of interference).

[76] For examples of judgments where the test is used, although only briefly, *see* Mémoli v. Argentina, Preliminary Objections, Merits, Reparations, and Costs, Judgment, Inter-Am. Ct. H.R. (ser. C) No. 265, paras. 179-180 (Aug. 22, 2013); Furlan and Family v. Argentina, Preliminary Objections, Merits, Reparations, and Costs, Judgment, Inter-Am. Ct. H.R. (ser. C) No. 246, para. 222 (Aug. 31, 2012).

B. MEANING OF "JUST COMPENSATION"

Article 21(2) is clear that deprivation of property demands payment of "just compensation." In the land expropriation case *Salvador Chiriboga v. Ecuador*, the Tribunal examined this principle. The Court held that "just compensation" must be "prompt, adequate and effective."[77] This is a demanding standard known as the Hull formula, which since the 1930s has been contested by communist regimes and developing countries.[78]

Still, the Inter-American criteria for "just compensation" may not be as supportive of property owners as it first appears. According to the Tribunal, for "adequate" compensation in expropriation matters, States must contemplate "the [market] value of the property prior to the [expropriation]," but also provide a "fair balance between the general interest and the individual interest."[79] In this way, the Court does not fully accept market value, a standard frequently required in international law.[80] Alejandra Gonza rightly questions the "fair balance" factor, which adds to the calculus an element of arbitrariness.[81] In the *Salvador Chiriboga* reparations judgment, the Court then used this opaque combination of market value and "fair balance" to determine the amount of compensation due to the petitioner.

Appraisals for the valuable park property were vigorously debated by the parties and judges in *Salvador Chiriboga*; the Court finally ordered that Ecuador pay nearly 19 million dollars in compensation.[82] With its ambiguous balancing procedure, the Tribunal appears intent on maintaining some limits on economic compensation, especially in cases such as *Salvador Chiriboga*, which threaten to impose dramatic financial consequences on States. These compensation approaches will be increasingly tested in the Inter-American System, as Latin America has experienced a surge of nationalizations and expropriations.[83]

---

[77] Salvador Chiriboga v. Ecuador, Preliminary Objections and Merits, Judgment, Inter-Am. Ct. H.R. (ser. C) No. 179, para. 96 (May 6, 2008).

[78] Ursula Kriebaum & August Reinisch, *Right to Property, in* MAX PLANCK ENCYCLOPEDIA OF PUBLIC INTERNATIONAL LAW (2009), at para. 24.

[79] Salvador Chiriboga v. Ecuador, Preliminary Objections and Merits, Judgment, Inter-Am. Ct. H.R. (ser. C) No. 179, para. 98 (May 6, 2008). The Court added that interest should also be paid from the "date that the victim actually lost the right to enjoy possession of the property." *Id.* para. 100.

[80] *See* Kriebaum & Reinisch, *supra* note 78, at para. 29 (stating that international law often requires that the amount of compensation should be equivalent to the fair market value of the expropriated property immediately before the expropriation took place).

[81] *See* Gonza, *supra* note 43, at 519.

[82] Salvador Chiriboga v. Ecuador, Reparations and Costs, Judgment, Inter-Am. Ct. H.R. (ser. C) No. 222, para. 84 (Mar. 3, 2011).

[83] *See, e.g.*, Sara Miller Llana & Whitney Eulich, *Brazil, Venezuela, and Mexico: Three Ways to Nationalize Oil*, THE CHRISTIAN SCI. MONITOR, May 12, 2012, http://www.csmonitor.com/World/Americas/2012/0512/Brazil-Venezuela-and-Mexico-three-ways-to-nationalize-oil; Simon Romero, *In Brazil and Elsewhere, Dismay at Argentina's Nationalization Move*, N.Y. TIMES, Apr. 18, 2012, http://www.nytimes.com/2012/04/19/world/americas/dismay-over-argentinas-nationalization-plan.html?_r=0.

The "fair balance" factor derives from the European Court's case law and distinct circumstances.[84] As noted above, Protocol 1 to the European Convention does not expressly provide for compensation, and the Strasbourg Tribunal accordingly grants much latitude to States with respect to their assessments of appropriate compensation and property value, if compensation is required at all.[85] In contrast, Article 21 of the American Convention, after extensive debate, was eventually designed to guarantee "just compensation" upon the deprivation of many forms of property. As a result, the Inter-American Tribunal should exercise caution in applying European standards in this area.

C. MEANING OF "REASONS OF PUBLIC UTILITY OR SOCIAL INTEREST"

The Tribunal has characterized "reasons of public utility or social interest" of Article 21(2) as those that "allow a better development of the democratic society."[86] In considering the phrase's meaning, the Court has referred to its jurisprudence on "general interest," a concept found in Article 30 of the Convention:

> the requirement that the laws be enacted for reasons of general interest means they must have been adopted for the "general welfare" . . . a concept that must be interpreted as an integral element of public order (*ordre public*) in democratic states, the main purpose of which is "the protection of the essential rights of man and the creation of circumstances that will permit him to achieve spiritual and material progress and attain happiness."[87]

The Court's willingness to freely associate "public utility" and "social interest" with its views on "general interest" and "general welfare" indicates that it would likely attribute similar meaning to "the interest of society," the phrase found in Article 21(1). That is, for the Tribunal, it is improbable that "interest of society" and "public utility or social interest" refer to different concepts. A predictably acceptable "social" objective is found in *Salvador Chiriboga*. The petitioner's parcel was to be used for a public park; thus, the State's occupation was considered "a legitimate public use" to establish "a recreational and ecological protected area" for the city of Quito.[88]

Yet the Inter-American Court is more demanding than the European Tribunal when assessing "reasons of public utility or social interest." The European Court will rarely

---

[84] Sporrong and Lönnroth v. Sweden, Eur. Ct. H.R., App. No. 7151/75 and No. 7152/75 (Sept. 23, 1982).

[85] *See* HARRIS, O'BOYLE & WARBRICK, *supra* note 4, at 889-890.

[86] Salvador Chiriboga v. Ecuador, Preliminary Objections and Merits, Judgment, Inter-Am. Ct. H.R. (ser. C) No. 179, para. 73 (May 6, 2008).

[87] The Word "Laws" in Article 30 of the American Convention on Human Rights, Advisory Opinion OC-6/86, Inter-Am. Ct. H.R. (ser. A) No. 6, para. 29 (May 9, 1986).

[88] Salvador Chiriboga v. Ecuador, Preliminary Objections and Merits, Judgment, Inter-Am. Ct. H.R. (ser. C) No. 179, para. 76 (May 6, 2008).

challenge a State's claim that the property interference was in the "public interest," the standard of Protocol 1. In the Inter-American judgment *Palamara Iribarne v. Chile*, the State seized copies of a book that was critical of the Chilean Navy; electronic files containing the book were also destroyed. In its decision, the Court considered the testimony of two expert witnesses, who had stated that the book's contents did not endanger national security concerns. The experts had conceded that the account "undoubtedly affect[ed] the institutional interest" of the Navy; however, the Inter-American Tribunal concluded that a mere "institutional interest" did not justify a deprivation of property under Article 21(2).[89]

Similarly, in the earlier case *Ivcher Bronstein v. Peru*, the Court discarded a "public utility or social interest" when the State blocked a majority shareholder's rights to a media company.[90] The petitioner, also the company's chairman of the board, had angered President Alberto Fujimori's administration by approving television programs that exposed wrongful government acts. In fact, broadcasting the critical programs, over government opposition, was very much in line with Peruvian society interests.

The Tribunal unjustifiably evaded the concepts of "public utility" and "social interest" in two pension cases. In a pair of judgments against Peru, *Five Pensioners* and *Acevedo Buendía* et al., it found that the State had arbitrarily reduced the petitioners' pension amounts, violating Article 21.[91] Yet, as Tara Melish points out, the Court did not recognize that the modification in pension regimes may have been motivated by legitimate objectives of social reform or exigency.[92] The Tribunal neither explored the reductions as such nor engaged in a balancing test to determine whether the restrictions were proportionate. Had it done so, it is conceivable that the State's measures would have been deemed consistent with social interests—although not necessarily passing the proportionality test.[93] In fact, in a subsequent judgment, *Furlan and Family v. Argentina*, the Court accepted that a national law, which restricted compensation awards against the State, pursued the legitimate purpose of addressing a "serious economic crisis that affected several rights of individuals."[94]

---

[89] Palamara Iribarne v. Chile, Merits, Reparations, Costs, Judgment, Inter-Am. Ct. H.R. (ser. C) No. 135, para. 109 (Nov. 22, 2005).

[90] Ivcher Bronstein v. Peru, Merits, Reparations, and Costs, Judgment, Inter-Am. Ct. H.R. (ser. C) No. 74, para. 129 (Feb. 6, 2001).

[91] "Five Pensioners" v. Peru, Merits, Reparations, and Costs, Judgment, Inter-Am. Ct. H.R. (ser. C) No. 98, para. 121 (Feb. 28, 2003); Acevedo Buendía et al. ("Discharged & Retired Employees of the Office of the Comptroller") v. Peru, Preliminary Objection, Merits, Reparations, and Costs, Judgment, Inter-Am. Ct. H.R. (ser. C) No. 198, paras. 88-91 (July 1, 2009).

[92] *See* Tara J. Melish, *The Inter-American Court of Human Rights: Beyond Progressivity*, *in* Social Rights Jurisprudence: Emerging Trends in Comparative and International Law 398–99 (Malcolm Langford ed., 2008).

[93] *See id.* at 399.

[94] Furlan and Family v. Argentina, Preliminary Objections, Merits, Reparations, and Costs, Judgment, Inter-Am. Ct. H.R. (ser. C) No. 246, para. 222 (Aug. 31, 2012) (holding, however, that the law's application in the case was not appropriate due to the petitioner's disabilities and, as a result, the right to property was violated).

D. Meaning of "In the Cases and According to the Forms Established by Law"

Pursuant to Article 21(2), deprivation of property is only acceptable "in the cases and according to the forms established by law." In *Ivcher Bronstein v. Peru*, as noted above, the State suspended a majority shareholder's rights to a media company.[95] This was accomplished by "creating temporary . . . courts and appointing judges to them at the time that the facts of the case *sub judice* occurred."[96] Baruch Ivcher Bronstein unsuccessfully defended himself in this hastily-arranged system, which clearly had not been previously established by law. Consequently, the Court considered that there was "no indication" that the decision against him "was adopted according to the law."[97] The resulting "deprivation" of his rights, according to the Tribunal, breached Article 21, paragraphs 1 and 2.[98]

However, *Salvador Chiriboga* shows a malleable approach to this provision. There, the Court held, "it is not necessary that every cause for deprivation or restriction to the right to property be embodied in the law . . . but that it is essential that such law and its application respect the essential content of the right to property."[99] It remains to be seen whether this pliable reading, which does not seem warranted by the terms of Article 21(2), is followed by subsequent judgments. Gonza observes that this interpretation—coupled with the "fair balance" factor employed by the Court—signals increasing deference to States.[100] Even the European Court, which grants States much flexibility in this area, insists that property interferences be based on national law and that the legislation in question be "accessible, precise, and foreseeable."[101]

E. Specific Approaches to Limitations

In the following two scenarios, the Court has offered specific guidance to States on permissible and unacceptable restrictions on the right to property.

1. Restrictions during Criminal Investigations and Police Action

In *Chaparro Álvarez and Lapo Íñiguez v. Ecuador*, the Court considered procedures for the seizure of property in connection with a criminal investigation.[102] If there is no less

---

[95] Ivcher Bronstein v. Peru, Merits, Reparations, and Costs, Judgment, Inter-Am. Ct. H.R. (ser. C) No. 74, para. 129 (Feb. 6, 2001).

[96] *Id.* para. 114.

[97] *Id.* para. 130.

[98] *Id.*

[99] Salvador Chiriboga v. Ecuador, Preliminary Objections and Merits, Judgment, Inter-Am. Ct. H.R. (ser. C) No. 179, para. 65 (May 6, 2008).

[100] *See* Gonza, *supra* note 43, at 530.

[101] Carbonara and Ventura v. Italy, Eur. Ct. H.R., App. No. 24638/94, para. 91 (May 30, 2000).

[102] *See also* Tibi v. Ecuador, Preliminary Objections, Merits, Reparations, and Costs, Judgment, Inter-Am. Ct. H.R. (ser. C) No. 114 (Sept. 7, 2004).

restrictive measure available, the State may seize property "when there is clear evidence of its connection to the offense," and "provided that it is necessary to guarantee the investigation and the payment of the applicable pecuniary responsibilities, or to avoid the loss or deterioration of the evidence."[103] Furthermore, seizures must be ordered and "supervised by judicial officials"; if the reasons "that justified the [seizure] cease to exist, the judge must assess the pertinence of maintaining the restriction, even before the proceedings are concluded."[104]

If the seizure is no longer justified, the property must be immediately returned, or the restriction would become disproportionate.[105] States have "the legal obligation to return the confiscated property in the condition in which it was at the time of its reception, except for normal deterioration owing to legitimate use."[106] The Tribunal has added that acquitted persons cannot be obligated to pay charges or fees for the return of their property.[107]

The Court has emphasized that low-income individuals suffer disproportionately when their property is seized or destroyed in state security operations. In *Uzcátegui* et al. *v. Venezuela*, police officers, while conducting an arrest, damaged the victims' home and belongings.[108] The Tribunal stated that given "the socioeconomic status and vulnerability of the Uzcátegui family, the damage to their property during the raid had a far greater impact than it would have had for other family groups with other means."[109]

2. Protective Framework for Traditional Territories

The Inter-American System has seen increasing numbers of cases where States and private companies have sought to extract natural resources or develop commercial projects on lands belonging to indigenous peoples and Afro-Latin communities.[110] According to the

---

[103] Chaparro Álvarez and Lapo Íñiguez v. Ecuador, Preliminary Objections, Merits, Reparations, and Costs, Judgment, Inter-Am. Ct. H.R. (ser. C) No. 170, para. 188 (Nov. 21, 2007).

[104] *Id.*

[105] *Id.*

[106] *Id.* para. 211.

[107] *Id.* para. 193.

[108] Uzcátegui et al. v. Venezuela, Merits and Reparations, Judgment, Inter-Am. Ct. H.R. (ser. C) No. 249, para. 203 (Sept. 3, 2012).

[109] *Id.* para. 204.

[110] In addition to the Inter-American Court, the Inter-American Commission on Human Rights has dealt with such cases on several occasions. For example, in 2011, the Commission called for Brazil to halt construction on a large hydroelectic power plant that endangered indigenous communities. PM 382/10: Indigenous Communities of the Xingu River Basin, Pará, Brazil (2011), *available at* www.oas.org/en/iachr/decisions/precautionary.asp. For more Commission jurisprudence on the topic, *see* Inter-American Commission on Human Rights, Indigenous Peoples, Afro-Descendent Communities, and Natural Resources: Human Rights Protection in the Context of Extraction, Exploitation, and Development Activities, OEA/Ser.L/V/II., Doc. 47/15, 31 Dec. 2015, *available at* http://www.oas.org/en/iachr/reports/pdfs/ExtractiveIndustries2016.pdf; Inter-American Commission on Human Rights, Indigenous and Tribal Peoples' Rights over Their Ancestral

Saramaka v. Suriname judgment, in order to ensure that concessions do not comprise "a denial of their traditions and customs in a way that endangers the very survival of the group and of its members," States must comply with three "safeguards."[111] First, the State must ensure "the effective participation of the [community], in conformity with their customs and traditions, regarding any development, investment, exploration or extraction plan" within the territory.[112] Second, the State must guarantee that the community will receive "a reasonable benefit" from any such project.[113] Third, States must prevent concessions "unless and until independent and technically capable entities, with the State's supervision, perform a prior environmental and social impact assessment."[114]

To ensure "effective" and "meaningful" participation, the Court has held that States have "a duty to actively consult" with the community, which requires "good-faith" efforts starting at the "early stages" of the development plan.[115] Any possible environmental and

---

Lands and Natural Resources: Norms and Jurisprudence of the Inter-American Human Rights System, OEA/Ser.L/V/II., Doc. 56/09, Dec. 30, 2009, *available at* http://www.oas.org/en/iachr/indigenous/docs/pdf/AncestralLands.pdf. For a review of the Court's indigenous cases, *see* Oswaldo Ruiz Chiriboga & Gina Donoso, *Los Pueblos Indígenas y Tribales ante la Corte Interamericana de Derechos Humanos, in* La Convención Americana sobre Derechos Humanos Comentada 947–1026 (2014).

[111] Saramaka People v. Suriname, Preliminary Objections, Merits, Reparations, and Costs, Judgment, Inter-Am. Ct. H.R. (ser. C) No. 172, para. 128 (Nov. 28, 2007). *See also* Kaliña and Lokono Peoples v. Suriname, Merits, Reparations and Costs, Judgment, Inter-Am. Ct. H.R. (ser. C) No. 309, para. 201 (Nov. 25, 2015). Note that the Court has emphasized that "the term 'survival' in this context signifies much more than physical survival"; it refers to the community's ability to maintain its traditional way of life and its special relationship with its territory. Saramaka People v. Suriname, Interpretation of the Judgment on Preliminary Objections, Merits, Reparations, and Costs, Judgment, Inter-Am. Ct. H.R. (ser. C) No. 185, para. 37 (Aug. 12, 2008).

[112] Saramaka People v. Suriname, Preliminary Objections, Merits, Reparations, and Costs, Judgment, Inter-Am. Ct. H.R. (ser. C) No. 172, para. 129 (Nov. 28, 2007).

[113] *Id.*

[114] *Id.* In its August 2008 judgment interpreting the *Saramaka* decision, the Court stated that the studies must "conform to the relevant international standards and best practices," such as the Akwé:Kon Guidelines for the Conduct of Cultural, Environmental and Social Impact Assessments. Saramaka People v. Suriname, Interpretation of the Judgment on Preliminary Objections, Merits, Reparations, and Costs, Judgment, Inter-Am. Ct. H.R. (ser. C) No. 185, para. 41 (Aug. 12, 2008).

[115] Saramaka People v. Suriname, Preliminary Objections, Merits, Reparations, and Costs, Judgment, Inter-Am. Ct. H.R. (ser. C) No. 172, para. 133 (Nov. 28, 2007). In its August 2008 judgment interpreting *Saramaka*, the Court held that the original judgment had required the State to consult with the Saramaka people "regarding at least the following six issues: (1) the process of delimiting, demarcating and granting collective title over the territory of the Saramaka people; (2) the process of granting the members of the Saramaka people legal recognition of their collective juridical capacity, pertaining to the community to which they belong; (3) the process of adopting legislative, administrative, and other measures as may be required to recognize, protect, guarantee, and give legal effect to the right of the members of the Saramaka people to the territory they have traditionally used and occupied; (4) the process of adopting legislative, administrative and other measures necessary to recognize and ensure the right of the Saramaka people to be effectively consulted, in accordance with their traditions and customs; (5) regarding the results of prior environmental and social impact assessments, and (6) regarding any proposed restrictions of the Saramaka people's property rights, particularly regarding proposed development or investment plans in or affecting Saramaka territory." Saramaka People v. Suriname, Interpretation of the Judgment on Preliminary Objections, Merits, Reparations, and Costs, Judgment, Inter-Am. Ct. H.R. (ser. C) No. 185, para. 16 (Aug. 12, 2008).

health risks must be communicated promptly to the community.[116] The consultations "should take account" of "traditional methods of decision-making"; for example, it is the indigenous community, not the State, who must decide which person or persons will represent the community in the process.[117]

Although all consultations must have "the objective of reaching an agreement," the Court requires States to obtain consent only in certain circumstances.[118] With regard to "large-scale development or investment projects that would have a major impact" within indigenous territory, States have "a duty not only to consult" with the affected community, "*but also to obtain [its] free, prior, and informed consent*, according to [its] customs and traditions."[119] The Court alternately described such projects as "major development or investment plans that may have a profound impact on the property rights of [the community] to a large part of their territory."[120]

In general, when land disputes arise between indigenous communities and other private parties, the Tribunal has held that a "restriction of the right of private individuals to private property might be necessary to attain the collective objective of preserving [indigenous] cultural identities in a democratic and pluralist society."[121] However, the Court added that "this does not mean that every time there is a conflict between [private individuals and indigenous communities] the latter must prevail over the former."[122] Still, the Tribunal places the burden upon States to resolve these matters with special regard to the unique indigenous relationship with ancestral land.[123] Only when States "are unable, for concrete and justified reasons, to . . . return traditional territory and communal resources to indigenous populations" are alternative measures of reparation then pursued.[124]

It is hoped that many of these concepts will be further developed, as more communal land cases arrive in San José. At present, for example, it is unclear which precise circumstances trigger the three *Saramaka* safeguards: effective participation, impact assessments, and "reasonable benefits" from the project. The Court unfortunately hints at situations where these measures might not be demanded. If a State or company seeks

---

[116] Saramaka People v. Suriname, Preliminary Objections, Merits, Reparations, and Costs, Judgment, Inter-Am. Ct. H.R. (ser. C) No. 172, para. 133 (Nov. 28, 2007).

[117] *Id.*

[118] *Id.*

[119] *Id.* para. 134 (emphasis added).

[120] *Id.* para. 137.

[121] Yakye Axa Indigenous Cmty. v. Paraguay, Merits, Reparations, and Costs, Judgment, Inter-Am. Ct. H.R. (ser. C) No. 125, para. 148 (June 17, 2005).

[122] *Id.* para. 149.

[123] *See* Xákmok Kásek Indigenous Community v. Paraguay, 2010 Inter-Am. Ct. H.R. (ser. C) No. 214, para. 284 (Aug. 24, 2010) ("State authorities must . . . [take] very much into account the special relationship that the indigenous have with their lands for preserving their culture and survival.").

[124] Yakye Axa Indigenous Cmty. v. Paraguay, Merits, Reparations, and Costs, Judgment, Inter-Am. Ct. H.R. (ser. C) No. 125, para. 149 (June 17, 2005). *See also* Kuna Indigenous People of Madungandi and Embera

to extract a natural resource that has not been "traditionally used" by the resident indigenous community, and that extraction would not affect "vital" community resources, it is uncertain whether the Tribunal still requires the safeguards.[125] Of course, there is no reliable manner to determine "traditional" resources—however the Court conceives of that term—and likely consequences for the community without a previous consultation with the indigenous group, in conjunction with a full impact analysis.[126]

Even when the safeguards apply, they offer only limited support. It is true that *Sarayaku v. Ecuador*, a Court judgment from 2012, expanded the applicability of consultation rights, extending them to "any administrative and legislative measures that may affect [indigenous and tribal] rights."[127] But there are too many opportunities to exploit the safeguards.[128] A State might conduct consultations, commission impact studies, and even provide the affected community some form of benefit. It could then mostly ignore the information gathered and damage ancestral lands and resources—while still in compliance with the Court's requirements.[129] Furthermore, even the *Saramaka* requirement for consent, activated when communities face "large-scale development or investment projects," offers insufficient protection for indigenous peoples.[130] A small-scale operation that destroys a sacred site could devastate a community, yet it would not likely require consent by the Court.[131]

Thomas Antkowiak has argued that attempts to enhance the three safeguards will likely not solve the fundamental problem.[132] When a State disregards these protections, under Article 21, a mere property violation will result. In fact, under a property framework, a violation may not be found at all, especially if States begin to defend themselves

---

Indigenous People of Bayano and their Members v. Panama, Preliminary Objections, Merits, Reparations, and Costs, Judgment, Inter-Am. Ct. H.R. (ser. C) No. 284, para. 120 (Oct. 14, 2014) (explaining that the State provided the community alternative lands because the ancestral territories had been flooded).

125 Saramaka People v. Suriname, Preliminary Objections, Merits, Reparations, and Costs, Judgment, Inter-Am. Ct. H.R. (ser. C) No. 172, para. 155 (Nov. 28, 2007).

126 *See* Thomas M. Antkowiak, *Rights, Resources, and Rhetoric: Indigenous Peoples and the Inter-American Court*, 35 U. PA. J. INT'L L. 113, 167 (2013).

127 Kichwa Indigenous People of Sarayaku v. Ecuador, Merits and Reparations, Judgment Inter.-Am. Ct. H.R. (ser. C) No. 245, para. 166 (June 27, 2012). The *Sarayaku* Court even regarded the right to consultation as a "general principle of international law." *Id.* para. 164. The *Sarayaku* judgment acknowledged *Saramaka*'s three safeguards: effective participation, reasonable benefits, and the impact assessment. Nevertheless, it did not examine the concept of benefits, and the Court's standard on consent was ignored.

128 *See* Antkowiak, *supra* note 126, at 170.

129 *See id.*

130 *See* Pasqualucci, *supra* note 26, at 98 ("[The standard] seems to give states leeway to grant smaller for-profit logging and mining concessions that could still negatively impact indigenous communities.").

131 *See* Lyng v. Nw. Indian Cemetery Protective Ass'n, 485 U.S. 439 (1988) (providing a real example of such a scenario). In *Lyng*, the U.S. government sought to build a short road through sacred sites of Native Americans. Justice Brennan, in a blistering dissent, wrote: "I find it difficult, however, to imagine conduct more insensitive to religious needs than the Government's determination to build a marginally useful road in the face of uncontradicted evidence that the road will render the practice of respondents' religion impossible." *Id.* at 477.

132 *See* Antkowiak, *supra* note 126, at 171.

more strenuously before the Court. Many tribunals and government agencies readily presume that State land actions are permissible, even in indigenous cases.[133]

For these reasons, rather than solely relying upon the modest right to property, Antkowiak has urged a robust right-to-life framework to protect ancestral lands and resources.[134] This would expand upon the Court's concept of *vida digna* (right to a dignified life) to affirm that a collective right to dignified life is at stake in these cases.[135] In other words, in the context of traditional territories, a State should be held to a more rigorous standard consistent with the Convention's Article 4 (Right to Life)—rather than the limited Article 21, where restrictions are routine and States are granted wide latitude. In concrete terms, a right-to-life standard could require effective participation, impact assessments, and *mutually-acceptable*—not merely "reasonable"—benefits for *all* projects to proceed on ancestral territories.[136] Effective participation, moreover, must require the free, prior, and informed consent of the communities concerned.[137] An invariable consent requirement is only rational, as a State cannot merely "consult" a community about initiatives that impact its rights to life, livelihood, and cultural integrity.[138]

---

[133] *See, e.g.*, Harris, O'Boyle & Warbrick, *supra* note 4, at 877 (describing the European Court's significant deference to States on property matters); Lynda J. Oswald, *The Role of Deference in Judicial Review of Public Use Determinations*, 39 B.C. Envtl. Aff. L. Rev. 243, 245 (2012) (noting "the traditional deference given by [U.S.] courts to legislative determinations of the need to take property by eminent domain"); Dinah Shelton, *Self-Determination in Regional Human Rights Law: From Kosovo to Cameroon*, 105 Am. J. Int'l L. 60, 77 (2011) ("[G]overnments routinely claim that a public interest in economic development overrides indigenous property rights.").

[134] *See* Antkowiak, *supra* note 126, at 179–81.

[135] For more on the right to *vida digna, see* this volume's chapter on the right to life.

[136] *See* Antkowiak, *supra* note 126, at 185.

[137] *See id.*

[138] *See id.* Some commentators are justifiably skeptical even of consent requirements, because they "assume that indigenous peoples are in a position to make meaningful choices." Engle, *supra* note 65, at 205. Informed by indigenous peoples and others, the Inter-American Court will need to clarify further how States may secure legitimate consent. Through coercion, fraud, and illicit payments, corporate and government representatives have usurped traditional decision-making processes and divided communities in attempts to gain approval for projects. *See, e.g.*, Kichwa Indigenous People of Sarayaku v. Ecuador, Merits and Reparations, Judgment, Inter-Am. Ct. H.R. (ser. C) No. 245, paras. 186, 194, 203 (June 27, 2012).

9

Reparations

Article 63

1. *If the Court finds that there has been a violation of a right or freedom protected by this Convention, the Court shall rule that the injured party be ensured the enjoyment of his right or freedom that was violated. It shall also rule, if appropriate, that the consequences of the measure or situation that constituted the breach of such right or freedom be remedied and that fair compensation be paid to the injured party.*
2. *In cases of extreme gravity and urgency, and when necessary to avoid irreparable damage to persons, the Court shall adopt such provisional measures as it deems pertinent in matters it has under consideration. With respect to a case not yet submitted to the Court, it may act at the request of the Commission.*

Chapter 9 Contents

I. Introduction 287
II. Background 289
III. The "Injured Party" of Article 63(1) and Related Topics 290
IV. Monetary Remedies 292
A. Pecuniary Damages 292

B. Moral Damages 296
1. In General 296
2. Community Development Programs 299
V. Non-Monetary Remedies 300
A. Background 300
B. Restitution 301
C. Rehabilitation 303
D. Recognition of Responsibility and Apologies 304
E. Memorials and Commemorations 304
F. Reform of Legislation and Policy, Training Programs 305
VI. Legal Fees and Expenses 307
VII. Supervision and Compliance with the Court's Judgments 308
A. Binding and Final Nature of Judgments 308
B. Introduction to Supervision 310
C. Cases of Noncompliance 311
D. Compliance Rates 313
VIII. Provisional Measures of Article 63(2) 314

I. Introduction

Interpreting the expansive provisions of Article 63(1), the Inter-American Court has repeatedly held that "any violation of an international obligation that has caused damage entails the obligation to repair it adequately."[1] The Tribunal has established that "reparations must be related to the facts of the case, the violations that have been declared, the damage proven, and the measures requested to repair the respective damage."[2] For the Court, then, "general requests" with little factual or legal foundation are insufficient, as they impede an analysis of "their purpose, reasonableness, and scope."[3]

The Inter-American Court's contemporary remedial approach comprises measures of restitution, rehabilitation, satisfaction, and guarantees of non-repetition, in conjunction with pecuniary and nonpecuniary damages. Although punitive damages have been avoided, legal fees and expenses are customarily granted.[4] The Court's potent approach to redress pursues the *restitutio in integrum* principle of the Permanent Court of International Justice's landmark *Factory at Chorzów* judgment, which held that "reparation must, as far as possible, wipe out all the consequences of the illegal act and reestablish the situation which would, in all probability, have existed if that act had not been committed."[5] In fact, the Inter-American Court has often cited this enduring principle when assessing reparations.[6]

The Inter-American Commission and the UN Human Rights Committee, although non-binding entities, reinforce the Court's broad remedial approach through their various recommendations to States.[7] This robust concept of reparations has also been

---

[1] *E.g.*, Radilla Pacheco v. Mexico, Preliminary Objections, Merits, Reparations, and Costs, Judgment, Inter-Am. Ct. H.R. (ser. C) No. 209, para. 327 (Nov. 23, 2009); Velásquez Rodríguez v. Honduras, Judgment (ser. C) No. 7, para. 25 (July 21, 1989).

[2] *E.g.*, Norín Catrimán et al. (Leaders, members and activist of the Mapuche Indigenous People) v. Chile, Merits, Reparations, and Costs, Judgment, Inter-Am. Ct. H.R. (ser. C) No. 279, para. 411 (May 29, 2014); Ticona Estrada et al. v. Bolivia. Merits, Reparations and Costs. Judgment (ser. C), No. 191 para. 110 (Nov. 27, 2008).

[3] *E.g.*, Fernández-Ortega et al. v. Mexico, Inter-Am. Ct. H.R. (ser. C) No. 215, para. 274 (Aug. 30, 2010); González et al. ("Cotton Field") v. Mexico, Inter-Am. Ct. H.R. (ser. C) No. 205, para. 493 (Nov. 16, 2009).

[4] *E.g.*, Garrido and Baigorria v. Argentina, Reparations and Costs, Judgment, Inter-Am. Ct. H.R. (ser. C) No. 39, paras. 43–44 (Aug. 27, 1998); Godínez Cruz v. Honduras, Reparations and Costs, Judgment, Inter-Am. Ct. H.R. (ser. C) No. 8, para. 36 (July 21, 1989).

[5] Factory at Chorzów (Germ. v. Pol.), 1928 P.C.I.J. (ser. A) No. 17, at 47 (Sept. 13).

[6] *E.g.*, Cruz Sánchez et al. v. Peru, Preliminary Objections, Merits, Reparations, Costs, Judgment, Inter-Am. Ct. H.R. (ser. C) No. 292, para. 452 (Apr. 17, 2015); Moiwana Cmty. v. Suriname, Inter-Am. Ct. H.R. (ser. C) No. 124, para. 170 (June 15, 2005).

[7] *See, e.g.*, Gallo et al. v. Argentina, Case 12.632, Inter-Am. Comm'n H.R., Report No. 43/15, OEA/Ser.L/V/II.155, doc. 23, para. 315 (2015) (recommending a variety of remedies); U.N. Int'l. Covenant on Civil & Political Rights, *The Nature of the General Legal Obligation Imposed on States Parties to the Covenant*, para. 16, U.N. Doc. CCPR/C/21/Rev.1/Add.13 (Mar. 29, 2004) (affirming that reparation to victims not only entails compensation, but also "can involve restitution, rehabilitation and measures of satisfaction, such as public apologies, public memorials, guarantees of non-repetition and changes in relevant laws and practices, as well as bringing to justice the perpetrators of human rights violations.").

adopted by other UN instruments and institutions.[8] For its part, the African Court on Human and Peoples' Rights has remedial powers comparable to its Inter-American peer.[9] However, it is not yet clear to what extent the African Court will fulfill its potential.[10]

In contrast, the European Court of Human Rights has historically favored only declaratory relief and monetary compensation.[11] Although it is true that its remedial authority appears somewhat limited, pursuant to Article 41 of the European Convention,[12] the European Court's approach has been overly cautious.[13] During the past 15 years, divergences from this narrow path have occurred, as the European Tribunal has sporadically ordered the restoration of liberty, the return of property, and legislative reform.[14] Nevertheless, these intermittent judgments do not approximate the Inter-American Court's reparative model, which consistently requires a wide variety of equitable remedies—often elaborated in substantial detail.

---

[8] For example, the Rome Statute of the International Criminal Court requires the establishment of "principles relating to reparations to, or in respect of, victims, including restitution, compensation and rehabilitation." Rome Statute of the International Criminal Court art. 75(1), July 17, 1998, 2187 U.N.T.S. 3. The International Convention for the Protection of All Persons from Enforced Disappearance provides for compensation, restitution, rehabilitation, satisfaction, and guarantees of non-repetition. International Convention for the Protection of All Persons from Enforced Disappearance, G.A. Res. 61/177, U.N. Doc. A/Res/61/177, art. 24 (Jan. 12, 2007).

[9] Article 27 of the Protocol to the African Charter provides: "if the Court finds that there has been violation of a human or peoples' rights, it shall make appropriate orders to remedy the violation, including the payment of fair compensation or reparation." Protocol to the African Charter on Human and Peoples' Rights on the Establishment of an African Court on Human and Peoples' Rights (June 9, 1998), OAU doc. OAU/LEG/EXP/AFCHPR/PROT (III).

[10] The African Court of Justice and Human Rights, for its part, has a similar remedial authority. Its Protocol reads: "the Court may, if it considers that there was a violation of a human or peoples' right, order any appropriate measures in order to remedy the situation, including granting fair compensation." African Union, Protocol on the Statute of the African Court of Justice and Human Rights, art. 45, July 1, 2008, *available at* http://www.peaceau.org/uploads/protocol-statute-african-court-justice-and-human-rights-en.pdf.

[11] *See, e.g.*, David Harris, Michael O'Boyle & Colin Warbrick, Law of the European Convention on Human Rights 157-158 (3d ed. 2014).

[12] Article 41 of the European Convention provides that, upon the finding of a violation, if domestic law "allows only partial reparation to be made, the Court shall, if necessary, afford just satisfaction to the injured party." European Convention, art. 41. *See also* Council of Europe's Report on the Inter-American Specialized Conference on Human Rights (1969).

[13] The European Court's interpretation of the term "just satisfaction" has been criticized as being too narrow. Dinah Shelton explains that the term "satisfaction" in international practice has never been restricted to monetary compensation, and argues that the European Court can rely on the "inherent powers of international tribunals" to provide victims various reparations. Dinah Shelton, Remedies in International Human Rights Law 280 (2d ed. 2005).

[14] *See, e.g.*, Laurence R. Helfer, *Redesigning the European Court of Human Rights: Embeddedness as a Deep Structural Principle of the European Human Rights Regime*, 19 Eur. J. Int'l L. 125, 147–49 (2008); Valerio Colandrea, *On the Power of the European Court of Human Rights to Order Specific Non-monetary Measures: Some Remarks in Light of the* Assanidze, Broniowski *and* Sejdovic *Cases*, 7 Hum. Rts. L. Rev. 396, 410–11 (2007); Philip Leach, *Beyond the Bug River: New Approaches to Redress by the ECHR*, 148 Eur. Hum. Rts. L. Rev. (2005).

Of course, the Inter-American Court's reparations are not without their flaws. As for non-monetary remedies, the Court at times could require more intensive victim engagement in the design and implementation of reparations.[15] Still, the Court's non-monetary reparations generally respond to victims' preferences for restoration, and even contemplate the complex realities of certain victim populations.[16] On the other hand, as discussed below, the Tribunal's inconsistent monetary reparations invite scrutiny. Particularly in the judgments involving groups, such as indigenous communities, the Court does not always respond to substantiated claims for monetary damages by both individuals and collectivities.[17] If it neglects well-founded requests for material or moral compensation, the Court will compromise both individual and collective rights.

II. Background

The drafters of the American Convention at the San José Conference intended for the Inter-American Court to have extensive remedial powers.[18] The preliminary proposal for the Convention, prepared by the Inter-American Commission, only referred to the Court's competence to grant an "amount of compensation" in the case of a violation.[19] However, the Conference's Committee II acted swiftly to expand the provision.[20] When adopting the final text, a plenary session even removed the qualifying language "to the extent possible" to make Article 63(1)'s first sentence stronger.[21]

As for the second paragraph of Article 63, the Inter-American Commission's preliminary draft for the Convention did not grant the Court competence to order provisional measures. Article 63(2) was added at the proposal of the Costa Rican delegate during the Third Plenary Session.[22] The delegate reasoned that the capacity to act in urgent situations was common to many of the globe's tribunals.[23] Since the 1980s, the Inter-American

---

[15] *See* Thomas M. Antkowiak, *A Dark Side of Virtue: The Inter-American Court and Reparations for Indigenous Peoples*, 25 DUKE J. COMP. & INT'L L. 1, 52 (2014).

[16] *Id.*

[17] *Id.* at 64.

[18] *See* Report of Committee II "Organs of Protection and General Provisions," Rapporteur Robert J. Redington, Doc. 71 (English) Rev. 1 (1969); p. 468, Doc 84, Discurso del Presidente de la Conferencia Especializada Interamericana sobre Derechos Humanos, Fernando Lara (1969). *See also* Baena-Ricardo v. Panama, Inter-Am. Ct. H.R. (ser. C) No. 104, para. 89 (Nov. 28, 2003).

[19] Draft Inter-American Convention on Protection of Human Rights, art. 52, Doc. 5 (English), Sept. 22, 1969.

[20] *See* Report of Committee II "Organs of Protection and General Provisions," Rapporteur Robert J. Redington, Doc. 71 (English) Rev. 1 (1969).

[21] P. 457, Minutes of the Third Plenary Session, Doc 83 (1969).

[22] *Id.*

[23] P. 361, Minutes of the 6th Session of Committee II, Doc. 85 (1969). The delegate, José Luis Redondo-Gómez, advanced these arguments during the sixth session of Committee II; they were not accepted at that point. However, he successfully reintroduced his proposal during the plenary session.

Court has ordered numerous provisional measures for the protection of both individuals and groups of persons.

III. The "Injured Party" of Article 63(1) and Related Topics

When the Court declares individuals or whole communities[24] to be victims of human rights violations, they become "injured parties" under the American Convention and beneficiaries of reparations.[25] In certain cases, family members may also be considered victims of rights violations and, thus, injured parties deserving of reparation. For example, in cases of extrajudicial executions, forced disappearances, and torture, the Tribunal will often decide that family members of the "main" victim have suffered violations of the right to mental and moral integrity, Article 5 of the Convention.[26] Another common scenario is a prolonged denial of justice by national courts and institutions; in these situations the Court may find violations of Articles 8 (Right to a Fair Trial) and 25 (Right to Judicial Protection)—as well as Article 5, depending upon the circumstances—with respect to those family members who have actively pursued judicial remedies on behalf of their relative.[27]

During its early years, the Court did not consider family members as victims in this manner.[28] Yet now it has affirmed that there is a rebuttable presumption of an Article 5(1)

---

[24] In *Sarayaku v. Ecuador*, the Court, for the first time, held that the indigenous community *itself* suffered human rights violations. *See* Kichwa Indigenous People of Sarayaku v. Ecuador, Merits and Reparations, Judgment Inter.-Am. Ct. H.R. (ser. C) No. 245, para. 341 (June 27, 2012). This holding appears to disregard the American Convention's Article 1, the central provision that obligates States Parties to respect and ensure the treaty's rights to "all persons subject to their jurisdiction"—with "person" defined as "every human being." In this sharp break with the past, the *Sarayaku* Court apparently adopted a wider definition of "person," perhaps following the views of institutions such as the U.N. Committee on Economic, Social and Cultural Rights. *See* Comm. on Econ., Soc. and Cultural Rights, Gen. Comment No. 21: Right of Everyone to Take Part in Cultural Life, para. 9, UN Doc. E/C.12/GC/21 (Dec. 21, 2009) ("[T]he Committee recognizes that the term 'everyone' in the first line of article 15 may denote the individual or the collective. . . .").

[25] American Convention, art. 63(1).

[26] *E.g.*, Rochac Hernandez et al. v. El Salvador, Merits, Reparations, and Costs, Judgment, Inter-Am. Ct. H.R. (ser. C) No. 285, para. 122 (Oct. 14, 2014) (forced disappearance); Gómez Paquiyauri Brothers v. Peru, Merits, Reparations, and Costs, Judgment, Inter-Am. Ct. H.R. (ser. C) No. 110, paras. 118–119 (July 8, 2004) (extrajudicial executions); Tibi v. Ecuador, Preliminary Objections, Merits, Reparations, and Costs, Judgment, Inter-Am. Ct. H.R. (ser. C) No. 114, paras. 160–162 (Sept. 7, 2004) (torture).

[27] *E.g.*, Mack Chang v. Guatemala, Merits, Reparations, and Costs, Judgment, Inter-Am. Ct. H.R. (ser. C) No. 101, para. 218 (Nov. 25, 2003); Bámaca Velásquez v. Guatemala, Merits, Judgment, Inter-Am. Ct. H.R. (ser. C) No. 70, para. 196 (Nov. 25, 2000).

[28] Formerly, family members would frequently receive non-pecuniary reparations for suffering endured, but they would not be found as victims of an Article 5(1) violation. *See* White Van" (Paniagua Morales et al.) v. Guatemala, Merits, Judgment, Inter-Am. Ct. H.R. (ser. C) No. 37, paras. 126–136 (Mar. 8, 1998) (no violations found with respect to family members); White Van" (Paniagua Morales et al.) v. Guatemala, Reparations and Costs, Judgment, Inter-Am. Ct. H.R. (ser. C) No. 76, paras. 85, 229 (May 25, 2001) (family members nevertheless receive non-pecuniary reparations for suffering).

violation with regard to parents, children, spouses, and permanent companions, provided that the principal victim has suffered a severe violation such as forced disappearance, extrajudicial execution, or torture.[29] Other petitioners—including siblings with some exceptions[30]—must submit evidence demonstrating a close relationship.[31] Violations of Articles 8 and 25 require evidence of involvement in judicial processes burdened with undue delays or irregularities.

Generally, a person must be fully identified before the Court to qualify as an injured party.[32] In multiple-petitioner cases, however, the process of victim identification has continued after the submission of the case to the Tribunal.[33] The Court has accepted requests by petitioners and the Commission to supplement the list of alleged victims originally submitted, as long as the State was guaranteed its right of defense.[34] Ultimately, in recognition of the complexities posed by large cases such as massacres, the Court revised its Rules of Procedure to formally allow this practice on a case-by-case basis: "When it has not been possible to identify one or more of the alleged victims . . . because [the case] concerns massive or collective violations, the Tribunal shall decide whether to consider those individuals as victims."[35]

On occasion, injured parties before the Court already received a measure of reparation through domestic procedures. The Tribunal will evaluate such "procedures and results" in order to determine "whether the compensation awarded meets the criteria of being

---

[29] Valle Jaramillo et al. v. Colombia, Merits, Reparations, and Costs, Judgment, Inter-Am. Ct. H.R. (ser. C) No. 192, para. 119 (Nov. 27, 2008).

[30] More recently, the Court has held that a rebuttable presumption of an Article 5(1) violation also applies to the siblings of disappeared victims, "unless the contrary is revealed by the specific circumstances of the case." *E.g.*, Osorio Rivera and Family v. Peru, Preliminary Objections, Merits, Reparations, and Costs, Judgment, Inter-Am. Ct. H.R. (ser. C) No. 274, para. 227 (Nov. 26, 2013); Guidel Alvarez et al. ("Diario Militar") v. Guatemala, Merits, Reparations, and Costs, Judgment, Inter-Am. Ct. H.R. (ser. C) No. 253, para. 286 (Nov. 20, 2012).

[31] *E.g.*, Cruz Sánchez et al. v. Peru, Preliminary Objections, Merits, Reparations, Costs, Judgment, Inter-Am. Ct. H.R. (ser. C) No. 292, para. 445 (Apr. 17, 2015). In *Mack Chang v. Guatemala*, a cousin of the murdered victim was himself considered a victim of an Article 5(1) violation. Mack Chang v. Guatemala, Merits, Reparations, and Costs, Judgment, Inter-Am. Ct. H.R. (ser. C) No. 101, paras. 233, 244 (Nov. 25, 2003).

[32] *E.g.*, Moiwana Cmty. v. Suriname, Inter-Am. Ct. H.R. (ser. C) No. 124, para. 177 (June 15, 2005); "Juvenile Reeducation Institute" v. Paraguay, Preliminary Objections, Merits, Reparations, and Costs, Judgment, Inter-Am. Ct. H.R. (ser. C) No. 112, paras. 107–109 (Sept. 2, 2004).

[33] Mapiripán Massacre v. Colombia, Inter-Am. Ct. H.R. (ser. C) No. 134, para. 137 (Sept. 15, 2005). In *Mapiripán*, the Court actually found violations and ordered remedies with respect to still-unidentified victims. According to the Tribunal, Colombia's deficient investigation of a State-sponsored massacre rendered the identification of many victims impossible at the time of the Court's judgment.

[34] *E.g.*, Moiwana Cmty. v. Suriname, Inter-Am. Ct. H.R. (ser. C) No. 124, paras. 71-74 (June 15, 2005); "Juvenile Reeducation Institute" v. Paraguay, Preliminary Objections, Merits, Reparations, and Costs, Judgment, Inter-Am. Ct. H.R. (ser. C) No. 112, paras. 110–111 (Sept. 2, 2004). In fact, additional victim names were permitted over a State's objections, in consideration of credible evidence in the record and the case's particular circumstances. Gutiérrez Soler v. Colombia, Inter-Am. Ct. H.R. (ser. C) No. 132, para. 58 (Sept. 12, 2005).

[35] Rules of Procedure of the Inter-American Court of Human Rights, entered into force 1 January 2010, Art. 35(2), approved by the Court during its LXXXV Regular Period of Sessions, held November 16–28, 2009.

objective, reasonable and effective to make adequate reparation" for the specific rights violations found in the Court's judgment.[36] If not, the Court will order additional reparations. In any event, "adequate and integral reparation cannot be reduced to the payment of compensation" and will also require non-monetary remedies, as described below.[37]

IV. Monetary Remedies

A. PECUNIARY DAMAGES

Pecuniary damages, according to the Court, address "the loss of, or detriment to, the income of the victims, the expenses incurred as a result of the facts, and the consequences of a pecuniary nature that have a causal nexus to the facts of the case."[38] In this way, the Tribunal has consistently granted pecuniary damages for lost earnings, actual damages, and consequential damages.

The lost earnings calculation for a deceased victim originally involved a number of factors: age, life expectancy, salary, and regular bonuses, among others.[39] Yet during the last several years, the Tribunal has shown a preference for determining both lost earnings and other damages in equity,[40] resisting more transparent calculations and current economic methodologies to assess a victim's earnings capacity.[41] Sergio García Ramírez has defended the use of equity as a flexible approach for the many cases where petitioners can only offer scant documentation; also, an equitable estimate could improve upon the Court's previous lost earnings formula.[42] That calculation uniformly deducted

---

[36] *E.g.*, Rodriguez Vera et al. (Persons Disappeared from the Palace of Justice) v. Colombia, Preliminary Objections, Merits, Reparations, and Costs, Judgment, Inter-Am. Ct. H.R. (ser. C) No. 287, para. 593 (Nov. 14, 2014); Cepeda Vargas v. Colombia, Preliminary Objections, Merits, Reparations, and Costs, Judgment, Inter-Am. Ct. H.R. (ser. C.) No. 213, paras. 139–140 (May 26, 2010).

[37] *E.g.*, Rodriguez Vera et al. (Persons Disappeared from the Palace of Justice) v. Colombia, Preliminary Objections, Merits, Reparations, and Costs, Judgment, Inter-Am. Ct. H.R. (ser. C) No. 287, para. 549 (Nov. 14, 2014); Mapiripán Massacre v. Colombia, Merits, Reparations, and Costs, Judgment, Inter-Am. Ct. H.R. (ser. C) No. 134, para. 214 (Sept. 15, 2005).

[38] *E.g.*, Rodriguez Vera et al. (Persons Disappeared from the Palace of Justice) v. Colombia, Preliminary Objections, Merits, Reparations, and Costs, Judgment, Inter-Am. Ct. H.R. (ser. C) No. 287, para. 591 (Nov. 14, 2014); Río Negro Massacres v. Guatemala, Inter-Am. Ct. H.R. (ser. C) No. 250, para. 307 (Sept. 4, 2012).

[39] *E.g.*, Caracazo v. Venezuela, Reparations and Costs, Judgment, Inter-Am. Ct. H.R. (ser. C) No. 95, para. 88 (Aug. 29, 2002); Caballero Delgado and Santana v. Colombia, Reparations and Costs, Judgment, Inter-Am. Ct. H.R. (ser. C) No. 31, para. 40 (Jan. 29, 1997).

[40] *See* Sergio García Ramírez, *La Jurisprudencia de la Corte Interamericana de Derechos Humanos en Materia de Reparaciones*, *in* LA CORTE INTERAMERICANA DE DERECHOS HUMANOS: UN CUARTO DE SIGLO 1, 47 (2005), *available at* http://www.corteidh.or.cr/docs/libros/cuarto%20de%20siglo.pdf; JO M. PASQUALUCCI, THE PRACTICE AND PROCEDURE OF THE INTER-AMERICAN COURT OF HUMAN RIGHTS 230–35 (2d ed. 2013).

[41] *See, e.g.*, STAN OWINGS, UNDERSTANDING EARNING CAPACITY ASSESSMENT AND EARNING CAPACITY OPTIONS 69–109 (2009) (reviewing the numerous factors that are currently considered in assessing earnings capacity).

[42] *See* García Ramírez, *supra* note 40, at 48 (citing Bámaca Velásquez v. Guatemala, Inter-Am. Ct. H.R. (ser. C) No. 91, para. 4 (Feb. 22, 2002) (separate opinion of Judge García Ramírez)).

25 percent of earnings for personal expenses—an amount criticized as too large for indigent victims.[43]

When determining pecuniary damages in equity, the Court will take into account plausible information submitted by petitioners, even if documentation is lacking, and objective factors such as minimum wage for lost earnings.[44] For example, the Tribunal not infrequently hears cases of farmers who offer little evidence of their income and assets. In two judgments against Mexico, *Fernández Ortega* and *Rosendo Cantú*, the Tribunal found that the petitioners were unable to farm owing to several rights violations. It determined lost earnings in equity as $5,500, taking into account "the annual value of the harvest produced" from their parcels of land; some petitioners had estimated the harvest value as $5,468, but did not submit corroborating documentation.[45] Yet this basic approach has not always been applied. In *Sarayaku v. Ecuador*, petitioners provided information about the community's production of yuca and its approximate value; yet there is little indication that these data points were seriously considered by the Court.[46]

Under the heading of "indirect" or "consequential" damages, the Court has compensated victims for a variety of expenses, for example: costs associated with personal security, exile to another country, criminal investigations, searches for missing persons, transportation, lodging, and funerals.[47] This category is very broad, often including, for instance, expenses for medical and psychological treatment.[48] As such consequences may have a direct relationship with the violations at issue, the terminology used in some official English translations of judgments—"indirect" and "consequential"—appears inaccurate.[49] In fact, *daño emergente*, the Spanish term that is used by both the

[43] *Id.*

[44] *See* PASQUALUCCI, *supra* note 40, at 230–31; García Ramírez, *supra* note 40, at 47.

[45] Fernández Ortega et al. v. Mexico, Inter-Am. Ct. H.R. (ser. C) No. 215, paras. 285–286 (Aug. 30, 2010); Rosendo Cantú v. Mexico, Inter-Am. Ct. H.R. (ser. C) No. 216, para. 274 (Aug. 31, 2010). *See also* Cabrera García and Montiel Flores v. Mexico, Inter-Am. Ct. H.R. (ser. C) No. 220, para. 253 (Nov. 26, 2010) (taking a similar approach); Kuna Indigenous People of Madungandi and Embera Indigenous People of Bayano and their Members v. Panama, Preliminary Objections, Merits, Reparations, and Costs, Judgment, Inter-Am. Ct. H.R. (ser. C) No. 284 (Oct. 14, 2014) (granting significant economic damages).

[46] Sarayaku Community's Brief containing Pleadings, Motions, and Evidence, p. 118 (copy provided by the Inter-American Court's Secretariat and on file with authors).

[47] *E.g.*, Radilla Pacheco v. Mexico, Preliminary Objections, Merits, Reparations, and Costs, Judgment, Inter-Am. Ct. H.R. (ser. C) No. 209, para. 368 (Nov. 23, 2009); Carpio Nicolle et al. v. Guatemala, Merits, Reparations, and Costs, Judgment, Inter-Am. Ct. H.R. (ser. C) No. 117, paras. 110-111 (Nov. 22, 2004).

[48] *E.g.*, Tibi v. Ecuador, Preliminary Objections, Merits, Reparations, and Costs, Judgment, Inter-Am. Ct. H.R. (ser. C) No. 114, para. 237 (Sept. 7, 2004); Carpio Nicolle et al. v. Guatemala, Merits, Reparations, and Costs, Judgment, Inter-Am. Ct. H.R. (ser. C) No. 117, paras. 112-113 (Nov. 22, 2004).

[49] Black's Law Dictionary defines "consequential damages" as "losses that do not flow directly and immediately from an injurious act but that result indirectly from the act" (compare with "actual damages," defined as "an amount awarded to a complainant to compensate for a proven injury or loss; damages that repay actual losses.—Also termed compensatory damages"). BLACK'S LAW DICTIONARY (Bryan A. Garner ed. 1996).

Court and many national tribunals for this concept, generally refers to "actual" or "real" damages.[50]

For years, the Tribunal has awarded compensation for victims' medical and psychological expenses. It also may order an additional amount for future expenses, if continued treatment is proven to be necessary.[51] Oddly, the Court has sporadically placed these future medical expenses under non-pecuniary, or moral, damages.[52] After 2004, the Tribunal has not commonly ordered specific sums for future medical and psychological expenses, although such an order is possible.[53]

Occasionally, the Court has awarded pecuniary compensation under a separate heading, known as *daño patrimonial familiar*, which expressly recognizes harm to a family's assets or estate.[54] This generally occurs in cases of persecution, where families have had to flee their homes and establish themselves again in other communities, often abroad. As one would expect, employment and schooling have been severely disrupted in these scenarios. The Tribunal looks for "a substantial change" in the family's "conditions and quality of life that are a direct consequence of the acts that can be attributed to the State."[55] If this standard is not met, the Court may still order the more typical monetary and non-monetary reparations.[56]

In cases that require challenging calculations for damages, the Tribunal has remitted matters to domestic institutions for resolution.[57] For example, in *Ivcher Bronstein v. Peru*, the Court left determinations of profits that a majority shareholder would have earned to

---

[50] *See, e.g.*, Universidad Nacional Autónoma de México Instituto de Investigaciones Jurídicas, Diccionario de Derecho Procesal Constitucional y Convencional (2014).

[51] *E.g.*, Molina Theissen v. Guatemala, Inter-Am. Ct. H.R. (ser. C) No. 108, para. 71 (July 3, 2004) (included under non-pecuniary damages); Bulacio v. Argentina, Inter-Am. Ct. H.R. (ser. C) No. 100, para. 100 (Sept. 18, 2003) (included under non-pecuniary damages).

[52] *Id.*

[53] *See* Section V(C) *infra* on rehabilitation measures. For future medical expenses, *see e.g.*, Bayarri v. Argentina, Preliminary Objection, Merits, Reparations, and Costs, Judgment, Inter-Am. Ct. H.R. (ser. C) No. 187, para. 142 (Oct. 30, 2008).

[54] *E.g.*, Gutiérrez Soler v. Colombia, Merits, Reparations, and Costs, Judgment, Inter-Am. Ct. H.R. (ser. C) No. 132, paras. 77–78 (Sept. 12, 2005); Molina Theissen, Reparations (Art. 63(1) American Convention on Human Rights), Judgment (ser. C), No. 108, para. 59 (July 3, 2004).

[55] Gutiérrez and Family v. Argentina, Merits, Reparations, and Costs, Judgment, Inter-Am. Ct. H.R. (ser. C) No. 271, para. 93 (Nov. 25, 2013). The Court has also discussed how human rights violations can disrupt an individual victim's life plan or "life project" (*proyecto de vida*). However, these consequences are generally not addressed within a separate "life project" category in reparations. *But see* Gutiérrez Soler v. Colombia, Merits, Reparations, and Costs, Judgment, Inter-Am. Ct. H.R. (ser. C) No. 132, para. 89 (Sept. 12, 2005); Loayza Tamayo v. Peru, 1998 Inter-Am. Ct. H.R. (ser. C) No. 42, paras. 147-54 (Nov. 27, 1998).

[56] *Id.* para. 94 (finding that the alleged "damage to the family wealth" was "not a direct consequence of these violations, and that, in this case, it is subsumed within the amounts for pecuniary and non-pecuniary damage").

[57] *E.g.*, "Five Pensioners" v. Peru, Merits, Reparations, and Costs, Judgment, Inter-Am. Ct. H.R. (ser. C) No. 98, para. 178 (Feb. 28, 2003); Cesti Hurtado v. Peru, Reparations and Costs, 2001 Inter-Am. Ct. H.R. (ser. C) No. 78, paras. 46-47 (May 31, 2001).

"the competent national authorities."[58] In its judgments regarding wrongful termination of employment, it has also deferred to domestic law for pecuniary compensation.[59]

In *Salvador Chiriboga v. Ecuador*, the Court held a separate reparations phase to evaluate varying assessments of an expropriated property; some of these valuation studies had been produced during domestic proceedings.[60] As previously noted in this volume, the Court did not accept market value as the principal standard for the expensive land at issue, despite the usual practice in international law.[61] It held that, for "adequate compensation" in expropriation matters, states should contemplate the property's market value, *but also provide a "fair balance between the general interest and the [owner's] interest."*[62] This ambiguous balancing test reflects the Court's increased use of discretion and equity to determine several types of material damages and compensation.

In this way, the Court's determination of pecuniary damages has become opaque and prone to unpredictable—and unfortunate—results.[63] In *Saramaka People v. Suriname*, the State had granted logging concessions in the petitioners' traditional territory.[64] The Court found that "a considerable quantity of valuable timber was extracted" without any compensation, and the community was "left with a legacy of environmental destruction."[65] In response, the Court ordered Suriname to pay $75,000 for the timber taken and related property damage.[66] The Court determined the amount "based on equitable grounds," without explaining its calculations further.[67]

---

[58] Ivcher Bronstein v. Peru, Merits, Reparations, and Costs, Judgment, Inter-Am. Ct. H.R. (ser. C) No. 74, para. 191 (Feb. 6, 2001).

[59] *E.g.*, Acevedo Jaramillo et al. v. Peru, Preliminary Objections, Merits, Reparations, and Costs, Judgment, Inter-Am. Ct. H.R. (ser. C) No. 144, para. 300 (Feb. 7, 2006); Baena Ricardo et al. v. Panama, Merits, Reparations, and Costs, Judgment, Inter-Am. Ct. H.R. (ser. C) No. 72, para. 214 (Feb. 2, 2001).

[60] Salvador Chiriboga v. Ecuador, Reparations and Costs, Judgment, Inter-Am. Ct. H.R. (ser. C) No. 222 (Mar. 3, 2011).

[61] International law frequently requires that the amount of compensation should be equivalent to the fair market value of the expropriated property immediately before the expropriation took place. *See, e.g.*, Ursula Kriebaum & August Reinisch, *Right to Property*, *in* MAX PLANCK ENCYCLOPEDIA OF PUBLIC INTERNATIONAL LAW (2009), at paras. 1, 29.

[62] Salvador Chiriboga v. Ecuador, Reparations and Costs, Judgment, Inter-Am. Ct. H.R. (ser. C) No. 222, para. 98 (Mar. 3, 2011) (emphasis added). The Court added that interest should also be paid from the "date that the victim actually lost the right to enjoy possession of the property." *Id.* at para. 100. For further discussion, *see* this volume's chapter on the right to property.

[63] Cristián Correa states that the Court's increased use of equity has resulted in inconsistent monetary damages, concluding that "this situation constitutes a weakness in its case law." Cristián Correa, *Artículo 63: Reparaciones y Medidas Provisionales*, *in* LA CONVENCIÓN AMERICANA SOBRE DERECHOS HUMANOS COMENTADA 859 (Christian Steiner & Patricia Uribe eds., 2014) (translation by authors).

[64] Saramaka People v. Suriname, Inter-Am. Ct. H.R. (ser. C) No. 172, para. 153 (Nov. 28, 2007).

[65] *Id.* para 153.

[66] The judgment added that amount to a $600,000 community development fund, which it established to redress the "suffering and distress" of the Saramaka community. *Id.* para. 200.

[67] *Id.* para. 199.

However, the Saramaka community's expert—who possessed 35 years of experience assessing environmental and social impacts—had "conservatively" estimated the extracted timber's market value as over 10 million dollars.[68] The expert's conclusions on forest damage and timber value appear to have gone largely ignored. Despite the Court's acceptance of "environmental destruction" and the petitioners' calls for market value compensation, the judgment set a very disappointing standard for pecuniary damages and thus undermined the community's rights to its land and resources.[69] It may also discourage petitioners from obtaining costly expert assessments, if it is uncertain that the Tribunal will seriously consider them. Nevertheless, petitioners must submit as much evidence as possible to substantiate pecuniary damages, in order to curtail the Court's discretion and eventually secure fair reparations.

B. MORAL DAMAGES

1. In General

To redress moral damages, the Court generally orders both monetary and non-monetary remedies. Moral harm is defined as "the suffering and affliction caused to the direct victim and to his next of kin, the impairment of values that are of great significance to the individual, as well as the alterations of a non-pecuniary nature in the living conditions of the victims or their families."[70] The Court determines cash compensation under this category "through reasonable application of judicial discretion and equity."[71] Non-monetary measures, for their part, are ordered "to commemorate and dignify victims, as well as to avoid the repetition of human rights violations."[72] We consider such non-monetary remedies in the following section.

The Court presumes moral damages in several instances, such as in cases of cruel, inhuman, or degrading treatment; "aggressions"; arbitrary detention; and when an individual suffers the loss of a close family member.[73] It has generally ordered between approximately

---

[68] Affidavit of Dr. Robert Goodland, Expert Witness, para. 34 (Apr. 27, 2007), *available at* http://www.corteidh.or.cr/casos.cfm.

[69] Saramaka People v. Suriname, Inter-Am. Ct. H.R. (ser. C) No. 172, para. 153 (Nov. 28, 2007). For more analysis on this point, *see* Antkowiak, *supra* note 15, at 68–70.

[70] *E.g.*, Rodriguez Vera et al. (Persons Disappeared from the Palace of Justice) v. Colombia, Preliminary Objections, Merits, Reparations, and Costs, Judgment, Inter-Am. Ct. H.R. (ser. C) No. 287, para. 600 (Nov. 14, 2014); Río Negro Massacres v. Guatemala, Inter-Am. Ct. H.R. (ser. C) No. 250, para. 307 (Sept. 4, 2012).

[71] *E.g.*, Moiwana Cmty. v. Suriname, Inter-Am. Ct. H.R. (ser. C) No. 124, para. 191 (June 15, 2005); Serrano Cruz Sisters v. El Salvador, Inter-Am. Ct. H.R. (ser. C) No. 120, para. 156 (Mar. 1, 2005).

[72] Moiwana Cmty. v. Suriname, Inter-Am. Ct. H.R. (ser. C) No. 124, para. 191 (June 15, 2005).

[73] *E.g.*, Maritza Urrutia v. Guatemala, Merits, Reparations, and Costs, Judgment, Inter-Am. Ct. H.R. (ser. C) No. 103, para. 168 (Nov. 27, 2003); Berenson Mejía v. Peru, Inter-Am. Ct. H.R. (ser. C) No. 119, para. 237 (Nov. 25, 2004). Citing to various Court judgments, Jo Pasqualucci states, "evidence is not necessary to prove non-pecuniary damages to a person who has been subject to cruel, inhuman, and degrading treatment, extrajudicial execution, forced disappearance, or arbitrary detention." PASQUALUCCI, *supra* note 40, at 236.

$50,000 and $100,000 for forced disappearances,[74] acts of torture,[75] and extrajudicial executions.[76] In addition, close family members who suffered intensely in these situations have received similar amounts.[77] The Tribunal usually orders less compensation for other rights violations.

Because most victims in Court judgments have experienced a series of abuses, and all situations are unique, it is difficult to precisely determine how a specific violation is "quantified" in terms of moral damages. The judges take into account various factors impacting each particular victim, and also consider similar precedents from the Tribunal's case law.[78] However, although a case-by-case approach is justifiable, at times the moral damages for the same type of violation will fluctuate excessively among judgments.

Occasionally, the Court orders only minimal damages, despite proof of moral harm. In fact, a few judgments involving confirmed criminals as victims required no monetary compensation at all for moral damages.[79] Although such a result is not without

---

[74] *See, e.g.*, Rodriguez Vera et al. (Persons Disappeared from the Palace of Justice) v. Colombia, Preliminary Objections, Merits, Reparations, and Costs, Judgment, Inter-Am. Ct. H.R. (ser. C) No. 287, para. 603 (Nov. 14, 2014) ($100,000 ordered for forced disappearance); Gómez Palomino v. Peru, Merits, Reparations, and Costs, Judgment, Inter-Am. Ct. H.R. (ser. C) No. 136 (Nov. 22, 2005) ($100,000 ordered for forced disappearance); Goiburú et al. v. Paraguay, Merits, Reparations, and Costs, Judgment, Inter-Am. Ct. H.R. (ser. C) No. 153 (Sept. 22, 2006) ($50,000 ordered for forced disappearance).

[75] *See, e.g.*, Espinoza Gonzales v. Peru, Preliminary Objections, Merits, Reparations, Costs, Judgment, Inter-Am. Ct. H.R. (ser. C) No. 289, para. 334 (Nov. 20, 2014) ($60,000 ordered for torture); Fernandez Ortega et al. v. Mexico, Preliminary Objections, Merits, Reparations, and Costs, Judgment, Inter-Am. Ct. H.R. (ser. C) No. 215 (Aug. 30, 2010) ($50,000 ordered for torture); Bueno Alves v. Argentina, Merits, Reparations, and Costs, Judgment, Inter-Am. Ct. H.R. (Ser. C) No. 164 (May 11, 2007) ($100,000 ordered for torture).

[76] *See, e.g.*, Gutiérrez and Family v. Argentina, Merits, Reparations, and Costs, Judgment, Inter-Am. Ct. H.R. (ser. C) No. 271, para. 186 (Nov. 25, 2013) ($75,000 ordered for an extrajudicial execution); Escué Zapata v. Colombia, Merits, Reparations, and Costs, Judgment, Inter-Am. Ct. H.R. (ser. C) No. 165 (July 4, 2007) ($50,000 ordered for an extrajudicial execution); Cepeda Vargas v. Colombia, Preliminary Objections, Merits, Reparations, and Costs, Judgment, Inter-Am. Ct. H.R. (ser. C.) No. 213 (May 26, 2010) ($80,000 ordered for an extrajudicial execution).

[77] *See, e.g.*, Gómez Palomino v. Peru, Merits, Reparations, and Costs, Judgment, Inter-Am. Ct. H.R. (ser. C) No. 136 (Nov. 22, 2005) (victim's mother and daughter each received $80,000); Rodriguez Vera et al. v. Colombia, Preliminary Objections, Merits, Reparations, and Costs, Judgment, Inter-Am. Ct. H.R. (ser. C) No. 287 (Nov. 14, 2014) (close family members each received $80,000). In fact, in *Mack Chang*, the victim's daughter received $110,000, nearly three times what her executed mother was ordered. Mack Chang v. Guatemala, Merits, Reparations, and Costs, Judgment, Inter-Am. Ct. H.R. (ser. C) No. 101 (Nov. 25, 2003).

[78] *See* Rodriguez Vera et al. v. Colombia, Preliminary Objections, Merits, Reparations, and Costs, Judgment, Inter-Am. Ct. H.R. (ser. C) No. 287, para. 603 (Nov. 14, 2014) ("Based on the compensation ordered by the Inter-American Court in other cases of forced disappearance of persons, as well as on the circumstances of this case, the significance, nature and gravity of the violations committed, the suffering caused to the victims and their families, the time that has passed since the events occurred, and their actual impunity, the Court finds it pertinent to establish, in equity, the sum of US$100,000").

[79] Cruz Sánchez et al. v. Peru, Preliminary Objections, Merits, Reparations, Costs, Judgment, Inter-Am. Ct. H.R. (ser. C) No. 292, paras. 145, 483 (Apr. 17, 2015) (involving a member of a terrorist organization that participated, and died, in a violent operation in Peru); Raxcacó Reyes v. Guatemala, Merits, Reparations, and Costs, Judgment, Inter-Am. Ct. H.R. (ser. C) No. 133, para. 131 (Sept. 15, 2005) (involving an individual who was convicted of kidnapping and suffered rights violations); Fermín Ramírez v. Guatemala, Merits, Reparations,

international precedent,[80] it seems problematic considering that all victims of rights violations are entitled to adequate redress—and preferably to those reparations that correspond to their situation and needs.[81] Another important factor for monetary damages appears to be the number of potential beneficiaries in a case. The Court generally reduces moral damages in judgments with larger numbers of victims.[82] That is, in multiple-petitioner cases, victims may, regrettably, obtain less monetary compensation than they would have received in a smaller case. This is likely done to make the payment of reparations more feasible for the respondent State.[83]

In these cases, the Court often requires substantial non-monetary reparations, frequently of a collective nature, as described below. There is no doubt that several of these remedies, such as public apologies, offer powerful redress on both communal and individual levels. Nevertheless, the Court's inconsistent monetary damages are troubling: if human rights are not enforced with sufficient remedies, the rights are diminished or even disregarded entirely.[84]

Particularly in the large cases, the Court is faced with limitations and difficult choices for reparations. Thomas Antkowiak has urged the Court to fully adopt a "victim-centered approach"[85] and "empower victims to define the restoration that matters to them."[86] Although victims' demands cannot always be met, Antkowiak maintains that their priorities must be understood—and then channeled into reparations consistent with the proven violations.[87] To illustrate, when a petitioner shows moral harm and expresses the

---

and Costs, Judgment, Inter-Am. Ct. H.R. (ser. C) No. 126, para. 130 (June 20, 2005) (involving an individual who was convicted of murder and suffered rights violations).

[80] *See, e.g.*, McCann and Others v. the United Kingdom, Eur. Ct. H.R., App. No. 18984/91(Sept. 27, 1995).

[81] *See* discussion of a "victim-centered" remedial approach in the following paragraphs.

[82] *See* Thomas M. Antkowiak, *Remedial Approaches to Human Rights Violations: The Inter-American Court of Human Rights and Beyond*, 46 Colum. J. Transnat'l L. 351, 397–99 (2008). In some group cases, victims have requested and proven individual moral damages, but did not receive any Court order for compensation. *E.g.*, "Juvenile Reeducation Institute" v. Paraguay, Inter-Am. Ct. H.R. (ser. C) No. 112, paras. 297, 309 (Sept. 2, 2004) (granting compensation to only certain categories of victims, despite compensation requests for all victims); Ituango Massacres v. Colombia, Inter-Am. Ct. H.R. (ser. C) No. 148, paras. 381, 397 (July 1, 2006) (same).

[83] *See* Carlos M. Beristain, Diálogos sobre la Reparación: Experiencias en el sistema interamericano de derechos humanos, Vol. II 178 (2008) (quoting a current Inter-American Court judge, who stated: "If you have to compensate three hundred people, you have to think realistically about a [judgment] of millions [of dollars against] the State, which possibly will not comply. So you need to find in equity an amount that helps the victim . . . and that does not make the State react negatively.") (translation by authors).

[84] *See, e.g.*, Daryl J. Levinson, *Rights Essentialism and Remedial Equilibration*, 99 Colum. L. Rev. 857, 887 (1999) ("rights can be effectively enlarged, abridged, or eviscerated by expanding, contracting, or eliminating remedies"); Richard H. Fallon, Jr., *The Linkage between Justiciability and Remedies—and Their Connections to Substantive Rights*, 92 Va. L. Rev. 633, 685–86 (2006) ("the more extensive and potent the enforcement mechanisms, the more valuable a right becomes").

[85] Thomas M. Antkowiak, *An Emerging Mandate for International Courts: Victim-Centered Remedies and Restorative Justice*, 47 Stan. J. Int'l L. 279, 281–92 (2011); Antkowiak, *supra* note 15, at 52.

[86] John Braithwaite, Restorative Justice and Responsive Regulation 46 (2002).

[87] Antkowiak, *supra* note 15, at 4. To fully assess relevant evidence and victim priorities, separate hearings on reparations may be required.

preference for a reasonable cash payment over other forms of reparation, some degree of individualized compensation must be provided—notwithstanding the size of the case.[88] Under these circumstances, even with modest sums the Court will expressly affirm individual and collective rights.[89]

2. Community Development Programs

For years now, the Court has established development funds for communities who have been displaced, attacked, or otherwise threatened.[90] The funds, at times reaching over 1 million dollars,[91] are often ordered as a collective remedy for moral damages.[92] Community leaders have frequently asked for these funds, although often with the condition that they be deployed in accordance with their modes of governance and customs.[93] Before *Sarayaku v. Ecuador*, nevertheless, the Court placed restrictions upon the funds. For example, *Saramaka People v. Suriname* provided that the fund "will serve to

[88] The sum should not be presented as full compensation for suffering, as in these terms it will certainly disappoint. *See* Pablo de Greiff, *Justice and Reparations*, *in* THE HANDBOOK OF REPARATIONS 451, 466 (Pablo de Greiff ed., 2006). The Court should openly recognize that it is reducing monetary reparations for pragmatic reasons. As Paul Gewirtz argued, "by candidly acknowledging that they are providing something less than a full remedy, courts leave the unfulfilled right as a beacon. This leaves open the possibility that at some point the courts will be able to furnish a more complete remedy." Paul Gewirtz, *Remedies and Resistance*, 92 YALE L.J. 585, 673 (1983).

[89] Eric Yamamoto states that individual payments and "economic justice" are "key to a personal and public sense of 'reconciliation achieved.'" Eric K. Yamamoto, *Forum on Public Policy: A Journal of the Oxford Round Table*, Vol. 2010, No. 4, Dec. 2010. Even a modest payment could have much significance, based on an understanding that "in our system of justice, when damage occurs money is paid." Yael Danieli, *Justice and Reparation: Steps in the Process of Healing*, *in* REINING IN IMPUNITY FOR INTERNATIONAL CRIMES AND SERIOUS VIOLATIONS OF FUNDAMENTAL HUMAN RIGHTS 303, 309 (Christopher C. Joyner ed., 1998).

[90] This section summarizes selected analysis in an article by this book's author Thomas M. Antkowiak, *A Dark Side of Virtue*, *supra* note 15, at 77.

[91] In *Sarayaku v. Ecuador*, the Court allocated $1,250,000 to the community development fund for "the suffering caused to the People and to their cultural identity." Kichwa Indigenous People of Sarayaku v. Ecuador, Merits and Reparations, Judgment, Inter-Am. Ct. H.R. (ser. C) No. 245, para. 323 (June 27, 2012). For other substantial development funds, *see, e.g.*, Sawhoyamaxa Indigenous Cmty. v. Paraguay, Merits, Reparations, and Costs, Judgment, Inter-Am. Ct. H.R. (ser. C) No. 146, para. 224 (Mar. 29, 2006) ($1,000,000); Yakye Axa Indigenous Cmty. v. Paraguay, Merits, Reparations, and Costs, Inter-Am. Ct. H.R. (ser. C) No. 125, para. 205 (June 17, 2005) ($950,000); Moiwana Cmty. v. Suriname, Inter-Am. Ct. H.R. (ser. C) No. 124, para. 214 (June 15, 2005) ($1,200,000).

[92] This approach began in *Mayagna (Sumo) Awas Tingni v. Nicaragua*. Mayagna (Sumo) Awas Tingni Cmty. v. Nicaragua, Inter-Am. Ct. H.R. (ser. C) No. 79, para. 167 (Aug. 31, 2001). In *Saramaka*, the fund was to redress the "denigration of their basic cultural and spiritual values" and "alterations to the very fabric of their society." Saramaka People v. Suriname, Inter-Am. Ct. H.R. (ser. C) No. 172, para. 201 (Nov. 28, 2007). *But see* Kaliña and Lokono Peoples v. Suriname, Merits, Reparations and Costs, Judgment, Inter-Am. Ct. H.R. (ser. C) No. 309, para. 295 (Nov. 25, 2015) (establishing a community development fund "as compensation for the pecuniary and non-pecuniary damage suffered").

[93] *See, e.g.*, Saramaka People v. Suriname, Inter-Am. Ct. H.R. (ser. C) No. 172, para. 192 (Nov. 28, 2007) ("all determined and implemented with the informed participation and consent of the Saramaka people").

finance educational, housing, agricultural, and health projects, as well as provide electricity and drinking water, if necessary, for the benefit of the Saramaka people."[94] Decisions to use these development funds were left to "implementation committees" composed of one representative appointed by the community, another by the State, and a third jointly named by the community and the government.[95]

In *Sarayaku* the Court finally abandoned this approach, granting the community full control over the assets. Such a reform was vital, because these funds serve as reparations for human rights violations. Regardless of how one chooses to conceptualize the programs, as material or moral redress, they cannot impose constraints on victims.

Defining the development funds as moral reparations affords the Court a dubious flexibility. By not characterizing the programs as material damages, it need not concern itself with market value or financial and technical evidence. Rather, the Tribunal can control non-pecuniary awards to an extent, as subjective estimates of "pain and suffering." Standards for moral damages, furthermore, are relatively modest in the Court's case law, as reviewed above. In this way, a non-pecuniary framework allows the Court to limit high-priced judgments against States. Consequently, defendant States, which already owe the communities some level of social investment and face far more expensive possibilities, have not strongly objected to the Court's questionable approach.[96]

V. Non-Monetary Remedies

A. BACKGROUND

One of the defining characteristics of the Inter-American Court's contemporary case law is its emphasis upon non-monetary remedies, in direct response to victims' repeated petitions.[97] The Court is the only international body with binding jurisdiction that has consistently ordered the full range of such measures, in conjunction with cash

[94] *Id.* para. 201. Some commentators have suggested that the Court's development programs may go too far, because they relate to social, economic, and cultural rights not fully established in the American Convention. *See* Iris T. Figueroa, *Remedies without Rights?: Reparations and ESC Rights in the Inter-American System* (May 2010), *available at* http://works.bepress.com/iris_figueroa/1.

[95] *Id.* para. 202. This committee in *Saramaka* follows other judgments such as *Moiwana* and *Yakye Axa*. Moiwana Cmty. v. Suriname, Inter-Am. Ct. H.R. (ser. C) No. 124, para. 215 (June 15, 2005); Yakye Axa Indigenous Cmty. v. Paraguay, Inter-Am. Ct. H.R. (ser. C) No. 125, para. 206 (June 17, 2005).

[96] The Inter-American Commission has held that reparations "must not be confused with the provision of basic social services that the State is bound to provide in any case by virtue of its obligations in the field of economic, social and cultural rights." Inter-Am. Comm'n on H.R., Indigenous and Tribal Peoples' Rights over Their Ancestral Lands and Natural Resources: Norms and Jurisprudence of the Inter-American Human Rights System, para. 243, Doc. No. 56/09, OEA/Ser.L/V/II (2009), *available at* http://www.oas.org/en/iachr/indigenous/docs/pdf/AncestralLands.pdf. *See also* Naomi Roht-Arriaza, *Reparations Decisions and Dilemmas*, 27 HASTINGS INT'L & COMP. L. REV. 157, 188 (2004) ("Human rights groups have objected to this conflation of obligations as an abdication of the state's legal obligation to respond to past injustices").

[97] This section summarizes and updates selected analysis in an article by this book's author Thomas M. Antkowiak, *Remedial Approaches to Human Rights Violations*, *supra* note 82, at 365–87.

compensation.[98] Below we review examples from the following non-monetary remedies ordered by the Tribunal: restitution, rehabilitation, apologies, memorials, legislative reform, and training programs for State officials.

The Court also calls for criminal investigation and prosecution in many judgments. It holds that these requirements derive from a State's general obligation to respect and ensure human rights, as established in the American Convention's Article 1(1).[99] Thus, investigation and prosecution—and other measures that seek to stop or prevent recurrence of violations—originate in Article 1 and are technically independent from a State Party's duty to redress individual victims, found in Article 63. The International Law Commission has also drawn this conceptual distinction, contrasting individual reparations with measures such as prosecution, cessation, and legal reform.[100] In any event, it is impossible to deny that all of these measures have crucial reparative effects on the individual level, providing satisfaction due to victims and family members.[101]

B. RESTITUTION

The Court has demanded the restitution of employment, including cases involving over 200 employees.[102] Judgments have also ordered the restitution of property, from intellectual property to ancestral lands. In *Ivcher Bronstein v. Peru*, the Court obligated the State "to enable [the victim] . . . to recover the use and enjoyment of his rights as majority shareholder" of his media company, after such rights were suspended by Peruvian authorities.[103] In *Cantos v. Argentina*, the State was required "to lift the attachments, general property encumbrances and other measures that were ordered against the properties and business assets" of José María Cantos.[104] In *Palamara Iribarne v. Chile*, the State had prevented a

---

[98] By the end of 2001, the Tribunal's current approach to expansive non-monetary redress was nearly developed. Up until the late 1990s, however, the Court generally limited its non-monetary remedies, with the exception of the judgment *Aloeboetoe v. Suriname*. *See* Aloeboetoe v. Suriname, Inter-Am. Ct. H.R. (ser. C) No. 11, paras. 11–15 (Sept. 10, 1993).

[99] Velásquez Rodríguez v. Honduras, Inter-Am. Ct. H.R. (ser. C) No. 4, paras. 166–167, 178–181 (July 29, 1988).

[100] Draft Articles on the Responsibility of States for Internationally Wrongful Acts, arts. 30-31, Report of the International Law Commission on the Work of its Fifty-third Session, U.N. GAOR, 56th Sess., Supp. No. 10, U.N. Doc. A/56/10 (2001), *available at* http://legal.un.org/ilc/texts/instruments/english/commentaries/9_6_2001.pdf.

[101] In *19 Merchants v. Colombia*, a medical doctor interviewed the many family members of the disappeared victims. He testified before the Inter-American Court that these family members showed a "fundamental need" that the facts be investigated and that the crimes be punished, so that they could move on with their lives. 19 Merchants v. Colombia, Merits, Reparations, and Costs, Judgment, Inter-Am. Ct. H.R. (ser. C) No. 109, para. 72(g) (July 5, 2004).

[102] *E.g.*, Baena Ricardo v. Panama, Inter-Am. Ct. H.R. (ser. C) No. 72, para. 214(7) (Feb. 2, 2001); De la Cruz Flores v. Peru, Inter-Am. Ct. H.R. (ser. C) No. 115, paras. 169–171 (Nov. 18, 2004).

[103] Ivcher Bronstein v. Peru, Inter-Am. Ct. H.R. (ser. C) No. 74, para. 191 (Feb. 6, 2001).

[104] Cantos v. Argentina, Inter-Am. Ct. H.R. (July 6, 2009) (Order on Supervision of Compliance with Judgments).

retired admiral from publishing his critical account of the Chilean Navy.[105] The judgment ordered Chile to return the seized copies and to allow the publication of the work.[106]

In several cases before the Court, indigenous and tribal communities sought to recover or protect their traditional lands.[107] In response, the Tribunal has not only endorsed the communities' rights to their territories, but it has also required the establishment of domestic laws and procedures to make such rights effective.[108] The Court discourages States from furnishing alternate lands or monetary compensation.[109] In these judgments, the Tribunal recognizes that the ancestral territory represents a "perpetual resource" with spiritual, cultural, and economic dimensions that sustain both present and future generations.[110] In addition to land restitution and legislative/administrative reforms, the Tribunal has required cleanup and reforestation of damaged lands and resources.[111] The Court has also ordered States to guarantee the safety of community members who fear returning to their homes.[112]

As noted elsewhere in this volume, the Tribunal frequently hears cases involving due process violations. Procedural abuses have resulted in Court orders to reverse criminal convictions,[113] grant retrials,[114] cancel death sentences,[115] expunge criminal records,[116]

---

105 Palamara Iribarne v. Chile, Inter-Am. Ct. H.R. (ser. C) No. 135 (Nov. 22, 2005).

106 *Id.* para. 269(9).

107 *See also* this volume's chapter on the right to property.

108 Saramaka People v. Suriname, Inter-Am. Ct. H.R. (ser. C) No. 172, para. 194(c) (Nov. 28, 2007) (ordering that Suriname "remove or amend the legal provisions that impede protection of the right to property of the members of the Saramaka people and adopt, in its domestic legislation, and through prior, effective and fully informed consultations with the Saramaka people, legislative, administrative, and other measures as may be required to recognize, protect, guarantee and give legal effect to the right of the members of the Saramaka people to hold collective title of the territory they have traditionally used and occupied"). *See also* Gaetano Pentassuglia, *Towards a Jurisprudential Articulation of Indigenous Land Rights*, 22 EUR. J. INT'L L. 165, 171 (2011) ("the [Court] has converted indigenous property rights into a state's obligation to delimit, demarcate, and title the lands in question, thereby requiring an effective domestic procedure to realize those rights").

109 *See* Garifuna Punta Piedra Community and its Members v. Honduras, Preliminary Objections, Merits, Reparations and Costs, Judgment, Inter-Am. Ct. H.R. (ser. C) No. 304, para. 325 (Oct. 8, 2015) (stressing that alternate lands may only be granted in "exceptional" circumstances); Xákmok Kásek Indigenous Community v. Paraguay, Inter-Am. Ct. H.R. (ser. C) No. 214, para. 284 (Aug. 24, 2010) ("State authorities must . . . [take] very much into account the special relationship that the indigenous have with their lands for preserving their culture and survival.").

110 *See* Moiwana Cmty. v. Suriname, Inter-Am. Ct. H.R. (ser. C) No. 124, para. 133 (June 15, 2005) (recognizing the "all-encompassing relationship" between communities and their traditional territories).

111 For a distinctive order requiring cleanup and reforestation, *see* Indigenous Community Kichwa of Sarayaku v. Ecuador, 2012 Inter. Am. Ct. H.R. (ser. C) No. 245, para. 294 (June 27, 2012).

112 *E.g.*, Ituango Massacres v. Colombia, Inter-Am. Ct. H.R. (ser. C) No. 148, para. 404 (July 1, 2006); Moiwana Cmty. v. Suriname, Inter-Am. Ct. H.R. (ser. C) No. 124, para. 212 (June 15, 2005).

113 *E.g.*, Herrera Ulloa v. Costa Rica, Inter-Am. Ct. H.R. (ser. C) No. 107, para. 195 (July 2, 2004); Cantoral Benavides v. Peru, Inter-Am. Ct. H.R. (ser. C) No. 88, paras. 77–78 (Dec. 3, 2001).

114 *E.g.*, Fermín Ramírez v. Guatemala, Inter-Am. Ct. H.R. (ser. C) No. 126, para. 138(7) (July 20, 2005); Hilaire v. Trinidad & Tobago, Inter-Am. Ct. H.R. (ser. C) No. 94, para. 223(9) (July 21, 2002).

115 *E.g.*, Fermín Ramírez v. Guatemala, Inter-Am. Ct. H.R. (ser. C) No. 126, para. 138(9) (July 20, 2005); Hilaire v. Trinidad & Tobago, Inter-Am. Ct. H.R. (ser. C) No. 94, para. 223(11) (July 21, 2002).

116 *E.g.*, Acosta Calderon v. Ecuador, Inter-Am. Ct. H.R. (ser. C) No. 129, para. 175(7) (June 24, 2005); Suárez Rosero v. Ecuador, Inter-Am. Ct. H.R. (ser. C) No. 44, para. 113(1) (Jan. 20, 1999).

and waive fines.[117] On only rare occasions have due process violations led the Court to demand the release of detainees.[118]

C. REHABILITATION

When appropriate, the Court currently requires the offending State to provide, through its national health institutions, free medical and psychological care to victims and their family members.[119] Without cash grants for future medical expenses, however, victims do not have the option to select often superior private health facilities. The Tribunal still appears to prefer the State provider model, particularly in judgments concerning multiple victims.[120] Yet it has specified that if the State lacks sufficiently "specialized" health institutions, private facilities must be used.[121] The Court occasionally grants a specific sum for future medical expenses, especially for victims who no longer reside in the defendant State.[122]

The Tribunal has required full university scholarships (or similar) for a case's principal victim.[123] Other judgments have provided once-detained individuals with opportunities to update their professional skills through funded courses.[124] More recently, close family

---

[117] *E.g.*, Berenson Mejía v. Peru, Inter-Am. Ct. H.R. (ser. C) No. 119, para. 248(5) (Nov. 25, 2004); Suárez Rosero v. Ecuador, Inter-Am. Ct. H.R. (ser. C) No. 44, para.113(1) (Jan. 20, 1999).

[118] Norín Catrimán et al. (Leaders, members, and activists of the Mapuche Indigenous People) v. Chile, Merits, Reparations, and Costs, Judgment, Inter-Am. Ct. H.R. (ser. C) No. 279, para. 422 (May 29, 2014); Loayza Tamayo v. Peru, Inter-Am. Ct. H.R. (ser. C) No. 33, para. 84 (Sept. 17, 1997). In contrast, victims were not ordered released, despite due process violations, in several judgments. *See, e.g.*, Berenson Mejía v. Peru, Inter-Am. Ct. H.R. (ser. C) No. 119 (Nov. 25, 2004); Castillo Pertruzzi v. Peru, Inter-Am. Ct. H.R. (ser. C) No. 41 (May 30, 1999).

[119] *E.g.*, Espinoza Gonzales v. Peru, Preliminary Objections, Merits, Reparations, Costs, Judgment, Inter-Am. Ct. H.R. (ser. C) No. 289, paras. 314–316 (Nov. 20, 2014); 19 Merchants v. Colombia, Merits, Reparations, and Costs, Judgment, Inter-Am. Ct. H.R. (ser. C) No. 109, para. 278 (July 5, 2004).

[120] *E.g.*, Rodriguez Vera et al. (Persons Disappeared from the Palace of Justice) v. Colombia, Preliminary Objections, Merits, Reparations, and Costs, Judgment, Inter-Am. Ct. H.R. (ser. C) No. 287, para. 567 (Nov. 14, 2014); 19 Merchants v. Colombia, Merits, Reparations, and Costs, Judgment, Inter-Am. Ct. H.R. (ser. C) No. 109, para. 278 (July 5, 2004). *Juvenile Reeducation Institute v. Paraguay* deserves special mention, as the Court required a psychological treatment program for over 3,000 victims. "Juvenile Reeducation Institute" v. Paraguay, Inter-Am. Ct. H.R. (ser. C) No. 112, paras. 318–320 (Sept. 2, 2004).

[121] *E.g.*, Rodriguez Vera et al. (Persons Disappeared from the Palace of Justice) v. Colombia, Preliminary Objections, Merits, Reparations, and Costs, Judgment, Inter-Am. Ct. H.R. (ser. C) No. 287, para. 567 (Nov. 14, 2014); Rochac Hernandez et al. v. El Salvador, Merits, Reparations, and Costs, Judgment, Inter-Am. Ct. H.R. (ser. C) No. 285, para. 220 (Oct. 14, 2014).

[122] *E.g.*, Rodriguez Vera et al. (Persons Disappeared from the Palace of Justice) v. Colombia, Preliminary Objections, Merits, Reparations, and Costs, Judgment, Inter-Am. Ct. H.R. (ser. C) No. 287, para. 569 (Nov. 14, 2014); Bayarri v. Argentina, Preliminary Objections, Merits, Reparations, and Costs, Judgment, Inter-Am. Ct. H.R. (ser. C) No. 187, para. 142 (Oct. 30, 2008).

[123] *E.g.*, Rosendo Cantú v. Mexico, Inter-Am. Ct. H.R. (ser. C) No. 216, para. 257 (August 31, 2010) ("either in technical or university studies"); Cantoral Benavides v. Peru, Inter-Am. Ct. H.R. (ser. C) No. 88, para. 80 (Dec. 3, 2001).

[124] *E.g.*, García Asto v. Peru, Inter-Am. Ct. H.R. (ser. C) No. 137, para. 281 (Nov. 25, 2005); De la Cruz Flores v. Peru, Inter-Am. Ct. H.R. (ser. C) No. 115, para. 170 (Nov. 18, 2004).

members of persons who were extrajudicially killed, tortured, or disappeared have been granted scholarships to "public institutions" for "all the costs of their education until the completion of their higher education, either in technical or university studies."[125]

D. Recognition of Responsibility and Apologies

The Court first required an apology in *Cantoral Benavides*.[126] The order has become more demanding, often requiring a public ceremony with the participation of top government officials.[127] Over the last 15 years, the public recognition of wrongdoing has become one of the Court's foremost remedies.

A similar reparation is the partial publication of Court judgments (or official summaries) in national newspapers and government websites, as well as their announcement over radio broadcasts and television programs.[128] The Court has ordered their translation into native languages of victim populations, when applicable.[129] It has required some form of publication or announcement by the offending State in almost every judgment since 2001.

E. Memorials and Commemorations

In addition to the public ceremonies and other measures mentioned above, the Court has ordered a variety of commemorations. *Villagrán Morales v. Guatemala*, the well-known "street children" case, required that Guatemala name a school after the five adolescents killed by state security forces, an order repeated in future cases involving young victims.[130] In *Mack Chang v. Guatemala*, the Tribunal ordered the State to establish an annual scholarship in honor of Myrna Mack Chang, a sociologist murdered by State

[125] *E.g.*, Rosendo Cantú v. Mexico, Inter-Am. Ct. H.R. (ser. C) No. 216, para. 257 (Aug. 31, 2010); Fernández Ortega et al. v. Mexico, Inter-Am. Ct. H.R. (ser. C) No. 215, para. 264 (Aug. 30, 2010).

[126] Cantoral Benavides v. Peru, Inter-Am. Ct. H.R. (ser. C) No. 88, para. 81 (Dec. 3, 2001).

[127] *E.g.*, Rodriguez Vera et al. (Persons Disappeared from the Palace of Justice) v. Colombia, Preliminary Objections, Merits, Reparations, and Costs, Judgment, Inter-Am. Ct. H.R. (ser. C) No. 287, paras. 572–573 (Nov. 14, 2014); Osorio Rivera and Family v. Peru, Preliminary Objections, Merits, Reparations, and Costs, Judgment, Inter-Am. Ct. H.R. (ser. C) No. 274, para. 264 (Nov. 26, 2013). *Mack Chang* was the first case to require the participation of high-ranking State officials. Mack Chang v. Guatemala, 2003 Inter-Am. Ct. H.R. (ser. C) No. 101, para. 278 (Nov. 25, 2003).

[128] *E.g.*, Rodriguez Vera et al. (Persons Disappeared from the Palace of Justice) v. Colombia, Preliminary Objections, Merits, Reparations, and Costs, Judgment, Inter-Am. Ct. H.R. (ser. C) No. 287, paras. 572–573 (Nov. 14, 2014); Serrano Cruz Sisters v. El Salvador, Inter-Am. Ct. H.R. (ser. C) No. 120, para. 195 (Mar. 1 2005).

[129] *E.g.*, Río Negro Massacres v. Guatemala, Inter-Am. Ct. H.R. (ser. C) No. 250 paras. 277–278 (Sept. 4, 2012); Plan de Sánchez Massacre *v.* Guatemala, Reparations, Judgment, Inter-Am. Ct. H.R. (ser. C) No. 116, paras. 100–103 (Nov. 19, 2004).

[130] *E.g.*, Gómez Paquiyauri Bros. v. Peru, Inter-Am. Ct. H.R. (ser. C) No. 110, para. 236 (July 8, 2004); Molina Theissen v. Guatemala, Inter-Am. Ct. H.R (ser. C) No. 108, para. 88 (July 3, 2004).

agents.[131] The Court also required that Guatemala name a street or square in Guatemala City after the victim, and place a plaque near the site of her death.[132] More recently, the Tribunal required a national day of remembrance for the disappeared children of El Salvador's internal conflict,[133] and ordered States to fund the production of documentaries, "because initiatives of this kind are significant both for the preservation of the memory and the satisfaction of the victims, and also for the recovery and restitution of the historical memory in a democratic society."[134]

Monuments are often required in the cases involving massacres of communities; the Court, in its better orders, has demanded close consultation with the survivors as to the design, content, and location.[135] *Río Negro Massacres v. Guatemala* concerned five brutal attacks by the Guatemalan military against indigenous communities.[136] Among other reparations, the judgment called for a program "for the rescue, promotion, dissemination and conservation of . . . ancestral customs and practices, based on the values, principles and philosophies of the Maya Achí people."[137] The Court even approved the victims' request for the construction of a museum to "honor the memory of the numerous victims of the internal armed conflict."[138]

F. REFORM OF LEGISLATION AND POLICY, TRAINING PROGRAMS

The Court declined requests to order changes to national legislation until the 1999 case *Castillo Petruzzi v. Peru*.[139] Since then, it has required constitutional and legislative reform a number of times, with varying specificity. Judgments have mandated States to conform legislation and policy to international standards in a number of areas, such as

---

[131] Mack Chang v. Guatemala, Inter-Am. Ct. H.R. (ser. C) No. 101, paras. 126, 146, 285 (Nov. 25, 2003).

[132] *Id.* para. 286. Although orders to name streets or plazas after victims are not common, the order resurfaced in *Baldeón García v. Peru*, Inter-Am. Ct. H.R. (ser. C) No. 147, para. 205 (Apr. 6, 2006).

[133] Serrano Cruz Sisters v. El Salvador, Merits, Reparations, and Costs, Judgment, Inter-Am. Ct. H.R. (ser. C) No. 120 (Mar. 1, 2005).

[134] *E.g.*, Rodriguez Vera et al. (Persons Disappeared from the Palace of Justice) v. Colombia, Preliminary Objections, Merits, Reparations, and Costs, Judgment, Inter-Am. Ct. H.R. (ser. C) No. 287, paras. 572–573 (Nov. 14, 2014); Guidel Alvarez et al. ("Diario Militar") v. Guatemala, Merits, Reparations, and Costs, Judgment, Inter-Am. Ct. H.R. (ser. C) No. 253, para. 345 (Nov. 20, 2012).

[135] *Mapiripán Massacre v. Colombia*, Inter-Am. Ct. H.R. (ser. C) No. 134 (Sept. 15, 2005), and *Pueblo Bello Massacre v. Colombia*, Inter-Am. Ct. H.R. (ser. C) No. 140 (Jan. 31, 2006), do not require such consultation with victims, although numerous other judgments have mandated this measure. *See, e.g.*, Río Negro Massacres v. Guatemala, Preliminary Objections, Merits, Reparations, and Costs, Judgment, Inter-Am. Ct. H.R. (ser. C) No. 250, para. 285 (Sept. 4, 2012); Ituango Massacres v. Colombia, Inter-Am. Ct. H.R. (ser. C) No. 148 (July 1, 2006); Moiwana Cmty. v. Suriname, Inter-Am. Ct. H.R. (ser. C) No. 124 (June 15, 2005).

[136] Río Negro Massacres v. Guatemala, Preliminary Objections, Merits, Reparations, and Costs, Judgment, Inter-Am. Ct. H.R. (ser. C) No. 250 (Sept. 4, 2012).

[137] *Id.* para. 285.

[138] *Id.* para. 279.

[139] Castillo Petruzzi v. Peru, Inter-Am. Ct. H.R. (ser. C) No. 52 (May 30, 1999).

freedom of expression,[140] indigenous land rights,[141] forced disappearance of persons,[142] due process rights,[143] voting regulations,[144] gender and sexual violence,[145] migrant rights,[146] prison conditions,[147] access to information,[148] and jurisdiction of military courts.[149] It should be noted that bills introduced to Congress by the executive branch are not sufficient to count for compliance; the Court requires the State's enactment of legislation.[150]

As for training programs and courses, those directed to national security forces are the most typical in the Court's case law.[151] However, in recent years other groups have been targeted as well, such as prosecutors, judges, prison officials, and health professionals associated with State institutions.[152]

---

[140] *E.g.*, Kimel v. Argentina, Merits, Reparations, and Costs, Judgment, Inter-Am. Ct. H.R. (ser. C) No. 177, para. 128 (May 2, 2008); "The Last Temptation of Christ" (Olmedo Bustos et al.) v. Chile, Inter-Am. Ct. H.R. (ser. C) No. 73, paras. 97–98 (Feb. 5, 2001).

[141] *E.g.*, Saramaka People v. Suriname, Inter-Am. Ct. H.R. (ser. C) No. 172, para. 214 (Nov. 28, 2007); Mayagna (Sumo) Awas Tingni Cmty. v. Nicaragua, Inter-Am. Ct. H.R. (ser. C) No. 79, para. 164 (Aug. 31, 2001).

[142] *E.g.*, Bámaca Velásquez v. Guatemala, Monitoring Compliance with Judgment, Order of the Court, Inter-Am. Ct. H.R. (Jan. 27, 2009) (insisting upon precise information on legislative reform directly related to forced disappearances, the subject matter of the case); Gómez Palomino v. Peru, Inter-Am. Ct. H.R. (ser. C) No. 136, para. 149 (Nov. 22, 2005).

[143] *E.g.*, Fermín Ramírez v. Guatemala, Merits, Reparations, and Costs, Judgment, Inter-Am. Ct. H.R. (ser. C) No. 126, para. 130 (June 20, 2005); Herrera Ulloa v. Costa Rica, Inter-Am. Ct. H.R. (ser. C) No. 107, para. 198 (July 2, 2004).

[144] YATAMA v. Nicaragua, Inter-Am. Ct. H.R. (ser. C) No. 127, paras. 258–259 (June 23, 2005).

[145] *E.g.*, Espinoza Gonzales v. Peru, Preliminary Objections, Merits, Reparations, Costs, Judgment, Inter-Am. Ct. H.R. (ser. C) No. 289, para. 322 (Nov. 20, 2014); Rosendo Cantú et al. v. Mexico, Preliminary Objections, Merits, Reparations, and Costs, Judgment, Inter-Am. Ct. H.R. (ser. C) No. 216, para. 242 (Aug. 31, 2010).

[146] Vélez Loor v. Panama, Preliminary Objections, Merits, Reparations, and Costs, Judgment, Inter-Am. Ct. H.R. (ser. C) No. 218, para. 272 (Nov. 23, 2010). *See also* Rights & Guarantees of Children in the Context of Migration and/or in Need of International Protection, Advisory Opinion OC-21/14, Inter-Am. Ct. H.R. (ser. A) No. 21 (Aug. 19, 2014); Juridical Condition & Rights of the Undocumented Migrants, Advisory Opinion OC-18/03, Inter-Am. Ct. H.R. (ser. A) No. 18 (Sept. 17, 2003).

[147] *E.g.*, Pacheco Teruel et al. v. Honduras, Merits, Reparations, and Costs, Judgment, Inter-Am. Ct. H.R. (ser. C) No. 241, para. 68 (Apr. 27, 2012); Montero Aranguren (Detention Center of Catia) v. Venezuela, Inter-Am. Ct. H.R. (ser. C) No. 150, paras. 145–146 (July 5, 2006).

[148] Claude Reyes et al. v. Chile, Merits, Reparations, and Costs, Judgment, Inter-Am. Ct. H.R. (ser. C) No. 151, para. 163 (Sept. 19, 2006).

[149] *E.g.*, Rosendo Cantú et al. v. Mexico, Preliminary Objections, Merits, Reparations, and Costs, Judgment, Inter-Am. Ct. H.R. (ser. C) No. 216, paras. 222–223 (Aug. 31, 2010); Palamara Iribarne v. Chile, Inter-Am. Ct. H.R. (ser. C) No. 135, paras. 256–257 (Nov. 22, 2005).

[150] *E.g.*, Goiburú et al. v. Paraguay, Monitoring Compliance with Judgment, Order of the Court, Inter-Am. Ct. H.R. (Nov. 19, 2009); Gómez Palomino v. Peru, Monitoring Compliance with Judgment, Order of the Court, Inter-Am. Ct. H.R. (July 1, 2009).

[151] *E.g.*, Vélez Restrepo and relatives v. Colombia, Inter-Am. Ct. H.R. (ser. C) No. 248, para. 277 (Sept. 3, 2012); Blanco Romero v. Venezuela, Inter-Am. Ct. H.R. (ser. C) No. 138, para. 106 (Nov. 28, 2005).

[152] *E.g.*, Espinoza Gonzales v. Peru, Inter-Am. Ct. H.R. (ser. C) No. 289, para. 327 (Nov. 20, 2014) (prosecutors and judges); Gutiérrez Soler v. Colombia, Inter-Am. Ct. H.R. (ser. C) No. 132, paras. 106–110 (Sept. 12, 2005) (training for police, judges, prosecutors, and health professionals working in State institutions).

VI. Legal Fees and Expenses

When States are found responsible for human rights violations, the Court customarily awards legal fees and expenses because, according to the Tribunal, they "form part of the concept of reparation" under Article 63.[153] It compensates for costs incurred in the case's litigation before national authorities, as well as before the Inter-American Commission and Court. The determination is made in equity, "taking into account the expenses indicated by the parties" as well as their accompanying documentation and justifications, "provided that their *quantum* is reasonable."[154] On occasion, the Court has awarded future legal expenses that the victims are likely to encounter.[155]

The Tribunal shows restraint in this area, dismissing those claims that "do not have a direct and exclusive relationship with the litigation" of the case.[156] Reimbursement requests for general overhead costs and advocacy activities not closely related to a case have been rejected.[157] The Court varies in its method for reimbursement: at times it conveys the sums to the victims; on other occasions, States are ordered to pay the attorneys or legal organizations directly.[158] Also, the Tribunal currently provides for additional expenses and fees incurred during a judgment's compliance stage.[159]

Compensation awarded under this category often appears unreasonably low, rendering litigation before the Inter-American System prohibitively expensive for many individual attorneys and even organizations.[160] For example, in *Yean and Bosico v. the*

---

[153] *E.g.*, Espinoza Gonzales v. Peru, Preliminary Objections, Merits, Reparations, Costs, Judgment, Inter-Am. Ct. H.R. (ser. C) No. 289, para. 337 (Nov. 20, 2014); Argüelles et al. v. Argentina, Preliminary Objections, Merits, Reparations, and Costs, Judgment, Inter-Am. Ct. H.R. (ser. C) No. 288, paras. 295–296 (Nov. 20, 2014).

[154] Espinoza Gonzales v. Peru, Preliminary Objections, Merits, Reparations, Costs, Judgment, Inter-Am. Ct. H.R. (ser. C) No. 289, para. 337 (Nov. 20, 2014).

[155] *E.g.*, Cepeda Vargas v. Colombia, Preliminary Objections, Merits, Reparations, and Costs, Judgment, Inter-Am. Ct. H.R. (ser. C.) No. 213, para. 259 (May 26, 2010); Mack Chang v. Guatemala, Merits, Reparations, and Costs, Judgment, Inter-Am. Ct. H.R. (ser. C) No. 101, para. 292 (Nov. 25, 2003).

[156] *E.g.*, Radilla Pacheco v. Mexico, Preliminary Objections, Merits, Reparations, and Costs, Judgment, Inter-Am. Ct. H.R. (ser. C) No. 209, para. 382 (Nov. 23, 2009); Cesti Hurtado v. Peru, Reparations and Costs, 2001 Inter-Am. Ct. H.R. (ser. C) No. 78, para. 72 (May 31, 2001).

[157] Radilla Pacheco v. Mexico, Preliminary Objections, Merits, Reparations, and Costs, Judgment, Inter-Am. Ct. H.R. (ser. C) No. 209, para. 382 (Nov. 23, 2009).

[158] *E.g., id.* para. 385; Yean and Bosico v. Dominican Republic, Preliminary Objections, Merits, Reparations, and Costs, Judgment, Inter-Am. Ct. H.R. (ser. C) No. 130, para. 250 (Sept. 8, 2005). Pasqualucci concludes that the Court prefers that States directly pay legal representatives in the cases with many victims. PASQUALUCCI, *supra* note 40, at 244. *But see* Espinoza Gonzales v. Peru, Preliminary Objections, Merits, Reparations, Costs, Judgment, Inter-Am. Ct. H.R. (ser. C) No. 289, para. 339 (Nov. 20, 2014) (directly to legal organizations in a case with only three victims).

[159] *E.g.*, Espinoza Gonzales v. Peru, Preliminary Objections, Merits, Reparations, Costs, Judgment, Inter-Am. Ct. H.R. (ser. C) No. 289, para. 339 (Nov. 20, 2014); Ibsen Cardenas and Ibsen Peña v. Bolivia, Merits, Reparations, and Costs, Judgment, Inter-Am. Ct. H.R. (ser. C) No. 217, para. 291 (Sept. 1, 2010).

[160] There are a few exceptional cases, where substantial legal fees and expenses were granted. *See* Kuna Indigenous People of Madungandi and Embera Indigenous People of Bayano and their Members v. Panama, Preliminary Objections, Merits, Reparations, and Costs, Judgment, Inter-Am. Ct. H.R. (ser. C) No. 284, para. 253 (Oct.

Dominican Republic, three legal organizations requested approximately $90,000 for fees and expenses incurred over five years of work, but were awarded only $6,000 in total.[161] As a means to enhance access to justice, the Victims' Legal Assistance Fund was established in 2008.[162] The Fund, supported by voluntary contributions, provides financial assistance to petitioners who have proven that they lack sufficient economic resources to litigate.[163] Moreover, if the Court has appointed an "Inter-American Defender" for a petitioner who lacks legal representation, the public defender can also be compensated from the Fund.[164] If the Tribunal eventually finds the State responsible for rights violations in a case where the Fund was deployed, the State is ordered to reimburse the Fund directly.[165]

VII. Supervision and Compliance with the Court's Judgments

A. BINDING AND FINAL NATURE OF JUDGMENTS

Article 68(1) of the Convention forms the cornerstone of the Inter-American System's enforcement authority: "The States Parties to the Convention undertake to comply with the judgment of the Court in any case to which they are parties." A State Party to the Convention "must comply with its international treaty obligations in good faith (*pacta sunt servanda*)," including all substantive and procedural obligations.[166] When a State flouts a Court judgment against it, the State violates the Convention yet again: first, for its original rights abuses, and then for its breach of Article 68.[167]

14, 2014); Mack Chang v. Guatemala, Merits, Reparations, and Costs, Judgment, Inter-Am. Ct. H.R. (ser. C) No. 101, para. 291 (Nov. 25, 2003).

161 Yean and Bosico v. Dominican Republic, Preliminary Objections, Merits, Reparations, and Costs, Judgment, Inter-Am. Ct. H.R. (ser. C) No. 130, paras. 246–250 (Sept. 8, 2005).

162 Rules for the Operation of the Victims' Legal Assistance Fund of The Inter-American Court of Human Rights, entered into force on June 1, 2010, art. 2 ("Alleged victims who wish to access the Victims' Legal Assistance Fund shall so inform the Court in the brief containing pleadings, motions, and evidence. These alleged victims must indicate, by means of a sworn affidavit and other probative evidence that will satisfy the Tribunal, that they lack the economic resources necessary to cover the cost of litigation before the Inter-American Court, and state precisely the aspects of their participation in proceedings that require use of the resources of the Victims' Legal Assistance Fund."), *available at* http://www.corteidh.or.cr/docs/regla_victimas/victimas_eng.pdf.

163 *Id.*

164 Rules of Procedure of the Inter-American Court of Human Rights, art. 37.

165 Rules for the Operation of the Victims' Legal Assistance Fund of The Inter-American Court of Human Rights, art. 5.

166 *E.g.*, Baena Ricardo et al. v. Panama, Competence, Judgment, Inter-Am. Ct. H.R. (ser. C) No. 104, paras. 61, 66 (Nov. 28, 2003) ("This principle is applicable not only with regard to the substantive norms of the human rights treaties . . . but also with regard to the procedural norms, such as those referring to compliance with the decisions of the Court); Bulacio v. Argentina, Merits, Reparations, and Costs, Judgment, Inter-Am. Ct. H.R. (ser. C) No. 100, para. 117 (Sept. 18, 2003).

167 *See* Antonio Cançado Trindade, *Informe: Bases para un Proyecto de Protocolo a la Convención Americana sobre Derechos Humanos para Fortalecer su Mecanismo de Protección, in* 2 EL SISTEMA INTERAMERICANO DE PROTECCIÓN DE LOS DERECHOS HUMANOS EN EL UMBRAL DEL SIGLO XXI 48 (2003).

The Tribunal has explained that all of its "decisions"—from judgments on the merits to orders on provisional measures—are obligatory.[168] The Court has drawn upon the authority of Article 68, among other provisions, to supervise compliance and issue binding orders on judgment implementation.[169] It has insisted on numerous occasions that such State obligations may not be altered or mitigated "by invoking provisions or difficulties of domestic law."[170]

Furthermore, the Court's judgments on preliminary objections, merits, and reparations are final. As no appeal is available, States "must promptly and fully comply with such judgments."[171] The Tribunal has explained that the protection of the Convention's human rights requires proceedings that are "as brief as possible" and not subject to the "excessive formalities" of domestic law, which often provides for varied opportunities to challenge judicial rulings.[172]

Parties to a Court case may only request the clarification of judgments pursuant to the Convention's Article 67.[173] States, the Inter-American Commission, and individual petitioners have all requested interpretations of judgments; such a request does not suspend any effects of the judgment.[174] According to the Court's Rules of Procedure, the request for interpretation "shall state with precision questions relating to the meaning or scope of the judgment."[175] The Tribunal has stressed that requests "should not be used as a means

---

[168] Baena Ricardo et al. v. Panama, Competence, Judgment, Inter-Am. Ct. H.R. (ser. C) No. 104, para. 61 (Nov. 28, 2003) (holding "the obligation to comply with the provisions of the Court's decisions corresponds to a basic principle of the law on the international responsibility of the State"). Note also that the Spanish version of Article 68(1) refers to a broader term, the Court's "decision," rather than only its "judgment." Article 68(1) in Spanish provides: "*Los Estados Partes en la Convención se comprometen a cumplir la decisión de la Corte en todo caso en que sean partes.*"

[169] *Id.* para. 101.

[170] *E.g.*, *id.* para. 61; Bulacio v. Argentina, Merits, Reparations, and Costs, Judgment, Inter-Am. Ct. H.R. (ser. C) No. 100, paras. 72, 118 (Sept. 18, 2003).

[171] *E.g.*, Supervision of Compliance with Judgments (Applicability of Article 65 of the American Convention on Human Rights), Order of the Court, Inter-Am. Ct. H.R. (June 29, 2005), "Whereas" para. 2; Baena Ricardo et al. v. Panama, Competence, Judgment, Inter-Am. Ct. H.R. (ser. C) No. 104, para. 60 (Nov. 28, 2003). If the Court is not sitting, the Court's president may take certain decisions, such as whether to issue urgent protective measures. Those decisions, as well as decisions by chambers of Court judges—which would never include judgments—may be appealed to the full Court. Rules of Procedure of the Inter-American Court, arts. 27(6) and 31(2) ("Decisions of the Presidency that are not merely procedural may be appealed from to the Court").

[172] Castillo Paéz v. Peru, Order of the Court, Inter-Am. Ct. H.R. (Sept. 10, 1996), "Considering" para. 7.

[173] The International Court of Justice, the European Court of Human Rights, and the African Court of Justice and Human Rights have similar faculties of interpretation. *See* Statute of the International Court of Justice, art. 60; Rules of the European Court, Rule 79; Protocol on the Statute of the African Court of Justice and Human Rights, art. 47.

[174] Rules of Procedure of the Inter-American Court, art. 68(4). The petition must be made within 90 days from the judgment's notification. American Convention, art. 67. Upon considering the petition for interpretation, the Tribunal "shall be composed, whenever possible, of the same judges who delivered the judgment whose interpretation is being sought." Rules of Procedure of the Inter-American Court, art. 68(3).

[175] Rules of Procedure of the Inter-American Court, Article 68(1). Still, the interpretation of a judgment's "meaning or scope" leaves considerable discretion to the Court. Although its interpretation rulings have provided

of contesting" or modifying the judgment.[176] Attempts to question the Court's holding, reasoning, or evaluation of evidence—disguised as requests pursuant to Article 67—are routinely rejected.[177] However, when earnest misunderstandings are held by the parties, the Tribunal should grant prompt clarification to facilitate the judgment's implementation. It also should act quickly to correct errors, as provided by the Court's revised Rules of Procedure.[178]

B. INTRODUCTION TO SUPERVISION

The Court has monitored compliance with its rulings since its first judgments on reparations in 1989.[179] It currently supervises over 150 cases.[180] Not surprisingly, the Tribunal has recognized that this has become "one of [its] most demanding activities."[181] This is not only because the caseload continues to increase. As discussed above, the Court often requires a range of non-monetary reparations measures in each judgment, along with pecuniary compensation. Many remedies ordered are complex and resource intensive; as a result, they require both time and constant vigilance to achieve fulfillment.

The Court's monitoring process primarily involves written submissions.[182] The Inter-American Commission and petitioners respond to a periodic State report on compliance, and the Tribunal issues a subsequent order. Starting in 2007, in situations of delay or

key clarifications in some cases, in other instances the Court's intervention may have been ill-advised or inconsistent. *See* HÉCTOR FAÚNDEZ LEDESMA, THE INTER-AMERICAN SYSTEM FOR THE PROTECTION OF HUMAN RIGHTS: INSTITUTIONAL AND PROCEDURAL ASPECTS 874 (3d ed. 2007).

[176] *E.g.*, Abrill Alosilla et al. v. Peru, Interpretation of the Judgment on Merits, Reparations, and Costs, Inter-Am. Ct. H.R. (ser. C) No. 235, para. 10 (Nov. 21, 2011); Fernández Ortega et al. v. Mexico, Interpretation of the Judgment on Preliminary Objection, Merits, Reparations, and Costs, Inter-Am. Ct. H.R. (ser. C) No. 224, para. 11 (May 15, 2011).

[177] The Court has proven reluctant to grant requests for interpretation. In 2011 alone, the Court declined to interpret judgments on four occasions. Still, the Tribunal considered that issues raised by the State in *Saramaka People v. Suriname* "indicated that the State requires further guidance in order to fully comply with the Court's orders." Saramaka People v. Suriname, Interpretation of the Judgment on Preliminary Objections, Merits, Reparations, and Costs, Inter-Am. Ct. H.R. (ser. C) No. 185, para. 10 (Aug. 12, 2008).

[178] Rules of Procedure of the Inter-American Court, art. 76 ("The Court may, on its own motion or at the request of any of the parties to the case, within one month of the notice of the judgment or order, rectify obvious mistakes, clerical errors, or errors in calculation."). Commentators have argued that the Tribunal, like other international courts, should allow for a request for revision if a new fact is later discovered that would have been decisive in the judgment. *See* FAÚNDEZ LEDESMA, *supra* note 175, at 879–880; PASQUALUCCI, *supra* note 40, at 219.

[179] Baena Ricardo et al. v. Panama, Competence, Judgment, Inter-Am. Ct. H.R. (ser. C) No. 104, para. 107 (Nov. 28, 2003).

[180] INTER-AMERICAN COURT OF HUMAN RIGHTS, ANNUAL REPORT 2015, at 56-57, *available at* http://www.corteidh.or.cr/sitios/informes/docs/ENG/eng_2015.pdf.

[181] *Id.* at 55.

[182] *See* INTER-AMERICAN COURT OF HUMAN RIGHTS, ANNUAL REPORT 2007, at 40 (indicating that the Court started to hold hearings on compliance in 2007), *available at* http://www.corteidh.or.cr/informes.cfm.

complexity, the Court began to call the parties to private hearings, or even to public hearings under exceptional circumstances.[183] In all cases, the Tribunal seeks to resolve disputes between the parties by issuing binding instructions, which are often quite detailed, on how the reparations orders should be fulfilled.

In 2003, Panama challenged the Court's competence to supervise judgments. It argued that such monitoring is a "post-judgment stage" that "is not included in the norms that regulate the jurisdiction and procedure of the Court."[184] Although it was true that the Convention, the Court's Statute, and its Rules of Procedure did not refer to supervision methods,[185] the Tribunal strenuously defended its ability to monitor compliance with judgments and provisional measures.[186] The Court affirmed its jurisdiction to supervise compliance on the basis of several Convention provisions[187] and the legal principles of *compétence de la competence* and *opinio juris communis*.[188]

C. CASES OF NONCOMPLIANCE

The Court actively supervises nearly all of those cases that it has not closed due to full compliance. However, a fraction of judgments is no longer monitored because States have refused to carry out some or all remedies ordered. In these instances, the Court has decided to "apply Article 65" of the American Convention and emphasize a lack of compliance in its annual report to the OAS General Assembly.[189] For example, the Court's 2012 Annual Report informed that it had "established the refusal of Venezuela to comply with . . . the case of *Apitz Barbera* et al."[190] As a consequence, the Tribunal

---

[183] *See* Article 69 of the Court's Rules of Procedure. The Court will also hold hearings that concern multiple judgments against a specific State, in order to address a common reparations order that is particularly challenging. *See, e.g.*, Medical and Psychological Reparations Measures Ordered in Nine Colombian Cases, Monitoring Compliance with Judgment, Order of the Court, Inter-Am. Ct. H.R. (Feb. 8, 2012).

[184] Baena Ricardo et al. v. Panama, Competence, Judgment, Inter-Am. Ct. H.R. (ser. C) No. 104, para. 53 (Nov. 28, 2003).

[185] *Id.* para. 105.

[186] *See also* Order on Provisional Measures with respect to Venezuela, Inter-Am. Ct. H.R. (May 4, 2004) (affirming the Court's binding jurisdiction and competence to monitor compliance with provisional measures), *available at* http://www.corteidh.or.cr/medidas.cfm.

[187] The Court grounded its position on several Convention provisions, such as Articles 29, 33, 62, and 65. Baena Ricardo et al. v. Panama, Competence, Judgment, Inter-Am. Ct. H.R. (ser. C) No. 104, paras. 93–95 (Nov. 28, 2003).

[188] Citing to the principle of *compétence de la compétence*, the Court asserted "the authority inherent in its attributions to determine the scope of its own competence." *Id.* para. 68. Further, it argued that an "*opinio juris communis* has been revealed because these States have shown a general and repeated attitude of accepting [its] monitoring function" and following its instructions during the supervision phase. *Id.* para. 102.

[189] Applicability of Article 65 of the American Convention on Human Rights, Monitoring Compliance with Judgment, Order of the Court, Inter-Am. Ct. H.R., para. 9 (June 29, 2005), *available at* http://www.corteidh.or.cr/docs/supervisiones/general_29_06_05_ing.doc. The Court's standards for the application of Article 65 are opaque.

[190] Inter-American Court of Human Rights, Annual Report 2012, at 62, *available at* http://www.corteidh.or.cr/informes.cfm.

requested the OAS General Assembly to "urge" that Venezuela comply.[191] The Court has requested similar action of the General Assembly with respect to disregarded provisional measures.[192]

A 2005 Court order held that, once the Tribunal has "applied" Article 65, it would not continue demanding State reports, presumably to ease its work burden.[193] If the States do not subsequently "demonstrate before the Tribunal [their] compliance with the pending provisions" of the judgments, the Court will continue to highlight the cases in its annual reports.[194] Although it is understandable that the Tribunal wants to streamline its supervision efforts, one wonders if this is the optimal solution. In conjunction with reporting to the General Assembly, it would appear that continued Court demands upon derelict States—over time and through successive governmental administrations—would increase pressure.

Even when troublesome matters are finally specified to the OAS political bodies, more obstacles await. The General Assembly has not effectively fostered compliance with specific Court cases.[195] Court judges have lamented that States can ultimately block the Assembly from discussing and acting upon cases of noncompliance.[196] To fully implement the Court's judgments and remedial orders, the General Assembly's instructions to noncomplying States should become more frequent, assertive, and detailed.

---

[191] *Id.*

[192] Inter-American Court of Human Rights, Annual Report 1998, at 31, *available at* http://www.corteidh.or.cr/informes.cfm (stating Trinidad and Tobago "has not complied with its decision regarding the provisional measures adopted in the *James* et al. Case, and as a result requests that the General Assembly urge that the Republic of Trinidad and Tobago comply with the Orders of the Court.").

[193] Applicability of Article 65 of the American Convention on Human Rights, Monitoring Compliance with Judgment, Order of the Court, Inter-Am. Ct. H.R. (June 29, 2005).

[194] *Id.*

[195] *See* Open Society Justice Initiative, From Judgment to Justice: Implementing International and Regional Human Rights Decisions 77–78 (2010) (noting the General Assembly's ineffectual resolutions); Pasqualucci, *supra* note 40, at 305 ("The General Assembly does not take action to influence those States that have not complied"); James L. Cavallaro & Stephanie Erin Brewer, *Reevaluating Regional Human Rights Litigation in the Twenty-First Century: The Case of the Inter-American Court,* 102 Am. J. Int'l L. 768, 783–84 (2008) (stressing the insufficient OAS support for the Court).

[196] Separate Opinion of Judge Manuel Ventura Robles, paras. 9, 26, Caesar v. Trinidad & Tobago, Merits, Reparations, and Costs, Judgment, Inter-Am. Ct. H.R. (ser. C) No. 123 (Mar. 11, 2005). As a result, some have proposed amendments to the American Convention; Judges Cançado Trindade and Ventura Robles have recommended that a permanent working group be established to monitor State compliance and to ensure that the General Assembly will address problematic Court cases. *Id.* paras. 31, 33. *See also* Cançado Trindade, *supra* note 167, at 47–48 (urging that the following sentence should be added to the end of Article 65: "The General Assembly shall convey [the cases of noncompliance] to the Permanent Council, which shall study and prepare a report on the matter, in order for the General Assembly to adopt a decision thereon").

D. COMPLIANCE RATES

Compliance rates for Court reparations have been variable, but respectable as a whole.[197] One study found that States fully paid pecuniary and nonpecuniary damages between 40 and 50 percent of the time;[198] the Tribunal itself has estimated as high as 80 percent compliance with such orders.[199] Paying damages, from technical and logistical standpoints, is one of the more straightforward reparations a State can accomplish.

In contrast, compliance with non-monetary remedies has varied widely by measure. Orders to clear criminal records, publish judgments, issue apologies, and establish training courses for State officials have fared well. Yet States have poorly implemented directives to investigate and punish perpetrators, return traditional lands, and carry out sprawling programs for medical and psychological rehabilitation.

Two variables, management and domestic politics, appear to explain these compliance results.[200] Clearing a petitioner's criminal record or waiving a fine, for example, has been accomplished nearly without fail by States. Little coordination between governmental entities and few resources are needed for such tasks. The procedure for compliance would also seem relatively simple.[201] When managerial and technical demands increase, compliance rates decline. It is not surprising that insufficient progress has been made implementing the Court's more complex requirements for healthcare programs. Similar difficulties are found when the Court orders community development initiatives, prison renovations, or the return of traditional lands. These efforts often require high levels of institutional coordination, technical knowledge, financial resources, and significant time for completion.

In this way, there seem to be two key factors for understanding compliance with Court cases: management and domestic politics. When easily-managed reparations are not

---

[197] This section summarizes selected data and analysis in an article by this book's author Thomas M. Antkowiak, *An Emerging Mandate for International Courts, supra* note 85, at 304–09.

[198] Darren Hawkins & Wade Jacoby, "Partial Compliance: A Comparison of the European and Inter-American Courts for Human Rights." Paper prepared for delivery at the 2008 Annual Meeting of the American Political Science Association.

[199] INTER-AMERICAN COURT OF HUMAN RIGHTS, ANNUAL REPORT 2010, at 12, *available at* http://www.corteidh.or.cr/informes.cfm (estimating "approximately" 80 percent State compliance with orders for monetary damages).

[200] The Former Executive Secretary of the Inter-American Commission on Human Rights, Santiago Canton, and the author of a leading study on the Inter-American System, Carlos Beristain, have concluded that institutional capacity and political will are key for compliance. *See* Santiago Canton, *Conference: Reparations in the Inter-American System: A Comparative Approach*, 56 AM. U.L. REV. 1375, 1454 (2007); BERISTAIN, *supra* note 83, at 531–32.

[201] This assumes adequate national procedures and the cooperation of local authorities, such as judges. *See* Alexandra Huneeus, *Courts Resisting Courts: Lessons from the Inter-American Court's Struggle to Enforce Human Rights*, 44 CORNELL INT'L L.J. 101, 152–55 (2011) (referring to some national courts as a "vexing source of non-compliance" and urging "partnerships with local justice systems" to expedite the fulfillment of Court remedies).

completed, one would expect domestic politics to hold the blame. Moreover, as remedial orders require increasingly unpopular or complex state action, delays with compliance typically follow. For this reason, two of the least successful Court orders are criminal investigations and finding/returning missing corpses. Such investigations can implicate powerful members of society; further, they require substantial technical expertise, as well as persistence and courage.[202]

The Court faces a number of challenges as it promotes compliance with its judgments. Still, there have been good-faith efforts and significant achievements across all categories of the Tribunal's reparations. Governments have reformed their constitutions, high-ranking officials have publicly apologized for abuses, and thousands of victims have received substantial, individualized measures responding to their preferences and needs. In addition, the Court's own exacting method of determining whether reparations measures are fulfilled drives down its compliance rates; consequently, such rates do not sufficiently reflect the Tribunal's impact upon States.[203] As procedures and institutions are firmly established at the national level, subsequent Court judgments will likely achieve faster compliance.

VIII. Provisional Measures of Article 63(2)

In cases of gravity and urgency already before the Court, the Tribunal may, on its own motion, adopt provisional measures to avoid irreparable damage to persons.[204] Similarly, victims or alleged victims, or their representatives, may request provisional measures, provided that they are related to the subject matter of the Court case.[205] But if the matter has not yet been submitted to the Tribunal, it may only act at the request of the Inter-American Commission.[206] Of course, the Court can only order provisional measures against those States that have accepted its jurisdiction.

As already noted, the Court has asserted that Article 63(2) confers an "obligatory character" upon its orders for provisional measures.[207] Both the International Court of Justice and

---

[202] *See* BERISTAIN, *supra* note 83, at 382–85 (discussing the many demands concerning the exhumation and identification of remains). *See also* Principles on the Effective Prevention and Investigation of Extra-legal, Arbitrary and Summary Executions, E.S.C. Res. 1989/65, U.N. Doc. E/1989/89 (May 24, 1989).

[203] *See* Yuval Shany, *Compliance with Decisions of International Courts as Indicative of Their Effectiveness: A Goal-Based Analysis* (Int'l Law Forum Research Paper No. 04-10, Oct. 2010), *available at* http://papers.ssrn.com/sol3/papers.cfm?abstract_id=1697488; OPEN SOCIETY JUSTICE INITIATIVE, *supra* note 195, at 63 (describing the Court's "tremendous and positive impact on the . . . region").

[204] American Convention, art. 63(2); Rules of Procedure of the Inter-American Court on Human Rights (2009), art. 27(1).

[205] Rules of Procedure of the Inter-American Court on Human Rights (2009), art. 27(3).

[206] Rules of Procedure of the Inter-American Court on Human Rights (2009), art. 27(2).

[207] Constitutional Court v. Peru, Provisional Measures, Order of the Court, Inter-Am. Ct. H.R. (Aug. 14, 2000), Fourteenth "Considering."

the European Court of Human Rights have weaker mandates on this point: they may "indicate to the parties" appropriate interim measures.[208] The ICJ's Statute also locates provisional measures in the chapter on procedure instead of jurisdiction, which led States to challenge their binding nature.[209] In contrast, the American Convention grants the Court a stronger foundation: it "shall adopt" pertinent measures.[210] Moreover, Article 63 is found squarely within the Convention's section on the Tribunal's "Jurisdiction and Functions."[211] Of course, all three international Courts now have affirmed their provisional measures to be binding.[212]

When the Inter-American Court is not in session, its president may order "urgent" measures, which eventually are reviewed and, if applicable, approved by the Court as provisional measures.[213] Generally, the Court acts to protect the rights to life and personal integrity; in addition, it has ordered measures to safeguard, among others: the rights to personal liberty, property, and due process of law; the freedoms of expression and movement; and the rights of children.[214]

For measures to issue, a prima facie showing of extreme seriousness and urgency is required. If the State does not respond to such allegations, the Tribunal presumes the standard has been met.[215] The Court and its presidents have constantly emphasized that the adoption of either urgent or provisional measures does not constitute a decision on the merits of the matter.

Provisional measures have protected, among others, alleged victims of Court cases and their family members, witnesses, human rights advocates, members of indigenous communities, prisoners, journalists, political candidates, judicial officials, immigrants under orders of deportation, and individuals sentenced to capital punishment.[216] Prior to 2000, the Court required all beneficiaries to be identified by name.[217] However, in the *Matter*

---

[208] PASQUALUCCI, *supra* note 40, at 254(citing Article 41 of the Statute of the International Court of Justice and Rule 39 of the Rules of the European Court).

[209] *Id.*

[210] American Convention, art. 63(2).

[211] American Convention, Section 2.

[212] LaGrand Case (Germany v. United States of America), 2001 ICJ Reports No. 104 (Merits) (Judgment 27 June); Mamatkulov and Abdurasulovic v. Turkey, Eur. Ct. H.R., App. Nos. 46827/99 and 46951/99, paras. 109–111 (Feb. 6, 2003). *See generally* EVA RIETER, PREVENTING IRREPARABLE HARM: PROVISIONAL MEASURES IN INTERNATIONAL HUMAN RIGHTS ADJUDICATION (2010).

[213] Rules of Procedure of the Inter-American Court on Human Rights (2009), art. 27(6).

[214] *See* CLARA BURBANO HERRERA, PROVISIONAL MEASURES IN THE CASE LAW OF THE INTER-AMERICAN COURT OF HUMAN RIGHTS 52–53 (2010); Matter of "*El Nacional*" and "*Así es la Noticia*" Newspapers regarding Venezuela, Inter-Am. Ct. H.R. (protecting freedom of expression); Matter of the Sarayaku Indigenous Community regarding Ecuador, Inter-Am. Ct. H.R. (protecting freedom of movement). All of the Court's provisional measures are available at http://www.corteidh.or.cr/cf/Jurisprudencia2/busqueda_medidas_provisionales.cfm?lang=en.

[215] Matter of A.J. and Others regarding Haiti, Order of the Inter-American Court of Human Rights, Inter-Am. Ct. H.R. (Sept. 21, 2009).

[216] *See* BURBANO HERRERA, *supra* note 214, at 68–85.

[217] Peace Community of San José de Apartadó regarding Colombia, Order of the Inter-American Court of Human Rights, Inter-Am. Ct. H.R., at 15 (Nov. 24, 2000).

of the Peace Community of San José de Apartadó, the Tribunal established that provisional measures may be applied to persons under a common situation of risk, whether individually identified or not.[218] If identification were required of every person, the Court reasoned, its action in urgent circumstances would be delayed or prevented entirely.[219] As a result, the Tribunal has subsequently issued orders to protect entire indigenous and ethnic communities,[220] as well as incarcerated populations, and groups of employees working for newspapers, television stations, and human rights organizations.[221]

[218] *Id.* para. 7 ("Considerando").

[219] Concurring Opinion of Sergio García Ramírez, Matter of "Globovisión" Television Station regarding Venezuela, Order of the Inter-American Court of Human Rights, Inter-Am. Ct. H.R. (Sept. 4, 2004).

[220] Yet the Court more recently has shown caution when considering emergency petitions to protect ancestral lands. *See* Saramaka People regarding Suriname, Order of the Inter-American Court of Human Rights, Inter-Am. Ct. H.R. (Sept. 4, 2013) (rejecting community's request for provisional measures, but requesting "a complete, detailed and specific report on the alleged award of the mining concession on the Saramaka territory"); Four Ngöbe Indigenous Communities regarding Panama, Order of the Inter-American Court of Human Rights, Inter-Am. Ct. H.R. (May 28, 2010) (refusing the request for provisional measures to protect ancestral lands from flooding).

[221] *E.g.*, Matter of Miguel Agustín Pro Juárez Human Rights Center et al. regarding Mexico, Inter-Am. Ct. H.R. (protecting the employees of a human rights organization); Matter of Mack Chang regarding Guatemala, Inter-Am. Ct. H.R. (protecting employees of the Mack Foundation).

APPENDIX

List of Inter-American Court Judgments by American Convention Article: Articles 2–26

Presented in reverse chronological order through February 2016. The judgment or advisory opinion is included if it makes a mention, however brief, of indicated Article.

ARTICLE 2: DOMESTIC LEGAL EFFECTS

1. Duque v. Colombia, Preliminary Objections, Merits, Reparations and Costs, Judgment, Inter-Am. Ct. H.R. (ser. C) No. 310 (Feb. 26, 2016).
2. Kaliña and Lokono Peoples v. Suriname, Merits, Reparations and Costs, Judgment, Inter-Am. Ct. H.R. (ser. C) No. 309 (Nov. 25, 2015).
3. Quispialaya Vilcapoma v. Peru, Preliminary Objections, Merits, Reparations and Costs, Judgment, Inter-Am. Ct. H.R. (ser. C) No. 308 (Nov. 23, 2015).
4. Velasquez Paiz et al. v. Guatemala, Preliminary Objections, Merits, Reparations and Costs, Judgment, Inter-Am. Ct. H.R. (ser. C) No. 307 (Nov. 19, 2015).
5. Community Garifuna Triunfo de la Cruz and its Members v. Honduras, Merits, Reparations and Costs, Judgment, Inter-Am. Ct. H.R. (ser. C) No. 305 (Oct. 8, 2015).
6. Garifuna Punta Piedra Community and its Members v. Honduras, Preliminary Objections, Merits, Reparations and Costs, Judgment, Inter-Am. Ct. H.R. (ser. C) No. 304 (Oct. 8, 2015).
7. Lopez Lone et al. v. Honduras, Preliminary Objection, Merits, Reparations and Costs, Judgment, Inter-Am. Ct. H.R. (ser. C) No. 302 (Oct. 5, 2015).
8. Galindo Cardenas et al. v. Peru, Preliminary Objections, Merits, Reparations and Costs, Judgment, Inter-Am. Ct. H.R. (ser. C) No. 301 (Oct. 2, 2015).

The American Convention on Human Rights. Thomas M. Antkowiak and Alejandra Gonza.

9. Omar Humberto Maldonado Vargas et al v. Chile, Merits, Reparations, Costs, Judgment, Inter-Am. Ct. H.R. (ser. C) No. 300 (Sept. 2, 2015).
10. Wong Ho Wing v. Peru, Preliminary Objection, Merits, Reparations and Costs, Judgment, Inter-Am. Ct. H.R. (ser. C) No. 297 (June 30, 2015).
11. Canales Huapaya et al v. Peru, Preliminary Objections, Merits, Reparations, Costs, Judgment, (ser. C) No. 296 (June 24, 2015).
12. Espinoza Gonzales v. Peru, Interpretation of the Judgment on Preliminary Objections, Merits, Reparations and Costs, Judgment, Inter-Am. Ct. H.R. (ser. C) No. 295 (June 23, 2015).
13. Cruz Sánchez et al. v. Peru, Preliminary Objections, Merits, Reparations, Costs, Judgment, Inter-Am. Ct. H.R. (ser. C) No. 292 (Apr. 17, 2015).
14. J. v. Peru, Interpretation of the Judgment on Preliminary Objection, Merits, Reparations, and Costs, Judgment, Inter-Am. Ct. H.R. (ser. C) No. 291 (Nov. 20, 2014).
15. Osorio Rivera and Family v. Peru, Interpretation of the Judgment on Preliminary Objection, Merits, Reparations, and Costs, Judgment, Inter-Am. Ct. H.R. (ser. C) No. 290 (Nov. 20, 2014).
16. Argüelles et al. v. Argentina, Preliminary Objections, Merits, Reparations, and Costs, Judgment, Inter-Am. Ct. H.R. (ser. C) No. 288 (Nov. 20, 2014).
17. Tarazona Arrieta et al. v. Peru, Preliminary Objections, Merits, Reparations, and Costs, Judgment, Inter-Am. Ct. H.R. (ser. C) No. 286 (Oct. 15, 2014).
18. Kuna Indigenous People of Madungandi and Embera Indigenous People of Bayano and their Members v. Panama, Preliminary Objections, Merits, Reparations, and Costs, Judgment, Inter-Am. Ct. H.R. (ser. C) No. 284 (Oct. 14, 2014).
19. Expelled Dominicans and Haitians v. Dominican Republic, Preliminary Objections, Merits, Reparations, and Costs, Judgment, Inter-Am. Ct. H.R. (ser. C) No. 282 (Aug. 28, 2014).
20. Landaeta Meijias Brothers et al. v. Venezuela, Preliminary Objections, Merits, Reparations, and Costs, Judgment, Inter-Am. Ct. H.R. (ser. C) No. 281 (Aug. 27, 2014).
21. Rights & Guar. of Children in the Context of Migration and/or in Need of Int'l Prot., Advisory Opinion OC-21/14, Inter-Am. Ct. H.R. (ser. A) No. 21 (Aug. 19, 2014).
22. Norín Catrimán et al. (Leaders, members, and activist of the Mapuche Indigenous People) v. Chile, Merits, Reparations, and Costs, Judgment, Inter-Am. Ct. H.R. (ser. C) No. 279 (May 29, 2014).
23. Brewer Carías v. Venezuela, Preliminary Objections, Judgment, Inter-Am. Ct. H.R. (ser. C) No. 278 (May 26, 2014).
24. Veliz Franco et al. v. Guatemala, Preliminary Objections, Merits, and Reparations, Judgment, Inter-Am. Ct. H.R. (ser. C) No. 277 (May 19, 2014).
25. Liakat Ali Alibux v. Suriname, Preliminary Objections, Merits, Reparations, and Costs, Judgment, Inter-Am. Ct. H.R. (ser. C) No. 276 (Jan. 30, 2014).
26. J. v. Peru, Preliminary Objections, Merits, Reparations, and Costs, Judgment, Inter-Am. Ct. H.R. (ser. C) No. 275 (Nov. 27, 2013).
27. Osorio Rivera and Family v. Peru, Preliminary Objections, Merits, Reparations, and Costs, Judgment, Inter-Am. Ct. H.R. (ser. C) No. 274 (Nov. 26, 2013).
28. Garcia Cruz and Sanchez Silvestre v. Mexico, Merits, Reparations, and Costs, Judgment, Inter-Am. Ct. H.R. (ser. C) No. 273 (Nov. 26, 2013).

29. Pacheco Tineo Family v. Bolivia, Preliminary Objections, Merits, Reparations, and Costs, Judgment, Inter-Am. Ct. H.R. (ser. C) No. 272 (Nov. 25, 2013).
30. Afro-Descendant Communities Displaced from the Cacarica River Basin (Operation Genesis) v. Colombia, Preliminary Objections, Merits, Reparations, and Costs, Judgment, Inter-Am. Ct. H.R. (ser. C) No. 270 (Nov. 20, 2013).
31. Luna Lopez v. Honduras, Merits, Reparations, and Costs, Judgment, Inter-Am. Ct. H.R. (ser. C) No. 269 (Oct. 10, 2013).
32. Constitutional Tribunal (Camba Campos et al.) v. Ecuador, Preliminary Objections, Merits, Reparations, and Costs, Judgment, Inter-Am. Ct. H.R. (ser. C) No. 268 (Aug. 28, 2013).
33. Garcia Lucero et al. v. Chile, Preliminary Objections, Merits, and Reparations, Judgment, Inter-Am. Ct. H.R. (ser. C) No. 267 (Aug. 28, 2013).
34. Supreme Court of Justice (Quintana Coello et al.) v. Ecuador, Preliminary Objections, Merits, Reparations, and Costs, Judgment, Inter-Am. Ct. H.R. (ser. C) No. 266 (Aug. 23, 2013).
35. Memoli v. Argentina, Preliminary Objections, Merits, Reparations, and Costs, Judgment, Inter-Am. Ct. H.R. (ser. C) No. 265 (Aug. 22, 2013).
36. Mendoza et al. v. Argentina, Preliminary Objections, Merits, and Reparations, Judgment, Inter-Am. Ct. H.R. (ser. C) No. 260 (May 14, 2013).
37. Santo Domingo Massacre v. Colombia, Preliminary Objections, Merits, and Reparations, Judgment, Inter-Am. Ct. H.R. (ser. C) No. 259 (Nov. 30, 2012).
38. García and Family Members v. Guatemala, Merits, Reparations, and Costs, Judgment, Inter-Am. Ct. H.R. (ser. C) No. 258 (Nov. 29, 2012).
39. Artavia Murillo et al. (In-vitro Fertilization) v. Costa Rica, Preliminary Objections, Merits, Reparations, and Costs, Judgment, Inter-Am. Ct. H.R. (ser. C) No. 257 (Nov. 28, 2012).
40. Mohamed v. Argentina, Preliminary Objections, Merits, Reparations, and Costs, Judgment, Inter-Am. Ct. H.R. (ser. C) No. 255 (Nov. 23, 2012).
41. Gudiel Alvarez et al. ("Diario Militar") v. Guatemala, Merits, Reparations, and Costs, Judgment, Inter-Am. Ct. H.R. (ser. C) No. 253 (Nov. 20, 2012).
42. Massacres of El Mozote and Nearby Places v. El Salvador, Merits, Reparations, and Costs, Judgment, Inter-Am. Ct. H.R. (ser. C) No. 252 (Oct. 25, 2012).
43. Nadege Dorzema et al. v. Dominican Republic, Merits, Reparations, and Costs, Judgment, Inter-Am. Ct. H.R. (ser. C) No. 251 (Oct. 24, 2012).
44. Uzcátegui et al. v. Venezuela, Merits and Reparations, Judgment, Inter-Am. Ct. H.R. (ser. C) No. 249 (Sept. 3, 2012).
45. Vélez Restrepo and Family v. Colombia, Preliminary Objections, Merits, Reparations, and Costs, Judgment, Inter-Am. Ct. H.R. (ser. C) No. 248 (Sept. 3, 2012).
46. Palma Mendoza et al. v. Ecuador, Preliminary Objections and Merits, Judgment, Inter-Am. Ct. H.R. (ser. C) No. 247 (Sept. 3, 2012).
47. Furlan and Family v. Argentina, Preliminary Objections, Merits, Reparations, and Costs, Judgment, Inter-Am. Ct. H.R. (ser. C) No. 246 (Aug. 31, 2012).
48. Kichwa Indigenous People of Sarayaku v. Ecuador, Merits and Reparations, Judgment Inter.-Am. Ct. H.R. (ser. C) No. 245 (June 27, 2012).
49. Díaz Peña v. Venezuela, Preliminary Objections, Merits, Reparations, and Costs, Judgment, Inter-Am. Ct. H.R. (ser. C) No. 244 (June 26, 2012).

50. Pacheco Teruel et al. v. Honduras, Merits, Reparations, and Costs, Judgment, Inter-Am. Ct. H.R. (ser. C) No. 241 (Apr. 27, 2012).
51. Gonzalez Medina and Family v. Dominican Republic, Preliminary Objections, Merits, Reparations, and Costs, Judgment, Inter-Am. Ct. H.R. (ser. C) No. 240 (Feb. 27, 2012).
52. Fontevecchia and D`Amico v. Argentina, Merits, Reparations, and Costs, Judgment, Inter-Am. Ct. H.R. (ser. C) No. 238 (Nov. 29, 2011).
53. López Mendoza v. Venezuela, Merits, Reparations, and Costs, Judgment,Inter-Am. Ct. H.R. (ser. C) No. 233 (Sept. 1, 2011).
54. Torres Millacura et al. v. Argentina, Merits, Reparations, and Costs, Judgment, Inter-Am. Ct. H.R. (ser. C) No. 229 (Aug. 26, 2011).
55. Mejía Idrovo v. Ecuador, Preliminary Objections, Merits, Reparations, and Costs, Judgment, Inter-Am. Ct. H.R. (ser. C) No. 228 (July 5, 2011).
56. Chocrón Chocrón v. Venezuela, Preliminary Objections, Merits, Reparations, and Costs, Judgment, Inter-Am. Ct. H.R. (ser. C) No. 227 (July 1, 2011).
57. Rosendo Cantu et al. v. Mexico, Interpretation of Judgment of Preliminary Objections, Merits, Reparations, and Costs, Judgment, Inter-Am. Ct. H.R. (ser. C) No. 225 (May 15, 2011).
58. Salvador Chiriboga v. Ecuador, Reparations and Costs, Judgment, Inter-Am. Ct. H.R. (ser. C) No. 222 (Mar. 3, 2011).
59. Gelman v. Uruguay, Merits and Reparations, Judgment, Inter-Am. Ct. H.R. (ser. C) No. 221 (Feb. 24, 2011).
60. Cabrera García and Montiel Flores v. Mexico, Preliminary Objections, Merits, Reparations, and Costs, Judgment, Inter-Am. Ct. H.R. (ser. C) No. 220 (Nov. 26, 2010).
61. Gomes Lund et al. ("Guerrilha do Araguaia") v. Brazil, Preliminary Objections, Merits, Reparations, and Costs, Judgment, Inter-Am. Ct. H.R. (ser. C) No. 219 (Nov. 24, 2010).
62. Vélez Loor v. Panama, Preliminary Objections, Merits, Reparations, and Costs, Judgment, Inter-Am. Ct. H.R. (ser. C) No. 218 (Nov. 23, 2010).
63. Ibsen Cardenas and Ibsen Peña v. Bolivia, Merits, Reparations, and Costs, Judgment, Inter-Am. Ct. H.R. (ser. C) No. 217 (Sept. 1, 2010).
64. Rosendo Cantu et al. v. Mexico, Preliminary Objections, Merits, Reparations, and Costs, Judgment, Inter-Am. Ct. H.R. (ser. C) No. 216 (Aug. 31, 2010).
65. Fernandez Ortega et al. v. Mexico, Preliminary Objections, Merits, Reparations, and Costs, Judgment, Inter-Am. Ct. H.R. (ser. C) No. 215 (Aug. 30, 2010).
66. Xákmok Kásek Indigenous Cmty. v. Paraguay, Merits, Reparations, and Costs, Judgment, Inter-Am. Ct. H.R. (ser. C) No. 214 (Aug. 24, 2010).
67. Cepeda Vargas v. Colombia, Preliminary Objections, Merits, Reparations, and Costs, Judgment, Inter-Am. Ct. H.R. (ser. C.) No. 213 (May 26, 2010).
68. Chitay Nech et al. v. Guatemala, Preliminary Objections, Merits, Reparations, and Costs, Judgment, Inter-Am. Ct. H.R. (ser. C) No. 212 (May 25, 2010).
69. "Las Dos Erres" Massacre v. Guatemala, Preliminary Objections, Merits, Reparations, and Costs, Judgment, Inter-Am. Ct. H.R. (ser. C) No. 211 (Nov. 24, 2009).
70. Radilla Pacheco v. Mexico, Preliminary Objections, Merits, Reparations, and Costs, Judgment, Inter-Am. Ct. H.R. (ser. C) No. 209 (Nov. 23, 2009).
71. Usón Ramírez v. Venezuela, Preliminary Objection, Merits, Reparations, and Costs, Judgment, Inter-Am. Ct. H.R. (ser. C) No. 207 (Nov. 20, 2009).
72. Barreto Leiva v. Venezuela, Merits, Reparations, and Costs, Judgment, Inter-Am. Ct. H.R. (ser. C) No. 206 (Nov. 17, 2009).

73. González et al. ("Cotton Field") v. Mexico, Preliminary Objections, Merits, Reparations, and Costs, Judgment, Inter-Am. Ct. H.R. (ser. C) No. 205 (Nov. 16, 2009).
74. DaCosta Cadogan v. Barbados, Preliminary Objections, Merits, Reparations, and Costs, Judgment, Inter-Am. Ct. H.R. (ser. C) No. 204 (Sept. 24, 2009).
75. Garibaldi v. Brazil, Preliminary Objections, Merits, Reparations, and Costs, Judgment, Inter-Am. Ct. H.R. (ser. C) No. 203 (Sept. 23, 2009).
76. Anzualdo Castro v. Peru, Preliminary Objections, Merits, Reparations, and Costs, Judgment, Inter-Am. Ct. H.R. (ser. C) No. 202 (Sept. 22, 2009).
77. Escher et al v. Brazil, Preliminary Objections, Merits, Reparations, and Costs, Judgment, Inter-Am. Ct. H.R. (ser. C) No. 200 (July 6, 2009).
78. Ticona Estrada et al. v. Bolivia, Interpretation of the Judgment on Merits, Reparations, and Costs, Judgment, Inter-Am. Ct. H.R. (ser. C) No. 199 (July 1, 2009).
79. Reverón Trujillo v. Venezuela, Preliminary Objections, Merits, Reparations, and Costs, Judgment, Inter-Am. Ct. H.R. (ser. C) No. 197 (June 30, 2009).
80. Kawas Fernández v. Honduras, Merits, Reparations, and Costs, Judgment, Inter-Am. Ct. H.R. (ser. C) No. 196 (Apr. 3, 2009).
81. Perozo et al. v. Venezuela, Preliminary Objections, Merits, Reparations, and Costs, Judgment, Inter-Am. Ct. H.R. (ser. C) No. 195 (Jan. 28, 2009).
82. Ríos et al. v. Venezuela, Preliminary Objections, Merits, Reparations, and Costs, Judgment, Inter-Am. Ct. H.R. (ser. C) No. 194 (Jan. 28, 2009).
83. Tristán Donoso v. Panama, Preliminary Objections, Merits, Reparations, and Costs, Judgment, Inter-Am. Ct. H.R. (ser. C) No. 193 (Jan. 27, 2009).
84. Ticona Estrada et al. v. Bolivia, Merits, Reparations, and Costs, Judgment, Inter-Am. Ct. H.R. (ser. C) No. 191 (Nov. 27, 2008).
85. Heliodoro Portugal v. Panama, Preliminary Objections, Merits, Reparations, and Costs, Judgment, Inter-Am. Ct. H.R. (ser. C) No. 186 (Aug. 12, 2008).
86. Saramaka People v. Suriname, Interpretation of the Judgment on Preliminary Objections, Merits, Reparations, and Costs, Judgment, Inter-Am. Ct. H.R. (ser. C) No. 185 (Aug. 12, 2008).
87. Castañeda Gutman v. Mexico, Preliminary Objections, Merits, Reparations, and Costs, Judgment, Inter-Am. Ct. H.R. (ser. C) No. 184 (Aug. 6, 2008).
88. Albán Cornejo et al. v. Ecuador, Interpretation of the Judgment on Merits, Reparations, and Costs, Judgment, Inter-Am. Ct. H.R. (ser. C) No. 183 (Aug. 5, 2008).
89. Apitz Barbera et al. ("First Court of Administrative Disputes") v. Venezuela, Preliminary Objection, Merits, Reparations, and Costs, Judgment, Inter-Am. Ct. H.R. (ser. C) No. 182 (Aug. 5, 2008).
90. Neptune v. Haiti, Merits, Reparations, and Costs, Judgment, Inter-Am. Ct. H.R. (ser. C) No. 180 (May 6, 2008).
91. Salvador Chiriboga v. Ecuador, Preliminary Objections and Merits, Judgment, Inter-Am. Ct. H.R. (ser. C) No. 179 (May 6, 2008).
92. Kimel v. Argentina, Merits, Reparations, and Costs, Judgment, Inter-Am. Ct. H.R. (ser. C) No. 177 (May 2, 2008).
93. Dismissed Cong. Emp. (Aguado Alfaro et al.) v. Peru, Request for Interpretation of the Judgment on Preliminary Objections, Merits, Reparations, and Costs, Judgment, Inter-Am. Ct. H.R. (ser. C) No. 174 (Nov. 30, 2007).
94. La Cantuta v. Peru, Interpretation of the Judgment on Merits, Reparations, and Costs, Judgment, Inter-Am. Ct. H.R. (ser. C) No. 173 (Nov. 30, 2007).

95. Saramaka People v. Suriname, Preliminary Objections, Merits, Reparations, and Costs, Judgment, Inter-Am. Ct. H.R. (ser. C) No. 172 (Nov. 28, 2007).
96. Albán Cornejo et al. v. Ecuador, Merits, Reparations, and Costs, Judgment, Inter-Am. Ct. H.R. (ser. C) No. 171 (Nov. 22, 2007).
97. Chaparro Álvarez & Lapo Íñiguez v. Ecuador, Preliminary Objections, Merits, Reparations, and Costs, Judgment, Inter-Am. Ct. H.R. (ser. C) No. 170 (Nov. 21, 2007).
98. Boyce et al. v. Barbados, Preliminary Objections, Merits, Reparations, and Costs, Judgment, Inter-Am. Ct. H.R. (ser. C) No. 169 (Nov. 20, 2007).
99. Zambrano Vélez et al. v. Ecuador, Merits, Reparations, and Costs, Judgment, Inter-Am. Ct. H.R. (ser. C) No. 166 (July 4, 2007).
100. Rochela Massacre v. Colombia, Merits, Reparations, and Costs, Judgment, Inter-Am. Ct. H.R. (ser. C) No. 163 (May 11, 2007).
101. La Cantuta v. Peru, Merits, Reparations, and Costs, Judgment, Inter-Am. Ct. H.R. (ser. C) No. 162 (Nov. 29, 2006).
102. Dismissed Cong. Emp. (Aguado Alfaro et al.) v. Peru, Preliminary Objections, Merits, Reparations, and Costs, Judgment, Inter-Am. Ct H.R. (ser. C) No. 158 (Nov. 24, 2006).
103. Almonacid Arellano et al. v. Chile, Preliminary Objections, Merits, Reparations, and Costs, Judgment, Inter-Am. Ct. H.R. (ser. C) No. 154 (Sept. 26, 2006).
104. Claude Reyes et al. v. Chile, Merits, Reparations, and Costs, Judgment, Inter-Am. Ct. H.R. (ser. C) No. 151 (Sept. 19, 2006).
105. Montero Aranguren et al. (Det. Ctr. of Catia) v. Venezuela, Preliminary Objection, Merits, Reparations, and Costs, Judgment, Inter-Am. Ct. H.R. (ser. C) No. 150 (July 5, 2006).
106. Sawhoyamaxa Indigenous Cmty. v. Paraguay, Merits, Reparations, and Costs, Judgment, Inter-Am. Ct. H.R. (ser. C) No. 146 (Mar. 29, 2006).
107. Acevedo Jaramillo et al. v. Peru, Preliminary Objections, Merits, Reparations, and Costs, Judgment, Inter-Am. Ct. H.R. (ser. C) No. 144 (Feb. 7, 2006).
108. Raxcacó Reyes v. Guatemala, Interpretation of the Judgment of Merits, Reparations, and Costs, Judgment, Inter-Am. Ct. H.R. (ser. C) No. 143 (Feb. 6, 2006).
109. Yakye Axa Indigenous Cmty. v. Paraguay, Interpretation of the Judgment of Merits, Reparations, and Costs, Judgment, Inter-Am. Ct. H.R. (ser. C) No. 142 (Feb. 6, 2006).
110. Blanco Romero et al. v. Venezuela, Merits, Reparations, and Costs, Judgment, Inter-Am. Ct. H.R. (ser. C) No. 138 (Nov. 28, 2005).
111. Gómez Palomino v. Peru, Merits, Reparations, and Costs, Judgment, Inter-Am. Ct. H.R. (ser. C) No. 136 (Nov. 22, 2005).
112. Palamara Iribarne v. Chile, Merits, Reparations, Costs, Judgment, Inter-Am. Ct. H.R. (ser. C) No. 135 (Nov. 22, 2005).
113. Raxcacó Reyes v. Guatemala, Merits, Reparations, and Costs, Judgment, Inter-Am. Ct. H.R. (ser. C) No. 133 (Sept. 15, 2005).
114. Acosta Calderón v. Ecuador, Merits, Reparations, and Costs, Judgment, Inter-Am. Ct. H.R. (ser. C) No. 129 (June 24, 2005).
115. Berenson Mejía v. Peru, Interpretation of the Judgment of Merits, Reparations, and Costs, Judgment, Inter-Am. Ct. H.R. (ser. C) No. 128 (June 23, 2005).
116. YATAMA v. Nicaragua, Preliminary Objections, Merits, Reparations, and Costs, Judgment, Inter-Am. Ct. H.R. (ser. C) No. 127 (June 23, 2005).

117. Fermín Ramírez v. Guatemala, Merits, Reparations, and Costs, Judgment, Inter-Am. Ct. H.R. (ser. C) No. 126 (June 20, 2005).
118. Yakye Axa Indigenous Cmty. v. Paraguay, Merits, Reparations, and Costs, Judgment, Inter-Am. Ct. H.R. (ser. C) No. 125 (June 17, 2005).
119. Caesar v. Trinidad & Tobago, Merits, Reparations, and Costs, Judgment, Inter-Am. Ct. H.R. (ser. C) No. 123 (Mar. 11, 2005).
120. Berenson Mejia v. Peru, Merits, Reparations, and Costs, Judgment, Inter-Am. Ct. H.R. (ser. C) No. 119 (Nov. 25, 2004).
121. De La Cruz Flores v. Peru, Merits, Reparations, and Costs, Judgment, Inter-Am. Ct. H.R. (ser. C) No. 115 (Nov. 18, 2004).
122. Tibi v. Ecuador, Preliminary Objections, Merits, Reparations, and Costs, Judgment, Inter-Am. Ct. H.R. (ser. C) No. 114 (Sept. 7, 2004).
123. Campo Dodd v. Mexico, Preliminary Objections, Judgment, Inter-Am. Ct. H.R. (ser. C) No. 113 (Sept. 3, 2004).
124. "Juvenile Reeducation Institute" v. Paraguay, Preliminary Objections, Merits, Reparations, and Costs, Judgment, Inter-Am. Ct. H.R. (ser. C) No. 112 (Sept. 2, 2004).
125. Canese v. Paraguay, Merits, Reparations, and Costs, Judgment, Inter-Am. Ct. H.R. (ser. C) No. 111 (Aug. 31, 2004).
126. Molina Theissen v. Guatemala, Reparations and Costs, Judgment, Inter-Am. Ct. H.R. (ser. C) No. 108 (July 3, 2004).
127. Herrera Ulloa v. Costa Rica, Preliminary Objections, Merits, Reparations, and Costs, Judgment, Inter-Am. Ct. H.R. (ser. C) No. 107 (July 2, 2004).
128. Molina Theissen v. Guatemala, Merits, Judgment, Inter-Am. Ct. H.R. (ser. C) No. 106 (May 4, 2004).
129. Baena Ricardo et al. v. Panama, Competence, Judgment, Inter-Am. Ct. H.R. (ser. C) No. 104 (Nov. 28, 2003).
130. Sánchez v. Honduras, Interpretation of the Judgment of Preliminary Objection, Merits, and Reparations, Judgment, Inter-Am. Ct. H.R. (ser. C) No. 102 (Nov. 26, 2003).
131. Bulacio v. Argentina, Merits, Reparations, and Costs, Judgment, Inter-Am. Ct. H.R. (ser. C) No. 100 (Sept. 18, 2003).
132. Sánchez v. Honduras, Preliminary Objection, Merits, Reparations, and Costs, Judgment, Inter-Am. Ct. H.R. (ser. C) No. 99 (June 7, 2003).
133. Juridical Condition & Rights of the Undocumented Migrants, Advisory Opinion OC-18/03, Inter-Am. Ct. H.R. (ser. A) No. 18 (Sept. 17, 2003).
134. "Five Pensioners" v. Peru, Merits, Reparations, and Costs, Judgment, Inter-Am. Ct. H.R. (ser. C) No. 98 (Feb. 28, 2003).
135. Cantos v. Argentina, Merits, Reparations, and Costs, Judgment, Inter-Am. Ct. H.R. (ser. C) No. 97 (Nov. 28, 2002).
136. Caracazo v. Venezuela, Reparations and Costs, Judgment, Inter-Am. Ct. H.R. (ser. C) No. 95 (Aug. 29, 2002).
137. Juridical Condition & Human Rights of the Child, Advisory Opinion OC-17/02, Inter-Am. Ct. H.R. (ser. A) No. 17 (Aug. 28, 2002).
138. Hilaire, Constantine, and Benjamin et al. v. Trinidad & Tobago, Merits, Reparations, and Costs, Judgment, Inter-Am. Ct. H.R. (ser. C) No. 94 (June 21, 2002).

139. Trujillo Oroza v. Bolivia, Reparations and Costs, Judgment, Inter-Am. Ct. H.R. (ser. C) No. 92 (Feb. 27, 2002).
140. Bámaca Velásquez v. Guatemala, Reparations and Costs, Judgment, Inter-Am. Ct. H.R. (ser. C) No. 91 (Feb. 22, 2002).
141. Cantoral Benavides v. Peru, Reparations and Costs, Judgment, Inter-Am. Ct. H.R. (ser. C) No. 88 (Dec. 3, 2001).
142. Barrios Altos v. Peru, Reparations and Costs, Judgment, Inter-Am. Ct. H.R. (ser. C) No. 87 (Nov. 30, 2001).
143. Barrios Altos v. Peru, Interpretation of the Judgment of Merits, Judgment, Inter-Am. Ct. H.R. (ser. C) No. 83 (Sept. 3, 2001).
144. Constantine et al. v. Trinidad & Tobago, Preliminary Objections, Judgment, Inter-Am. Ct. H.R. (ser. C) No. 82 (Sept. 1, 2001).
145. Benjamin et al. v. Trinidad & Tobago, Preliminary Objections, Judgment, Inter-Am. Ct. H.R. (ser. C) No. 81 (Sept. 1, 2001).
146. Hilaire v. Trinidad & Tobago, Preliminary Objections, Judgment, Inter-Am. Ct. H.R. (ser. C) No. 80 (Sept. 1, 2001).
147. Mayagna (Sumo) Awas Tingni Cmty. v. Nicaragua, Merits, Reparations, and Costs, Judgment, Inter-Am. Ct. H.R. (ser. C) No. 79 (Aug. 31, 2001).
148. Cesti Hurtado v. Peru, Reparations and Costs, 2001 Inter-Am. Ct. H.R. (ser. C) No. 78 (May 31, 2001).
149. "Street Children" (Villagrán Morales et al.) v. Guatemala, Reparations and Costs, Judgment, Inter-Am. Ct. H.R. (ser. C) No. 77 (May 26, 2001).
150. "White Van" (Paniagua Morales et al.) v. Guatemala, Reparations and Costs, Judgment, Inter-Am. Ct. H.R. (ser. C) No. 76 (May 25, 2001).
151. Barrios Altos v. Peru, Merits, Judgment, Inter-Am. Ct. H.R. (ser. C) No. 75 (Mar. 14, 2001).
152. "The Last Temptation of Christ" (Olmedo Bustos et al.) v. Chile, Merits, Reparations, and Costs, Judgment, Inter-Am. Ct. H.R. (ser. C) No. 73 (Feb. 5, 2001).
153. Baena Ricardo et al. v. Panama, Merits, Reparations, and Costs, Judgment, Inter-Am. Ct. H.R. (ser. C) No. 72 (Feb. 2, 2001).
154. Cantoral Benavides v. Peru, Merits, Judgment, Inter-Am. Ct. H.R. (ser. C) No. 69 (Aug. 18, 2000).
155. Durand and Ugarte v. Peru, Merits, Judgment, Inter-Am. Ct. H.R. (ser. C) No. 68 (Aug. 16, 2000).
156. Mayagna (Sumo) Awas Tingni Cmty. v. Nicaragua, Preliminary Objections, Judgment, Inter-Am. Ct. H.R. (ser. C) No. 66 (Feb. 1, 2000).
157. Cesti Hurtado v. Peru, Request for Interpretation of the Judgment of Merits, Order of the Court, Inter-Am. Ct. H.R. (ser. C) No. 62 (Nov. 19, 1999).
158. Baena Ricardo et al. v. Panama, Preliminary Objections, Judgment, Inter-Am. Ct. H.R. (ser. C) No. 61 (Nov. 18, 1999).
159. Caracazo v. Venezuela, Merits, Judgment, Inter-Am. Ct. H.R. (ser. C) No. 58 (Nov. 11, 1999).
160. Cesti Hurtado v. Peru, Merits, Judgment, Inter-Am. Ct. H.R. (ser. C) No. 56 (Sept. 29, 1999).
161. Constitutional Court v. Peru, Competence, Judgment, Inter-Am. Ct. H.R. (ser. C) No. 55 (Sept. 24, 1999).
162. Castillo Petruzzi et al. v. Peru, Merits, Reparations, and Costs, Judgment, Inter-Am. Ct. H.R. (ser. C) No. 52 (May 30, 1999).

163. Blake v. Guatemala, Reparations and Costs, Judgment, Inter-Am. Ct. H.R. (ser. C) No. 48 (Jan. 22, 1999).
164. Suárez Rosero v. Ecuador, Reparations and Costs, Judgment, Inter-Am. Ct. H.R. (ser. C) No. 44 (Jan. 20, 1999).
165. Castillo Páez v. Peru, Reparations and Costs, Judgment, Inter-Am. Ct. H.R. (ser. C) No. 43 (Nov. 27, 1998).
166. Loayza Tamayo v. Peru, Reparations and Costs, Judgment, Inter-Am. Ct. H.R. (ser. C) No. 42 (Nov. 27, 1998).
167. Castillo Petruzzi et al. v. Peru, Preliminary Objections, Judgment, Inter-Am. Ct. H.R. (ser. C) No. 41 (Sept. 4, 1998).
168. Cantoral Benavides v. Peru, Preliminary Objections, Judgment, Inter-Am. Ct. H.R. (ser. C) No. 40 (Sept. 3, 1998).
169. Genie Lacayo v. Nicaragua, Application for Judicial Review of the Judgment of Merits, Reparations, and Costs, Order of the Court, Inter-Am. Ct. H.R. (ser. C) No. 45 (Sept. 13, 1997).
170. Suárez Rosero v. Ecuador, Merits, Judgment, Inter-Am. Ct. H.R. (ser. C) No. 35 (Nov. 12, 1997).
171. Caballero Delgado & Santana v. Colombia, Reparations and Costs, Judgment, Inter-Am. Ct. H.R. (ser. C) No. 31 (Jan. 29, 1997).
172. Genie Lacayo v. Nicaragua, Merits, Reparations, and Costs, Judgment, Inter-Am. Ct. H.R. (ser. C) No. 30 (Jan. 29, 1997).
173. Neira Alegría et al. v. Peru, Reparations and Costs, Judgment, Inter-Am. Ct. H.R. (ser. C) No. 29 (Sept. 19, 1996).
174. El Amparo v. Venezuela, Reparations and Costs, Judgment, Inter-Am. Ct. H.R. (ser. C) No. 28 (Sept. 14, 1996).
175. Caballero Delgado and Santana v. Colombia, Merits, Judgment, Inter-Am. Ct. H.R. (ser. C) No. 22 (Dec. 8, 1995).
176. Genie Lacayo v. Nicaragua, Preliminary Objections, Judgment, Inter-Am. Ct. H.R. (ser. C) No. 21 (Jan. 27, 1995).
177. El Amparo v. Venezuela, Merits, Judgment, Inter-Am. Ct. H.R. (ser. C) No. 19 (Jan. 18, 1995).
178. Maqueda v. Argentina, Preliminary Objections, Order of the Court, Inter-Am. Ct. H.R. (ser. C) No. 18 (Jan. 17, 1995).
179. Int'l Responsibility for the Promulgation & Enforcement of Laws in Violation of the Convention (Arts. 1 & 2 of the Am. Convention on Human Rights), Advisory Opinion OC-14/94, Inter-Am. Ct. H.R. (ser. A) No. 14 (Dec. 9, 1994).
180. Caballero Delgado and Santana v. Colombia, Preliminary Objections, Judgment, Inter-Am. Ct. H.R. (ser. C) No. 17 (Jan. 21, 1994).
181. Gangaram Panday v. Suriname, Merits, Reparations, and Costs, Judgment, Inter-Am. Ct. H.R. (ser. C) No. 16 (Jan. 21, 1994).
182. Aloeboetoe et al. v. Suriname, Reparations and Costs, Judgment, Inter-Am. Ct. H.R. (ser. C) No. 15 (Sept. 10, 1993).
183. Cayara v. Peru, Preliminary Objections, Judgment, Inter-Am. Ct. H.R. (ser. C) No. 14 (Feb. 3, 1993).
184. Neira Alegría et al. v. Peru, Preliminary Objections, Judgment, Inter-Am. Ct. H.R. (ser. C) No. 13 (Dec. 11, 1991).

185. Gangaram Panday v. Suriname, Preliminary Objections, Judgment, Inter-Am. Ct. H.R. (ser. C) No. 12 (Dec. 4, 1991).
186. Aloeboetoe et al. v. Suriname, Merits, Judgment, Inter-Am. Ct. H.R. (ser. C) No. 11 (Dec. 4, 1991).
187. Velasquez Rodriguez v. Honduras, Merits, Judgment, Inter-Am. Ct. H.R. (ser. C) No. 4 (July 29, 1988).
188. Enforceability of the Right to Reply or Corr. (Arts. 14(1), 1(1), & 2 Am. Convention on Human Rights), Advisory Opinion OC-7/85, Inter-Am. Ct. H.R. (ser. A) No. 7 (Aug. 29, 1986).
189. Proposed Amendments of the Naturalization Provisions of the Constitution of Costa Rica, Advisory Opinion OC-4/84, Inter-Am. Ct. H.R. (ser. A) No. 4 (Jan. 19, 1984).
190. Effect of Reservations on the Entry into Force of the Am. Convention on Human Rights (Arts. 74 and 75), Advisory Opinion) C-2/82, Inter-Am. Ct. H.R. (ser. A) No. 2 (Sept. 24, 1982).

ARTICLE 3: RIGHT TO JURIDICAL PERSONALITY

1. Kaliña and Lokono Peoples v. Suriname, Merits, Reparations and Costs, Judgment, Inter-Am. Ct. H.R. (ser. C) No. 309 (Nov. 25, 2015).
2. Case of Peasant Community of Santa Barbara v. Peru, Preliminary Objections, Merits, Reparations and Costs, Judgment, Inter-Am. Ct. H.R. (ser. C) No. 299 (Sept. 1, 2015).
3. Rochac Hernandez et al. v. El Salvador, Merits, Reparations, and Costs, Judgment, Inter-Am. Ct. H.R. (ser. C) No. 285 (Oct. 14, 2014).
4. Expelled Dominicans and Haitians v. Dominican Republic, Preliminary Objections, Merits, Reparations, and Costs, Judgment, Inter-Am. Ct. H.R. (ser. C) No. 282 (Aug. 28, 2014).
5. J. v. Peru, Preliminary Objections, Merits, Reparations, and Costs, Judgment, Inter-Am. Ct. H.R. (ser. C) No. 275 (Nov. 27, 2013). [footnote].
6. Osorio Rivera & Family v. Peru, Preliminary Objections, Merits, Reparations, and Costs, Judgment, Inter-Am. Ct. H.R. (ser. C) No. 274 (Nov. 26, 2013).
7. Mendoza et al. v. Argentina, Preliminary Objections, Merits, and Reparations, Judgment, Inter-Am. Ct. H.R. (ser. C) No. 260 (May 14, 2013).
8. García and Family Members v. Guatemala, Merits, Reparations, and Costs, Judgment, Inter-Am. Ct. H.R. (ser. C) No. 258 (Nov. 29, 2012).
9. Gudiel Alvarez et al. ("Diario Militar") v. Guatemala, Merits, Reparations, and Costs, Judgment, Inter-Am. Ct. H.R. (ser. C) No. 253 (Nov. 20, 2012).
10. Río Negro Massacres v. Guatemala, Preliminary Objections, Merits, Reparations, and Costs, Judgment, Inter-Am. Ct. H.R. (ser. C) No. 250 (Sept. 4, 2012).
11. Gonzalez Medina & Family v. Dominican Republic, Preliminary Objections, Merits, Reparations, and Costs, Judgment, Inter-Am. Ct. H.R. (ser. C) No. 240 (Feb. 27, 2012).
12. Contreras et. al. v. El Salvador, Merits, Reparations, and Costs, Judgment, Inter-Am. Ct. H.R. (ser. C) No. 232 (Aug. 31, 2011).
13. Torres Millacura et al. v. Argentina, Merits, Reparations, and Costs, Judgment, Inter-Am. Ct. H.R. (ser. C) No. 229 (Aug. 26, 2011).
14. Gelman v. Uruguay, Merits and Reparations, Judgment, Inter-Am. Ct. H.R. (ser. C) No. 221 (Feb. 24, 2011).

15. Gomes Lund et al. ("Guerrilha do Araguaia") v. Brazil, Preliminary Objections, Merits, Reparations, and Costs, Judgment, Inter-Am. Ct. H.R. (ser. C) No. 219 (Nov. 24, 2010).
16. Ibsen Cardenas and Ibsen Peña v. Bolivia, Merits, Reparations, and Costs, Judgment, Inter-Am. Ct. H.R. (ser. C) No. 217 (Sept. 1, 2010).
17. Xákmok Kásek Indigenous Cmty. v. Paraguay, Merits, Reparations, and Costs, Judgment, Inter-Am. Ct. H.R. (ser. C) No. 214 (Aug. 24, 2010).
18. Chitay Nech et al. v. Guatemala, Preliminary Objections, Merits, Reparations, and Costs, Judgment, Inter-Am. Ct. H.R. (ser. C) No. 212 (May 25, 2010).
19. Radilla Pacheco v. Mexico, Preliminary Objections, Merits, Reparations, and Costs, Judgment, Inter-Am. Ct. H.R. (ser. C) No. 209 (Nov. 23, 2009).
20. Anzualdo Castro v. Peru, Preliminary Objections, Merits, Reparations, and Costs, Judgment, Inter-Am. Ct. H.R. (ser. C) No. 202 (Sept. 22, 2009).
21. Ticona Estrada et al. v. Bolivia, Merits, Reparations, and Costs, Judgment, Inter-Am. Ct. H.R. (ser. C) No. 191 (Nov. 27, 2008).
22. Saramaka People v. Suriname, Interpretation of the Judgment on Preliminary Objections, Merits, Reparations, and Costs, Judgment, Inter-Am. Ct. H.R. (ser. C) No. 185 (Aug. 12, 2008).
23. Saramaka People v. Suriname, Preliminary Objections, Merits, Reparations, and Costs, Judgment, Inter-Am. Ct. H.R. (ser. C) No. 172 (Nov. 28, 2007).
24. La Cantuta v. Peru, Merits, Reparations, and Costs, Judgment, Inter-Am. Ct. H.R. (ser. C) No. 162 (Nov. 29, 2006).
25. Sawhoyamaxa Indigenous Cmty. v. Paraguay, Merits, Reparations, and Costs, Judgment, Inter-Am. Ct. H.R. (ser. C) No. 146 (Mar. 29, 2006).
26. Yean and Bosico v. Dominican Republic, Preliminary Objections, Merits, Reparations, and Costs, Judgment, Inter-Am. Ct. H.R. (ser. C) No. 130 (Sept. 8, 2005).
27. Juridical Condition & Human Rights of the Child, Advisory Opinion OC-17/02, Inter-Am. Ct. H.R. (ser. A) No. 17 (Aug. 28, 2002).
28. Trujillo Oroza v. Bolivia, Reparations and Costs, Judgment, Inter-Am. Ct. H.R. (ser. C) No. 92 (Feb. 27, 2002).
29. Bámaca Velásquez v. Guatemala, Reparations and Costs, Judgment, Inter-Am. Ct. H.R. (ser. C) No. 91 (Feb. 22, 2002).
30. Bámaca Velásquez v. Guatemala, Merits, Judgment, Inter-Am. Ct. H.R. (ser. C) No. 70 (Nov. 25, 2000).
31. Trujillo Oroza v. Bolivia, Merits, Judgment, Inter-Am. Ct. H.R. (ser. C) No. 64 (Jan. 26, 2000).
32. Garrido and Baigorria v. Argentina, Reparations and Costs, Judgment, Inter-Am. Ct. H.R. (ser. C) No. 39 (Aug. 27, 1998).
33. Benavides Cevallos v. Ecuador, Merits, Reparations, and Costs, Judgment, Inter-Am. Ct. H.R. (ser. C) No. 38 (June 19, 1998).
34. Blake v. Guatemala, Preliminary Objections, Judgment, Inter-Am. Ct. H.R. (ser. C) No. 27 (July 2, 1996).
35. Judicial Guarantees in States of Emergency (Arts. 27(2), 25, and 8 American Convention on Human Rights), Advisory Opinion OC-9/87, Inter-Am. Ct. H.R. (ser. A) No. 9 (Oct. 6, 1987).
36. Habeas Corpus in Emergency Situations (Arts. 27(2), 25(1), and 7(6) American Convention on Human Rights), Advisory Opinion OC-8/87, Inter-Am. Ct. H.R. (ser. A) No. 8 (Jan. 30, 1987).

ARTICLE 4: RIGHT TO LIFE

1. Duque v. Colombia, Preliminary Objections, Merits, Reparations and Costs, Judgment, Inter-Am. Ct. H.R. (ser. C) No. 310 (Feb. 26, 2016).
2. Velasquez Paiz et al. v. Guatemala, Preliminary Objections, Merits, Reparations and Costs, Judgment, Inter-Am. Ct. H.R. (ser. C) No. 307 (Nov. 19, 2015).
3. Garcia Ibarra et al. v. Ecuador, Preliminary Objections, Merits, Reparations and Costs, Judgment, Inter-Am. Ct. H.R. (ser. C) No. 306 (Nov. 17, 2015).
4. Community Garifuna Triunfo de la Cruz & its Members v. Honduras, Merits, Reparations and Costs, Judgment, Inter-Am. Ct. H.R. (ser. C) No. 305 (Oct. 8, 2015).
5. Garifuna Punta Piedra Community and its Members v. Honduras, Preliminary Objections, Merits, Reparations and Costs, Judgment, Inter-Am. Ct. H.R. (ser. C) No. 304 (Oct. 8, 2015).
6. Case of Peasant Community of Santa Barbara v. Peru, Preliminary Objections, Merits, Reparations and Costs, Judgment, Inter-Am. Ct. H.R. (ser. C) No. 299 (Sept. 1, 2015).
7. Gonzales Lluy et al. v. Ecuador, Preliminary Objections, Merits, Reparations and Costs, Judgment, Inter-Am. Ct. H.R. (ser. C) No. 298 (September 1, 2015).
8. Wong Ho Wing v. Peru, Preliminary Objection, Merits, Reparations and Costs, Judgment, Inter-Am. Ct. H.R. (ser. C) No. 297 (June 30, 2015).
9. Canales Huapaya et al v. Peru, Preliminary Objections, Merits, Reparations, Costs, Judgment, Inter-Am. Ct. H.R. (ser. C) No. 296 (June 24, 2015).
10. Cruz Sánchez et al. v. Peru, Preliminary Objections, Merits, Reparations, Costs, Judgment, Inter-Am. Ct. H.R. (ser. C) No. 292 (Apr. 17, 2015).
11. Rodriguez Vera et al. (Persons Disappeared from the Palace of Justice) v. Colombia, Preliminary Objections, Merits, Reparations, and Costs, Judgment, Inter-Am. Ct. H.R. (ser. C) No. 287 (Nov. 14, 2014).
12. Tarazona Arrieta et al. v. Peru, Preliminary Objections, Merits, Reparations, and Costs, Judgment, Inter-Am. Ct. H.R. (ser. C) No. 286 (Oct. 15, 2014).
13. Rochac Hernandez et al. v. El Salvador, Merits, Reparations, and Costs, Judgment, Inter-Am. Ct. H.R. (ser. C) No. 285 (Oct. 14, 2014).
14. Human Rights Defender et al. v. Guatemala, Preliminary Objections, Merits, Reparations, and Costs, Judgment, Inter-Am. Ct. H.R. (ser. C) No. 283 (Aug. 28, 2014).
15. Landaeta Meijias Brothers et al. v. Venezuela, Preliminary Objections, Merits, Reparations, and Costs, Judgment, Inter-Am. Ct. H.R. (ser. C) No. 281 (Aug. 27, 2014).
16. Rights & Guar. of Children in the Context of Migration and/or in Need of Int'l Prot., Advisory Opinion OC-21/14, Inter-Am. Ct. H.R. (ser. A) No. 21 (Aug. 19, 2014).
17. Veliz Franco et al. v. Guatemala, Preliminary Objections, Merits, and Reparations, Judgment, Inter-Am. Ct. H.R. (ser. C) No. 277 (May 19, 2014).
18. Liakat Ali Alibux v. Suriname, Preliminary Objections, Merits, Reparations, and Costs, Judgment, Inter-Am. Ct. H.R. (ser. C) No. 276 (Jan. 30, 2014).
19. J. v. Peru, Preliminary Objections, Merits, Reparations, and Costs, Judgment, Inter-Am. Ct. H.R. (ser. C) No. 275 (Nov. 27, 2013). [footnote].
20. Osorio Rivera and Family v. Peru, Preliminary Objections, Merits, Reparations, and Costs, Judgment, Inter-Am. Ct. H.R. (ser. C) No. 274 (Nov. 26, 2013).
21. Gutiérrez and Family v. Argentina, Merits, Reparations, and Costs, Judgment, Inter-Am. Ct. H.R. (ser. C) No. 271 (Nov. 25, 2013).

22. Afro-Descendant Communities Displaced from the Cacarica River Basin (Operation Genesis) v. Colombia, Preliminary Objections, Merits, Reparations, and Costs, Judgment, Inter-Am. Ct. H.R. (ser. C) No. 270 (Nov. 20, 2013).
23. Luna Lopez v. Honduras, Merits, Reparations, and Costs, Judgment, Inter-Am. Ct. H.R. (ser. C) No. 269 (Oct. 10, 2013).
24. Massacre of Santo Domingo v. Colombia, Request for Interpretation of the Judgment on Preliminary Objections, Merits, Reparations, and Costs, Judgment, Inter-Am. Ct. H.R. (ser. C) No. 263 (Aug. 19, 2013).
25. Mendoza et al. v. Argentina, Preliminary Objections, Merits, and Reparations, Judgment, Inter-Am. Ct. H.R. (ser. C) No. 260 (May 14, 2013).
26. Santo Domingo Massacre v. Colombia, Preliminary Objections, Merits, and Reparations, Judgment, Inter-Am. Ct. H.R. (ser. C) No. 259 (Nov. 30, 2012).
27. García and Family Members v. Guatemala, Merits, Reparations, and Costs, Judgment, Inter-Am. Ct. H.R. (ser. C) No. 258 (Nov. 29, 2012).
28. Artavia Murillo et al. (In-vitro Fertilization) v. Costa Rica, Preliminary Objections, Merits, Reparations, and Costs, Judgment, Inter-Am. Ct. H.R. (ser. C) No. 257 (Nov. 28, 2012).
29. Castillo González et al. v. Venezuela, Merits, Judgment, Inter-Am. Ct. H.R. (ser. C) No. 256 (Nov. 27, 2012).
30. Gudiel Alvarez et al. ("Diario Militar") v. Guatemala, Merits, Reparations, and Costs, Judgment, Inter-Am. Ct. H.R. (ser. C) No. 253 (Nov. 20, 2012).
31. Massacres of El Mozote and Nearby Places v. El Salvador, Merits, Reparations, and Costs, Judgment, Inter-Am. Ct. H.R. (ser. C) No. 252 (Oct. 25, 2012).
32. Nadege Dorzema et al. v. Dominican Republic, Merits, Reparations, and Costs, Judgment, Inter-Am. Ct. H.R. (ser. C) No. 251 (Oct. 24, 2012).
33. Río Negro Massacres v. Guatemala, Preliminary Objections, Merits, Reparations, and Costs, Judgment, Inter-Am. Ct. H.R. (ser. C) No. 250 (Sept. 4, 2012).
34. Uzcátegui et al. v. Venezuela, Merits and Reparations, Judgment, Inter-Am. Ct. H.R. (ser. C) No. 249 (Sept. 3, 2012).
35. Palma Mendoza et al. v. Ecuador, Preliminary Objections and Merits, Judgment, Inter-Am. Ct. H.R. (ser. C) No. 247 (Sept. 3, 2012).
36. Kichwa Indigenous People of Sarayaku v. Ecuador, Merits and Reparations, Judgment Inter.-Am. Ct. H.R. (ser. C) No. 245 (June 27, 2012).
37. Díaz Peña v. Venezuela, Preliminary Objections, Merits, Reparations, and Costs, Judgment, Inter-Am. Ct. H.R. (ser. C) No. 244 (June 26, 2012).
38. Pacheco Teruel et al. v. Honduras, Merits, Reparations, and Costs, Judgment, Inter-Am. Ct. H.R. (ser. C) No. 241 (Apr. 27, 2012).
39. Gonzalez Medina and Family v. Dominican Republic, Preliminary Objections, Merits, Reparations, and Costs, Judgment, Inter-Am. Ct. H.R. (ser. C) No. 240 (Feb. 27, 2012).
40. Barrios Family v. Venezuela, Merits, Reparations, and Costs, Judgment, Inter-Am. Ct. H.R. (ser. C) No. 237 (Nov. 24, 2011).
41. Contreras et. al. v. El Salvador, Merits, Reparations, and Costs, Judgment, Inter-Am. Ct. H.R. (ser. C) No. 232 (Aug. 31, 2011).
42. Torres Millacura et al. v. Argentina, Merits, Reparations, and Costs, Judgment, Inter-Am. Ct. H.R. (ser. C) No. 229 (Aug. 26, 2011).

43. Vera Vera et al. v. Ecuador, Preliminary Objections, Merits, Reparations, and Costs, Judgment, Inter-Am. Ct. H.R. (ser. C) No. 226 (May 19, 2011).
44. Gelman v. Uruguay, Merits and Reparations, Judgment, Inter-Am. Ct. H.R. (ser. C) No. 221 (Feb. 24, 2011).
45. Gomes Lund et al. ("Guerrilha do Araguaia") v. Brazil, Preliminary Objections, Merits, Reparations, and Costs, Judgment, Inter-Am. Ct. H.R. (ser. C) No. 219 (Nov. 24, 2010).
46. Ibsen Cardenas and Ibsen Peña v. Bolivia, Merits, Reparations, and Costs, Judgment, Inter-Am. Ct. H.R. (ser. C) No. 217 (Sept. 1, 2010).
47. Xákmok Kásek Indigenous Cmty. v. Paraguay, Merits, Reparations, and Costs, Judgment, Inter-Am. Ct. H.R. (ser. C) No. 214 (Aug. 24, 2010).
48. Cepeda Vargas v. Colombia, Preliminary Objections, Merits, Reparations, and Costs, Judgment, Inter-Am. Ct. H.R. (ser. C.) No. 213 (May 26, 2010).
49. Chitay Nech et al. v. Guatemala, Preliminary Objections, Merits, Reparations, and Costs, Judgment, Inter-Am. Ct. H.R. (ser. C) No. 212 (May 25, 2010).
50. "Las Dos Erres" Massacre v. Guatemala, Preliminary Objections, Merits, Reparations, and Costs, Judgment, Inter-Am. Ct. H.R. (ser. C) No. 211 (Nov. 24, 2009).
51. Radilla Pacheco v. Mexico, Preliminary Objections, Merits, Reparations, and Costs, Judgment, Inter-Am. Ct. H.R. (ser. C) No. 209 (Nov. 23, 2009).
52. González et al. ("Cotton Field") v. Mexico, Preliminary Objections, Merits, Reparations, and Costs, Judgment, Inter-Am. Ct. H.R. (ser. C) No. 205 (Nov. 16, 2009).
53. DaCosta Cadogan v. Barbados, Preliminary Objections, Merits, Reparations, and Costs, Judgment, Inter-Am. Ct. H.R. (ser. C) No. 204 (Sept. 24, 2009).
54. Garibaldi v. Brazil, Preliminary Objections, Merits, Reparations, and Costs, Judgment, Inter-Am. Ct. H.R. (ser. C) No. 203 (Sept. 23, 2009).
55. Anzualdo Castro v. Peru, Preliminary Objections, Merits, Reparations, and Costs, Judgment, Inter-Am. Ct. H.R. (ser. C) No. 202 (Sept. 22, 2009).
56. Kawas Fernández v. Honduras, Merits, Reparations, and Costs, Judgment, Inter-Am. Ct. H.R. (ser. C) No. 196 (Apr. 3, 2009).
57. Valle Jaramillo et al. v. Colombia, Merits, Reparations, and Costs, Judgment, Inter-Am. Ct. H.R. (ser. C) No. 192 (Nov. 27, 2008).
58. Ticona Estrada et al. v. Bolivia, Merits, Reparations, and Costs, Judgment, Inter-Am. Ct. H.R. (ser. C) No. 191 (Nov. 27, 2008).
59. Tiu Tojín v. Guatemala, Merits, Reparations, and Costs, Judgment, Inter-Am. Ct. H.R. (ser. C) No. 190 (Nov. 26, 2008).
60. Heliodoro Portugal v. Panama, Preliminary Objections, Merits, Reparations, and Costs, Judgment, Inter-Am. Ct. H.R. (ser. C) No. 186 (Aug. 12, 2008).
61. Albán Cornejo et al. v. Ecuador, Merits, Reparations, and Costs, Judgment, Inter-Am. Ct. H.R. (ser. C) No. 171 (Nov. 22, 2007).
62. Boyce et al. v. Barbados, Preliminary Objections, Merits, Reparations, and Costs, Judgment, Inter-Am. Ct. H.R. (ser. C) No. 169 (Nov. 20, 2007).
63. García Prieto et al. v. El Salvador, Preliminary Objections, Merits, Reparations, and Costs, Judgment, Inter-Am. Ct. H.R. (ser. C) No. 168 (Nov. 20, 2007).
64. Cantoral Huamaní and García Santa Cruz v. Peru, Preliminary Objections, Merits, Reparations, and Costs, Judgment, Inter-Am. Ct. H.R. (ser. C) No. 167 (July 10, 2007).

65. Zambrano Vélez et al. v. Ecuador, Merits, Reparations, and Costs, Judgment, Inter-Am. Ct. H.R. (ser. C) No. 166 (July 4, 2007).
66. Escué Zapata v. Colombia, Merits, Reparations, and Costs, Judgment, Inter-Am. Ct. H.R. (ser. C) No. 165 (July 4, 2007).
67. Rochela Massacre v. Colombia, Merits, Reparations, and Costs, Judgment, Inter-Am. Ct. H.R. (ser. C) No. 163 (May 11, 2007).
68. La Cantuta v. Peru, Merits, Reparations, and Costs, Judgment, Inter-Am. Ct. H.R. (ser. C) No. 162 (Nov. 29, 2006).
69. Miguel Castro Castro Prison v. Peru, Merits, Reparations, and Costs, Judgment, Inter-Am. Ct. H.R. (ser. C) No. 160 (Nov. 25, 2006).
70. Vargas Areco v. Paraguay, Merits, Reparations, and Costs, Judgment, Inter-Am. Ct. H.R. (ser. C) No. 155 (Sept. 26, 2006).
71. Goiburú et al. v. Paraguay, Merits, Reparations, and Costs, Judgment, Inter-Am. Ct. H.R. (ser. C) No. 153 (Sept. 22, 2006).
72. Servellón García et al. v. Honduras, Merits, Reparations, and Costs, Judgment, Inter-Am. Ct. H.R. (ser. C) No. 152 (Sept. 21, 2006).
73. Montero Aranguren et al. (Det. Ctr. of Catia) v. Venezuela, Preliminary Objection, Merits, Reparations, and Costs, Judgment, Inter-Am. Ct. H.R. (ser. C) No. 150 (July 5, 2006).
74. Ximenes Lopes v. Brazil, Merits, Reparations, and Costs, Judgment, Inter-Am. Ct. H.R. (ser. C) No. 149 (July 4, 2006).
75. Ituango Massacres v. Colombia, Preliminary Objections, Merits, Reparations, and Costs, Judgment, Inter-Am. Ct. H.R. (ser. C) No. 148 (July 1, 2006).
76. Baldeón García v. Peru, Merits, Reparations, and Costs, Judgment, Inter-Am. Ct. H.R. (ser. C) No. 147 (Apr. 6, 2006).
77. Sawhoyamaxa Indigenous Cmty. v. Paraguay, Merits, Reparations, and Costs, Judgment, Inter-Am. Ct. H.R. (ser. C) No. 146 (Mar. 29, 2006).
78. Raxcacó Reyes v. Guatemala, Interpretation of the Judgment of Merits, Reparations, and Costs, Judgment, Inter-Am. Ct. H.R. (ser. C) No. 143 (Feb. 6, 2006).
79. Yakye Axa Indigenous Cmty. v. Paraguay, Interpretation of the Judgment of Merits, Reparations, and Costs, Judgment, Inter-Am. Ct. H.R. (ser. C) No. 142 (Feb. 6, 2006).
80. Pueblo Bello Massacre v. Colombia, Merits, Reparations, and Costs, Judgment, Inter-Am. Ct. H.R. (ser. C) No. 140 (Jan. 31, 2006).
81. Ximenes Lopes v. Brazil, Preliminary Objections, Judgment, Inter-Am. Ct. H.R. (ser. C) No. 139 (Nov. 30, 2005).
82. Blanco Romero et al. v. Venezuela, Merits, Reparations, and Costs, Judgment, Inter-Am. Ct. H.R. (ser. C) No. 138 (Nov. 28, 2005).
83. Gómez Palomino v. Peru, Merits, Reparations, and Costs, Judgment, Inter-Am. Ct. H.R. (ser. C) No. 136 (Nov. 22, 2005).
84. Mapiripán Massacre v. Colombia, Merits, Reparations, and Costs, Judgment, Inter-Am. Ct. H.R. (ser. C) No. 134 (Sept. 15, 2005).
85. Raxcacó Reyes v. Guatemala, Merits, Reparations, and Costs, Judgment, Inter-Am. Ct. H.R. (ser. C) No. 133 (Sept. 15, 2005).
86. Serrano Cruz Sisters v. El Salvador, Interpretation of the Judgment of Merits, Reparations, and Costs, Judgment, Inter-Am. Ct. H.R. (ser. C) No. 131 (Sept. 9, 2005).

87. Fermín Ramírez v. Guatemala, Merits, Reparations, and Costs, Judgment, Inter-Am. Ct. H.R. (ser. C) No. 126 (June 20, 2005).
88. Yakye Axa Indigenous Cmty. v. Paraguay, Merits, Reparations, and Costs, Judgment, Inter-Am. Ct. H.R. (ser. C) No. 125 (June 17, 2005).
89. Mapiripán Massacre v. Colombia, Preliminary Objections, Judgment, Inter-Am. Ct. H.R. (ser. C) No. 122 (Mar. 7, 2005).
90. Huilca Tecse v. Peru, Merits, Reparations, and Costs, Judgment, Inter-Am. Ct. H.R. (ser. C) No. 121 (Mar. 3, 2005).
91. Serrano Cruz Sisters v. El Salvador, Merits, Reparations, and Costs, Judgment, Inter-Am. Ct. H.R. (ser. C) No. 120 (Mar. 1, 2005).
92. Serrano Cruz Sisters v. El Salvador, Preliminary Objections, Judgment, Inter-Am. Ct. H.R. (ser. C) No. 118 (Nov. 23, 2004).
93. Carpio Nicolle et al. v. Guatemala, Merits, Reparations, and Costs, Judgment, Inter-Am. Ct. H.R. (ser. C) No. 117 (Nov. 22, 2004).
94. "Juvenile Reeducation Institute" v. Paraguay, Preliminary Objections, Merits, Reparations, and Costs, Judgment, Inter-Am. Ct. H.R. (ser. C) No. 112 (Sept. 2, 2004).
95. Gómez Paquiyauri Brothers v. Peru, Merits, Reparations, and Costs, Judgment, Inter-Am. Ct. H.R. (ser. C) No. 110 (July 8, 2004).
96. 19 Merchants v. Colombia, Merits, Reparations, and Costs, Judgment, Inter-Am. Ct. H.R. (ser. C) No. 109 (July 5, 2004).
97. Molina Theissen v. Guatemala, Reparations and Costs, Judgment, Inter-Am. Ct. H.R. (ser. C) No. 108 (July 3, 2004).
98. Molina Theissen v. Guatemala, Merits, Judgment, Inter-Am. Ct. H.R. (ser. C) No. 106 (May 4, 2004).
99. Sánchez v. Honduras, Interpretation of the Judgment of Preliminary Objection, Merits, and Reparations, Judgment, Inter-Am. Ct. H.R. (ser. C) No. 102 (Nov. 26, 2003).
100. Mack Chang v. Guatemala, Merits, Reparations, and Costs, Judgment, Inter-Am. Ct. H.R. (ser. C) No. 101 (Nov. 25, 2003).
101. Bulacio v. Argentina, Merits, Reparations, and Costs, Judgment, Inter-Am. Ct. H.R. (ser. C) No. 100 (Sept. 18, 2003).
102. Sánchez v. Honduras, Preliminary Objection, Merits, Reparations, and Costs, Judgment, Inter-Am. Ct. H.R. (ser. C) No. 99 (June 7, 2003).
103. Las Palmeras v. Colombia, Reparations and Costs, Judgment, Inter-Am. Ct. H.R. (ser. C) No. 96 (Nov. 26, 2002).
104. Caracazo v. Venezuela, Reparations and Costs, Judgment, Inter-Am. Ct. H.R. (ser. C) No. 95 (Aug. 29, 2002).
105. Juridical Condition & Human Rights of the Child, Advisory Opinion OC-17/02, Inter-Am. Ct. H.R. (ser. A) No. 17 (Aug. 28, 2002).
106. Hilaire, Constantine, and Benjamin et al. v. Trinidad & Tobago, Merits, Reparations, and Costs, Judgment, Inter-Am. Ct. H.R. (ser. C) No. 94 (June 21, 2002).
107. 19 Merchants v. Colombia, Preliminary Objection, Judgment, Inter-Am. Ct. H.R. (ser. C) No. 93 (June 12, 2002).
108. Trujillo Oroza v. Bolivia, Reparations and Costs, Judgment, Inter-Am. Ct. H.R. (ser. C) No. 92 (Feb. 27, 2002).
109. Bámaca Velásquez v. Guatemala, Reparations and Costs, Judgment, Inter-Am. Ct. H.R. (ser. C) No. 91 (Feb. 22, 2002).

110. Las Palmeras v. Colombia, Merits, Judgment, Inter-Am. Ct. H.R. (Ser. C) No. 90 (Dec. 6, 2001).
111. Durand and Ugarte v. Peru, Reparations and Costs, Judgment, Inter-Am. Ct. H.R. (ser. C) No. 89 (Dec. 3, 2001).
112. Barrios Altos v. Peru, Reparations and Costs, Judgment, Inter-Am. Ct. H.R. (ser. C) No. 87 (Nov. 30, 2001).
113. Cantos v. Argentina, Preliminary Objections, Judgment, Inter-Am. Ct. H.R. (ser. C) No. 85 (Sept. 7, 2001). [footnote]
114. Constantine et al. v. Trinidad & Tobago, Preliminary Objections, Judgment, Inter-Am. Ct. H.R. (ser. C) No. 82 (Sept. 1, 2001).
115. Benjamin et al. v. Trinidad & Tobago, Preliminary Objections, Judgment, Inter-Am. Ct. H.R. (ser. C) No. 81 (Sept. 1, 2001).
116. Hilaire v. Trinidad & Tobago, Preliminary Objections, Judgment, Inter-Am. Ct. H.R. (ser. C) No. 80 (Sept. 1, 2001).
117. Mayagna (Sumo) Awas Tingni Cmty. v. Nicaragua, Merits, Reparations, and Costs, Judgment, Inter-Am. Ct. H.R. (ser. C) No. 79 (Aug. 31, 2001).
118. "Street Children" (Villagrán Morales et al.) v. Guatemala, Reparations and Costs, Judgment, Inter-Am. Ct. H.R. (ser. C) No. 77 (May 26, 2001).
119. "White Van" (Paniagua Morales et al.) v. Guatemala, Reparations and Costs, Judgment, Inter-Am. Ct. H.R. (ser. C) No. 76 (May 25, 2001).
120. Barrios Altos v. Peru, Merits, Judgment, Inter-Am. Ct. H.R. (ser. C) No. 75 (Mar. 14, 2001).
121. Bámaca Velásquez v. Guatemala, Merits, Judgment, Inter-Am. Ct. H.R. (ser. C) No. 70 (Nov. 25, 2000).
122. Durand and Ugarte v. Peru, Merits, Judgment, Inter-Am. Ct. H.R. (ser. C) No. 68 (Aug. 16, 2000).
123. Las Palmeras v. Colombia, Preliminary Objections, Judgment, Inter-Am. Ct. H.R. (ser. C) No. 67 (Feb. 4, 2000).
124. Trujillo Oroza v. Bolivia, Merits, Judgment, Inter-Am. Ct. H.R. (ser. C) No. 64 (Jan. 26, 2000).
125. "Street Children" (Villagrán Morales et al.) v. Guatemala, Merits, Judgment, Inter-Am. Ct. H.R. (ser. C) No. 63 (Nov. 19, 1999).
126. Caracazo v. Venezuela, Merits, Judgment, Inter-Am. Ct. H.R. (ser. C) No. 58 (Nov. 11, 1999).
127. Right to Information on Consular Assistance in the Framework of the Guarantees of the Due Process of Law, Advisory Opinion OC-16/99, Inter-Am. Ct. H.R. (ser. A) No. 16 (Oct. 1, 1999).
128. Durand and Ugarte v. Peru, Preliminary Objections, Judgment, Inter-Am. Ct. H.R. (ser. C) No. 50 (May 28, 1999).
129. Blake v. Guatemala, Reparations and Costs, Judgment, Inter-Am. Ct. H.R. (ser. C) No. 48 (Jan. 22, 1999).
130. Castillo Páez v. Peru, Reparations and Costs, Judgment, Inter-Am. Ct. H.R. (ser. C) No. 43 (Nov. 27, 1998).
131. Garrido and Baigorria v. Argentina, Reparations and Costs, Judgment, Inter-Am. Ct. H.R. (ser. C) No. 39 (Aug. 27, 1998).
132. Benavides Cevallos v. Ecuador, Merits, Reparations, and Costs, Judgment, Inter-Am. Ct. H.R. (ser. C) No. 38 (June 19, 1998).
133. Blake v. Guatemala, Merits, Judgment, Inter-Am. Ct. H.R. (ser. C) No. 36 (Jan. 24, 1998).

134. Castillo Páez v. Peru, Merits, Judgment, Inter-Am. Ct. H.R. (ser. C) No. 34 (Nov. 3, 1997).
135. "Street Children" (Villagrán Morales et al.) v. Guatemala, Preliminary Objections, Judgment, Inter-Am. Ct. H.R. (ser. C) No. 32 (Sept. 11, 1997).
136. Caballero Delgado and Santana v. Colombia, Reparations and Costs, Judgment, Inter-Am. Ct. H.R. (ser. C) No. 31 (Jan. 29, 1997).
137. Neira Alegría et al. v. Peru, Reparations and Costs, Judgment, Inter-Am. Ct. H.R. (ser. C) No. 29 (Sept. 19, 1996).
138. El Amparo v. Venezuela, Reparations and Costs, Judgment, Inter-Am. Ct. H.R. (ser. C) No. 28 (Sept. 14, 1996).
139. Blake v. Guatemala, Preliminary Objections, Judgment, Inter-Am. Ct. H.R. (ser. C) No. 27 (July 2, 1996).
140. Garrido and Baigorria v. Argentina, Merits, Judgment, Inter-Am. Ct. H.R. (ser. C) No. 26 (Feb. 2, 1996).
141. Castillo Páez v. Peru, Preliminary Objections, Judgment, Inter-Am. Ct. H.R. (ser. C) No. 24 (Jan. 30, 1996).
142. "White Van" (Paniagua Morales et al.) v. Guatemala, Preliminary Objections, Judgment, Inter-Am. Ct. H.R. (ser. C) No. 23 (Jan. 25, 1996).
143. Caballero Delgado and Santana v. Colombia, Merits, Judgment, Inter-Am. Ct. H.R. (ser. C) No. 22 (Dec. 8, 1995).
144. Genie Lacayo v. Nicaragua, Preliminary Objections, Judgment, Inter-Am. Ct. H.R. (ser. C) No. 21 (Jan. 27, 1995).
145. Neira Alegría et al. v. Peru, Merits, Judgment, Inter-Am. Ct. H.R. (ser. C) No. 20 (Jan. 19, 1995).
146. El Amparo v. Venezuela, Merits, Judgment, Inter-Am. Ct. H.R. (ser. C) No. 19 (Jan. 18, 1995).
147. Int'l Responsibility for the Promulgation & Enforcement of Laws in Violation of the Convention (Arts. 1 & 2 of the Am. Convention on Human Rights), Advisory Opinion OC-14/94, Inter-Am. Ct. H.R. (ser. A) No. 14 (Dec. 9, 1994).
148. Caballero Delgado and Santana v. Colombia, Preliminary Objections, Judgment, Inter-Am. Ct. H.R. (ser. C) No. 17 (Jan. 21, 1994).
149. Gangaram Panday v. Suriname, Merits, Reparations, and Costs, Judgment, Inter-Am. Ct. H.R. (ser. C) No. 16 (Jan. 21, 1994).
150. Aloeboetoe et al. v. Suriname, Reparations and Costs, Judgment, Inter-Am. Ct. H.R. (ser. C) No. 15 (Sept. 10, 1993).
151. Cayara v. Peru, Preliminary Objections, Judgment, Inter-Am. Ct. H.R. (ser. C) No. 14 (Feb. 3, 1993).
152. Neira Alegría et al. v. Peru, Preliminary Objections, Judgment, Inter-Am. Ct. H.R. (ser. C) No. 13 (Dec. 11, 1991).
153. Gangaram Panday v. Suriname, Preliminary Objections, Judgment, Inter-Am. Ct. H.R. (ser. C) No. 12 (Dec. 4, 1991).
154. Aloeboetoe et al. v. Suriname, Merits, Judgment, Inter-Am. Ct. H.R. (ser. C) No. 11 (Dec. 4, 1991).
155. Fairén Garbi and Solís Corrales v. Honduras, Merits, Judgment, Inter-Am. Ct. H.R. (ser. C) No. 6 (Mar. 15, 1989).

156. Godínez Cruz v. Honduras, Merits, Judgment, Inter-Am. Ct. H.R. (ser. C) No. 5 (Jan. 20, 1989).
157. Velásquez Rodríguez v. Honduras, Merits, Judgment, Inter-Am. Ct. H.R. (ser. C) No. 4 (July 29, 1988).
158. Judicial Guarantees in States of Emergency (Arts. 27(2), 25, and 8 American Convention on Human Rights), Advisory Opinion OC-9/87, Inter-Am. Ct. H.R. (ser. A) No. 9 (Oct. 6, 1987).
159. Godínez Cruz v. Honduras, Preliminary Objections, Judgment, Inter-Am. Ct. H.R. (ser. C) No. 3 (June 26, 1987).
160. Fairén Garbi and Solís Corrales v. Honduras, Preliminary Objections, Judgment, Inter-Am. Ct. H.R. (ser. C) No. 2 (June 26, 1987).
161. Velásquez Rodríguez v. Honduras, Preliminary Objections, Judgment, Inter-Am. Ct. H.R. (ser. C) No. 1 (June 26, 1987).
162. Habeas Corpus in Emergency Situations (Arts. 27(2), 25(1), and 7(6) American Convention on Human Rights), Advisory Opinion OC-8/87, Inter-Am. Ct. H.R. (ser. A) No. 8 (Jan. 30, 1987).
163. Restrictions to the Death Penalty (Arts. 4(2) and 4(4) American Convention on Human Rights), Advisory Opinion OC-3/83, Inter-Am. Ct. H.R. (ser. A) No. 3 (Sept. 8, 1983).
164. In the Matter of Viviana Gallardo et al., Inter-Am. Ct. H.R. (ser. A) No. 101 (July 15, 1981).

ARTICLE 5: RIGHT TO HUMANE TREATMENT

1. Duque v. Colombia, Preliminary Objections, Merits, Reparations and Costs, Judgment, Inter-Am. Ct. H.R. (ser. C) No. 310 (Feb. 26, 2016).
2. Quispialaya Vilcapoma v. Peru, Preliminary Objections, Merits, Reparations and Costs, Judgment, Inter-Am. Ct. H.R. (ser. C) No. 308 (Nov. 23, 2015).
3. Velasquez Paiz et al. v. Guatemala, Preliminary Objections, Merits, Reparations and Costs, Judgment, Inter-Am. Ct. H.R. (ser. C) No. 307 (Nov. 19, 2015).
4. Garcia Ibarra et al. v. Ecuador, Preliminary Objections, Merits, Reparations and Costs, Judgment, Inter-Am. Ct. H.R. (ser. C) No. 306 (Nov. 17, 2015).
5. Ruano Torres et al. v. El Salvador, Merits, Reparations and Costs, Judgment, Inter-Am. Ct. H.R. (ser. C) No. 303 (Oct. 5, 2015).
6. Lopez Lone et al. v. Honduras, Preliminary Objection, Merits, Reparations and Costs, Judgment, Inter-Am. Ct. H.R. (ser. C) No. 302 (Oct. 5, 2015).
7. Galindo Cardenas et al. v. Peru, Preliminary Objections, Merits, Reparations and Costs, Judgment, Inter-Am. Ct. H.R. (ser. C) No. 301 (Oct. 2, 2015).
8. Case of Peasant Community of Santa Barbara v. Peru, Preliminary Objections, Merits, Reparations and Costs, Judgment, Inter-Am. Ct. H.R. (ser. C) No. 299 (Sept. 1, 2015).
9. Gonzales Lluy et al. v. Ecuador, Preliminary Objections, Merits, Reparations and Costs, Judgment, Inter-Am. Ct. H.R. (ser. C) No. 298 (Sept. 1, 2015).
10. Wong Ho Wing v. Peru, Preliminary Objection, Merits, Reparations and Costs, Judgment, Inter-Am. Ct. H.R. (ser. C) No. 297 (June 30, 2015).
11. Canales Huapaya et al. v. Peru, Preliminary Objections, Merits, Reparations, Costs, Judgment (ser. C) No. 296 (June 24, 2015).

12. Espinoza Gonzales v. Peru, Interpretation of the Judgment on Preliminary Objections, Merits, Reparations and Costs, Judgment, Inter-Am. Ct. H.R. (ser. C) No. 295 (June 23, 2015).
13. Cruz Sánchez et al. v. Peru, Preliminary Objections, Merits, Reparations, Costs, Judgment, Inter-Am. Ct. H.R. (ser. C) No. 292 (Apr. 17, 2015).
14. J. v. Peru, Interpretation of the Judgment on Preliminary Objection, Merits, Reparations, and Costs, Judgment, Inter-Am. Ct. H.R. (ser. C) No. 291 (Nov. 20, 2014).
15. Espinoza Gonzales v. Peru, Preliminary Objections, Merits, Reparations, and Costs, Judgment, Inter-Am. Ct. H.R. (ser. C) No. 289 (Nov. 20, 2014).
16. Argüelles et al. v. Argentina, Preliminary Objections, Merits, Reparations, and Costs, Judgment, Inter-Am. Ct. H.R. (ser. C) No. 288 (Nov. 20, 2014).
17. Rodriguez Vera et al. (Persons Disappeared from the Palace of Justice) v. Colombia, Preliminary Objections, Merits, Reparations, and Costs, Judgment, Inter-Am. Ct. H.R. (ser. C) No. 287 (Nov. 14, 2014).
18. Tarazona Arrieta et al. v. Peru, Preliminary Objections, Merits, Reparations, and Costs, Judgment, Inter-Am. Ct. H.R. (ser. C) No. 286 (Oct. 15, 2014).
19. Rochac Hernandez et al. v. El Salvador, Merits, Reparations, and Costs, Judgment, Inter-Am. Ct. H.R. (ser. C) No. 285 (Oct. 14, 2014).
20. Human Rights Defender et al. v. Guatemala, Preliminary Objections, Merits, Reparations, and Costs, Judgment, Inter-Am. Ct. H.R. (ser. C) No. 283 (Aug. 28, 2014).
21. Expelled Dominicans and Haitians v. Dominican Republic, Preliminary Objections, Merits, Reparations, and Costs, Judgment, Inter-Am. Ct. H.R. (ser. C) No. 282 (Aug. 28, 2014).
22. Landaeta Meijias Brothers et al. v. Venezuela, Preliminary Objections, Merits, Reparations, and Costs, Judgment, Inter-Am. Ct. H.R. (ser. C) No. 281 (Aug. 27, 2014).
23. Rights & Guar. of Children in the Context of Migration and/or in Need of Int'l Prot., Advisory Opinion OC-21/14, Inter-Am. Ct. H.R. (ser. A) No. 21 (Aug. 19, 2014).
24. Norín Catrimán et al. (Leaders, members, and Activists of the Mapuche Indigenous People) v. Chile, Merits, Reparations, and Costs, Judgment, Inter-Am. Ct. H.R. (ser. C) No. 279 (May 29, 2014).
25. Veliz Franco et al. v. Guatemala, Preliminary Objections, Merits, and Reparations, Judgment, Inter-Am. Ct. H.R. (ser. C) No. 277 (May 19, 2014).
26. Liakat Ali Alibux v. Suriname, Preliminary Objections, Merits, Reparations, and Costs, Judgment, Inter-Am. Ct. H.R. (ser. C) No. 276 (Jan. 30, 2014). [footnote]
27. J. v. Peru, Preliminary Objections, Merits, Reparations, and Costs, Judgment, Inter-Am. Ct. H.R. (ser. C) No. 275 (Nov. 27, 2013).
28. Osorio Rivera and Family v. Peru, Preliminary Objections, Merits, Reparations, and Costs, Judgment, Inter-Am. Ct. H.R. (ser. C) No. 274 (Nov. 26, 2013).
29. Garcia Cruz and Sanchez Silvestre v. Mexico, Merits, Reparations, and Costs, Judgment, Inter-Am. Ct. H.R. (ser. C) No. 273 (Nov. 26, 2013).
30. Pacheco Tineo Family v. Bolivia, Preliminary Objections, Merits, Reparations, and Costs, Judgment, Inter-Am. Ct. H.R. (ser. C) No. 272 (Nov. 25, 2013).
31. Gutiérrez and Family v. Argentina, Merits, Reparations, and Costs, Judgment, Inter-Am. Ct. H.R. (ser. C) No. 271 (Nov. 25, 2013).
32. Afro-Descendant Communities Displaced from the Cacarica River Basin (Operation Genesis) v. Colombia, Preliminary Objections, Merits, Reparations, and Costs, Judgment, Inter-Am. Ct. H.R. (ser. C) No. 270 (Nov. 20, 2013).

33. Luna Lopez v. Honduras, Merits, Reparations, and Costs, Judgment, Inter-Am. Ct. H.R. (ser. C) No. 269 (Oct. 10, 2013).
34. Garcia Lucero et al. v. Chile, Preliminary Objections, Merits, and Reparations, Judgment, Inter-Am. Ct. H.R. (ser. C) No. 267 (Aug. 28, 2013).
35. Massacre of Santo Domingo v. Colombia, Request for Interpretation of the Judgment on Preliminary Objections, Merits, Reparations, and Costs, Judgment, Inter-Am. Ct. H.R. (ser. C) No. 263 (Aug. 19, 2013).
36. Suárez Peralta v. Ecuador, Preliminary Objections, Merits, Reparations, and Costs, Judgment, Inter-Am. Ct. H.R. (ser. C) No. 261 (May 21, 2013).
37. Mendoza et al. v. Argentina, Preliminary Objections, Merits, and Reparations, Judgment, Inter-Am. Ct. H.R. (ser. C) No. 260 (May 14, 2013).
38. Santo Domingo Massacre v. Colombia, Preliminary Objections, Merits, and Reparations, Judgment, Inter-Am. Ct. H.R. (ser. C) No. 259 (Nov. 30, 2012).
39. García and Family Members v. Guatemala, Merits, Reparations, and Costs, Judgment, Inter-Am. Ct. H.R. (ser. C) No. 258 (Nov. 29, 2012).
40. Artavia Murillo et al. (In-vitro Fertilization) v. Costa Rica, Preliminary Objections, Merits, Reparations, and Costs, Judgment, Inter-Am. Ct. H.R. (ser. C) No. 257 (Nov. 28, 2012).
41. Castillo González et al. v. Venezuela, Merits, Judgment, Inter-Am. Ct. H.R. (ser. C) No. 256 (Nov. 27, 2012).
42. Gudiel Alvarez et al. ("Diario Militar") v. Guatemala, Merits, Reparations, and Costs, Judgment, Inter-Am. Ct. H.R. (ser. C) No. 253 (Nov. 20, 2012).
43. Massacres of El Mozote and Nearby Places v. El Salvador, Merits, Reparations, and Costs, Judgment, Inter-Am. Ct. H.R. (ser. C) No. 252 (Oct. 25, 2012).
44. Nadege Dorzema et al. v. Dominican Republic, Merits, Reparations, and Costs, Judgment, Inter-Am. Ct. H.R. (ser. C) No. 251 (Oct. 24, 2012).
45. Río Negro Massacres v. Guatemala, Preliminary Objections, Merits, Reparations, and Costs, Judgment, Inter-Am. Ct. H.R. (ser. C) No. 250 (Sept. 4, 2012).
46. Uzcátegui et al. v. Venezuela, Merits and Reparations, Judgment, Inter-Am. Ct. H.R. (ser. C) No. 249 (Sept. 3, 2012).
47. Vélez Restrepo and Family v. Colombia, Preliminary Objections, Merits, Reparations, and Costs, Judgment, Inter-Am. Ct. H.R. (ser. C) No. 248 (Sept. 3, 2012).
48. Palma Mendoza et al. v. Ecuador, Preliminary Objections and Merits, Judgment, Inter-Am. Ct. H.R. (ser. C) No. 247 (Sept. 3, 2012).
49. Furlan and Family v. Argentina, Preliminary Objections, Merits, Reparations, and Costs, Judgment, Inter-Am. Ct. H.R. (ser. C) No. 246 (Aug. 31, 2012).
50. Kichwa Indigenous People of Sarayaku v. Ecuador, Merits and Reparations, Judgment Inter.-Am. Ct. H.R. (ser. C) No. 245 (June 27, 2012).
51. Díaz Peña v. Venezuela, Preliminary Objections, Merits, Reparations, and Costs, Judgment, Inter-Am. Ct. H.R. (ser. C) No. 244 (June 26, 2012).
52. Pacheco Teruel et al. v. Honduras, Merits, Reparations, and Costs, Judgment, Inter-Am. Ct. H.R. (ser. C) No. 241 (Apr. 27, 2012).
53. Gonzalez Medina and Family v. Dominican Republic, Preliminary Objections, Merits, Reparations, and Costs, Judgment, Inter-Am. Ct. H.R. (ser. C) No. 240 (Feb. 27, 2012).
54. Barrios Family v. Venezuela, Merits, Reparations, and Costs, Judgment, Inter-Am. Ct. H.R. (ser. C) No. 237 (Nov. 24, 2011).

55. Lysias Fleury et al. v. Haiti, Merits and Reparations, Judgment, Inter-Am. Ct. H.R. (ser. C) No. 236 (Nov. 23, 2011).
56. Contreras et. al. v. El Salvador, Merits, Reparations, and Costs, Judgment, Inter-Am. Ct. H.R. (ser. C) No. 232 (Aug. 31, 2011).
57. Torres Millacura et al. v. Argentina, Merits, Reparations, and Costs, Judgment, Inter-Am. Ct. H.R. (ser. C) No. 229 (Aug. 26, 2011).
58. Vera Vera et al. v. Ecuador, Preliminary Objections, Merits, Reparations, and Costs, Judgment, Inter-Am. Ct. H.R. (ser. C) No. 226 (May 19, 2011).
59. Rosendo Cantu et al. v. Mexico, Interpretation of Judgment of Preliminary Objections, Merits, Reparations, and Costs, Judgment, Inter-Am. Ct. H.R. (ser. C) No. 225 (May 15, 2011).
60. Fernandez Ortega et al. v. Mexico, Interpretation of Judgment of Preliminary Objection, Merits, Reparations, and Costs, Judgment, Inter-Am. Ct. H.R. (ser. C) No. 224 (May 15, 2011).
61. Gelman v. Uruguay, Merits and Reparations, Judgment, Inter-Am. Ct. H.R. (ser. C) No. 221 (Feb. 24, 2011).
62. Cabrera García and Montiel Flores v. Mexico, Preliminary Objections, Merits, Reparations, and Costs, Judgment, Inter-Am. Ct. H.R. (ser. C) No. 220 (Nov. 26, 2010).
63. Gomes Lund et al. ("Guerrilha do Araguaia") v. Brazil, Preliminary Objections, Merits, Reparations, and Costs, Judgment, Inter-Am. Ct. H.R. (ser. C) No. 219 (Nov. 24, 2010).
64. Vélez Loor v. Panama, Preliminary Objections, Merits, Reparations, and Costs, Judgment, Inter-Am. Ct. H.R. (ser. C) No. 218 (Nov. 23, 2010).
65. Ibsen Cardenas and Ibsen Peña v. Bolivia, Merits, Reparations, and Costs, Judgment, Inter-Am. Ct. H.R. (ser. C) No. 217 (Sept. 1, 2010).
66. Rosendo Cantu et al. v. Mexico, Preliminary Objections, Merits, Reparations, and Costs, Judgment, Inter-Am. Ct. H.R. (ser. C) No. 216 (Aug. 31, 2010).
67. Fernandez Ortega et al. v. Mexico, Preliminary Objections, Merits, Reparations, and Costs, Judgment, Inter-Am. Ct. H.R. (ser. C) No. 215 (Aug. 30, 2010).
68. Xákmok Kásek Indigenous Cmty. v. Paraguay, Merits, Reparations, and Costs, Judgment, Inter-Am. Ct. H.R. (ser. C) No. 214 (Aug. 24, 2010).
69. Cepeda Vargas v. Colombia, Preliminary Objections, Merits, Reparations, and Costs, Judgment, Inter-Am. Ct. H.R. (ser. C.) No. 213 (May 26, 2010).
70. Chitay Nech et al. v. Guatemala, Preliminary Objections, Merits, Reparations, and Costs, Judgment, Inter-Am. Ct. H.R. (ser. C) No. 212 (May 25, 2010).
71. "Las Dos Erres" Massacre v. Guatemala, Preliminary Objections, Merits, Reparations, and Costs, Judgment, Inter-Am. Ct. H.R. (ser. C) No. 211 (Nov. 24, 2009).
72. Radilla Pacheco v. Mexico, Preliminary Objections, Merits, Reparations, and Costs, Judgment, Inter-Am. Ct. H.R. (ser. C) No. 209 (Nov. 23, 2009).
73. González et al. ("Cotton Field") v. Mexico, Preliminary Objections, Merits, Reparations, and Costs, Judgment, Inter-Am. Ct. H.R. (ser. C) No. 205 (Nov. 16, 2009).
74. DaCosta Cadogan v. Barbados, Preliminary Objections, Merits, Reparations, and Costs, Judgment, Inter-Am. Ct. H.R. (ser. C) No. 204 (Sept. 24, 2009).
75. Garibaldi v. Brazil, Preliminary Objections, Merits, Reparations, and Costs, Judgment, Inter-Am. Ct. H.R. (ser. C) No. 203 (Sept. 23, 2009).

76. Anzualdo Castro v. Peru, Preliminary Objections, Merits, Reparations, and Costs, Judgment, Inter-Am. Ct. H.R. (ser. C) No. 202 (Sept. 22, 2009).
77. Valle Jaramillo et al. v. Colombia, Interpretation of the Judgment on the Merits, Reparations, and Costs, Judgment, Inter-Am. Ct. H.R. (ser. C) No. 201 (July 7, 2009).
78. Reverón Trujillo v. Venezuela, Preliminary Objections, Merits, Reparations, and Costs, Judgment, Inter-Am. Ct. H.R. (ser. C) No. 197 (June 30, 2009).
79. Kawas Fernández v. Honduras, Merits, Reparations, and Costs, Judgment, Inter-Am. Ct. H.R. (ser. C) No. 196 (Apr. 3, 2009).
80. Perozo et al. v. Venezuela, Preliminary Objections, Merits, Reparations, and Costs, Judgment, Inter-Am. Ct. H.R. (ser. C) No. 195 (Jan. 28, 2009).
81. Ríos et al. v. Venezuela, Preliminary Objections, Merits, Reparations, and Costs, Judgment, Inter-Am. Ct. H.R. (ser. C) No. 194 (Jan. 28, 2009).
82. Valle Jaramillo et al. v. Colombia, Merits, Reparations, and Costs, Judgment, Inter-Am. Ct. H.R. (ser. C) No. 192 (Nov. 27, 2008).
83. Ticona Estrada et al. v. Bolivia, Merits, Reparations, and Costs, Judgment, Inter-Am. Ct. H.R. (ser. C) No. 191 (Nov. 27, 2008).
84. Tiu Tojín v. Guatemala, Merits, Reparations, and Costs, Judgment, Inter-Am. Ct. H.R. (ser. C) No. 190 (Nov. 26, 2008).
85. Bayarri v. Argentina, Preliminary Objection, Merits, Reparations, and Costs, Judgment, Inter-Am. Ct. H.R. (ser. C) No. 187 (Oct. 30, 2008).
86. Heliodoro Portugal v. Panama, Preliminary Objections, Merits, Reparations, and Costs, Judgment, Inter-Am. Ct. H.R. (ser. C) No. 186 (Aug. 12, 2008).
87. Albán Cornejo et al. v. Ecuador, Interpretation of the Judgment on Merits, Reparations, and Costs, Judgment, Inter-Am. Ct. H.R. (ser. C) No. 183 (Aug. 5, 2008).
88. Miguel Castro Castro Prison v. Peru, Interpretation of the Judgment on Merits, Reparations, and Costs, Judgment, Inter-Am. Ct. H.R. (ser. C) No. 181 (Aug. 2, 2008).
89. Neptune v. Haiti, Merits, Reparations, and Costs, Judgment, Inter-Am. Ct. H.R. (ser. C) No. 180 (May 6, 2008).
90. La Cantuta v. Peru, Interpretation of the Judgment on Merits, Reparations, and Costs, Judgment, Inter-Am. Ct. H.R. (ser. C) No. 173 (Nov. 30, 2007).
91. Albán Cornejo et al. v. Ecuador, Merits, Reparations, and Costs, Judgment, Inter-Am. Ct. H.R. (ser. C) No. 171 (Nov. 22, 2007).
92. Chaparro Álvarez and Lapo Íñiguez v. Ecuador, Preliminary Objections, Merits, Reparations, and Costs, Judgment, Inter-Am. Ct. H.R. (ser. C) No. 170 (Nov. 21, 2007).
93. Boyce et al. v. Barbados, Preliminary Objections, Merits, Reparations, and Costs, Judgment, Inter-Am. Ct. H.R. (ser. C) No. 169 (Nov. 20, 2007).
94. García Prieto et al. v. El Salvador, Preliminary Objections, Merits, Reparations, and Costs, Judgment, Inter-Am. Ct. H.R. (ser. C) No. 168 (Nov. 20, 2007).
95. Cantoral Huamaní and García Santa Cruz v. Peru, Preliminary Objections, Merits, Reparations, and Costs, Judgment, Inter-Am. Ct. H.R. (ser. C) No. 167 (July 10, 2007).
96. Escué Zapata v. Colombia, Merits, Reparations, and Costs, Judgment, Inter-Am. Ct. H.R. (ser. C) No. 165 (July 4, 2007).
97. Bueno Alves v. Argentina, Merits, Reparations, and Costs, Judgment, Inter-Am. Ct. H.R. (Ser. C) No. 164 (May 11, 2007).

98. Rochela Massacre v. Colombia, Merits, Reparations, and Costs, Judgment, Inter-Am. Ct. H.R. (ser. C) No. 163 (May 11, 2007).
99. La Cantuta v. Peru, Merits, Reparations, and Costs, Judgment, Inter-Am. Ct. H.R. (ser. C) No. 162 (Nov. 29, 2006).
100. Miguel Castro Castro Prison v. Peru, Merits, Reparations, and Costs, Judgment, Inter-Am. Ct. H.R. (ser. C) No. 160 (Nov. 25, 2006).
101. Pueblo Bello Massacre v. Colombia, Interpretation of the Judgment of Merits, Reparations, and Costs, Judgment, Inter-Am. Ct. H.R. (ser. C) No. 159 (Nov. 25, 2006).
102. Vargas Areco v. Paraguay, Merits, Reparations, and Costs, Judgment, Inter-Am. Ct. H.R. (ser. C) No. 155 (Sept. 26, 2006).
103. Goiburú et al. v. Paraguay, Merits, Reparations, and Costs, Judgment, Inter-Am. Ct. H.R. (ser. C) No. 153 (Sept. 22, 2006).
104. Servellón García et al. v. Honduras, Merits, Reparations, and Costs, Judgment, Inter-Am. Ct. H.R. (ser. C) No. 152 (Sept. 21, 2006).
105. Montero Aranguren et al. (Det. Ctr. of Catia) v. Venezuela, Preliminary Objection, Merits, Reparations, and Costs, Judgment, Inter-Am. Ct. H.R. (ser. C) No. 150 (July 5, 2006).
106. Ximenes Lopes v. Brazil, Merits, Reparations, and Costs, Judgment, Inter-Am. Ct. H.R. (ser. C) No. 149 (July 4, 2006).
107. Ituango Massacres v. Colombia, Preliminary Objections, Merits, Reparations, and Costs, Judgment, Inter-Am. Ct. H.R. (ser. C) No. 148 (July 1, 2006).
108. Baldeón García v. Peru, Merits, Reparations, and Costs, Judgment, Inter-Am. Ct. H.R. (ser. C) No. 147 (Apr. 6, 2006).
109. Sawhoyamaxa Indigenous Cmty. v. Paraguay, Merits, Reparations, and Costs, Judgment, Inter-Am. Ct. H.R. (ser. C) No. 146 (Mar. 29, 2006).
110. Moiwana Cmty. v. Suriname, Interpretation of the Judgment of Merits, Reparations, and Costs, Judgment, Inter-Am. Ct. H.R. (ser. C) No. 145 (Feb. 8, 2006).
111. Raxcacó Reyes v. Guatemala, Interpretation of the Judgment of Merits, Reparations, and Costs, Judgment, Inter-Am. Ct. H.R. (ser. C) No. 143 (Feb. 6, 2006).
112. López Álvarez v. Honduras, Merits, Reparations, and Costs, Judgment, Inter-Am. Ct. H.R. (ser. C) No. 141 (Feb. 1, 2006).
113. Pueblo Bello Massacre v. Colombia, Merits, Reparations, and Costs, Judgment, Inter-Am. Ct. H.R. (ser. C) No. 140 (Jan. 31, 2006).
114. Ximenes Lopes v. Brazil, Preliminary Objections, Judgment, Inter-Am. Ct. H.R. (ser. C) No. 139 (Nov. 30, 2005).
115. Blanco Romero et al. v. Venezuela, Merits, Reparations, and Costs, Judgment, Inter-Am. Ct. H.R. (ser. C) No. 138 (Nov. 28, 2005).
116. García Asto and Ramírez Rojas v. Peru, Preliminary Objection, Merits, Reparations, and Costs, Judgment, Inter-Am. Ct. H.R. (ser. C) No. 137 (Nov. 25, 2005).
117. Gómez Palomino v. Peru, Merits, Reparations, and Costs, Judgment, Inter-Am. Ct. H.R. (ser. C) No. 136 (Nov. 22, 2005).
118. Mapiripán Massacre v. Colombia, Merits, Reparations, and Costs, Judgment, Inter-Am. Ct. H.R. (ser. C) No. 134 (Sept. 15, 2005).
119. Raxcacó Reyes v. Guatemala, Merits, Reparations, and Costs, Judgment, Inter-Am. Ct. H.R. (ser. C) No. 133 (Sept. 15, 2005).

120. Gutiérrez Soler v. Colombia, Merits, Reparations, and Costs, Judgment, Inter-Am. Ct. H.R. (ser. C) No. 132 (Sept. 12, 2005).
121. Serrano Cruz Sisters v. El Salvador, Interpretation of the Judgment of Merits, Reparations, and Costs, Judgment, Inter-Am. Ct. H.R. (ser. C) No. 131 (Sept. 9, 2005).
122. Yean and Bosico v. Dominican Republic, Preliminary Objections, Merits, Reparations, and Costs, Judgment, Inter-Am. Ct. H.R. (ser. C) No. 130 (Sept. 8, 2005).
123. Acosta Calderón v. Ecuador, Merits, Reparations, and Costs, Judgment, Inter-Am. Ct. H.R. (ser. C) No. 129 (June 24, 2005).
124. Fermín Ramírez v. Guatemala, Merits, Reparations, and Costs, Judgment, Inter-Am. Ct. H.R. (ser. C) No. 126 (June 20, 2005).
125. Moiwana Cmty. v. Suriname, Preliminary Objections, Merits, Reparations, and Costs, Judgment, Inter-Am. Ct. H.R. (ser. C) No. 124 (June 15, 2005).
126. Caesar v. Trinidad & Tobago, Merits, Reparations, and Costs, Judgment, Inter-Am. Ct. H.R. (ser. C) No. 123 (Mar. 11, 2005).
127. Mapiripán Massacre v. Colombia, Preliminary Objections, Judgment, Inter-Am. Ct. H.R. (ser. C) No. 122 (Mar. 7, 2005).
128. Serrano Cruz Sisters v. El Salvador, Merits, Reparations, and Costs, Judgment, Inter-Am. Ct. H.R. (ser. C) No. 120 (Mar. 1, 2005).
129. Berenson Mejia v. Peru, Merits, Reparations, and Costs, Judgment, Inter-Am. Ct. H.R. (ser. C) No. 119 (Nov. 25, 2004).
130. Serrano Cruz Sisters v. El Salvador, Preliminary Objections, Judgment, Inter-Am. Ct. H.R. (ser. C) No. 118 (Nov. 23, 2004).
131. Carpio Nicolle et al. v. Guatemala, Merits, Reparations, and Costs, Judgment, Inter-Am. Ct. H.R. (ser. C) No. 117 (Nov. 22, 2004).
132. Plan de Sánchez Massacre v. Guatemala, Reparations, Judgment, Inter-Am. Ct. H.R. (ser. C) No. 116 (Nov. 19, 2004).
133. De La Cruz Flores v. Peru, Merits, Reparations, and Costs, Judgment, Inter-Am. Ct. H.R. (ser. C) No. 115 (Nov. 18, 2004).
134. Tibi v. Ecuador, Preliminary Objections, Merits, Reparations, and Costs, Judgment, Inter-Am. Ct. H.R. (ser. C) No. 114 (Sept. 7, 2004).
135. Campo Dodd v. Mexico, Preliminary Objections, Judgment, Inter-Am. Ct. H.R. (ser. C) No. 113 (Sept. 3, 2004).
136. "Juvenile Reeducation Institute" v. Paraguay, Preliminary Objections, Merits, Reparations, and Costs, Judgment, Inter-Am. Ct. H.R. (ser. C) No. 112 (Sept. 2, 2004).
137. Gómez Paquiyauri Brothers v. Peru, Merits, Reparations, and Costs, Judgment, Inter-Am. Ct. H.R. (ser. C) No. 110 (July 8, 2004).
138. 19 Merchants v. Colombia, Merits, Reparations, and Costs, Judgment, Inter-Am. Ct. H.R. (ser. C) No. 109 (July 5, 2004).
139. Molina Theissen v. Guatemala, Reparations and Costs, Judgment, Inter-Am. Ct. H.R. (ser. C) No. 108 (July 3, 2004).
140. Molina Theissen v. Guatemala, Merits, Judgment, Inter-Am. Ct. H.R. (ser. C) No. 106 (May 4, 2004).
141. Plan de Sánchez Massacre v. Guatemala, Merits, Judgment, Inter-Am. Ct. H.R. (ser. C) No. 105 (Apr. 29, 2004).

142. Maritza Urrutia v. Guatemala, Merits, Reparations, and Costs, Judgment, Inter-Am. Ct. H.R. (ser. C) No. 103 (Nov. 27, 2003).
143. Sánchez v. Honduras, Interpretation of the Judgment of Preliminary Objection, Merits, and Reparations, Judgment, Inter-Am. Ct. H.R. (ser. C) No. 102 (Nov. 26, 2003).
144. Mack Chang v. Guatemala, Merits, Reparations, and Costs, Judgment, Inter-Am. Ct. H.R. (ser. C) No. 101 (Nov. 25, 2003).
145. Bulacio v. Argentina, Merits, Reparations, and Costs, Judgment, Inter-Am. Ct. H.R. (ser. C) No. 100 (Sept. 18, 2003).
146. Sánchez v. Honduras, Preliminary Objection, Merits, Reparations, and Costs, Judgment, Inter-Am. Ct. H.R. (ser. C) No. 99 (June 7, 2003).
147. Caracazo v. Venezuela, Reparations and Costs, Judgment, Inter-Am. Ct. H.R. (ser. C) No. 95 (Aug. 29, 2002).
148. Juridical Condition & Human Rights of the Child, Advisory Opinion OC-17/02, Inter-Am. Ct. H.R. (ser. A) No. 17 (Aug. 28, 2002).
149. Hilaire, Constantine, and Benjamin et al. v. Trinidad & Tobago, Merits, Reparations, and Costs, Judgment, Inter-Am. Ct. H.R. (ser. C) No. 94 (June 21, 2002).
150. 19 Merchants v. Colombia, Preliminary Objection, Judgment, Inter-Am. Ct. H.R. (ser. C) No. 93 (June 12, 2002).
151. Trujillo Oroza v. Bolivia, Reparations and Costs, Judgment, Inter-Am. Ct. H.R. (ser. C) No. 92 (Feb. 27, 2002).
152. Bámaca Velásquez v. Guatemala, Reparations and Costs, Judgment, Inter-Am. Ct. H.R. (ser. C) No. 91 (Feb. 22, 2002).
153. Durand and Ugarte v. Peru, Reparations and Costs, Judgment, Inter-Am. Ct. H.R. (ser. C) No. 89 (Dec. 3, 2001).
154. Cantoral Benavides v. Peru, Reparations and Costs, Judgment, Inter-Am. Ct. H.R. (ser. C) No. 88 (Dec. 3, 2001).
155. Barrios Altos v. Peru, Reparations and Costs, Judgment, Inter-Am. Ct. H.R. (ser. C) No. 87 (Nov. 30, 2001).
156. Cantos v. Argentina, Preliminary Objections, Judgment, Inter-Am. Ct. H.R. (ser. C) No. 85 (Sept. 7, 2001).
157. Constantine et al. v. Trinidad & Tobago, Preliminary Objections, Judgment, Inter-Am. Ct. H.R. (ser. C) No. 82 (Sept. 1, 2001).
158. Benjamin et al. v. Trinidad & Tobago, Preliminary Objections, Judgment, Inter-Am. Ct. H.R. (ser. C) No. 81 (Sept. 1, 2001).
159. Hilaire v. Trinidad & Tobago, Preliminary Objections, Judgment, Inter-Am. Ct. H.R. (ser. C) No. 80 (Sept. 1, 2001).
160. Cesti Hurtado v. Peru, Reparations and Costs, 2001 Inter-Am. Ct. H.R. (ser. C) No. 78 (May 31, 2001).
161. "Street Children" (Villagrán Morales et al.) v. Guatemala, Reparations and Costs, Judgment, Inter-Am. Ct. H.R. (ser. C) No. 77 (May 26, 2001).
162. "White Van" (Paniagua Morales et al.) v. Guatemala, Reparations and Costs, Judgment, Inter-Am. Ct. H.R. (ser. C) No. 76 (May 25, 2001).
163. Barrios Altos v. Peru, Merits, Judgment, Inter-Am. Ct. H.R. (ser. C) No. 75 (Mar. 14, 2001).
164. Bámaca Velásquez v. Guatemala, Merits, Judgment, Inter-Am. Ct. H.R. (ser. C) No. 70 (Nov. 25, 2000).

165. Cantoral Benavides v. Peru, Merits, Judgment, Inter-Am. Ct. H.R. (ser. C) No. 69 (Aug. 18, 2000).
166. Durand and Ugarte v. Peru, Merits, Judgment, Inter-Am. Ct. H.R. (ser. C) No. 68 (Aug. 16, 2000).
167. Trujillo Oroza v. Bolivia, Merits, Judgment, Inter-Am. Ct. H.R. (ser. C) No. 64 (Jan. 26, 2000).
168. "Street Children" (Villagrán Morales et al.) v. Guatemala, Merits, Judgment, Inter-Am. Ct. H.R. (ser. C) No. 63 (Nov. 19, 1999).
169. Cesti Hurtado v. Peru, Request for Interpretation of the Judgment of Merits, Order of the Court, Inter-Am. Ct. H.R. (ser. C) No. 62 (Nov. 19, 1999).
170. Caracazo v. Venezuela, Merits, Judgment, Inter-Am. Ct. H.R. (ser. C) No. 58 (Nov. 11, 1999).
171. Cesti Hurtado v. Peru, Merits, Judgment, Inter-Am. Ct. H.R. (ser. C) No. 56 (Sept. 29, 1999).
172. Castillo Petruzzi et al. v. Peru, Merits, Reparations, and Costs, Judgment, Inter-Am. Ct. H.R. (ser. C) No. 52 (May 30, 1999).
173. Cesti Hurtado v. Peru, Preliminary Objections, Judgment, Inter-Am. Ct. H.R. (ser. C) No. 49 (Jan. 26, 1999).
174. Blake v. Guatemala, Reparations and Costs, Judgment, Inter-Am. Ct. H.R. (ser. C) No. 48 (Jan. 22, 1999).
175. Loayza Tamayo v. Peru, Interpretation of the Judgment of Merits, Order of the Court, Inter-Am. Ct. H.R. (ser. C) No. 47 (Mar. 8, 1998).
176. Suárez Rosero v. Ecuador, Reparations and Costs, Judgment, Inter-Am. Ct. H.R. (ser. C) No. 44 (Jan. 20, 1999).
177. Castillo Páez v. Peru, Reparations and Costs, Judgment, Inter-Am. Ct. H.R. (ser. C) No. 43 (Nov. 27, 1998).
178. Loayza Tamayo v. Peru, Reparations and Costs, Judgment, Inter-Am. Ct. H.R. (ser. C) No. 42 (Nov. 27, 1998).
179. Castillo Petruzzi et al. v. Peru, Preliminary Objections, Judgment, Inter-Am. Ct. H.R. (ser. C) No. 41 (Sept. 4, 1998).
180. Cantoral Benavides v. Peru, Preliminary Objections, Judgment, Inter-Am. Ct. H.R. (ser. C) No. 40 (Sept. 3, 1998).
181. Garrido and Baigorria v. Argentina, Reparations and Costs, Judgment, Inter-Am. Ct. H.R. (ser. C) No. 39 (Aug. 27, 1998).
182. Benavides Cevallos v. Ecuador, Merits, Reparations, and Costs, Judgment, Inter-Am. Ct. H.R. (ser. C) No. 38 (June 19, 1998).
183. Blake v. Guatemala, Merits, Judgment, Inter-Am. Ct. H.R. (ser. C) No. 36 (Jan. 24, 1998).
184. Suárez Rosero v. Ecuador, Merits, Judgment, Inter-Am. Ct. H.R. (ser. C) No. 35 (Nov. 12, 1997).
185. Castillo Páez v. Peru, Merits, Judgment, Inter-Am. Ct. H.R. (ser. C) No. 34 (Nov. 3, 1997).
186. Loayza Tamayo v. Peru, Merits, Judgment, Inter-Am. Ct. H.R. (ser. C) No. 33 (Sept. 17, 1997).
187. "Street Children" (Villagrán Morales et al.) v. Guatemala, Preliminary Objections, Judgment, Inter-Am. Ct. H.R. (ser. C) No. 32 (Sept. 11, 1997).
188. Caballero Delgado and Santana v. Colombia, Reparations and Costs, Judgment, Inter-Am. Ct. H.R. (ser. C) No. 31 (Jan. 29, 1997).

189. Genie Lacayo v. Nicaragua, Merits, Reparations, and Costs, Judgment, Inter-Am. Ct. H.R. (ser. C) No. 30 (Jan. 29, 1997).
190. Neira Alegría et al. v. Peru, Reparations and Costs, Judgment, Inter-Am. Ct. H.R. (ser. C) No. 29 (Sept. 19, 1996).
191. El Amparo v. Venezuela, Reparations and Costs, Judgment, Inter-Am. Ct. H.R. (ser. C) No. 28 (Sept. 14, 1996).
192. Garrido and Baigorria v. Argentina, Merits, Judgment, Inter-Am. Ct. H.R. (ser. C) No. 26 (Feb. 2, 1996).
193. Loayza Tamayo v. Peru, Preliminary Objections, Judgment, Inter-Am. Ct. H.R. (ser. C) No. 25 (Jan. 31, 1996).
194. Castillo Páez v. Peru, Preliminary Objections, Judgment, Inter-Am. Ct. H.R. (ser. C) No. 24 (Jan. 30, 1996).
195. "White Van" (Paniagua Morales et al.) v. Guatemala, Preliminary Objections, Judgment, Inter-Am. Ct. H.R. (ser. C) No. 23 (Jan. 25, 1996).
196. Caballero Delgado and Santana v. Colombia, Merits, Judgment, Inter-Am. Ct. H.R. (ser. C) No. 22 (Dec. 8, 1995).
197. Genie Lacayo v. Nicaragua, Preliminary Objections, Judgment, Inter-Am. Ct. H.R. (ser. C) No. 21 (Jan. 27, 1995).
198. Neira Alegría et al. v. Peru, Merits, Judgment, Inter-Am. Ct. H.R. (ser. C) No. 20 (Jan. 19, 1995).
199. El Amparo v. Venezuela, Merits, Judgment, Inter-Am. Ct. H.R. (ser. C) No. 19 (Jan. 18, 1995).
200. Caballero Delgado and Santana v. Colombia, Preliminary Objections, Judgment, Inter-Am. Ct. H.R. (ser. C) No. 17 (Jan. 21, 1994).
201. Gangaram Panday v. Suriname, Merits, Reparations, and Costs, Judgment, Inter-Am. Ct. H.R. (ser. C) No. 16 (Jan. 21, 1994).
202. Aloeboetoe et al. v. Suriname, Reparations and Costs, Judgment, Inter-Am. Ct. H.R. (ser. C) No. 15 (Sept. 10, 1993).
203. Cayara v. Peru, Preliminary Objections, Judgment, Inter-Am. Ct. H.R. (ser. C) No. 14 (Feb. 3, 1993).
204. Gangaram Panday v. Suriname, Preliminary Objections, Judgment, Inter-Am. Ct. H.R. (ser. C) No. 12 (Dec. 4, 1991).
205. Aloeboetoe et al. v. Suriname, Merits, Judgment, Inter-Am. Ct. H.R. (ser. C) No. 11 (Dec. 4, 1991).
206. Fairén Garbi and Solís Corrales v. Honduras, Merits, Judgment, Inter-Am. Ct. H.R. (ser. C) No. 6 (Mar. 15, 1989).
207. Godínez Cruz v. Honduras, Merits, Judgment, Inter-Am. Ct. H.R. (ser. C) No. 5 (Jan. 20, 1989).
208. Velásquez Rodríguez v. Honduras, Merits, Judgment, Inter-Am. Ct. H.R. (ser. C) No. 4 (July 29, 1988).
209. Judicial Guarantees in States of Emergency (Arts. 27(2), 25, and 8 American Convention on Human Rights), Advisory Opinion OC-9/87, Inter-Am. Ct. H.R. (ser. A) No. 9 (Oct. 6, 1987).
210. Godínez Cruz v. Honduras, Preliminary Objections, Judgment, Inter-Am. Ct. H.R. (ser. C) No. 3 (June 26, 1987).

211. Fairén Garbi and Solís Corrales v. Honduras, Preliminary Objections, Judgment, Inter-Am. Ct. H.R. (ser. C) No. 2 (June 26, 1987).
212. Velásquez Rodríguez v. Honduras, Preliminary Objections, Judgment, Inter-Am. Ct. H.R. (ser. C) No. 1 (June 26, 1987).
213. Habeas Corpus in Emergency Situations (Arts. 27(2), 25(1), and 7(6) American Convention on Human Rights), Advisory Opinion OC-8/87, Inter-Am. Ct. H.R. (ser. A) No. 8 (Jan. 30, 1987).
214. In the Matter of Viviana Gallardo et al., Inter-Am. Ct. H.R. (ser. A) No. 101 (July 15, 1981).

ARTICLE 6: FREEDOM FROM SLAVERY

1. Case of Peasant Community of Santa Barbara v. Peru, Preliminary Objections, Merits, Reparations and Costs, Judgment, Inter-Am. Ct. H.R. (ser. C) No. 299 (Sept. 1, 2015).
2. Espinoza Gonzales v. Peru, Interpretation of the Judgment on Preliminary Objections, Merits, Reparations and Costs, Judgment, Inter-Am. Ct. H.R. (ser. C) No. 295 (June 23, 2015).
3. J. v. Peru, Preliminary Objections, Merits, Reparations, and Costs, Judgment, Inter-Am. Ct. H.R. (ser. C) No. 275 (Nov. 27, 2013). [footnote]
4. Mendoza et al. v. Argentina, Preliminary Objections, Merits, and Reparations, Judgment, Inter-Am. Ct. H.R. (ser. C) No. 260 (May 14, 2013).
5. Río Negro Massacres v. Guatemala, Preliminary Objections, Merits, Reparations, and Costs, Judgment, Inter-Am. Ct. H.R. (ser. C) No. 250 (Sept. 4, 2012).
6. Ituango Massacres v. Colombia, Preliminary Objections, Merits, Reparations, and Costs, Judgment, Inter-Am. Ct. H.R. (ser. C) No. 148 (July 1, 2006).
7. Judicial Guarantees in States of Emergency (Arts. 27(2), 25, and 8 American Convention on Human Rights), Advisory Opinion OC-9/87, Inter-Am. Ct. H.R. (ser. A) No. 9 (Oct. 6, 1987).
8. Habeas Corpus in Emergency Situations (Arts. 27(2), 25(1), and 7(6) American Convention on Human Rights), Advisory Opinion OC-8/87, Inter-Am. Ct. H.R. (ser. A) No. 8 (Jan. 30, 1987).

ARTICLE 7: RIGHT TO PERSONAL LIBERTY

1. Ruano Torres et al. v. El Salvador, Merits, Reparations and Costs, Judgment, Inter-Am. Ct. H.R. (ser. C) No. 303 (Oct. 5, 2015).
2. Lopez Lone et al. v. Honduras, Preliminary Objection, Merits, Reparations and Costs, Judgment, Inter-Am. Ct. H.R. (ser. C) No. 302 (Oct. 5, 2015).
3. Galindo Cardenas et al. v. Peru, Preliminary Objections, Merits, Reparations and Costs, Judgment, Inter-Am. Ct. H.R. (ser. C) No. 301 (Oct. 2, 2015).
4. Case of Peasant Community of Santa Barbara v. Peru, Preliminary Objections, Merits, Reparations and Costs, Judgment, Inter-Am. Ct. H.R. (ser. C) No. 299 (Sept. 1, 2015).
5. Wong Ho Wing v. Peru, Preliminary Objection, Merits, Reparations and Costs, Judgment, Inter-Am. Ct. H.R. (ser. C) No. 297 (June 30, 2015).
6. Espinoza Gonzales v. Peru, Preliminary Objections, Merits, Reparations, and Costs, Judgment, Inter-Am. Ct. H.R. (ser. C) No. 289 (Nov. 20, 2014).
7. Argüelles et al. v. Argentina, Preliminary Objections, Merits, Reparations, and Costs, Judgment, Inter-Am. Ct. H.R. (ser. C) No. 288 (Nov. 20, 2014).

8. Rodriguez Vera et al. (Persons Disappeared from the Palace of Justice) v. Colombia, Preliminary Objections, Merits, Reparations, and Costs, Judgment, Inter-Am. Ct. H.R. (ser. C) No. 287 (Nov. 14, 2014).
9. Rochac Hernandez et al. v. El Salvador, Merits, Reparations, and Costs, Judgment, Inter-Am. Ct. H.R. (ser. C) No. 285 (Oct. 14, 2014).
10. Expelled Dominicans and Haitians v. Dominican Republic, Preliminary Objections, Merits, Reparations, and Costs, Judgment, Inter-Am. Ct. H.R. (ser. C) No. 282 (Aug. 28, 2014).
11. Landaeta Meijias Brothers et al. v. Venezuela, Preliminary Objections, Merits, Reparations, and Costs, Judgment, Inter-Am. Ct. H.R. (ser. C) No. 281 (Aug. 27, 2014).
12. Rights & Guar. of Children in the Context of Migration and/or in Need of Int'l Prot., Advisory Opinion OC-21/14, Inter-Am. Ct. H.R. (ser. A) No. 21 (Aug. 19, 2014).
13. Norín Catrimán et al. (Leaders, members, and activists of the Mapuche Indigenous People) v. Chile, Merits, Reparations, and Costs, Judgment, Inter-Am. Ct. H.R. (ser. C) No. 279 (May 29, 2014).
14. Brewer Carías v. Venezuela, Preliminary Objections, Judgment, Inter-Am. Ct. H.R. (ser. C) No. 278 (May 26, 2014).
15. Veliz Franco et al. v. Guatemala, Preliminary Objections, Merits, and Reparations, Judgment, Inter-Am. Ct. H.R. (ser. C) No. 277 (May 19, 2014).
16. Liakat Ali Alibux v. Suriname, Preliminary Objections, Merits, Reparations, and Costs, Judgment, Inter-Am. Ct. H.R. (ser. C) No. 276 (Jan. 30, 2014).
17. J. v. Peru, Preliminary Objections, Merits, Reparations, and Costs, Judgment, Inter-Am. Ct. H.R. (ser. C) No. 275 (Nov. 27, 2013).
18. Osorio Rivera and Family v. Peru, Preliminary Objections, Merits, Reparations, and Costs, Judgment, Inter-Am. Ct. H.R. (ser. C) No. 274 (Nov. 26, 2013).
19. Garcia Cruz and Sanchez Silvestre v. Mexico, Merits, Reparations, and Costs, Judgment, Inter-Am. Ct. H.R. (ser. C) No. 273 (Nov. 26, 2013).
20. Pacheco Tineo Family v. Bolivia, Preliminary Objections, Merits, Reparations, and Costs, Judgment, Inter-Am. Ct. H.R. (ser. C) No. 272 (Nov. 25, 2013).
21. Mendoza et al. v. Argentina, Preliminary Objections, Merits, and Reparations, Judgment, Inter-Am. Ct. H.R. (ser. C) No. 260 (May 14, 2013).
22. García and Family Members v. Guatemala, Merits, Reparations, and Costs, Judgment, Inter-Am. Ct. H.R. (ser. C) No. 258 (Nov. 29, 2012).
23. Artavia Murillo et al. (In-vitro Fertilization) v. Costa Rica, Preliminary Objections, Merits, Reparations, and Costs, Judgment, Inter-Am. Ct. H.R. (ser. C) No. 257 (Nov. 28, 2012).
24. Gudiel Alvarez et al. ("Diario Militar") v. Guatemala, Merits, Reparations, and Costs, Judgment, Inter-Am. Ct. H.R. (ser. C) No. 253 (Nov. 20, 2012).
25. Massacres of El Mozote and Nearby Places v. El Salvador, Merits, Reparations, and Costs, Judgment, Inter-Am. Ct. H.R. (ser. C) No. 252 (Oct. 25, 2012).
26. Nadege Dorzema et al. v. Dominican Republic, Merits, Reparations, and Costs, Judgment, Inter-Am. Ct. H.R. (ser. C) No. 251 (Oct. 24, 2012).
27. Río Negro Massacres v. Guatemala, Preliminary Objections, Merits, Reparations, and Costs, Judgment, Inter-Am. Ct. H.R. (ser. C) No. 250 (Sept. 4, 2012).
28. Uzcátegui et al. v. Venezuela, Merits and Reparations, Judgment, Inter-Am. Ct. H.R. (ser. C) No. 249 (Sept. 3, 2012).

29. Palma Mendoza et al. v. Ecuador, Preliminary Objections and Merits, Judgment, Inter-Am. Ct. H.R. (ser. C) No. 247 (Sept. 3, 2012).
30. Kichwa Indigenous People of Sarayaku v. Ecuador, Merits and Reparations, Judgment Inter.-Am. Ct. H.R. (ser. C) No. 245 (June 27, 2012).
31. Díaz Peña v. Venezuela, Preliminary Objections, Merits, Reparations, and Costs, Judgment, Inter-Am. Ct. H.R. (ser. C) No. 244 (June 26, 2012).
32. Pacheco Teruel et al. v. Honduras, Merits, Reparations, and Costs, Judgment, Inter-Am. Ct. H.R. (ser. C) No. 241 (Apr. 27, 2012).
33. Gonzalez Medina and Family v. Dominican Republic, Preliminary Objections, Merits, Reparations, and Costs, Judgment, Inter-Am. Ct. H.R. (ser. C) No. 240 (Feb. 27, 2012).
34. Barrios Family v. Venezuela, Merits, Reparations, and Costs, Judgment, Inter-Am. Ct. H.R. (ser. C) No. 237 (Nov. 24, 2011).
35. Lysias Fleury et al. v. Haiti, Merits and Reparations, Judgment, Inter-Am. Ct. H.R. (ser. C) No. 236 (Nov. 23, 2011).
36. Contreras et. al. v. El Salvador, Merits, Reparations, and Costs, Judgment, Inter-Am. Ct. H.R. (ser. C) No. 232 (Aug. 31, 2011).
37. Torres Millacura et al. v. Argentina, Merits, Reparations, and Costs, Judgment, Inter-Am. Ct. H.R. (ser. C) No. 229 (Aug. 26, 2011).
38. Gelman v. Uruguay, Merits and Reparations, Judgment, Inter-Am. Ct. H.R. (ser. C) No. 221 (Feb. 24, 2011).
39. Cabrera García and Montiel Flores v. Mexico, Preliminary Objections, Merits, Reparations, and Costs, Judgment, Inter-Am. Ct. H.R. (ser. C) No. 220 (Nov. 26, 2010).
40. Gomes Lund et al. ("Guerrilha do Araguaia") v. Brazil, Preliminary Objections, Merits, Reparations, and Costs, Judgment, Inter-Am. Ct. H.R. (ser. C) No. 219 (Nov. 24, 2010).
41. Vélez Loor v. Panama, Preliminary Objections, Merits, Reparations, and Costs, Judgment, Inter-Am. Ct. H.R. (ser. C) No. 218 (Nov. 23, 2010).
42. Ibsen Cardenas and Ibsen Peña v. Bolivia, Merits, Reparations, and Costs, Judgment, Inter-Am. Ct. H.R. (ser. C) No. 217 (Sept. 1, 2010).
43. Fernandez Ortega et al. v. Mexico, Preliminary Objections, Merits, Reparations, and Costs, Judgment, Inter-Am. Ct. H.R. (ser. C) No. 215 (Aug. 30, 2010).
44. Chitay Nech et al. v. Guatemala, Preliminary Objections, Merits, Reparations, and Costs, Judgment, Inter-Am. Ct. H.R. (ser. C) No. 212 (May 25, 2010).
45. Radilla Pacheco v. Mexico, Preliminary Objections, Merits, Reparations, and Costs, Judgment, Inter-Am. Ct. H.R. (ser. C) No. 209 (Nov. 23, 2009).
46. Usón Ramírez v. Venezuela, Preliminary Objection, Merits, Reparations, and Costs, Judgment, Inter-Am. Ct. H.R. (ser. C) No. 207 (Nov. 20, 2009).
47. Barreto Leiva v. Venezuela, Merits, Reparations, and Costs, Judgment, Inter-Am. Ct. H.R. (ser. C) No. 206 (Nov. 17, 2009).
48. González et al. ("Cotton Field") v. Mexico, Preliminary Objections, Merits, Reparations, and Costs, Judgment, Inter-Am. Ct. H.R. (ser. C) No. 205 (Nov. 16, 2009).
49. Anzualdo Castro v. Peru, Preliminary Objections, Merits, Reparations, and Costs, Judgment, Inter-Am. Ct. H.R. (ser. C) No. 202 (Sept. 22, 2009).
50. Valle Jaramillo et al. v. Colombia, Merits, Reparations, and Costs, Judgment, Inter-Am. Ct. H.R. (ser. C) No. 192 (Nov. 27, 2008).

51. Ticona Estrada et al. v. Bolivia, Merits, Reparations, and Costs, Judgment, Inter-Am. Ct. H.R. (ser. C) No. 191 (Nov. 27, 2008).
52. Tiu Tojín v. Guatemala, Merits, Reparations, and Costs, Judgment, Inter-Am. Ct. H.R. (ser. C) No. 190 (Nov. 26, 2008).
53. Bayarri v. Argentina, Preliminary Objection, Merits, Reparations, and Costs, Judgment, Inter-Am. Ct. H.R. (ser. C) No. 187 (Oct. 30, 2008).
54. Heliodoro Portugal v. Panama, Preliminary Objections, Merits, Reparations, and Costs, Judgment, Inter-Am. Ct. H.R. (ser. C) No. 186 (Aug. 12, 2008).
55. Neptune v. Haiti, Merits, Reparations, and Costs, Judgment, Inter-Am. Ct. H.R. (ser. C) No. 180 (May 6, 2008).
56. Chaparro Álvarez and Lapo Íñiguez v. Ecuador, Preliminary Objections, Merits, Reparations, and Costs, Judgment, Inter-Am. Ct. H.R. (ser. C) No. 170 (Nov. 21, 2007).
57. Cantoral Huamaní and García Santa Cruz v. Peru, Preliminary Objections, Merits, Reparations, and Costs, Judgment, Inter-Am. Ct. H.R. (ser. C) No. 167 (July 10, 2007).
58. Zambrano Vélez et al. v. Ecuador, Merits, Reparations, and Costs, Judgment, Inter-Am. Ct. H.R. (ser. C) No. 166 (July 4, 2007).
59. Escué Zapata v. Colombia, Merits, Reparations, and Costs, Judgment, Inter-Am. Ct. H.R. (ser. C) No. 165 (July 4, 2007).
60. Bueno Alves v. Argentina, Merits, Reparations, and Costs, Judgment, Inter-Am. Ct. H.R. (Ser. C) No. 164 (May 11, 2007).
61. Rochela Massacre v. Colombia, Merits, Reparations, and Costs, Judgment, Inter-Am. Ct. H.R. (ser. C) No. 163 (May 11, 2007).
62. La Cantuta v. Peru, Merits, Reparations, and Costs, Judgment, Inter-Am. Ct. H.R. (ser. C) No. 162 (Nov. 29, 2006).
63. Miguel Castro Castro Prison v. Peru, Merits, Reparations, and Costs, Judgment, Inter-Am. Ct. H.R. (ser. C) No. 160 (Nov. 25, 2006).
64. Goiburú et al. v. Paraguay, Merits, Reparations, and Costs, Judgment, Inter-Am. Ct. H.R. (ser. C) No. 153 (Sept. 22, 2006).
65. Servellón García et al. v. Honduras, Merits, Reparations, and Costs, Judgment, Inter-Am. Ct. H.R. (ser. C) No. 152 (Sept. 21, 2006).
66. Ituango Massacres v. Colombia, Preliminary Objections, Merits, Reparations, and Costs, Judgment, Inter-Am. Ct. H.R. (ser. C) No. 148 (July 1, 2006).
67. Baldeón García v. Peru, Merits, Reparations, and Costs, Judgment, Inter-Am. Ct. H.R. (ser. C) No. 147 (Apr. 6, 2006).
68. López Álvarez v. Honduras, Merits, Reparations, and Costs, Judgment, Inter-Am. Ct. H.R. (ser. C) No. 141 (Feb. 1, 2006).
69. Pueblo Bello Massacre v. Colombia, Merits, Reparations, and Costs, Judgment, Inter-Am. Ct. H.R. (ser. C) No. 140 (Jan. 31, 2006).
70. Blanco Romero et al. v. Venezuela, Merits, Reparations, and Costs, Judgment, Inter-Am. Ct. H.R. (ser. C) No. 138 (Nov. 28, 2005).
71. García Asto and Ramírez Rojas v. Peru, Preliminary Objection, Merits, Reparations, and Costs, Judgment, Inter-Am. Ct. H.R. (ser. C) No. 137 (Nov. 25, 2005).
72. Gómez Palomino v. Peru, Merits, Reparations, and Costs, Judgment, Inter-Am. Ct. H.R. (ser. C) No. 136 (Nov. 22, 2005).

73. Palamara Iribarne v. Chile, Merits, Reparations, Costs, Judgment, Inter-Am. Ct. H.R. (ser. C) No. 135 (Nov. 22, 2005).
74. Mapiripán Massacre v. Colombia, Merits, Reparations, and Costs, Judgment, Inter-Am. Ct. H.R. (ser. C) No. 134 (Sept. 15, 2005).
75. Gutiérrez Soler v. Colombia, Merits, Reparations, and Costs, Judgment, Inter-Am. Ct. H.R. (ser. C) No. 132 (Sept. 12, 2005).
76. Acosta Calderón v. Ecuador, Merits, Reparations, and Costs, Judgment, Inter-Am. Ct. H.R. (ser. C) No. 129 (June 24, 2005).
77. Mapiripán Massacre v. Colombia, Preliminary Objections, Judgment, Inter-Am. Ct. H.R. (ser. C) No. 122 (Mar. 7, 2005).
78. Berenson Mejia v. Peru, Merits, Reparations, and Costs, Judgment, Inter-Am. Ct. H.R. (ser. C) No. 119 (Nov. 25, 2004).
79. Serrano Cruz Sisters v. El Salvador, Preliminary Objections, Judgment, Inter-Am. Ct. H.R. (ser. C) No. 118 (Nov. 23, 2004).
80. De La Cruz Flores v. Peru, Merits, Reparations, and Costs, Judgment, Inter-Am. Ct. H.R. (ser. C) No. 115 (Nov. 18, 2004).
81. Tibi v. Ecuador, Preliminary Objections, Merits, Reparations, and Costs, Judgment, Inter-Am. Ct. H.R. (ser. C) No. 114 (Sept. 7, 2004).
82. Campo Dodd v. Mexico, Preliminary Objections, Judgment, Inter-Am. Ct. H.R. (ser. C) No. 113 (Sept. 3, 2004).
83. "Juvenile Reeducation Institute" v. Paraguay, Preliminary Objections, Merits, Reparations, and Costs, Judgment, Inter-Am. Ct. H.R. (ser. C) No. 112 (Sept. 2, 2004).
84. Gómez Paquiyauri Brothers v. Peru, Merits, Reparations, and Costs, Judgment, Inter-Am. Ct. H.R. (ser. C) No. 110 (July 8, 2004).
85. 19 Merchants v. Colombia, Merits, Reparations, and Costs, Judgment, Inter-Am. Ct. H.R. (ser. C) No. 109 (July 5, 2004).
86. Molina Theissen v. Guatemala, Reparations and Costs, Judgment, Inter-Am. Ct. H.R. (ser. C) No. 108 (July 3, 2004).
87. Molina Theissen v. Guatemala, Merits, Judgment, Inter-Am. Ct. H.R. (ser. C) No. 106 (May 4, 2004).
88. Maritza Urrutia v. Guatemala, Merits, Reparations, and Costs, Judgment, Inter-Am. Ct. H.R. (ser. C) No. 103 (Nov. 27, 2003).
89. Sánchez v. Honduras, Interpretation of the Judgment of Preliminary Objection, Merits, and Reparations, Judgment, Inter-Am. Ct. H.R. (ser. C) No. 102 (Nov. 26, 2003).
90. Bulacio v. Argentina, Merits, Reparations, and Costs, Judgment, Inter-Am. Ct. H.R. (ser. C) No. 100 (Sept. 18, 2003).
91. Sánchez v. Honduras, Preliminary Objection, Merits, Reparations, and Costs, Judgment, Inter-Am. Ct. H.R. (ser. C) No. 99 (June 7, 2003).
92. Caracazo v. Venezuela, Reparations and Costs, Judgment, Inter-Am. Ct. H.R. (ser. C) No. 95 (Aug. 29, 2002).
93. Juridical Condition & Human Rights of the Child, Advisory Opinion OC-17/02, Inter-Am. Ct. H.R. (ser. A) No. 17 (Aug. 28, 2002).
94. Hilaire, Constantine, and Benjamin et al. v. Trinidad & Tobago, Merits, Reparations, and Costs, Judgment, Inter-Am. Ct. H.R. (ser. C) No. 94 (June 21, 2002).

95. 19 Merchants v. Colombia, Preliminary Objection, Judgment, Inter-Am. Ct. H.R. (ser. C) No. 93 (June 12, 2002).
96. Trujillo Oroza v. Bolivia, Reparations and Costs, Judgment, Inter-Am. Ct. H.R. (ser. C) No. 92 (Feb. 27, 2002).
97. Bámaca Velásquez v. Guatemala, Reparations and Costs, Judgment, Inter-Am. Ct. H.R. (ser. C) No. 91 (Feb. 22, 2002).
98. Durand and Ugarte v. Peru, Reparations and Costs, Judgment, Inter-Am. Ct. H.R. (ser. C) No. 89 (Dec. 3, 2001).
99. Cantoral Benavides v. Peru, Reparations and Costs, Judgment, Inter-Am. Ct. H.R. (ser. C) No. 88 (Dec. 3, 2001).
100. Constantine et al. v. Trinidad & Tobago, Preliminary Objections, Judgment, Inter-Am. Ct. H.R. (ser. C) No. 82 (Sept. 1, 2001).
101. Benjamin et al. v. Trinidad & Tobago, Preliminary Objections, Judgment, Inter-Am. Ct. H.R. (ser. C) No. 81 (Sept. 1, 2001).
102. Hilaire v. Trinidad & Tobago, Preliminary Objections, Judgment, Inter-Am. Ct. H.R. (ser. C) No. 80 (Sept. 1, 2001).
103. Cesti Hurtado v. Peru, Reparations and Costs, 2001 Inter-Am. Ct. H.R. (ser. C) No. 78 (May 31, 2001).
104. "Street Children" (Villagrán Morales et al.) v. Guatemala, Reparations and Costs, Judgment, Inter-Am. Ct. H.R. (ser. C) No. 77 (May 26, 2001).
105. "White Van" (Paniagua Morales et al.) v. Guatemala, Reparations and Costs, Judgment, Inter-Am. Ct. H.R. (ser. C) No. 76 (May 25, 2001).
106. "The Last Temptation of Christ" (Olmedo Bustos et al.) v. Chile, Merits, Reparations, and Costs, Judgment, Inter-Am. Ct. H.R. (ser. C) No. 73 (Feb. 5, 2001).
107. Bámaca Velásquez v. Guatemala, Merits, Judgment, Inter-Am. Ct. H.R. (ser. C) No. 70 (Nov. 25, 2000).
108. Cantoral Benavides v. Peru, Merits, Judgment, Inter-Am. Ct. H.R. (ser. C) No. 69 (Aug. 18, 2000).
109. Durand and Ugarte v. Peru, Merits, Judgment, Inter-Am. Ct. H.R. (ser. C) No. 68 (Aug. 16, 2000).
110. Cesti Hurtado v. Peru, Interpretation of the Judgment of Merits, Judgment, Inter-Am. Ct. H.R. (ser. C) No. 65 (Jan. 29, 2000).
111. Trujillo Oroza v. Bolivia, Merits, Judgment, Inter-Am. Ct. H.R. (ser. C) No. 64 (Jan. 26, 2000).
112. "Street Children" (Villagrán Morales et al.) v. Guatemala, Merits, Judgment, Inter-Am. Ct. H.R. (ser. C) No. 63 (Nov. 19, 1999).
113. Cesti Hurtado v. Peru, Request for Interpretation of the Judgment of Merits, Order of the Court, Inter-Am. Ct. H.R. (ser. C) No. 62 (Nov. 19, 1999).
114. Caracazo v. Venezuela, Merits, Judgment, Inter-Am. Ct. H.R. (ser. C) No. 58 (Nov. 11, 1999).
115. Cesti Hurtado v. Peru, Merits, Judgment, Inter-Am. Ct. H.R. (ser. C) No. 56 (Sept. 29, 1999).
116. Castillo Petruzzi et al. v. Peru, Merits, Reparations, and Costs, Judgment, Inter-Am. Ct. H.R. (ser. C) No. 52 (May 30, 1999).
117. Durand and Ugarte v. Peru, Preliminary Objections, Judgment, Inter-Am. Ct. H.R. (ser. C) No. 50 (May 28, 1999).

118. Cesti Hurtado v. Peru, Preliminary Objections, Judgment, Inter-Am. Ct. H.R. (ser. C) No. 49 (Jan. 26, 1999).
119. Loayza Tamayo v. Peru, Interpretation of the Judgment of Merits, Order of the Court, Inter-Am. Ct. H.R. (ser. C) No. 47 (Mar. 8, 1998).
120. Suárez Rosero v. Ecuador, Reparations and Costs, Judgment, Inter-Am. Ct. H.R. (ser. C) No. 44 (Jan. 20, 1999).
121. Castillo Páez v. Peru, Reparations and Costs, Judgment, Inter-Am. Ct. H.R. (ser. C) No. 43 (Nov. 27, 1998).
122. Loayza Tamayo v. Peru, Reparations and Costs, Judgment, Inter-Am. Ct. H.R. (ser. C) No. 42 (Nov. 27, 1998).
123. Cantoral Benavides v. Peru, Preliminary Objections, Judgment, Inter-Am. Ct. H.R. (ser. C) No. 40 (Sept. 3, 1998).
124. Garrido and Baigorria v. Argentina, Reparations and Costs, Judgment, Inter-Am. Ct. H.R. (ser. C) No. 39 (Aug. 27, 1998).
125. Benavides Cevallos v. Ecuador, Merits, Reparations, and Costs, Judgment, Inter-Am. Ct. H.R. (ser. C) No. 38 (June 19, 1998).
126. "White Van" (Paniagua Morales et al.) v. Guatemala, Merits, Judgment, Inter-Am. Ct. H.R. (ser. C) No. 37 (Mar. 8, 1998).
127. Blake v. Guatemala, Merits, Judgment, Inter-Am. Ct. H.R. (ser. C) No. 36 (Jan. 24, 1998).
128. Suárez Rosero v. Ecuador, Merits, Judgment, Inter-Am. Ct. H.R. (ser. C) No. 35 (Nov. 12, 1997).
129. Castillo Páez v. Peru, Merits, Judgment, Inter-Am. Ct. H.R. (ser. C) No. 34 (Nov. 3, 1997).
130. Loayza Tamayo v. Peru, Merits, Judgment, Inter-Am. Ct. H.R. (ser. C) No. 33 (Sept. 17, 1997).
131. "Street Children" (Villagrán Morales et al.) v. Guatemala, Preliminary Objections, Judgment, Inter-Am. Ct. H.R. (ser. C) No. 32 (Sept. 11, 1997).
132. Caballero Delgado and Santana v. Colombia, Reparations and Costs, Judgment, Inter-Am. Ct. H.R. (ser. C) No. 31 (Jan. 29, 1997).
133. Genie Lacayo v. Nicaragua, Merits, Reparations, and Costs, Judgment, Inter-Am. Ct. H.R. (ser. C) No. 30 (Jan. 29, 1997).
134. Neira Alegría et al. v. Peru, Reparations and Costs, Judgment, Inter-Am. Ct. H.R. (ser. C) No. 29 (Sept. 19, 1996).
135. Blake v. Guatemala, Preliminary Objections, Judgment, Inter-Am. Ct. H.R. (ser. C) No. 27 (July 2, 1996).
136. Garrido and Baigorria v. Argentina, Merits, Judgment, Inter-Am. Ct. H.R. (ser. C) No. 26 (Feb. 2, 1996).
137. Loayza Tamayo v. Peru, Preliminary Objections, Judgment, Inter-Am. Ct. H.R. (ser. C) No. 25 (Jan. 31, 1996).
138. Castillo Páez v. Peru, Preliminary Objections, Judgment, Inter-Am. Ct. H.R. (ser. C) No. 24 (Jan. 30, 1996).
139. "White Van" (Paniagua Morales et al.) v. Guatemala, Preliminary Objections, Judgment, Inter-Am. Ct. H.R. (ser. C) No. 23 (Jan. 25, 1996).
140. Caballero Delgado and Santana v. Colombia, Merits, Judgment, Inter-Am. Ct. H.R. (ser. C) No. 22 (Dec. 8, 1995).

141. Neira Alegría et al. v. Peru, Merits, Judgment, Inter-Am. Ct. H.R. (ser. C) No. 20 (Jan. 19, 1995).
142. Caballero Delgado and Santana v. Colombia, Preliminary Objections, Judgment, Inter-Am. Ct. H.R. (ser. C) No. 17 (Jan. 21, 1994).
143. Gangaram Panday v. Suriname, Merits, Reparations, and Costs, Judgment, Inter-Am. Ct. H.R. (ser. C) No. 16 (Jan. 21, 1994).
144. Aloeboetoe et al. v. Suriname, Reparations and Costs, Judgment, Inter-Am. Ct. H.R. (ser. C) No. 15 (Sept. 10, 1993).
145. Cayara v. Peru, Preliminary Objections, Judgment, Inter-Am. Ct. H.R. (ser. C) No. 14 (Feb. 3, 1993).
146. Neira Alegría et al. v. Peru, Preliminary Objections, Judgment, Inter-Am. Ct. H.R. (ser. C) No. 13 (Dec. 11, 1991).
147. Gangaram Panday v. Suriname, Preliminary Objections, Judgment, Inter-Am. Ct. H.R. (ser. C) No. 12 (Dec. 4, 1991).
148. Aloeboetoe et al. v. Suriname, Merits, Judgment, Inter-Am. Ct. H.R. (ser. C) No. 11 (Dec. 4, 1991).
149. Fairén Garbi and Solís Corrales v. Honduras, Merits, Judgment, Inter-Am. Ct. H.R. (ser. C) No. 6 (Mar. 15, 1989).
150. Godínez Cruz v. Honduras, Merits, Judgment, Inter-Am. Ct. H.R. (ser. C) No. 5 (Jan. 20, 1989).
151. Velásquez Rodríguez v. Honduras, Merits, Judgment, Inter-Am. Ct. H.R. (ser. C) No. 4 (July 29, 1988).
152. Judicial Guarantees in States of Emergency (Arts. 27(2), 25, and 8 American Convention on Human Rights), Advisory Opinion OC-9/87, Inter-Am. Ct. H.R. (ser. A) No. 9 (Oct. 6, 1987).
153. Godínez Cruz v. Honduras, Preliminary Objections, Judgment, Inter-Am. Ct. H.R. (ser. C) No. 3 (June 26, 1987).
154. Fairén Garbi and Solís Corrales v. Honduras, Preliminary Objections, Judgment, Inter-Am. Ct. H.R. (ser. C) No. 2 (June 26, 1987).
155. Velásquez Rodríguez v. Honduras, Preliminary Objections, Judgment, Inter-Am. Ct. H.R. (ser. C) No. 1 (June 26, 1987).
156. Habeas Corpus in Emergency Situations (Arts. 27(2), 25(1), and 7(6) American Convention on Human Rights), Advisory Opinion OC-8/87, Inter-Am. Ct. H.R. (ser. A) No. 8 (Jan. 30, 1987).

ARTICLE 8: RIGHT TO A FAIR TRIAL

Article 8(1)

1. Duque v. Colombia, Preliminary Objections, Merits, Reparations and Costs, Judgment, Inter-Am. Ct. H.R. (ser. C) No. 310 (Feb. 26, 2016).
2. Quispialaya Vilcapoma v. Peru, Preliminary Objections, Merits, Reparations and Costs, Judgment, Inter-Am. Ct. H.R. (ser. C) No. 308 (Nov. 23, 2015).
3. Velasquez Paiz et al. v. Guatemala, Preliminary Objections, Merits, Reparations and Costs, Judgment, Inter-Am. Ct. H.R. (ser. C) No. 307 (Nov. 19, 2015).

4. Garcia Ibarra et al. v. Ecuador, Preliminary Objections, Merits, Reparations and Costs, Judgment, Inter-Am. Ct. H.R. (ser. C) No. 306 (Nov. 17, 2015).
5. Community Garifuna Triunfo de la Cruz & its Members v. Honduras, Merits, Reparations and Costs, Judgment, Inter-Am. Ct. H.R. (ser. C) No. 305 (Oct. 8, 2015).
6. Garifuna Punta Piedra Community and its Members v. Honduras, Preliminary Objections, Merits, Reparations and Costs, Judgment, Inter-Am. Ct. H.R. (ser. C) No. 304 (Oct. 8, 2015).
7. Ruano Torres et al. v. El Salvador, Merits, Reparations and Costs, Judgment, Inter-Am. Ct. H.R. (ser. C) No. 303 (Oct. 5, 2015).
8. Lopez Lone et al. v. Honduras, Preliminary Objection, Merits, Reparations and Costs, Judgment, Inter-Am. Ct. H.R. (ser. C) No. 302 (Oct. 5, 2015).
9. Galindo Cardenas et al. v. Peru, Preliminary Objections, Merits, Reparations and Costs, Judgment, Inter-Am. Ct. H.R. (ser. C) No. 301 (Oct. 2, 2015).
10. Omar Humberto Maldonado Vargas et al v. Chile, Merits, Reparations, Costs, Judgment, Inter-Am. Ct. H.R. (ser. C) No. 300 (Sept. 2, 2015).
11. Case of Peasant Community of Santa Barbara v. Peru, Preliminary Objections, Merits, Reparations and Costs, Judgment, Inter-Am. Ct. H.R. (ser. C) No. 299 (Sept. 1, 2015).
12. Gonzales Lluy et al. v. Ecuador, Preliminary Objections, Merits, Reparations and Costs, Judgment, Inter-Am. Ct. H.R. (ser. C) No. 298 (Sept. 1, 2015).
13. Wong Ho Wing v. Peru, Preliminary Objection, Merits, Reparations and Costs, Judgment, Inter-Am. Ct. H.R. (ser. C) No. 297 (June 30, 2015).
14. Canales Huapaya et al. v. Peru, Preliminary Objections, Merits, Reparations, Costs, Judgment, (ser. C) No. 296 (June 24, 2015).
15. Espinoza Gonzales v. Peru, Interpretation of the Judgment on Preliminary Objections, Merits, Reparations and Costs, Judgment, Inter-Am. Ct. H.R. (ser. C) No. 295 (June 23, 2015).
16. Granier et al. (Radio Caracas Television) v. Venezuela, Preliminary Objections, Merits, Reparations, Costs, Judgment, Inter-Am. Ct. H.R. (ser. C) No. 293 (June 22, 2015).
17. Cruz Sánchez et al. v. Peru, Preliminary Objections, Merits, Reparations, Costs, Judgment, Inter-Am. Ct. H.R. (ser. C) No. 292 (Apr. 17, 2015).
18. J. v. Peru, Interpretation of the Judgment on Preliminary Objection, Merits, Reparations, and Costs, Judgment, Inter-Am. Ct. H.R. (ser. C) No. 291 (Nov. 20, 2014).
19. Osorio Rivera and Family v. Peru, Interpretation of the Judgment on Preliminary Objection, Merits, Reparations, and Costs, Judgment, Inter-Am. Ct. H.R. (ser. C) No. 290 (Nov. 20, 2014).
20. Espinoza Gonzales v. Peru, Preliminary Objections, Merits, Reparations, and Costs, Judgment, Inter-Am. Ct. H.R. (ser. C) No. 289 (Nov. 20, 2014).
21. Argüelles et al. v. Argentina, Preliminary Objections, Merits, Reparations, and Costs, Judgment, Inter-Am. Ct. H.R. (ser. C) No. 288 (Nov. 20, 2014).
22. Rodriguez Vera et al. (Persons Disappeared from the Palace of Justice) v. Colombia, Preliminary Objections, Merits, Reparations, and Costs, Judgment, Inter-Am. Ct. H.R. (ser. C) No. 287 (Nov. 14, 2014).
23. Tarazona Arrieta et al. v. Peru, Preliminary Objections, Merits, Reparations, and Costs, Judgment, Inter-Am. Ct. H.R. (ser. C) No. 286 (Oct. 15, 2014).
24. Rochac Hernandez et al. v. El Salvador, Merits, Reparations, and Costs, Judgment, Inter-Am. Ct. H.R. (ser. C) No. 285 (Oct. 14, 2014).

25. Kuna Indigenous People of Madungandi and Embera Indigenous People of Bayano & their Members v. Panama, Preliminary Objections, Merits, Reparations, and Costs, Judgment, Inter-Am. Ct. H.R. (ser. C) No. 284 (Oct. 14, 2014).
26. Human Rights Defender et al. v. Guatemala, Preliminary Objections, Merits, Reparations, and Costs, Judgment, Inter-Am. Ct. H.R. (ser. C) No. 283 (Aug. 28, 2014).
27. Expelled Dominicans and Haitians v. Dominican Republic, Preliminary Objections, Merits, Reparations, and Costs, Judgment, Inter-Am. Ct. H.R. (ser. C) No. 282 (Aug. 28, 2014).
28. Landaeta Meijias Brothers et al. v. Venezuela, Preliminary Objections, Merits, Reparations, and Costs, Judgment, Inter-Am. Ct. H.R. (ser. C) No. 281 (Aug. 27, 2014).
29. Norín Catrimán et al. (Leaders, members, and activists of the Mapuche Indigenous People) v. Chile, Merits, Reparations, and Costs, Judgment, Inter-Am. Ct. H.R. (ser. C) No. 279 (May 29, 2014).
30. Veliz Franco et al. v. Guatemala, Preliminary Objections, Merits, and Reparations, Judgment, Inter-Am. Ct. H.R. (ser. C) No. 277 (May 19, 2014).
31. Liakat Ali Alibux v. Suriname, Preliminary Objections, Merits, Reparations, and Costs, Judgment, Inter-Am. Ct. H.R. (ser. C) No. 276 (Jan. 30, 2014).
32. J. v. Peru, Preliminary Objections, Merits, Reparations, and Costs, Judgment, Inter-Am. Ct. H.R. (ser. C) No. 275 (Nov. 27, 2013).
33. Osorio Rivera and Family v. Peru, Preliminary Objections, Merits, Reparations, and Costs, Judgment, Inter-Am. Ct. H.R. (ser. C) No. 274 (Nov. 26, 2013).
34. Pacheco Tineo Family v. Bolivia, Preliminary Objections, Merits, Reparations, and Costs, Judgment, Inter-Am. Ct. H.R. (ser. C) No. 272 (Nov. 25, 2013).
35. Gutiérrez and Family v. Argentina, Merits, Reparations, and Costs, Judgment, Inter-Am. Ct. H.R. (ser. C) No. 271 (Nov. 25, 2013).
36. Afro-Descendant Communities Displaced From the Cacarica River Basin (Operation Genesis) v. Colombia, Preliminary Objections, Merits, Reparations, and Costs, Judgment, Inter-Am. Ct. H.R. (ser. C) No. 270 (Nov. 20, 2013).
37. Luna Lopez v. Honduras, Merits, Reparations, and Costs, Judgment, Inter-Am. Ct. H.R. (ser. C) No. 269 (Oct. 10, 2013).
38. Constitutional Tribunal (Camba Campos et al.) v. Ecuador, Preliminary Objections, Merits, Reparations, and Costs, Judgment, Inter-Am. Ct. H.R. (ser. C) No. 268 (Aug. 28, 2013).
39. Garcia Lucero et al. v. Chile, Preliminary Objections, Merits, and Reparations, Judgment, Inter-Am. Ct. H.R. (ser. C) No. 267 (Aug. 28, 2013).
40. Supreme Court of Justice (Quintana Coello et al.) v. Ecuador, Preliminary Objections, Merits, Reparations, and Costs, Judgment, Inter-Am. Ct. H.R. (ser. C) No. 266 (Aug. 23, 2013).
41. Memoli v. Argentina, Preliminary Objections, Merits, Reparations, and Costs, Judgment, Inter-Am. Ct. H.R. (ser. C) No. 265 (Aug. 22, 2013).
42. Suárez Peralta v. Ecuador, Preliminary Objections, Merits, Reparations, and Costs, Judgment, Inter-Am. Ct. H.R. (ser. C) No. 261 (May 21, 2013).
43. Mendoza et al. v. Argentina, Preliminary Objections, Merits, and Reparations, Judgment, Inter-Am. Ct. H.R. (ser. C) No. 260 (May 14, 2013).
44. Santo Domingo Massacre v. Colombia, Preliminary Objections, Merits, and Reparations, Judgment, Inter-Am. Ct. H.R. (ser. C) No. 259 (Nov. 30, 2012).

45. García and Family Members v. Guatemala, Merits, Reparations, and Costs, Judgment, Inter-Am. Ct. H.R. (ser. C) No. 258 (Nov. 29, 2012).
46. Mohamed v. Argentina, Preliminary Objections, Merits, Reparations, and Costs, Judgment, Inter-Am. Ct. H.R. (ser. C) No. 255 (Nov. 23, 2012).
47. Gudiel Alvarez et al. ("Diario Militar") v. Guatemala, Merits, Reparations, and Costs, Judgment, Inter-Am. Ct. H.R. (ser. C) No. 253 (Nov. 20, 2012).
48. Massacres of El Mozote and Nearby Places v. El Salvador, Merits, Reparations, and Costs, Judgment, Inter-Am. Ct. H.R. (ser. C) No. 252 (Oct. 25, 2012).
49. Nadege Dorzema et al. v. Dominican Republic, Merits, Reparations, and Costs, Judgment, Inter-Am. Ct. H.R. (ser. C) No. 251 (Oct. 24, 2012).
50. Río Negro Massacres v. Guatemala, Preliminary Objections, Merits, Reparations, and Costs, Judgment, Inter-Am. Ct. H.R. (ser. C) No. 250 (Sept. 4, 2012).
51. Uzcátegui et al. v. Venezuela, Merits and Reparations, Judgment, Inter-Am. Ct. H.R. (ser. C) No. 249 (Sept. 3, 2012).
52. Vélez Restrepo and Family v. Colombia, Preliminary Objections, Merits, Reparations, and Costs, Judgment, Inter-Am. Ct. H.R. (ser. C) No. 248 (Sept. 3, 2012).
53. Palma Mendoza et al. v. Ecuador, Preliminary Objections and Merits, Judgment, Inter-Am. Ct. H.R. (ser. C) No. 247 (Sept. 3, 2012).
54. Furlan and Family v. Argentina, Preliminary Objections, Merits, Reparations, and Costs, Judgment, Inter-Am. Ct. H.R. (ser. C) No. 246 (Aug. 31, 2012).
55. Kichwa Indigenous People of Sarayaku v. Ecuador, Merits and Reparations, Judgment Inter.-Am. Ct. H.R. (ser. C) No. 245 (June 27, 2012).
56. Díaz Peña v. Venezuela, Preliminary Objections, Merits, Reparations, and Costs, Judgment, Inter-Am. Ct. H.R. (ser. C) No. 244 (June 26, 2012).
57. Barbani Duarte et al. v. Uruguay, Request for Interpretation of the Judgment of Merits, Reparations, and Costs, Judgment, Inter-Am. Ct. H.R. (ser. C) No. 243 (June 26, 2012).
58. Fornerón and Daughter v. Argentina, Merits, Reparations, and Costs, Judgment, Inter-Am. Ct. H.R. (ser. C) No. 242 (Apr. 27, 2012).
59. Atala Riffo and Daughters v. Chile, Merits, Reparations, and Costs, Judgment, Inter-Am. Ct. H.R. (ser. C) No. 239 (Feb. 24, 2012).
60. Lysias Fleury et al. v. Haiti, Merits and Reparations, Judgment, Inter-Am. Ct. H.R. (ser. C) No. 236 (Nov. 23, 2011).
61. Barbani Duarte et al. v. Uruguay, Merits, Reparations, and Costs, Judgment, Inter. Am. Ct. H.R. (ser. C) No. 234 (Oct. 13, 2011).
62. López Mendoza v. Venezuela, Merits, Reparations, and Costs, Judgment,Inter-Am. Ct. H.R. (ser. C) No. 233 (Sept. 1, 2011).
63. Contreras et. al. v. El Salvador, Merits, Reparations, and Costs, Judgment, Inter-Am. Ct. H.R. (ser. C) No. 232 (Aug. 31, 2011).
64. Grande v. Argentina, Preliminary Objections and Merits, Judgment, Inter-Am. Ct. H.R. (ser. C) No. 231 (Aug. 31, 2011).
65. Torres Millacura et al. v. Argentina, Merits, Reparations, and Costs, Judgment, Inter-Am. Ct. H.R. (ser. C) No. 229 (Aug. 26, 2011).
66. Mejía Idrovo v. Ecuador, Preliminary Objections, Merits, Reparations, and Costs, Judgment, Inter-Am. Ct. H.R. (ser. C) No. 228 (July 5, 2011).

67. Chocrón Chocrón v. Venezuela, Preliminary Objections, Merits, Reparations, and Costs, Judgment, Inter-Am. Ct. H.R. (ser. C) No. 227 (July 1, 2011).
68. Vera Vera et al. v. Ecuador, Preliminary Objections, Merits, Reparations, and Costs, Judgment, Inter-Am. Ct. H.R. (ser. C) No. 226 (May 19, 2011).
69. Rosendo Cantu et al. v. Mexico, Interpretation of Judgment of Preliminary Objections, Merits, Reparations, and Costs, Judgment, Inter-Am. Ct. H.R. (ser. C) No. 225 (May 15, 2011).
70. Fernandez Ortega et al. v. Mexico, Interpretation of Judgment of Preliminary Objection, Merits, Reparations, and Costs, Judgment, Inter-Am. Ct. H.R. (ser. C) No. 224 (May 15, 2011).
71. Salvador Chiriboga v. Ecuador, Reparations and Costs, Judgment, Inter-Am. Ct. H.R. (ser. C) No. 222 (Mar. 3, 2011).
72. Gelman v. Uruguay, Merits and Reparations, Judgment, Inter-Am. Ct. H.R. (ser. C) No. 221 (Feb. 24, 2011).
73. Cabrera García and Montiel Flores v. Mexico, Preliminary Objections, Merits, Reparations, and Costs, Judgment, Inter-Am. Ct. H.R. (ser. C) No. 220 (Nov. 26, 2010).
74. Gomes Lund et al. ("Guerrilha do Araguaia") v. Brazil, Preliminary Objections, Merits, Reparations, and Costs, Judgment, Inter-Am. Ct. H.R. (ser. C) No. 219 (Nov. 24, 2010).
75. Vélez Loor v. Panama, Preliminary Objections, Merits, Reparations, and Costs, Judgment, Inter-Am. Ct. H.R. (ser. C) No. 218 (Nov. 23, 2010).
76. Ibsen Cardenas and Ibsen Peña v. Bolivia, Merits, Reparations, and Costs, Judgment, Inter-Am. Ct. H.R. (ser. C) No. 217 (Sept. 1, 2010).
77. Rosendo Cantu et al. v. Mexico, Preliminary Objections, Merits, Reparations, and Costs, Judgment, Inter-Am. Ct. H.R. (ser. C) No. 216 (Aug. 31, 2010).
78. Fernandez Ortega et al. v. Mexico, Preliminary Objections, Merits, Reparations, and Costs, Judgment, Inter-Am. Ct. H.R. (ser. C) No. 215 (Aug. 30, 2010).
79. Xákmok Kásek Indigenous Cmty. v. Paraguay, Merits, Reparations, and Costs, Judgment, Inter-Am. Ct. H.R. (ser. C) No. 214 (Aug. 24, 2010).
80. Cepeda Vargas v. Colombia, Preliminary Objections, Merits, Reparations, and Costs, Judgment, Inter-Am. Ct. H.R. (ser. C.) No. 213 (May 26, 2010).
81. "Las Dos Erres" Massacre v. Guatemala, Preliminary Objections, Merits, Reparations, and Costs, Judgment, Inter-Am. Ct. H.R. (ser. C) No. 211 (Nov. 24, 2009).
82. Radilla Pacheco v. Mexico, Preliminary Objections, Merits, Reparations, and Costs, Judgment, Inter-Am. Ct. H.R. (ser. C) No. 209 (Nov. 23, 2009).
83. Escher et al. v. Brazil, Interpretation of the Judgment on Preliminary Objections, Merits, Reparations, and Costs, Judgment, Inter-Am. Ct. H.R. (ser. C) No. 208 (Nov. 20, 2009).
84. Usón Ramírez v. Venezuela, Preliminary Objections, Merits, Reparations, and Costs, Judgment, Inter-Am. Ct. H.R. (ser. C) No. 207 (Nov. 20, 2009).
85. Barreto Leiva v. Venezuela, Merits, Reparations, and Costs, Judgment, Inter-Am. Ct. H.R. (ser. C) No. 206 (Nov. 17, 2009).
86. González et al. ("Cotton Field") v. Mexico, Preliminary Objections, Merits, Reparations, and Costs, Judgment, Inter-Am. Ct. H.R. (ser. C) No. 205 (Nov. 16, 2009).
87. DaCosta Cadogan v. Barbados, Preliminary Objections, Merits, Reparations, and Costs, Judgment, Inter-Am. Ct. H.R. (ser. C) No. 204 (Sept. 24, 2009).

88. Garibaldi v. Brazil, Preliminary Objections, Merits, Reparations, and Costs, Judgment, Inter-Am. Ct. H.R. (ser. C) No. 203 (Sept. 23, 2009).
89. Anzualdo Castro v. Peru, Preliminary Objections, Merits, Reparations, and Costs, Judgment, Inter-Am. Ct. H.R. (ser. C) No. 202 (Sept. 22, 2009).
90. Valle Jaramillo et al. v. Colombia, Interpretation of the Judgment on the Merits, Reparations, and Costs, Judgment, Inter-Am. Ct. H.R. (ser. C) No. 201 (July 7, 2009).
91. Escher et al v. Brazil, Preliminary Objections, Merits, Reparations, and Costs, Judgment, Inter-Am. Ct. H.R. (ser. C) No. 200 (July 6, 2009).
92. Reverón Trujillo v. Venezuela, Preliminary Objections, Merits, Reparations, and Costs, Judgment, Inter-Am. Ct. H.R. (ser. C) No. 197 (June 30, 2009).
93. Kawas Fernández v. Honduras, Merits, Reparations, and Costs, Judgment, Inter-Am. Ct. H.R. (ser. C) No. 196 (Apr. 3, 2009).
94. Tristán Donoso v. Panama, Preliminary Objections, Merits, Reparations, and Costs, Judgment, Inter-Am. Ct. H.R. (ser. C) No. 193 (Jan. 27, 2009).
95. Valle Jaramillo et al. v. Colombia, Merits, Reparations, and Costs, Judgment, Inter-Am. Ct. H.R. (ser. C) No. 192 (Nov. 27, 2008).
96. Ticona Estrada et al. v. Bolivia, Merits, Reparations, and Costs, Judgment, Inter-Am. Ct. H.R. (ser. C) No. 191 (Nov. 27, 2008).
97. Tiu Tojín v. Guatemala, Merits, Reparations, and Costs, Judgment, Inter-Am. Ct. H.R. (ser. C) No. 190 (Nov. 26, 2008).
98. García Prieto et al. v. El Salvador, Interpretation of the Judgment on Preliminary Objections, Merits, Reparations, and Costs, Judgment, Inter-Am. Ct. H.R. (ser. C) No. 188 (Nov. 24, 2008).
99. Bayarri v. Argentina, Preliminary Objection, Merits, Reparations, and Costs, Judgment, Inter-Am. Ct. H.R. (ser. C) No. 187 (Oct. 30, 2008).
100. Heliodoro Portugal v. Panama, Preliminary Objections, Merits, Reparations, and Costs, Judgment, Inter-Am. Ct. H.R. (ser. C) No. 186 (Aug. 12, 2008).
101. Castañeda Gutman v. Mexico, Preliminary Objections, Merits, Reparations, and Costs, Judgment, Inter-Am. Ct. H.R. (ser. C) No. 184 (Aug. 6, 2008).
102. Albán Cornejo et al. v. Ecuador, Interpretation of the Judgment on Merits, Reparations, and Costs, Judgment, Inter-Am. Ct. H.R. (ser. C) No. 183 (Aug. 5, 2008).
103. Apitz Barbera et al. ("First Court of Administrative Disputes") v. Venezuela, Preliminary Objection, Merits, Reparations, and Costs, Judgment, Inter-Am. Ct. H.R. (ser. C) No. 182 (Aug. 5, 2008).
104. Neptune v. Haiti, Merits, Reparations, and Costs, Judgment, Inter-Am. Ct. H.R. (ser. C) No. 180 (May 6, 2008).
105. Salvador Chiriboga v. Ecuador, Preliminary Objections and Merits, Judgment, Inter-Am. Ct. H.R. (ser. C) No. 179 (May 6, 2008).
106. Kimel v. Argentina, Merits, Reparations, and Costs, Judgment, Inter-Am. Ct. H.R. (ser. C) No. 177 (May 2, 2008).
107. Dismissed Cong. Emp. (Aguado Alfaro et al.) v. Peru, Request for Interpretation of the Judgment on Preliminary Objections, Merits, Reparations, and Costs, Judgment, Inter-Am. Ct. H.R. (ser. C) No. 174 (Nov. 30, 2007).
108. La Cantuta v. Peru, Interpretation of the Judgment on Merits, Reparations, and Costs, Judgment, Inter-Am. Ct. H.R. (ser. C) No. 173 (Nov. 30, 2007).

109. Albán Cornejo et al. v. Ecuador, Merits, Reparations, and Costs, Judgment, Inter-Am. Ct. H.R. (ser. C) No. 171 (Nov. 22, 2007).
110. Chaparro Álvarez and Lapo Íñiguez v. Ecuador, Preliminary Objections, Merits, Reparations, and Costs, Judgment, Inter-Am. Ct. H.R. (ser. C) No. 170 (Nov. 21, 2007).
111. García Prieto et al. v. El Salvador, Preliminary Objections, Merits, Reparations, and Costs, Judgment, Inter-Am. Ct. H.R. (ser. C) No. 168 (Nov. 20, 2007).
112. Cantoral Huamaní and García Santa Cruz v. Peru, Preliminary Objections, Merits, Reparations, and Costs, Judgment, Inter-Am. Ct. H.R. (ser. C) No. 167 (July 10, 2007).
113. Zambrano Vélez et al. v. Ecuador, Merits, Reparations, and Costs, Judgment, Inter-Am. Ct. H.R. (ser. C) No. 166 (July 4, 2007).
114. Escué Zapata v. Colombia, Merits, Reparations, and Costs, Judgment, Inter-Am. Ct. H.R. (ser. C) No. 165 (July 4, 2007).
115. Bueno Alves v. Argentina, Merits, Reparations, and Costs, Judgment, Inter-Am. Ct. H.R. (Ser. C) No. 164 (May 11, 2007).
116. Rochela Massacre v. Colombia, Merits, Reparations, and Costs, Judgment, Inter-Am. Ct. H.R. (ser. C) No. 163 (May 11, 2007).
117. La Cantuta v. Peru, Merits, Reparations, and Costs, Judgment, Inter-Am. Ct. H.R. (ser. C) No. 162 (Nov. 29, 2006).
118. Nogueira de Carvalho et al. v. Brazil, Preliminary Objections and Merits, Judgment, Inter-Am. Ct. H.R. (ser. C) No. 161 (Nov. 28, 2006).
119. Miguel Castro Castro Prison v. Peru, Merits, Reparations, and Costs, Judgment, Inter-Am. Ct. H.R. (ser. C) No. 160 (Nov. 25, 2006).
120. Dismissed Cong. Emp. (Aguado Alfaro et al.) v. Peru, Preliminary Objections, Merits, Reparations, and Costs, Judgment, Inter-Am. Ct H.R. (ser. C) No. 158 (Nov. 24, 2006).
121. Vargas Areco v. Paraguay, Merits, Reparations, and Costs, Judgment, Inter-Am. Ct. H.R. (ser. C) No. 155 (Sept. 26, 2006).
122. Almonacid Arellano et al. v. Chile, Preliminary Objections, Merits, Reparations, and Costs, Judgment, Inter-Am. Ct. H.R. (ser. C) No. 154 (Sept. 26, 2006).
123. Goiburú et al. v. Paraguay, Merits, Reparations, and Costs, Judgment, Inter-Am. Ct. H.R. (ser. C) No. 153 (Sept. 22, 2006).
124. Servellón García et al. v. Honduras, Merits, Reparations, and Costs, Judgment, Inter-Am. Ct. H.R. (ser. C) No. 152 (Sept. 21, 2006).
125. Claude Reyes et al. v. Chile, Merits, Reparations, and Costs, Judgment, Inter-Am. Ct. H.R. (ser. C) No. 151 (Sept. 19, 2006).
126. Montero Aranguren et al. (Det. Ctr. of Catia) v. Venezuela, Preliminary Objection, Merits, Reparations, and Costs, Judgment, Inter-Am. Ct. H.R. (ser. C) No. 150 (July 5, 2006).
127. Ximenes Lopes v. Brazil, Merits, Reparations, and Costs, Judgment, Inter-Am. Ct. H.R. (ser. C) No. 149 (July 4, 2006).
128. Ituango Massacres v. Colombia, Preliminary Objections, Merits, Reparations, and Costs, Judgment, Inter-Am. Ct. H.R. (ser. C) No. 148 (July 1, 2006).
129. Baldeón García v. Peru, Merits, Reparations, and Costs, Judgment, Inter-Am. Ct. H.R. (ser. C) No. 147 (Apr. 6, 2006).
130. Sawhoyamaxa Indigenous Cmty. v. Paraguay, Merits, Reparations, and Costs, Judgment, Inter-Am. Ct. H.R. (ser. C) No. 146 (Mar. 29, 2006).

131. Moiwana Cmty. v. Suriname, Interpretation of the Judgment of Merits, Reparations, and Costs, Judgment, Inter-Am. Ct. H.R. (ser. C) No. 145 (Feb. 8, 2006).
132. Acevedo Jaramillo et al. v. Peru, Preliminary Objections, Merits, Reparations, and Costs, Judgment, Inter-Am. Ct. H.R. (ser. C) No. 144 (Feb. 7, 2006).
133. López Álvarez v. Honduras, Merits, Reparations, and Costs, Judgment, Inter-Am. Ct. H.R. (ser. C) No. 141 (Feb. 1, 2006).
134. Pueblo Bello Massacre v. Colombia, Merits, Reparations, and Costs, Judgment, Inter-Am. Ct. H.R. (ser. C) No. 140 (Jan. 31, 2006).
135. Blanco Romero et al. v. Venezuela, Merits, Reparations, and Costs, Judgment, Inter-Am. Ct. H.R. (ser. C) No. 138 (Nov. 28, 2005).
136. García Asto and Ramírez Rojas v. Peru, Preliminary Objection, Merits, Reparations, and Costs, Judgment, Inter-Am. Ct. H.R. (ser. C) No. 137 (Nov. 25, 2005).
137. Gómez Palomino v. Peru, Merits, Reparations, and Costs, Judgment, Inter-Am. Ct. H.R. (ser. C) No. 136 (Nov. 22, 2005).
138. Palamara Iribarne v. Chile, Merits, Reparations, Costs, Judgment, Inter-Am. Ct. H.R. (ser. C) No. 135 (Nov. 22, 2005).
139. Mapiripán Massacre v. Colombia, Merits, Reparations, and Costs, Judgment, Inter-Am. Ct. H.R. (ser. C) No. 134 (Sept. 15, 2005).
140. Raxcacó Reyes v. Guatemala, Merits, Reparations, and Costs, Judgment, Inter-Am. Ct. H.R. (ser. C) No. 133 (Sept. 15, 2005).
141. Gutiérrez Soler v. Colombia, Merits, Reparations, and Costs, Judgment, Inter-Am. Ct. H.R. (ser. C) No. 132 (Sept. 12, 2005).
142. Serrano Cruz Sisters v. El Salvador, Interpretation of the Judgment of Merits, Reparations, and Costs, Judgment, Inter-Am. Ct. H.R. (ser. C) No. 131 (Sept. 9, 2005).
143. Acosta Calderón v. Ecuador, Merits, Reparations, and Costs, Judgment, Inter-Am. Ct. H.R. (ser. C) No. 129 (June 24, 2005).
144. Berenson Mejía v. Peru, Interpretation of the Judgment of Merits, Reparations, and Costs, Judgment, Inter-Am. Ct. H.R. (ser. C) No. 128 (June 23, 2005).
145. YATAMA v. Nicaragua, Preliminary Objections, Merits, Reparations, and Costs, Judgment, Inter-Am. Ct. H.R. (ser. C) No. 127 (June 23, 2005).
146. Fermín Ramírez v. Guatemala, Merits, Reparations, and Costs, Judgment, Inter-Am. Ct. H.R. (ser. C) No. 126 (June 20, 2005).
147. Yakye Axa Indigenous Cmty. v. Paraguay, Merits, Reparations, and Costs, Judgment, Inter-Am. Ct. H.R. (ser. C) No. 125 (June 17, 2005).
148. Moiwana Cmty. v. Suriname, Preliminary Objections, Merits, Reparations, and Costs, Judgment, Inter-Am. Ct. H.R. (ser. C) No. 124 (June 15, 2005).
149. Caesar v. Trinidad & Tobago, Merits, Reparations, and Costs, Judgment, Inter-Am. Ct. H.R. (ser. C) No. 123 (Mar. 11, 2005).
150. Mapiripán Massacre v. Colombia, Preliminary Objections, Judgment, Inter-Am. Ct. H.R. (ser. C) No. 122 (Mar. 7, 2005).
151. Serrano Cruz Sisters v. El Salvador, Merits, Reparations, and Costs, Judgment, Inter-Am. Ct. H.R. (ser. C) No. 120 (Mar. 1, 2005).
152. Berenson Mejia v. Peru, Merits, Reparations, and Costs, Judgment, Inter-Am. Ct. H.R. (ser. C) No. 119 (Nov. 25, 2004).

153. Carpio Nicolle et al. v. Guatemala, Merits, Reparations, and Costs, Judgment, Inter-Am. Ct. H.R. (ser. C) No. 117 (Nov. 22, 2004).
154. Plan de Sánchez Massacre v. Guatemala, Reparations, Judgment, Inter-Am. Ct. H.R. (ser. C) No. 116 (Nov. 19, 2004).
155. De La Cruz Flores v. Peru, Merits, Reparations, and Costs, Judgment, Inter-Am. Ct. H.R. (ser. C) No. 115 (Nov. 18, 2004).
156. Tibi v. Ecuador, Preliminary Objections, Merits, Reparations, and Costs, Judgment, Inter-Am. Ct. H.R. (ser. C) No. 114 (Sept. 7, 2004).
157. Campo Dodd v. Mexico, Preliminary Objections, Judgment, Inter-Am. Ct. H.R. (ser. C) No. 113 (Sept. 3, 2004).
158. "Juvenile Reeducation Institute" v. Paraguay, Preliminary Objections, Merits, Reparations, and Costs, Judgment, Inter-Am. Ct. H.R. (ser. C) No. 112 (Sept. 2, 2004).
159. Canese v. Paraguay, Merits, Reparations, and Costs, Judgment, Inter-Am. Ct. H.R. (ser. C) No. 111 (Aug. 31, 2004).
160. Gómez Paquiyauri Brothers v. Peru, Merits, Reparations, and Costs, Judgment, Inter-Am. Ct. H.R. (ser. C) No. 110 (July 8, 2004).
161. 19 Merchants v. Colombia, Merits, Reparations, and Costs, Judgment, Inter-Am. Ct. H.R. (ser. C) No. 109 (July 5, 2004).
162. Herrera Ulloa v. Costa Rica, Preliminary Objections, Merits, Reparations, and Costs, Judgment, Inter-Am. Ct. H.R. (ser. C) No. 107 (July 2, 2004).
163. Plan de Sánchez Massacre v. Guatemala, Merits, Judgment, Inter-Am. Ct. H.R. (ser. C) No. 105 (Apr. 29, 2004).
164. Baena Ricardo et al. v. Panama, Competence, Judgment, Inter-Am. Ct. H.R. (ser. C) No. 104 (Nov. 28, 2003).
165. Maritza Urrutia v. Guatemala, Merits, Reparations, and Costs, Judgment, Inter-Am. Ct. H.R. (ser. C) No. 103 (Nov. 27, 2003).
166. Sánchez v. Honduras, Interpretation of the Judgment of Preliminary Objection, Merits, and Reparations, Judgment, Inter-Am. Ct. H.R. (ser. C) No. 102 (Nov. 26, 2003).
167. Mack Chang v. Guatemala, Merits, Reparations, and Costs, Judgment, Inter-Am. Ct. H.R. (ser. C) No. 101 (Nov. 25, 2003).
168. Sánchez v. Honduras, Preliminary Objection, Merits, Reparations, and Costs, Judgment, Inter-Am. Ct. H.R. (ser. C) No. 99 (June 7, 2003).
169. Juridical Condition & Rights of the Undocumented Migrants, Advisory Opinion OC-18/03, Inter-Am. Ct. H.R. (ser. A) No. 18 (Sept. 17, 2003).
170. "Five Pensioners" v. Peru, Merits, Reparations, and Costs, Judgment, Inter-Am. Ct. H.R. (ser. C) No. 98 (Feb. 28, 2003).
171. Cantos v. Argentina, Merits, Reparations, and Costs, Judgment, Inter-Am. Ct. H.R. (ser. C) No. 97 (Nov. 28, 2002).
172. Las Palmeras v. Colombia, Reparations and Costs, Judgment, Inter-Am. Ct. H.R. (ser. C) No. 96 (Nov. 26, 2002).
173. Caracazo v. Venezuela, Reparations and Costs, Judgment, Inter-Am. Ct. H.R. (ser. C) No. 95 (Aug. 29, 2002).
174. Hilaire, Constantine, and Benjamin et al. v. Trinidad & Tobago, Merits, Reparations, and Costs, Judgment, Inter-Am. Ct. H.R. (ser. C) No. 94 (June 21, 2002).

175. 19 Merchants v. Colombia, Preliminary Objection, Judgment, Inter-Am. Ct. H.R. (ser. C) No. 93 (June 12, 2002).
176. Trujillo Oroza v. Bolivia, Reparations and Costs, Judgment, Inter-Am. Ct. H.R. (ser. C) No. 92 (Feb. 27, 2002).
177. Las Palmeras v. Colombia, Merits, Judgment, Inter-Am. Ct. H.R. (Ser. C) No. 90 (Dec. 6, 2001).
178. Durand and Ugarte v. Peru, Reparations and Costs, Judgment, Inter-Am. Ct. H.R. (ser. C) No. 89 (Dec. 3, 2001).
179. Cantoral Benavides v. Peru, Reparations and Costs, Judgment, Inter-Am. Ct. H.R. (ser. C) No. 88 (Dec. 3, 2001).
180. Barrios Altos v. Peru, Interpretation of the Judgment of Merits, Judgment, Inter-Am. Ct. H.R. (ser. C) No. 83 (Sept. 3, 2001).
181. Constantine et al. v. Trinidad & Tobago, Preliminary Objections, Judgment, Inter-Am. Ct. H.R. (ser. C) No. 82 (Sept. 1, 2001).
182. Benjamin et al. v. Trinidad & Tobago, Preliminary Objections, Judgment, Inter-Am. Ct. H.R. (ser. C) No. 81 (Sept. 1, 2001).
183. Cesti Hurtado v. Peru, Reparations and Costs, 2001 Inter-Am. Ct. H.R. (ser. C) No. 78 (May 31, 2001).
184. "Street Children" (Villagrán Morales et al.) v. Guatemala, Reparations and Costs, Judgment, Inter-Am. Ct. H.R. (ser. C) No. 77 (May 26, 2001).
185. "White Van" (Paniagua Morales et al.) v. Guatemala, Reparations and Costs, Judgment, Inter-Am. Ct. H.R. (ser. C) No. 76 (May 25, 2001).
186. Barrios Altos v. Peru, Merits, Judgment, Inter-Am. Ct. H.R. (ser. C) No. 75 (Mar. 14, 2001).
187. Ivcher Bronstein v. Peru, Merits, Reparations, and Costs, Judgment, Inter-Am. Ct. H.R. (ser. C) No. 74 (Feb. 6, 2001).
188. Baena Ricardo et al. v. Panama, Merits, Reparations, and Costs, Judgment, Inter-Am. Ct. H.R. (ser. C) No. 72 (Feb. 2, 2001).
189. Constitutional Court v. Peru, Merits, Reparations, and Costs, Judgment, Inter-Am. Ct. H.R. (ser. C) No. 71 (Jan. 31, 2001).
190. Cantoral Benavides v. Peru, Merits, Judgment, Inter-Am. Ct. H.R. (ser. C) No. 69 (Aug. 18, 2000).
191. Durand and Ugarte v. Peru, Merits, Judgment, Inter-Am. Ct. H.R. (ser. C) No. 68 (Aug. 16, 2000).
192. Trujillo Oroza v. Bolivia, Merits, Judgment, Inter-Am. Ct. H.R. (ser. C) No. 64 (Jan. 26, 2000).
193. "Street Children" (Villagrán Morales et al.) v. Guatemala, Merits, Judgment, Inter-Am. Ct. H.R. (ser. C) No. 63 (Nov. 19, 1999).
194. Cesti Hurtado v. Peru, Request for Interpretation of the Judgment of Merits, Order of the Court, Inter-Am. Ct. H.R. (ser. C) No. 62 (Nov. 19, 1999).
195. Caracazo v. Venezuela, Merits, Judgment, Inter-Am. Ct. H.R. (ser. C) No. 58 (Nov. 11, 1999).
196. Cesti Hurtado v. Peru, Merits, Judgment, Inter-Am. Ct. H.R. (ser. C) No. 56 (Sept. 29, 1999).
197. Constitutional Court v. Peru, Competence, Judgment, Inter-Am. Ct. H.R. (ser. C) No. 55 (Sept. 24, 1999).

198. Ivcher Bronstein v. Peru, Competence, Judgment, Inter-Am. Ct. H.R. (ser. C) No. 54 (Sept. 24, 1999).
199. Castillo Petruzzi et al. v. Peru, Merits, Reparations, and Costs, Judgment, Inter-Am. Ct. H.R. (ser. C) No. 52 (May 30, 1999).
200. Cesti Hurtado v. Peru, Preliminary Objections, Judgment, Inter-Am. Ct. H.R. (ser. C) No. 49 (Jan. 26, 1999).
201. Blake v. Guatemala, Reparations and Costs, Judgment, Inter-Am. Ct. H.R. (ser. C) No. 48 (Jan. 22, 1999).
202. Loayza Tamayo v. Peru, Interpretation of the Judgment of Merits, Order of the Court, Inter-Am. Ct. H.R. (ser. C) No. 47 (Mar. 8, 1998).
203. Genie Lacayo v. Nicaragua, Application for Judicial Review of the Judgment of Merits, Reparations, and Costs, Order of the Court, Inter-Am. Ct. H.R. (ser. C) No. 45 (Sept. 13, 1997).
204. Loayza Tamayo v. Peru, Reparations and Costs, Judgment, Inter-Am. Ct. H.R. (ser. C) No. 42 (Nov. 27, 1998).
205. Castillo Petruzzi et al. v. Peru, Preliminary Objections, Judgment, Inter-Am. Ct. H.R. (ser. C) No. 41 (Sept. 4, 1998).
206. Cantoral Benavides v. Peru, Preliminary Objections, Judgment, Inter-Am. Ct. H.R. (ser. C) No. 40 (Sept. 3, 1998).
207. Garrido and Baigorria v. Argentina, Reparations and Costs, Judgment, Inter-Am. Ct. H.R. (ser. C) No. 39 (Aug. 27, 1998).
208. "White Van" (Paniagua Morales et al.) v. Guatemala, Merits, Judgment, Inter-Am. Ct. H.R. (ser. C) No. 37 (Mar. 8, 1998).
209. Blake v. Guatemala, Merits, Judgment, Inter-Am. Ct. H.R. (ser. C) No. 36 (Jan. 24, 1998).
210. Suárez Rosero v. Ecuador, Merits, Judgment, Inter-Am. Ct. H.R. (ser. C) No. 35 (Nov. 12, 1997).
211. Loayza Tamayo v. Peru, Merits, Judgment, Inter-Am. Ct. H.R. (ser. C) No. 33 (Sept. 17, 1997).
212. Caballero Delgado and Santana v. Colombia, Reparations and Costs, Judgment, Inter-Am. Ct. H.R. (ser. C) No. 31 (Jan. 29, 1997).
213. Genie Lacayo v. Nicaragua, Merits, Reparations, and Costs, Judgment, Inter-Am. Ct. H.R. (ser. C) No. 30 (Jan. 29, 1997).
214. El Amparo v. Venezuela, Reparations and Costs, Judgment, Inter-Am. Ct. H.R. (ser. C) No. 28 (Sept. 14, 1996).
215. Garrido and Baigorria v. Argentina, Merits, Judgment, Inter-Am. Ct. H.R. (ser. C) No. 26 (Feb. 2, 1996).
216. Genie Lacayo v. Nicaragua, Preliminary Objections, Judgment, Inter-Am. Ct. H.R. (ser. C) No. 21 (Jan. 27, 1995).
217. El Amparo v. Venezuela, Merits, Judgment, Inter-Am. Ct. H.R. (ser. C) No. 19 (Jan. 18, 1995).
218. Maqueda v. Argentina, Preliminary Objections, Order of the Court, Inter-Am. Ct. H.R. (ser. C) No. 18 (Jan. 17, 1995).
219. Judicial Guarantees in States of Emergency (Arts. 27(2), 25, and 8 American Convention on Human Rights), Advisory Opinion OC-9/87, Inter-Am. Ct. H.R. (ser. A) No. 9 (Oct. 6, 1987).

Article 8(2)–(5)

1. Ruano Torres et al. v. El Salvador, Merits, Reparations and Costs, Judgment, Inter-Am. Ct. H.R. (ser. C) No. 303 (Oct. 5, 2015).
2. Galindo Cardenas et al. v. Peru, Preliminary Objections, Merits, Reparations and Costs, Judgment, Inter-Am. Ct. H.R. (ser. C) No. 301 (Oct. 2, 2015).
3. Granier et al. (Radio Caracas Television) v. Venezuela, Preliminary Objections, Merits, Reparations, Costs, Judgment, Inter-Am. Ct. H.R. (ser. C) No. 293 (June 22, 2015).
4. J. v. Peru, Interpretation of the Judgment on Preliminary Objection, Merits, Reparations, and Costs, Judgment, Inter-Am. Ct. H.R. (ser. C) No. 291 (Nov. 20, 2014). [8(4)]
5. Argüelles et al. v. Argentina, Preliminary Objections, Merits, Reparations, and Costs, Judgment, Inter-Am. Ct. H.R. (ser. C) No. 288 (Nov. 20, 2014). [8(2), 8(3)]
6. Rights & Guar. of Children in the Context of Migration and/or in Need of Int'l Prot., Advisory Opinion OC-21/14, Inter-Am. Ct. H.R. (ser. A) No. 21 (Aug. 19, 2014). [8(2)]
7. Norín Catrimán et al. (Leaders, members, and activists of the Mapuche Indigenous People) v. Chile, Merits, Reparations, and Costs, Judgment, Inter-Am. Ct. H.R. (ser. C) No. 279 (May 29, 2014). [8(2), 8(4), 8(5)]
8. Liakat Ali Alibux v. Suriname, Preliminary Objections, Merits, Reparations, and Costs, Judgment, Inter-Am. Ct. H.R. (ser. C) No. 276 (Jan. 30, 2014). [8(2)]
9. J. v. Peru, Preliminary Objections, Merits, Reparations, and Costs, Judgment, Inter-Am. Ct. H.R. (ser. C) No. 275 (Nov. 27, 2013). [8(2), 8(4), 8(5)]
10. Garcia Cruz and Sanchez Silvestre v. Mexico, Merits, Reparations, and Costs, Judgment, Inter-Am. Ct. H.R. (ser. C) No. 273 (Nov. 26, 2013). [8(2), 8(3)]
11. Pacheco Tineo Family v. Bolivia, Preliminary Objections, Merits, Reparations, and Costs, Judgment, Inter-Am. Ct. H.R. (ser. C) No. 272 (Nov. 25, 2013). [8(2)]
12. Gutiérrez and Family v. Argentina, Merits, Reparations, and Costs, Judgment, Inter-Am. Ct. H.R. (ser. C) No. 271 (Nov. 25, 2013). [8(4)]
13. Constitutional Tribunal (Camba Campos et al.) v. Ecuador, Preliminary Objections, Merits, Reparations, and Costs, Judgment, Inter-Am. Ct. H.R. (ser. C) No. 268 (Aug. 28, 2013). [8(2), 8(4)]
14. Supreme Court of Justice (Quintana Coello et al.) v. Ecuador, Preliminary Objections, Merits, Reparations, and Costs, Judgment, Inter-Am. Ct. H.R. (ser. C) No. 266 (Aug. 23, 2013). [8(2)]
15. Mendoza et al. v. Argentina, Preliminary Objections, Merits, and Reparations, Judgment, Inter-Am. Ct. H.R. (ser. C) No. 260 (May 14, 2013). [8(2)]
16. Mohamed v. Argentina, Preliminary Objections, Merits, Reparations, and Costs, Judgment, Inter-Am. Ct. H.R. (ser. C) No. 255 (Nov. 23, 2012). [8(2), 8(4)]
17. Furlan and Family v. Argentina, Preliminary Objections, Merits, Reparations, and Costs, Judgment, Inter-Am. Ct. H.R. (ser. C) No. 246 (Aug. 31, 2012). [8(2)]
18. López Mendoza v. Venezuela, Merits, Reparations, and Costs, Judgment,Inter-Am. Ct. H.R. (ser. C) No. 233 (Sept. 1, 2011). [8(4)]
19. Grande v. Argentina, Preliminary Objections and Merits, Judgment, Inter-Am. Ct. H.R. (ser. C) No. 231 (Aug. 31, 2011). [8(2)]
20. Rosendo Cantu et al. v. Mexico, Interpretation of Judgment of Preliminary Objections, Merits, Reparations, and Costs, Judgment, Inter-Am. Ct. H.R. (ser. C) No. 225 (May 15, 2011). [8(2)]

21. Fernandez Ortega et al. v. Mexico, Interpretation of Judgment of Preliminary Objection, Merits, Reparations, and Costs, Judgment, Inter-Am. Ct. H.R. (ser. C) No. 224 (May 15, 2011). [8(2)]
22. Cabrera García and Montiel Flores v. Mexico, Preliminary Objections, Merits, Reparations, and Costs, Judgment, Inter-Am. Ct. H.R. (ser. C) No. 220 (Nov. 26, 2010). [8(2), 8(3)]
23. Vélez Loor v. Panama, Preliminary Objections, Merits, Reparations, and Costs, Judgment, Inter-Am. Ct. H.R. (ser. C) No. 218 (Nov. 23, 2010). [8(2)]
24. Usón Ramírez v. Venezuela, Preliminary Objection, Merits, Reparations, and Costs, Judgment, Inter-Am. Ct. H.R. (ser. C) No. 207 (Nov. 20, 2009). [8(2)]
25. Barreto Leiva v. Venezuela, Merits, Reparations, and Costs, Judgment, Inter-Am. Ct. H.R. (ser. C) No. 206 (Nov. 17, 2009).
26. DaCosta Cadogan v. Barbados, Preliminary Objections, Merits, Reparations, and Costs, Judgment, Inter-Am. Ct. H.R. (ser. C) No. 204 (Sept. 24, 2009). [8(2)]
27. Tristán Donoso v. Panama, Preliminary Objections, Merits, Reparations, and Costs, Judgment, Inter-Am. Ct. H.R. (ser. C) No. 193 (Jan. 27, 2009). [8(2)]
28. Bayarri v. Argentina, Preliminary Objection, Merits, Reparations, and Costs, Judgment, Inter-Am. Ct. H.R. (ser. C) No. 187 (Oct. 30, 2008). [8(2)]
29. Neptune v. Haiti, Merits, Reparations, and Costs, Judgment, Inter-Am. Ct. H.R. (ser. C) No. 180 (May 6, 2008). [8(2)]
30. Kimel v. Argentina, Merits, Reparations, and Costs, Judgment, Inter-Am. Ct. H.R. (ser. C) No. 177 (May 2, 2008). [8(2)]
31. Chaparro Álvarez and Lapo Íñiguez v. Ecuador, Preliminary Objections, Merits, Reparations, and Costs, Judgment, Inter-Am. Ct. H.R. (ser. C) No. 170 (Nov. 21, 2007). [8(2)]
32. Boyce et al. v. Barbados, Preliminary Objections, Merits, Reparations, and Costs, Judgment, Inter-Am. Ct. H.R. (ser. C) No. 169 (Nov. 20, 2007). [8(2)]
33. Servellón García et al. v. Honduras, Merits, Reparations, and Costs, Judgment, Inter-Am. Ct. H.R. (ser. C) No. 152 (Sept. 21, 2006). [8(2)]
34. López Álvarez v. Honduras, Merits, Reparations, and Costs, Judgment, Inter-Am. Ct. H.R. (ser. C) No. 141 (Feb. 1, 2006). [8(2)]
35. García Asto and Ramírez Rojas v. Peru, Preliminary Objection, Merits, Reparations, and Costs, Judgment, Inter-Am. Ct. H.R. (ser. C) No. 137 (Nov. 25, 2005). [8(2)]
36. Palamara Iribarne v. Chile, Merits, Reparations, Costs, Judgment, Inter-Am. Ct. H.R. (ser. C) No. 135 (Nov. 22, 2005). [8(2)]
37. Gutiérrez Soler v. Colombia, Merits, Reparations, and Costs, Judgment, Inter-Am. Ct. H.R. (ser. C) No. 132 (Sept. 12, 2005). [8(2), 8(3)]
38. Acosta Calderón v. Ecuador, Merits, Reparations, and Costs, Judgment, Inter-Am. Ct. H.R. (ser. C) No. 129 (June 24, 2005). [8(2)]
39. Berenson Mejía v. Peru, Interpretation of the Judgment of Merits, Reparations, and Costs, Judgment, Inter-Am. Ct. H.R. (ser. C) No. 128 (June 23, 2005). [8(2)]
40. Fermín Ramírez v. Guatemala, Merits, Reparations, and Costs, Judgment, Inter-Am. Ct. H.R. (ser. C) No. 126 (June 20, 2005). [8(2)]
41. Yakye Axa Indigenous Cmty. v. Paraguay, Merits, Reparations, and Costs, Judgment, Inter-Am. Ct. H.R. (ser. C) No. 125 (June 17, 2005). [8(2)]
42. Berenson Mejia v. Peru, Merits, Reparations, and Costs, Judgment, Inter-Am. Ct. H.R. (ser. C) No. 119 (Nov. 25, 2004). [8(2), 8(4), 8(5)]

43. Tibi v. Ecuador, Preliminary Objections, Merits, Reparations, and Costs, Judgment, Inter-Am. Ct. H.R. (ser. C) No. 114 (Sept. 7, 2004). [8(2)]
44. Campo Dodd v. Mexico, Preliminary Objections, Judgment, Inter-Am. Ct. H.R. (ser. C) No. 113 (Sept. 3, 2004). [8(2), 8(3)]
45. "Juvenile Reeducation Institute" v. Paraguay, Preliminary Objections, Merits, Reparations, and Costs, Judgment, Inter-Am. Ct. H.R. (ser. C) No. 112 (Sept. 2, 2004). [8(2)]
46. Canese v. Paraguay, Merits, Reparations, and Costs, Judgment, Inter-Am. Ct. H.R. (ser. C) No. 111 (Aug. 31, 2004). [8(2)]
47. Herrera Ulloa v. Costa Rica, Preliminary Objections, Merits, Reparations, and Costs, Judgment, Inter-Am. Ct. H.R. (ser. C) No. 107 (July 2, 2004). [8(2)]
48. Baena Ricardo et al. v. Panama, Competence, Judgment, Inter-Am. Ct. H.R. (ser. C) No. 104 (Nov. 28, 2003). [8(2)]
49. Maritza Urrutia v. Guatemala, Merits, Reparations, and Costs, Judgment, Inter-Am. Ct. H.R. (ser. C) No. 103 (Nov. 27, 2003). [8(2), 8(3)]
50. Juridical Condition & Rights of the Undocumented Migrants, Advisory Opinion OC-18/03, Inter-Am. Ct. H.R. (ser. A) No. 18 (Sept. 17, 2003). [8(2)]
51. Juridical Condition & Human Rights of the Child, Advisory Opinion OC-17/02, Inter-Am. Ct. H.R. (ser. A) No. 17 (Aug. 28, 2002). [8(2), 8(3), 8(4), 8(5)]
52. Hilaire, Constantine, and Benjamin et al. v. Trinidad & Tobago, Merits, Reparations, and Costs, Judgment, Inter-Am. Ct. H.R. (ser. C) No. 94 (June 21, 2002). [8(2)]
53. Cantoral Benavides v. Peru, Reparations and Costs, Judgment, Inter-Am. Ct. H.R. (ser. C) No. 88 (Dec. 3, 2001). [8(2), 8(5)]
54. Constantine et al. v. Trinidad & Tobago, Preliminary Objections, Judgment, Inter-Am. Ct. H.R. (ser. C) No. 82 (Sept. 1, 2001). [8(2)]
55. Benjamin et al. v. Trinidad & Tobago, Preliminary Objections, Judgment, Inter-Am. Ct. H.R. (ser. C) No. 81 (Sept. 1, 2001). [8(2)]
56. Cesti Hurtado v. Peru, Reparations and Costs, 2001 Inter-Am. Ct. H.R. (ser. C) No. 78 (May 31, 2001). [8(2)]
57. "The Last Temptation of Christ" (Olmedo Bustos et al.) v. Chile, Merits, Reparations, and Costs, Judgment, Inter-Am. Ct. H.R. (ser. C) No. 73 (Feb. 5, 2001). [8(4)]
58. Ivcher Bronstein v. Peru, Merits, Reparations, and Costs, Judgment, Inter-Am. Ct. H.R. (ser. C) No. 74 (Feb. 6, 2001). [8(2)]
59. Baena Ricardo et al. v. Panama, Merits, Reparations, and Costs, Judgment, Inter-Am. Ct. H.R. (ser. C) No. 72 (Feb. 2, 2001). [8(2)]
60. Constitutional Court v. Peru, Merits, Reparations, and Costs, Judgment, Inter-Am. Ct. H.R. (ser. C) No. 71 (Jan. 31, 2001). [8(2)]
61. Cantoral Benavides v. Peru, Merits, Judgment, Inter-Am. Ct. H.R. (ser. C) No. 69 (Aug. 18, 2000). [8(2), 8(3), 8(4), 8(5)]
62. Cesti Hurtado v. Peru, Request for Interpretation of the Judgment of Merits, Order of the Court, Inter-Am. Ct. H.R. (ser. C) No. 62 (Nov. 19, 1999). [8(2)]
63. Cesti Hurtado v. Peru, Merits, Judgment, Inter-Am. Ct. H.R. (ser. C) No. 56 (Sept. 29, 1999). [8(2)]
64. Constitutional Court v. Peru, Competence, Judgment, Inter-Am. Ct. H.R. (ser. C) No. 55 (Sept. 24, 1999). [8(2)]

65. Castillo Petruzzi et al. v. Peru, Merits, Reparations, and Costs, Judgment, Inter-Am. Ct. H.R. (ser. C) No. 52 (May 30, 1999). [8(2), 8(3), 8(5)]
66. Cesti Hurtado v. Peru, Preliminary Objections, Judgment, Inter-Am. Ct. H.R. (ser. C) No. 49 (Jan. 26, 1999). [8(2)]
67. Loayza Tamayo v. Peru, Interpretation of the Judgment of Merits, Order of the Court, Inter-Am. Ct. H.R. (ser. C) No. 47 (Mar. 8, 1998). [8(1), 8(2), 8(3), 8(4)]
68. Loayza Tamayo v. Peru, Reparations and Costs, Judgment, Inter-Am. Ct. H.R. (ser. C) No. 42 (Nov. 27, 1998). [8(2), 8(3), 8(4)]
69. Cantoral Benavides v. Peru, Preliminary Objections, Judgment, Inter-Am. Ct. H.R. (ser. C) No. 40 (Sept. 3, 1998). [8(2), 8(4)]
70. Reports of the Inter-American Commission on Human Rights (Art. 51 American Convention on Human Rights), Advisory Opinion OC-15/97, Inter-Am. Ct. H.R. (ser. A) No. 15 (Nov. 14, 1997). [8(2)]
71. Suárez Rosero v. Ecuador, Merits, Judgment, Inter-Am. Ct. H.R. (ser. C) No. 35 (Nov. 12, 1997). [8(2)]
72. Loayza Tamayo v. Peru, Merits, Judgment, Inter-Am. Ct. H.R. (ser. C) No. 33 (Sept. 17, 1997). [8(2), 8(3), 8(4)]
73. "Street Children" (Villagrán Morales et al.) v. Guatemala, Preliminary Objections, Judgment, Inter-Am. Ct. H.R. (ser. C) No. 32 (Sept. 11, 1997). [8(4)]
74. Maqueda v. Argentina, Preliminary Objections, Order of the Court, Inter-Am. Ct. H.R. (ser. C) No. 18 (Jan. 17, 1995). [8(2)]
75. Int'l Responsibility for the Promulgation & Enforcement of Laws in Violation of the Convention (Arts. 1 & 2 of the Am. Convention on Human Rights), Advisory Opinion OC-14/94, Inter-Am. Ct. H.R. (ser. A) No. 14 (Dec. 9, 1994). [8(2)]
76. Certain Attributes of the Inter-American Commission on Human Rights (Arts. 41, 42, 44, 46, 47, 50 and 51 of the American Convention on Human Rights), Advisory Opinion OC-13/93, Inter-Am. Ct. H.R. (ser. A) No. 13 (July 16, 1993). [8(2)]
77. Compatibility of Draft Legislation with Article 8(2)(h) of the American Convention on Human Rights, Advisory Opinion OC-12/91, Inter-Am. Ct. H.R. (ser. A) No. 12 (Dec. 6, 1991). [8(2)]
78. Exceptions to the Exhaustion of Domestic Remedies (Arts. 46(1), 46(2)(a), and 46(2)(b) American Convention on Human Rights), Advisory Opinion OC-11/90, Inter-Am. Ct. H.R. (ser. A) No. 11 (Aug. 10, 1990). [8(2)]

ARTICLE 9: FREEDOM FROM EX POST FACTO LAWS

1. Lopez Lone et al. v. Honduras, Preliminary Objection, Merits, Reparations and Costs, Judgment, Inter-Am. Ct. H.R. (ser. C) No. 302 (Oct. 5, 2015).
2. Galindo Cardenas et al. v. Peru, Preliminary Objections, Merits, Reparations and Costs, Judgment, Inter-Am. Ct. H.R. (ser. C) No. 301 (Oct. 2, 2015).
3. Espinoza Gonzales v. Peru, Preliminary Objections, Merits, Reparations, and Costs, Judgment, Inter-Am. Ct. H.R. (ser. C) No. 289 (Nov. 20, 2014).
4. Argüelles et al. v. Argentina, Preliminary Objections, Merits, Reparations, and Costs, Judgment, Inter-Am. Ct. H.R. (ser. C) No. 288 (Nov. 20, 2014).

5. Expelled Dominicans and Haitians v. Dominican Republic, Preliminary Objections, Merits, Reparations, and Costs, Judgment, Inter-Am. Ct. H.R. (ser. C) No. 282 (Aug. 28, 2014). [footnote]
6. Norín Catrimán et al. (Leaders, members, and activists of the Mapuche Indigenous People) v. Chile, Merits, Reparations, and Costs, Judgment, Inter-Am. Ct. H.R. (ser. C) No. 279 (May 29, 2014).
7. Liakat Ali Alibux v. Suriname, Preliminary Objections, Merits, Reparations, and Costs, Judgment, Inter-Am. Ct. H.R. (ser. C) No. 276 (Jan. 30, 2014).
8. J. v. Peru, Preliminary Objections, Merits, Reparations, and Costs, Judgment, Inter-Am. Ct. H.R. (ser. C) No. 275 (Nov. 27, 2013).
9. Pacheco Tineo Family v. Bolivia, Preliminary Objections, Merits, Reparations, and Costs, Judgment, Inter-Am. Ct. H.R. (ser. C) No. 272 (Nov. 25, 2013).
10. Constitutional Tribunal (Camba Campos et al.) v. Ecuador, Preliminary Objections, Merits, Reparations, and Costs, Judgment, Inter-Am. Ct. H.R. (ser. C) No. 268 (Aug. 28, 2013).
11. Supreme Court of Justice (Quintana Coello et al.) v. Ecuador, Preliminary Objections, Merits, Reparations, and Costs, Judgment, Inter-Am. Ct. H.R. (ser. C) No. 266 (Aug. 23, 2013).
12. Memoli v. Argentina, Preliminary Objections, Merits, Reparations, and Costs, Judgment, Inter-Am. Ct. H.R. (ser. C) No. 265 (Aug. 22, 2013).
13. Mendoza et al. v. Argentina, Preliminary Objections, Merits, and Reparations, Judgment, Inter-Am. Ct. H.R. (ser. C) No. 260 (May 14, 2013).
14. Mohamed v. Argentina, Preliminary Objections, Merits, Reparations, and Costs, Judgment, Inter-Am. Ct. H.R. (ser. C) No. 255 (Nov. 23, 2012).
15. Uzcátegui et al. v. Venezuela, Merits and Reparations, Judgment, Inter-Am. Ct. H.R. (ser. C) No. 249 (Sept. 3, 2012).
16. Pacheco Teruel et al. v. Honduras, Merits, Reparations, and Costs, Judgment, Inter-Am. Ct. H.R. (ser. C) No. 241 (Apr. 27, 2012).
17. Gomes Lund et al. ("Guerrilha do Araguaia") v. Brazil, Preliminary Objections, Merits, Reparations, and Costs, Judgment, Inter-Am. Ct. H.R. (ser. C) No. 219 (Nov. 24, 2010).
18. Vélez Loor v. Panama, Preliminary Objections, Merits, Reparations, and Costs, Judgment, Inter-Am. Ct. H.R. (ser. C) No. 218 (Nov. 23, 2010).
19. Usón Ramírez v. Venezuela, Preliminary Objection, Merits, Reparations, and Costs, Judgment, Inter-Am. Ct. H.R. (ser. C) No. 207 (Nov. 20, 2009).
20. Tristán Donoso v. Panama, Preliminary Objections, Merits, Reparations, and Costs, Judgment, Inter-Am. Ct. H.R. (ser. C) No. 193 (Jan. 27, 2009).
21. Neptune v. Haiti, Merits, Reparations, and Costs, Judgment, Inter-Am. Ct. H.R. (ser. C) No. 180 (May 6, 2008).
22. Kimel v. Argentina, Merits, Reparations, and Costs, Judgment, Inter-Am. Ct. H.R. (ser. C) No. 177 (May 2, 2008).
23. García Asto and Ramírez Rojas v. Peru, Preliminary Objection, Merits, Reparations, and Costs, Judgment, Inter-Am. Ct. H.R. (ser. C) No. 137 (Nov. 25, 2005).
24. Palamara Iribarne v. Chile, Merits, Reparations, Costs, Judgment, Inter-Am. Ct. H.R. (ser. C) No. 135 (Nov. 22, 2005).

25. Berenson Mejía v. Peru, Interpretation of the Judgment of Merits, Reparations, and Costs, Judgment, Inter-Am. Ct. H.R. (ser. C) No. 128 (June 23, 2005).
26. Fermín Ramírez v. Guatemala, Merits, Reparations, and Costs, Judgment, Inter-Am. Ct. H.R. (ser. C) No. 126 (June 20, 2005).
27. Berenson Mejia v. Peru, Merits, Reparations, and Costs, Judgment, Inter-Am. Ct. H.R. (ser. C) No. 119 (Nov. 25, 2004).
28. De La Cruz Flores v. Peru, Merits, Reparations, and Costs, Judgment, Inter-Am. Ct. H.R. (ser. C) No. 115 (Nov. 18, 2004).
29. Canese v. Paraguay, Merits, Reparations, and Costs, Judgment, Inter-Am. Ct. H.R. (ser. C) No. 111 (Aug. 31, 2004).
30. Baena Ricardo et al. v. Panama, Competence, Judgment, Inter-Am. Ct. H.R. (ser. C) No. 104 (Nov. 28, 2003).
31. Juridical Condition & Human Rights of the Child, Advisory Opinion OC-17/02, Inter-Am. Ct. H.R. (ser. A) No. 17 (Aug. 28, 2002).
32. Cantoral Benavides v. Peru, Reparations and Costs, Judgment, Inter-Am. Ct. H.R. (ser. C) No. 88 (Dec. 3, 2001).
33. Baena Ricardo et al. v. Panama, Merits, Reparations, and Costs, Judgment, Inter-Am. Ct. H.R. (ser. C) No. 72 (Feb. 2, 2001).
34. Cantoral Benavides v. Peru, Merits, Judgment, Inter-Am. Ct. H.R. (ser. C) No. 69 (Aug. 18, 2000).
35. Baena Ricardo et al. v. Panama, Preliminary Objections, Judgment, Inter-Am. Ct. H.R. (ser. C) No. 61 (Nov. 18, 1999).
36. Castillo Petruzzi et al. v. Peru, Merits, Reparations, and Costs, Judgment, Inter-Am. Ct. H.R. (ser. C) No. 52 (May 30, 1999).
37. Garrido and Baigorria v. Argentina, Reparations and Costs, Judgment, Inter-Am. Ct. H.R. (ser. C) No. 39 (Aug. 27, 1998).
38. Habeas Corpus in Emergency Situations (Arts. 27(2), 25(1), and 7(6) American Convention on Human Rights), Advisory Opinion OC-8/87, Inter-Am. Ct. H.R. (ser. A) No. 8 (Jan. 30, 1987).
39. Restrictions to the Death Penalty (Arts. 4(2) and 4(4) American Convention on Human Rights), Advisory Opinion OC-3/83, Inter-Am. Ct. H.R. (ser. A) No. 3 (Sept. 8, 1983).

ARTICLE 10: RIGHT TO COMPENSATION

1. Argüelles et al. v. Argentina, Preliminary Objections, Merits, Reparations, and Costs, Judgment, Inter-Am. Ct. H.R. (ser. C) No. 288 (Nov. 20, 2014).
2. Grande v. Argentina, Preliminary Objections and Merits, Judgment, Inter-Am. Ct. H.R. (ser. C) No. 231 (Aug. 31, 2011).
3. Baena Ricardo et al. v. Panama, Competence, Judgment, Inter-Am. Ct. H.R. (ser. C) No. 104 (Nov. 28, 2003).
4. Cantos v. Argentina, Preliminary Objections, Judgment, Inter-Am. Ct. H.R. (ser. C) No. 85 (Sept. 7, 2001).
5. Baena Ricardo et al. v. Panama, Merits, Reparations, and Costs, Judgment, Inter-Am. Ct. H.R. (ser. C) No. 72 (Feb. 2, 2001).
6. Baena Ricardo et al. v. Panama, Preliminary Objections, Judgment, Inter-Am. Ct. H.R. (ser. C) No. 61 (Nov. 18, 1999).

ARTICLE 11: RIGHT TO PRIVACY

1. Velasquez Paiz et al. v. Guatemala, Preliminary Objections, Merits, Reparations and Costs, Judgment, Inter-Am. Ct. H.R. (ser. C) No. 307 (Nov. 19, 2015).
2. Lopez Lone et al. v. Honduras, Preliminary Objection, Merits, Reparations and Costs, Judgment, Inter-Am. Ct. H.R. (ser. C) No. 302 (Oct. 5, 2015).
3. Case of Peasant Community of Santa Barbara v. Peru, Preliminary Objections, Merits, Reparations and Costs, Judgment, Inter-Am. Ct. H.R. (ser. C) No. 299 (Sept. 1, 2015).
4. Espinoza Gonzales v. Peru, Interpretation of the Judgment on Preliminary Objections, Merits, Reparations and Costs, Judgment, Inter-Am. Ct. H.R. (ser. C) No. 295 (June 23, 2015).
5. J. v. Peru, Interpretation of the Judgment on Preliminary Objection, Merits, Reparations, and Costs, Judgment, Inter-Am. Ct. H.R. (ser. C) No. 291 (Nov. 20, 2014).
6. Espinoza Gonzales v. Peru, Preliminary Objections, Merits, Reparations, and Costs, Judgment, Inter-Am. Ct. H.R. (ser. C) No. 289 (Nov. 20, 2014).
7. Rodriguez Vera et al. (Persons Disappeared from the Palace of Justice) v. Colombia, Preliminary Objections, Merits, Reparations, and Costs, Judgment, Inter-Am. Ct. H.R. (ser. C) No. 287 (Nov. 14, 2014).
8. Rochac Hernandez et al. v. El Salvador, Merits, Reparations, and Costs, Judgment, Inter-Am. Ct. H.R. (ser. C) No. 285 (Oct. 14, 2014).
9. Expelled Dominicans and Haitians v. Dominican Republic, Preliminary Objections, Merits, Reparations, and Costs, Judgment, Inter-Am. Ct. H.R. (ser. C) No. 282 (Aug. 28, 2014).
10. Rights & Guar. of Children in the Context of Migration and/or in Need of Int'l Prot., Advisory Opinion OC-21/14, Inter-Am. Ct. H.R. (ser. A) No. 21 (Aug. 19, 2014).
11. Brewer Carías v. Venezuela, Preliminary Objections, Judgment Inter-Am. Ct. H.R. (ser. C) No. 278 (May 26, 2014).
12. Veliz Franco et al. v. Guatemala, Preliminary Objections, Merits, and Reparations, Judgment, Inter-Am. Ct. H.R. (ser. C) No. 277 (May 19, 2014).
13. Liakat Ali Alibux v. Suriname, Preliminary Objections, Merits, Reparations, and Costs, Judgment, Inter-Am. Ct. H.R. (ser. C) No. 276 (Jan. 30, 2014).
14. J. v. Peru, Preliminary Objections, Merits, Reparations, and Costs, Judgment, Inter-Am. Ct. H.R. (ser. C) No. 275 (Nov. 27, 2013).
15. Afro-Descendant Communities Displaced From the Cacarica River Basin (Operation Genesis) v. Colombia, Preliminary Objections, Merits, Reparations, and Costs, Judgment, Inter-Am. Ct. H.R. (ser. C) No. 270 (Nov. 20, 2013).
16. Memoli v. Argentina, Preliminary Objections, Merits, Reparations, and Costs, Judgment, Inter-Am. Ct. H.R. (ser. C) No. 265 (Aug. 22, 2013).
17. Santo Domingo Massacre v. Colombia, Preliminary Objections, Merits, and Reparations, Judgment, Inter-Am. Ct. H.R. (ser. C) No. 259 (Nov. 30, 2012).
18. Artavia Murillo et al. (In-vitro Fertilization) v. Costa Rica, Preliminary Objections, Merits, Reparations, and Costs, Judgment, Inter-Am. Ct. H.R. (ser. C) No. 257 (Nov. 28, 2012).
19. Castillo González et al. v. Venezuela, Merits, Judgment, Inter-Am. Ct. H.R. (ser. C) No. 256 (Nov. 27, 2012).
20. Gudiel Alvarez et al. ("Diario Militar") v. Guatemala, Merits, Reparations, and Costs, Judgment, Inter-Am. Ct. H.R. (ser. C) No. 253 (Nov. 20, 2012).

21. Massacres of El Mozote and Nearby Places v. El Salvador, Merits, Reparations, and Costs, Judgment, Inter-Am. Ct. H.R. (ser. C) No. 252 (Oct. 25, 2012).
22. Río Negro Massacres v. Guatemala, Preliminary Objections, Merits, Reparations, and Costs, Judgment, Inter-Am. Ct. H.R. (ser. C) No. 250 (Sept. 4, 2012).
23. Uzcátegui et al. v. Venezuela, Merits and Reparations, Judgment, Inter-Am. Ct. H.R. (ser. C) No. 249 (Sept. 3, 2012).
24. Vélez Restrepo and Family v. Colombia, Preliminary Objections, Merits, Reparations, and Costs, Judgment, Inter-Am. Ct. H.R. (ser. C) No. 248 (Sept. 3, 2012).
25. Díaz Peña v. Venezuela, Preliminary Objections, Merits, Reparations, and Costs, Judgment, Inter-Am. Ct. H.R. (ser. C) No. 244 (June 26, 2012).
26. Atala Riffo and Daughters v. Chile, Merits, Reparations, and Costs, Judgment, Inter-Am. Ct. H.R. (ser. C) No. 239 (Feb. 24, 2012).
27. Fontevecchia and D`Amico v. Argentina, Merits, Reparations, and Costs, Judgment, Inter-Am. Ct. H.R. (ser. C) No. 238 (Nov. 29, 2011).
28. Barrios Family v. Venezuela, Merits, Reparations, and Costs, Judgment, Inter-Am. Ct. H.R. (ser. C) No. 237 (Nov. 24, 2011).
29. Rosendo Cantu et al. v. Mexico, Preliminary Objections, Merits, Reparations, and Costs, Judgment, Inter-Am. Ct. H.R. (ser. C) No. 216 (Aug. 31, 2010).
30. Fernandez Ortega et al. v. Mexico, Preliminary Objections, Merits, Reparations, and Costs, Judgment, Inter-Am. Ct. H.R. (ser. C) No. 215 (Aug. 30, 2010).
31. Contreras et. al. v. El Salvador, Merits, Reparations, and Costs, Judgment, Inter-Am. Ct. H.R. (ser. C) No. 232 (Aug. 31, 2011).
32. Cepeda Vargas v. Colombia, Preliminary Objections, Merits, Reparations, and Costs, Judgment, Inter-Am. Ct. H.R. (ser. C.) No. 213 (May 26, 2010).
33. Usón Ramírez v. Venezuela, Preliminary Objection, Merits, Reparations, and Costs, Judgment, Inter-Am. Ct. H.R. (ser. C) No. 207 (Nov. 20, 2009).
34. Escher et al v. Brazil, Preliminary Objections, Merits, Reparations, and Costs, Judgment, Inter-Am. Ct. H.R. (ser. C) No. 200 (July 6, 2009).
35. González et al. ("Cotton Field") v. Mexico, Preliminary Objections, Merits, Reparations, and Costs, Judgment, Inter-Am. Ct. H.R. (ser. C) No. 205 (Nov. 16, 2009).
36. Tristán Donoso v. Panama, Preliminary Objections, Merits, Reparations, and Costs, Judgment, Inter-Am. Ct. H.R. (ser. C) No. 193 (Jan. 27, 2009).
37. Kimel v. Argentina, Merits, Reparations, and Costs, Judgment, Inter-Am. Ct. H.R. (ser. C) No. 177 (May 2, 2008).
38. Valle Jaramillo et al. v. Colombia, Merits, Reparations, and Costs, Judgment, Inter-Am. Ct. H.R. (ser. C) No. 192 (Nov. 27, 2008).
39. García Prieto et al. v. El Salvador, Preliminary Objections, Merits, Reparations, and Costs, Judgment, Inter-Am. Ct. H.R. (ser. C) No. 168 (Nov. 20, 2007).
40. Escué Zapata v. Colombia, Merits, Reparations, and Costs, Judgment, Inter-Am. Ct. H.R. (ser. C) No. 165 (July 4, 2007).
41. Bueno Alves v. Argentina, Merits, Reparations, and Costs, Judgment, Inter-Am. Ct. H.R. (ser. C) No. 164 (May 11, 2007).
42. Miguel Castro Castro Prison v. Peru, Merits, Reparations, and Costs, Judgment, Inter-Am. Ct. H.R. (ser. C) No. 160 (Nov. 25, 2006).

43. Ituango Massacres v. Colombia, Preliminary Objections, Merits, Reparations, and Costs, Judgment, Inter-Am. Ct. H.R. (ser. C) No. 148 (July 1, 2006).
44. García Asto and Ramírez Rojas v. Peru, Preliminary Objection, Merits, Reparations, and Costs, Judgment, Inter-Am. Ct. H.R. (ser. C) No. 137 (Nov. 25, 2005).
45. Berenson Mejia v. Peru, Merits, Reparations, and Costs, Judgment, Inter-Am. Ct. H.R. (ser. C) No. 119 (Nov. 25, 2004).
46. Plan de Sánchez Massacre v. Guatemala, Reparations, Judgment, Inter-Am. Ct. H.R. (ser. C) No. 116 (Nov. 19, 2004).
47. Gómez Paquiyauri Brothers v. Peru, Merits, Reparations, and Costs, Judgment, Inter-Am. Ct. H.R. (ser. C) No. 110 (July 8, 2004).
48. Plan de Sánchez Massacre v. Guatemala, Merits, Judgment, Inter-Am. Ct. H.R. (ser. C) No. 105 (Apr. 29, 2004).
49. Maritza Urrutia v. Guatemala, Merits, Reparations, and Costs, Judgment, Inter-Am. Ct. H.R. (ser. C) No. 103 (Nov. 27, 2003).
50. Cantos v. Argentina, Preliminary Objections, Judgment, Inter-Am. Ct. H.R. (ser. C) No. 85 (Sept. 7, 2001).
51. Mayagna (Sumo) Awas Tingni Cmty. v. Nicaragua, Merits, Reparations, and Costs, Judgment, Inter-Am. Ct. H.R. (ser. C) No. 79 (Aug. 31, 2001).
52. Cesti Hurtado v. Peru, Reparations and Costs, 2001 Inter-Am. Ct. H.R. (ser. C) No. 78 (May 31, 2001).
53. Cesti Hurtado v. Peru, Request for Interpretation of the Judgment of Merits, Order of the Court, Inter-Am. Ct. H.R. (ser. C) No. 62 (Nov. 19, 1999).
54. Cesti Hurtado v. Peru, Merits, Judgment, Inter-Am. Ct. H.R. (ser. C) No. 56 (Sept. 29, 1999).
55. Cesti Hurtado v. Peru, Preliminary Objections, Judgment, Inter-Am. Ct. H.R. (ser. C) No. 49 (Jan. 26, 1999).
56. Suárez Rosero v. Ecuador, Merits, Judgment, Inter-Am. Ct. H.R. (ser. C) No. 35 (Nov. 12, 1997).
57. Enforceability of the Right to Reply or Corr. (Arts. 14(1), 1(1), and 2 Am. Convention on Human Rights), Advisory Opinion OC-7/85, Inter-Am. Ct. H.R. (ser. A) No. 7 (Aug. 29, 1986).

ARTICLE 12: FREEDOM OF CONSCIENCE AND RELIGION

1. Velasquez Paiz et al. v. Guatemala, Preliminary Objections, Merits, Reparations and Costs, Judgment, Inter-Am. Ct. H.R. (ser. C) No. 307 (Nov. 19, 2015).
2. Rodriguez Vera et al. (Persons Disappeared from the Palace of Justice) v. Colombia, Preliminary Objections, Merits, Reparations, and Costs, Judgment, Inter-Am. Ct. H.R. (ser. C) No. 287 (Nov. 14, 2014).
3. Rights & Guar. of Children in the Context of Migration and/or in Need of Int'l Prot., Advisory Opinion OC-21/14, Inter-Am. Ct. H.R. (ser. A) No. 21 (Aug. 19, 2014). [footnote]
4. J. v. Peru, Preliminary Objections, Merits, Reparations, and Costs, Judgment, Inter-Am. Ct. H.R. (ser. C) No. 275 (Nov. 27, 2013).
5. García and Family Members v. Guatemala, Merits, Reparations, and Costs, Judgment, Inter-Am. Ct. H.R. (ser. C) No. 258 (Nov. 29, 2012).

6. Río Negro Massacres v. Guatemala, Preliminary Objections, Merits, Reparations, and Costs, Judgment, Inter-Am. Ct. H.R. (ser. C) No. 250 (Sept. 4, 2012).
7. Castañeda Gutman v. Mexico, Preliminary Objections, Merits, Reparations, and Costs, Judgment, Inter-Am. Ct. H.R. (ser. C) No. 184 (Aug. 6, 2008).
8. Miguel Castro Castro Prison v. Peru, Merits, Reparations, and Costs, Judgment, Inter-Am. Ct. H.R. (ser. C) No. 160 (Nov. 25, 2006).
9. Yean and Bosico v. Dominican Republic, Preliminary Objections, Merits, Reparations, and Costs, Judgment, Inter-Am. Ct. H.R. (ser. C) No. 130 (Sept. 8, 2005).
10. Plan de Sánchez Massacre v. Guatemala, Reparations, Judgment, Inter-Am. Ct. H.R. (ser. C) No. 116 (Nov. 19, 2004).
11. Plan de Sánchez Massacre v. Guatemala, Merits, Judgment, Inter-Am. Ct. H.R. (ser. C) No. 105 (Apr. 29, 2004).
12. Mayagna (Sumo) Awas Tingni Cmty. v. Nicaragua, Merits, Reparations, and Costs, Judgment, Inter-Am. Ct. H.R. (ser. C) No. 79 (Aug. 31, 2001).
13. "The Last Temptation of Christ" (Olmedo Bustos et al.) v. Chile, Merits, Reparations, and Costs, Judgment, Inter-Am. Ct. H.R. (ser. C) No. 73 (Feb. 5, 2001).
14. Judicial Guarantees in States of Emergency (Arts. 27(2), 25, and 8 American Convention on Human Rights), Advisory Opinion OC-9/87, Inter-Am. Ct. H.R. (ser. A) No. 9 (Oct. 6, 1987).
15. Habeas Corpus in Emergency Situations (Arts. 27(2), 25(1), and 7(6) American Convention on Human Rights), Advisory Opinion OC-8/87, Inter-Am. Ct. H.R. (ser. A) No. 8 (Jan. 30, 1987).

ARTICLE 13: FREEDOM OF THOUGHT AND EXPRESSION

1. Kaliña and Lokono Peoples v. Suriname, Merits, Reparations and Costs, Judgment, Inter-Am. Ct. H.R. (ser. C) No. 309 (Nov. 25, 2015).
2. Velasquez Paiz et al. v. Guatemala, Preliminary Objections, Merits, Reparations and Costs, Judgment, Inter-Am. Ct. H.R. (ser. C) No. 307 (Nov. 19, 2015).
3. Lopez Lone et al. v. Honduras, Preliminary Objection, Merits, Reparations and Costs, Judgment, Inter-Am. Ct. H.R. (ser. C) No. 302 (Oct. 5, 2015).
4. Granier et al. (Radio Caracas Television) v. Venezuela, Preliminary Objections, Merits, Reparations, Costs, Judgment, Inter-Am. Ct. H.R. (ser. C) No. 293 (June 22, 2015).
5. Cruz Sánchez et al. v. Peru, Preliminary Objections, Merits, Reparations, Costs, Judgment, Inter-Am. Ct. H.R. (ser. C) No. 292 (Apr. 17, 2015).
6. Rodriguez Vera et al. (Persons Disappeared from the Palace of Justice) v. Colombia, Preliminary Objections, Merits, Reparations, and Costs, Judgment, Inter-Am. Ct. H.R. (ser. C) No. 287 (Nov. 14, 2014).
7. Rights & Guar. of Children in the Context of Migration and/or in Need of Int'l Prot., Advisory Opinion OC-21/14, Inter-Am. Ct. H.R. (ser. A) No. 21 (Aug. 19, 2014). [footnote]
8. Norín Catrimán et al. (Leaders, members, and activists of the Mapuche Indigenous People) v. Chile, Merits, Reparations, and Costs, Judgment, Inter-Am. Ct. H.R. (ser. C) No. 279 (May 29, 2014).
9. Brewer Carías v. Venezuela, Preliminary Objections, Judgment Inter-Am. Ct. H.R. (ser. C) No. 278 (May 26, 2014).
10. Memoli v. Argentina, Preliminary Objections, Merits, Reparations, and Costs, Judgment, Inter-Am. Ct. H.R. (ser. C) No. 265 (Aug. 22, 2013).

11. García and Family Members v. Guatemala, Merits, Reparations, and Costs, Judgment, Inter-Am. Ct. H.R. (ser. C) No. 258 (Nov. 29, 2012).
12. Castillo González et al. v. Venezuela, Merits, Judgment, Inter-Am. Ct. H.R. (ser. C) No. 256 (Nov. 27, 2012).
13. Gudiel Alvarez et al. ("Diario Militar") v. Guatemala, Merits, Reparations, and Costs, Judgment, Inter-Am. Ct. H.R. (ser. C) No. 253 (Nov. 20, 2012).
14. Massacres of El Mozote and Nearby Places v. El Salvador, Merits, Reparations, and Costs, Judgment, Inter-Am. Ct. H.R. (ser. C) No. 252 (Oct. 25, 2012).
15. Nadege Dorzema et al. v. Dominican Republic, Merits, Reparations, and Costs, Judgment, Inter-Am. Ct. H.R. (ser. C) No. 251 (Oct. 24, 2012).
16. Uzcátegui et al. v. Venezuela, Merits and Reparations, Judgment, Inter-Am. Ct. H.R. (ser. C) No. 249 (Sept. 3, 2012).
17. Vélez Restrepo and Family v. Colombia, Preliminary Objections, Merits, Reparations, and Costs, Judgment, Inter-Am. Ct. H.R. (ser. C) No. 248 (Sept. 3, 2012).
18. Kichwa Indigenous People of Sarayaku v. Ecuador, Merits and Reparations, Judgment Inter.-Am. Ct. H.R. (ser. C) No. 245 (June 27, 2012).
19. Gonzalez Medina and Family v. Dominican Republic, Preliminary Objections, Merits, Reparations, and Costs, Judgment, Inter-Am. Ct. H.R. (ser. C) No. 240 (Feb. 27, 2012).
20. Fontevecchia and D`Amico v. Argentina, Merits, Reparations, and Costs, Judgment, Inter-Am. Ct. H.R. (ser. C) No. 238 (Nov. 29, 2011).
21. Barrios Family v. Venezuela, Merits, Reparations, and Costs, Judgment, Inter-Am. Ct. H.R. (ser. C) No. 237 (Nov. 24, 2011).
22. Contreras et. al. v. El Salvador, Merits, Reparations, and Costs, Judgment, Inter-Am. Ct. H.R. (ser. C) No. 232 (Aug. 31, 2011).
23. Gelman v. Uruguay, Merits and Reparations, Judgment, Inter-Am. Ct. H.R. (ser. C) No. 221 (Feb. 24, 2011).
24. Gomes Lund et al. ("Guerrilha do Araguaia") v. Brazil, Preliminary Objections, Merits, Reparations, and Costs, Judgment, Inter-Am. Ct. H.R. (ser. C) No. 219 (Nov. 24, 2010).
25. Cepeda Vargas v. Colombia, Preliminary Objections, Merits, Reparations, and Costs, Judgment, Inter-Am. Ct. H.R. (ser. C.) No. 213 (May 26, 2010).
26. "Las Dos Erres" Massacre v. Guatemala, Preliminary Objections, Merits, Reparations, and Costs, Judgment, Inter-Am. Ct. H.R. (ser. C) No. 211 (Nov. 24, 2009).
27. Radilla Pacheco v. Mexico, Preliminary Objections, Merits, Reparations, and Costs, Judgment, Inter-Am. Ct. H.R. (ser. C) No. 209 (Nov. 23, 2009).
28. Usón Ramírez v. Venezuela, Preliminary Objection, Merits, Reparations, and Costs, Judgment, Inter-Am. Ct. H.R. (ser. C) No. 207 (Nov. 20, 2009).
29. Anzualdo Castro v. Peru, Preliminary Objections, Merits, Reparations, and Costs, Judgment, Inter-Am. Ct. H.R. (ser. C) No. 202 (Sept. 22, 2009).
30. Perozo et al. v. Venezuela, Preliminary Objections, Merits, Reparations, and Costs, Judgment, Inter-Am. Ct. H.R. (ser. C) No. 195 (Jan. 28, 2009).
31. Ríos et al. v. Venezuela, Preliminary Objections, Merits, Reparations, and Costs, Judgment, Inter-Am. Ct. H.R. (ser. C) No. 194 (Jan. 28, 2009).
32. Tristán Donoso v. Panama, Preliminary Objections, Merits, Reparations, and Costs, Judgment, Inter-Am. Ct. H.R. (ser. C) No. 193 (Jan. 27, 2009).

33. Valle Jaramillo et al. v. Colombia, Merits, Reparations, and Costs, Judgment, Inter-Am. Ct. H.R. (ser. C) No. 192 (Nov. 27, 2008).
34. Heliodoro Portugal v. Panama, Preliminary Objections, Merits, Reparations, and Costs, Judgment, Inter-Am. Ct. H.R. (ser. C) No. 186 (Aug. 12, 2008).
35. Castañeda Gutman v. Mexico, Preliminary Objections, Merits, Reparations, and Costs, Judgment, Inter-Am. Ct. H.R. (ser. C) No. 184 (Aug. 6, 2008). [Alleged but not analyzed]
36. Kimel v. Argentina, Merits, Reparations, and Costs, Judgment, Inter-Am. Ct. H.R. (ser. C) No. 177 (May 2, 2008).
37. Albán Cornejo et al. v. Ecuador, Merits, Reparations, and Costs, Judgment, Inter-Am. Ct. H.R. (ser. C) No. 171 (Nov. 22, 2007).
38. Rochela Massacre v. Colombia, Merits, Reparations, and Costs, Judgment, Inter-Am. Ct. H.R. (ser. C) No. 163 (May 11, 2007).
39. Miguel Castro Castro Prison v. Peru, Merits, Reparations, and Costs, Judgment, Inter-Am. Ct. H.R. (ser. C) No. 160 (Nov. 25, 2006).
40. Claude Reyes et al. v. Chile, Merits, Reparations, and Costs, Judgment, Inter-Am. Ct. H.R. (ser. C) No. 151 (Sept. 19, 2006).
41. López Álvarez v. Honduras, Merits, Reparations, and Costs, Judgment, Inter-Am. Ct. H.R. (ser. C) No. 141 (Feb. 1, 2006).
42. Pueblo Bello Massacre v. Colombia, Merits, Reparations, and Costs, Judgment, Inter-Am. Ct. H.R. (ser. C) No. 140 (Jan. 31, 2006).
43. García Asto and Ramírez Rojas v. Peru, Preliminary Objection, Merits, Reparations, and Costs, Judgment, Inter-Am. Ct. H.R. (ser. C) No. 137 (Nov. 25, 2005).
44. Palamara Iribarne v. Chile, Merits, Reparations, Costs, Judgment, Inter-Am. Ct. H.R. (ser. C) No. 135 (Nov. 22, 2005).
45. Serrano Cruz Sisters v. El Salvador, Preliminary Objections, Judgment, Inter-Am. Ct. H.R. (ser. C) No. 118 (Nov. 23, 2004).
46. Carpio Nicolle et al. v. Guatemala, Merits, Reparations, and Costs, Judgment, Inter-Am. Ct. H.R. (ser. C) No. 117 (Nov. 22, 2004).
47. Plan de Sánchez Massacre v. Guatemala, Reparations, Judgment, Inter-Am. Ct. H.R. (ser. C) No. 116 (Nov. 19, 2004).
48. Canese v. Paraguay, Merits, Reparations, and Costs, Judgment, Inter-Am. Ct. H.R. (ser. C) No. 111 (Aug. 31, 2004).
49. Herrera Ulloa v. Costa Rica, Preliminary Objections, Merits, Reparations, and Costs, Judgment, Inter-Am. Ct. H.R. (ser. C) No. 107 (July 2, 2004).
50. Plan de Sánchez Massacre v. Guatemala, Merits, Judgment, Inter-Am. Ct. H.R. (ser. C) No. 105 (Apr. 29, 2004).
51. Maritza Urrutia v. Guatemala, Merits, Reparations, and Costs, Judgment, Inter-Am. Ct. H.R. (ser. C) No. 103 (Nov. 27, 2003).
52. Barrios Altos v. Peru, Merits, Judgment, Inter-Am. Ct. H.R. (ser. C) No. 75 (Mar. 14, 2001).
53. Ivcher Bronstein v. Peru, Merits, Reparations, and Costs, Judgment, Inter-Am. Ct. H.R. (ser. C) No. 74 (Feb. 6, 2001).
54. "The Last Temptation of Christ" (Olmedo Bustos et al.) v. Chile, Merits, Reparations, and Costs, Judgment, Inter-Am. Ct. H.R. (ser. C) No. 73 (Feb. 5, 2001).
55. Bámaca Velásquez v. Guatemala, Merits, Judgment, Inter-Am. Ct. H.R. (ser. C) No. 70 (Nov. 25, 2000). [Alleged but not analyzed]

56. Ivcher Bronstein v. Peru, Competence, Judgment, Inter-Am. Ct. H.R. (ser. C) No. 54 (Sept. 24, 1999).
57. Blake v. Guatemala, Merits, Judgment, Inter-Am. Ct. H.R. (ser. C) No. 36 (Jan. 24, 1998).
58. Blake v. Guatemala, Preliminary Objections, Judgment, Inter-Am. Ct. H.R. (ser. C) No. 27 (July 2, 1996).
59. Enforceability of the Right to Reply or Corr. (Arts. 14(1), 1(1), and 2 Am. Convention on Human Rights), Advisory Opinion OC-7/85, Inter-Am. Ct. H.R. (ser. A) No. 7 (Aug. 29, 1986).
60. Compulsory Membership in an Association Prescribed by Law for the Practice of Journalism (Arts. 13 and 29 American Convention on Human Rights), Advisory Opinion OC-5/85, Inter-Am. Ct. H.R. (ser. A) No. 5 (Nov. 13, 1985).

ARTICLE 14: RIGHT OF REPLY

1. "The Last Temptation of Christ" (Olmedo Bustos et al.) v. Chile, Merits, Reparations, and Costs, Judgment, Inter-Am. Ct. H.R. (ser. C) No. 73 (Feb. 5, 2001).
2. Cantos v. Argentina, Preliminary Objections, Judgment, Inter-Am. Ct. H.R. (ser. C) No. 85 (Sept. 7, 2001). [footnote]
3. Enforceability of the Right to Reply or Corr. (Arts. 14(1), 1(1), and 2 Am. Convention on Human Rights), Advisory Opinion OC-7/85, Inter-Am. Ct. H.R. (ser. A) No. 7 (Aug. 29, 1986).

ARTICLE 15: RIGHT OF ASSEMBLY

1. Lopez Lone et al. v. Honduras, Preliminary Objection, Merits, Reparations and Costs, Judgment, Inter-Am. Ct. H.R. (ser. C) No. 302 (Oct. 5, 2015).
2. Rights & Guar. of Children in the Context of Migration and/or in Need of Int'l Prot., Advisory Opinion OC-21/14, Inter-Am. Ct. H.R. (ser. A) No. 21 (Aug. 19, 2014). [footnote]
3. Díaz Peña v. Venezuela, Preliminary Objections, Merits, Reparations, and Costs, Judgment, Inter-Am. Ct. H.R. (ser. C) No. 244 (June 26, 2012).
4. Escher et al v. Brazil, Preliminary Objections, Merits, Reparations, and Costs, Judgment, Inter-Am. Ct. H.R. (ser. C) No. 200 (July 6, 2009).
5. Castañeda Gutman v. Mexico, Preliminary Objections, Merits, Reparations, and Costs, Judgment, Inter-Am. Ct. H.R. (ser. C) No. 184 (Aug. 6, 2008).
6. Baena Ricardo et al. v. Panama, Competence, Judgment, Inter-Am. Ct. H.R. (ser. C) No. 104 (Nov. 28, 2003).
7. Baena Ricardo et al. v. Panama, Merits, Reparations, and Costs, Judgment, Inter-Am. Ct. H.R. (ser. C) No. 72 (Feb. 2, 2001).
8. Baena Ricardo et al. v. Panama, Preliminary Objections, Judgment, Inter-Am. Ct. H.R. (ser. C) No. 61 (Nov. 18, 1999).

ARTICLE 16: FREEDOM OF ASSOCIATION

1. Lopez Lone et al. v. Honduras, Preliminary Objection, Merits, Reparations and Costs, Judgment, Inter-Am. Ct. H.R. (ser. C) No. 302 (Oct. 5, 2015).
2. Human Rights Defender et al. v. Guatemala, Preliminary Objections, Merits, Reparations, and Costs, Judgment, Inter-Am. Ct. H.R. (ser. C) No. 283 (Aug. 28, 2014).

3. Rights & Guar. of Children in the Context of Migration and/or in Need of Int'l Prot., Advisory Opinion OC-21/14, Inter-Am. Ct. H.R. (ser. A) No. 21 (Aug. 19, 2014).
4. García and Family Members v. Guatemala, Merits, Reparations, and Costs, Judgment, Inter-Am. Ct. H.R. (ser. C) No. 258 (Nov. 29, 2012).
5. Castillo González et al. v. Venezuela, Merits, Judgment, Inter-Am. Ct. H.R. (ser. C) No. 256 (Nov. 27, 2012).
6. Gudiel Alvarez et al. ("Diario Militar") v. Guatemala, Merits, Reparations, and Costs, Judgment, Inter-Am. Ct. H.R. (ser. C) No. 253 (Nov. 20, 2012).
7. Río Negro Massacres v. Guatemala, Preliminary Objections, Merits, Reparations, and Costs, Judgment, Inter-Am. Ct. H.R. (ser. C) No. 250 (Sept. 4, 2012).
8. Lysias Fleury et al. v. Haiti, Merits and Reparations, Judgment, Inter-Am. Ct. H.R. (ser. C) No. 236 (Nov. 23, 2011).
9. Fernandez Ortega et al. v. Mexico, Preliminary Objections, Merits, Reparations, and Costs, Judgment, Inter-Am. Ct. H.R. (ser. C) No. 215 (Aug. 30, 2010).
10. Cepeda Vargas v. Colombia, Preliminary Objections, Merits, Reparations, and Costs, Judgment, Inter-Am. Ct. H.R. (ser. C.) No. 213 (May 26, 2010).
11. Escher et al v. Brazil, Preliminary Objections, Merits, Reparations, and Costs, Judgment, Inter-Am. Ct. H.R. (ser. C) No. 200 (July 6, 2009).
12. Kawas Fernández v. Honduras, Merits, Reparations, and Costs, Judgment, Inter-Am. Ct. H.R. (ser. C) No. 196 (Apr. 3, 2009).
13. Castañeda Gutman v. Mexico, Preliminary Objections, Merits, Reparations, and Costs, Judgment, Inter-Am. Ct. H.R. (ser. C) No. 184 (Aug. 6, 2008).
14. Cantoral Huamaní and García Santa Cruz v. Peru, Preliminary Objections, Merits, Reparations, and Costs, Judgment, Inter-Am. Ct. H.R. (ser. C) No. 167 (July 10, 2007).
15. Acevedo Jaramillo et al. v. Peru, Preliminary Objections, Merits, Reparations, and Costs, Judgment, Inter-Am. Ct. H.R. (ser. C) No. 144 (Feb. 7, 2006).
16. López Álvarez v. Honduras, Merits, Reparations, and Costs, Judgment, Inter-Am. Ct. H.R. (ser. C) No. 141 (Feb. 1, 2006).
17. YATAMA v. Nicaragua, Preliminary Objections, Merits, Reparations, and Costs, Judgment, Inter-Am. Ct. H.R. (ser. C) No. 127 (June 23, 2005).
18. Huilca Tecse v. Peru, Merits, Reparations, and Costs, Judgment, Inter-Am. Ct. H.R. (ser. C) No. 121 (Mar. 3, 2005).
19. Plan de Sánchez Massacre v. Guatemala, Reparations, Judgment, Inter-Am. Ct. H.R. (ser. C) No. 116 (Nov. 19, 2004).
20. Plan de Sánchez Massacre v. Guatemala, Merits, Judgment, Inter-Am. Ct. H.R. (ser. C) No. 105 (Apr. 29, 2004).
21. Baena Ricardo et al. v. Panama, Competence, Judgment, Inter-Am. Ct. H.R. (ser. C) No. 104 (Nov. 28, 2003).
22. Mayagna (Sumo) Awas Tingni Cmty. v. Nicaragua, Merits, Reparations, and Costs, Judgment, Inter-Am. Ct. H.R. (ser. C) No. 79 (Aug. 31, 2001).
23. Baena Ricardo et al. v. Panama, Merits, Reparations, and Costs, Judgment, Inter-Am. Ct. H.R. (ser. C) No. 72 (Feb. 2, 2001).
24. Baena Ricardo et al. v. Panama, Preliminary Objections, Judgment, Inter-Am. Ct. H.R. (ser. C) No. 61 (Nov. 18, 1999).

ARTICLE 17: RIGHTS OF THE FAMILY

1. Case of Peasant Community of Santa Barbara v. Peru, Preliminary Objections, Merits, Reparations and Costs, Judgment, Inter-Am. Ct. H.R. (ser. C) No. 299 (Sept. 1, 2015).
2. Rochac Hernandez et al. v. El Salvador, Merits, Reparations, and Costs, Judgment, Inter-Am. Ct. H.R. (ser. C) No. 285 (Oct. 14, 2014).
3. Expelled Dominicans and Haitians v. Dominican Republic, Preliminary Objections, Merits, Reparations, and Costs, Judgment, Inter-Am. Ct. H.R. (ser. C) No. 282 (Aug. 28, 2014).
4. Rights & Guar. of Children in the Context of Migration and/or in Need of Int'l Prot., Advisory Opinion OC-21/14, Inter-Am. Ct. H.R. (ser. A) No. 21 (Aug. 19, 2014).
5. Norín Catrimán et al. (Leaders, members, and activists of the Mapuche Indigenous People) v. Chile, Merits, Reparations, and Costs, Judgment, Inter-Am. Ct. H.R. (ser. C) No. 279 (May 29, 2014).
6. J. v. Peru, Preliminary Objections, Merits, Reparations, and Costs, Judgment, Inter-Am. Ct. H.R. (ser. C) No. 275 (Nov. 27, 2013).
7. Pacheco Tineo Family v. Bolivia, Preliminary Objections, Merits, Reparations, and Costs, Judgment, Inter-Am. Ct. H.R. (ser. C) No. 272 (Nov. 25, 2013).
8. Afro-Descendant Communities Displaced From the Cacarica River Basin (Operation Genesis) v. Colombia, Preliminary Objections, Merits, Reparations, and Costs, Judgment, Inter-Am. Ct. H.R. (ser. C) No. 270 (Nov. 20, 2013).
9. Mendoza et al. v. Argentina, Preliminary Objections, Merits, and Reparations, Judgment, Inter-Am. Ct. H.R. (ser. C) No. 260 (May 14, 2013).
10. García and Family Members v. Guatemala, Merits, Reparations, and Costs, Judgment, Inter-Am. Ct. H.R. (ser. C) No. 258 (Nov. 29, 2012).
11. Artavia Murillo et al. (In-vitro Fertilization) v. Costa Rica, Preliminary Objections, Merits, Reparations, and Costs, Judgment, Inter-Am. Ct. H.R. (ser. C) No. 257 (Nov. 28, 2012).
12. Gudiel Alvarez et al. ("Diario Militar") v. Guatemala, Merits, Reparations, and Costs, Judgment, Inter-Am. Ct. H.R. (ser. C) No. 253 (Nov. 20, 2012).
13. Río Negro Massacres v. Guatemala, Preliminary Objections, Merits, Reparations, and Costs, Judgment, Inter-Am. Ct. H.R. (ser. C) No. 250 (Sept. 4, 2012).
14. Vélez Restrepo and Family v. Colombia, Preliminary Objections, Merits, Reparations, and Costs, Judgment, Inter-Am. Ct. H.R. (ser. C) No. 248 (Sept. 3, 2012).
15. Fornerón and Daughter v. Argentina, Merits, Reparations, and Costs, Judgment, Inter-Am. Ct. H.R. (ser. C) No. 242 (Apr. 27, 2012).
16. Gonzalez Medina & Family v. Dominican Republic, Preliminary Objections, Merits, Reparations, and Costs, Judgment, Inter-Am. Ct. H.R. (ser. C) No. 240 (Feb. 27, 2012).
17. Atala Riffo and Daughters v. Chile, Merits, Reparations, and Costs, Judgment, Inter-Am. Ct. H.R. (ser. C) No. 239 (Feb. 24, 2012).
18. Barrios Family v. Venezuela, Merits, Reparations, and Costs, Judgment, Inter-Am. Ct. H.R. (ser. C) No. 237 (Nov. 24, 2011).
19. Contreras et. al. v. El Salvador, Merits, Reparations, and Costs, Judgment, Inter-Am. Ct. H.R. (ser. C) No. 232 (Aug. 31, 2011).
20. Gelman v. Uruguay, Merits and Reparations, Judgment, Inter-Am. Ct. H.R. (ser. C) No. 221 (Feb. 24, 2011).

21. Fernandez Ortega et al. v. Mexico, Preliminary Objections, Merits, Reparations, and Costs, Judgment, Inter-Am. Ct. H.R. (ser. C) No. 215 (Aug. 30, 2010). [footnote]
22. Chitay Nech et al. v. Guatemala, Preliminary Objections, Merits, Reparations, and Costs, Judgment, Inter-Am. Ct. H.R. (ser. C) No. 212 (May 25, 2010).
23. "Las Dos Erres" Massacre v. Guatemala, Preliminary Objections, Merits, Reparations, and Costs, Judgment, Inter-Am. Ct. H.R. (ser. C) No. 211 (Nov. 24, 2009).
24. Valle Jaramillo et al. v. Colombia, Merits, Reparations, and Costs, Judgment, Inter-Am. Ct. H.R. (ser. C) No. 192 (Nov. 27, 2008).
25. Albán Cornejo et al. v. Ecuador, Merits, Reparations, and Costs, Judgment, Inter-Am. Ct. H.R. (ser. C) No. 171 (Nov. 22, 2007).
26. López Álvarez v. Honduras, Merits, Reparations, and Costs, Judgment, Inter-Am. Ct. H.R. (ser. C) No. 141 (Feb. 1, 2006).
27. García Asto and Ramírez Rojas v. Peru, Preliminary Objection, Merits, Reparations, and Costs, Judgment, Inter-Am. Ct. H.R. (ser. C) No. 137 (Nov. 25, 2005).
28. Serrano Cruz Sisters v. El Salvador, Interpretation of the Judgment of Merits, Reparations, and Costs, Judgment, Inter-Am. Ct. H.R. (ser. C) No. 131 (Sept. 9, 2005).
29. Yean and Bosico v. Dominican Republic, Preliminary Objections, Merits, Reparations, and Costs, Judgment, Inter-Am. Ct. H.R. (ser. C) No. 130 (Sept. 8, 2005).
30. Fermín Ramírez v. Guatemala, Merits, Reparations, and Costs, Judgment, Inter-Am. Ct. H.R. (ser. C) No. 126 (June 20, 2005).
31. Serrano Cruz Sisters v. El Salvador, Merits, Reparations, and Costs, Judgment, Inter-Am. Ct. H.R. (ser. C) No. 120 (Mar. 1, 2005).
32. Serrano Cruz Sisters v. El Salvador, Preliminary Objections, Judgment, Inter-Am. Ct. H.R. (ser. C) No. 118 (Nov. 23, 2004).
33. Tibi v. Ecuador, Preliminary Objections, Merits, Reparations, and Costs, Judgment, Inter-Am. Ct. H.R. (ser. C) No. 114 (Sept. 7, 2004).
34. "Juvenile Reeducation Institute" v. Paraguay, Preliminary Objections, Merits, Reparations, and Costs, Judgment, Inter-Am. Ct. H.R. (ser. C) No. 112 (Sept. 2, 2004).
35. Gómez Paquiyauri Brothers v. Peru, Merits, Reparations, and Costs, Judgment, Inter-Am. Ct. H.R. (ser. C) No. 110 (July 8, 2004).
36. Molina Theissen v. Guatemala, Reparations and Costs, Judgment, Inter-Am. Ct. H.R. (ser. C) No. 108 (July 3, 2004).
37. Molina Theissen v. Guatemala, Merits, Judgment, Inter-Am. Ct. H.R. (ser. C) No. 106 (May 4, 2004).
38. Cantos v. Argentina, Preliminary Objections, Judgment, Inter-Am. Ct. H.R. (ser. C) No. 85 (Sept. 7, 2001).
39. Mayagna (Sumo) Awas Tingni Cmty. v. Nicaragua, Merits, Reparations, and Costs, Judgment, Inter-Am. Ct. H.R. (ser. C) No. 79 (Aug. 31, 2001).
40. Cesti Hurtado v. Peru, Preliminary Objections, Judgment, Inter-Am. Ct. H.R. (ser. C) No. 49 (Jan. 26, 1999).
41. Suárez Rosero v. Ecuador, Merits, Judgment, Inter-Am. Ct. H.R. (ser. C) No. 35 (Nov. 12, 1997).
42. Castillo Páez v. Peru, Merits, Judgment, Inter-Am. Ct. H.R. (ser. C) No. 34 (Nov. 3, 1997).
43. Judicial Guarantees in States of Emergency (Arts. 27(2), 25, and 8 American Convention on Human Rights), Advisory Opinion OC-9/87, Inter-Am. Ct. H.R. (ser. A) No. 9 (Oct. 6, 1987).

44. Habeas Corpus in Emergency Situations (Arts. 27(2), 25(1), and 7(6) American Convention on Human Rights), Advisory Opinion OC-8/87, Inter-Am. Ct. H.R. (ser. A) No. 8 (Jan. 30, 1987).
45. Proposed Amendments of the Naturalization Provisions of the Constitution of Costa Rica, Advisory Opinion OC-4/84, Inter-Am. Ct. H.R. (ser. A) No. 4 (Jan. 19, 1984).

ARTICLE 18: RIGHT TO A NAME

1. Rochac Hernandez et al. v. El Salvador, Merits, Reparations, and Costs, Judgment, Inter-Am. Ct. H.R. (ser. C) No. 285 (Oct. 14, 2014). [footnote]
2. Expelled Dominicans and Haitians v. Dominican Republic, Preliminary Objections, Merits, Reparations, and Costs, Judgment, Inter-Am. Ct. H.R. (ser. C) No. 282 (Aug. 28, 2014).
3. J. v. Peru, Preliminary Objections, Merits, Reparations, and Costs, Judgment, Inter-Am. Ct. H.R. (ser. C) No. 275 (Nov. 27, 2013). [footnote]
4. García and Family Members v. Guatemala, Merits, Reparations, and Costs, Judgment, Inter-Am. Ct. H.R. (ser. C) No. 258 (Nov. 29, 2012).
5. Río Negro Massacres v. Guatemala, Preliminary Objections, Merits, Reparations, and Costs, Judgment, Inter-Am. Ct. H.R. (ser. C) No. 250 (Sept. 4, 2012).
6. Contreras et al. v. El Salvador, Merits, Reparations, and Costs, Judgment, Inter-Am. Ct. H.R. (ser. C) No. 232 (Aug. 31, 2011).
7. Gelman v. Uruguay, Merits and Reparations, Judgment, Inter-Am. Ct. H.R. (ser. C) No. 221 (Feb. 24, 2011).
8. "Las Dos Erres" Massacre v. Guatemala, Preliminary Objections, Merits, Reparations, and Costs, Judgment, Inter-Am. Ct. H.R. (ser. C) No. 211 (Nov. 24, 2009).
9. Serrano Cruz Sisters v. El Salvador, Interpretation of the Judgment of Merits, Reparations, and Costs, Judgment, Inter-Am. Ct. H.R. (ser. C) No. 131 (Sept. 9, 2005).
10. Yean and Bosico v. Dominican Republic, Preliminary Objections, Merits, Reparations, and Costs, Judgment, Inter-Am. Ct. H.R. (ser. C) No. 130 (Sept. 8, 2005).
11. Serrano Cruz Sisters v. El Salvador, Merits, Reparations, and Costs, Judgment, Inter-Am. Ct. H.R. (ser. C) No. 120 (Mar. 1, 2005).
12. Serrano Cruz Sisters v. El Salvador, Preliminary Objections, Judgment, Inter-Am. Ct. H.R. (ser. C) No. 118 (Nov. 23, 2004).
13. Judicial Guarantees in States of Emergency (Arts. 27(2), 25, and 8 American Convention on Human Rights), Advisory Opinion OC-9/87, Inter-Am. Ct. H.R. (ser. A) No. 9 (Oct. 6, 1987).
14. Habeas Corpus in Emergency Situations (Arts. 27(2), 25(1), and 7(6) American Convention on Human Rights), Advisory Opinion OC-8/87, Inter-Am. Ct. H.R. (ser. A) No. 8 (Jan. 30, 1987).

ARTICLE 19: RIGHTS OF THE CHILD

1. Garcia Ibarra et al. v. Ecuador, Preliminary Objections, Merits, Reparations and Costs, Judgment, Inter-Am. Ct. H.R. (ser. C) No. 306 (Nov. 17, 2015).
2. Case of Peasant Community of Santa Barbara v. Peru, Preliminary Objections, Merits, Reparations and Costs, Judgment, Inter-Am. Ct. H.R. (ser. C) No. 299 (Sept. 1, 2015).
3. Gonzales Lluy et al. v. Ecuador, Preliminary Objections, Merits, Reparations and Costs, Judgment, Inter-Am. Ct. H.R. (ser. C) No. 298 (Sept. 1, 2015).

4. Rochac Hernandez et al. v. El Salvador, Merits, Reparations, and Costs, Judgment, Inter-Am. Ct. H.R. (ser. C) No. 285 (Oct. 14, 2014).
5. Human Rights Defender et al. v. Guatemala, Preliminary Objections, Merits, Reparations, and Costs, Judgment, Inter-Am. Ct. H.R. (ser. C) No. 283 (Aug. 28, 2014).
6. Expelled Dominicans and Haitians v. Dominican Republic, Preliminary Objections, Merits, Reparations, and Costs, Judgment, Inter-Am. Ct. H.R. (ser. C) No. 282 (Aug. 28, 2014).
7. Landaeta Meijias Brothers et al. v. Venezuela, Preliminary Objections, Merits, Reparations, and Costs, Judgment, Inter-Am. Ct. H.R. (ser. C) No. 281 (Aug. 27, 2014).
8. Rights & Guar. of Children in the Context of Migration and/or in Need of Int'l Prot., Advisory Opinion OC-21/14, Inter-Am. Ct. H.R. (ser. A) No. 21 (Aug. 19, 2014).
9. Veliz Franco et al. v. Guatemala, Preliminary Objections, Merits, and Reparations, Judgment, Inter-Am. Ct. H.R. (ser. C) No. 277 (May 19, 2014).
10. Pacheco Tineo Family v. Bolivia, Preliminary Objections, Merits, Reparations, and Costs, Judgment, Inter-Am. Ct. H.R. (ser. C) No. 272 (Nov. 25, 2013).
11. Afro-Descendant Communities Displaced From the Cacarica River Basin (Operation Genesis) v. Colombia, Preliminary Objections, Merits, Reparations, and Costs, Judgment, Inter-Am. Ct. H.R. (ser. C) No. 270 (Nov. 20, 2013).
12. Mendoza et al. v. Argentina, Preliminary Objections, Merits, and Reparations, Judgment, Inter-Am. Ct. H.R. (ser. C) No. 260 (May 14, 2013).
13. Santo Domingo Massacre v. Colombia, Preliminary Objections, Merits, and Reparations, Judgment, Inter-Am. Ct. H.R. (ser. C) No. 259 (Nov. 30, 2012).
14. García and Family Members v. Guatemala, Merits, Reparations, and Costs, Judgment, Inter-Am. Ct. H.R. (ser. C) No. 258 (Nov. 29, 2012).
15. Castillo González et al. v. Venezuela, Merits, Judgment, Inter-Am. Ct. H.R. (ser. C) No. 256 (Nov. 27, 2012).
16. Gudiel Alvarez et al. ("Diario Militar") v. Guatemala, Merits, Reparations, and Costs, Judgment, Inter-Am. Ct. H.R. (ser. C) No. 253 (Nov. 20, 2012).
17. Massacres of El Mozote and Nearby Places v. El Salvador, Merits, Reparations, and Costs, Judgment, Inter-Am. Ct. H.R. (ser. C) No. 252 (Oct. 25, 2012).
18. Río Negro Massacres v. Guatemala, Preliminary Objections, Merits, Reparations, and Costs, Judgment, Inter-Am. Ct. H.R. (ser. C) No. 250 (Sept. 4, 2012).
19. Uzcátegui et al. v. Venezuela, Merits and Reparations, Judgment, Inter-Am. Ct. H.R. (ser. C) No. 249 (Sept. 3, 2012).
20. Vélez Restrepo and Family v. Colombia, Preliminary Objections, Merits, Reparations, and Costs, Judgment, Inter-Am. Ct. H.R. (ser. C) No. 248 (Sept. 3, 2012).
21. Furlan and Family v. Argentina, Preliminary Objections, Merits, Reparations, and Costs, Judgment, Inter-Am. Ct. H.R. (ser. C) No. 246 (Aug. 31, 2012).
22. Fornerón and Daughter v. Argentina, Merits, Reparations, and Costs, Judgment, Inter-Am. Ct. H.R. (ser. C) No. 242 (Apr. 27, 2012).
23. Gonzalez Medina and Family v. Dominican Republic, Preliminary Objections, Merits, Reparations, and Costs, Judgment, Inter-Am. Ct. H.R. (ser. C) No. 240 (Feb. 27, 2012).
24. Atala Riffo & Daughters v. Chile, Merits, Reparations, and Costs, Judgment, Inter-Am. Ct. H.R. (ser. C) No. 239 (Feb. 24, 2012).
25. Barrios Family v. Venezuela, Merits, Reparations, and Costs, Judgment, Inter-Am. Ct. H.R. (ser. C) No. 237 (Nov. 24, 2011).

26. Contreras et. al. v. El Salvador, Merits, Reparations, and Costs, Judgment, Inter-Am. Ct. H.R. (ser. C) No. 232 (Aug. 31, 2011).
27. Torres Millacura et al. v. Argentina, Merits, Reparations, and Costs, Judgment, Inter-Am. Ct. H.R. (ser. C) No. 229 (Aug. 26, 2011).
28. Gelman v. Uruguay, Merits and Reparations, Judgment, Inter-Am. Ct. H.R. (ser. C) No. 221 (Feb. 24, 2011).
29. Rosendo Cantu et al. v. Mexico, Preliminary Objections, Merits, Reparations, and Costs, Judgment, Inter-Am. Ct. H.R. (ser. C) No. 216 (Aug. 31, 2010).
30. Fernandez Ortega et al. v. Mexico, Preliminary Objections, Merits, Reparations, and Costs, Judgment, Inter-Am. Ct. H.R. (ser. C) No. 215 (Aug. 30, 2010).
31. Xákmok Kásek Indigenous Cmty. v. Paraguay, Merits, Reparations, and Costs, Judgment, Inter-Am. Ct. H.R. (ser. C) No. 214 (Aug. 24, 2010).
32. Chitay Nech et al. v. Guatemala, Preliminary Objections, Merits, Reparations, and Costs, Judgment, Inter-Am. Ct. H.R. (ser. C) No. 212 (May 25, 2010).
33. "Las Dos Erres" Massacre v. Guatemala, Preliminary Objections, Merits, Reparations, and Costs, Judgment, Inter-Am. Ct. H.R. (ser. C) No. 211 (Nov. 24, 2009).
34. González et al. ("Cotton Field") v. Mexico, Preliminary Objections, Merits, Reparations, and Costs, Judgment, Inter-Am. Ct. H.R. (ser. C) No. 205 (Nov. 16, 2009).
35. Tiu Tojín v. Guatemala, Merits, Reparations, and Costs, Judgment, Inter-Am. Ct. H.R. (ser. C) No. 190 (Nov. 26, 2008).
36. Yean and Bosico v. Dominican Republic, Interpretation of the Judgment of Preliminary Objections, Merits, Reparations, and Costs, Judgment, Inter-Am. Ct. H.R. (ser. C) No. 156 (Nov. 23, 2006).
37. Servellón García et al. v. Honduras, Merits, Reparations, and Costs, Judgment, Inter-Am. Ct. H.R. (ser. C) No. 152 (Sept. 21, 2006).
38. Ituango Massacres v. Colombia, Preliminary Objections, Merits, Reparations, and Costs, Judgment, Inter-Am. Ct. H.R. (ser. C) No. 148 (July 1, 2006).
39. Pueblo Bello Massacre v. Colombia, Merits, Reparations, and Costs, Judgment, Inter-Am. Ct. H.R. (ser. C) No. 140 (Jan. 31, 2006).
40. Mapiripán Massacre v. Colombia, Merits, Reparations, and Costs, Judgment, Inter-Am. Ct. H.R. (ser. C) No. 134 (Sept. 15, 2005).
41. Serrano Cruz Sisters v. El Salvador, Interpretation of the Judgment of Merits, Reparations, and Costs, Judgment, Inter-Am. Ct. H.R. (ser. C) No. 131 (Sept. 9, 2005).
42. Yean and Bosico v. Dominican Republic, Preliminary Objections, Merits, Reparations, and Costs, Judgment, Inter-Am. Ct. H.R. (ser. C) No. 130 (Sept. 8, 2005).
43. Yakye Axa Indigenous Cmty. v. Paraguay, Merits, Reparations, and Costs, Judgment, Inter-Am. Ct. H.R. (ser. C) No. 125 (June 17, 2005).
44. Mapiripán Massacre v. Colombia, Preliminary Objections, Judgment, Inter-Am. Ct. H.R. (ser. C) No. 122 (Mar. 7, 2005).
45. Serrano Cruz Sisters v. El Salvador, Merits, Reparations, and Costs, Judgment, Inter-Am. Ct. H.R. (ser. C) No. 120 (Mar. 1, 2005).
46. Serrano Cruz Sisters v. El Salvador, Preliminary Objections, Judgment, Inter-Am. Ct. H.R. (ser. C) No. 118 (Nov. 23, 2004).
47. Carpio Nicolle et al. v. Guatemala, Merits, Reparations, and Costs, Judgment, Inter-Am. Ct. H.R. (ser. C) No. 117 (Nov. 22, 2004).

48. "Juvenile Reeducation Institute" v. Paraguay, Preliminary Objections, Merits, Reparations, and Costs, Judgment, Inter-Am. Ct. H.R. (ser. C) No. 112 (Sept. 2, 2004).
49. Gómez Paquiyauri Brothers v. Peru, Merits, Reparations, and Costs, Judgment, Inter-Am. Ct. H.R. (ser. C) No. 110 (July 8, 2004).
50. Molina Theissen v. Guatemala, Reparations and Costs, Judgment, Inter-Am. Ct. H.R. (ser. C) No. 108 (July 3, 2004).
51. Molina Theissen v. Guatemala, Merits, Judgment, Inter-Am. Ct. H.R. (ser. C) No. 106 (May 4, 2004).
52. Maritza Urrutia v. Guatemala, Merits, Reparations, and Costs, Judgment, Inter-Am. Ct. H.R. (ser. C) No. 103 (Nov. 27, 2003).
53. Bulacio v. Argentina, Merits, Reparations, and Costs, Judgment, Inter-Am. Ct. H.R. (ser. C) No. 100 (Sept. 18, 2003).
54. Juridical Condition & Human Rights of the Child, Advisory Opinion OC-17/02, Inter-Am. Ct. H.R. (ser. A) No. 17 (Aug. 28, 2002).
55. "Street Children" (Villagrán Morales et al.) v. Guatemala, Reparations and Costs, Judgment, Inter-Am. Ct. H.R. (ser. C) No. 77 (May 26, 2001).
56. "Street Children" (Villagrán Morales et al.) v. Guatemala, Merits, Judgment, Inter-Am. Ct. H.R. (ser. C) No. 63 (Nov. 19, 1999).
57. "Street Children" (Villagrán Morales et al.) v. Guatemala, Preliminary Objections, Judgment, Inter-Am. Ct. H.R. (ser. C) No. 32 (Sept. 11, 1997).
58. Judicial Guarantees in States of Emergency (Arts. 27(2), 25, and 8 American Convention on Human Rights), Advisory Opinion OC-9/87, Inter-Am. Ct. H.R. (ser. A) No. 9 (Oct. 6, 1987).
59. Habeas Corpus in Emergency Situations (Arts. 27(2), 25(1), and 7(6) American Convention on Human Rights), Advisory Opinion OC-8/87, Inter-Am. Ct. H.R. (ser. A) No. 8 (Jan. 30, 1987).

ARTICLE 20: RIGHT TO NATIONALITY

1. Expelled Dominicans and Haitians v. Dominican Republic, Preliminary Objections, Merits, Reparations, and Costs, Judgment, Inter-Am. Ct. H.R. (ser. C) No. 282 (Aug. 28, 2014).
2. Rights & Guar. of Children in the Context of Migration and/or in Need of Int'l Prot., Advisory Opinion OC-21/14, Inter-Am. Ct. H.R. (ser. A) No. 21 (Aug. 19, 2014). [footnote]
3. J. v. Peru, Preliminary Objections, Merits, Reparations, and Costs, Judgment, Inter-Am. Ct. H.R. (ser. C) No. 275 (Nov. 27, 2013). [footnote]
4. Gelman v. Uruguay, Merits and Reparations, Judgment, Inter-Am. Ct. H.R. (ser. C) No. 221 (Feb. 24, 2011).
5. Zambrano Vélez et al. v. Ecuador, Merits, Reparations, and Costs, Judgment, Inter-Am. Ct. H.R. (ser. C) No. 166 (July 4, 2007).
6. Yean and Bosico v. Dominican Republic, Interpretation of the Judgment of Preliminary Objections, Merits, Reparations, and Costs, Judgment, Inter-Am. Ct. H.R. (ser. C) No. 156 (Nov. 23, 2006).
7. Yean and Bosico v. Dominican Republic, Preliminary Objections, Merits, Reparations, and Costs, Judgment, Inter-Am. Ct. H.R. (ser. C) No. 130 (Sept. 8, 2005).
8. Ivcher Bronstein v. Peru, Merits, Reparations, and Costs, Judgment, Inter-Am. Ct. H.R. (ser. C) No. 74 (Feb. 6, 2001).
9. Durand and Ugarte v. Peru, Merits, Judgment, Inter-Am. Ct. H.R. (ser. C) No. 68 (Aug. 16, 2000).

10. Ivcher Bronstein v. Peru, Competence, Judgment, Inter-Am. Ct. H.R. (ser. C) No. 54 (Sept. 24, 1999).
11. Castillo Petruzzi et al. v. Peru, Merits, Reparations, and Costs, Judgment, Inter-Am. Ct. H.R. (ser. C) No. 52 (May 30, 1999).
12. Castillo Petruzzi et al. v. Peru, Preliminary Objections, Judgment, Inter-Am. Ct. H.R. (ser. C) No. 41 (Sept. 4, 1998).
13. Judicial Guarantees in States of Emergency (Arts. 27(2), 25, and 8 American Convention on Human Rights), Advisory Opinion OC-9/87, Inter-Am. Ct. H.R. (ser. A) No. 9 (Oct. 6, 1987).
14. Habeas Corpus in Emergency Situations (Arts. 27(2), 25(1), and 7(6) American Convention on Human Rights), Advisory Opinion OC-8/87, Inter-Am. Ct. H.R. (ser. A) No. 8 (Jan. 30, 1987).
15. Proposed Amendments of the Naturalization Provisions of the Constitution of Costa Rica, Advisory Opinion OC-4/84, Inter-Am. Ct. H.R. (ser. A) No. 4 (Jan. 19, 1984).

ARTICLE 21: RIGHT TO PROPERTY

1. Kaliña and Lokono Peoples v. Suriname, Merits, Reparations and Costs, Judgment, Inter-Am. Ct. H.R. (ser. C) No. 309 (Nov. 25, 2015).
2. Community Garifuna Triunfo de la Cruz & its Members v. Honduras, Merits, Reparations and Costs, Judgment, Inter-Am. Ct. H.R. (ser. C) No. 305 (Oct. 8, 2015).
3. Garifuna Punta Piedra Community and its Members v. Honduras, Preliminary Objections, Merits, Reparations and Costs, Judgment, Inter-Am. Ct. H.R. (ser. C) No. 304 (Oct. 8, 2015).
4. Kuna Indigenous People of Madungandi and Embera Indigenous People of Bayano & their Members v. Panama, Preliminary Objections, Merits, Reparations, and Costs, Judgment, Inter-Am. Ct. H.R. (ser. C) No. 284 (Oct. 14, 2014).
5. Expelled Dominicans and Haitians v. Dominican Republic, Preliminary Objections, Merits, Reparations, and Costs, Judgment, Inter-Am. Ct. H.R. (ser. C) No. 282 (Aug. 28, 2014).
6. Liakat Ali Alibux v. Suriname, Preliminary Objections, Merits, Reparations, and Costs, Judgment, Inter-Am. Ct. H.R. (ser. C) No. 276 (Jan. 30, 2014).
7. Afro-Descendant Communities Displaced From the Cacarica River Basin (Operation Genesis) v. Colombia, Preliminary Objections, Merits, Reparations, and Costs, Judgment, Inter-Am. Ct. H.R. (ser. C) No. 270 (Nov. 20, 2013).
8. Memoli v. Argentina, Preliminary Objections, Merits, Reparations, and Costs, Judgment, Inter-Am. Ct. H.R. (ser. C) No. 265 (Aug. 22, 2013).
9. Massacre of Santo Domingo v. Colombia, Request for Interpretation of the Judgment on Preliminary Objections, Merits, Reparations, and Costs, Judgment, Inter-Am. Ct. H.R. (ser. C) No. 263 (Aug. 19, 2013).
10. Mendoza et al. v. Argentina, Preliminary Objections, Merits, and Reparations, Judgment, Inter-Am. Ct. H.R. (ser. C) No. 260 (May 14, 2013).
11. Santo Domingo Massacre v. Colombia, Preliminary Objections, Merits, and Reparations, Judgment, Inter-Am. Ct. H.R. (ser. C) No. 259 (Nov. 30, 2012).
12. Massacres of El Mozote and Nearby Places v. El Salvador, Merits, Reparations, and Costs, Judgment, Inter-Am. Ct. H.R. (ser. C) No. 252 (Oct. 25, 2012).
13. Río Negro Massacres v. Guatemala, Preliminary Objections, Merits, Reparations, and Costs, Judgment, Inter-Am. Ct. H.R. (ser. C) No. 250 (Sept. 4, 2012).

14. Uzcátegui et al. v. Venezuela, Merits and Reparations, Judgment, Inter-Am. Ct. H.R. (ser. C) No. 249 (Sept. 3, 2012).
15. Furlan and Family v. Argentina, Preliminary Objections, Merits, Reparations, and Costs, Judgment, Inter-Am. Ct. H.R. (ser. C) No. 246 (Aug. 31, 2012).
16. Kichwa Indigenous People of Sarayaku v. Ecuador, Merits and Reparations, Judgment Inter.-Am. Ct. H.R. (ser. C) No. 245 (June 27, 2012).
17. Barrios Family v. Venezuela, Merits, Reparations, and Costs, Judgment, Inter-Am. Ct. H.R. (ser. C) No. 237 (Nov. 24, 2011).
18. Barbani Duarte et al. v. Uruguay, Merits, Reparations, and Costs, Judgment, Inter. Am. Ct. H.R. (ser. C) No. 234 (Oct. 13, 2011).
19. Salvador Chiriboga v. Ecuador, Interpretation of the Judgment on Reparations and Costs, Judgment, Inter-Am. Ct. H.R. (ser. C) No. 230 (Aug. 29, 2011).
20. Abrill Alosilla et al. v. Peru, Merits, Reparations, and Costs, Judgment, Inter-Am. Ct. H.R. (ser. C) No. 223 (Mar. 4, 2011).
21. Salvador Chiriboga v. Ecuador, Reparations and Costs, Judgment, Inter-Am. Ct. H.R. (ser. C) No. 222 (Mar. 3, 2011).
22. Fernandez Ortega et al. v. Mexico, Preliminary Objections, Merits, Reparations, and Costs, Judgment, Inter-Am. Ct. H.R. (ser. C) No. 215 (Aug. 30, 2010). [footnote]
23. Xákmok Kásek Indigenous Cmty. v. Paraguay, Merits, Reparations, and Costs, Judgment, Inter-Am. Ct. H.R. (ser. C) No. 214 (Aug. 24, 2010).
24. Chitay Nech et al. v. Guatemala, Preliminary Objections, Merits, Reparations, and Costs, Judgment, Inter-Am. Ct. H.R. (ser. C) No. 212 (May 25, 2010).
25. "Las Dos Erres" Massacre v. Guatemala, Preliminary Objections, Merits, Reparations, and Costs, Judgment, Inter-Am. Ct. H.R. (ser. C) No. 211 (Nov. 24, 2009).
26. Acevedo Buendía et al. ("Discharged & Retired Employees of the Office of the Comptroller") v. Peru, Interpretation of the Judgment on the Preliminary Objection, Merits, Reparations, and Costs, Judgment, Inter-Am. Ct. H.R. (ser. C) No. 210 (Nov. 24, 2009).
27. Acevedo Buendía et al. ("Discharged & Retired Employees of the Office of the Comptroller") v. Peru, Preliminary Objection, Merits, Reparations, and Costs, Judgment, Inter-Am. Ct. H.R. (ser. C) No. 198 (July 1, 2009).
28. Perozo et al. v. Venezuela, Preliminary Objections, Merits, Reparations, and Costs, Judgment, Inter-Am. Ct. H.R. (ser. C) No. 195 (Jan. 28, 2009).
29. Saramaka People v. Suriname, Interpretation of the Judgment on Preliminary Objections, Merits, Reparations, and Costs, Judgment, Inter-Am. Ct. H.R. (ser. C) No. 185 (Aug. 12, 2008)
30. Salvador Chiriboga v. Ecuador, Preliminary Objections and Merits, Judgment, Inter-Am. Ct. H.R. (ser. C) No. 179 (May 6, 2008).
31. Saramaka People v. Suriname, Preliminary Objections, Merits, Reparations, and Costs, Judgment, Inter-Am. Ct. H.R. (ser. C) No. 172 (Nov. 28, 2007).
32. Chaparro Álvarez and Lapo Íñiguez v. Ecuador, Preliminary Objections, Merits, Reparations, and Costs, Judgment, Inter-Am. Ct. H.R. (ser. C) No. 170 (Nov. 21, 2007).
33. Ituango Massacres v. Colombia, Preliminary Objections, Merits, Reparations, and Costs, Judgment, Inter-Am. Ct. H.R. (ser. C) No. 148 (July 1, 2006).
34. Sawhoyamaxa Indigenous Cmty. v. Paraguay, Merits, Reparations, and Costs, Judgment, Inter-Am. Ct. H.R. (ser. C) No. 146 (Mar. 29, 2006).
35. Moiwana Cmty. v. Suriname, Interpretation of the Judgment of Merits, Reparations, and Costs, Judgment, Inter-Am. Ct. H.R. (ser. C) No. 145 (Feb. 8, 2006).

36. Yakye Axa Indigenous Cmty. v. Paraguay, Interpretation of the Judgment of Merits, Reparations, and Costs, Judgment, Inter-Am. Ct. H.R. (ser. C) No. 142 (Feb. 6, 2006).
37. Palamara Iribarne v. Chile, Merits, Reparations, Costs, Judgment, Inter-Am. Ct. H.R. (ser. C) No. 135 (Nov. 22, 2005).
38. Yakye Axa Indigenous Cmty. v. Paraguay, Merits, Reparations, and Costs, Judgment, Inter-Am. Ct. H.R. (ser. C) No. 125 (June 17, 2005).
39. Moiwana Cmty. v. Suriname, Preliminary Objections, Merits, Reparations, and Costs, Judgment, Inter-Am. Ct. H.R. (ser. C) No. 124 (June 15, 2005).
40. Plan de Sánchez Massacre v. Guatemala, Reparations, Judgment, Inter-Am. Ct. H.R. (ser. C) No. 116 (Nov. 19, 2004).
41. Tibi v. Ecuador, Preliminary Objections, Merits, Reparations, and Costs, Judgment, Inter-Am. Ct. H.R. (ser. C) No. 114 (Sept. 7, 2004).
42. Plan de Sánchez Massacre v. Guatemala, Merits, Judgment, Inter-Am. Ct. H.R. (ser. C) No. 105 (Apr. 29, 2004).
43. "Five Pensioners" v. Peru, Merits, Reparations, and Costs, Judgment, Inter-Am. Ct. H.R. (ser. C) No. 98 (Feb. 28, 2003).
44. Cantos v. Argentina, Preliminary Objections, Judgment, Inter-Am. Ct. H.R. (ser. C) No. 85 (Sept. 7, 2001).
45. Mayagna (Sumo) Awas Tingni Cmty. v. Nicaragua, Merits, Reparations, and Costs, Judgment, Inter-Am. Ct. H.R. (ser. C) No. 79 (Aug. 31, 2001).
46. Cesti Hurtado v. Peru, Reparations and Costs, 2001 Inter-Am. Ct. H.R. (ser. C) No. 78 (May 31, 2001).
47. Ivcher Bronstein v. Peru, Merits, Reparations, and Costs, Judgment, Inter-Am. Ct. H.R. (ser. C) No. 74 (Feb. 6, 2001).
48. Mayagna (Sumo) Awas Tingni Cmty. v. Nicaragua, Preliminary Objections, Judgment, Inter-Am. Ct. H.R. (ser. C) No. 66 (Feb. 1, 2000).
49. Cesti Hurtado v. Peru, Interpretation of the Judgment of Merits, Judgment, Inter-Am. Ct. H.R. (ser. C) No. 65 (Jan. 29, 2000).
50. Cesti Hurtado v. Peru, Request for Interpretation of the Judgment of Merits, Order of the Court, Inter-Am. Ct. H.R. (ser. C) No. 62 (Nov. 19, 1999).
51. Cesti Hurtado v. Peru, Merits, Judgment, Inter-Am. Ct. H.R. (ser. C) No. 56 (Sept. 29, 1999).
52. Ivcher Bronstein v. Peru, Competence, Judgment, Inter-Am. Ct. H.R. (ser. C) No. 54 (Sept. 24, 1999).
53. Cesti Hurtado v. Peru, Preliminary Objections, Judgment, Inter-Am. Ct. H.R. (ser. C) No. 49 (Jan. 26, 1999).
54. Neira Alegría et al. v. Peru, Preliminary Objections, Judgment, Inter-Am. Ct. H.R. (ser. C) No. 13 (Dec. 11, 1991).

ARTICLE 22: FREEDOM OF MOVEMENT AND RESIDENCE

1. Velasquez Paiz et al. v. Guatemala, Preliminary Objections, Merits, Reparations and Costs, Judgment, Inter-Am. Ct. H.R. (ser. C) No. 307 (Nov. 19, 2015).
2. Rodriguez Vera et al. (Persons Disappeared from the Palace of Justice) v. Colombia, Preliminary Objections, Merits, Reparations, and Costs, Judgment, Inter-Am. Ct. H.R. (ser. C) No. 287 (Nov. 14, 2014).

3. Kuna Indigenous People of Madungandi and Embera Indigenous People of Bayano and their Members v. Panama, Preliminary Objections, Merits, Reparations, and Costs, Judgment, Inter-Am. Ct. H.R. (ser. C) No. 284 (Oct. 14, 2014).
4. Human Rights Defender et al. v. Guatemala, Preliminary Objections, Merits, Reparations, and Costs, Judgment, Inter-Am. Ct. H.R. (ser. C) No. 283 (Aug. 28, 2014).
5. Expelled Dominicans and Haitians v. Dominican Republic, Preliminary Objections, Merits, Reparations, and Costs, Judgment, Inter-Am. Ct. H.R. (ser. C) No. 282 (Aug. 28, 2014).
6. Rights & Guar. of Children in the Context of Migration and/or in Need of Int'l Prot., Advisory Opinion OC-21/14, Inter-Am. Ct. H.R. (ser. A) No. 21 (Aug. 19, 2014).
7. Brewer Carías v. Venezuela, Preliminary Objections, Judgment Inter-Am. Ct. H.R. (ser. C) No. 278 (May 26, 2014).
8. Liakat Ali Alibux v. Suriname, Preliminary Objections, Merits, Reparations, and Costs, Judgment, Inter-Am. Ct. H.R. (ser. C) No. 276 (Jan. 30, 2014).
9. Pacheco Tineo Family v. Bolivia, Preliminary Objections, Merits, Reparations, and Costs, Judgment, Inter-Am. Ct. H.R. (ser. C) No. 272 (Nov. 25, 2013).
10. Afro-Descendant Communities Displaced From the Cacarica River Basin (Operation Genesis) v. Colombia, Preliminary Objections, Merits, Reparations, and Costs, Judgment, Inter-Am. Ct. H.R. (ser. C) No. 270 (Nov. 20, 2013).
11. Garcia Lucero et al. v. Chile, Preliminary Objections, Merits, and Reparations, Judgment, Inter-Am. Ct. H.R. (ser. C) No. 267 (Aug. 28, 2013).
12. Massacre of Santo Domingo v. Colombia, Request for Interpretation of the Judgment on Preliminary Objections, Merits, Reparations, and Costs, Judgment, Inter-Am. Ct. H.R. (ser. C) No. 263 (Aug. 19, 2013).
13. Santo Domingo Massacre v. Colombia, Preliminary Objections, Merits, and Reparations, Judgment, Inter-Am. Ct. H.R. (ser. C) No. 259 (Nov. 30, 2012).
14. Gudiel Alvarez et al. ("Diario Militar") v. Guatemala, Merits, Reparations, and Costs, Judgment, Inter-Am. Ct. H.R. (ser. C) No. 253 (Nov. 20, 2012).
15. Massacres of El Mozote and Nearby Places v. El Salvador, Merits, Reparations, and Costs, Judgment, Inter-Am. Ct. H.R. (ser. C) No. 252 (Oct. 25, 2012).
16. Nadege Dorzema et al. v. Dominican Republic, Merits, Reparations, and Costs, Judgment, Inter-Am. Ct. H.R. (ser. C) No. 251 (Oct. 24, 2012).
17. Río Negro Massacres v. Guatemala, Preliminary Objections, Merits, Reparations, and Costs, Judgment, Inter-Am. Ct. H.R. (ser. C) No. 250 (Sept. 4, 2012).
18. Vélez Restrepo and Family v. Colombia, Preliminary Objections, Merits, Reparations, and Costs, Judgment, Inter-Am. Ct. H.R. (ser. C) No. 248 (Sept. 3, 2012).
19. Kichwa Indigenous People of Sarayaku v. Ecuador, Merits and Reparations, Judgment Inter.-Am. Ct. H.R. (ser. C) No. 245 (June 27, 2012).
20. Barrios Family v. Venezuela, Merits, Reparations, and Costs, Judgment, Inter-Am. Ct. H.R. (ser. C) No. 237 (Nov. 24, 2011).
21. Lysias Fleury et al. v. Haiti, Merits and Reparations, Judgment, Inter-Am. Ct. H.R. (ser. C) No. 236 (Nov. 23, 2011).
22. Cepeda Vargas v. Colombia, Preliminary Objections, Merits, Reparations, and Costs, Judgment, Inter-Am. Ct. H.R. (ser. C.) No. 213 (May 26, 2010).
23. Chitay Nech et al. v. Guatemala, Preliminary Objections, Merits, Reparations, and Costs, Judgment, Inter-Am. Ct. H.R. (ser. C) No. 212 (May 25, 2010).

24. Valle Jaramillo et al. v. Colombia, Interpretation of the Judgment on the Merits, Reparations, and Costs, Judgment, Inter-Am. Ct. H.R. (ser. C) No. 201 (July 7, 2009).
25. Valle Jaramillo et al. v. Colombia, Merits, Reparations, and Costs, Judgment, Inter-Am. Ct. H.R. (ser. C) No. 192 (Nov. 27, 2008).
26. Castañeda Gutman v. Mexico, Preliminary Objections, Merits, Reparations, and Costs, Judgment, Inter-Am. Ct. H.R. (ser. C) No. 184 (Aug. 6, 2008).
27. Ituango Massacres v. Colombia, Preliminary Objections, Merits, Reparations, and Costs, Judgment, Inter-Am. Ct. H.R. (ser. C) No. 148 (July 1, 2006).
28. Moiwana Cmty. v. Suriname, Interpretation of the Judgment of Merits, Reparations, and Costs, Judgment, Inter-Am. Ct. H.R. (ser. C) No. 145 (Feb. 8, 2006).
29. Pueblo Bello Massacre v. Colombia, Merits, Reparations, and Costs, Judgment, Inter-Am. Ct. H.R. (ser. C) No. 140 (Jan. 31, 2006).
30. Mapiripán Massacre v. Colombia, Merits, Reparations, and Costs, Judgment, Inter-Am. Ct. H.R. (ser. C) No. 134 (Sept. 15, 2005).
31. Moiwana Cmty. v. Suriname, Preliminary Objections, Merits, Reparations, and Costs, Judgment, Inter-Am. Ct. H.R. (ser. C) No. 124 (June 15, 2005).
32. Mapiripán Massacre v. Colombia, Preliminary Objections, Judgment, Inter-Am. Ct. H.R. (ser. C) No. 122 (Mar. 7, 2005).
33. Canese v. Paraguay, Merits, Reparations, and Costs, Judgment, Inter-Am. Ct. H.R. (ser. C) No. 111 (Aug. 31, 2004).
34. Juridical Condition & Rights of the Undocumented Migrants, Advisory Opinion OC-18/03, Inter-Am. Ct. H.R. (ser. A) No. 18 (Sept. 17, 2003).
35. Mayagna (Sumo) Awas Tingni Cmty. v. Nicaragua, Merits, Reparations, and Costs, Judgment, Inter-Am. Ct. H.R. (ser. C) No. 79 (Aug. 31, 2001).
36. Blake v. Guatemala, Merits, Judgment, Inter-Am. Ct. H.R. (ser. C) No. 36 (Jan. 24, 1998).
37. Blake v. Guatemala, Preliminary Objections, Judgment, Inter-Am. Ct. H.R. (ser. C) No. 27 (July 2, 1996).

ARTICLE 23: RIGHT TO PARTICIPATE IN GOVERNMENT

1. Kaliña and Lokono Peoples v. Suriname, Merits, Reparations and Costs, Judgment, Inter-Am. Ct. H.R. (ser. C) No. 309 (Nov. 25, 2015).
2. Lopez Lone et al. v. Honduras, Preliminary Objection, Merits, Reparations and Costs, Judgment, Inter-Am. Ct. H.R. (ser. C) No. 302 (Oct. 5, 2015).
3. Argüelles et al. v. Argentina, Preliminary Objections, Merits, Reparations, and Costs, Judgment, Inter-Am. Ct. H.R. (ser. C) No. 288 (Nov. 20, 2014).
4. Human Rights Defender et al. v. Guatemala, Preliminary Objections, Merits, Reparations, and Costs, Judgment, Inter-Am. Ct. H.R. (ser. C) No. 283 (Aug. 28, 2014).
5. Norín Catrimán et al. (Leaders, members, and activists of the Mapuche Indigenous People) v. Chile, Merits, Reparations, and Costs, Judgment, Inter-Am. Ct. H.R. (ser. C) No. 279 (May 29, 2014).
6. J. v. Peru, Preliminary Objections, Merits, Reparations, and Costs, Judgment, Inter-Am. Ct. H.R. (ser. C) No. 275 (Nov. 27, 2013). [footnote]
7. Luna Lopez v. Honduras, Merits, Reparations, and Costs, Judgment, Inter-Am. Ct. H.R. (ser. C) No. 269 (Oct. 10, 2013).

8. Constitutional Tribunal (Camba Campos et al.) v. Ecuador, Preliminary Objections, Merits, Reparations, and Costs, Judgment, Inter-Am. Ct. H.R. (ser. C) No. 268 (Aug. 28, 2013).
9. Supreme Court of Justice (Quintana Coello et al.) v. Ecuador, Preliminary Objections, Merits, Reparations, and Costs, Judgment, Inter-Am. Ct. H.R. (ser. C) No. 266 (Aug. 23, 2013).
10. Memoli v. Argentina, Preliminary Objections, Merits, Reparations, and Costs, Judgment, Inter-Am. Ct. H.R. (ser. C) No. 265 (Aug. 22, 2013).
11. García and Family Members v. Guatemala, Merits, Reparations, and Costs, Judgment, Inter-Am. Ct. H.R. (ser. C) No. 258 (Nov. 29, 2012).
12. Gudiel Alvarez et al. ("Diario Militar") v. Guatemala, Merits, Reparations, and Costs, Judgment, Inter-Am. Ct. H.R. (ser. C) No. 253 (Nov. 20, 2012).
13. Kichwa Indigenous People of Sarayaku v. Ecuador, Merits and Reparations, Judgment Inter.-Am. Ct. H.R. (ser. C) No. 245 (June 27, 2012).
14. López Mendoza v. Venezuela, Merits, Reparations, and Costs, Judgment,Inter-Am. Ct. H.R. (ser. C) No. 233 (Sept. 1, 2011).
15. Chocrón Chocrón v. Venezuela, Preliminary Objections, Merits, Reparations, and Costs, Judgment, Inter-Am. Ct. H.R. (ser. C) No. 227 (July 1, 2011).
16. Cepeda Vargas v. Colombia, Preliminary Objections, Merits, Reparations, and Costs, Judgment, Inter-Am. Ct. H.R. (ser. C.) No. 213 (May 26, 2010).
17. Chitay Nech et al. v. Guatemala, Preliminary Objections, Merits, Reparations, and Costs, Judgment, Inter-Am. Ct. H.R. (ser. C) No. 212 (May 25, 2010).
18. Reverón Trujillo v. Venezuela, Preliminary Objections, Merits, Reparations, and Costs, Judgment, Inter-Am. Ct. H.R. (ser. C) No. 197 (June 30, 2009).
19. Castañeda Gutman v. Mexico, Preliminary Objections, Merits, Reparations, and Costs, Judgment, Inter-Am. Ct. H.R. (ser. C) No. 184 (Aug. 6, 2008).
20. Apitz Barbera et al. ("First Court of Administrative Disputes") v. Venezuela, Preliminary Objection, Merits, Reparations, and Costs, Judgment, Inter-Am. Ct. H.R. (ser. C) No. 182 (Aug. 5, 2008).
21. Claude Reyes et al. v. Chile, Merits, Reparations, and Costs, Judgment, Inter-Am. Ct. H.R. (ser. C) No. 151 (Sept. 19, 2006).
22. YATAMA v. Nicaragua, Preliminary Objections, Merits, Reparations, and Costs, Judgment, Inter-Am. Ct. H.R. (ser. C) No. 127 (June 23, 2005).
23. Carpio Nicolle et al. v. Guatemala, Merits, Reparations, and Costs, Judgment, Inter-Am. Ct. H.R. (ser. C) No. 117 (Nov. 22, 2004).
24. Mayagna (Sumo) Awas Tingni Cmty. v. Nicaragua, Merits, Reparations, and Costs, Judgment, Inter-Am. Ct. H.R. (ser. C) No. 79 (Aug. 31, 2001).
25. Constitutional Court v. Peru, Merits, Reparations, and Costs, Judgment, Inter-Am. Ct. H.R. (ser. C) No. 71 (Jan. 31, 2001).
26. Constitutional Court v. Peru, Competence, Judgment, Inter-Am. Ct. H.R. (ser. C) No. 55 (Sept. 24, 1999).
27. Certain Attributes of the Inter-American Commission on Human Rights (Arts. 41, 42, 44, 46, 47, 50, and 51 of the American Convention on Human Rights), Advisory Opinion OC-13/93, Inter-Am. Ct. H.R. (ser. A) No. 13 (July 16, 1993).
28. Exceptions to the Exhaustion of Domestic Remedies (Arts. 46(1), 46(2)(a), and 46(2)(b) American Convention on Human Rights), Advisory Opinion OC-11/90, Inter-Am. Ct. H.R. (ser. A) No. 11 (Aug. 10, 1990).

29. Judicial Guarantees in States of Emergency (Arts. 27(2), 25, and 8 American Convention on Human Rights), Advisory Opinion OC-9/87, Inter-Am. Ct. H.R. (ser. A) No. 9 (Oct. 6, 1987).
30. Habeas Corpus in Emergency Situations (Arts. 27(2), 25(1), and 7(6) American Convention on Human Rights), Advisory Opinion OC-8/87, Inter-Am. Ct. H.R. (ser. A) No. 8 (Jan. 30, 1987).

ARTICLE 24: RIGHT TO EQUAL PROTECTION

1. Duque v. Colombia, Preliminary Objections, Merits, Reparations and Costs, Judgment, Inter-Am. Ct. H.R. (ser. C) No. 310 (Feb. 26, 2016).
2. Velasquez Paiz et al. v. Guatemala, Preliminary Objections, Merits, Reparations and Costs, Judgment, Inter-Am. Ct. H.R. (ser. C) No. 307 (Nov. 19, 2015).
3. Gonzales Lluy et al. v. Ecuador, Preliminary Objections, Merits, Reparations and Costs, Judgment, Inter-Am. Ct. H.R. (ser. C) No. 298 (Sept. 1, 2015).
4. Canales Huapaya et al. v. Peru, Preliminary Objections, Merits, Reparations, Costs, Judgment, Inter-Am. Ct. H.R. (ser. C) No. 296 (June 24, 2015).
5. Espinoza Gonzales v. Peru, Interpretation of the Judgment on Preliminary Objections, Merits, Reparations and Costs, Judgment, Inter-Am. Ct. H.R. (ser. C) No. 295 (June 23, 2015).
6. Granier et al. (Radio Caracas Television) v. Venezuela, Preliminary Objections, Merits, Reparations, Costs, Judgment, Inter-Am. Ct. H.R. (ser. C) No. 293 (June 22, 2015).
7. Argüelles et al. v. Argentina, Preliminary Objections, Merits, Reparations, and Costs, Judgment, Inter-Am. Ct. H.R. (ser. C) No. 288 (Nov. 20, 2014).
8. Kuna Indigenous People of Madungandi and Embera Indigenous People of Bayano and their Members v. Panama, Preliminary Objections, Merits, Reparations, and Costs, Judgment, Inter-Am. Ct. H.R. (ser. C) No. 284 (Oct. 14, 2014).
9. Expelled Dominicans and Haitians v. Dominican Republic, Preliminary Objections, Merits, Reparations, and Costs, Judgment, Inter-Am. Ct. H.R. (ser. C) No. 282 (Aug. 28, 2014).
10. Norín Catrimán et al. (Leaders, members, and activists of the Mapuche Indigenous People) v. Chile, Merits, Reparations, and Costs, Judgment, Inter-Am. Ct. H.R. (ser. C) No. 279 (May 29, 2014).
11. Brewer Carías v. Venezuela, Preliminary Objections, Judgment Inter-Am. Ct. H.R. (ser. C) No. 278 (May 26, 2014).
12. Veliz Franco et al. v. Guatemala, Preliminary Objections, Merits, and Reparations, Judgment, Inter-Am. Ct. H.R. (ser. C) No. 277 (May 19, 2014).
13. Liakat Ali Alibux v. Suriname, Preliminary Objections, Merits, Reparations, and Costs, Judgment, Inter-Am. Ct. H.R. (ser. C) No. 276 (Jan. 30, 2014). [footnote]
14. Afro-Descendant Communities Displaced From the Cacarica River Basin (Operation Genesis) v. Colombia, Preliminary Objections, Merits, Reparations, and Costs, Judgment, Inter-Am. Ct. H.R. (ser. C) No. 270 (Nov. 20, 2013).
15. Constitutional Tribunal (Camba Campos et al.) v. Ecuador, Preliminary Objections, Merits, Reparations, and Costs, Judgment, Inter-Am. Ct. H.R. (ser. C) No. 268 (Aug. 28, 2013).
16. Supreme Court of Justice (Quintana Coello et al.) v. Ecuador, Preliminary Objections, Merits, Reparations, and Costs, Judgment, Inter-Am. Ct. H.R. (ser. C) No. 266 (Aug. 23, 2013).
17. Memoli v. Argentina, Preliminary Objections, Merits, Reparations, and Costs, Judgment, Inter-Am. Ct. H.R. (ser. C) No. 265 (Aug. 22, 2013).

18. Mendoza et al. v. Argentina, Preliminary Objections, Merits, and Reparations, Judgment, Inter-Am. Ct. H.R. (ser. C) No. 260 (May 14, 2013).
19. Artavia Murillo et al. (In-vitro Fertilization) v. Costa Rica, Preliminary Objections, Merits, Reparations, and Costs, Judgment, Inter-Am. Ct. H.R. (ser. C) No. 257 (Nov. 28, 2012).
20. Nadege Dorzema et al. v. Dominican Republic, Merits, Reparations, and Costs, Judgment, Inter-Am. Ct. H.R. (ser. C) No. 251 (Oct. 24, 2012).
21. Río Negro Massacres v. Guatemala, Preliminary Objections, Merits, Reparations, and Costs, Judgment, Inter-Am. Ct. H.R. (ser. C) No. 250 (Sept. 4, 2012).
22. Díaz Peña v. Venezuela, Preliminary Objections, Merits, Reparations, and Costs, Judgment, Inter-Am. Ct. H.R. (ser. C) No. 244 (June 26, 2012).
23. Atala Riffo and Daughters v. Chile, Merits, Reparations, and Costs, Judgment, Inter-Am. Ct. H.R. (ser. C) No. 239 (Feb. 24, 2012).
24. Barbani Duarte et al. v. Uruguay, Merits, Reparations, and Costs, Judgment, Inter. Am. Ct. H.R. (ser. C) No. 234 (Oct. 13, 2011).
25. López Mendoza v. Venezuela, Merits, Reparations, and Costs, Judgment, Inter-Am. Ct. H.R. (ser. C) No. 233 (Sept. 1, 2011).
26. Mejía Idrovo v. Ecuador, Preliminary Objections, Merits, Reparations, and Costs, Judgment, Inter-Am. Ct. H.R. (ser. C) No. 228 (July 5, 2011).
27. Rosendo Cantu et al. v. Mexico, Interpretation of Judgment of Preliminary Objections, Merits, Reparations, and Costs, Judgment, Inter-Am. Ct. H.R. (ser. C) No. 225 (May 15, 2011).
28. Fernandez Ortega et al. v. Mexico, Interpretation of Judgment of Preliminary Objection, Merits, Reparations, and Costs, Judgment, Inter-Am. Ct. H.R. (ser. C) No. 224 (May 15, 2011).
29. Salvador Chiriboga v. Ecuador, Reparations and Costs, Judgment, Inter-Am. Ct. H.R. (ser. C) No. 222 (Mar. 3, 2011).
30. Vélez Loor v. Panama, Preliminary Objections, Merits, Reparations, and Costs, Judgment, Inter-Am. Ct. H.R. (ser. C) No. 218 (Nov. 23, 2010).
31. Ibsen Cardenas and Ibsen Peña v. Bolivia, Merits, Reparations, and Costs, Judgment, Inter-Am. Ct. H.R. (ser. C) No. 217 (Sept. 1, 2010).
32. Rosendo Cantu et al. v. Mexico, Preliminary Objections, Merits, Reparations, and Costs, Judgment, Inter-Am. Ct. H.R. (ser. C) No. 216 (Aug. 31, 2010).
33. Fernandez Ortega et al. v. Mexico, Preliminary Objections, Merits, Reparations, and Costs, Judgment, Inter-Am. Ct. H.R. (ser. C) No. 215 (Aug. 30, 2010).
34. Chitay Nech et al. v. Guatemala, Preliminary Objections, Merits, Reparations, and Costs, Judgment, Inter-Am. Ct. H.R. (ser. C) No. 212 (May 25, 2010).
35. Perozo et al. v. Venezuela, Preliminary Objections, Merits, Reparations, and Costs, Judgment, Inter-Am. Ct. H.R. (ser. C) No. 195 (Jan. 28, 2009).
36. Ríos et al. v. Venezuela, Preliminary Objections, Merits, Reparations, and Costs, Judgment, Inter-Am. Ct. H.R. (ser. C) No. 194 (Jan. 28, 2009).
37. Castañeda Gutman v. Mexico, Preliminary Objections, Merits, Reparations, and Costs, Judgment, Inter-Am. Ct. H.R. (ser. C) No. 184 (Aug. 6, 2008).
38. Apitz Barbera et al. ("First Court of Administrative Disputes") v. Venezuela, Preliminary Objection, Merits, Reparations, and Costs, Judgment, Inter-Am. Ct. H.R. (ser. C) No. 182 (Aug. 5, 2008).

39. Salvador Chiriboga v. Ecuador, Preliminary Objections and Merits, Judgment, Inter-Am. Ct. H.R. (ser. C) No. 179 (May 6, 2008).
40. Bueno Alves v. Argentina, Merits, Reparations, and Costs, Judgment, Inter-Am. Ct. H.R. (ser. C) No. 164 (May 11, 2007).
41. Yean and Bosico v. Dominican Republic, Interpretation of the Judgment of Preliminary Objections, Merits, Reparations, and Costs, Judgment, Inter-Am. Ct. H.R. (ser. C) No. 156 (Nov. 23, 2006).
42. López Álvarez v. Honduras, Merits, Reparations, and Costs, Judgment, Inter-Am. Ct. H.R. (ser. C) No. 141 (Feb. 1, 2006).
43. Yean and Bosico v. Dominican Republic, Preliminary Objections, Merits, Reparations, and Costs, Judgment, Inter-Am. Ct. H.R. (ser. C) No. 130 (Sept. 8, 2005).
44. YATAMA v. Nicaragua, Preliminary Objections, Merits, Reparations, and Costs, Judgment, Inter-Am. Ct. H.R. (ser. C) No. 127 (June 23, 2005).
45. Plan de Sánchez Massacre v. Guatemala, Reparations, Judgment, Inter-Am. Ct. H.R. (ser. C) No. 116 (Nov. 19, 2004).
46. De La Cruz Flores v. Peru, Merits, Reparations, and Costs, Judgment, Inter-Am. Ct. H.R. (ser. C) No. 115 (Nov. 18, 2004).
47. Plan de Sánchez Massacre v. Guatemala, Merits, Judgment, Inter-Am. Ct. H.R. (ser. C) No. 105 (Apr. 29, 2004).
48. Juridical Condition & Rights of the Undocumented Migrants, Advisory Opinion OC-18/03, Inter-Am. Ct. H.R. (ser. A) No. 18 (Sept. 17, 2003).
49. Juridical Condition & Human Rights of the Child, Advisory Opinion OC-17/02, Inter-Am. Ct. H.R. (ser. A) No. 17 (Aug. 28, 2002).
50. Cantos v. Argentina, Preliminary Objections, Judgment, Inter-Am. Ct. H.R. (ser. C) No. 85 (Sept. 7, 2001).
51. Baena Ricardo et al. v. Panama, Preliminary Objections, Judgment, Inter-Am. Ct. H.R. (ser. C) No. 61 (Nov. 18, 1999).
52. Genie Lacayo v. Nicaragua, Application for Judicial Review of the Judgment of Merits, Reparations, and Costs, Order of the Court, Inter-Am. Ct. H.R. (ser. C) No. 45 (Sept. 13, 1997).
53. Genie Lacayo v. Nicaragua, Merits, Reparations, and Costs, Judgment, Inter-Am. Ct. H.R. (ser. C) No. 30 (Jan. 29, 1997).
54. El Amparo v. Venezuela, Reparations and Costs, Judgment, Inter-Am. Ct. H.R. (ser. C) No. 28 (Sept. 14, 1996).
55. "White Van" (Paniagua Morales et al.) v. Guatemala, Preliminary Objections, Judgment, Inter-Am. Ct. H.R. (ser. C) No. 23 (Jan. 25, 1996).
56. Genie Lacayo v. Nicaragua, Preliminary Objections, Judgment, Inter-Am. Ct. H.R. (ser. C) No. 21 (Jan. 27, 1995).
57. El Amparo v. Venezuela, Merits, Judgment, Inter-Am. Ct. H.R. (ser. C) No. 19 (Jan. 18, 1995).
58. Certain Attributes of the Inter-American Commission on Human Rights (Arts. 41, 42, 44, 46, 47, 50, and 51 of the American Convention on Human Rights), Advisory Opinion OC-13/93, Inter-Am. Ct. H.R. (ser. A) No. 13 (July 16, 1993).
59. Proposed Amendments of the Naturalization Provisions of the Constitution of Costa Rica, Advisory Opinion OC-4/84, Inter-Am. Ct. H.R. (ser. A) No. 4 (Jan. 19, 1984).

ARTICLE 25: RIGHT TO JUDICIAL PROTECTION

1. Duque v. Colombia, Preliminary Objections, Merits, Reparations and Costs, Judgment, Inter-Am. Ct. H.R. (ser. C) No. 310 (Feb. 26, 2016).
2. Kaliña and Lokono Peoples v. Suriname, Merits, Reparations and Costs, Judgment, Inter-Am. Ct. H.R. (ser. C) No. 309 (Nov. 25, 2015).
3. Quispialaya Vilcapoma v. Peru, Preliminary Objections, Merits, Reparations and Costs, Judgment, Inter-Am. Ct. H.R. (ser. C) No. 308 (Nov. 23, 2015).
4. Velasquez Paiz et al. v. Guatemala, Preliminary Objections, Merits, Reparations and Costs, Judgment, Inter-Am. Ct. H.R. (ser. C) No. 307 (Nov. 19, 2015).
5. Garcia Ibarra et al. v. Ecuador, Preliminary Objections, Merits, Reparations and Costs, Judgment, Inter-Am. Ct. H.R. (ser. C) No. 306 (Nov. 17, 2015).
6. Community Garifuna Triunfo de la Cruz and its Members v. Honduras, Merits, Reparations and Costs, Judgment, Inter-Am. Ct. H.R. (ser. C) No. 305 (Oct. 8, 2015).
7. Garifuna Punta Piedra Community and its Members v. Honduras, Preliminary Objections, Merits, Reparations and Costs, Judgment, Inter-Am. Ct. H.R. (ser. C) No. 304 (Oct. 8, 2015).
8. Ruano Torres et al. v. El Salvador, Merits, Reparations and Costs, Judgment, Inter-Am. Ct. H.R. (ser. C) No. 303 (Oct. 5, 2015).
9. Lopez Lone et al. v. Honduras, Preliminary Objection, Merits, Reparations and Costs, Judgment, Inter-Am. Ct. H.R. (ser. C) No. 302 (Oct. 5, 2015).
10. Galindo Cardenas et al. v. Peru, Preliminary Objections, Merits, Reparations and Costs, Judgment, Inter-Am. Ct. H.R. (ser. C) No. 301 (Oct. 2, 2015).
11. Omar Humberto Maldonado Vargas et al. v. Chile, Merits, Reparations, Costs, Judgment, Inter-Am. Ct. H.R. (ser. C) No. 300 (Sept. 2, 2015).
12. Case of Peasant Community of Santa Barbara v. Peru, Preliminary Objections, Merits, Reparations and Costs, Judgment, Inter-Am. Ct. H.R. (ser. C) No. 299 (Sept. 1, 2015).
13. Gonzales Lluy et al. v. Ecuador, Preliminary Objections, Merits, Reparations and Costs, Judgment, Inter-Am. Ct. H.R. (ser. C) No. 298 (Sept. 1, 2015).
14. Wong Ho Wing v. Peru, Preliminary Objection, Merits, Reparations and Costs, Judgment, Inter-Am. Ct. H.R. (ser. C) No. 297 (June 30, 2015).
15. Canales Huapaya et al. v. Peru, Preliminary Objections, Merits, Reparations, Costs, Judgment, Inter-Am. Ct. H.R. (ser. C) No. 296 (June 24, 2015).
16. Espinoza Gonzales v. Peru, Interpretation of the Judgment on Preliminary Objections, Merits, Reparations and Costs, Judgment, Inter-Am. Ct. H.R. (ser. C) No. 295 (June 23, 2015).
17. Granier et al. (Radio Caracas Television) v. Venezuela, Preliminary Objections, Merits, Reparations, Costs, Judgment, Inter-Am. Ct. H.R. (ser. C) No. 293 (June 22, 2015).
18. Cruz Sánchez et al. v. Peru, Preliminary Objections, Merits, Reparations, Costs, Judgment, Inter-Am. Ct. H.R. (ser. C) No. 292 (Apr. 17, 2015).
19. Osorio Rivera and Family v. Peru, Interpretation of the Judgment on Preliminary Objection, Merits, Reparations, and Costs, Judgment, Inter-Am. Ct. H.R. (ser. C) No. 290 (Nov. 20, 2014).
20. Espinoza Gonzales v. Peru, Preliminary Objections, Merits, Reparations, and Costs, Judgment, Inter-Am. Ct. H.R. (ser. C) No. 289 (Nov. 20, 2014).
21. Argüelles et al. v. Argentina, Preliminary Objections, Merits, Reparations, and Costs, Judgment, Inter-Am. Ct. H.R. (ser. C) No. 288 (Nov. 20, 2014).

22. Rodriguez Vera et al. (Persons Disappeared from the Palace of Justice) v. Colombia, Preliminary Objections, Merits, Reparations, and Costs, Judgment, Inter-Am. Ct. H.R. (ser. C) No. 287 (Nov. 14, 2014).
23. Tarazona Arrieta et al. v. Peru, Preliminary Objections, Merits, Reparations, and Costs, Judgment, Inter-Am. Ct. H.R. (ser. C) No. 286 (Oct. 15, 2014).
24. Rochac Hernandez et al. v. El Salvador, Merits, Reparations, and Costs, Judgment, Inter-Am. Ct. H.R. (ser. C) No. 285 (Oct. 14, 2014).
25. Kuna Indigenous People of Madungandi and Embera Indigenous People of Bayano and their Members v. Panama, Preliminary Objections, Merits, Reparations, and Costs, Judgment, Inter-Am. Ct. H.R. (ser. C) No. 284 (Oct. 14, 2014).
26. Human Rights Defender et al. v. Guatemala, Preliminary Objections, Merits, Reparations, and Costs, Judgment, Inter-Am. Ct. H.R. (ser. C) No. 283 (Aug. 28, 2014).
27. Expelled Dominicans and Haitians v. Dominican Republic, Preliminary Objections, Merits, Reparations, and Costs, Judgment, Inter-Am. Ct. H.R. (ser. C) No. 282 (Aug. 28, 2014).
28. Landaeta Meijias Brothers et al. v. Venezuela, Preliminary Objections, Merits, Reparations, and Costs, Judgment, Inter-Am. Ct. H.R. (ser. C) No. 281 (Aug. 27, 2014).
29. Rights & Guar. of Children in the Context of Migration and/or in Need of Int'l Prot., Advisory Opinion OC-21/14, Inter-Am. Ct. H.R. (ser. A) No. 21 (Aug. 19, 2014).
30. Brewer Carías v. Venezuela, Preliminary Objections, Judgment Inter-Am. Ct. H.R. (ser. C) No. 278 (May 26, 2014).
31. Veliz Franco et al. v. Guatemala, Preliminary Objections, Merits, and Reparations, Judgment, Inter-Am. Ct. H.R. (ser. C) No. 277 (May 19, 2014).
32. Liakat Ali Alibux v. Suriname, Preliminary Objections, Merits, Reparations, and Costs, Judgment, Inter-Am. Ct. H.R. (ser. C) No. 276 (Jan. 30, 2014).
33. J. v. Peru, Preliminary Objections, Merits, Reparations, and Costs, Judgment, Inter-Am. Ct. H.R. (ser. C) No. 275 (Nov. 27, 2013).
34. Osorio Rivera and Family v. Peru, Preliminary Objections, Merits, Reparations, and Costs, Judgment, Inter-Am. Ct. H.R. (ser. C) No. 274 (Nov. 26, 2013).
35. Garcia Cruz and Sanchez Silvestre v. Mexico, Merits, Reparations, and Costs, Judgment, Inter-Am. Ct. H.R. (ser. C) No. 273 (Nov. 26, 2013).
36. Pacheco Tineo Family v. Bolivia, Preliminary Objections, Merits, Reparations, and Costs, Judgment, Inter-Am. Ct. H.R. (ser. C) No. 272 (Nov. 25, 2013).
37. Gutiérrez and Family v. Argentina, Merits, Reparations, and Costs, Judgment, Inter-Am. Ct. H.R. (ser. C) No. 271 (Nov. 25, 2013).
38. Afro-Descendant Communities Displaced From the Cacarica River Basin (Operation Genesis) v. Colombia, Preliminary Objections, Merits, Reparations, and Costs, Judgment, Inter-Am. Ct. H.R. (ser. C) No. 270 (Nov. 20, 2013).
39. Luna Lopez v. Honduras, Merits, Reparations, and Costs, Judgment, Inter-Am. Ct. H.R. (ser. C) No. 269 (Oct. 10, 2013).
40. Constitutional Tribunal (Camba Campos et al.) v. Ecuador, Preliminary Objections, Merits, Reparations, and Costs, Judgment, Inter-Am. Ct. H.R. (ser. C) No. 268 (Aug. 28, 2013).
41. Garcia Lucero et al. v. Chile, Preliminary Objections, Merits, and Reparations, Judgment, Inter-Am. Ct. H.R. (ser. C) No. 267 (Aug. 28, 2013).
42. Supreme Court of Justice (Quintana Coello et al.) v. Ecuador, Preliminary Objections, Merits, Reparations, and Costs, Judgment, Inter-Am. Ct. H.R. (ser. C) No. 266 (Aug. 23, 2013).

43. Memoli v. Argentina, Preliminary Objections, Merits, Reparations, and Costs, Judgment, Inter-Am. Ct. H.R. (ser. C) No. 265 (Aug. 22, 2013).
44. Suárez Peralta v. Ecuador, Preliminary Objections, Merits, Reparations, and Costs, Judgment, Inter-Am. Ct. H.R. (ser. C) No. 261 (May 21, 2013).
45. Mendoza et al. v. Argentina, Preliminary Objections, Merits, and Reparations, Judgment, Inter-Am. Ct. H.R. (ser. C) No. 260 (May 14, 2013).
46. Santo Domingo Massacre v. Colombia, Preliminary Objections, Merits, and Reparations, Judgment, Inter-Am. Ct. H.R. (ser. C) No. 259 (Nov. 30, 2012).
47. García and Family Members v. Guatemala, Merits, Reparations, and Costs, Judgment, Inter-Am. Ct. H.R. (ser. C) No. 258 (Nov. 29, 2012).
48. Castillo González et al. v. Venezuela, Merits, Judgment, Inter-Am. Ct. H.R. (ser. C) No. 256 (Nov. 27, 2012).
49. Mohamed v. Argentina, Preliminary Objections, Merits, Reparations, and Costs, Judgment, Inter-Am. Ct. H.R. (ser. C) No. 255 (Nov. 23, 2012).
50. Gudiel Alvarez et al. ("Diario Militar") v. Guatemala, Merits, Reparations, and Costs, Judgment, Inter-Am. Ct. H.R. (ser. C) No. 253 (Nov. 20, 2012).
51. Massacres of El Mozote and Nearby Places v. El Salvador, Merits, Reparations, and Costs, Judgment, Inter-Am. Ct. H.R. (ser. C) No. 252 (Oct. 25, 2012).
52. Nadege Dorzema et al. v. Dominican Republic, Merits, Reparations, and Costs, Judgment, Inter-Am. Ct. H.R. (ser. C) No. 251 (Oct. 24, 2012).
53. Río Negro Massacres v. Guatemala, Preliminary Objections, Merits, Reparations, and Costs, Judgment, Inter-Am. Ct. H.R. (ser. C) No. 250 (Sept. 4, 2012).
54. Uzcátegui et al. v. Venezuela, Merits and Reparations, Judgment, Inter-Am. Ct. H.R. (ser. C) No. 249 (Sept. 3, 2012).
55. Vélez Restrepo and Family v. Colombia, Preliminary Objections, Merits, Reparations, and Costs, Judgment, Inter-Am. Ct. H.R. (ser. C) No. 248 (Sept. 3, 2012).
56. Palma Mendoza et al. v. Ecuador, Preliminary Objections and Merits, Judgment, Inter-Am. Ct. H.R. (ser. C) No. 247 (Sept. 3, 2012).
57. Furlan and Family v. Argentina, Preliminary Objections, Merits, Reparations, and Costs, Judgment, Inter-Am. Ct. H.R. (ser. C) No. 246 (Aug. 31, 2012).
58. Kichwa Indigenous People of Sarayaku v. Ecuador, Merits and Reparations, Judgment Inter.-Am. Ct. H.R. (ser. C) No. 245 (June 27, 2012).
59. Díaz Peña v. Venezuela, Preliminary Objections, Merits, Reparations, and Costs, Judgment, Inter-Am. Ct. H.R. (ser. C) No. 244 (June 26, 2012).
60. Fornerón and Daughter v. Argentina, Merits, Reparations, and Costs, Judgment, Inter-Am. Ct. H.R. (ser. C) No. 242 (Apr. 27, 2012).
61. Pacheco Teruel et al. v. Honduras, Merits, Reparations, and Costs, Judgment, Inter-Am. Ct. H.R. (ser. C) No. 241 (Apr. 27, 2012).
62. Gonzalez Medina and Family v. Dominican Republic, Preliminary Objections, Merits, Reparations, and Costs, Judgment, Inter-Am. Ct. H.R. (ser. C) No. 240 (Feb. 27, 2012).
63. Atala Riffo and Daughters v. Chile, Merits, Reparations, and Costs, Judgment, Inter-Am. Ct. H.R. (ser. C) No. 239 (Feb. 24, 2012).
64. Barrios Family v. Venezuela, Merits, Reparations, and Costs, Judgment, Inter-Am. Ct. H.R. (ser. C) No. 237 (Nov. 24, 2011).

65. Lysias Fleury et al. v. Haiti, Merits and Reparations, Judgment, Inter-Am. Ct. H.R. (ser. C) No. 236 (Nov. 23, 2011).
66. Barbani Duarte et al. v. Uruguay, Merits, Reparations, and Costs, Judgment, Inter. Am. Ct. H.R. (ser. C) No. 234 (Oct. 13, 2011).
67. López Mendoza v. Venezuela, Merits, Reparations, and Costs, Judgment,Inter-Am. Ct. H.R. (ser. C) No. 233 (Sept. 1, 2011).
68. Contreras et. al. v. El Salvador, Merits, Reparations, and Costs, Judgment, Inter-Am. Ct. H.R. (ser. C) No. 232 (Aug. 31, 2011).
69. Grande v. Argentina, Preliminary Objections and Merits, Judgment, Inter-Am. Ct. H.R. (ser. C) No. 231 (Aug. 31, 2011).
70. Torres Millacura et al. v. Argentina, Merits, Reparations, and Costs, Judgment, Inter-Am. Ct. H.R. (ser. C) No. 229 (Aug. 26, 2011).
71. Mejía Idrovo v. Ecuador, Preliminary Objections, Merits, Reparations, and Costs, Judgment, Inter-Am. Ct. H.R. (ser. C) No. 228 (July 5, 2011).
72. Chocrón Chocrón v. Venezuela, Preliminary Objections, Merits, Reparations, and Costs, Judgment, Inter-Am. Ct. H.R. (ser. C) No. 227 (July 1, 2011).
73. Vera Vera et al. v. Ecuador, Preliminary Objections, Merits, Reparations, and Costs, Judgment, Inter-Am. Ct. H.R. (ser. C) No. 226 (May 19, 2011).
74. Rosendo Cantu et al. v. Mexico, Interpretation of Judgment of Preliminary Objections, Merits, Reparations, and Costs, Judgment, Inter-Am. Ct. H.R. (ser. C) No. 225 (May 15, 2011).
75. Fernandez Ortega et al. v. Mexico, Interpretation of Judgment of Preliminary Objection, Merits, Reparations, and Costs, Judgment, Inter-Am. Ct. H.R. (ser. C) No. 224 (May 15, 2011).
76. Abrill Alosilla et al. v. Peru, Merits, Reparations, and Costs, Judgment, Inter-Am. Ct. H.R. (ser. C) No. 223 (Mar. 4, 2011).
77. Salvador Chiriboga v. Ecuador, Reparations and Costs, Judgment, Inter-Am. Ct. H.R. (ser. C) No. 222 (Mar. 3, 2011).
78. Gelman v. Uruguay, Merits and Reparations, Judgment, Inter-Am. Ct. H.R. (ser. C) No. 221 (Feb. 24, 2011).
79. Cabrera García and Montiel Flores v. Mexico, Preliminary Objections, Merits, Reparations, and Costs, Judgment, Inter-Am. Ct. H.R. (ser. C) No. 220 (Nov. 26, 2010).
80. Gomes Lund et al. ("Guerrilha do Araguaia") v. Brazil, Preliminary Objections, Merits, Reparations, and Costs, Judgment, Inter-Am. Ct. H.R. (ser. C) No. 219 (Nov. 24, 2010).
81. Vélez Loor v. Panama, Preliminary Objections, Merits, Reparations, and Costs, Judgment, Inter-Am. Ct. H.R. (ser. C) No. 218 (Nov. 23, 2010).
82. Ibsen Cardenas and Ibsen Peña v. Bolivia, Merits, Reparations, and Costs, Judgment, Inter-Am. Ct. H.R. (ser. C) No. 217 (Sept. 1, 2010).
83. Rosendo Cantu et al. v. Mexico, Preliminary Objections, Merits, Reparations, and Costs, Judgment, Inter-Am. Ct. H.R. (ser. C) No. 216 (Aug. 31, 2010).
84. Fernandez Ortega et al. v. Mexico, Preliminary Objections, Merits, Reparations, and Costs, Judgment, Inter-Am. Ct. H.R. (ser. C) No. 215 (Aug. 30, 2010).
85. Xákmok Kásek Indigenous Cmty. v. Paraguay, Merits, Reparations, and Costs, Judgment, Inter-Am. Ct. H.R. (ser. C) No. 214 (Aug. 24, 2010).

86. Cepeda Vargas v. Colombia, Preliminary Objections, Merits, Reparations, and Costs, Judgment, Inter-Am. Ct. H.R. (ser. C.) No. 213 (May 26, 2010).
87. Chitay Nech et al. v. Guatemala, Preliminary Objections, Merits, Reparations, and Costs, Judgment, Inter-Am. Ct. H.R. (ser. C) No. 212 (May 25, 2010).
88. "Las Dos Erres" Massacre v. Guatemala, Preliminary Objections, Merits, Reparations, and Costs, Judgment, Inter-Am. Ct. H.R. (ser. C) No. 211 (Nov. 24, 2009).
89. Acevedo Buendía et al. ("Discharged & Retired Employees of the Office of the Comptroller") v. Peru, Interpretation of the Judgment on the Preliminary Objection, Merits, Reparations, and Costs, Judgment, Inter-Am. Ct. H.R. (ser. C) No. 210 (Nov. 24, 2009).
90. Radilla Pacheco v. Mexico, Preliminary Objections, Merits, Reparations, and Costs, Judgment, Inter-Am. Ct. H.R. (ser. C) No. 209 (Nov. 23, 2009).
91. Escher et al. v. Brazil, Interpretation of the Judgment on Preliminary Objections, Merits, Reparations, and Costs, Judgment, Inter-Am. Ct. H.R. (ser. C) No. 208 (Nov. 20, 2009).
92. Usón Ramírez v. Venezuela, Preliminary Objection, Merits, Reparations, and Costs, Judgment, Inter-Am. Ct. H.R. (ser. C) No. 207 (Nov. 20, 2009).
93. Barreto Leiva v. Venezuela, Merits, Reparations, and Costs, Judgment, Inter-Am. Ct. H.R. (ser. C) No. 206 (Nov. 17, 2009).
94. González et al. ("Cotton Field") v. Mexico, Preliminary Objections, Merits, Reparations, and Costs, Judgment, Inter-Am. Ct. H.R. (ser. C) No. 205 (Nov. 16, 2009).
95. DaCosta Cadogan v. Barbados, Preliminary Objections, Merits, Reparations, and Costs, Judgment, Inter-Am. Ct. H.R. (ser. C) No. 204 (Sept. 24, 2009).
96. Garibaldi v. Brazil, Preliminary Objections, Merits, Reparations, and Costs, Judgment, Inter-Am. Ct. H.R. (ser. C) No. 203 (Sept. 23, 2009).
97. Anzualdo Castro v. Peru, Preliminary Objections, Merits, Reparations, and Costs, Judgment, Inter-Am. Ct. H.R. (ser. C) No. 202 (Sept. 22, 2009).
98. Valle Jaramillo et al. v. Colombia, Interpretation of the Judgment on the Merits, Reparations, and Costs, Judgment, Inter-Am. Ct. H.R. (ser. C) No. 201 (July 7, 2009).
99. Escher et al v. Brazil, Preliminary Objections, Merits, Reparations, and Costs, Judgment, Inter-Am. Ct. H.R. (ser. C) No. 200 (July 6, 2009).
100. Acevedo Buendía et al. ("Discharged & Retired Employees of the Office of the Comptroller") v. Peru, Preliminary Objection, Merits, Reparations, and Costs, Judgment, Inter-Am. Ct. H.R. (ser. C) No. 198 (July 1, 2009).
101. Reverón Trujillo v. Venezuela, Preliminary Objections, Merits, Reparations, and Costs, Judgment, Inter-Am. Ct. H.R. (ser. C) No. 197 (June 30, 2009).
102. Kawas Fernández v. Honduras, Merits, Reparations, and Costs, Judgment, Inter-Am. Ct. H.R. (ser. C) No. 196 (Apr. 3, 2009).
103. Perozo et al. v. Venezuela, Preliminary Objections, Merits, Reparations, and Costs, Judgment, Inter-Am. Ct. H.R. (ser. C) No. 195 (Jan. 28, 2009).
104. Ríos et al. v. Venezuela, Preliminary Objections, Merits, Reparations, and Costs, Judgment, Inter-Am. Ct. H.R. (ser. C) No. 194 (Jan. 28, 2009).
105. Tristán Donoso v. Panama, Preliminary Objections, Merits, Reparations, and Costs, Judgment, Inter-Am. Ct. H.R. (ser. C) No. 193 (Jan. 27, 2009).
106. Valle Jaramillo et al. v. Colombia, Merits, Reparations, and Costs, Judgment, Inter-Am. Ct. H.R. (ser. C) No. 192 (Nov. 27, 2008).

107. Ticona Estrada et al. v. Bolivia, Merits, Reparations, and Costs, Judgment, Inter-Am. Ct. H.R. (ser. C) No. 191 (Nov. 27, 2008).
108. Tiu Tojín v. Guatemala, Merits, Reparations, and Costs, Judgment, Inter-Am. Ct. H.R. (ser. C) No. 190 (Nov. 26, 2008).
109. García Prieto et al. v. El Salvador, Interpretation of the Judgment on Preliminary Objections, Merits, Reparations, and Costs, Judgment, Inter-Am. Ct. H.R. (ser. C) No. 188 (Nov. 24, 2008).
110. Bayarri v. Argentina, Preliminary Objection, Merits, Reparations, and Costs, Judgment, Inter-Am. Ct. H.R. (ser. C) No. 187 (Oct. 30, 2008).
111. Heliodoro Portugal v. Panama, Preliminary Objections, Merits, Reparations, and Costs, Judgment, Inter-Am. Ct. H.R. (ser. C) No. 186 (Aug. 12, 2008).
112. Castañeda Gutman v. Mexico, Preliminary Objections, Merits, Reparations, and Costs, Judgment, Inter-Am. Ct. H.R. (ser. C) No. 184 (Aug. 6, 2008).
113. Albán Cornejo et al. v. Ecuador, Interpretation of the Judgment on Merits, Reparations, and Costs, Judgment, Inter-Am. Ct. H.R. (ser. C) No. 183 (Aug. 5, 2008).
114. Apitz Barbera et al. ("First Court of Administrative Disputes") v. Venezuela, Preliminary Objection, Merits, Reparations, and Costs, Judgment, Inter-Am. Ct. H.R. (ser. C) No. 182 (Aug. 5, 2008).
115. Neptune v. Haiti, Merits, Reparations, and Costs, Judgment, Inter-Am. Ct. H.R. (ser. C) No. 180 (May 6, 2008).
116. Salvador Chiriboga v. Ecuador, Preliminary Objections and Merits, Judgment, Inter-Am. Ct. H.R. (ser. C) No. 179 (May 6, 2008).
117. Kimel v. Argentina, Merits, Reparations, and Costs, Judgment, Inter-Am. Ct. H.R. (ser. C) No. 177 (May 2, 2008).
118. Dismissed Cong. Emp. (Aguado Alfaro et al.) v. Peru, Request for Interpretation of the Judgment on Preliminary Objections, Merits, Reparations, and Costs, Judgment, Inter-Am. Ct. H.R. (ser. C) No. 174 (Nov. 30, 2007).
119. La Cantuta v. Peru, Interpretation of the Judgment on Merits, Reparations, and Costs, Judgment, Inter-Am. Ct. H.R. (ser. C) No. 173 (Nov. 30, 2007).
120. Saramaka People v. Suriname, Preliminary Objections, Merits, Reparations, and Costs, Judgment, Inter-Am. Ct. H.R. (ser. C) No. 172 (Nov. 28, 2007).
121. Albán Cornejo et al. v. Ecuador, Merits, Reparations, and Costs, Judgment, Inter-Am. Ct. H.R. (ser. C) No. 171 (Nov. 22, 2007).
122. Chaparro Álvarez and Lapo Íñiguez v. Ecuador, Preliminary Objections, Merits, Reparations, and Costs, Judgment, Inter-Am. Ct. H.R. (ser. C) No. 170 (Nov. 21, 2007).
123. Boyce et al. v. Barbados, Preliminary Objections, Merits, Reparations, and Costs, Judgment, Inter-Am. Ct. H.R. (ser. C) No. 169 (Nov. 20, 2007).
124. García Prieto et al. v. El Salvador, Preliminary Objections, Merits, Reparations, and Costs, Judgment, Inter-Am. Ct. H.R. (ser. C) No. 168 (Nov. 20, 2007).
125. Cantoral Huamaní and García Santa Cruz v. Peru, Preliminary Objections, Merits, Reparations, and Costs, Judgment, Inter-Am. Ct. H.R. (ser. C) No. 167 (July 10, 2007).
126. Zambrano Vélez et al. v. Ecuador, Merits, Reparations, and Costs, Judgment, Inter-Am. Ct. H.R. (ser. C) No. 166 (July 4, 2007).
127. Escué Zapata v. Colombia, Merits, Reparations, and Costs, Judgment, Inter-Am. Ct. H.R. (ser. C) No. 165 (July 4, 2007).

128. Bueno Alves v. Argentina, Merits, Reparations, and Costs, Judgment, Inter-Am. Ct. H.R. (ser. C) No. 164 (May 11, 2007).
129. Rochela Massacre v. Colombia, Merits, Reparations, and Costs, Judgment, Inter-Am. Ct. H.R. (ser. C) No. 163 (May 11, 2007).
130. La Cantuta v. Peru, Merits, Reparations, and Costs, Judgment, Inter-Am. Ct. H.R. (ser. C) No. 162 (Nov. 29, 2006).
131. Nogueira de Carvalho et al. v. Brazil, Preliminary Objections and Merits, Judgment, Inter-Am. Ct. H.R. (ser. C) No. 161 (Nov. 28, 2006).
132. Miguel Castro Castro Prison v. Peru, Merits, Reparations, and Costs, Judgment, Inter-Am. Ct. H.R. (ser. C) No. 160 (Nov. 25, 2006).
133. Pueblo Bello Massacre v. Colombia, Interpretation of the Judgment of Merits, Reparations, and Costs, Judgment, Inter-Am. Ct. H.R. (ser. C) No. 159 (Nov. 25, 2006).
134. Dismissed Cong. Emp. (Aguado Alfaro et al.) v. Peru, Preliminary Objections, Merits, Reparations, and Costs, Judgment, Inter-Am. Ct H.R. (ser. C) No. 158 (Nov. 24, 2006).
135. Vargas Areco v. Paraguay, Merits, Reparations, and Costs, Judgment, Inter-Am. Ct. H.R. (ser. C) No. 155 (Sept. 26, 2006).
136. Almonacid Arellano et al. v. Chile, Preliminary Objections, Merits, Reparations, and Costs, Judgment, Inter-Am. Ct. H.R. (ser. C) No. 154 (Sept. 26, 2006).
137. Goiburú et al. v. Paraguay, Merits, Reparations, and Costs, Judgment, Inter-Am. Ct. H.R. (ser. C) No. 153 (Sept. 22, 2006).
138. Servellón García et al. v. Honduras, Merits, Reparations, and Costs, Judgment, Inter-Am. Ct. H.R. (ser. C) No. 152 (Sept. 21, 2006).
139. Claude Reyes et al. v. Chile, Merits, Reparations, and Costs, Judgment, Inter-Am. Ct. H.R. (ser. C) No. 151 (Sept. 19, 2006).
140. Montero Aranguren et al. (Det. Ctr. of Catia) v. Venezuela, Preliminary Objection, Merits, Reparations, and Costs, Judgment, Inter-Am. Ct. H.R. (ser. C) No. 150 (July 5, 2006).
141. Ximenes Lopes v. Brazil, Merits, Reparations, and Costs, Judgment, Inter-Am. Ct. H.R. (ser. C) No. 149 (July 4, 2006).
142. Ituango Massacres v. Colombia, Preliminary Objections, Merits, Reparations, and Costs, Judgment, Inter-Am. Ct. H.R. (ser. C) No. 148 (July 1, 2006).
143. Baldeón García v. Peru, Merits, Reparations, and Costs, Judgment, Inter-Am. Ct. H.R. (ser. C) No. 147 (Apr. 6, 2006).
144. Sawhoyamaxa Indigenous Cmty. v. Paraguay, Merits, Reparations, and Costs, Judgment, Inter-Am. Ct. H.R. (ser. C) No. 146 (Mar. 29, 2006).
145. Moiwana Cmty. v. Suriname, Interpretation of the Judgment of Merits, Reparations, and Costs, Judgment, Inter-Am. Ct. H.R. (ser. C) No. 145 (Feb. 8, 2006).
146. Acevedo Jaramillo et al. v. Peru, Preliminary Objections, Merits, Reparations, and Costs, Judgment, Inter-Am. Ct. H.R. (ser. C) No. 144 (Feb. 7, 2006).
147. Raxcacó Reyes v. Guatemala, Interpretation of the Judgment of Merits, Reparations, and Costs, Judgment, Inter-Am. Ct. H.R. (ser. C) No. 143 (Feb. 6, 2006).
148. Yakye Axa Indigenous Cmty. v. Paraguay, Interpretation of the Judgment of Merits, Reparations, and Costs, Judgment, Inter-Am. Ct. H.R. (ser. C) No. 142 (Feb. 6, 2006).
149. López Álvarez v. Honduras, Merits, Reparations, and Costs, Judgment, Inter-Am. Ct. H.R. (ser. C) No. 141 (Feb. 1, 2006).
150. Pueblo Bello Massacre v. Colombia, Merits, Reparations, and Costs, Judgment, Inter-Am. Ct. H.R. (ser. C) No. 140 (Jan. 31, 2006).

151. Ximenes Lopes v. Brazil, Preliminary Objections, Judgment, Inter-Am. Ct. H.R. (ser. C) No. 139 (Nov. 30, 2005).
152. Blanco Romero et al. v. Venezuela, Merits, Reparations, and Costs, Judgment, Inter-Am. Ct. H.R. (ser. C) No. 138 (Nov. 28, 2005).
153. García Asto and Ramírez Rojas v. Peru, Preliminary Objection, Merits, Reparations, and Costs, Judgment, Inter-Am. Ct. H.R. (ser. C) No. 137 (Nov. 25, 2005).
154. Gómez Palomino v. Peru, Merits, Reparations, and Costs, Judgment, Inter-Am. Ct. H.R. (ser. C) No. 136 (Nov. 22, 2005).
155. Palamara Iribarne v. Chile, Merits, Reparations, Costs, Judgment, Inter-Am. Ct. H.R. (ser. C) No. 135 (Nov. 22, 2005).
156. Mapiripán Massacre v. Colombia, Merits, Reparations, and Costs, Judgment, Inter-Am. Ct. H.R. (ser. C) No. 134 (Sept. 15, 2005).
157. Raxcacó Reyes v. Guatemala, Merits, Reparations, and Costs, Judgment, Inter-Am. Ct. H.R. (ser. C) No. 133 (Sept. 15, 2005).
158. Gutiérrez Soler v. Colombia, Merits, Reparations, and Costs, Judgment, Inter-Am. Ct. H.R. (ser. C) No. 132 (Sept. 12, 2005).
159. Serrano Cruz Sisters v. El Salvador, Interpretation of the Judgment of Merits, Reparations, and Costs, Judgment, Inter-Am. Ct. H.R. (ser. C) No. 131 (Sept. 9, 2005).
160. Yean and Bosico v. Dominican Republic, Preliminary Objections, Merits, Reparations, and Costs, Judgment, Inter-Am. Ct. H.R. (ser. C) No. 130 (Sept. 8, 2005).
161. Acosta Calderón v. Ecuador, Merits, Reparations, and Costs, Judgment, Inter-Am. Ct. H.R. (ser. C) No. 129 (June 24, 2005).
162. YATAMA v. Nicaragua, Preliminary Objections, Merits, Reparations, and Costs, Judgment, Inter-Am. Ct. H.R. (ser. C) No. 127 (June 23, 2005).
163. Fermín Ramírez v. Guatemala, Merits, Reparations, and Costs, Judgment, Inter-Am. Ct. H.R. (ser. C) No. 126 (June 20, 2005).
164. Yakye Axa Indigenous Cmty. v. Paraguay, Merits, Reparations, and Costs, Judgment, Inter-Am. Ct. H.R. (ser. C) No. 125 (June 17, 2005).
165. Moiwana Cmty. v. Suriname, Preliminary Objections, Merits, Reparations, and Costs, Judgment, Inter-Am. Ct. H.R. (ser. C) No. 124 (June 15, 2005).
166. Caesar v. Trinidad & Tobago, Merits, Reparations, and Costs, Judgment, Inter-Am. Ct. H.R. (ser. C) No. 123 (Mar. 11, 2005).
167. Mapiripán Massacre v. Colombia, Preliminary Objections, Judgment, Inter-Am. Ct. H.R. (ser. C) No. 122 (Mar. 7, 2005).
168. Huilca Tecse v. Peru, Merits, Reparations, and Costs, Judgment, Inter-Am. Ct. H.R. (ser. C) No. 121 (Mar. 3, 2005).
169. Serrano Cruz Sisters v. El Salvador, Merits, Reparations, and Costs, Judgment, Inter-Am. Ct. H.R. (ser. C) No. 120 (Mar. 1, 2005).
170. Serrano Cruz Sisters v. El Salvador, Preliminary Objections, Judgment, Inter-Am. Ct. H.R. (ser. C) No. 118 (Nov. 23, 2004).
171. Carpio Nicolle et al. v. Guatemala, Merits, Reparations, and Costs, Judgment, Inter-Am. Ct. H.R. (ser. C) No. 117 (Nov. 22, 2004).
172. Plan de Sánchez Massacre v. Guatemala, Reparations, Judgment, Inter-Am. Ct. H.R. (ser. C) No. 116 (Nov. 19, 2004).
173. Tibi v. Ecuador, Preliminary Objections, Merits, Reparations, and Costs, Judgment, Inter-Am. Ct. H.R. (ser. C) No. 114 (Sept. 7, 2004).

174. Campo Dodd v. Mexico, Preliminary Objections, Judgment, Inter-Am. Ct. H.R. (ser. C) No. 113 (Sept. 3, 2004).
175. "Juvenile Reeducation Institute" v. Paraguay, Preliminary Objections, Merits, Reparations, and Costs, Judgment, Inter-Am. Ct. H.R. (ser. C) No. 112 (Sept. 2, 2004).
176. Gómez Paquiyauri Brothers v. Peru, Merits, Reparations, and Costs, Judgment, Inter-Am. Ct. H.R. (ser. C) No. 110 (July 8, 2004).
177. 19 Merchants v. Colombia, Merits, Reparations, and Costs, Judgment, Inter-Am. Ct. H.R. (ser. C) No. 109 (July 5, 2004).
178. Molina Theissen v. Guatemala, Reparations and Costs, Judgment, Inter-Am. Ct. H.R. (ser. C) No. 108 (July 3, 2004).
179. Herrera Ulloa v. Costa Rica, Preliminary Objections, Merits, Reparations, and Costs, Judgment, Inter-Am. Ct. H.R. (ser. C) No. 107 (July 2, 2004).
180. Molina Theissen v. Guatemala, Merits, Judgment, Inter-Am. Ct. H.R. (ser. C) No. 106 (May 4, 2004).
181. Plan de Sánchez Massacre v. Guatemala, Merits, Judgment, Inter-Am. Ct. H.R. (ser. C) No. 105 (Apr. 29, 2004).
182. Baena Ricardo et al. v. Panama, Competence, Judgment, Inter-Am. Ct. H.R. (ser. C) No. 104 (Nov. 28, 2003).
183. Maritza Urrutia v. Guatemala, Merits, Reparations, and Costs, Judgment, Inter-Am. Ct. H.R. (ser. C) No. 103 (Nov. 27, 2003).
184. Sánchez v. Honduras, Interpretation of the Judgment of Preliminary Objection, Merits, and Reparations, Judgment, Inter-Am. Ct. H.R. (ser. C) No. 102 (Nov. 26, 2003).
185. Mack Chang v. Guatemala, Merits, Reparations, and Costs, Judgment, Inter-Am. Ct. H.R. (ser. C) No. 101 (Nov. 25, 2003).
186. Bulacio v. Argentina, Merits, Reparations, and Costs, Judgment, Inter-Am. Ct. H.R. (ser. C) No. 100 (Sept. 18, 2003).
187. Sánchez v. Honduras, Preliminary Objection, Merits, Reparations, and Costs, Judgment, Inter-Am. Ct. H.R. (ser. C) No. 99 (June 7, 2003).
188. "Five Pensioners" v. Peru, Merits, Reparations, and Costs, Judgment, Inter-Am. Ct. H.R. (ser. C) No. 98 (Feb. 28, 2003).
189. Cantos v. Argentina, Merits, Reparations, and Costs, Judgment, Inter-Am. Ct. H.R. (ser. C) No. 97 (Nov. 28, 2002).
190. Las Palmeras v. Colombia, Reparations and Costs, Judgment, Inter-Am. Ct. H.R. (ser. C) No. 96 (Nov. 26, 2002).
191. Caracazo v. Venezuela, Reparations and Costs, Judgment, Inter-Am. Ct. H.R. (ser. C) No. 95 (Aug. 29, 2002).
192. Juridical Condition & Human Rights of the Child, Advisory Opinion OC-17/02, Inter-Am. Ct. H.R. (ser. A) No. 17 (Aug. 28, 2002).
193. Hilaire, Constantine, and Benjamin et al. v. Trinidad & Tobago, Merits, Reparations, and Costs, Judgment, Inter-Am. Ct. H.R. (ser. C) No. 94 (June 21, 2002).
194. 19 Merchants v. Colombia, Preliminary Objection, Judgment, Inter-Am. Ct. H.R. (ser. C) No. 93 (June 12, 2002).
195. Trujillo Oroza v. Bolivia, Reparations and Costs, Judgment, Inter-Am. Ct. H.R. (ser. C) No. 92 (Feb. 27, 2002).
196. Bámaca Velásquez v. Guatemala, Reparations and Costs, Judgment, Inter-Am. Ct. H.R. (ser. C) No. 91 (Feb. 22, 2002).

197. Las Palmeras v. Colombia, Merits, Judgment, Inter-Am. Ct. H.R. (Ser. C) No. 90 (Dec. 6, 2001).
198. Durand and Ugarte v. Peru, Reparations and Costs, Judgment, Inter-Am. Ct. H.R. (ser. C) No. 89 (Dec. 3, 2001).
199. Cantoral Benavides v. Peru, Reparations and Costs, Judgment, Inter-Am. Ct. H.R. (ser. C) No. 88 (Dec. 3, 2001).
200. Barrios Altos v. Peru, Reparations and Costs, Judgment, Inter-Am. Ct. H.R. (ser. C) No. 87 (Nov. 30, 2001).
201. Cantos v. Argentina, Preliminary Objections, Judgment, Inter-Am. Ct. H.R. (ser. C) No. 85 (Sept. 7, 2001).
202. Barrios Altos v. Peru, Interpretation of the Judgment of Merits, Judgment, Inter-Am. Ct. H.R. (ser. C) No. 83 (Sept. 3, 2001).
203. Constantine et al. v. Trinidad & Tobago, Preliminary Objections, Judgment, Inter-Am. Ct. H.R. (ser. C) No. 82 (Sept. 1, 2001).
204. Benjamin et al. v. Trinidad & Tobago, Preliminary Objections, Judgment, Inter-Am. Ct. H.R. (ser. C) No. 81 (Sept. 1, 2001).
205. Hilaire v. Trinidad & Tobago, Preliminary Objections, Judgment, Inter-Am. Ct. H.R. (ser. C) No. 80 (Sept. 1, 2001).
206. Mayagna (Sumo) Awas Tingni Cmty. v. Nicaragua, Merits, Reparations, and Costs, Judgment, Inter-Am. Ct. H.R. (ser. C) No. 79 (Aug. 31, 2001).
207. Cesti Hurtado v. Peru, Reparations and Costs, 2001 Inter-Am. Ct. H.R. (ser. C) No. 78 (May 31, 2001).
208. "Street Children" (Villagrán Morales et al.) v. Guatemala, Reparations and Costs, Judgment, Inter-Am. Ct. H.R. (ser. C) No. 77 (May 26, 2001).
209. "White Van" (Paniagua Morales et al.) v. Guatemala, Reparations and Costs, Judgment, Inter-Am. Ct. H.R. (ser. C) No. 76 (May 25, 2001).
210. Barrios Altos v. Peru, Merits, Judgment, Inter-Am. Ct. H.R. (ser. C) No. 75 (Mar. 14, 2001).
211. Ivcher Bronstein v. Peru, Merits, Reparations, and Costs, Judgment, Inter-Am. Ct. H.R. (ser. C) No. 74 (Feb. 6, 2001).
212. Baena Ricardo et al. v. Panama, Merits, Reparations, and Costs, Judgment, Inter-Am. Ct. H.R. (ser. C) No. 72 (Feb. 2, 2001).
213. Constitutional Court v. Peru, Merits, Reparations, and Costs, Judgment, Inter-Am. Ct. H.R. (ser. C) No. 71 (Jan. 31, 2001).
214. Bámaca Velásquez v. Guatemala, Merits, Judgment, Inter-Am. Ct. H.R. (ser. C) No. 70 (Nov. 25, 2000).
215. Cantoral Benavides v. Peru, Merits, Judgment, Inter-Am. Ct. H.R. (ser. C) No. 69 (Aug. 18, 2000).
216. Durand and Ugarte v. Peru, Merits, Judgment, Inter-Am. Ct. H.R. (ser. C) No. 68 (Aug. 16, 2000).
217. Las Palmeras v. Colombia, Preliminary Objections, Judgment, Inter-Am. Ct. H.R. (ser. C) No. 67 (Feb. 4, 2000).
218. Mayagna (Sumo) Awas Tingni Cmty. v. Nicaragua, Preliminary Objections, Judgment, Inter-Am. Ct. H.R. (ser. C) No. 66 (Feb. 1, 2000).
219. Cesti Hurtado v. Peru, Interpretation of the Judgment of Merits, Judgment, Inter-Am. Ct. H.R. (ser. C) No. 65 (Jan. 29, 2000).

220. Trujillo Oroza v. Bolivia, Merits, Judgment, Inter-Am. Ct. H.R. (ser. C) No. 64 (Jan. 26, 2000).
221. "Street Children" (Villagrán Morales et al.) v. Guatemala, Merits, Judgment, Inter-Am. Ct. H.R. (ser. C) No. 63 (Nov. 19, 1999).
222. Cesti Hurtado v. Peru, Request for Interpretation of the Judgment of Merits, Order of the Court, Inter-Am. Ct. H.R. (ser. C) No. 62 (Nov. 19, 1999).
223. Baena Ricardo et al. v. Panama, Preliminary Objections, Judgment, Inter-Am. Ct. H.R. (ser. C) No. 61 (Nov. 18, 1999).
224. Caracazo v. Venezuela, Merits, Judgment, Inter-Am. Ct. H.R. (ser. C) No. 58 (Nov. 11, 1999).
225. Cesti Hurtado v. Peru, Merits, Judgment, Inter-Am. Ct. H.R. (ser. C) No. 56 (Sept. 29, 1999).
226. Constitutional Court v. Peru, Competence, Judgment, Inter-Am. Ct. H.R. (ser. C) No. 55 (Sept. 24, 1999).
227. Ivcher Bronstein v. Peru, Competence, Judgment, Inter-Am. Ct. H.R. (ser. C) No. 54 (Sept. 24, 1999).
228. Castillo Petruzzi et al. v. Peru, Merits, Reparations, and Costs, Judgment, Inter-Am. Ct. H.R. (ser. C) No. 52 (May 30, 1999).
229. Durand and Ugarte v. Peru, Preliminary Objections, Judgment, Inter-Am. Ct. H.R. (ser. C) No. 50 (May 28, 1999).
230. Cesti Hurtado v. Peru, Preliminary Objections, Judgment, Inter-Am. Ct. H.R. (ser. C) No. 49 (Jan. 26, 1999).
231. Blake v. Guatemala, Reparations and Costs, Judgment, Inter-Am. Ct. H.R. (ser. C) No. 48 (Jan. 22, 1999).
232. Loayza Tamayo v. Peru, Interpretation of the Judgment of Merits, Order of the Court, Inter-Am. Ct. H.R. (ser. C) No. 47 (Mar. 8, 1998).
233. Genie Lacayo v. Nicaragua, Application for Judicial Review of the Judgment of Merits, Reparations, and Costs, Order of the Court, Inter-Am. Ct. H.R. (ser. C) No. 45 (Sept. 13, 1997).
234. Suárez Rosero v. Ecuador, Reparations and Costs, Judgment, Inter-Am. Ct. H.R. (ser. C) No. 44 (Jan. 20, 1999).
235. Castillo Páez v. Peru, Reparations and Costs, Judgment, Inter-Am. Ct. H.R. (ser. C) No. 43 (Nov. 27, 1998).
236. Loayza Tamayo v. Peru, Reparations and Costs, Judgment, Inter-Am. Ct. H.R. (ser. C) No. 42 (Nov. 27, 1998).
237. Castillo Petruzzi et al. v. Peru, Preliminary Objections, Judgment, Inter-Am. Ct. H.R. (ser. C) No. 41 (Sept. 4, 1998).
238. Cantoral Benavides v. Peru, Preliminary Objections, Judgment, Inter-Am. Ct. H.R. (ser. C) No. 40 (Sept. 3, 1998).
239. Garrido and Baigorria v. Argentina, Reparations and Costs, Judgment, Inter-Am. Ct. H.R. (ser. C) No. 39 (Aug. 27, 1998).
240. Benavides Cevallos v. Ecuador, Merits, Reparations, and Costs, Judgment, Inter-Am. Ct. H.R. (ser. C) No. 38 (June 19, 1998).
241. "White Van" (Paniagua Morales et al.) v. Guatemala, Merits, Judgment, Inter-Am. Ct. H.R. (ser. C) No. 37 (Mar. 8, 1998).
242. Blake v. Guatemala, Merits, Judgment, Inter-Am. Ct. H.R. (ser. C) No. 36 (Jan. 24, 1998).

243. Suárez Rosero v. Ecuador, Merits, Judgment, Inter-Am. Ct. H.R. (ser. C) No. 35 (Nov. 12, 1997).
244. Castillo Páez v. Peru, Merits, Judgment, Inter-Am. Ct. H.R. (ser. C) No. 34 (Nov. 3, 1997).
245. Loayza Tamayo v. Peru, Merits, Judgment, Inter-Am. Ct. H.R. (ser. C) No. 33 (Sept. 17, 1997).
246. "Street Children" (Villagrán Morales et al.) v. Guatemala, Preliminary Objections, Judgment, Inter-Am. Ct. H.R. (ser. C) No. 32 (Sept. 11, 1997).
247. Caballero Delgado and Santana v. Colombia, Reparations and Costs, Judgment, Inter-Am. Ct. H.R. (ser. C) No. 31 (Jan. 29, 1997).
248. Genie Lacayo v. Nicaragua, Merits, Reparations, and Costs, Judgment, Inter-Am. Ct. H.R. (ser. C) No. 30 (Jan. 29, 1997).
249. Neira Alegría et al. v. Peru, Reparations and Costs, Judgment, Inter-Am. Ct. H.R. (ser. C) No. 29 (Sept. 19, 1996).
250. El Amparo v. Venezuela, Reparations and Costs, Judgment, Inter-Am. Ct. H.R. (ser. C) No. 28 (Sept. 14, 1996).
251. Blake v. Guatemala, Preliminary Objections, Judgment, Inter-Am. Ct. H.R. (ser. C) No. 27 (July 2, 1996).
252. Garrido and Baigorria v. Argentina, Merits, Judgment, Inter-Am. Ct. H.R. (ser. C) No. 26 (Feb. 2, 1996).
253. Loayza Tamayo v. Peru, Preliminary Objections, Judgment, Inter-Am. Ct. H.R. (ser. C) No. 25 (Jan. 31, 1996).
254. Castillo Páez v. Peru, Preliminary Objections, Judgment, Inter-Am. Ct. H.R. (ser. C) No. 24 (Jan. 30, 1996).
255. "White Van" (Paniagua Morales et al.) v. Guatemala, Preliminary Objections, Judgment, Inter-Am. Ct. H.R. (ser. C) No. 23 (Jan. 25, 1996).
256. Caballero Delgado and Santana v. Colombia, Merits, Judgment, Inter-Am. Ct. H.R. (ser. C) No. 22 (Dec. 8, 1995).
257. Genie Lacayo v. Nicaragua, Preliminary Objections, Judgment, Inter-Am. Ct. H.R. (ser. C) No. 21 (Jan. 27, 1995).
258. Neira Alegría et al. v. Peru, Merits, Judgment, Inter-Am. Ct. H.R. (ser. C) No. 20 (Jan. 19, 1995).
259. El Amparo v. Venezuela, Merits, Judgment, Inter-Am. Ct. H.R. (ser. C) No. 19 (Jan. 18, 1995).
260. Maqueda v. Argentina, Preliminary Objections, Order of the Court, Inter-Am. Ct. H.R. (ser. C) No. 18 (Jan. 17, 1995).
261. Caballero Delgado and Santana v. Colombia, Preliminary Objections, Judgment, Inter-Am. Ct. H.R. (ser. C) No. 17 (Jan. 21, 1994).
262. Gangaram Panday v. Suriname, Merits, Reparations, and Costs, Judgment, Inter-Am. Ct. H.R. (ser. C) No. 16 (Jan. 21, 1994).
263. Aloeboetoe et al. v. Suriname, Reparations and Costs, Judgment, Inter-Am. Ct. H.R. (ser. C) No. 15 (Sept. 10, 1993).
264. Certain Attributes of the Inter-American Commission on Human Rights (Arts. 41, 42, 44, 46, 47, 50, and 51 of the American Convention on Human Rights), Advisory Opinion OC-13/93, Inter-Am. Ct. H.R. (ser. A) No. 13 (July 16, 1993).
265. Cayara v. Peru, Preliminary Objections, Judgment, Inter-Am. Ct. H.R. (ser. C) No. 14 (Feb. 3, 1993).

266. Neira Alegría et al. v. Peru, Preliminary Objections, Judgment, Inter-Am. Ct. H.R. (ser. C) No. 13 (Dec. 11, 1991).
267. Gangaram Panday v. Suriname, Preliminary Objections, Judgment, Inter-Am. Ct. H.R. (ser. C) No. 12 (Dec. 4, 1991).
268. Aloeboetoe et al. v. Suriname, Merits, Judgment, Inter-Am. Ct. H.R. (ser. C) No. 11 (Dec. 4, 1991).
269. Judicial Guarantees in States of Emergency (Arts. 27(2), 25, and 8 American Convention on Human Rights), Advisory Opinion OC-9/87, Inter-Am. Ct. H.R. (ser. A) No. 9 (Oct. 6, 1987).
270. Habeas Corpus in Emergency Situations (Arts. 27(2), 25(1), and 7(6) American Convention on Human Rights), Advisory Opinion OC-8/87, Inter-Am. Ct. H.R. (ser. A) No. 8 (Jan. 30, 1987).

ARTICLE 26: PROGRESSIVE DEVELOPMENT

1. Gonzales Lluy et al. v. Ecuador, Preliminary Objections, Merits, Reparations and Costs, Judgment, Inter-Am. Ct. H.R. (ser. C) No. 298 (Sept. 1, 2015).
2. Rights & Guar. of Children in the Context of Migration and/or in Need of Int'l Prot., Advisory Opinion OC-21/14, Inter-Am. Ct. H.R. (ser. A) No. 21 (Aug. 19, 2014). [footnote]
3. Pacheco Tineo Family v. Bolivia, Preliminary Objections, Merits, Reparations, and Costs, Judgment, Inter-Am. Ct. H.R. (ser. C) No. 272 (Nov. 25, 2013).
4. Mendoza et al. v. Argentina, Preliminary Objections, Merits, and Reparations, Judgment, Inter-Am. Ct. H.R. (ser. C) No. 260 (May 14, 2013). [footnote]
5. Furlan and Family v. Argentina, Preliminary Objections, Merits, Reparations, and Costs, Judgment, Inter-Am. Ct. H.R. (ser. C) No. 246 (Aug. 31, 2012).
6. Kichwa Indigenous People of Sarayaku v. Ecuador, Merits and Reparations, Judgment Inter.-Am. Ct. H.R. (ser. C) No. 245 (June 27, 2012).
7. Torres Millacura et al. v. Argentina, Merits, Reparations, and Costs, Judgment, Inter-Am. Ct. H.R. (ser. C) No. 229 (Aug. 26, 2011).
8. Acevedo Buendía et al. ("Discharged & Retired Employees of the Office of the Comptroller") v. Peru, Preliminary Objection, Merits, Reparations, and Costs, Judgment, Inter-Am. Ct. H.R. (ser. C) No. 198 (July 1, 2009).
9. Dismissed Cong. Emp. (Aguado Alfaro et al.) v. Peru, Preliminary Objections, Merits, Reparations, and Costs, Judgment, Inter-Am. Ct H.R. (ser. C) No. 158 (Nov. 24, 2006).
10. Acevedo Jaramillo et al. v. Peru, Preliminary Objections, Merits, Reparations, and Costs, Judgment, Inter-Am. Ct. H.R. (ser. C) No. 144 (Feb. 7, 2006).
11. Yean and Bosico v. Dominican Republic, Preliminary Objections, Merits, Reparations, and Costs, Judgment, Inter-Am. Ct. H.R. (ser. C) No. 130 (Sept. 8, 2005).
12. Yakye Axa Indigenous Cmty. v. Paraguay, Merits, Reparations, and Costs, Judgment, Inter-Am. Ct. H.R. (ser. C) No. 125 (June 17, 2005).
13. "Juvenile Reeducation Institute" v. Paraguay, Preliminary Objections, Merits, Reparations, and Costs, Judgment, Inter-Am. Ct. H.R. (ser. C) No. 112 (Sept. 2, 2004).
14. "Five Pensioners" v. Peru, Merits, Reparations, and Costs, Judgment, Inter-Am. Ct. H.R. (ser. C) No. 98 (Feb. 28, 2003).

Index

abortion, 60, 73–75. *See also* "conception"; reproductive rights
access to justice, right of, 224–25
access to information, right of, 241–42
Acevedo Buendía et al. *v. Peru*, 223, 277
Acosta Calderón v. Ecuador, 151, 158, 163, 166, 219
Additional Protocol to the American Convention on Human Rights in the area of Economic, Social, and Cultural Rights. *See* Protocol of San Salvador
African Charter on Human and Peoples' Rights (African Charter), 22, 34, 57, 58, 103, 141, 218, 231, 265, 288n9
African Court of Justice and Human Rights, 288
Afro-Descendant Communities Displaced from the Cacarica River v. Colombia, 88, 115
Aguado Alfaro et al. *v. Peru*, 219
Albán Cornejo et al. *v. Ecuador*, 193
American Convention on Human Rights. *See also specific topics*
  outline, 6–7
American Declaration on the Rights and Duties of Man, 5–7, 9, 10, 74, 231, 260n235, 265
amnesty laws, 3, 25, 67, 95
amparo, 218–20. *See also* judicial protection
  Article 7(6) and, 167–68, 216
  Article 25 and, 25, 168, 216, 217, 225, 227, 228
  Cecilia Medina on, 220, 225
  central function, 216
  habeas corpus and, 25, 167–68, 221, 227
  overview, 25, 216
anonymous witnesses, testimony of
  used in prosecutions, 205–6
Apitz Barbera et al. *v. Venezuela*, 37, 40, 44, 193, 311
appeal, right to, 208–11
Arab Charter on Human Rights (Arab Charter), 34, 57–59, 103, 218, 231, 265
arbitrariness principle, 156–57. *See also* liberty, general requirements to deprive
arbitrary deprivation of life, 75. *See also under* life, right to
  of imprisoned individuals, 89–92
arbitrary detention, pretrial detention as, 157–60
armed forces, honor and reputation of, 252–53
Artavia Murillo et al. *v. Costa Rica*, 21, 57, 72–75
Article 1 (Obligation to Respect Rights), 20
  Article 1(1), 18, 20, 36n25, 40, 61, 225–26, 301
  Article 24 and, 36–40

Article 2 (Domestic Legal Effects), 66, 155, 273n68
Article 4 (Right to Life), 21–22, 57–59, 130n208. *See also* life, right to
  Article 4(1), 61, 72
  background, 59–61
  scope of protection, 72–100
Article 5 (Right to Humane Treatment), 22–23, 89, 103–5, 211. *See also* humane treatment, right to
  Article 5(3) (no extension of punishment beyond the convicted individual), 132
  Article 5(4) (separate location and treatment for unconvicted persons in detention), 132–34
  Article 5(5) (separate proceedings and facilities for children in criminal justice system), 134–35
  Article 5(6) ("reform and social readaptation" of prisoners), 135–37
  background, 105–6
  scope of protection, 106–32
    violations to personal integrity below the threshold of Article 5(2), 127–30
  State obligations to ensure the rights of, 130–32
Article 7 (Right to Personal Liberty), 23–24, 141–42. *See also* liberty, right to personal
  Article 7(2), Court's increasing reluctance to find violations of, 154–55
  Article 7(4) (reasons for detention and notification of charges), 162–64
  Article 7(5) (judicial supervision), 164–67
  Article 7(6) (right to habeas corpus), 167–69, 216
  Article 7(7) (no one shall be detained for debt), 143, 169
  background, 142–43
  Inter-American Commission on Human Rights (IACHR) and, 131, 144–45, 157, 159
  requirements of paragraphs 4, 5, and 6, 162–69
  scope of protection, 143–69
Article 8 (Right to a Fair Trial), 174. *See also* due process; trial, right to a (fair)
  Article 8(1), 178–94
  Article 8(2) and the right to be presumed innocent, 194–96
    Article 8(2)(a) (right to be assisted by a translator or interpreter), 196–97
    Article 8(2)(b) (prior notification in detail of charges), 197–99
    Article 8(2)(c) (adequate time and means for preparation of defense), 199–200
    Article 8(2)(d) (rights to defend oneself, to counsel, and to communicate with counsel), 200–202
    Article 8(2)(e) (right to be assisted by counsel provided by State), 199, 201–4
    Article 8(2)(f) (right of defense to present and examine witnesses), 204–6
    Article 8(2)(g) (right not to be compelled to be a witness against oneself), 206–8
    Article 8(2)(h) (right to appeal a judgment to a higher court), 208–11
  Article 8(3) (coercion and confessions), 206–8
  Article 8(4) (prohibition against double jeopardy), 211–13
  Article 8(5) (public criminal proceedings), 213–14
  background, 177–78
  combining Article 25 and, 225–27
  meaning of "competent, independent, and impartial tribunal, previously established by law," 188–94
  similarities among human rights treaties, 174–76
  variances among human rights systems, 176–77
Article 9 (Freedom from Ex Post Facto Laws), 6n23
Article 11 (Right to Privacy), 119
Article 13 (Freedom of Thought and Expression), 25–26, 231–34. *See also* freedom of expression
  Article 13(1), cases of persecution leading to violations of, 259–60
  Article 13(5), 260–61
  background, 234–35
  scope of protection, 235–42
    the meaning of "everyone," 235–36
Article 21 (Right to Property), 26–27, 265–66. *See also* property, right to
  background, 267–68
  scope of protection, 268–73
Article 24 (Right to Equal Protection), 20–21, 32–35
  Article 1 and, 36–40
  background, 35–36
  scope of protection, 36–53

Article 25 (Right to Judicial Protection), 25, 216–18
Article 25(1) (simple, prompt, and effective remedies)
"effective" remedies, 220–22
"simple" and "prompt" remedies, 218–20
Article 25(2) (enforcement of national judgments), 216, 223
background, 216–18
the Court's current, broader view of, 227–28
Article 26 (Progressive Development), 6
Article 27 (Suspension of Guarantees), 83, 152
Article 29 (Restrictions Regarding Interpretation), 15, 15n87
Article 30 (Scope of Restrictions), 276
Article 63, 12, 19–20, 287–89. *See also* reparations
Article 63(2), provisional measures, 314–16
background, 289–90
the "injured" party of Article 63(1) and related topics, 290–92
asylum seekers, 81n189, 182, 182n77
Atala Riffo and Daughters v. Chile, 239
Article 24 and, 37, 50, 52
and the court's current approach to discrimination, 37, 49–53
attorney, right to an. *See* counsel

Bámaca Velázquez v. Guatemala, 86–87
Barreto Leiva v. Venezuela, 199–201
Bayarri v. Argentina, 110, 112, 131, 145n41, 161, 165, 167, 168, 219–20, 226
Belém do Pará, Convention of. *See* Convention of Belém do Pará
Benham v. The United Kingdom, 175
Berenson Mejía v. Peru, 212–14
Blake v. Guatemala, 94–96
Boyce et al. *v. Barbados*, 80n180, 121, 125
Brewer Carías, Allan, 219
Bronstein, Ivcher, 194, 257–58
Bueno Alves v. Argentina, 112

Cabrera García and Montiel Flores v. Mexico, 208n288
Caesar v. Trinidad and Tobago, 120
Caldas, Roberto, 239n71
Camba Campos et al. *v. Ecuador*, 190
Cançado Trindade, Antonio, 16n100, 94–95, 312n196
Canese v. Paraguay, 205, 238n63, 253
Cantoral Benavides v. Peru, 118n113, 214, 304
Cantos, José María, 301
capital punishment. *See* death penalty; executions
Castillo Páez v. Peru, 222
Castillo Petruzzi et al. *v. Peru*, 194, 199, 201, 209, 305
Castro Castro Prison v. Peru. *See Miguel Castro Castro Prison v. Peru*
censorship
defined, 244–47
Cesti Hurtado v. Peru, 154, 268
Chaparro Álvarez and Lapo Íñiguez v. Ecuador, 147, 154, 165, 201, 203, 211n318, 274n72, 278
charges, notification of, 162–64, 197–99
Charter of Fundamental Rights of the European Union (EU Charter), 34, 103n4, 141, 218, 266
Chávez, Hugo, 3, 44–45, 258–59
children
in criminal justice system, separate proceedings and facilities for, 134–35
due process protections for child migrants, 182n76
humane treatment of, 127
life imprisonment of, 121
UN Convention on the Rights of the Child, 15, 134, 160
Claude Reyes et al. *v. Chile*, 179, 183, 241–42
coerced evidence and coerced testimony, 25, 130, 206–8
commemorations, 304–5
communal property, rights to, 271–73
community development programs, 299–300
commutation of sentence, right to apply for, 81–82
compensation
just, 275–76
for medical expenses, 293, 294, 303
"competent" tribunal, 188–89
compliance and supervision of Court's judgments, 310–14
binding and final nature of judgments, 308–10
cases of noncompliance, 311–12
compliance rates, 313–14
"conception," moment of
and the right to life, 21, 57, 60, 61, 72, 73, 75n144

confessions, coerced, 207, 208. *See also* coerced evidence and coerced testimony
consequential damages, 293–94. *See also* pecuniary damages
  defined, 293, 293n49
Constitutional Court v. Peru, 193, 219
consular assistance, right to effective access to, 25, 79, 163, 210–11
contempt, laws of, 249, 252
Convention Against Torture (CAT), 103, 104, 108–9, 111, 115–17
Convention of Belém do Pará, 8, 14, 15, 23, 105, 118, 119, 131
  Article 7, 120, 131
Convention on the Elimination of All Forms of Discrimination Against Women, 41–42
Convention on the Rights of the Child, 15, 134, 160
corporal punishment, 120
Correa, Cristián, 295n63
counsel, right to, 175, 178, 201–4
crimes, categories of, 77, 78
cruel treatment. *See* Article 5
Cruz, Anahís, 45
Cruz Sánchez et al. *v. Peru*, 88, 89, 188–89

DaCosta Cadogan v. Barbados, 80, 203–5
daño emergente, 293–94
death, reasonable presumption of, 94, 96
death penalty, 21, 58–60, 69n99, 76, 120–21. *See also* Article 4; executions
  due process requirements, 78–81
  Inter-American Commission on Human Rights (IACHR) and, 76n149, 77, 79, 81
  "mandatory," 76–78
  "only for the most serious crimes," 77
  Protocol to the American Convention on Human Rights to Abolish the Death Penalty, 7–8, 58
  right to apply for pardon, amnesty, or commutation, 81–82
"death row phenomenon," 121
debt, detention for, 142, 143, 169
Declaration on the Protection of All Persons from Enforced Disappearance, 93
degrading treatment, 107, 118, 120, 121. *See also* Article 5; humane treatment
  defined, 118
  investigation and prevention of, 130–32
detention. *See also* Guantanamo Bay detention camp; imprisoned individuals; liberty; pretrial detention
  European Convention on Human Rights and, 142, 143, 158, 162
  Inter-American Commission on Human Rights (IACHR) on, 133, 157, 159
  reasons for, 162–63
  separate location and treatment for unconvicted persons in, 132–34
  State obligation to register detentions, 153–54
  without judicial warrant (exceptional cases), 151–53
detention conditions and practices, 90–91, 122–25. *See also* Article 5; detention
dignified life/dignified existence. *See vida digna*
disadvantaged groups, discrimination against, 45–48. *See also* discrimination
discrimination. *See also* Article 24
  assessment of
    Atala Riffo and the court's approach to discrimination, 49–53
    definitions and State obligations, 40–43
    progression of the court's case law, 43–49
  Atala Riffo and Daughters v. Chile and the court's approach to, 37, 49–53
  International Covenant on Civil and Political Rights (ICCPR) and, 33–34
  in law and in fact, 43–44, 48–49
    disadvantaged groups, 45–48
    perceived political opponents, 44–45
double jeopardy, prohibition against, 177, 211–13. *See also* Article 8: Article 8(4)
due diligence, 19, 19n117, 22, 65–66, 66n74, 69–71, 120, 152, 184, 186, 224–25, 226n419
  defined, 19, 19n117
due process, 69, 174–75, 178–83 . *See also* Article 8; *specific topics*
  criminal proceedings and, 194–214
  death penalty and, 78–81
  deportation/expulsion proceedings and, 181–82
  "due guarantees" and, 181–83
  European Convention on Human Rights on, 176–77, 218, 223
  European Court of Human Rights on, 175, 176, 226
  impartiality and, 191

right to, 24–25, 181
warrants and, 150
United Nations (UN) and, 175
due process violations, Court cases involving reparations for, 302–3
duress, exclusion of evidence obtained under, 25, 208. *See also* coerced evidence and coerced testimony

equality, right to, 32–33. *See also* Article 24
and the right to be presumed innocent, 196
sexual orientation and, 239
equal protection, right to, 32–33. *See also* Article 24
assessment of discrimination and, 40–53
Espinoza Gonzáles v. Peru, 111–14, 116, 122–23, 227
EU Charter of Fundamental Rights, 34, 103n4, 141, 218, 266
European Convention on Human Rights, 58–60, 161n162
Article 3, 103
Article 5, 131, 141–43, 148
Article 6, 176, 177
Article 10, 233n21
Article 13, 218
Article 41, 288
detention and, 142, 143, 158, 162
on double jeopardy, 177
on due process, 176–77, 218, 223
freedom of expression and, 231, 260
on humane treatment, 103
procedural breaches to, 131, 226
on property rights, 265, 266
Protocol 1, 276
Protocol 7, 177
on reasonable suspicion, 158
right to liberty and, 141, 142, 148
European Court of Human Rights, 14, 16, 161n162, 266, 276–78
burden of proof required by, 85
discrimination and, 41, 49, 51
on due process, 175, 176, 226
equality, suspect categories, and, 49, 51
freedom of expression and, 16, 26, 231, 233, 241, 248–49, 253
on human dignity, 99n330, 103
on humane treatment, 22, 103, 104, 118
on property rights, 16, 265, 266, 276–78
on reasonable suspicion, 158
on reparations, 288, 315
right to liberty and, 163, 166n193
right to life and, 21, 57–58, 71–73, 85, 91
on right to personal security, 141, 146
torture and, 22, 103, 104, 111, 116, 118n113, 120, 126
UN Convention Against Torture (CAT) and, 111
European Union (EU). *See* EU Charter of Fundamental Rights
executions, 74, 94, 95, 121. *See also* death penalty
extrajudicial, 24, 62, 71, 89–91, 97, 115, 128, 129n202, 144, 180, 186, 187, 224, 290, 291, 297
of juvenile offenders, 81
staying, 21, 76, 81
Expelled Dominicans and Haitians v. Dominican Republic, 38, 52, 129, 130, 222n390
ex post facto laws, 6, 6n23

Factory at Chorzów, 287
fair balance between general interest and individual interest ("fair balance" factor), 275, 276, 278, 295
Fermin Ramirez v. Guatemala, 79, 80, 82
Fernández Ortega et al. *v.* Mexico, 47–48, 293
fetus. *See* Article 4; "conception"; life, right to
"Five Pensioners" v. Peru, 277
Fontevecchia and D'Amico v. Argentina, 247–48, 256
forced disappearances, 17, 21, 24, 125–26, 128, 180
access to justice and, 224
arbitrariness principle and, 156–57
arbitrary deprivations of life and, 75
Article 4 and, 71, 74
Article 5 and, 126, 156–57
Article 7 and, 126, 144, 156, 157
Article 25 and, 222, 224
defined, 93
habeas corpus and, 168, 221
overview, 92–94
right to life, *ratione temporis* jurisdiction, and, 94–97
search operations and, 70–71

freedom of expression. *See also* Article 13
European Court of Human Rights and, 16, 26, 231, 233, 241, 248–49, 253
International Covenant on Civil and Political Rights (ICCPR) and, 231, 234–35, 260
limitations to, 243–44
incitements to violence, 260–61
"indirect" restrictions, 257–59
prior censorship, 244–47
subsequent imposition of liability, 247–57
protected expression, 237–39
requirements for sanctions on, 247–49
right of access to State-held information, 241–42
safeguards for journalists, 239–41
State obligations regarding, 232–33
Fujimori, Alberto, 3n4, 277
Furlan and Family v. Argentina, 187, 277

García Asto and Ramírez Rojas v. Peru, 132
García Ramírez, Sergio, 254
Gelman v. Uruguay, 74
gender violence, 119–20. *See also* sexual violence; women; rape
general interest and general welfare, 276
Geneva Conventions, 87, 89, 269
Genie Lacayo v. Nicaragua, 184
Globovisión, 236, 261
Gonzales Lluy et al. *v. Ecuador*, 63
González et al. *("Cotton Field") v. Mexico*, 15, 47, 114–16, 119n126, 131n219, 227
Gonzalez Medina and Family v. Dominican Republic, 96
Granier et al. *(Radio Caracas Television) v. Venezuela*, 258, 261
Guantanamo Bay detention camp, 17, 111n62, 194, 222
guarantees of non-repetition, 19, 287
Gutiérrez and Family v. Argentina, 129n202
Gutiérrez Soler v. Colombia, 146n56

habeas corpus. *See also* Article 7: Article 7(6)
amparo and, 25, 167–68, 221, 227
health care. *See* medical care for detained persons
hearing, right to a, 178–81. *See also* trial: right to a (fair)
Heliodoro Portugal v. Panama, 96
Herrera Ulloa v. Costa Rica, 175, 209, 253
Hilaire, Constantine and Benjamin et al. *v. Trinidad and Tobago*, 79, 81–82, 120–21
humane treatment. *See also* inhuman treatment
European Court of Human Rights on, 22, 103, 104, 118
right to. *See also* Article 5; Inter-American Convention to Prevent and Punish Torture; torture
Bayarri v. Argentina and, 226
as a broad right with uncertain parameters, 106–8
considerations of evidence and proof, 116–17
cruel, inhuman, or degrading punishment or treatment, 117–27, 130–32
Espinoza Gonzales v. Peru, 227
State obligations to ensure, 130–32
State-sanctioned punishment and, 120–21
threats of "severe physical injuries," 126
violations to personal integrity below the threshold of Article 5(2), 127–30
Human Rights Committee (HRC) of United Nations, 39, 77, 104, 117, 141, 147, 161n162, 175
human rights treaties, 12, 34. *See also specific treaties*
specialized, 8
Hurtado, Cesti, 154

"impartial" tribunal, 188, 191–93
imprisoned individuals
arbitrary deprivation of life of, 89–90
detention conditions and health care, 90–91
security operations in prisons, 91–92
"reform and social readaptation" of, 135–37
incommunicado detention, 123
"independent" tribunal, 190–91, 193
inhuman treatment, 104, 107, 118, 121. *See also* Article 5; humane treatment
vs. degrading treatment, 118
investigation and prevention of, 130–32
State-sanctioned punishment and, 120
threats of "severe physical injuries" as, 126
vs. torture, 22, 103, 104, 107n29, 118n113
innocence, presumption of, 194–96
Inter-American Commission on Human Rights (IACHR), 2, 5, 86, 279n110, 287. *See also specific topics*
Article 7 and, 131, 144–45, 157, 159
Article 25 and, 216, 222
censorship and, 246
on criminal laws to limit speech, 249
death penalty and, 76n149, 77, 79, 81

on "death row phenomenon," 121
Declaration of Principles on Freedom of Expression ("Principles"), 231, 236
draft of American Convention on Human Rights, 6, 35, 36, 59–61
functions, 1, 7–11
on gender violence, 119–20
on Guantánamo Bay, 17
on immigration detention, 133
Inter-American Court of Human Rights and, 13–14, 26
movement to "reform" the, 3
overview, 8–11
petitions before, 9
on pretrial detention, 157, 159
on right to life, 59, 74–75
settlement procedure, 9
Special Rapporteur on Freedom of Expression (Special Rapporteur), 194n179, 237, 239, 248–50, 259–61
terrorism and, 194, 222
on torture, 105, 111n62, 115
Inter-American Convention on Forced Disappearance of Persons (IACFDP), 8, 14
Inter-American Convention on the Prevention, Punishment and Eradication of Violence against Women. *See* Convention of Belém do Pará
Inter-American Convention to Prevent and Punish Torture (IACPPT), 8, 115, 131
Article 1, 109, 131
Article 3, 115
Article 6, 109, 131
Article 8, 109, 131
definitions of torture and, 103, 108–11
three-part test for torture and, 110, 111
UN Convention Against Torture (CAT) and, 103, 108–9, 111
violations of, 15, 109–10, 116, 131
Inter-American Court of Human Rights. *See also specific topics*
advisory opinions, 12–13
assessment of evidence and burden of proof, 17–18
contentious cases, 11–12
factors for understanding compliance with, 313–14
functions, 7
Inter-American Commission on Human Rights and, 13–14, 26
overview, 11–13
ratione materiae, ratione temporis, ratione personae, and *ratione loci* jurisdiction, 14–17
Inter-American Human Rights System, impact and importance of, 2–5
Inter-American jurisprudence, key developments and critiques of, 18–27
Inter-American Specialized Conference on Human Rights, 6
International Convention on the Elimination of All Forms of Racial Discrimination, 41–42
International Court of Justice (ICJ), 315
International Covenant on Civil and Political Rights (ICCPR), 7
American Convention's Article 5 and, 103
American Convention's Article 8 and, 177, 212
Article 1, 269
Article 2, 39
Article 2(3), 216–18
Article 6, 59–60
Article 7, 103, 118n112
Article 9, 141, 142
Article 10, 105
Article 19(1), 235
Article 20, 260n234
Article 26, 33–36, 39
Article 27, 269
discrimination and, 33–34
due process and, 174, 176, 177
equal protection and, 33
freedom of expression and, 231, 234–35, 260
property rights and, 269
right to liberty and, 141–43, 148, 156
right to life and, 57–60, 98n325
interpreter, right to be assisted by an, 196–97
Ituango Massacres v. Colombia, 64, 126, 269–70
Ivcher Bronstein v. Peru, 194, 257–58, 277, 278, 294–95, 301

J. v. Peru, 119, 214
judicial protection
boundaries of, 224–28
right to, 215–17. *See also* Article 8; Article 25
amparo and, 25, 168, 216, 217, 225, 227, 228
due process and, 224, 228
warrants and, 150

judicial supervision, 151
brought "before a judge or other officer authorized by law," 164–66
judicial warrants, 150–51
detentions without, 151–53
jus cogens norms, 20, 32, 57, 93, 107
"just compensation," meaning of, 275–76
justice, right of access to, 224–25
Juvenile Reeducation Institute v. Paraguay, 90, 98, 134, 135n246, 136, 159–60

Karner v. Austria, 51
Kichwa Indigenous People of Sarayaku v. Ecuador. See Sarayaku v. Ecuador
Kimel v. Argentina, 239n66, 241, 253–56
Kuna Indigenous People of Madungandi and Embera Indigenous People of Bayano v. Panama, 186, 228

Landaeta Meijias Brothers et al. *v. Venezuela*, 84, 85, 187
Lapo Íñiguez, Freddy, 203
Las Dos Erres Massacre v. Guatemala, 185
Las Palmeras v. Colombia, 86
"The Last Temptation of Christ" (Olmedo Bustos et al.*) v. Chile*, 245–46
legal counsel. *See* counsel
legality principle, 200, 247–48. *See also under* liberty, general requirements to deprive
and use of lethal force, 83, 84
lesbian, gay, bisexual, trans and intersex (LGBTI) persons. *See also* sexual orientation
incitements to violence against, 261
lethal force, use of
in armed conflicts, 86–89
in law enforcement scenarios, 82–83
burden of proof, 85
principles of legality, necessity, and proportionality, 83–85
State duties after the use of force, 85–86
lex specialis (in situations of armed conflict), 86, 222
Liakat Ali Alibux v. Suriname, 210n309
liberty
of accused persons, presumption of innocence and, 195
defined, 143–44
deprivation of, 122. *See also* liberty, general requirements to deprive
children and, 134
forced disappearance and, 93, 125
right to legal counsel and, 175, 178
threat of, 143
personal integrity and, 106
right to notification and, 198
right to personal, 141–142. *See also* Article 7
European Convention on Human Rights and, 141, 142, 148
International Covenant on Civil and Political Rights (ICCPR) and, 141–43, 148, 156
right to personal security and, 146–48
right to physical, 143–46
liberty, general requirements to deprive. *See also* liberty: deprivation of
arbitrariness principle, 156
forced disappearances, 156–57
methodological problems, 160–62
pretrial detention as arbitrary detention, 157–60
legality principle, 148
Court's increasing reluctance to find violations of Article 7(2), 154–55
detention time limit and orders for release, 154
methodological problems, 160–62
ordered by a competent judicial authority, 150–53
pretrial detention as illegal detention, 154
restriction of liberty always the exception, 148–50
State obligation to register detentions, 153–54
life, right to. *See also* Article 4
and the concept of *vida digna*, 97–100
duty to ensure (or "protect") the, 65–72
duty to respect the, 62–65
European Court of Human Rights and, 21, 57–58, 71–73, 85, 91
extensive State obligations to respect and ensure the, 61–62
meaning of "every person," 72, 73
meaning of "in general, from the moment of conception," 72–75. *See also* "conception"
meaning of "no one shall be arbitrarily deprived" of life, 75–97
right to communal property and, 283

Loayza Tamayo v. Peru, 123, 212
López, Marino, 115
López Álvarez v. Honduras, 39, 46, 48, 168, 184, 220, 239
López Lone et al. *v. Honduras*, 259
López Mendoza v. Venezuela, 199n221
Luna López, Carlos, 67–68

Mack Chang v. Guatemala, 69n99, 128n199, 297n77, 304–5
Mamere v. France, 253n182
Mapiripán Massacre v. Colombia, 227, 291n33
Maritza Urrutia v. Guatemala, 113, 207
Massacres of El Mozote and Nearby Places v. El Salvador, 63, 126
Matter of the Peace Community of San José de Apartadó, 315–16
Matus Acuña et al. *v. Chile*, 246–47
Mayagna (Sumo) Awas Tingni v. Nicaragua, 27, 269, 271
medical care for detained persons, failure to provide, 90–91, 98, 116, 122, 165
medical expenses, compensation for, 293, 294, 303
Medina Quiroga, Cecilia, 226
  on *amparo*, 220
  Article 7 and, 146–47, 155, 166
  Article 8 and, 181, 214, 225, 227
  Article 25 and, 220, 225–27
  on *Claude Reyes* et al. *v. Chile*, 179n52
  on detainees and the right to personal security, 146–47
  on *Espinoza Gonzáles v. Peru*, 116, 154–55
  on right to trial "within a reasonable time," 166
Melish, Tara, 277
Mémoli v. Argentina, 238nn63–64, 241, 248, 254–55
memorials, 304–5
Mendoza et al. *v. Argentina*, 112, 121, 137
Menem, Carlos, 256
mental health evaluations of defendants, 205
Miguel Castro Castro Prison v. Peru, 91, 113, 114, 118, 119
"minimum guarantees," 196
Mohamed v. Argentina, 210
Moiwana Community v. Suriname, 272
Montero Aranguren et al *v. Venezuela*, 92
moral damages, 296–300
moral harm, defined, 296
Movimiento para la Revolución Tupac Amaru (MRTA), 88–89

Nadege Dorzema et al. *v. Dominican Republic*, 84, 85
ne bis in idem principle, 211, 212. *See also* double jeopardy
necessity, principle of, 83, 84
Neira Alegría et al. *v. Peru*, 92
New York Times Co. v. Sullivan, 231n1
19 Merchants v. Colombia, 301n101
non-discrimination, 32. *See also* discrimination
non-retroactivity principle.
  of Vienna Convention on the Law of Treaties, 16
Norín Catrimán et al. *v. Chile*, 51–52, 53n141, 130n207, 155, 158, 160, 205–6, 209
notification of charges, 162–64

offensive content, prohibitions against, 245–47
Olmedo Bustos et al. *v. Chile*, 245–46
Organization of American States (OAS), 4–6
  Charter, 5, 6, 8
  General Assembly, 11, 311–12
  Member States, 6, 8, 9, 12
Osorio Rivera and Family v. Peru, 152–53
overcrowding in detention, 123–25

Pacheco Teruel et al *v. Honduras*, 91, 124, 136, 155
Pacheco Tineo Family v. Bolivia, 197
"pain and suffering," remedies for, 300
Palamara Iribarne v. Chile, 154, 164n180, 189n131, 199, 246, 252, 277, 301–2
Paniagua Morales v. Guatemala, 109, 151
pardon, right to apply for a, 81–82
Pasqualucci, Jo, 296n73
pecuniary damages, 292–96
Perozo et al. *v. Venezuela*, 9n40, 44–45, 232n14, 236, 261
persecution leading to violations of Article 13(1), cases of, 259–60
political opponents, perceived
  discrimination perpetrated by, 44–45
Portugal, Heliodoro, 96
precautionary measures, 9, 17n104, 75, 76n149, 81, 222
presumption of innocence, right to the, 194–96

pretrial detention. *See also* time limits for (pretrial) detention
as arbitrary detention, 157–60
detention in immigration proceedings, 159
risks to the criminal proceeding, 158–59
sufficient evidence of criminal responsibility, 158
defined, 157
as illegal detention, 154
of special sectors of the population, 159–60
prevent, duty to, 65–66. *See also* humane treatment
through legal regulation, 66–67
"prevention and protection measures" in threatening circumstances, duty to adopt, 67–69, 92, 132
"previously established by law" (tribunals), 193–94
prisoners. *See* detention; imprisoned individuals
privacy, right to, 119
pro homine interpretation of the Convention, 2, 39
property, restitution of, 295, 301–2
property, right to. *See also* Article 21
European Court of Human Rights on, 16, 265, 266, 276–78
group rights, 266
indigenous property rights, 15, 271–73, 279–83, 302n108
limitations to the
meaning of "in the cases and according to the forms established by law," 278
meaning of "just compensation," 275–76
meaning of "reasons of public utility or social interest," 276–77
protective framework for traditional territories, 279–83
restrictions during criminal investigations and police action, 278–79
right to property not absolute, 273–74
many forms of property recognized, 268–71
rights to communal property, 271–73
proportionality test for the use of lethal force, 83–85
protection
equal. *See* Article 24
judicial. *See* Article 25
Protocol of San Salvador, 7, 14, 72
Protocol to the American Convention on Human Rights to Abolish the Death Penalty, 7–8, 58
provisional measures, 11, 12, 289–90, 309, 311, 312, 314–16
abortion and, 75
psychiatric health evaluations of defendants, 205
public criminal proceedings, 213–14
public officials, honor and reputation of, 253–55
public utility, reasons of, 276–77
punishment. *See also* Article 5; humane treatment; investigate and punish; *specific topics*
no extension of punishment beyond the convicted individual, 132
State-sanctioned, 120–21

Quintana Coello et al. *v. Ecuador*, 190

Radilla Pacheco v. Mexico, 67, 96, 189
Radio Caracas Televisión (RCTV), 258, 261
rape, 47, 113–14. *See also* sexual violence
ratione loci jurisdiction, 17, 188
ratione materiae (subject matter) jurisdiction, 14, 188
ratione personae jurisdiction, 16, 188
ratione temporis (temporal) jurisdiction, 16, 188
right to life and, 94–97
Raxcacó Reyes v. Guatemala, 76, 77, 82, 121, 136
RCTV (Radio Caracas Televisión), 258, 261
reasonableness standard, 19, 65–66. *See also* due diligence
reasonable presumption of death, 94, 96
reasonable suspicion, 158
rehabilitation. *See also under* reparations: non-monetary remedies
criminal, 134–35
reparations. *See also* Article 63
legal fees and expenses, 307–8
monetary remedies
moral damages, 296–300
pecuniary damages, 292–96
non-monetary remedies
background, 300–301
memorials and commemorations, 304–5
recognition of responsibility and apologies, 304
reform of legislation and policy, training programs, 305–6
rehabilitation, 303–4
restitution, 295, 301–3
supervision and compliance with Court's judgments, 310–14

reproductive rights, 72. *See also* abortion; "conception"
restitutio in integrum principle, 287
restitution, 301–3
of property, 295, 301–2
Reverón Trujillo v. Venezuela, 190
Ricardo Canese v. Paraguay, 205, 238n63, 253
right-to-life framework to protect ancestral lands and resources, 283
Río Negro Massacres v. Guatemala, 305
Ríos et al. *v. Venezuela*, 44, 45, 261
Robles Espinoza, Rodolfo, 253n174
Rochela Massacre v. Colombia, 62–63
Rodriguez Vera et al. *v. Colombia*, 89n258, 112, 187n124, 297n78
Rosendo Cantú et al. *v.* Mexico, 47–48, 293

Salvador Chiriboga v. Ecuador, 275, 276, 278
San Salvador, Protocol of, 7, 14, 72
Santo Domingo Massacre v. Colombia, 87
Saramaka People v. Suriname, 266, 269, 272nn65–66, 280–82, 295–96, 299–300, 302n108, 310n177, 316n220
Sarayaku v. Ecuador, 64n66, 282, 290n24, 293, 299, 300
satisfaction, 19, 20, 40, 44, 69, 287, 288nn12–13, 301, 305
security, right to personal, 141, 146–48
seizure of property. *See also* property
in connection with criminal investigations, 278–79
self-incrimination, right against, 206–8
Serrano Cruz Sisters v. El Salvador, 95
sexual orientation
discrimination based on, 41, 49–51
freedom of expression, right to equality, and, 239
propaganda, hate speech, and, 261
sexual violence, 117–20. *See also* rape
Shelton, Dinah, 288n13
social interest, reasons of, 276–77
Special Rapporteur on Freedom of Expression (Special Rapporteur), 194n179, 237, 239, 248–50, 259–61
State obligations/State duties, 6, 12, 18–19, 309. *See also* Article 4; due diligence; *specific topics*
after the use of force, 85–86
Article 1 and, 35, 223, 225–26
Article 5 and, 130–32
Article 8 and, 224
Article 25 and, 224
Article 25(2) and, 216, 223
deprivation of property and, 274
discrimination and, 40–43
equality law and, 42
expansion of, 18–20, 23, 35
freedom of expression and, 232
gender violence and, 120
Inter-American Convention to Prevent and Punish Torture (IACPPT) and, 131
to investigate and punish human rights abuses, 19, 24, 62, 65, 68–72, 120, 130–31, 180, 224–26, 313
negative, 22, 61, 232
positive, 19, 22, 61, 65, 104, 232
to protect life "by law," 66–67
to protect personal integrity, 104
to provide medical care for detainees, 91. *See also* medical care for detained persons
to register detentions, 153–54
to respect and ensure rights, 18–19
when using force, 128n193
Suárez Rosero v. Ecuador, 166, 167
suspect categories/classifications, 48–49, 51, 52

terrorism, Inter-American Commission on Human Rights (IACHR) and, 194, 222
Tibi, Daniel, 112
Tibi v. Ecuador, 109n42, 110n46, 112, 204n258
time limits for (pretrial) detention, 154, 160
right to be tried "within a reasonable time," 166, 174, 175, 177–78, 183–88
Torres Millacura et al. *v. Argentina*, 155, 161n163
torture. *See also* Article 5; Inter-American Convention to Prevent and Punish Torture
definitions of and criteria for, 110–14
European Court of Human Rights and, 22, 103, 104, 111, 116, 118n113, 120, 126
vs. inhuman/degrading treatment, 22, 103, 104, 107n29, 118n113
involvement of State actors as a requirement for, 114–16
UN Convention Against Torture (CAT), 103, 104, 108–9, 111, 115–17
translator, right to be assisted by a, 196–97

treaties. *See* human rights treaties
trial
right to a (fair), 24–25. *See also* Article 8
meaning of "with due guarantees," 181–83
"within a reasonable time," 166–67, 183–88

United Nations (UN)
Charter, 32
Convention Against Torture (CAT), 103, 104, 108–9, 111, 115–17
Convention on the Rights of the Child, 15, 134, 160
Declaration on the Protection of All Persons from Enforced Disappearance, 93
due process and, 175
Human Rights Committee (HRC), 39, 77, 104, 117, 141, 147, 161n162, 175
purposes/objectives, 32
Working Group on Enforced or Involuntary Disappearances, 97
Universal Declaration of Human Rights, 5, 32, 34, 231, 265
Urrutia, Maritza, 113, 207
Usón Ramírez v. Venezuela, 189n132, 192, 248–49, 251n164, 252–53, 255
Uzcátegui et al. *v. Venezuela*, 130n208, 250n159, 279

Valle Jaramillo et al. *v. Colombia*, 126, 147n63, 184, 186
Velásquez Paiz et al. *v. Guatemala*, 239n71
Velásquez Rodríguez v. Honduras, 12, 19, 21, 71, 92–94, 224, 226
Vélez Loor v. Panama, 48, 124, 133, 159, 163, 175, 177, 201–2, 211
Ventura Robles, Manuel, 312n196
Vera Vera et al. *v. Ecuador*, 91
Verbitsky, Horacio, 249
victim-centered approach, 2, 298
Victims' Legal Assistance Fund, 308
vida digna (right to a dignified life), 97–100, 283
Vienna Convention on the Law of Treaties, non-retroactivity principle of, 16
Villagrán Morales et al. *v. Guatemala*, 98, 109, 127, 304
violence. *See also specific topics*
incitements to, and freedom of expression, 260–61
Vivanco, José Miguel, 2n3

warrants. *See* judicial warrants
"without delay" (*sin demora*) principle, 165, 167, 168, 210, 219–20, 223
witnesses
right of defense to present and examine, 204–6
testimony of anonymous, 205–6
women
discrimination against, 41–42
violence against, 118–20. *See also* Convention of Belém do Pará; gender violence; rape; sexual violence
Wong Ho Wing v. Peru, 160

Xákmok Kásek Indigenous Community, 185, 272n64, 272n66, 281n123, 302n109
Ximenes Lopes v. Brazil, 63–65

Yakye Axa Indigenous Community v. Paraguay, 269
Yamamoto, Eric, 299n89
YATAMA v. Nicaragua, 37, 38, 46–48
Yean and Bosico v. Dominican Republic, 39, 45, 48, 307–8
Yvon Neptune v. Haiti, 133

Zambrano Vélez et al. *v. Ecuador*, 88n251
Zelaya, Manuel, 259

www.ingramcontent.com/pod-product-compliance
Ingram Content Group UK Ltd.
Pitfield, Milton Keynes, MK11 3LW, UK
UKHW020843150926
475595UK00004B/131

9 780199 989683